Build Your Own Pentium III PC

Aubrey Pilgrim

McGraw-Hill
New York   San Francisco   Washington, D.C.
Auckland   Bogotá   Caracas   Lisbon   London
Madrid   Mexico City   Milan   Montreal   New Delhi
San Juan   Singapore   Sydney   Tokyo   Toronto

McGraw-Hill

A Division of The McGraw·Hill Companies

Copyright © 2000 by The McGraw-Hill Companies, Inc. All rights reserved. Printed in the United States of America. Except as permitted under the United States Copyright Act of 1976, no part of this publication may be reproduced or distributed in any form or by any means, or stored in a data base or retrieval system, without the prior written permission of the publisher.

3 4 5 6 7 8 9 0 AGM/AGM 0 4 3 2 1 0

0-07-135201-5

The sponsoring editor for this book was Michael Sprague, the editing supervisor was Scott Amerman, and the production supervisor was Clare Stanley. It was set in Century Schoolbook by Priscilla Beer and Victoria Khavkina of McGraw-Hill's desktop composition unit in cooperation with Spring Point Publishing Services.

Printed and bound by Quebecor/Martinsburg.

 This book is printed on recycled, acid-free paper containing a minimum of 50% recycled de-inked fiber.

CONTENTS

Contents

Contents

Contents

Contents

Contents

Contents

PREFACE

Introduction

I began writing this Build Your Own and Save a Bundle series of books in 1986. At that time it was easy to save a bundle by building your own computer. A genuine IBM XT with 64KB of memory, two 360KB floppy disks, and a 10MB hard drive cost almost $5000. And that was when the dollar was worth about three times what it is worth today.

But times have changed all for the better. Today, computers are so inexpensive that some companies are actually giving them away. One company gave away over 10,000 systems. The only cost was that purchasers have to give them a lot of information about themselves and their shopping habits. They also have to look at several ads every time they turn on the computer.

So I have to be honest with you. You can save some money, but you may not be able to save a bundle by building your own. You should still consider doing it, however. You will definitely be able to save over the cost of a well-known, brand-name, store-bought system. It may not be much, but you will gain an enormous amount of knowledge about what is inside a computer. If you are fairly new to computers, building your own will take away a lot of the mystery. You will see how simple they are to assemble.

Why You Need a Computer

We are in the midst of the computer age. Today they are as necessary as indoor plumbing. We need computers not only in business but also in the home. If you are a student or have a child who is a student, then by all means you need a computer.

A recent issue of *Information Week* magazine estimated that there are 108.2 million PCs in this country and about 270 million men, women, and children. We are approaching the point where almost every home has a PC. Many homes now have at least two computers. What will your neighbors think if you don't have a PC?

One very big reason to have a computer is the Internet. In just a few years, it has brought about enormous changes in the way we communicate, entertain ourselves, gather information, and do business.

There are very few businesses that do not have a Web site. For most companies, to access their Web site, just type www.*companyname*.com.

Buying Instead of Building

You know you need a computer, but you may not have the money for a new one. But, again, computers are very inexpensive today. Even if you have to skip going to the opera a few times or to an NFL football game every weekend, save the money and build yourself a computer. You owe it to yourself and family to have a good computer. If you are in business, it is an essential tool.

You may feel a bit apprehensive about building your own. That is understandable considering what they can do. But, actually, it is very easy to assemble one. If you still feel that you don't want to put one together yourself, there are several good computers available now for under $500.

Of course, these low-price computers will not be as fast or as powerful as some of the high-cost ones, but a low-cost computer may be able to do all that you need to do at the moment. You can always upgrade and add to it later.

Even if you do take the easy way out and buy a preassembled unit, you still need this book. It can help you decide what peripherals you need and help you to understand how a computer works.

Upgrade and Save a Bundle

You may lust for a powerful 550MHz Pentium III, but you may not have the money at this time to buy all the components. No problem. There is a very inexpensive way to get your hands on one. Just upgrade an older system, such as a lowly 486 or a Pentium. In this computer age, a three-year-old 486 or Pentium is as ancient as a dinosaur, but with a few new components, it can be as good as brand-new. These old clunkers can be easily and rather inexpensively upgraded to be as good as the fastest and most powerful beast.

The best upgrade would be to pull out the old motherboard and install a new one. But motherboards have changed a bit, so you may have to buy a case and power supply. The new motherboards have the ports and other connectors grouped in such a way that the motherboard would not fit in the old case unless you took a hacksaw and made some extra holes in the back panel. Most of the new motherboards also mount differently. In the ancient days of the XT, they used brass stand-offs and screws to attach the motherboard to the case. They got away from that, and for several years, they used plastic stand-offs and two screws. Now they are back to using raised stand-offs and screws to attach the motherboards.

If you don't have an older computer, you might consider buying a used one. You can get some fantastic deals on some of them. You can then use this book to upgrade any of the older 486 or Pentium systems. Chapter 12 can show you how to do it.

The B-B Gene

Except for a few high-end applications, most people don't need a 550MHz computer or even a 500MHz system. If all you do is word processing, databases, or spreadsheets, you can get by very well with a low-cost 266MHz or 300MHz system. But if at all possible, go ahead and build the biggest and fastest computer you can possibly afford. I postulated in one of my earlier books that there is no doubt a gene in some people that causes them to insist on having the biggest and best. If and when this gene is proven, I suggested that it be named the B-B gene for *biggest* and *best*. I am a bit ashamed to admit it, but I am one of those people who is afflicted with this condition.

Unfortunately, I don't have the necessary money to satisfy all of my desires for the biggest and best. That is one reason why I build my own systems.

Don't Be a Pioneer

There is one other gene that resides in a lot of people. This one causes them to want to be the first with every new toy or device that is ever invented. This may not be a good idea because many of the new computer devices and software usually have a few bugs when first introduced. If at all possible, you should resist the urge to buy the first release of a product. It is best to wait until it has been proven that it will work as promised. Most of the components that are discussed in this book have been around long enough to have been proven. (Someone once said that pioneers often end up with arrows in their back. Buying a new product that doesn't work may cause as much pain as an arrow.)

One other very important reason to wait is that the initial price is usually very high when a product first comes out. The Pentium III 550HMz CPU that costs $800 today will cost about half that much six months later. Just a few months ago, the Intel Pentium II 450MHz CPU was the fastest and most powerful available. Its cost was about $1000. Today, it costs about $400. It will be even less by the time you read this.

You Can Do It

With this book as a guide, you can build a computer that will be very fast and powerful. It can be faster and more powerful than many of the multimillion dollar mainframes of just a few years ago. And it won't cost you a million dollars; you can do it for just a few hundred bucks.

This is truly a fantastic age that we are living in.

Ease of Assembly

You can build a powerful computer without having any advanced knowledge about electronics or computer science. Nor do you need to have an IQ that would qualify you to be a member of Mensa. Some of the most popular books on the market today are those written for "dummies." I know that you are not a dummy, but assembling a computer is so easy that even a dummy can do it. This book will show you how easy it is to assemble all the parts. There are lots of photos and clear instructions in the book. The beauty of assembling your own is that you can include only those items that you want.

One of the greatest benefits of building your own is that you will have a sense of accomplishment that is priceless. You will know what is inside your computer because you added it.

Computers are made up of discrete components. They all plug together somewhat like a toy Erector set. You can plug in dozens of different components; the components are all made to standards and are interchangeable. So you can shop around to find the best buy and not have to worry about whether it will work or not. This is one of the fantastic features that make computers so versatile and functional. No matter what you need a computer for, there are components available that will allow you to build it.

How Much Can You Save?

You will probably save some money in building your own computer, but the number-one reason to do it is to gain the experience. Since all my books have the subtitle "Save a Bundle," I am often asked how much one can save. The answer depends on a lot of factors, such as how well you shop, whether you want brand names, and the type of items you want to include.

Where you shop can make a big difference. Some stores have a lot of salespeople, are in a high-rent district, carry a lot of stock, and have a very high overhead. In order to make ends meet, their prices may be higher than a small shop in a low-rent district that has a low overhead.

Brand names also make a big difference. There are some people who must have the very latest clothing style. They may pay outrageous prices for a suit or dress just because it has a famous designer label. I buy clothes merely to hide my nakedness. Designer brand labels don't do anything for me. There are some people who are convinced that some of the brand-name computer components are superior to the no-name brands. But like clothes, in most cases, the no-name components will be all that you need to do the job.

Another reason to build your own is that you may not be able to afford all that you want at this time. You can build a basic system, then add to it as you can afford to. For instance, you may want a couple of 9.1GB hard drives. You may be able to afford only one at this time, or you may have to settle for a measly 6.4GB. You can always add a larger one later. Another bit of good news: If you wait a little while, the price of hard disk drives and most other components will go down.

So how much can you save? I put together a Pentium III 500MHz and an AMD 450MHz. There is actually very little difference in the power and speed of these two machines. I spent $2369 to build the Pentium III and $1314 to build the AMD K6-III. I saved $1055.

Again, one of the best ways to save is to upgrade an older computer as outlined in Chapter 12.

I know that you are anxious to get started, but if you are fairly new to computers, I hope that you will read about the various components in the first few chapters so that you will know what components to buy. Chapter 13 has the photos and instructions for assembling the computer after you have bought your components.

Obsolescence

Even if you buy or build the most powerful computer available, within a very short time it will be practically obsolete. At this moment, the 550MHz systems are the fastest, but by the time you read this, there will no doubt be several 600MHz systems on the market. Shortly after that, there will be 650MHz, then 700MHz systems. It won't be long until CPUs will operate at 1 gigahertz, or a billion cycles per second.

We toss these numbers around and usually don't think about the enormity of them. A device that turns itself on and off a million times per second is hard to imagine. It is even more difficult to imagine a device that turns itself on and off a million-million or one billion times per second. Or try to imagine yourself as Bill Gates, who has 100 billion dollars. It would take several lifetimes to even count that much money.

You may not want to build or buy anything, and instead wait for these newer, faster, and more powerful machines. But no matter how long you wait, there will always be an improved model out tomorrow. Think about all you would miss out on by waiting. And if you are in business or really need a computer now, go ahead and build it or buy it, and don't worry. Just upgrade it later.

AMD Athlon

Intel has been the ruler of the roost for a long time with the fastest and most powerful CPUs. AMD's new Athlon is about to change all that. The AMD Athlon will be discussed in Chapter 3, which is about CPUs and in Chapter 13, which shows how to assemble a unit.

A Brief Summary of Chapters

Chapter 1   What's Inside?

A brief description of each component needed in a computer. The PC is made up of discrete components that are usually just connected together by cables or connectors on a board.

Chapter 2   The Motherboard

The motherboard is the most important board in the system. they are all basically the same; however, some vendors differentiate their products in certain ways.

There is a major difference in the Pentium III motherboard and the AMD K6 and Cyrix MII motherboards in the way that the CPUs are installed. AMD and Cyrix use a square Socket 7/Zero Insertion Force (ZIF) sockets. Intel designed a new slot for the Pentium II CPUs, which is also used for the Pentium III CPUs.

You can easily upgrade a system by replacing the motherboard.

Chapter 3   The CPU

You have a choice of several CPUs. This chapter lists some of the facts about each of them.

Chapter 4   Memory

There are several types of memory. You must use whatever type the motherboard was designed to use.

Chapter 5   Floppy Drives and Disks

This chapter describes how floppy drives operate, as well as how disks are organized and formatted into tracks, sectors, and cylinders. Disk differences are also discussed.

Chapter 6   Choosing a Hard Disk Drive

This chapter discusses how hard drives operate and how they are formatted. Also covers IDE and SCSI hard disk differences.

Chapter 7   Backup: Disaster Prevention

Chapter 7 discusses why backup is critical, along with some methods of backup. Methods of recovery are also discussed.

Chapter 8   CD-ROM and DVD-ROM

Here we'll discuss how CD-ROMs operate. The operation of CD-ROM recordables and DVDs are also covered.

Chapter 9   Monitors and Adapters

Chapter 9 discusses how monitors operate, including differences in the CRT and the new LCD flat-panel monitors. Also covered is the need for adapters and how they operate.

Chapter 10   Input Devices

Chapter 10 covers several input devices, such as keyboards, mice, scanners, and digital camers, and how these devices operate.

Chapter 11   Communications

Here we'll discuss how modems and fax machines work.

Chapter 12   Upgrading an Older PC

As mentioned earlier in the introduction, you can save a lot of money by simply upgrading an older system. This chapter can show you how.

Chapter 13   Assembling Your Computer

This chapter provides complete instructions for assembling a computer, along with detailed photographs.

Chapter 14   The Internet

The Internet has brought about enormous changes in the last few short years. It has brought changes in the way we do business, in our entertainment, in ways that we can learn, in all kinds of information, in our society, and in just about all aspects of our lives. In this chapter we'll discuss how we can benefit from this important tool.

Chapter 15   Printers

The different types of printers, including dot-matrix, ink-jet, and laser, are discussed, along with how they operate.

Chapter 16   Essential Software

This chapter outlines just some of the software that is needed, including operating systems, word processing, database, and spreadsheet programs, and utilities. There are thousands of other miscellaneous programs that may be needed for specific applications.

I will also talk a bit about EULA (end-user license agreement) in this chapter. EULA is one reason that Bill Gates has 100 billion dollars at this time.

Chapter 17   How Your Computer Can Help You

Some advantages/disadvantages of handhelds and laptops are discussed. Also discussed are networks, and some home office and small business applications.

Chapter 18   Computer Sound and Music

Here we'll discuss how music is digitized, along with how you can use your computer to make sounds and music.

Chapter 19   Component Sources

There are several places where you can buy the components you need. In the larger cities there may be several large computer discount stores, as well as several small stores who will have most of the components needed. In larger cities, there may also be frequent swap meets and trade shows where several vendors offer components.

I do a lot of my shopping from ads in computer magazines, and I've listed several, along with catalogs. In addition, of course, many sites on the Internet offer computer components.

Chapter 20   Troubleshooting and Repairing Your PC

You will need to know how computers operate in order to diagnose and fix any problems. Old pros may want to skip the beginning part of the chapter. The rest of the chapter offers a few basic troubleshooting tips to help you find and fix most problems.

Glossary

Definitions of many computer terms are provided.

BUILD YOUR OWN
PENTIUM III PC

CHAPTER 1

What's Inside

I know that many of you may still be hesitant about building your own computer. You shouldn't be. Computers are a lot like an erector set. They are made up of components that just plug together. This chapter will briefly discuss some of the major components. More detailed discussions will be found in subsequent chapters.

A Real Success Story

Just a few years ago, while still in college, a young man built his own computer. Several students asked him to build one for them. He hired some help, formed a company, and today is head of a multimillion-dollar company. His name is Michael Dell.

At that time, IBM, Compaq, and all the other large companies sold their computers through their distributors. Many of the distributors had large showrooms, lots of salespersons, and high overhead. To pay for the sales commissions and other overhead, a little bit was added to the price of the computer.

Michael Dell's company did not have any distributors or fancy showrooms. They sold directly to the purchaser through mail order. So they could sell a computer for less than IBM and the other large companies.

The large companies have finally taken note of this and are now selling direct also. This puts them in direct competition with their distributors. This has not made the hundreds of distributors too happy. Many of these distributors have begun to assemble what they call "white boxes," which are boxed computers with no brand name on them.

Ever since I built my first IBM clone in 1985, I have been preaching that the brand name on a computer does not guarantee that it will work any better than a clone. Usually all the brand name guarantees is that it will cost more.

Competition

Of course, the added competition is a fantastic plus for the consumer, since computer prices keep shrinking. However, one major essential component has not gone down in price: the operating system software. Because Microsoft has almost no competition, the price of Windows goes up each year. You may not see this cost if you buy a computer that has Windows preloaded. But for businesses that have to pay a license fee for each computer they own, it can be quite hefty.

How Much Can You Save?

I saved a real bundle when I built my first IBM compatible in 1985. But because of the competition and factors listed above, you may not be able to save much today. IBM, Compaq, and the other large companies can buy components for much less than what you and I have to pay for them. They buy in large quantities and get very good discounts. They get to enjoy the benefits of economies of scale.

However, just because you may not be able to save a large amount does not mean that you should not build your own computer. With judicious shopping, you should be able to beat the prices of even the companies who assemble white boxes. After all, they have to make a profit and pay the employee assemblers, and must contend with other overhead costs as well.

So even without the discounts and benefits of economies of scale, you should be able to save some money. But saving money may not be your biggest benefit. Even if you don't save any money, by assembling your own, you will know what is inside your computer. It will be a learning experience that is well worthwhile.

Here is an example of how much I saved in putting together a Pentium III 500MHz and an AMD 450MHz:

Pentium III 500MHz		AMD K6-III 450MHz	
Motherboard and CPU	$ 845	Motherboard and CPU	$ 286
Case and Power Supply	$ 150	Case and Power Supply	$ 59
DVD	$ 300	DVD	$ 249
Monitor Adapter	$ 150	Monitor Adapter	$ 100
20Gb Hard Drive	$ 400	20Gb Hard Drive	$ 295
128Mb DIMM Memory	$ 199	128Mb DIMM Memory	$ 100
LS120 Floppy Drive	$ 95	LS120 Floppy Drive	$ 75
Speakers and Sound	$ 150	Speakers and Sound	$ 100
Keyboard	$ 45	Keyboard	$ 30
Mouse	$ 35	Mouse	$ 20
Total	$2369	Total	$1314

One of the reasons the Pentium III costs more is because it is new and the manufacturers can sell all they can make. If I had waited for a few months, I could have saved a bit on building it. I would have put together an AMD 500MHz system, but this chip was not available when I built my system. I could now pull out the 450MHz and replace it with a 500MHz, but the extra speed is not all that important for my work. An assembled equivalent system from a vendor would have added $300 to $400 to the overall cost of each system.

What Should You Build?

The Pentium II, AMD K6, and Cyrix models are still good computers, and they are very inexpensive. However, in many ways they are obsolete. By the time you read this, few, if any, major manufacturers will still be assembling them. They will be assembling Pentium IIIs and AMD K6-IIIs or AMD Athlons.

If you have more time than money and can afford to wait a few extra microseconds for a program to run, you can probably get by with a Pentium II. You should be able to find some fantastic bargains at this time. (Just don't let your neighbors know that you using an obsolete computer.)

Tools You May Need

Whether you build your own or buy a ready-made system, you should have a few basic tools. You will need some small screwdrivers, such as a few different-sized flat-blade screwdrivers and Phillips screwdrivers. Most of the computer systems use Phillips-type screws. Some use a Phillips-type head with a slot so that you can use either Phillips or a flat blade. In addition, some systems use Phillips screws that also have a hexagonal head. You can use a ¼-inch nutdriver on these type screws, which makes installing or removing them very easy.

If the screwdrivers are magnetized, it will help you to get the screws started. (**Caution!** Be very careful not to let a magnetized screwdriver or any magnet near your floppy disks. A magnet can erase them or partially destroy the data.)

A pair of long-nose pliers is absolutely essential when you are installing the small jumper blocks that are used to configure the motherboard. Most motherboards can now be used with dozens of different CPUs, but they need to have small jumpers installed to allow you to configure them. To move the jumper blocks with your fingers would be almost impossible. If you don't have a pair of long-nose pliers, you can use a pair of tweezers.

Long-nose pliers are also very handy for retrieving dropped screws. In addition, the flat portion of the long-nose blades are excellent for straightening the pins on integrated circuit (IC) chips or pins on connectors. They may not be absolutely necessary, but you may need a pair of standard pliers.

A flashlight or a good bench light is essential for troubleshooting and exploring your computer. A good magnifying glass may also come in handy for reading the types and part numbers on some of the chips.

Keep in mind, however, that you may not need any tools at all. Many of the new cases are built so that the sides of the case just snap together. Just press a tab and they come apart. Components such as disk drives fit in assemblies that also snap together.

Major Computer Components

Before you start building a computer, you should know what the inside of one looks like. If you have never looked inside, it may seem a bit formidable. You will see several cables, plug-in boards, disk drives, and electronic components. Figure 1-1 can give you an idea of what the inside of a computer looks like.

If you have an older computer, just pull the cover off and take a look. Most computers will look pretty much the same, whether an old 286 or a powerful Pentium III. There will be a large motherboard with several slots that will have other boards plugged into the slots. You will see several cables and connections to the motherboard and to the plug-in boards.

Some of the cables will be from the power supply to the motherboard and to the disk drives. Some of the cables will be from the floppy disk drive, the hard disk drive, and the CD-ROM or DVD drive. The cables will be plugged into upright pins on the motherboard or on a board that is plugged into a slot on the motherboard.

Figure 1-1
Inside a computer.

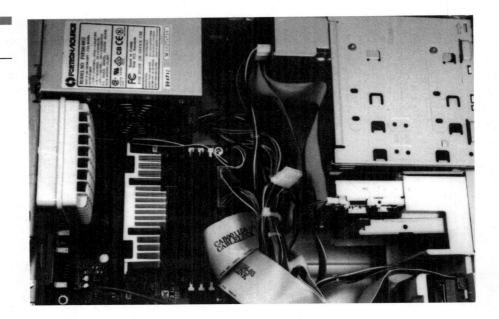

Minimum System Requirements

Here is a list of the major components needed for a minimum system. Later, you may also want to add several other components, such as one or two more hard drives, a network card, and several other goodies. But starting out with a minimum system is best.

Case and power supply

Motherboard with CPU and fan

Floppy drive

Hard drives

Keyboard

Mouse

Monitor and adapter board

Modem/fax board

CD-ROM drive

Sound card and speakers

Case and power supply

Optional Components

DVD-ROM drive

CD-R (CD-ROM-recordable drive)

Network adapter card

PC card slot

Digital camera adapter card

Peripheral components

Scanner

Digital camera

Printer

Speakers

USB products

Case and Power Supply

The power supply usually comes with the case. Most of the cases are fairly well standardized so that they will accommodate almost any motherboard. Before the advent of the Pentium II, the fan was mounted inside the power supply. Some of the systems now mount the fan outside the power supply. In addition, the fan is reversed. Older systems had the fan draw air from the front of the computer, pull it over the components, then exhaust it out the back of the case through a grill. The newer Pentium III systems have a separate fan that draws air in from the rear of the system and blows it over the CPU assembly, over the other components, and out the front grill of the case.

Because there is nothing inside them that can wear out, semiconductors and transistors should last for several lifetimes. They are, however, very susceptible to heat. Make sure they get as much cooling as possible. Heat is the enemy of semiconductors, so the CPU assembly has its own cooling fan.

The standard case is $6\frac{3}{4}$ inches wide. In order to accommodate the Pentium II CPU assemblies, some of the cases are $8\frac{5}{8}$ inches wide. Some of the Pentium III systems can be mounted in a standard case that is $6\frac{3}{4}$ inches wide. Most will be modified for the special fan that is needed.

The desktop-type case is still quite popular. Most desktop types are limited to three or four bays for mounting disk drives. If you want to install two hard disk drives, a 1.44MB floppy drive, and a CD-ROM drive, you will need one with at least four bays. At least two of the bays, those for the floppy disk and CD-ROM, should be accessible from the front.

Tower cases stand on one side. There are usually six screws on the back that hold the cover in place. On most tower cases, the front bezel has a groove that accepts the front part of the cover so that no screws are needed in the front.

Some cases are now built so that they do not need screws. They have catches and plastic devices that hold them together. Some of these do not even use screws to hold the disk drives in place.

The tower cases are very popular and handy, because they can sit on the floor and not use up any of your desktop space. The larger ones may have space for up to eight drive bays. This would provide room for up to four hard drives, a floppy, a tape backup, a couple of CD-ROM drives, and other items.

There are three sizes of tower-type cases: a mini tower for "baby sizes," a medium size for baby and standard sizes, and a large standard size. Tower cases are a bit more expensive than the standard- or the baby-sized cases.

The smaller sizes do not have as many bays for mounting drives. Most of the cases include a power supply with the cost. Make sure that any power supply is at least 200 watts; 300 watts is even better. When you buy a new case, it will come with several small bags of screws, stand-offs, cables, and other necessary mounting hardware. A case may cost from $40 to $100. Figure 1-2 shows some different-sized cases.

Figure 1-2
Some different-sized cases.

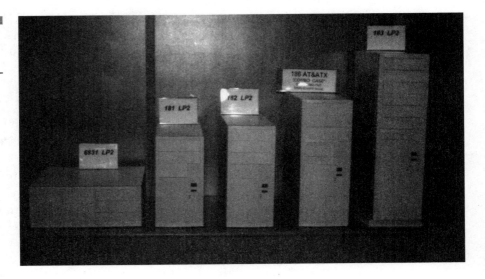

The Power Supply

If you have a desktop-type case, the power supply will be located in the right rear corner of the chassis. If you have a tower case, the power supply will be in the upper rear corner of the case. In either case, the power supply will have a metal cover around it. When your computer is running, except for your disk drives, the only noise you hear is the cooling fan in the power supply. On some systems, the cooling fan sucks air in from the front of the computer and forces it out through the grill in the back of the power supply. All holes in the computer and blank slots in the back panel should be covered so that the air is drawn only from the front grill of the computer and flows over the components. You should make sure that nothing in the front of the computer or the back of it impedes the airflow. The power supply usually has four screws on the back panel that holds it in place.

As mentioned, the newer ATX-type power supplies have a fan that is just the opposite of older systems. It pulls air in from the grill in back of the computer and forces it over the components and out the front grill.

Transforming the Voltage

Computer systems use direct current (DC). Original systems used DC voltages of 12VDC and 5VDC. The CPUs used 5 volts (5V). As more transistors were enclosed in the CPUs, the more current was used and the hotter the CPU became. Heat sinks and fans were used to keep the CPUs from burning up. The newer CPUs use a lower voltage such as 3V, 2.5V, or 2.2V. Because of the lower voltage, the total wattage is lowered, and the systems don't run quite as hot. But with the millions of transistors, they still need heat sinks and a special fan to keep them from burning up.

The voltage that is provided by the wall socket is usually 110V alternating current (AC). The computer power supply uses rectifiers and transformers to convert the AC voltage to the proper DC voltages. The motherboards have special circuits built in for providing the precise voltage and regulating it.

The AC voltage that comes from the wall plug is alternating at 60 cycles per second, or 60Hz. To transform 110V at 60Hz would require a large transformer. But a fairly small transformer can be used if the frequency is very high. Rectifiers can be used to transform the 60Hz AC voltage to a 120Hz chopped DC voltage. An oscillator circuit takes this 120Hz chopped voltage and changes the frequency to as high as 50,000Hz or more. The higher the frequency of the voltage, the smaller the transformer can be.

This high frequency is still 110V, which is much too high for our components. So the 110V is put through a small transformer that reduces it to the required 12V, 5V, and lesser voltages. Since the voltage that comes from the transformer is still AC voltage, it must be rectified and converted to DC voltage.

The 110V that is input into the power supply is the only voltage in your computer that might harm you. That is one reason for the cover over it. Another reason is to reduce any stray radiation that might emanate from the high-frequency conversion process.

Early IBMs and most clones had a switch on the side of the power supply for turning on the computer. This switch turned the AC on and off. Reaching around near the back of the computer to turn it on and off was a bit inconvenient, so most of the newer systems have a switch on the front panel. There is usually a four-wire electrical cord that goes from the power supply to the switch. Often when you buy a new case, this switch is not connected to the power cord. The switch will have four terminals for the power connection. The four power cords connect to the switch terminals with slip-on connectors. Two of the four wires in the power cord brings 110V volts from the wall socket to the switch; the other two return the switched voltage back to the power supply.

Care should be used in connecting the power to the switch. If it is not connected properly, it could cause a direct short across the power line. If you short the line out this way, you will see a lot of sparks, smoke, and maybe even a fire. You should get some documentation as to how the wires should be connected. In addition, the power supply may have a diagram showing how the switch should be connected.

Many of the newer ATX system motherboards have a "soft" power sense system built into them so the power can be turned on from the keyboard.

Power Strip

Because you will have your computer, a monitor, a printer, and perhaps three or four more units to be plugged into the wall outlet, you should buy a power strip that has at least five outlets. These strips usually have a circuit breaker in case of power overload. Some also have surge protection that can help protect your computer and the delicate electronics in it. Low-cost strips may cost as little as $5; others may cost $25 or more.

Power Distribution Panel

Even more convenient than a power strip is a power panel that is about 1 inch high and about the width and depth of a desktop computer case. Your computer or monitor can sit on top of it. I use a power panel that is about 15 inches square and has six individual lighted switches: one for the master input power, one for the computer, one for a monitor, one for a printer, and two for auxiliary devices. I can use the switches on the front of the panel to turn any of the devices on or off. It is very convenient and is rather inexpensive, at about $15.

Surge Protection

When large, heavy-duty electric motors and other electrical equipment is turned on, it sometimes creates a very high voltage spike in the nearby power lines. These surges can cause glitches and data corruption in your computer. A good surge protector can cause the spikes to be shunted to ground. Electrical storms can also cause surges in the power lines and telephone lines.

Some of the more-expensive power distribution panels have surge protection. Some also have sockets with surge protection for connecting a telephone line for a modem. If you are in an area where there are large, heavy-duty electric motors, they may send very high voltage surges through the line. These surges could severely damage your system. Surge protectors vary in quality. Some are very inexpensive but may not offer much protection. Many of the uninterruptible power supply (UPS) companies listed below also sell good-quality surge protectors.

The Need for Uninterruptible Power Supply

If you are working on data that is critical and you live in an area where there are a lot of electrical storms, power outages, or brownouts, you should install an uninterruptible power supply (UPS). When you are working on a file, it is loaded into random access memory (RAM). This memory is volatile; that is, if the power is interrupted, even for a brief fraction of a second, the RAM loses all of its memory. The data that is being worked on will disappear and be gone forever. A UPS can take over when the power is interrupted and keeps the computer running until it can be safely shut down.

Basically, the UPS is a battery that is kept charged up by the voltage from the wall socket. If there is an interruption of power, the electronic circuits immediately switch so that the battery supplies power to the computer.

Depending on the UPS model and the amount of wattage you are drawing from it, the UPS may be able to keep your system going for 10 to 15 minutes or more. This should give you plenty of time to close all your work and save it to disk. If you live in an area where there are electrical storms, then by all means you should have a good lightning rod installed as well. If a severe electrical storm occurs, even with a good lightning rod, you should turn off your computer and unplug it. Just one good bolt can zap your system and fry it to a crisp.

Figure 1-3 shows an uninterruptible power supply from American Power Conversion. This model is one of the better ones available. I live in the Los Angeles area, where lightning or thunderstorms are seldom a

Figure 1-3
An uninterruptible power supply.

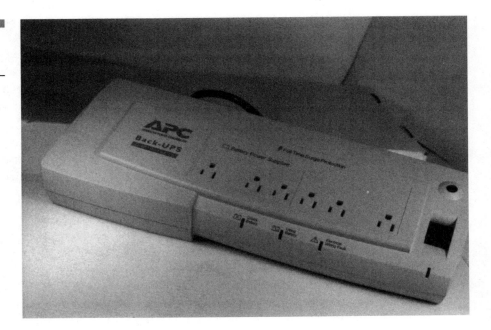

problem. However, we do have electrical problems once in a while. With my computer plugged into this unit, I never have to worry about losing data due to loss of power.

Several companies manufacture UPS systems. Following are just a few of them:

American Power Conversion
888 289-APCC
Ext. 8129
www.apcc.com

Best Power Technology
800 356-5794
http://bestpower.com

Deltec
800 854-2658
www.deltecpower.com

Exide Electronics
800 554-3448
www.exide.com/p-ups.htm

MGE UPS Systems
800-523-0142
www.mgeups.com

Tripp Lite
312 755-5400
http://tripplite.com

Visit their Web sites or call these companies for brochures and information.

Each of the companies listed above has several models to choose from. Basically, the different models will be designed for the amount of power or wattage that it will have to supply. In addition, some of the UPS systems, such as the one from American Power Conversion, may have several outlets so that you may not need a power strip. The expense of a UPS will be more than offset if it saves you even once from a disaster.

Motherboard

The large motherboard sits on the floor of the chassis of a desktop system or on the back of an upright tower case. There are usually eight slots on the motherboard for various types of plug-in boards. These usually include four or five Industry Standard Architecture (ISA)-type slots and three or four Peripheral Component Interconnect (PCI) slots.

Because they are much too slow for some of the newer faster systems, the older ISA-type boards are gradually being phased out. Eventually, the motherboard will have only PCI slots. Some of the boards that you may install in your computer include an adapter board for your monitor, a modem/fax board, a sound card, a network interface card (NIC), a SCSI adapter, and any of several others.

If you look at an ISA slot on a motherboard, you might notice that it is divided. The longer portion of the slot was the original standard 62-contact slot for 8-bit boards. When the 286 was developed, they added an additional 36-contact slot to the original for 16-bit boards. As you have probably deduced, an 8-bit plug-in board, even those designed for the antique XT, can also be used in the latest computer.

Each motherboard manufacturer tries to differentiate their product from the others. Basically, however, they are all the same, with just some slight differences among them. Of course, the type of CPU will be a determining factor in what motherboard you buy. Chapter 2 discusses motherboards in more detail.

Cost of Components

Again, with the exception of the motherboard and CPU, all of the PCs use the same basic components. Since the common components are all interchangeable, you can shop around for the best buys. You can peruse ads in computer magazines such as the *Computer Shopper*, *PC Magazine*, *PC World*, *PC Computing*, and others for an idea of what is available. These ads will also give you an idea of the cost of the various components and options. You can order the components through the mail, or if you live near a large city, you can find them at a swap meet or local store.

Putting a real cost on components is almost impossible. Prices change daily—usually in a downward direction. A few approximate costs are listed for comparison purposes. There are hundreds of different manufacturers and many, many options, so the prices will vary. Of course, brand names and the type of component will be a factor.

The cost of motherboards will vary widely depending on the brand name and manufacturer. The cost of the CPU will vary considerably depending on the operating frequency of the CPU: the higher the frequency, the higher the cost.

TABLE 1-1

Component Prices

Power supply and case	$35–150
Motherboard, no CPU	75–200
CPUs (AMD, Cyrix, Intel)	75–700
Monitor	200–1200
Monitor adapter	40–400
Memory, 32MB–64MB	75–150
Floppy drive, 1.4MB	25–50
Floppy drive, 120MB	75–100
Hard drive, 2GB–20GB	75–500
CD-ROM drive	50–100
DVD ROM	200–600
Keyboard	20–100
Mouse	10–60
Modem	50–100
Total	$1005–4410

Table 1-1 lists approximate prices of some common components. These prices are listed to give you an idea of what a basic system might cost at the time this is being written. Again, keep in mind that the prices will have changed, usually downward, by the time you read this.

As you can see, there can be quite a large variation in the cost. The cost will depend on several available options and whether the components are well-known brand names. There is also a large variation in cost from dealer to dealer. Some high-volume dealers may charge less than the smaller ones, so it will pay you to shop around a bit and compare prices.

Low-Cost Systems—White Boxes

You may see some systems advertised for $499, which is a fantastic price. Some dealers can afford low prices because they can get a large discount when buying in huge quantities. That is one of the advantages that some dealers will have over you. Because you are only buying in small quantities, you won't be able to get any discounts.

However, if you see an ad for a system at a very low price, be sure to read the ad very closely. Some low-cost systems are advertised without a monitor. The dealer may also cut corners in the capacity of the hard disk, the memory, and the quality of the components.

You won't see many brand-name systems being advertised for less than $500 at this time. (But they could be available by the time you read this.) Many dealers have begun to assemble no-name systems that are often shipped in white boxes with no brand name on them.

Buying rather than building one of these systems may be a good alternative if you don't have a lot of money. It may be a way to get started. You can always upgrade later and add whatever goodies you want.

The component cost figures listed above are only rough approximations. The market is so volatile that the prices can change overnight. If you are buying through the mail, you might even call or check out the advertised prices before ordering. Often the advertisements have to be made up one or two months before the magazine is published, so the prices could have changed considerably.

At one time, Intel was the only manufacturer of the x86-type CPUs. Now, however, Cyrix, AMD, IDT, and Rise Technology have x86 CPU clones on the market. Clone CPUs are equivalent to some of the Intel chips but usually sell for about 25 percent less than the Intel chips. This competition has forced the CPU prices down. When the CPU prices go down, the system prices usually go down as well. Chapter 3 discusses CPUs in more detail.

Memory

When a computer runs a program, the program is temporarily loaded into memory and processed there. When the processing is completed, it is then loaded back on the hard disk, printed out, or sent to wherever you want it to go.

At one time we got by with as little as 64KB of RAM memory. It is now difficult to run most programs with less than 32MB of RAM. Better yet is 64MB or 128MB. You can always start out with 32MB and add more later. You can never have too much memory.

On older systems, the memory chips were usually located in the left front quadrant of the motherboard. They used dual in-line package-type (DIP) chips. Chips to make 640KB used about one-fourth of the entire motherboard real estate.

Most systems today use single in-line memory module (SIMM) or dual in-line memory module (DIMM) type memory. These are small boards that have miniature chips on them. The board has an edge connector that plugs into special sockets on the motherboard. The SIMM and DIMM technologies allow up to 512MB or more memory in an area smaller than the 640KB required on the older motherboards that used DIP chips.

Chapter 4 goes into detail about the many types of memory.

Floppy Disk Drives

At one time an IBM 360KB floppy drive cost over $400. Today they are completely obsolete. You may still have some data on 360KB and 1.2MB floppies. If you insist on keeping these floppies, I recommend that you buy a 5¼-inch 1.2MB and a 3½-inch 1.44MB combination drive. The 1.2MB drive will read and write to both the 360KB and 1.2MB floppies. You may even have some old 3½-inch 720KB floppies with data on them. The 1.44MB drive will read and write to the 720KB, as well as to the 1.44MB.

Floppy drives have come a long way since the early days. One of the most popular floppy drives today can read and write to the 720KB and 1.44MB 3½-inch floppies, as well as to special formatted 120MB 3½-inch disks. The Sony Corporation has also developed a 200MB 3½-inch floppy drive.

See Chapter 5 for more details on floppy drives.

Hard Disk Drives

Most older systems used the MFM-, RLL-, or ESDI-type hard drives. They were physically large, clunky, and slow. They were also very limited in storage capacity.

One of my early hard disk drives was 40MB. It was 3 inches high, 6 inches wide, and 8 inches long. I paid almost $1000 for it ($1000 back then would be worth about $3000 today). Since DOS 2.0 could only handle 32MB, I had to buy special software in order to use the full 40MB. Then in 1995 I bought a 1.050-GB (gigabyte) drive for $740. It was 1 inch high, 4 inches wide, and 6 inches long. I can buy a 10.2GB drive today for less than $200.

There are several hard disk manufacturers with hundreds of different models, sizes, and types of hard disks. The older hard drives needed a controller board that plugs into one of the slots. Often companies other than the ones who manufactured the hard drives made the controllers. In those days, the disk controllers often cost almost as much as the hard drives.

Today, the integrated disk electronics (IDE) drives have all of the controller electronics on the drive itself. They still need an interface to the system, however. Older systems used a low-cost interface that plugged into one of the slots. This interface is now built in on most all motherboards as upright pins that accept the hard drive cable. In fact, most of them now have two sets of pins and can handle up to four IDE hard drives or a combination of hard drives and CD-ROM drives.

The Small Computer System Interface (SCSI, pronounced "scuzzy") also has all of its controller functions on the disk. It also needs an interface card, but a SCSI card can handle up to seven different devices. Installing an IDE hard drive and a SCSI hard drive is a good idea. One advantage of this type of system is that you can use the two drives to back up each other. It is possible that one of the drives may crash or fail, but not very likely that both will fail.

For your new computer, I recommend that you install at least a 6.8GB hard drive, or an even larger one if you can afford it. Most hard disk manufacturers are no longer manufacturing hard disk drives with a capacity less than 1GB.

See Chapter 6 for more details on hard drives.

Backup

Keeping copies or backups of all of your software programs and important or critical data is imperative. You never know when your hard disk may crash or have a failure. You can lose very important data a thousand different ways, so you should always have a current backup. There are many methods of backup; some use hardware and some require special software programs. See Chapter 7 for more details.

CD-ROM Drives

Your computer is not complete without a CD-ROM drive. Much of the available software now comes on CD-ROM. You cannot load Windows 95 or Windows 98 into your system without a CD-ROM drive.

An ideal system would be a CD-recorder drive and a DVD drive. Both of these drives will read standard CD-ROM disks and even audio CDs.

CD-ROM drives are discussed in more detail in Chapter 8.

Monitors

A large variety of monitors are available. You can buy a fairly good color monitor for about $250. Of course, a large screen, very high resolution monitor will cost more. The type of monitor you buy should match whatever you are using your computer for. If you are doing a lot of high-end graphics or computer-aided design (CAD), you need a large screen with high resolution.

A short time ago, the thin-film transistor (TFT) panels, such as those used in the better laptop computers, were very expensive. They are now fairly reasonable. These flat-panel thin monitors take up very little desk space. Eventually, they will replace the old CRT-type monitors.

Monitor Adapter

You will need a plug-in adapter board to drive the monitor. (Some motherboards have built-in adapters.) For standard VGA color you should be able to buy one for about $40. For very high resolution color, it may cost up to $500. Most of the newer systems have an Accelerated Graphics Port (AGP). This AGP slot accepts the new high-speed graphics boards that are replacing older monitor adapters.

See Chapter 9 for more details on monitors and adapters.

Keyboards

The keyboard cable is plugged into a connector that is mounted on the back of the motherboard and is accessible on the back panel. Because it is the main device for communicating with the computer, the keyboard is a very important component. Many brands of keyboards are available. Most of them have slight differences in the placement of the keys and the tactile feel, and many have special adjuncts such as trackballs, calculators, and keypads.

In addition to keyboards, to run Windows and other graphical user interface (GUI) programs, a mouse, trackball, or other pointing device is essential. Chapter 10 discusses keyboards and other input devices in detail.

Modems, FAX Devices, and Communications

With online services, you can use your computer to communicate with millions of other computers. You can download software from bulletin boards or send a low-cost FAX to millions of other FAX sites.

You will definitely need some communications hardware and software if you want to get the most from your computer. We discuss communications in Chapter 11.

Upgrading an Older System

You can save a lot of money by upgrading an older system. In most cases, you can use most of your older components. See Chapter 12 for more details.

System Assembly

After you have read all the chapters about the components and purchased the components, it is time to assemble them. Chapter 13 covers system assembly in detail.

USB Components

Most newer motherboards have a USB (universal serial bus) port. There are now dozens of USB components and products. They will be discussed in Chapter 2.

Printers

Your system is incomplete without a printer. Hundreds of different types and models are available. You will have lots of options when buying your printer. Types of printers include dot-matrix, lasers, ink-jets, and many others. Because some types are better for a particular application than others, your decision will depend on what you want to do with your computer and how much you want to spend.

Chapter 15 discusses the various types of printers.

The Internet

In just a few short years, the Internet has become one of the most important tools that we have today. It is a communications tool, an information tool, a tool for fun and entertainment, a business tool, a tool for learning, and it has a host of other uses. If for no other reason, you should have a computer for access to the Internet.

The Internet is discussed in Chapter 14.

Other Peripheral Components

Besides the components inside your computer case, you will need some peripheral components. We already listed the printer and the monitor. In addition, there are several common components that are not absolutely necessary for a system. If you don't need a lot of goodies at this time, you can buy the minimum components and add to your system later.

An external fax machine is essential for most businesses. A scanner is also necessary for most businesses and can be great for home use. You can get by without a sound card and speakers, but you would be missing out on an excellent reason to have a computer.

Software

You will also need software for your computer. Before you even turn it on, you will need operating software such as Windows 95, or 98.

Windows 2000 may be available by the time you read this. There are billions of dollars worth of off-the-shelf software that you can use. Some of the commercial programs may be a bit expensive. In lieu of these are inexpensive public-domain and shareware programs that can do just about everything the commercial programs do.

See Chapter 16 for more about software.

Some Applications

Hundreds of applications are available for the Pentium III computer, many ideal for both large businesses or for a small office/home office (SOHO). Some of the applications are listed in Chapter 17.

Other Ways Your Computer Can Help You

Your computer is extraordinarily versatile. Many boards and components are available so that you can configure it almost any way you want. See Chapter 17 for more on this topic.

Sound and Music

The computer is a fantastic tool for creating music or for just listening to it. Sound is also necessary for several computer applications. Sound is discussed in more detail in Chapter 19.

Sources

You need to know, of course, where to buy all of the components that you need to upgrade or repair your PC. If you live near a large city, there are probably local stores who sell the parts. The local vendors and computer stores will be most happy to help you. They may charge a bit more than a mail-order house, but if anything goes wrong, they will usually be very quick to help you or make it right.

In addition, in most large cities, there are frequent computer swaps. A computer swap is just a gathering of local vendors at a fairgrounds, stadium, or some other area. They usually set up booths and tables and present their wares. You can usually find all that you need at these meets. You can go from booth to booth and compare the components and prices. The prices are usually very competitive, and you may even be able to haggle a bit with the vendors.

The other good source for components is through mail order. Just check the ads in any computer magazine. Although at one time mail order could be a bit risky, it is very safe today.

If a price seems too good to be true, then the vendor has probably cut a few corners somewhere. There are some very good bargains out there, but you should be careful. Your best protection is to be fairly knowledge-able about the computer business. Computer magazines, along with books like the one you are holding, are some of the better sources for this knowledge.

Another excellent source of knowledge and help is local computer user groups. If you live near a large city, there will probably be several groups. Most of the people in these groups are very friendly and anxious to help you with any problem.

If you are fairly new to computing, be sure to read the chapters on floppy disk drives, hard disk drives, monitors, keyboards, and the major components before you buy your parts. Billions of dollars worth of products are available. Many of them are very similar in functionality and quality. What you buy should depend primarily on what you want your computer to do and how much you can afford to spend. If you are knowl-edgeable and you shop wisely, you can save a bundle.

Chapter 19 discusses the many sources and lists several magazines.

Troubleshooting

Computers are actually dumb machines. In most cases, there is only one way to do something right, but there may be thousands of ways that it can be done wrong. No book could cover all the possible things that can go wrong. However, there are a few things that can be done to find and fix most of the common problems.

Chapter 20 goes into detail about troubleshooting.

How Computers Work

This section is very basic. If you are an old pro, you may want to skip ahead. If you are a beginner, this may answer a lot of your questions as to how a computer works.

A computer is made up of circuits and boards that have resistors, capacitors, inductors, transistors, motors, and many other components. These components perform a useful function when electricity passes through them. The circuits are designed so that the paths of the electric currents are divided, controlled, and shunted to do the work that we want done. The transistors and other components can force the electrons to go to the memory, to a disk drive, to the printer, or wherever the software and hardware direct it to go.

Computers are possible only because of our ability to control voltages. We control small voltages, usually direct current voltages, by turning them on or off. So when the voltage is on, it can represent a 1; when it is off, it is a 0. With these two digits we can digitize a world of things, such as drawings, photos, movies, sound, speech, music, and virtual reality. In addition, once these objects are digitized we can compress them, add to them, delete portions, or manipulate them in hundreds of ways.

In fact, determining reality from virtual reality can sometimes be difficult. A good example was Forrest Gump having a conversation with JFK, who has been dead for several years. Since that movie, several others have been made, along with commercials that use long-deceased people (perhaps because they don't have to pay them any fees and residuals).

A short time ago, we couldn't do many of the things that we take for granted today; we just didn't have the computer power.

Computers and Electricity

Computers are possible because of electricity. Under the control of software and hardware, small electric on/off signal voltages are formed when we type from the keyboard. The absence or presence of magnetic bits on a hard or floppy disk can be detected and represented as on or off voltages. The small pits and lands on a CD-ROM disk can also be detected and represented as on or off voltages. The data sent or received over a telephone line from a fax or modem are just bits of on and off voltages. These on and off voltages are used to turn transistors on or off.

An electric charge is formed when there is an imbalance or an excess amount of electrons at one pole. Much like water flowing downhill to find its level, the excess electrons will flow through whatever path they can find to get to the other pole. Electricity is the lifeblood of a computer. Under the control of the software and hardware, small voltage signals are sent to different areas of the computer to accomplish the various tasks.

We cannot see electricity. We can only see the effects of it. And, of course, we can feel it. If it is a fairly high voltage, it can knock you on your fanny or even kill you.

All matter is made up of atoms. Atoms are made up of a nucleus that contains a given number of protons and neutrons, along with several electrons in orbits around the nucleus. The number of protons, neutrons, and electrons in the atom will depend on what the substance is. Ordinarily, the number of electrons in orbit around a nucleus balances the protons and neutrons in the nucleus. But electrons can be displaced from the orbits of some substances. When this happens, there is an imbalance. Just as water will seek its own level, an atom that is imbalanced will try to regain its balance.

Count Alessandro Volta of Italy (1745–1827) developed the first battery. We have improved batteries considerably since then, but they still use the same basic principle. We have also developed electric generators. We can use batteries and generators to create an imbalance of electrons. Batteries and other electric sources have two electrodes: a positive and a negative, or ground. The negative pole will have an excess of electrons. If we provide a path with no resistance between the electrodes, the excess electrons will rush through the path at almost the speed of light to get to the positive pole.

Most electric or electronic paths have varying amounts of resistance so that work or heat is created when the electrons pass through them. For instance, if a flashlight is turned on, electrons will pass through the bulb, which has a resistive filament. The heat generated by the electrons passing through the bulb will cause the filament to glow red-hot and create light. If the light is left on for a period of time, the excess electrons from the negative pole of the battery will pass through the bulb to the positive pole of the battery. Electrons will continue to flow until the amount of electrons at the negative and positive poles are equal. At this time there will be a perfect balance, and the battery will be dead. When a motor is placed in the path between the electrodes, the flow of electrons through the coils of wire around the rotor will create a magnetic force that will cause the rotor to spin.

Soon after the battery was developed, Georg Simon Ohm (1789–1854) discovered that there was a direct relationship between the amount of voltage, the resistance of the path, and the number of electrons passing through the path. Resistance (R) is equal to the voltage (E) divided by the current (I). This is known as Ohm's Law. Using Ohm's Law, if we know any two values, we can determine the other one. Electrons moving through a circuit can be measured in units called *amperes*. The ampere is a very large number of electrons that pass a given point in a given amount of time. It was named for French mathematician Andre Marie Ampere (1775–1836).

When presented with two or more resistive paths, the electricity obeys Ohm's Law exactly. Using Ohm's Law, circuits can be designed in thousands of ways to make electricity work for us by controlling and directing it to where we want it to go. We can control voltage with switches, transistors, resistors, capacitors, inductive coils, transformers, and various other electronic components.

Transistors and Computers

The first and foremost reason that we have computers today is because we have transistors. Three scientists working in the Bell Labs in the late 1940s discovered the transistor effect. The scientists, William Shockley, John Bardeen, and Walter Brattain, were awarded a Nobel Prize in 1956. (I believe that the importance of the discovery and development of the transistor should rank right up there alongside the discovery of the wheel and fire.)

A very basic computer, the Electronic Numerical Integrator and Computer (ENIAC), was developed in the early 1940s. There were no transistors in those days, so the computer used thousands of vacuum tubes and cost millions of dollars. It took several large rooms to house one of these computers. ENIAC was used during World War II to calculate cannon trajectories. It took 30 to 40 hours for hand calculations for each trajectory, but the new computer could do it in 30 seconds. This precursor could perform fewer functions than a present-day $2 calculator. Computers now can do the same trajectory calculations in about 30 billionths of a second, or 30 nanoseconds.

Technology made a quantum leap forward when the transistor was invented. So how do we get those transistors to work for us? We use software that instructs the computer to turn the transistors on and off to perform the various tasks. Although most software is something that is written, when it is typed into the computer from a keyboard, each time a key is depressed, it generates electrical pulses that turn the transistors on and off. When the software is loaded in from a disk, the magnetic flux of the disk is converted to electrical pulses that are identical to those created by the keyboard. The end result of all software applications, no matter how it is input into the computer, is to cause the generation of on and off voltages that control the transistors. Ordinarily, the more complex the software and the more transistors available, the more work that a computer can accomplish.

The transistor can act as a switch. It has three basic elements: the collector, the base, and the emitter. Suppose the collector of this transistor is connected to the positive pole of a 6V battery and the emitter is connected to the negative pole. No voltage or electrons will pass through the transistor. But if we connect a small voltage, as little as a millionth of a volt on the base of the transistor, it can act like a switch and allow a large number of electrons to flow through the transistor and anything that is connected between its collector and the battery. So a very small voltage on the base of a transistor can cause it to switch a much larger voltage on or off.

The transistor can also act as an amplifier. If the small voltage signal on the base of the transistor goes up gradually, then goes down, the transistor can cause a large voltage to go up and down in an exact replica of the input signal. When a radio or TV station broadcasts its signal, it throws a high voltage out into the air. By the time it gets to your radio or TV, it might only be a millionth of a volt. Using transistors, this voltage can be amplified in an exact replica of the original voltage signal so that it is strong enough to power a loudspeaker or to drive a 25,000V electron gun in a TV set.

The picture tube or cathode ray tube (CRT) of a TV or computer monitor is similar to a vacuum tube. Figure 1-4 is a diagram of an old-fashioned vacuum tube circuit and a transistor circuit. The transistor circuit can be thousands of times smaller and use only a fraction of the energy needed for the vacuum tube. The radio and TV voltages vary up and down and are called *analog voltages*. Figure 1-5 is a diagram of square waves and analog sine waves.

Computers use millions of transistors. The main chip or brain of a computer is the central processing unit (CPU). In addition to the CPU, there are several other chips and components on the motherboard with many more thousands of transistors.

The transistors in the CPU, those on the motherboard and those on the various plug-in boards and peripherals, all respond to signals or voltages that are fed to them from sources such as the keyboard, floppy

Figure 1-4
Vacuum tube and
transistor circuits.

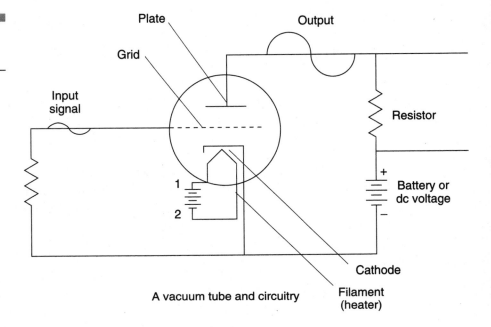

A vacuum tube and circuitry

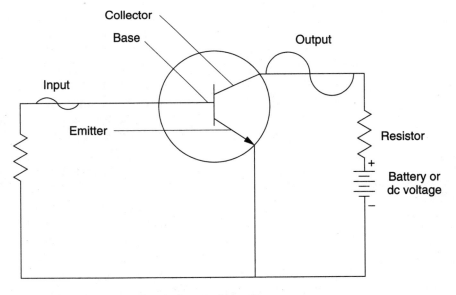

A transistor and circuitry

disk drives, hard disk drives, modems, scanners, or any of several other
input devices. The voltages used by computers are digital voltages that
have two states: off or on. If we have two switches or two transistors, we
can have four different states as follows: #1 off and #2 off, #1 on and #2
off, #1 off and #2 on, or #1 on and #2 on. If we have four transistors, we

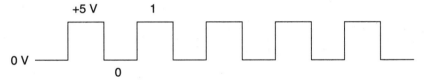

Figure 1-5
Square waves and
analog sine waves.

+5 V   1

0 V

0

Square waves representing 0s and 1s

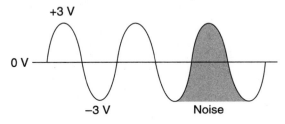

Analog voltage

can have 16 different states. If we double the amount of transistors to 8, which would be 2 to the power of 8 (2^8), we can have 256 different states. If we double the number to 16 (2^16) we can have 65536 different states. The different number of states goes up by the power of 2 with each additional transistor or switch. With 32 transistors, 4,294,967,296 different signals can be produced.

Computers work with 1s and 0s, or bits. (*Bit* is a contraction of *binary digit*.) It takes 8 bits to make 1 byte. It takes 8 bits or 1 byte to represent one letter of the alphabet or a single number. For certain digital states, we can assign a number or a letter of the alphabet. In our decimal system, we assign values to wherever the numeral happens to be. For instance, in the number 321, the 3 is in the hundred place, the 2 is in the ten place, and the 1 is in the one place. In the digital system, each place also has a value, but it works a bit differently than the decimal system. The right column is 1, the next is 2, the next is 4, then 8, then 16, 32, 64, 128, 256, and so on. Note that each new column toward the left doubles. Here is what the output of four different switches or transistors would look like:

0000 = 0 = all off

0001 = 1 (the 1 place)

0010 = 2 (the 2 place)

0011 = 3 (the 2 place + 1)

0100 = 4 (the 4 place)

0101 = 5 (the 4 place + 1)

0110 = 6 (the 4 place + 2)

0111 = 7 (the 4 place + 2 + 1)

1000 = 8 (the 8 place)

1001 = 9 (the 8 place + 1)

1010 = 10 (the 8 place + 2)

1011 = 11 (the 8 place + 2 + 1)

1100 = 12 (the 8 place + 4)

1101 = 13 (the 8 place + 4 + 1)

1110 = 14 (the 8 place + 4 + 2)

1111 = 15 (the 8 place + 4 + 2 + 1)

The ASCII Code

When the Teletype was developed, they used the digital system to devise a code so that messages could be sent over telephone wires. This was called the *American Standard Code for Information Interchange* (ASCII), pronounced "asskee." The original code was 128 different characters, which included all of the characters found on a typewriter keyboard, including punctuation and spaces.

If the letter A was typed on a Teletype keyboard, it would cause a voltage to be turned on and off to produce 100001, equivalent to decimal 65, to be sent over the Teletype wire. If a Teletype machine in another city was connected to this Teletype, the letter A would be typed out. If a B were typed, the signal 100020, or 66, would be produced. (The fourth place to the left is 16, the fifth is 32, and the sixth is 64, or 2^4, 2^5, and 2^6.)

This 128-character code worked very well for several years. Later, the ASCII code was extended by an additional 128 characters and symbols for a total of 256 or 2^8. The extended ASCII code uses smiling faces, playing card symbols, Greek letters, and several other symbols. If you would like to see what some of these symbols look like, at the DOS prompt, use the command TYPE to type out any command that has a .EXE or .COM extension. For instance, at the DOS prompt, type TYPE COMMAND.COM.

Software

If you type an A on a computer keyboard, like the Teletype, it causes a digital voltage to be created equivalent to 1000001 or 65 decimal. This would cause certain transistors inside the computer to be turned on or off and the A character would be displayed, stored, printed, or whatever the software told it to do.

Inputs

The computer keyboard creates digital voltages for each key that is typed. But there are other ways to input data to a computer. The floppy and hard disks have a magnetic coating very similar to the tape in a tape recorder. A small voltage is created when the data is read by the head. This voltage is then amplified and routed to wherever the software tells it to go.

We can also have inputs from such things as a mouse, a modem, a scanner, or a network. They all produce a digital voltage that is used by the software and hardware to accomplish a task. If an electronic circuit is designed properly, it should last several lifetimes. There is nothing in a semiconductor or transistor to wear out. But occasionally, too many electrons may find their way through a weakened component and cause it to heat up and burn out. Or for some reason the electrons may be shunted through a path or component where it shouldn't go. This may cause an intermittent, a partial, or a complete failure.

System Clock

The computer has a real-time clock and calendar that keeps track of the date and the time. But the computer also has a system clock that is much more precise than the real-time clock. Everything that a computer does is precisely timed. Crystal oscillators control the timing. The computer carries out each instruction in a certain number of clock cycles. On the early XT system, the clock operated at 4.77 million hertz (megahertz, abbreviated MHz), or cycles, per second. Even so, it often took several clock cycles, moving 8 bits at a time, to perform a single instruction. At this writing, the Pentium III can operate as fast as 550MHz and process several instructions per cycle. Eventually, CPUs will operate as high as 1GHz.

The foregoing material is rather simplified, but it may help you understand what is happening inside your computer.

Moore's Law

Several years ago, the then chairman of Intel Corporation, Gordon Moore, studied the microprocessor industry and noticed a very definite trend. He observed that the 286 had 125,000 transistors, more than three times the 29,000 in the XT. Very soon the 386 was introduced with 275,000 transistors, which more than doubled the 286. Soon afterward, the 486 with 1.2 million transistors was developed, followed by the Pentium with 3.1 million, and then the Pentium Pro with 5.5 million. The Pentium III has over 10 million transistors. The trend is that every 18 months or so, the number of transistors and computing power more than doubles. This trend has become so predictable that it is now known as Moore's Law. Intel said at one time that they would eventually have microprocessors with 100 million transistors. According to Moore's Law, it will only take another three or four generations to reach that level, which should occur sometime within the next five or six years.

So go ahead and build your computer to the very latest and enjoy the power and speed it can deliver. However, you should know that within a very short time your wonderful machine will be obsolete again. But not to worry. With this book you will learn how to deal with obsolescence by upgrading your computer.

2

The Motherboard

The motherboard is the largest and most important board in your system. It includes the central processing unit (CPU), all of the other chips and electronics, and slots for plug-in boards that make computing possible. Besides the CPU, the other very important chip on the motherboard is the chipset. The chipset will determine the kind of CPU, the frequency, and several other things that are used with the motherboard.

If you have an old system, you can upgrade to a Pentium III (PIII) class machine by replacing the motherboard. It is one of the easiest upgrades that you can make and can give you most of the benefits of a new system at a fairly reasonable cost. Figure 2-1 shows a Socket 7-type motherboard that can accept the AMD K6, Cyrix 6x86MX, or IDT C6 CPUs, as well as Pentium CPUs (but not the Pentium II or III CPUs).

Figure 2-1
A motherboard with a Socket 7. It has an AMD CPU installed in the upper left-hand corner.

If you are building a system from scratch, then the motherboard will be high on your list of components to buy. If you are upgrading an older system, the motherboard will also be one of the most important components on your shopping list.

When purchasing a motherboard, keep in mind that not all motherboards are created equal; there are hundreds of variations. Since most all vendors now have Web sites, before you buy a motherboard, you can log on to the particular vendor's site and check out the specifications.

The ATX Motherboard and Power Supply

Most of the cooling in a computer is from a small fan in the power supply. As mentioned in Chapter 1, the original power supply drew air in from the front grill and pulled it over the components. The newer ATX power supply draws air in from the back and blows it over the components. The power supply has a socket that can only be connected to a motherboard with an ATX socket. Figure 2-2 shows an ATX power connector for the motherboard. If you buy a motherboard for the Pentium class machines, be sure to check the power supply connector. Some of them still use the original connector, but most of the later models use the ATX socket. Figure 2-3 shows a motherboard with both connectors. All of the Pentium III motherboards now use the ATX socket.

The original power supply had two connectors with six wires each for

Figure 2-2
An ATX power
connector for the
motherboard.

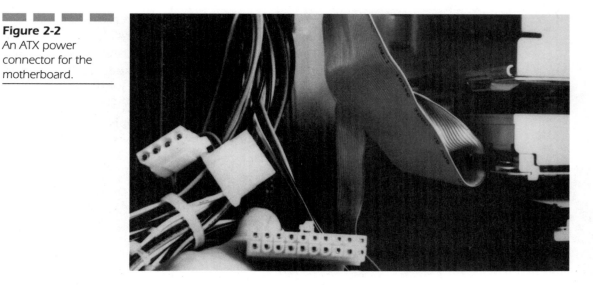

Figure 2-3
An older Socket 7
motherboard. The
two white connectors
in the lower left
corner are for both
ATX and old-style
power connectors.

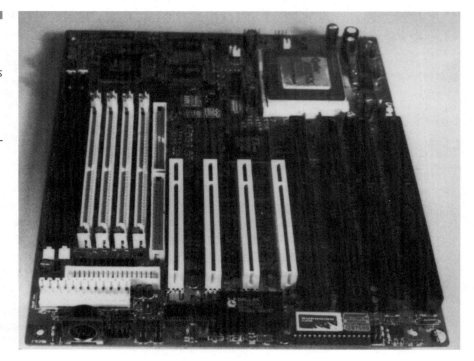

the inline motherboard socket. The power connectors plugged in side-by-side into the motherboard socket. If one was not careful, it was possible to plug them in backwards or improperly. This could be disastrous and ruin the motherboard. When properly plugged in, the four black ground wires should be in the center of the socket. If you have one of the old standard connectors, when the two halves are plugged in, the four black wires should be in the center. The ATX power supply has a connector that can only be plugged in properly to the motherboard socket.

If your new motherboard has an ATX socket, you can buy an ATX power supply for about $30 to $40. However, it would be better to buy a new case with the power supply already mounted for $60 to $70. The original systems power supply had an output of −5V, +5V, −12V, and +12V. The new ATX system has added 3.3V for the newer CPUs.

Soft Power

In older systems, an on/off switch was provided either on the front panel or on the side of the case. This switch has the incoming 110V to the power supply. The 110V goes directly to the power supply on the ATX systems. These power-supply systems provide Power_On and 5V_Standby signals. Power_On is a signal that Windows 95 and NT can use to power the system on or off. An option allows the keyboard to use these signals to power up or down. The low-current 5V_Standby signal is present at all times, even when the main system is powered down.

Motherboard Variations

Some motherboard manufacturers are building in several goodies such as sound, video, universal serial bus (USB), and SCSI. This integration saves precious slots and even the bit of money that it would cost for plug-in boards. Figure 2-4 shows the rear of my Pentium III motherboard with the small, round PS/2-type connectors for mouse and keyboard, two USB connectors, the parallel port for the printer, two serial port connectors, a joystick connector, and the sound connectors.

One reason for using the PS/2 connector for the mouse is that it saves having to use one of your two COM ports. However, a PS/2 mouse still uses one of the precious IRQs (interrupt requests). The PS/2 keyboard

Figure 2-4
A Pentium III mother-
board shows the
connectors for
mouse, keyboard,
printer, USB, serial
connectors, sound,
and joystick.

and mouse connectors may be side-by-side or stacked one on the other.
The mouse or keyboard can be plugged into either connector. Most of the
newer motherboards have a PS/2-type keyboard and mouse connector.
That means that you can't use an older standard keyboard and mouse
without an adapter. Several cable companies provide adapters that will
let you use the old keyboard and mouse. The adapters cost about $5
each. Not bad; but finding a vendor and ordering the parts takes time
and effort. It may be especially frustrating if you have ordered a motherboard through the mail, hoping to use it right away, but then find that
you either have to buy a new mouse and keyboard or some adapters.
Figure 2-5 shows a standard keyboard-to-PS/2 adapter on the right,
alongside two PS/2 connectors.

■■■ ■■ ■■ ■■

Figure 2-5
A standard keyboard-
to-PS/2 adapter on
the right, alongside
two PS/2-type
connectors.

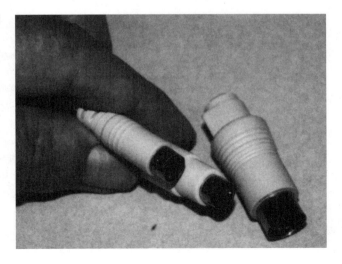

Most of the Pentium III and Super7 Socket motherboards now have USB connectors. This bus is simple to configure and will handle up to 127 devices. Although it will be the new standard, at this time, there are not many components available that can use the USB. However, more and more are being introduced every day.

Many local computer stores will have the adapters and cables that you need. But ordering by mail is often easier than going downtown and looking for something like this. Here are a few companies who can send you adapters for the PS/2 connectors and the USB cables and connectors:

ASP   800-445-6190

Belkin   310-898-1100

Cables to Go   800-826-7904

Monster Cable   415-871-6000

Primax Cables to Go   800-826-4000

QVS   313-641-6700

Jumpers

At one time there weren't many CPUs, and there were very few differences in the frequencies of the CPUs. Therefore, each CPU had a separate motherboard. In fact, some early motherboards actually came with the CPU soldered in place.

But now we have dozens and dozens of different CPUs, different frequencies, different voltages, and several other options. Rather than designing a motherboard for each type of CPU, most manufacturers now design their motherboards to accept a large number of different CPUs.

To configure the motherboard to accept a certain CPU type, jumpers and switches are used. A *jumper* is a small shorting bar that connects upright pins on the motherboard. If the CPU requires a certain voltage, it can be selected by the jumper system. The frequency can also be selected by jumpers. There are dozens of ways to configure the motherboard by use of jumpers. Figure 3-3 in the next chapter shows some jumpers. Some newer motherboards, such as those from ABIT (www.abit.com) have jumperless CPU settings.

DRAM Bus Frequency

When a program is run, it is loaded into the system memory, usually dynamic random access memory (DRAM). In order to process the program, the CPU does a lot of communicating with the DRAM. It does this over a special bus, called the *front side bus,* FSB. The bus frequency is usually a fraction of the internal frequency of the CPU. Until a short time ago, CPUs communicated over a 66MHz bus to go to and from the memory. Some systems, such as the Pentium 266 and Celeron, still use the 66MHz bus, but newer and faster CPUs now use a 100MHz FSB. So a Celeron 466MHz might not be as fast as a Pentium III at 450MHz.

PC-133

Several manufacturers have proposed a PC-133 motherboard bus standard. This would allow the PCI bus to memory and other peripherals to operate at 133MHz. The PC-133 standard will allow systems with 133MHz main memory, as compared to the current 100MHz standard. But Intel is committed to the much faster Direct Rambus Dynamic Random Access Memory (RDRAM) technology. However, there have been several problems getting the RDRAM to market. Many of the vendors don't want to wait. They want to adopt the PC-133 in the interim.

The PC-133 was developed by chipset vendor Via Technologies and partners, including several major PC and memory makers. The PC-133 specification also offers support for future processors with a 133MHz system bus interface. The PC-133 standard would also apply to motherboards designed for Celeron and Pentium III processors. In addition, Via has also developed a PC-133-compliant chipset for systems featuring Advanced Micro devices' K7 processor.

For more about memory bus frequency, see Table 3-2 in the next chapter.

ROM BIOS

Before the Plug-and-Play era, when you installed a hard drive, you had to tell the system configuration setup what type it was. You had to input the number of heads, sectors, and cylinders, along with other information. This had to be exact; otherwise, the hard disk would not operate. The manufacturers now put all this information in the circuitry of the hard drive. The BIOS in most newer systems can automatically detect this information and configure the system. But you may still want to input it yourself.

The configuration system also needs to be informed as to what kind of floppy drives you have. If you want to reset the time or date, you do it with the CMOS system setup. You should get some sort of documentation with your system or with a new motherboard that tells you what options you have when configuring your system through the BIOS.

You won't have to worry about read-only memory (ROM). ROM is memory that cannot ordinarily be altered or changed. ROM comes with the motherboard. The principal use of ROM in PCs today is for the basic input/output system (BIOS).

The BIOS chip is second in importance only to the CPU. Every time you turn your computer on, the BIOS does a power-on self test (POST). The BIOS checks all of the major components to make sure that they are operating properly. It also facilitates the transfer of data among peripherals. Many BIOS chips also have diagnostics and several utilities built in. BIOS sounds a bit like "boss," and that is its principal job.

The BIOS performs its important functions under the control of firmware programs. These programs are similar to software programs except that the ROM is actually made up of hundreds of transistors that are programmed to perform certain functions.

Until recently, the ROM BIOS programs were usually burned into electrically programmable read-only memory (EPROM) chips. Special devices were used to input a software program into the ROM chip. As the program voltages pass through the chip, the transistors are turned on and off to match the input program. When a normal transistor has voltage applied to it, it will turn on or off as long as the voltage is present. The EPROM transistors are different from ordinary transistors. When the EPROM transistors are turned on or off, they remain in that condition.

Fairly large programs and text can be stored on a ROM chip. The ROM BIOS for an early XT could be programmed onto a 64KB ROM chip. The ROM BIOS for newer systems need 512KB or more. All of the text in a large book can be stored in less than 512KB.

Flash Memory

Companies that manufacture the BIOS chips are constantly improving and adding new functionality to the BIOS. Most motherboards now come with the BIOS in a flash memory chip. The flash memory chips can be upgraded by software from a floppy disk or even downloaded by modem through the telephone line. Many motherboard companies have flash updates available on their Web sites.

Some Basic Information about Motherboards

In early 1985, I spent $2500 for a 286 motherboard. This was in the days when each dollar was worth about three times what it is today. This 286 was the latest, greatest, and most powerful desktop machine at that time. I still have it; if I tried, I couldn't even give that old motherboard away. Figure 2-6 shows my old 286 alongside a modern Socket 7-type motherboard.

The 286 motherboard was bigger than my XT motherboard, so I had to buy a bigger case. However, I was able to use almost all of the components from my old XT. The old XT ran at a piddling 4.77MHz. The new 286 ran at a blazing 6MHz. The new Pentium II runs at 450MHz. Today, a 450MHz motherboard and CPU costs about one-third as much as my

Figure 2-6
My old 286 on the left, alongside a Socket 7 motherboard.

early 286. I cannot say it often enough: these are fantastic times we are living in.

Motherboard Components

Besides the five to eight slot connectors for plug-in boards, the motherboard will have the CPU and several other chips, sockets, or slots for memory chips and upright pins for printer, mouse, and disk interface cable connections. The early AT (for Advanced Technology), or 286, from IBM was the "standard" size, or about one-third larger than the "baby" AT size of almost all motherboards today. My old 286 motherboard has over 150 separate chips on it. Soon after the 286 came out, a few companies started integrating several chips into a single package. They were called *very large-scale integration* (VLSI). Most motherboards now have just a few separate VLSI chips. With fewer chips, there is less chance of having solder problems, less chance of stray capacitance, less distance between the components, and much greater reliability. Manufacturing a board with fewer chips also costs much less.

Even with 150 separate chips on the old 286 motherboard, I still had to buy a separate board for the mouse and printer, along with a separate controller board for the floppy drives and one for the hard drives. Motherboards now have sets of upright pins for most of those functions. All that is needed are cables from components such as the disk drives, mouse, printer, or CD-ROM. The set of pins for the floppy drives can control two floppy disk drives. The two drives can be any floppies such as 360K, 1.2MB, 720KB, 1.44MB, or 2.88MB. I doubt that anyone would still use the old $5\frac{1}{4}$-inch 360KB and the 1.2MB drives or the obsolete 720KB drives. Most newer systems usually have a single 1.44MB drive. Many of the newer systems are not even including the 1.44 MB drive, but installing instead the LS120, a 120MB drive that can also read and write to the 1.44MB format.

The parallel port connector is for the printer or other parallel device. It has an enhanced parallel port (EPP) and an expanded capability port (ECP). The parallel port has eight lines and transmits one bit of data at a time on each line. Ordinarily, a parallel port only transmits data out, but these newer ports can be used for output or input. The EPP and ECP ports can transfer data at up to 1MB/second. The ports can be used not only for printers but also for tape backup drives, external hard drives, CD-ROMs, small local area networks, and several other new products.

The serial COM1 and COM2 ports have the 16550 universal asynchronous receiver-transmitter (UART). This UART is much faster than the earlier 16450 chips. Remember that each single on or off, or 0 and 1, are single bits. It takes 8 of these single bits to make 1 byte. Computers handle data in 8-bit bytes, or one word. But mice, modems, and several other peripherals are serial devices. They handle data 1 bit at a time. For output, the serial ports change the standard 8-bit bytes into single bits for transmission. When receiving data, it changes the single bits back into 8-bit bytes.

In addition to the COM ports, many of the newer motherboards now have a Small Computer System Interface (SCSI), a USB, sound chips, an Accelerated Graphics Port (AGP), Ultra DMA/33 IDE, and more built in. A new standard has also been developed, the Ultra66, which allows throughput at 66MHz. I recommend that you look for this improved board. Many hard drives are now manufactured to the Ultra66 and may not work on a standard motherboard without disabling the Ultra66. Western Digital at www.westerndigital.com has a utility that will allow you to enable or disable the Ultra66 specification.

Figure 2-7 shows a new Socket 7 motherboard alongside an older motherboard. Note that on the new motherboard, the keyboard, mouse, printer, serial, and USB ports are all in a group. With this grouping of the connectors and ports, you would not be able to use this new motherboard in one of the older cases.

Figure 2-7

A new Socket 7 motherboard on the right, alongside an older Socket 7. Note the connectors on the new one—only the connector on the old one is for the keyboard.

At a recent swap meet, I saw several of the old Socket 7 mother-boards. Since they were obsolete, the vendors were selling them at a very low price.

Expansion Slots

The motherboard usually lies on the floor of the chassis of a desktop case or on the right side of a tower case. Most motherboards have eight slots or connectors for plug-in boards. Almost all motherboards now have three or four Peripheral Component Interconnect (PCI) slots. In Figure 2-7, the four white slots are for PCI devices. A few years ago all the slots were Industry Standard Architecture (ISA) slots.

At one time all the early PC and XT motherboards had only five to eight expansion slots or connectors that accepted 8-bit plug-in boards. When the 286 was introduced, a second connector slot was added to the first slot for 16-bit add-in boards. The 16-bit boards made the computer much faster and more versatile than the original 8-bit systems, but the input/output (I/O) bus was still limited to 8MHz and up to 10MHz on some systems. At the present time, you will still find three or four 16-bit ISA slots on motherboards. These add-in boards still have an I/O frequency of 8MHz and up to 10MHz, even on those systems that have a 450MHz CPU. This limitation can be a severe bottleneck for some systems. To help solve the I/O speed problem, the Peripheral Component Interconnect (PCI) was developed. The PCI can operate at 33MHz or faster.

Intel and several other manufacturers have decided that the old ISA system is obsolete. According to a new specification that Intel and other manufacturers agreed to, SPEC99, new motherboards will have only PCI slots. There are still billions of dollars worth of 16-bit ISA boards in use and being manufactured. In many cases where speed is not critical, they do all that is necessary. Items that don't need the higher speed of the PCI include modems, sound cards, and some SCSI interface cards.

These boards are also inexpensive and readily available. I am not sure that the change to total PCI is a good thing. Keep in mind, however, the old legacy cards are being phased out. SPEC99 calls for new motherboards without the 16-bit slot connectors.

We never seem to have enough slots. There are so many different boards that we can use in them. Many companies are designing mother-boards with more built-in functions such as a soundboard, a monitor adapter, a SCSI interface, and USB. So there is less need for the expansion slots, especially the ISA slots.

Expansion Bus

The slot connectors have two rows of contacts that mate with both sides of the edge connector of the plug-in boards. Each contact in each slot is connected to the same contact on all of the other slots. This is called a *bus*. Since all of the slots have the same bus connections, a plug-in board may be inserted into any one of the slots.

A bus is more or less a generic term. It may be just etched circuits on a board, some wires, or anything that provides a signal path. There are several different types of buses: the input/output (I/O) bus, memory bus, ISA bus, PCI bus, and PC Card bus (formerly known as the Personal Computer Memory Card International Association, or PCM-CIA, bus).

A bus is also differentiated by the width or number of lines. The XT had an 8-bit bus and the 286 a 16-bit bus for accessing memory and for I/O. The 386 and 486 have a 32-bit memory bus, but the ISA boards still operate their I/O bus at 16 bits and are limited to a speed of 8MHz to 10MHz. This means that any board or peripheral that wanted to communicate with the CPU has to do so over the 16-bit I/O bus at a fairly low speed.

To help overcome this problem, the faster PCI systems were designed. But billions of dollars worth of hardware is still available for the older ISA-type systems. Many businesses and individuals still have large investments in the ISA hardware.

The PCI helps to overcome part of this bottleneck. Boards and components manufactured to the PCI specifications can operate at higher speeds. But none of the ISA boards will fit in the PCI slots, so manufacturers compromise and put both systems on the motherboards. Eventually, the ISA system will become completely obsolete, and the sockets will not be installed on the motherboards.

In the early days, the bus to the RAM operated at the same speed or frequency of the CPU. The early XT operated at 4.77MHz, and the first 286 increased to 6MHz. But as the frequency of the CPUs were doubled, then tripled, the RAM bus just couldn't match the CPU. The Pentium II can run as fast as 450MHz internally, but it cannot communicate with the system memory at this speed. At this time, the external frequency to memory is limited to 100MHz. For some systems such as the Celeron CPU, it is 66MHz. Eventually, the external bus will become 133MHz, or even 200MHz for some systems. A new PC-133 motherboard should be on the market by the time you read this.

One other thing that contributes to the higher speed of today's computer is that they have moved up from the original 8-bit-wide memory bus to some that are 64 bits wide. That is like moving from a one-lane country road up to a super freeway with eight 8-bit lanes.

The CPU

The computers are named according to the CPU that is mounted on the motherboard. The 286 had an 80286 CPU, the 386 an 80386 CPU, and the 486 an 80486 CPU. Intel tried but could not copyright the CPU numbers. So what should have been the 586 was called the Pentium, which they could copyright. (The word *Pentium* is derived from the Greek *pente* meaning "five.") Cyrix and AMD continued with the number scheme. Cyrix issued a 5x86, and AMD issued a K5. Cyrix now has a 6x86MX and AMD has a K6 that is equivalent to the Intel Pentium II. By the time you read this, AMD will have introduced their K7. Intel has introduced their Pentium III.

Within the latest CPU designations, there are several variations of the Pentium CPUs, including the Pentium MMX, the Pentium Pro, the Pentium II, and the Pentium III. CPUs are so important that the next chapter will be devoted to them.

Motherboard Memory

A Pentium III, or clone equivalent, motherboard should have slots, or provisions, for the installation of at least 128MB of RAM and up to 512MB of memory on board. Some motherboards may have four 72-contact slots for SIMMs and up to four 168-contact slots for DIMMs. Most of the newer motherboards will use DIMMs.

Before you order memory, make sure that you get the right type for your motherboard. Get the right speed, the right memory size, and the right physical size.

More about memory in Chapter 4.

Cache SRAM

When processing data, quite often the same data is used over and over again. Having to traverse the bus to retrieve the data can slow the system down considerably. Most CPUs now have a Level 1 (L1) cache built into the chip. Before Pentium II was introduced, most motherboards had provisions for a large Level 2 (L2) cache on the motherboard. Socket 7 motherboards still have provisions for an L2 cache on the motherboard. Older systems used discrete memory chips for the L2 cache; newer motherboards have a very large-scale integrated (VLSI) single chip for the L2 cache. Because it takes a finite amount of time for the CPU to go to the L2 on the motherboard, the Pentium II and Pentium III places a large L2 in the same package very close to the CPU. The new AMD K7 will also have a large L2 built-in cache in the same enclosure.

The CPU will look in the L1 cache first to see if the needed data is there. If not, it will look in the L2 cache. If it doesn't find the needed data in either L1 or L2, it will go to the main memory. If it is a large program that is being processed and there is not enough memory, some of it may be temporarily stored on the hard disk. The fastest processing is done when the needed data is in L1, the next-fastest is when it is in L2, and the next when in main memory. If the system has to go to the hard disk, it really slows down.

Not All Cache Is Equal

I recently attended a swap meet where there were about 300 vendors. One vendor was selling Socket 7 motherboards for $35. There were several on sale for as little as $60. One reason that some of the motherboards were so inexpensive is that they had very little onboard L2 cache. The better motherboards had a minimum L2 cache of 512KB. They were selling for about $80. For $100 there were some that had 1MB of L2 cache, and for $130 there were some with a 2MB L2 cache.

Other Motherboard Chips

Besides the CPU and memory chips, there are several other chips and systems on the motherboard.

Keyboard BIOS

The keyboard is a small computer in itself, and it has its own special BIOS chip. When you press a key on the keyboard, a scan code or signal is sent to the keyboard BIOS. Another signal is sent when the key is released. When two keys are pressed at the same time, it can detect which one was pressed first. It can also detect when a key is held down longer than normal, and it will start beeping at you. The last 20 keystrokes are stored in the keyboard memory and are continually flushed out and replaced by new keystrokes.

CMOS Battery

Every time you booted up the old PC and XT, you had to input the date and time. It is helpful if the time and date are correct, because every time a file is created, it includes the time and date. This makes determining which of two files is the later one very easy. Several companies made fortunes selling plug-in boards with a battery-operated clock. When the 286 was introduced, it had a battery-operated clock built onto the motherboard. The early systems used batteries that lasted about two or three years.

The batteries supply power for a complementary metal-oxide semiconductor (CMOS) transistor circuit. Besides keeping the date and time when the power is turned off, these low-power transistors keep the system configuration. It also keeps a record of what types of floppies, hard drives, monitor, and keyboard are used in the system. In some cases, it remembers what files or programs you were working on when the computer was turned off.

If your system does not keep accurate time, the battery may need to be replaced. The early IBM 286 ATs used a battery that cost over $30. Many of the clone builders designed a system that used low-cost alkaline batteries. Most systems used a tubular lithium battery that was soldered to the motherboard. This made it very difficult to replace. Modern systems use batteries that are easily replaced.

The batteries may last three years or more. One factor in battery life is how often you use your computer. While the computer is on, it draws its power from the wall socket. When it is off, the CMOS transistors must be kept alive by the lithium battery. If a system consistently loses time, it's possible that the battery needs to be replaced. If the battery goes completely dead, it will lose all of the CMOS configuration data. In

Figure 2-8

A Pentium III mother-
board. The round
device in the lower
right corner is a
lithium battery. The
AGP slot is just above
the four white PCI
slots.

the old days if you lost your CMOS configuration data, it would have
been disastrous. But today with Plug and Play, it is not much of a big
deal.

If you replace the battery, make sure that you install it the same way.
Make a diagram showing the + and − ends before you remove the battery. It is very easy to forget how a battery or other chip was installed.
Some of the batteries on the newer motherboards may be in a square
chip-like device that can be plugged into a socket. Many of the new
motherboards use a round lithium battery about the size of a quarter,
such as that shown in the lower corner of Figure 2-8 . They are inexpensive, very easy to replace, and usually last three or four years.

Timing

A computer depends on precise timing. Several of the chips on a motherboard control the frequency and timing circuits. The timing is so critical
that there are usually one or more crystals on the motherboard that
oscillate at a precise frequency to control the timing circuits. The crystals are usually in a small, oblong, shiny can.

DMA

The direct memory access (DMA) system allows some processing to take place without having to bother the CPU. For instance, the disk drives can exchange data directly with the RAM without having to go through the CPU. Many of the newer motherboards are now designed with an Ultra DMA/33 IDE hard drive protocol. This allows the hard drive to transfer data at up to 33MB/sec.

IRQ

The interrupt request (IRQ) system is a very important part of the computer. It can cause the system to interrupt whatever it is doing and take care of the request. Without the interrupts, nothing would get done. Even if the computer is doing nothing, it must be interrupted and told to perform a task.

There are 16 IRQs, numbered from 0 to 15. Each I/O device on the bus is given a unique IRQ number. Software can also perform interrupt requests. There is a priority system, and some interrupts take precedence over others.

TABLE 2-1

IRQ Assignments

IRQ	Address	Description	Detected
0	OCO8:0103	Timer click	Yes
1	OCO8:0113	Keyboard	Yes
2	OA7D:OO57	Second 8259A	Yes
3	E939:1FAD	COM2: COM4	COM2
4	OA7D:0087	COM1: COM3	COM1
5	OA7D:OO9F	LPT2:	No
6	OA7D:OOB7	Floppy disk	Yes
7	OO7O:O6F4	LPT1:	Yes
8	OA7D:OO52	Real-time clock	Yes
9	FOOO:EED3	Redirected IRQ2	Yes
13	FOOO:EEDC	Math coprocessor	Yes
14	OA7D:O117	Fixed disk	Yes

Sixteen IRQs may seem like a large number, but it isn't nearly enough. Several of the interrupts are reserved or used by the system, so they are not available. It would have been wonderful if the Pentium had provided about twice as many, but no such luck.

If you want to see how your system is using IRQs, in Windows 95/98, select `My Computer`, then click on `Control Panel`, then click on `Device Manager` and highlight `Computer`. Not only will this allow you to look at your IRQs, it will tell you about most of the other important elements in your computer.

Table 2-1 shows how the 16 IRQs might be used.

As you can see in the table, out of the 16 IRQs, 10, 11, 12, and 15 are not shown. Windows shows those that are in use but does not show those that are available. IRQ5 is for LPT2, but since I don't have a second printer attached, it could be used for other devices such as a mouse, a soundboard, or a network card.

UARTs and Serial Ports

Mice, modems, game controllers, sound controllers, fax boards, some printers, plotters, and many other devices communicate with the computer through a serial port. They operate with serial data. The data must be furnished over a single line with one bit following another. The computer operates with parallel data. It takes 8 bits to make 1 byte, so for 8 bits it will have 8 lines, and for 16 bits it will have 16 lines. Obviously, this data cannot be sent out over a modem or any of the other serial devices. The serial ports receive these 8-bit bytes, then convert them to single bits so that they can be transmitted over the phone lines or wherever. When receiving data from an outside source, it must be converted back to the 8-bit form. The conversion is done with a special universal asynchronous receiver-transmitter (UART) chip.

Ordinarily, only two serial ports can be used, and each requires a dedicated IRQ. COM1 uses IRQ4, and COM2 uses IRQ3. You may have four or more different serial devices that you would like to attach to your computer. It is possible to add two more virtual ports, COM3 and COM4, but they must share the COM1 and COM2 IRQ lines; COM3 uses IRQ4, and COM4 uses IRQ3. Some devices are rather selfish and don't like to share. You need special software in order to use COM3 and COM4.

The COM ports also have specific addresses in memory. COM1 uses

3F8h, COM2 uses 2F8h, COM3 uses 3E8h, and COM4 uses 2E8h. Life would be a whole lot simpler if only we had four or more dedicated IRQ lines for the COM ports. Of course, you would also need two more UART chips for the additional ports.

A large number of the problems encountered in adding or upgrading a system are due to the serial ports and IRQs. If a device conflicts with another one as to the assigned IRQ or memory address, neither device will work. (Refer to Table 2-1 to see how IRQs are assigned.) I have spent hours and hours trying to figure out why a new board would not operate.

Architecture

The architecture of the computer refers to the overall design and the components it uses. The architecture is also concerned with the type of bus that is used. The bus is the internal pathway over which data is sent from one part of the computer to another. The 8-bit systems use 8-bit parallel paths, 16 use 16, 32 use 32, and 64 use 64. The flow of data over a bus is often compared to the flow of traffic on a highway. If there are only two lanes, the flow of traffic may be limited. Adding more lanes can vastly improve the flow of traffic.

ISA

The Industry Standard Architecture (ISA) is what was once known as the IBM-compatible standard. IBM more or less abandoned the standard when they introduced their Micro Channel Architecture (MCA) in 1987. There were far more IBM-compatible clone computers in existence than computers manufactured by IBM. Since IBM was now directing most of its efforts toward the MCA, the clone makers took over the standard and changed the name.

An ISA computer can be anything from the oldest and slowest XT up to the newest and fastest Pentium. The old XT used an 8-bit bus, which means that eight parallel lines connected to the same pins on all of the slot connectors for plug-in boards. When IBM was developing the 286, it became apparent that an 8-bit bus was too slow and was clearly inadequate. So they devised a 16-bit slot connector by adding a second 36-contact connector in front of the original 62-contact connector. This was a brilliant innovation.

Compatibility

About 5 billion dollars worth of 8-bit hardware was in existence at the time IBM introduced their 16-bit AT 286. But with the 16-bit connector, either an 8-bit or 16-bit board can be used in a 16-bit system. The industry loved it because it did not make obsolete their present investment in plug-in boards.

This downward compatibility still exists even with the fastest and most powerful Pentium II. But there is a price to pay for the compatibility. The CPU operates over a special memory bus to communicate with RAM at the CPU's rated frequency. The 386 and 486 are 32-bit systems; the Pentium is a 64-bit. The 386 and 486 ISA systems communicate with the system RAM over a 32-bit bus back and forth to memory. But the system can only communicate with their plug-in boards and peripherals over a 16-bit bus.

Even though the ISA I/O bus is limited to a speed of about 8MHz and an I/O bus width of 16 parallel lines, and even though the Pentium III CPU may operate as fast as 550MHz internally, it will still run all previous ISA software and hardware. But the old legacy ISA bus and hardware are obsolete. The newer and faster systems are much better. Eventually ISA will be as dead as the dodo bird.

The Intel PCI Bus

The Intel Peripheral Component Interconnect (PCI) has become the standard on all new motherboards. In the past it was sometimes very frustrating when adding a plug-in board. Often you had to set several dip switches or jumpers so that it did not conflict with the assigned IRQs, serial and parallel ports, and DMA channels of other plug-in boards. Almost all boards and peripherals are now made to the Plug and Play specification.

The old ISA bus for I/O operates at about 8MHz. The PCI bus can operate at 33MHz or more.

PC Card Bus

Many personal and desktop computers now have a PC Card slot, formerly known as PCMCIA. The PCMCIA specification was originally developed for adding memory to laptop and notebook computers, using credit card-size memory cards. You might ask why anyone would want a desktop computer with a PC Card. The answer is because there are now many devices and components besides memory that can be plugged into this slot. Dozens more new devices and components are being developed every day. Adaptec has a SlimSCSI adapter that can be used with several SCSI devices.

A PC Card slot can be more useful than an extra slot on the motherboard. In order to change a board on the motherboard, you have to shut everything down, remove the cover, and then install the new board. On a PC Card slot, if you want to use a modem, just plug it in. You don't even have to shut off the power.

After you have finished with the modem or fax, plug in an Ethernet card, a hard disk, a sound card, a SCSI interface, or any of the other PC Card devices that are available. A PC Card slot can add a vast amount of utility and expansion capabilities to a computer.

Built-in Goodies

It is amazing how soon you can fill up all of the available slots on the motherboard. One way to get around having to use plug-in boards is to have many of the functions built in on the motherboard. At one time there were very few built-in functions. Most motherboards now have several built-in functions and utilities. One of the arguments against built-in functions is that the functions may become obsolete, or they may become defective. But, if necessary, the onboard functions can usually be disabled and replaced with a plug-in board. Following are some of the things that may be built in.

IDE Interface

Many motherboards now have the IDE interface for hard disks and a floppy disk controller built in on the motherboard. They have rows of pins protruding from the motherboard that will accept the ribbon cables from the drives.

SCSI Interface

Many of the Macintosh models have built-in SCSI interfaces. That is one of the reasons for their popularity. The PC industry has been lax in not following suit. SCSI is something that is essential, not only for multimedia, but also for many PC applications. A few motherboard manufacturers are now including a built-in SCSI interface.

Universal Serial Bus

The universal serial bus (USB) is being integrated on most new motherboards. Here is some information about it from the Intel Web site at www.intel.com:

> USB will allow users to connect up to 127 different peripherals all at once, using a single standard connector type. There will be no more guesswork about which serial or parallel port to choose, and nontechnical PC users will be able to say good-bye to DIP switches, jumpers, IRQ settings, DMA channels and I/O addresses. USB features hot insertion and removal, so users will be able to attach and detach peripherals anytime, without powering down their system. It will have a 12MB/s data rate.
>
> In fact, USB hardware solutions from Intel are so flexible, they will make it easy to connect with the fast-growing world of new and existing digital peripherals, computer telephony integration (CTI) applications and popular multi-user games. In addition, USB enjoys widespread support from the industry's leading suppliers of PCs, peripherals and software.
>
> Intel supports USB with PCI chipsets and the industry's first single-chip USB peripheral USB Controller. For those developing and marketing products for PCs, it's time to make your own connection with USB now.
>
> USB is an open and royalty-free specification with broad industry support. Compaq, Digital Equipment, IBM, Intel, MICROSOFT, NEC and Northern Telecom developed USB.
>
> The USB Implementers Forum consists of more than 250 semiconductor, computer, peripheral and software companies, providing marketing and technical support to help accelerate USB product development.
>
> For those people who have bought machines that do not have the USB built-in port, USB Host Adapter PCI boards are available from several manufacturers.

USB Peripherals

Several peripherals have been developed for the USB. More are hitting the market every day. The USB can handle up to 127 different devices, so things like a monitor, keyboard, mouse, scanner, printer, and any of several other peripherals can be attached to the USB. Instead of having several cables that connect to the motherboard, the USB will be the only one necessary.

You need Windows 98 to run most of the USB devices.

Printer Port

There are very few computers that are not tied to a printer of some sort. A few printers still use the serial port, but most printers today use one of the two parallel ports, LPT1 or LPT2. Some motherboards may come with short cables for the printer and COM ports. These printer and COM port cables have connectors that plug into the upright pins on the motherboard. The other end of the cables are usually attached to a bracket that mounts on the back of the case. The bracket will have connectors for external connections.

Game Ports

Many of the multifunction boards sold today have a game port for joysticks used with several of the games that are available. With the increased interest and popularity of multimedia, the game port has become almost mandatory. The game port connector may also be a set of upright pins on the motherboard. A short cable with a connector may be attached to the motherboard pins. The other end of the short connector may be attached to a bracket and connector for external connection.

Monitor Adapter

Every computer needs a board or adapter to drive the monitor. Some motherboards have had built-in monitor adapters for some time. They are great for many applications; however, the main problem is that the developers keep making the adapters faster, with better resolution, true colors, and increasing complexity. If your adapter is built in, then you are stuck with whatever resolution or functions that it provides. Most of the motherboards with built-in functions have jumpers or switches that will allow you to disable those functions so that a board can be plugged in to take over for the built-in functions.

Benchmarks

Benchmarks are tests designed to give a standard measure of performance that can be used to predict how well and how fast a computer will run actual applications. There are many factors that will affect the outcome of a benchmark test. Some of the factors are the computer CPU, the architecture, the design, system software, hardware, and many other combined characteristics of a computer.

There are several different benchmarks. Some are designed to test only a specific portion of a system.

Motherboard Sources and Specs

Later in this section is a short list of manufacturers of motherboards. If you have access to the Internet, by all means visit the sites listed. The computer industry changes so quickly that many things become obsolete overnight. If you buy a computer magazine such as *Computer Shopper* to check prices, the prices may have changed since the magazine was published. Vendors usually place their ads about a month before publication. Often the vendor will ask what catalog or magazine you are looking at and ask what price is quoted. Of course, that is the price they will charge, even though the prices may have dropped. You should call and ask them what the current price is before they ask you.

As mentioned, most all vendors now have Web sites. Their Web sites are usually up-to-date and can show you their products and specifications. Most of them will also have a photo of the product. The Web site will tell you just about everything you need to know, but they usually do not quote prices. Most of the sites will have e-mail addresses for the sales department if you want to know prices.

There are several motherboard vendors. Because each vendor tries to differentiate their product from the others, you will have several choices. As mentioned, the motherboard you choose should depend on what you want to use your computer for and how much money you want to spend. The type of CPU that you choose will also determine the type of motherboard you will need.

The less expensive systems use Socket 7 motherboards with a Zero Insertion Force (ZIF) socket. The Intel Pentium (not Pentium II or III), the AMD K6, the Cyrix 6x86M II, and the IDT C6 CPUs use motherboards with Socket 7. Some of the Celeron CPUs use a ZIF socket that is similar to the Socket 7, but the Celeron has more pins. Intel calls it Socket 370. The Pentium II- and Pentium III-type CPUs and some of the Celerons use a Single Edge Contact (S.E.C.) cartridge and plug into a slot on the motherboard, which Intel calls Slot 1. If you buy a motherboard with the Socket 370 on it, you will not be able to upgrade to the Pentium II or Pentium III. Micron and some of the other companies have designed a daughter card with a Socket 370 on it. The Celeron can be plugged into the daughter card, which can then be plugged into a Slot 1 connector. If later you decide to upgrade to a Pentium II or Pentium III, it will be no problem.

Intel's high-end Xeon CPU uses a slightly different connector called Slot 2. Table 3-4 in the next chapter lists the various motherboard sockets.

Hundreds of motherboards are available. The various CPUs require different configurations for supply voltages and frequency. The motherboards have jumpers and switches for the individual CPU configuration. These jumpers and switches allow you to configure the board for the particular CPU, the voltage, the frequency, the amount of memory, and several other utilities. Some of the newer motherboards have the ability to recognize, or autosense, the CPU type and automatically configure itself.

Sources for Motherboards

Since there are several Pentium motherboard manufacturers, the competition keeps the prices fairly reasonable. I do a lot of my buying and shopping by mail order. I look through computer magazines such as *Computer Shopper, PC World, PC Magazine,* and about 50 others and compare prices and products. The *Computer Shopper* and some of the other computer magazines have a section near the back where they list the products advertised for that month. The items are categorized and grouped by product type. The page number for each ad is listed so it is easy to find what you are looking for. This is a great help when you consider that the *Computer Shopper* may have over 1000 large, tabloid-sized pages.

If you live near a large city, there will probably be several computer dealers in the area. The local dealers may be a bit more expensive than mail order. But you can usually get better support and help if there is a problem. You can also see the product before you buy it.

In addition, there will probably be computer swap meets every so often in the larger cities. Many local dealers will meet at a large auditorium or fairgrounds and set up booths to sell their wares. It is very competitive, and most dealers usually offer very good prices and discounts.

You can go from booth to booth and compare prices and products. You might even be able to haggle a little bit.

I often go to swap meets even if I don't need anything. There is usually a large crowd and lots of excitement in the air. It's almost like a circus.

If you have access to the Internet, here are some Web sites that offer motherboards. The sites usually have lots of information that I can't possibly include in this book. Besides that, the products are changed and updated frequently. The Web sites can easily reflect late product changes.

Here are just a few sites:

Aberdeen
www.aberdeeninc.com
1-800-501-6502

ABIT Computer
www.abit.com
1-800-364-7232

AsusTek Computer
www.asus.com
1-510-739-3777

A-Trend Technology
www.a-trend.com
1-800-866-0188

Aventec
www.aventec.com
1-800-898-9494

Biostar Microtech Corp.
www.biostar-usa.com
1-510-226-6678

Elitegroup
http://www.ecsusa.com
1-888-327-2288

EPoX International
www.epox.com
1-714-990-8858

FIC
www.fica.com
1-800-878-4726

Intel Corp.
www.intel.com
1-408-765-8080

Iwill USA
www.iwillusa.com
1-714-258-4500

JM Computers
www.jmcomputers.com
1-800-331-2128

LPC Technology
www.lpc-tech.com
1-909-598-2710

M Technology
www.mtiusa.com
1-800-420-3636

Micronics (Diamond Corp.)
www.micronics.com
1-800-577-0977

QDI
www.qdigrp.com
1-510-668-4933

Shuttle Corp.
www.spacewalker.com
1-909-595-5060

TigerDirect
www.tigerdirect.com
1-800-364-9478

Tyan Computer
www.tyan.com
1-408-956-8000

There are many other companies and dealers for motherboards. Look in any of the computer magazines.

Some Motherboard Specifications

Most vendors publish their motherboard specifications on their Web sites. Motherboard manufacturers usually produce several different types with different chipsets and for different CPUs.

The manufacturers will have specifications and information about all of their products. Some of them even have an online manual for anyone who may not have gotten one or has lost it. They will also have technical support if you run into problems.

I have listed the specifications for some motherboards with different chipsets as an example of what you may find. I have listed a couple of specs for the Pentium II-type motherboards and one set for a Socket 7-type motherboard.

I recommend that you buy the motherboards with the 440BX chipsets, since they will be compatible with the 266MHz to the 450MHz and higher. These motherboards will also be compatible with the 66MHz front side bus (FSB) as well as the 100MHz. This is the bus between the CPU and memory. The motherboards with the 440LX and 440EX are limited in the FSB and CPU frequency they can handle. Intel has developed a new chipset 810 for the Celeron.

Internal Frequency vs. External Frequency

Strange things happen when a circuit operates at high frequencies. In a low-frequency circuit, the effects of stray capacitance and inductance can usually be ignored. But it is a very big factor in high-frequency circuits, and the higher the frequency, the more of a problem it becomes. In fact, it may be such a problem that a circuit will not operate at all. Devising high-frequency circuits is very difficult and costly. The distance between the components may also be a problem in high-frequency circuits. Even if the distance is only a half-inch or so, at a high frequency, a large portion of the signal may be lost.

The distance between transistors inside the CPU is very small. The capacitive and inductive effects are also small, so the frequency inside the CPU can be much faster than that in the external circuits. The conductive traces are also very small. At the present time, most CPUs have traces about 25 microns wide. Intel will go to 18 microns in their newer CPUs. The smaller traces will allow the CPU to operate at a higher frequency and use less wattage.

Built-in Functions

As mentioned, some motherboard manufacturers have built in several functions and utilities. In fact, so many functions are now being incorporated on the motherboard that some of the retailers are complaining that it is cutting down on their sales. Manufacturers are now building in sound, monitor adapters, SCSI controllers, network interfaces, and a host of other functions and utilities.

Advantages of Built-In Utilities

Having so many utilities built in on the motherboard can be handy. All computers need these utilities. This integration reduces, or even eliminates in some cases, the need for cables. Cables can be the source of many problems. Integration also reduces problems by reducing the number of solder joints and components. The more solder joints and components there are, the more chance for errors and failures.

Disadvantages of Built-Ins

The disadvantages are that if one of the utilities fail, the entire motherboard may have to be replaced. The motherboard is usually the most expensive component in the system. If the utilities are on plug-in boards and it fails, it is fairly inexpensive to replace the single board. Most all systems today that have built-in utilities have jumpers or switches that allow you to disable the built-in utility in case of failure, so that a board can be installed.

The biggest disadvantage of the proprietary systems is that technology does not stand still. The clone machines can be upgraded in thousands of ways with thousands of different components. But if you have one of the proprietary systems, you may not be able to do much to upgrade. You may be able to add a few things such as more memory or larger disk drives.

Another problem with built-ins is possible IRQ conflicts when you try to add boards. Each item such as sound, graphics, networks, and others that would normally be on a plug-in board requires the use of one of the 16 precious IRQs. Ordinarily, you can switch the IRQs of some add-in boards to avoid the conflicts. But many of the motherboards with built-in utilities and functions have their IRQs set in the BIOS, and it cannot be changed.

The Computer Reseller News Test Center in a recent issue of *Reseller News* lists some tips for buying a motherboard or a system that has built-in items:

1. Select motherboards that allow you to disable integrated devices.
2. Use motherboards and adapter cards that provide three to five IRQs and I/O addresses for each device.
3. Flash (update) the BIOS with the latest vendor BIOS.
4. Use Plug and Play cards, not the old legacy cards.
5. Select adapter cards that permit IRQ sharing, but not edge-triggered IRQ-compatible cards. The legacy cards usually send an edge-trigger signal to invoke an interrupt. Most of the legacy cards cannot share an IRQ. Most of the PCI cards can share IRQs.

One other tip that I would add is to make sure the motherboard has USB ports and an AGP slot.

Accelerated Graphics Port (AGP)

Almost all motherboards now have an extra slot for the Accelerated Graphics Port (AGP). You can see the AGP slot in Figure 2-8 just above the four white PCI slots.

Since AGP was an Intel proprietary system, the early Socket 7 motherboards did not have the AGP socket. A few low-cost Socket 7 motherboards being made today do not have AGP capability. But the Super Socket 7 motherboards, discussed below, now have the AGP socket.

The PCI bus is limited to 33MHz and can be a bottleneck for extensive graphics work. More and more applications are making use of full-motion video playback and 3D graphics, such as those found in games. This puts a heavy burden on the system. Intel developed the Accelerated Graphics Port to help solve this problem.

The AGP-1x operates at 66MHz, twice as fast as the PCI bus speed. As you might imagine, being able to run graphics at twice the speed possible with PCI is a fantastic advantage for those who do a lot of video work, 3D graphic design, and game playing. A newer AGP-2x mode will double the speed to 133MHz. A proposed AGP-4x mode will double the speed again to 266MHz.

In late 1997, Intel designed and developed the AGP socket and chipset for their Pentium II systems. Since it was proprietary, AMD, Cyrix, and IDT were not able to make use of this new system. In 1998, Via Technologies and several other companies developed compatible Accelerated Graphics Ports for AMD, Cyrix, and IDT, those systems that use the motherboards with Socket 7. They are called Super Socket 7 motherboards. This means that even the original Pentium CPU, which used Socket 7, can now be plugged into a Super Socket 7 motherboard with AGP.

If you are buying a Socket 7 motherboard, be sure to check to see if it has the AGP socket. Eventually all Socket 7 motherboards will have AGP, but some of the less expensive Socket 7 motherboards still do not have it. I hate to mention prices because they change so often, but at this time in early 1999, Socket 7 motherboards without AGP are selling for as little as $45; those with AGP are selling for as little as $55. All Pentium II and Pentium III motherboards have AGP. Some Pentium II motherboards are selling for as little as $65.

Several companies are manufacturing AGP plug-in boards. The AGP board has its own memory, which may be from 4MB up to 32MB or more. Of course, the more memory, the more the board will cost. The AGP systems are much faster and more powerful than the standard monitor adapters, or even the PCI monitor adapters. The AGP system has made the standard video adapter obsolete.

Here are just a few companies who make AGP boards:

Number Nine Revolution 3D AGP
    www.nine.com
    1-617-674-0009

Creative Labs
    www.soundblaster.com
    1-800-998-1000

ASUSTek 3DexPlorer V3000
    www.asus.com
    1-510-739-7777

Matrox Millennium
    www.matrox.com
    1-800-361-1408

ATI Xpert@Play
    www.atitech.com
    1-905-882-2600

S3 Savage3D
    www.s3.com
    1-408-588-8000

This is only a very short list; there are many others. Check computer magazines.

Chipset Specifications

One of the most important chips on the motherboard is the chipset. This is a chip that has up to 100 or more functions integrated into the single chip. Some of the functions are the bus controller, clock generator, system timer, interrupt controllers, DMA controllers, USB, and many others. In addition, the chipset may determine what CPU is used and its operational frequency.

Intel designs and releases new chipsets at about the same rate as they release new CPUs. Here are some of their Pentium II chipsets:

- *440FX* Released in May 1996 for the Pentium II, it had a bus speed of 66MHz. It supported Fast Page Mode (FPM), Extended Data Out (EDO), and Burst EDO (BEDO) memory. Maximum memory supported was 1GB.

- *440LX* Introduced in August of 1997, this chipset bus speed was 66MHz, and it supported FPM, EDO, and Synchronous DRAM (SDRAM), with a maximum memory of 1GB of EDO and 512MB of SDRAM. It also supported the new AGP socket.

- *440EX* Introduced in April of 1998, it has a bus speed of 66MHz and supports a maximum of 256MB of FPM, EDO, and SDRAM. It was designed to support the low-cost Celeron and Pentium II CPUs that operate from 266MHz up to 500MHz. It also supports the AGP.

- *810* Also developed for the Celeron, the 810 delivers better video, audio, and 3D graphics through Intel's Scalable Graphics Architecture. It will perform on a level with AGP 2-X graphics cards.

- *440BX* Introduced in April of 1998, this chipset has a bus speed of 66MHz and 100MHz. It supports FPM, EDO, and SDRAM memory up to 1GB. It also supports AGP and CPUs with frequencies to 450MHz and above. The 440BX is backward-compatible, so it will support the Pentium II and Celeron CPUs that operate from 266MHz to 500MHz. The motherboards with the 440BX chipset may cost a few dollars more, but if you can possibly afford it, buy it rather than a 440LX or a 440EX. Even if you are installing a 266MHz or Celeron 333MHz CPU, buy the 440BX motherboard. Later, if you decide to upgrade to a 400MHz, a 450MHz, or even a 500MHz, it will be no problem.

Motherboards with 440BX Chipsets

Following are a couple of examples of specifications for the 440BX motherboards from the EpoX Web site.

EPoX EP-BXT 440BX

The EPoX International (www.epox.com) has several different motherboards. Here is some info on one of the EpoX motherboards:

The EP-BXT is based on the Intel 440BX chipset, a chipset offering a 100MHz Bus Clock, supporting a single Slot-1 Pentium II CPU operating at 233-550MHz. It supports many advanced ACPI Power Management features meeting the requirements of PC97 specification and Microsoft's Windows 98, saving power usage in the system and peripherals. Moreover, the on-board Ultra DMA-33 hard drive interface combines the lower cost IDE form-factor with SCSI-like data transfers speeds up to a blistering 33MB/sec.

The built-in i740 graphics chipset is an AGP-compliant adapter providing an immediate doubling (or quadruple) in the maximum available 2D/3D Graphics Bandwidth without reducing performance of other PCI cards. AGP Technology also allows virtual reality applications to use as much texture buffer space as they need without expensive card or hardware upgrades. (i740 video adapter is built in the motherboard; therefore, no AGP slot is present.)

The on-board design of Yamaha YMF724E (PCI-based chipset), a leading sound chip, creates tremendous 3D enhanced sound effects for your system. The built-in specifications of OPL3 and MPU401 makes it compatible with the most popular FM-synthesizer and MIDI/JOYSTICK ports. Together with the compatibility of DOS/Windows Sound Blaster games, it will let you really enjoy the fun and entertainment from your applications.

The bundled feature USDM, another exclusive innovation from EPoX and supported by the EP-BXT, provides you the important real-time information to monitor and control your system for safer and more stable computing in mission-critical Enterprise, Internet, and Commerce applications.

- *Processor Support* (*CPU*): Intel Pentium II at 233-550MHz Slot 1 × 1
- *Chipset:* Intel 82440BX chipset with built-in i740 graphics.
- *Dram Modules:* 168-pin DIMM X 3 for SDRAM. Board does support EDO DIMM but only with Pentium II and NOT Deschutes! PC100-compliant memory required for proper use of 100MHz CPU bus speed (8ns or faster).
- *I/O Chip:* Winbond multi-super I/O W83977EF.

- *Expansion Slot:* 32-bit PCI Master Bus × 4 and, 16-bit ISA Bus × 2.
- *BIOS:* Supports Award Plug and Play BIOS and Flash EPROM.
- *Extended Function:*

    Supports USDM (Unified System Diagnostic Manager).
    Supports ESDJ (Easy Setting Dual Jumper).
    Supports KBPO (Keyboard Power-on) and "Hot-Key" Power-on.
    Supports External Modem Ring-in Power ON Function.
    Supports Fan Status/Voltage/Temperature.
    Supports Hardware Monitoring Function by LM78 and LM75.
    Supports WOL (Wake-On-LAN) function.

- *Form Factor:* ATX Size.
- *Onboard I/O:* Supports 1 FDD connector, 1 Parallel port (EPP, ECP) and 2 Serial ports.
- *Onboard PCI IDE:* PIO mode 3/4 & Ultra DMA-33 (Up to 4 IDE Devices).
- *I/O Connector:* Supports 1 PS/2 MOUSE and 1 PS/2 Style Keyboard.
- *USB:* Supports the Universal Serial Bus (USB) on-board.
- *BIOS:* Supports Award Plug & Play BIOS in Flash memory. Supports 120MB ATAPI Floppy Disk. Supports ZIP Disk Drive. Supports multi-boot from IDE, SCSI, CD-Rom and FDD.
- *Power Management:* Supports Hardware Sleep/Resume and SMM (System Management Mode).
- *Resume by Alarm:* Allows your system to turn on at a pre-selected time.
- *Power Loss Recovery:* In the event of a power outage your system will automatically turn itself back on without user intervention.
- *Desktop Management Interface (DMI):* Supports Desktop Management Interface (DMI) facilitating the management of desktop computers, hardware and software components and peripherals.

Unified System Diagnostic Management (USDM)

USDM is software that collects data from special hardware monitor chips on selected EPoX models. Chips typically used are the LM75/78 from National Semiconductors and the W83781D from Winbond. Although the two chips offer the same monitoring features (voltage, fan

RPMs, temperature, etc.), they are completely different in terms of design and implementation. Check your motherboard's documentation or EPoX's online technical support for which type of monitor chip is used in your EPoX motherboard.

The Unified System Diagnostic Management (USDM) system keeps watch on the essential elements on your motherboard. Here is some info from the EPoX Web site:

> Following the exclusive EPoX innovations of ESSJ (Easy Setting Single Jumper) and KBPO (Keyboard Power On), we are proud to announce another new innovation: USDM. USDM is another aid which we believe offers real benefits to our customers and added security to end users as well as adding value to the overall product. This document provides simplified instructions for understanding the installation process, and how this software works to provide you the important real-time information to monitor and control your system. By virtue of the On-Line Alarm/Warning system, it will protect you from damage due to overheating and over/undervoltage power supply, and provide regular updates of system operating characteristics.

The Control Page

Auto Update: Data is updated automatically to show the real-time information.

Enable Alarm: Warning alarm is activated.

Update Interval: Sets the timer interval and rate at which data will be updated.

Install on Task Bar: EPoX logo will be resident in the bottom of right-hand side.

The Temperature Page

CPU Temp: CPU temperature display and alarm setup.

CPU Fan: CPU cooling fan speed display in RPM (revolutions per minute).

System Temp: System chassis average.

Chassis Fan: System chassis fan speed display in RPM.

The Power Supply Page

CPU Voltage: CPU voltage display and alarm setup.

Power Level: Power supply voltage display and alarm setup.

Auxiliary Power Fan: Power supply fan speed display in RPM.

The On-line Windows

Alarm Condition: A system error message will display indicating the problem.

Choose Action: Suggestions given to solve current problem.

Micronics C400 440BX

Most all motherboard companies make a large variety of motherboards. Here are the specifications from the Micronics Web site for their C400 motherboard. Note that Micronics is now a part of the Diamond Multimedia Corp. (www.diamondmm.com).

Chipset:
Intel 440BX PIIX4e AGPset

Processor Support (Slot 1):
Intel Celeron®—233MHz to 466MHz
Intel Pentium® II—233MHz to 500MHz

Additional Features:
AGP graphics support
UltraDMA/33 Hard disk support
SDRAM memory support

Memory:
Three 168-pin DIMM sockets (3.3V unbuffered)
(2nd-level cache built into CPU)
up to 768MB of system memory
Support for 64-bit SDRAM
Support for 72-bit ECC* SDRAM
Memory bus runs between 66MHz and 100MHz, user selectable

Connectors:
Three 168-pin DIMM sockets (see Memory section)
Five 32-bit PCI slots
Two 16-bit ISA slots (one PCI/ISA shared)
One 32-bit 2X AGP slot

Peripheral Support Built-in:
Integrated I/O includes dual 16550-compatible serial ports

ECP/EPP-compatible parallel port
Floppy port
Dual USB ports
PS/2-style keyboard and mouse connectors
IrDA-compliant infrared connector

Advanced Features:
SB-LINK for legacy Sound Blaster card compatibility
Wake-on-LAN and Wake-on-RING cable headers
Smart Soft power control

BIOS Features:
Award PCI Plug and Play BIOS
APM 1.2 / ACPI / DMI 2.0 / Quick boot / Multi-boot II / SMI
Optional system hardware monitoring
Flash BIOS for free downloadable software upgrades

Operating System Support:
Windows® 95/98 and NT
MS-DOS ™ 5.0, 6.2
PC-DOS
OS/2™ Warp
NOVELL™
SCO®
UNIX®
ODT

The Micronics Tigercat 440LX Motherboard

The Tigercat is a single state-of-the-art Intel Pentium II solution with processors running at speeds of 233MHz up to 333MHz. Based on the Intel 440LX AGPset, Tigercat provides LM78 Microprocessor System Hardware Monitor support and Ultra DMA133 IDE hard drive protocol (up to 33MB/second transfer rate) support. Tigercat's flexibility is augmented by its support for the ISA, PCI, and AGP bus.

The AGP bus slot has greater bandwidth capacity, which provides a higher data transfer rate than the PCI bus. Other features include SDRAM (Synchronous Dynamic RAM) memory and Wake-on-LAN, which provides a way to access a local area or wide area network to turn on desktop PCs remotely. Manufacturing options include 16-bit Yamaha sound with wavetable synthesis.

Following are specifications from Micronics' Web site:

Processors:
Single Intel Slot 1
Intel Pentium II chip 233/266/300/333MHz
Integrated VRM

System Management:
Microprocessor System Hardware Monitor CPU temperature sensor CPU Fan Speed
Monitoring 3-pin header Chassis Intrusion 2-pin header Chassis Fan Speed
Monitoring 3-pin header Intel LANDesk_ Client Manager software (Ver. 3.0)
Wake-on LAN ready (3-pin header)

Expansion:
Four 32-bit PCI slots
Two 16-bit ISA slots
One is a shared PCI/ISA slot
One AGP

CPU Clock Select:
Support for 66MHz CPU bus speed configurations

Chipset:
Intel 440LX AGP set
Intel PIIX 4
SMC FDC37C68x Ultra I/O chip

Memory:
Four 3.3V unbuffered 64/72-bits 68-pin DIMM sockets
Maximum memory: 512MB for SDRAM
Maximum memory: 1GB for EDO
Supports EDO and SDRAM memory
ECC supported via chipset

PCI (Local Bus) IDE:
Ultra DMA/33 IDE

Two 40-pin IDE connectors (Primary and Secondary IDE)
Auto detection of add-in IDE board
Supports ATAPI devices
Multiple sector transfer support

Floppy:
Supports 360K to 2.88MB formats and LS-120
Auto detection of add-in floppy controllers

Sound (Manufacturing Option):
Yamaha OPL3 and OPL4
Sound Blaster-compatible, 16-bit stereo line-in, line-out, mic, and
    game/MIDI ports
4-pin CD-ROM audio header (ATAPI and SB)
4-pin modem audio header (ATAPI)
4-pin Line-in header (ATAPI)
Built-in wavetable (Yamaha OPL4ML)
Sound drivers OCR, Win 95/NT, OS/2)

Communication Ports:
Two 9-pin 16550-compatible serial ports
One 25-pin parallel port (ECP, EPP)
IrDA-compliant IR header
Two USB ports

Keyboard and Mouse:
PS/2-style keyboard and mouse connectors

BIOS:
Phoenix 4.06 BIOS on 2MB flash
PCI auto configuration
Plug and Play ready
APM1.2
Auto detection of memory size
Auto detection and display of EDO, ECC, and SDRAM memory
Auto configuration of DE hard disk types
SoftPowerDown
Multi-boot II
DMI/SMI/ACPI
Wake-on-LAN

Form factor:
ATX footprint (12″ × 9.6″)
Four-layer board
20-pin ATX power connector
Stack mouse/keyboard connectors
Stack three-output audio/game port connectors
Stack serials/parallel connectors

The Tigercat is extensively tested for compatibility under various operating systems, including OS/2 Warp, NOVELL, SCO, UNIX, ODT, Windows 95 and NT, MS-DOS versions 5.0 and 6.2, and PC-DOS.

Super Socket 7

Intel developed the AGP system for their Pentium II systems. Since the Socket 7 companies were in direct competition with their Pentium II, Intel had no interest in sharing the system. VIA Technologies (www. viatech.com) developed a clone chipset for the AGP system that can be used on Super7 motherboards. Via also developed a chipset, their VIA Apollo Pro, that is a clone of the 440BX. The Apollo Pro even surpasses the 440BX in that it allows 1GB of main memory, compared to 512MB for the 440BX.

Here are the specifications for an A-Trend Company motherboard with Super Socket 7:

ATC-5220 Via MVP3 100MHz Pentium Motherboard with
AGP Micro ATX Form Factor

Feature:
Socket 7 supporting Pentium level System Bus 100MH & AGP support

Processor:
Intel Pentium MMXTM and w/o MMXTM processors
AMD K6-2/K6/K5 processors
Cyrix M II/6x86MX processors
IBM 6x86MX processors
IDT WinChip C6/C6+ processors

Switching Regulator:
Built-in switching voltage regulator

Chipset:
VIA MVP3 AGPset (VT82C598AT and VT82C586B)
I/O chipset Winbond 83877

L2 Cache:
Onboard 512KB Pipeline Burst SRAM

System Memory:
Running AMD K6-2 & Cyrix M II processors with PC-100- compliant
   SDRAM DIMM memory only
Three 3.3V 168-pin DIMM sockets
2 SIMM memory sockets
Supports 8/16/64/128MB SDRAM module
Supports 4/8/16/64/128MB EDO DRAM module
Capacity 8MB to 384MB DRAM size

Bus selection:
Jumper setting for FSB/AGP/PCI clock selection:
66/66/33 or 100/66/63 or 83.5/66/33

PCI IDE:
2 × bus master DMA/33 IDE ports (up to four devices)

I/O Interface:
1 × floppy port (360KB ~ 2.88MB)
2 × serial port (16550 UART compatible)
1 × parallel port (EPP/ECP)
AT-style keyboard
Dual USB ports

Expansion Slots:
4 × PCI 32-bit slots, (PCI 2.1 compliant)
2 × ISA 16-bit slots
1 × AGP slots (1× & 2× Speed Mode, 66/133MHz)

Power Management:
PC 98-compliant, ACPI-compliant
Modem-RING-on
Power off by Windows 95 shutdown & PS-ON Power button

Form Factor:
ATX form factor, 30.5cm × 18.0cm (12″ × 7.08″)
AT and ATX power connectors on board

System BIOS:
1MB bit flash ROM
Award PCI BIOS with green, PnP, DMI, INT13 extension and antivirus
    functions
LS-120, ZIP, SCSI, and CD-ROM bootable
Multiple host bus clock selection—60/66/68.5/75/83.5/90/100MHz

Utility:
Ultra DMA/33 IDE enhanced driver
Award BIOS flash utility
VGART.VxD driver

Here are specifications for their 440Ex chipset:

**ATC-6150 Intel Pentium II 440EX AGPset Motherboard
Baby AT Form Factor**

Processor:
Pentium II 500 MHz and Celeron 266/466MHz processor.

Chipset:
Intel 440EX AGPset for Pentium II processor-based systems.
Supports AGP, ACPI, USB, SDRAM, and Ultra DMA/33, SMC 602 Ultra
    I/O chipset.

Feature:
Easy DIP switch installation for CPU frequency setup.
Hot-key recovery mechanism for power-on failure, the easiest way to
    reboot system during system power failure.
AT and ATX power supply connector on board.
Auto detected CPU core voltage.
User-friendly CPU installation auto detects Pentium II and Celeron
    processors' core voltages.

Wake-on-LAN:
Remotely wakes up system via network with Wake-on-LAN Ethernet card.

CPU Bus Clock and Bus Frequency Ratio:
60/66/75/83MHz and 2.0 × /3.5 × /4.0 × /4.5 × /5.0 × /5.5 × ratio.

System Memory:

Two 168-pin DIMM sockets for support up to 256MB SDRAM or 512MB
 EDO DRAM memory.

On Board:

Ultra Multi-I/O Winbond 2 83977 AW/EF, supports infrared transfer
 (IrDA TX/RX), FDC port, integrated keyboard controller, two 16550A
 serial ports, one EPP/ECP parallel port. AT-style keyboard connector.
Ultra DMA/33 IDE, 2 USB, PC/PCI audio cable connector supports.
Creative SB-LINK sound card mode. Two IrDA built-in switching voltage
 regulators.

Expansion Slots:

Three 32-bit PCI slots shared with two 16-bit ISA slots and one AGP.
Advanced BIOS, Year 2000-compliant. Meets PC 97 requirement. CPU
 clock installation.
Multiple host frequency selection, auto detects AT/ATX power type, Wake-
 on-LAN, energy saving/management, Plug and Play, DMI Int 13 extension, and antivirus functions.
Able to book storage drives, including LS120, ZIP SCSI, and CD-ROM
 drives.

Feature Options:

Intel LAN Desk Client Manager software, simplifies local and network
 management of desktop systems.

PC Health Monitoring:

Detects mainboard hardware health monitoring such as CPU temperature,
 fan speed, and system voltage. Particular signal sound for each detection.

CPU Protection:

Alerts CPU speed to slow down and alarm when overheating occurs.
CPU thermistor cable.

The Tyan S1571S Titan Turbo AT-2

This type of motherboard uses the intel 430TX chipset. It is over two
years old and is obsolete. I don't recommend buying it. I list it only for
comparison with the newer systems.

Here are the specifications from the Tyan Web site (www.tyan.com) for their S1571S motherboard with the Socket 7 that is suitable for the Pentium MMX, AMD, and Cyrix CPUs:

S1571S Titan Turbo AT-2 Pentium 75 to 233MHz System Board

Intel Pentium, Pentium MMX, AMD K6, and Cyrix 120+, 150+ and 166+

New switching power supply for complete CPU support

Five PCI and four ISA slots

Ultra DMA133 drive support and P10 modes 1

The S1571S is a quality, high-performance mainboard designed for Intel Pentium microprocessors. This mainboard utilizes the Intel 430TX chipset and can support CPU speeds of 75MHz through 233MHz. The S1571S will also support the Cyrix MII6x86 CPUs, AMD K6, and the Intel multimedia Pentium with MMX processor, both the P550 and P54CTB overdrive versions.

The S1571S's PCI local bus provides high-performance capabilities that are ideal for a wide range of demanding applications such as: CAD, CAM, CAE, networking, multiuser environments, database management, desktop publishing, image processing, and 3D animation. This integrated system board achieves high reliability with numerous features and yet is small enough to be supported in a NATH form factor.

Some of the features included are: on-board dual channel PCI PIO, DMA IDE and Ultra DMA33, on-board floppy controller, on-board high speed I/O, and on-board 512K burst SRAM.

Flexibility and expandability have been designed into the S1571S. With I/O and drive controller support built on-board, the five PCI and four ISA (one ISA and one PCI as a shared slot) slots are free for numerous add-on expansion cards.

Processor:

Pentium/Pentium MMX/AMD K6

Supports 75MHz through 233MHz, Cyrix/SGSIIBM 6x86 P120+, P150+, and P166+

#7 ZIF socket/wide voltage range

Intel 430TX

8-256MB, six 72-pin SIMM Sockets, two 168-pin DIMM sockets

Fast Page mode or EDO DRAM support, EDO DIMM and SDRAM support

Cache Memory:

On-board 512K burst cache

Expansion Slots:
Five 32-bit PCI bus mastering slots, four 16-bit ISA slots
One shared PCI/ISA slot—eight usable
On-board PCI bus mastering IDE—Two PCI Bus-Master enhanced IDE
    Ports 4 HDD plus EIDE CD-ROM support (four IDE devices total)
Ultra DMA/33 support
Bus mastering DMA modes 1 and 2
PIO modes 3 and 4

On-board I/O with IR:
Two floppy drives
Two serial ports (16550 UARTs)
One ECP/EPP parallel port
One IR (Infrared) I/O interface port
Two USB rev 1.2 port support

Flash BIOS:
Award standard, AMI BIOS available
Green PC compatible
Microsoft Plug and Play ready

Physical Dimensions:
Intel Baby AT (11″ × 8.8″) reduced form factor

Warranty:
Two years

Intel Pentium II Motherboards

Besides manufacturing and selling several billion dollars worth of chips each year, Intel also manufactures and sells motherboards. They design and build motherboards for their CPUs. Some of Intel's biggest CPU customers also make motherboards, and many of them are not too happy with the Intel competition.

You can see photos of Intel motherboards and chips on the Intel Web site at www.intel.com.

Dual Pentium III Motherboards

Several manufacturers have designed Pentium III motherboards with dual Slot 1s. Check with the motherboard vendors. You can build a dual Pentium III system with Xeon 550MHz CPUs for about $10,000. It could perform as well as a $100,000 minicomputer.

Using dual Socket 7 motherboards would allow you to build a very powerful machine for much less than the cost of building dual Pentium IIIs. Although I have not seen any dual Socket 7 motherboards myself, I have been told that there are a few companies making them, and, in fact, there may be several by the time you read this. One problem is that it takes a special chipset for a dual processor. At the present time only Intel has designed dual processor chipsets for their Pentium II, III, and Xeon chips.

At this writing, the AMD K7 has not been released. It is possible that some manufacturers may design a motherboard for the AMD Athlon with two slot A's.

Deciding What to Buy

One of the first things that you will have to decide is which motherboard you want. Or, if you are like me, you need to decide which one you want at a price you can afford.

I subscribe to several computer magazines. Most of them have articles and reviews of software and hardware. And, of course, they have lots of ads from stores that sell by mail. The ads give me a fairly good idea of the prices so that I know what I can afford. Mail order may be the best way to purchase your parts, especially if you don't live near a large city.

Usually, the larger cities have lots of computer stores. The San Francisco Bay area and the Los Angeles area have hundreds. There are also computer swap meets every weekend. If I need something, I will go to one of the swap meets and compare the prices at the various booths. I often take a pad along, write the prices down, then go back and make the best deal that I can. As mentioned, sometimes you can haggle with the vendors for a better price, especially if it is near closing time.

Replacing a Motherboard

Replacing a motherboard is very easy. Basically, it is the same whether it is an XT, 286, 386, 486, or Pentium. Chapter 12 contains some step-by-step instructions and photos. This is one of the more cost-effective upgrades you can perform.

I have an old AMD 233MHz system with a Socket 7 motherboard. Ordinarily, I could buy one of the faster AMD or Cyrix CPUs and just plug it in to easily upgrade the system. But the old motherboard was designed before anyone dreamed of 500MHz or 600MHz CPUs. Though a faster CPU could be installed, you could not set it to operate at the rated speed.

Ultra66—A New Motherboard Standard

I recently went to a swap meet and bought a new Socket 7 motherboard and an AMD K6-III 450MHz CPU. Then I noticed that the new motherboard had the USB, serial and parallel ports, the keyboard, and mouse connectors grouped so that this motherboard would not fit in my old case. Besides, this motherboard, and most all newer ones, now have the ATX power supply connector. So I bought a new case and power supply for $50.

There were lots of good bargains at the swap meet. I decided that I needed a larger hard disk. I bought 20GB and 13GB Western Digital hard disks. After spending an entire day trying to format the hard disks, I finally called the vendor, who told me that the hard disks were manufactured to the Ultra66 specification. The motherboard that I bought was not. He suggested that I access the Western Digital Web site at www.westerndigital.com and download their Ultra66 utility. This utility allows you to turn off the Ultra66 of the hard disks. They can then be formatted and used in any motherboard.

I was a bit teed-off about wasting so much time. Nowhere on the hard disk or the motherboard is there any mention of the Ultra66 specification.

Following is a list of some compatible Ultra66 motherboards:

Mfr.	Model	Chipset	BIOS
ABITAB	BX6INTEL	440BX AGPset	Award 4.51PG
ASUS	P2BINTEL	440BX AGPset	Award
ASUS	PCI/I-P54	INTEL 82430N	Award 4.51PG
ASUS	P/I-P6NP5	INTEL 440FX	Award 4.51PG
ECSSI	54P-AIO	SiS 501 chipset	
FIC	VA-503	VIA MVP3	
INTEL	VENUS	INTEL 440FX	AMI 1.00.04
INTEL	Seattle	INTEL 440FX	AMI
INTEL	XEON	INTEL 440GX	AMI
MSIMS	6111	INTEL 440LX	AMI V1.8
MSIMS	5169	ALI Aladdin5	
SOYO	SY-5	EASETEQ	

Several others will be on the market by the time you read this. The Ultra66 will be the new standard. Contact any of the larger motherboard vendors listed in the computer magazines.

Universal Serial Bus (USB) Frequently Asked Questions (FAQs)

Note: All information here was obtained from http://www.usb.org. This site is a service of the USB Implementers Forum staff, whose primary charter is to support the USB Implementers Forum member companies with developers conferences, spec technical support, and compatibility workshops. Their secondary charter is to provide the industry with available information to encourage development and understanding of USB.

1. *What is USB?*

   USB is the peripheral bus standard developed by PC and telecom industry leaders—Compaq, DEC, IBM, Intel, Microsoft, NEC and Northern Telecom—that will bring plug and play of computer peripherals outside the box, eliminating the need to install cards into dedicated computer slots and reconfigure the system. Personal computers equipped with USB will allow computer peripherals to be automatically configured as soon as they are physically attached—without the need to reboot or run setup. USB will also allow multiple devices—up to 127—to run simultaneously on a computer, with peripherals such as monitors and keyboards acting as additional plug-in sites, or hubs.

2. *What kind of peripherals will USB allow me to hook up to my PC?*
   You name it: monitor controls, audio IO devices, telephones, modems, keyboards, mice, 4x and 6x CD-ROM devices, joysticks, tape and floppy drives, imaging devices such as scanners and printers. USB's 12 megabit/s data rate will also accommodate a whole new generation of peripherals, including MPEG-2 video-based products, data gloves and digitizers. Also, since computer-telephony integration is expected to be a big growth area for PCs, USB will provide a low-cost interface for Integrated Services Digital Network (ISDN) and digital PBXs.

3. *How does it work?*
   Drawing its intelligence from the host PC, USB will detect when devices are added and removed. The bus automatically determines what host resource, including driver software and bus bandwidth, each peripheral needs and makes those resources available without user intervention. Users with a USB-equipped PC will be able to switch out compatible peripherals as needed as easily as they would plug in a lamp.

4. *Will I need to purchase special software to run USB peripherals?*
   The Windows operating system (since OSR 2.1 release on October 29, 1996) comes already equipped with the feature (called "drivers") that allows your PC to recognize USB peripherals. Ultimately, you will not need to purchase or install additional software for each new peripheral. However, new peripheral products (including those never-before-seen) may mean a gap between the peripheral availability and software upgrades. This may mean you receive a diskette with your new USB peripheral with the updated driver information.

5. *Will USB peripherals cost more?*
   USB peripherals will be competitively priced with the peripherals available on the market today.

6. *Is there a Mac version of the standard?*
   Yes.

7. *Are there USB products out right now?*
   Yes. Almost all new PC designs from major vendors shipping today have USB connections on the motherboard and the correct Win OS to make them work. There are also many products used to design and

build USB systems, such as connectors, chipsets and board-level computers. USB peripherals, including keyboards, monitors, mice and joysticks, are slowly starting to appear.

8. *How can USB be used between two hosts, like a laptop and a desktop?*
   The answer is a small adapter that would appear as a device to each USB system desiring connections. Two USB peripheral microcontrollers sharing a buffer memory would be a quick solution and could sell for under $50. The packaging could be as streamlined as a small blob (dongle) [see Glossary] in the middle of the cable or maybe even a slightly larger connector shell at one end and nothing in the middle of the cable. A cable like this could also perform hub functions for very little extra cost to produce a higher value product.

9. *How does USB compare with Sony's FireWire/IEEE 1394 standard?*
   They differ most in terms of application focus, availability, and price. The USB feature is available now and will address more traditional PC connections, like keyboards, mice, joysticks, and handheld scanners. However, USB's data rate (12 Mb/s) is more than adequate for many consumer applications including more-advanced computer game devices, high-fidelity audio and highly compressed video, like MPEG-1 and MPEG-2. Most importantly, the USB feature will add nothing to system cost.
   FireWire will only be available in low volume until late 1997. FireWire will target high-bandwidth consumer electronics connections to the PC—like digital camcorders, cameras, and digital video disc players.

10. *When it is available, will FireWire replace USB?*
   No. The two technologies target different peripheral connections and will therefore be complementary. When FireWire becomes more prevalent, in about two years, it will be up to individual consumers what features they want on their new PCs. It seems likely that, in the future, PCs will have both USB and FireWire connection ports.

11. *Who created USB anyway?*
   USB was developed by a group of seven companies that saw a need for an interconnect to enable the growth of the blossoming Computer Telephony Integration Industry. The seven promoters of the USB definition are Compaq, Digital Equipment Corp., IBM PC Co., Intel, Microsoft, NEC, and Northern Telecom.

12. *What are the Intellectual Property issues with USB, is there a license, what does it cost, what is the "Reciprocal Covenant Agreement" I've heard about?*

USB is royalty-free, the promoters that created the specification agreed to allow anyone to build products around the spec without any charge. The promoters have signed an IP agreement which promises there will be no lawsuits based on any IP incorporated within the specification. The Reciprocal Covenant Agreement is a copy of that agreement with a place for any implementer to sign and return to USB-IF administration in order to go on record as having seen and understood the agreement. The Reciprocal Covenant is made available to anyone (USB-IF member or not) to clarify the USB license agreement.

13. *What is the USB-IF?*
USB Implementers Forum is a support organization formed by the seven promoters of USB to help speed development of high-quality compatible devices using USB. The organization is administered by personnel supplied by the promoter companies and is funded by membership fees.

The organization is nonprofit and will use all funds for promotion of USB products or technical education of implementers of USB products. Most of the activities USB Implementers Forum sponsors will be organized to be breakeven events. Large presence shows such as COMDEX consume most of the organization's budget.

14. *What are the benefits of USB-IF?*
We are constantly looking for more ways to encourage and accelerate USB product development. The following list is a collection of benefits that USB-IF has committed to its members.
- Free vendor ID
- Free technical support
- Whitepapers, design guides, app notes, etc.
- Discounted attendance at developer conferences
- Participation in compatibility workshops
- Invitation to participate in marketing events
- Company listing in USB key contacts list
- Participation in USB committed products list
- Participation in industry discussion mail list
- Five free copies of each hardcopy spec (automatic distribution)

15. *Is the USB bus going to have a long-distance 50 to 200 meter extension (possibly fiber) for these large customers that need the capability?*
USB is intended for desktop (or laptop) peripheral interface; 200 meters seems like a rather large desktop. Still, many members' companies have talked about longer distance applications and are thinking of creating the products needed to accomplish them, such as an

extension device that looks like a hub to the USB bus from both sides, but utilizes another protocol (such as fiber) between the endpoints of the cable. Each end would translate USB electrical signaling to or from a long-distance signaling. While this is possible, there are issues regarding packet protocol and latency that must be considered to maintain USB compatibility.

16. *When a device is detached, its device driver is unloaded. If that device is reinserted, would its driver be reloaded?*
Yes, dynamic configuration and initialization by the OS includes automatically loading and unloading the drivers as needed.

17. *Are there any plans to increase the bus bandwidth of USB in the future to 2x, 3x?*
No, USB was designed for a desktop peripheral interface and has a performance/cost point for today's peripherals. A new interface, such as P1394, for future high-speed peripherals may develop.

18. *Can someone clarify the difference and applications for series "A" and series "B" connectors?*
The series "A" connector is intended for all USB devices, is a plug for a peripheral and a socket for a PC platform. In most cases a USB cable should be captive (molded in) to its peripheral. This saves connector cost, eliminates incompatibilities due to power drop in a cable and simplifies the user connection task. There are some cases where a captive cable is prohibitive. A very large, heavy device may not be able to tolerate dangling cables that cannot be removed and some devices that are only occasionally connected, but have a useful function when not connected are good examples. The series "B" connector was created for such applications. The two connector series are different to prevent connections that violate the USB architecture topology.

19. *What is the difference between a root hub and normal hub in terms of hardware and software?*
All hubs are identical from a software viewpoint (notwithstanding the powered and unpowered differences). A root hub is simply the first hub encountered during enumeration. In many implementations the root hub can be integrated into the same silicon as the host controller to save cost.

20. *Is USB a viable bus for peripherals like CD-R, tape or hard disk drives?*
The viability depends on the definition of acceptable performance point. If any of these devices are for frequent use, then I would want a permanent installation both for performance and mechanical integra-

tion. USB is not intended to be an inside-the-box, permanent connection for high-speed peripherals. If the use is occasional or is for a peripheral that is shared between many computers, I would think that USB performance would be more than sufficient. The convenience of USB and the ubiquitous connection that USB will bring would outweigh blazing transfer rates. Still, USB will provide CD transfer rates up to 4x or 6x drives (not enough for re-writeable drives) and better transfer rates than the typical LPT-connected tape drive, floppy drive or removable hard disk.

The CPU

There are several highly integrated chips on the motherboard, but the most important one is the central processing unit (CPU). It is the brains of the computer. In fact, it is so important that the whole computer system will be called by whatever CPU is installed on the motherboard. If you are building a Pentium III, Intel is your only choice. If you want to save a bit of money, you may want to build a K6-III or an AMD Athlon from Advanced Micro Devices (AMD). The AMD CPUs will do everything that the Pentium III will do.

In this chapter, I will discuss these two main CPUs briefly, then talk about the other choices you have. I will also talk a bit about how a CPU is made.

CPU Variations

At one time there were only three major auto manufacturers. I could recognize and name the year of every car on the road. Today there are dozens of auto makers and more models than any 10 people can remember. Similarly, at one time there was only one CPU, one speed, and one manufacturer. Today we only have four different CPU makers, but there are more CPU variations than automobile models.

Each company has several CPU variations and designations. Intel makes several variations of the Pentium CPUs, such as the Celeron, the Pentium II, the Pentium III, and the Xeon. CPU variations are usually based on the speed or frequency of the CPU.

CPUs become obsolete faster than yesterday's newspapers. The CPU business is much like the auto business. They constantly improve and add new functions to the CPUs and do everything possible to convince you that you cannot live without these new improvements.

The Pentium III Processor

The hottest CPU on the market at this time is the Pentium III, which was launched in January of 1999. Figure 3-1 shows the Pentium III. The Pentium III is just a slightly improved Pentium II. It uses the same Slot 1

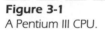
Figure 3-1
A Pentium III CPU.

for the plug-in board that has the CPU. The main difference between the Pentium II and the Pentium III is the 70 Katmai New Instructions (KNI). These instructions are now called Streaming SIMD (Single Instruction Multiple Data) Extensions. SIMD can tell a single program instruction to perform the same operation on two or more pieces of data. SIMD floating-point operations are very useful for graphics, polygons, lighting effects, physics models, and 3D games. The Streaming SIMD Extensions add to and enhance the MMX instructions.

The Pentium III processor integrates the best features of the P6 microarchitecture processors. The original Pentium processors were the P5 CPUs. Many of the cloners called them some version of *586*, since they were next in line from the 286, 386, and 486. Because Intel could not copyright those numbers, the clone companies used them to designate their clone CPUs. Intel could and did copyright the name *Pentium*.

The Pentium II should have been called a 686, and that in fact is what some of the cloners called it. Intel often refers to the Pentium as P5 and to the Pentium II as P6. So the Pentium III and the Celeron are not new architectures, but just an improvement of the P6 family.

When developing a new product, the companies go to great lengths to try to keep it secret. They often choose a code name that has nothing to do with the product. During development, the Pentium III was known by the code name *Katmai*, which is a volcanic mountain in the Alaskan Aleutian range.

Part of the enhancement technology in the Pentium III processor is that it offers SIMD Extensions. These are 70 new instructions enabling advanced imaging, 3D, streaming audio and video, and speech recognition applications. These new instructions were originally known as the KNI, or Katmai New Instructions. (You might still see some of the CPUs advertised as having KNI.) The Pentium III processor works with all PC software and is fully compatible with existing Intel Architecture-based software.

On certain multimedia and 3D benchmarks, the Pentium III shows substantial performance benefits. Compared with the Pentium II 450MHz, the Pentium III 450MHz shows between a 29 percent and up to 74 percent improvement using some of the benchmarks. The Pentium III demonstrates performance improvements in applications such as word-processing, presentation, and personal finance programs. It also shows improvements in running audio, video, imaging, and creativity applications. It works very well in 3D software, including games, and modeling and simulation applications, as well as Internet browsers and multimedia Web content.

Pentium III Serial Numbers

One of the new additions to the Pentium III is that Intel added an electronic serial number to the chip. According to Intel, this serial number enables the system or user to be identified by networks and applications, improving security in managed access to the Internet content and services. In addition, Intel says that it can be used for asset management, remote system load and configuration, and electronic document exchange.

This serial number caused a great hue and cry in the digital community. Many people pointed out that it could be used to take away a lot of privacy. Because of the privacy issue, Intel promised that the chip would be shipped with the serial number turned off. However, if a person or an employer desires the feature, it can be turned back on.

XEON

The Pentium III Xeon processor brand is similar to the Pentium III. It is designed to deliver high performance for mid-range and higher server and workstation applications. The Pentium III Xeon processor will provide quality computing solutions designed to fit your needs whether you're a business professional, hardcore gamer, Internet surfer, or a new PC user.

The Pentium III Xeon CPUs can be set up as two-way, four-way, and eight-way multiprocessing systems. They can be used for such things as power ISP Web servers, corporate ERP applications and networks, or to support multiterabyte data warehouses. There are many other high-end uses for the Xeon.

Intel Celeron CPU

Intel has always been interested in selling low-cost systems. When the 386 came out, they introduced a 386SX. Then when the 486 came out, they introduced a 486SX. Many power users sneered and looked down their noses at anyone who admitted that they used one of these systems. But they were a low-cost option and did most of what needed to be done.

In 1998 they introduced the low-cost Celeron. Figure 3-2 is an Intel Celeron, with the cover removed. If you took the cover off the Pentium III, it would look just like the Celeron. The Celeron was initially a 300MHz chip with no internal cache. The motherboard bus speed was

Figure 3-2
An Intel Celeron with the cover removed.

66MHz. Many people complained about how slow it was because it did not have a cache.

Intel listened and soon came out with faster models that had 128KB of L2 cache in the same cartridge. The cache operated at the same speed as the CPU, whereas the Pentium II L2 cache only operates at half the speed of the CPU. The main difference was that the Pentium II may have from 512KB and up to 1MB of cache.

The Celeron is now available at speeds up to 466MHz and can now operate at 100MHz on the motherboard bus. The Celeron 466MHz can run most applications as fast as the Pentium II 450MHz. One of the Web sites is advertising the Celeron 466MHz at $206.99 and the Pentium II 450MHz at $298.99. The Celeron has hastened the death of the Pentium II systems. Eventually, the Celeron will operate at 550MHz or even faster. It may be all that you need.

The Single Edge Connector Cartridge

Pentium II CPUs are installed on a circuit board with a Single Edge Contact (SEC) cartridge. The cartridge plugs into a special slot on the motherboard, which Intel calls Slot 1. Some of the Celeron CPUs use the same Slot 1 and are pin-compatible with the Pentium II and III. But Intel calls the Celeron cartridge a Single Edge Processor (SEP) package. There are people who stay awake nights dreaming up new acronyms—most of them are unnecessary.

The Pentium III has a slightly different heat sink and mounting cradle. It still mounts in Slot 1. Intel calls this slightly revised cartridge an SECC2.

The L2 cache on the Pentium II and III is mounted on the circuit board on each side of the CPU. The L2 cache is accessed at half the frequency of the CPU. Intel claimed that the reason they developed the Slot 1 was because they needed more space for the added cache and improvements to the Pentium II. But some of the more cynical believed that the reason was to freeze out some of the clones. Most of the cloners were using Socket 7 for their CPUs so they could be compatible with any of the Intel CPUs that used Socket 7. Intel patented the Slot 1 so the cloners could not make a product that was compatible with the Intel Pentium II or Pentium III.

The Celeron in Figure 3-2 uses Slot 1. But the whole idea of the Celeron was to provide an inexpensive CPU that would match the clones in cost. The SEC cartridge adds considerably to the cost of producing the Celeron. So most Celerons are now being produced in the Flat Plastic Pin Grid Array (FPPGA) for the Socket 370. Socket 370 is similar to Socket 7, except that it has more contacts.

Intel has recently announced that they will start producing the Pentium III in the FPPGA configuration for a socket that is similar to the Socket 370. They said that they would continue to support the Slot 1 configuration. This will save Intel a bit of money, but some vendors are not too happy. It just means that they will have to add yet another motherboard to their stock.

Intel 810 Chipset for Celeron CPUs

Intel has developed a new 810 chipset for Celeron processor-based PCs. It delivers better video, audio, and 3D graphics through Intel's Scalable Graphics Architecture. It allows the systems to work much better with the software for these applications. A later version, 810e, will allow the Pentium III and all Slot 1 chips to use this chipset.

Intel is developing new chipsets called 820 and 840 for the newer and faster CPUs. They should be available by the time you read this.

Meeting the Competition

Intel continues to cut the price of the Celeron in order to stay competitive with AMD. By the time you read this, the 466MHz Celeron will be selling for $137 in 1000 lots. But the cost of the Pentium III is still fairly high. A recent ad for a 466MHz Celeron system was $775; an equivalent system from the same company with a Pentium III 500MHz was $1695, or $920 more. The main difference was 34MHz and the Pentium III CPU.

Some Intel CPU Specifications

Following are specificiations for the Xeon, Pentium III, and Celeron processors:

Pentium III Xeon Processor

Clock speed: 450 to 550MHz

Performance data: Workstations, servers

L2 cache: 512KB to 2MB

Number of transistors: 7.5 million

Processor package style: Single Edge Contact (SEC) cartridge

System bus speed: 100MHz

System bus width: 8 bytes

Addressable memory: 64GB

Virtual memory: 64 terabytes

Package dimensions: Height 4.8″ × Width 6.0″ × Depth .73″

Typical use: Dual-processor workstations and servers

Pentium III Processor

Clock speeds: 450 to 550MHz; performance data

Number of transistors: 7.5 million (0.25 micron process)

Processor package style: Single Edge Contact (SEC) cartridge, 242 pins

Package dimensions: 5.505″ × 2.473″ × 0.647″

Bus speed: 100MHz

Bus width: 64-bit system bus

Addressable memory: 64GB

Typical use: Business and consumer PCs, one- and two-way servers and workstations

Celeron Processor

Clock speeds: 333 to 466MHz; performance data

Number of transistors: 7.5 million (0.25 micron process)

Processor package style: Single Edge Processor (SEP) package, 242 pins
Bus speed: 100MHz
Bus width: 64-bit system bus
Addressable memory: 4GB
Package dimensions: 5″ × 2.275″ × .208″
Typical use: Basic PCs

PR Hype

Intel, AMD, Cyrix, IDT, and Rise Technology all have Web sites with the latest information about their products. I am sure that you are aware that you must consider the source of the data and information placed there. In some cases, the actual truth may be stretched a bit and the facts colored somewhat. With this in mind, the Web sites are still an excellent information resource. Please note that the Web sites are constantly updated, so some of the information will have changed by the time you read this.

The AMD K6, Cyrix, IDT, and Rise Technology CPUs still use the motherboards with Socket 7. This is the motherboard that was designed for the original Pentium. When Intel introduced the Pentium II, they designed the Slot 1 system. The AMD Athlon will use a newly designed motherboard with Slot A, which is a bit similar to the Intel Slot 1.

Socket 7 compatibility makes for easier upgrades and faster time to market. AMD has stayed with Socket 7 compatibility for the AMD-K6 processor. Socket 7 can deliver sixth-generation performance within the industry's most cost-effective, widely used PC infrastructure (motherboards, chipsets, and BIOS). By working within the Socket 7 environment, PC manufacturers and resellers can leverage high-volume, low-cost system designs and mature infrastructure.

MMX and Pentium II

The Pentium was almost obsolete before Intel came up with the MMX addition in January of 1997. The MMX extension supports multimedia (most people thought MMX meant "MultiMedia eXtension," but Intel denied it). The set of 57 MMX instructions allows image processing, video conferencing, and 3D rendering for games. MMX helped to extend the life of the Pentium until the Pentium II was released in May of 1997.

The fifth-generation Pentium is obsolete, but there are millions of computers out there that are still using everything from the Pentium 60MHz and up to Pentium 166. Depending on what you want to do with your computer, they are still good systems.

The Pentium II was first released as a 233MHz, then 266MHz, then 300MHz. We now have Pentium II versions that operate as high as 450MHz. The early versions, up to 333MHz, all had a motherboard memory bus speed of 66MHz. The Pentium II 350MHz and later now have a 100MHz motherboard memory bus speed.

The Pentium II 450MHz will do just about everything that the Pentium III 450MHz does. The main difference is that the Pentium II does not have the extra Katmai New Instructions (KNI).

When the Pentium II was first introduced, I called several Intel distributors and tried to buy a 266MHz CPU. There were lots of 233MHz units available, but no one had a 266MHz unit. A few years ago at a large computer swap meet at the Los Angeles County Fairgrounds with over 300 booths, I found a dealer who had just sold his last 266MHz. There was another booth nearby that had one for sale at $860. I decided to look around a bit more, but no one else had the 266MHz units. About 20 minutes later I went back to the booth and the price had been raised from $860 to $870. I quickly bought it before they had a chance to raise the price even more. It was still a bargain even at that price. The Intel distributors had quoted me a price of $1130.

Today, about 30 months later, the Pentium II 266MHz CPU is obsolete. If you could find one, it probably wouldn't cost more than $50. The early Pentium II had a bus speed-to-main memory of only 66MHz. The later ones now have a bus speed of 100MHz and a CPU frequency as high as 450MHz or more. The faster Pentium II CPUs are still a good alternative and offer some real bargains. But they are being made obsolete by the Celeron and Pentium III.

The Future

Intel is working on the next-generation CPU, which is code named Merced, the name of a city in the San Juaquin Valley. It will use the 0.18-micron process and will be a 64-bit architecture. Closely following that CPU will be the McKinley, which will initially run at 1GHz and have twice the power of the Merced.

For more information about Intel, visit their Web site at www.intel.com.

The AMD-K6

The AMD-K6-III processor with 3DNow! technology incorporates AMD's TriLevel Cache design. It is ideal for today's consumer PC enthusiasts and business power users. The TriLevel Cache design of the AMD-K6-III provides one of the industry's largest maximum combined system caches. For more details on this technology, see the AMD press releases, below.

AMD Press Releases

Following are some press releases from the AMD Web site (www.amd.com).

About the K6-III

The AMD-K6-III processor with 3DNow! technology incorporates AMD's TriLevel Cache design to enable leading-edge performance for today's consumer PC enthusiasts and business power users. The innovative TriLevel Cache design maximizes the overall system performance of AMD-K6-III processor-based desktop PCs by delivering one of the industry's largest maximum combined system caches. This larger total cache results in higher system performance. The TriLevel Cache design includes a full-speed 64KB Level 1 (L1) cache (a standard feature of the AMD-K6 processor family), an internal full-speed backside 256KB Level 2 (L2) cache, and a 100-MHz frontside bus to an optional external Level 3 (L3) cache on the Super7™ motherboard. With a total of 320KB of combined L1 and L2 cache, the AMD-K6-III processor has more internal cache memory than any other x86 CPU available today.

The 21.3-million transistor AMD-K6-III processor is manufactured on AMD's 0.25-micron, five-layer-metal process technology using local interconnect and shallow trench isolation at AMD's Fab 25 wafer fabrication facility in Austin, Texas. The AMD-K6-III processor is packaged in a 100-MHz Super7 platform-compatible, 321-pin ceramic pin grid array (CPGA) package using C4 flip-chip interconnection technology.

About 3DNow! Technology

3DNow! technology, the first innovation to the x86 architecture that significantly enhances floating-point-intensive 3D graphics and multimedia applications, uses SIMD (Single Instruction Multiple Data) and other performance enhancements to enable a superior visual computing experience. Introduced as a key feature of the AMD-K6-2 processor in May 1998, 3DNow! technology has more than a nine-month time-to-market head start over competing CPU-based 3D enhancement technologies. The worldwide installed base of 3DNow! technology-enhanced PCs has grown to more than 12 million systems. AMD processors with 3DNow! technology span the complete range of desktop and mobile computing, from sub-$1,000 PCs to high-performance laptops based on the Mobile AMD-K6-2 processor to high-end multimedia desktop systems powered by the new AMD-K6-III processor.

Support for 3DNow! technology exists today in the leading industry-standard application programming interfaces (APIs), including Microsoft's DirectX 6.x and SGI's OpenGL APIs. In addition, numerous hardware and software products have been optimized for 3DNow! technology. Accolade, Activision, Criterion Studios, Digital Anvil, Eidos, GT Interactive, Gremlin, id Software, Interplay, Psygnosis, Rage, and 3DO have announced their support for 3DNow! technology in several of their forthcoming software titles. These publishers and developers join a growing list of software and hardware developers, including Microsoft, IBM, Epic Games, 3Dfx, and Matrox, that already support 3DNow! in their leading 3D graphics-intensive applications and hardware. New titles supporting 3DNow! technology continue to be added.

Specifications for AMD K6-II-450 Chip

Pin/socket: 321-pin (CPGA)/ZIF Socket 7
(P54C/P54CS/P55C MMX) Super7
Architecture: RISC86 Superscalar (level 6) (0.25 micron)
External Bus: 64-bit (pipelined) 100MHz
Bus/Core Ratio: 1/4.5
L1 Cache: Large on-chip split 64-KB level-one (L1) cache
　　—32-Kbyte instruction cache with additional 20Kbytes of predecode
　　cache

—32-Kbyte writeback dual-ported data cache

—Two-way set associative

—MESI protocol support

L2 Cache: No

Floating-Point Unit: Integrated, high-performance with low-latency add/multiply and single-cycle issue; high-performance IEEE 754-compatible and 854-compatible floating-point unit

3DNow! Technology: Additional instructions to improve 3D graphics and multimedia performance

Separate multiplier and ALU for superscalar instruction execution

Voltage: 2.4V

Additional Features: High-performance industry-standard multimedia extensions (MMX)

Full x86 instruction set optimization

6-stage pipelined

Register renaming

Dynamic branch prediction

16-entry/16byte target branch cache

8192-entry branch history table

95% prediction accuracy

Speculative execution

Out-of-order completion

Specifications for AMD K6-III-450 Chip

Pin/Socket: 321-Pin (CPGA) / ZIF Socket 7 (P54C/P54CS/P55C MMX) Super7

Architecture: Die size: 21.3 million transistors on 118 square mm die RISC86 Superscalar (level 6) (0.25 micron, five-layer-metal silicon)

External Bus: 64-bit (pipelined) 100MHz

Bus/Core Ratio: 1/4.5

L1 Cache : Large on-chip split 64-KB Level-1 (L1) cache

—32KB instruction cache with additional 20Kbytes of predecode cache

—32KB writeback dual-ported data cache

—Two-way set associative

—MESI protocol support

L2 Cache: Internal, full-speed backside 256KB Level-2 write-back cache

—Multiport internal cache design enabling simultaneous 64-bit reads/writes of L1 and L2 caches

—Four-way set associative L2 cache design enabling optimal data management and efficiency

Floating-Point Unit: Integrated, high-performance with low-latency add/multiply and single-cycle issue; high-performance IEEE 754-compatible and 854-compatible floating-point unit

3DNOW! Technology: 21 new SIMD instructions to improve 3D graphics and multimedia performance

—Peak operation of 4 floating-point operations per clock

—Separate multiplier and ALU for superscalar instruction execution

—Compatible with existing x86 operating system

Voltage: 2.4V core

Additional Features: TriLevel cache design with optional external Level-3 cache on Super7 motherboard

Enhanced superscalar MMX(TM) instruction execution with dual decode and dual execution pipelines

Full x86 instruction set optimization

Six-stage pipelined

Register renaming and data forwarding

Advanced two-level branch prediction

16-entry/16byte target branch cache

8192-entry branch history table

95% prediction accuracy

Speculative execution

Out-of-order completion

K6-III vs. Pentium III

Ziff-Davis's *PC Magazine* has a well-equipped test laboratory. They often invite vendors to send them systems, which they test and review for the magazine. They have several tests that they perform on systems. They can determine if one system is faster than another, even if it is only by a fraction of a microsecond. These reviews are a great way to know which systems perform better.

I have a K6-III 450MHz and a Pentium III 500MHz. I don't have all the facilities and equipment to do tests as elaborate as *PC Magazine* does. So I rely on their published tests to a great degree. One of their tests pitted a Pentium III 500MHz against an AMD 450MHz. In one of their Business Winstone 99 tests, the Pentium III 500MHz tested out at 24.7; the AMD 450MHz tested out at 24.5. In a 3D WinMark 99 test, the Pentium III 500MHz did a little better at 685, while the AMD 450MHz was 581.

Norton Utilities has a System Information (SI) utility that can run several tests on your system. It can then compare your system to a Pentium 166MHz, which has a score of 37.2, a Pentium II 233MHz, with 57.8, and a Pentium II 450MHz, with 204.8. My Pentium 500MHz has a Norton SI score of 228.5. My AMD K6-III 450MHz has a Norton SI of 215.4.

AMD Athlon

AMD has renamed the K7 as the AMD Athlon. They didn't say, but I suspect that it may have been for the same reason that Intel named their CPU "Pentium," rather than "586." The numbers *586* could not be copyrighted. *Pentium* and *Athlon* are copyrightable.

Here is a recent press release from AMD about the new AMD Athlon:

> "The all-new AMD-Athlon design features a number of compelling technological breakthroughs, including the industry's first mainstream 200 MHz system bus and the most architecturally advanced floating point capability ever delivered in an x86 microprocessor," said S. Atiq Raza, AMD executive vice president and chief technical officer.
>
> The Microsoft Windows compatible AMD Athlon processor with 3DNow! technology offers seventh-generation design features that distinguish it from previous generations of PC processors. These innovations include a nine-issue superscalar microarchitecture optimized for high clock frequency, a superscalar pipelined floating point unit, 128KB of on-chip level one (L1) cache, a programmable high-performance backside L2 cache interface, and a 200MHz Alpha EV6-compatible system bus interface with support for scalable multiprocessing.
>
> The AMD Athlon processor operates at clock frequencies of 500MHz, 550MHz and 600MHz. According to some of the benchmark tests, the Athlon has a 40% performance improvement over the equivalent Pentium III. AMD expects that they will have an Athlon built on the 0.18 micron process in a short time. They expect that the Athlon will operate in the gigahertz range. The AMD Athlon processor will leverage existing physical and mechanical PC infrastructure.

Of course, this competition will cause Intel to match and improve over the Athlon. They will also be trimming prices of their CPUs to match the AMD prices. (Isn't competition grand?)

L1 Cache

One of the AMD Athlon's major features is the 128KB Level-1 (L1) cache, four times as much as the Pentium II has, and twice as much L1 as AMD's K6 II. The L1 is accessed at the full CPU speed. The LI cache holds the most commonly used data while an application is being processed. The L1 cache is the first place the CPU looks for information. If the needed information is not in the L1, then it will look in the Level-2 cache.

L2 cache

Most L2 cache is on the motherboard. Even though the signal travels near the speed of light, it takes a finite amount of time to go back and forth to the motherboard. Intel designed the Pentium II and Pentium III so that the L2 cache is very close and is within the same enclosure as the CPU. But even being that close, the L2 cache usually runs at some fraction of the CPU speed.

The AMD Athlon will feature an "on-card" L2 cache similar to that found in the Pentium II and III. The speed of the L2 cache is configurable and may range from one-third clock speed all the way to full speed. The size of the L2 cache is currently limited to 512KB. It is expected that AMD will release later versions of the Athlon that may have up to 8MB of L2 cache. The Pentium III may have from 512KB L2 and up to 2MB. The more the cache, the more cash you will have to pay.

Slot A

The Socket 7 has some limitations. That is one reason Intel designed the Slot 1. Intel patented the Slot 1 design so that no one else can use it without permission and a proper license. And they were not about to give AMD or anyone else permission to use Slot 1. So AMD has designed a new Slot A for their new AMD Athlon. It will be a bit more expensive for the motherboard manufacturers, but no more expensive than it was for Intel to design Slot 1 motherboards for Pentium II. (It seems a bit ironic that Intel is giving up on their Slot 1 and going back to Socket 370 just when AMD is developing a Slot A.)

For up-to-date information about AMD, visit their Web site at www.amd.com.

Some Alternatives

Intel is the original and the foremost CPU maker in the world. Last year, they sold about 22 billion dollars worth of chips. A whole lot of that 22 billion was profit. They invest a lot of that profit in research and development. They also spent an enormous amount in advertising. The CPU clone makers have a very small piece of the pie and have very small profit margins. In order to compete, the clone makers have had to offer CPUs that are compatible with the Intel, are almost as fast and powerful as it, and are less expensive.

If you can get by with something a bit slower and less powerful, but a lot less expensive, you might want to look at the Cyrix CPUs.

Cyrix M II Processor

The M II processor is a high-performance CPU offering advanced processing on Windows 95 and other operating systems. The M II processor features MMX instructions, enhanced memory management unit, a 64KB internal cache, and other state-of-the-art architectural features to achieve higher performance and offer better value than competitive processors.

The M II processor features advanced circuit design for optimum performance. The M II is superscalar in that it contains two separate pipelines that allow multiple instructions to be processed at the same time. It features a 64KB internal cache, a two-level TLB, and a 512-entry BTB. The MMX-enhanced M II processor also contains a scratchpad RAM feature, supports performance monitoring, allows caching of both SMI code and SMI data, and features a superpipelined architecture that increases the number of pipeline stages to reduce timing constraints and increase frequency scalability. It delivers optimum 32-bit performance while running Windows 95, Windows NT, OS/2, DOS, UNIX, and other x86 operating systems.

The M II processor features a superpipelined architecture that increases the number of pipeline stages to reduce timing constraints and increase frequency scalability. Advanced architectural techniques include register renaming, out-of-order completion, data dependency removal, branch prediction, and speculative execution. These design innovations eliminate many data dependencies and resource conflicts to achieve higher performance when executing 32-bit software.

Enhanced Sixth-Generation Architecture

64KB on-chip unified L1 cache

Two-level TLB (16 entry L1 TLB, 384 entry L2 TLB)

Branch prediction with a 512-entry BTB

Enhanced memory management unit

Optimized for 32-bit code

80-bit floating-point unit

Superpipelined

Superscalar

Technical Specifications:

Clocking—2x, 2.5x, 3x, 3.5x, 4x flexible core/bus clock ratios

L1 cache—64KB; write-back; four-way associative, unified instruction and data; dual port address

Bus—64-bit external data bus; 32-bit pipelined address bus

Pin/socket—Socket 7 pinout-compatible (P55C)

Compatibility—Compatible with Windows 95, Windows NT, Windows, UNIX, OS/2, and many other operating systems; runs thousands of 16-bit and 32-bit applications, as well as the latest MMX-enhanced software

Floating-point unit—80-bit with 64-bit interface; parallel execution; x87 instruction set; IEEE-754 compatible

Voltage—2.9V core with 3.3V I/O

Power management

System Management Mode (SMM); hardware suspend; FPU auto-idle

The Cyrix Corp. has had a lot of problems. They merged with National Semiconductor, which should have given them a bit more clout. But National has recently decided to put the Cyrix division up for sale. Hopefully, someone will take it over and continue to offer low-cost alternatives. We definitely need the competition.

For up-to-date information, visit their Web site at www.cyrix.com.

IDT WinChip C6 Processor

Another company, the IDT Corporation (for Integrated Device Technology), has entered the CPU market with the WinChip C6. The Rise Technology Company also has a low-cost CPU. Each of these CPUs has a cost advantage, but they are usually not as fast or powerful as Intel's CPUs. However, not everybody needs an expensive Cadillac luxury automobile. A low-cost compact can get you to your destination just as well as a Cadillac. It may not be as comfortable, but a compact can get you there. Similarly, not everybody needs a 550MHz Pentium III. For most jobs, an IDT WinChip will do all that is needed. They may take a few milliseconds more to do some jobs, but you know the old saying, you probably have more time than money.

Of course, I know that the statement above has probably not changed your mind. I have no doubt that you are a lot like me and thousands of others. We want the most powerful, the fastest, the biggest, and the best. The following is what the IDT Web site has to say about the capabilities of their new microprocessors:

The IDT WinChip C6 is the first microprocessor from Centaur Technology, a subsidiary of IDT. Using a unique design approach, the IDT WinChip C6 delivers competitive performance, lower cost, and lower power dissipation than offerings from other x86 microprocessor suppliers. This combination of features is expected to shift the price/performance paradigm in the personal computer industry and will allow computer manufacturers to deliver higher value to the end customer. IDT WinChip C6 is targeted at the sub-$1000 desktop and sub-$2000 notebook product categories. The IDT WinChip C6 includes MMX-compatible instructions and is offered in processor speeds of 180MHz and 200MHz, with faster speeds to come.

Architecture The IDT WinChip C6 uses a unique design concept that goes back to the principles of RISC (Reduced Instruction Set Computing) architecture. This unique design approach focuses on optimizing the microprocessor for highly used simple instructions and improving the overall clock frequency. Memory performance is further improved by using large on-chip caches and sophisticated cache and translation algorithms to reduce bus utilization. In addition, the IDT WinChip C6 processor is highly optimized for small physical size, which results in lower manufacturing costs as well as lower power consumption.

Performance The IDT WinChip C6 offers competitive performance to Pentium with MMX technology, AMD-K6, and Cyrix 6x86MX microprocessors running Windows 95/98 business applications.

Power Dissipation IDT WinChip C6 power dissipation is much lower than other Pentium-class processors with MMX technology, making it suitable for mobile systems and the rapidly growing sub-$1000 PC product category. The WinChip C6 has a die size of only 88 square mm, or about .4 inches square. The smaller die area means lower production cost, lower power consumption, and less heat dissipation.

Compatibility   Centaur Technology has extensively tested the IDT WinChip C6 processor with x86 operating systems such as DOS, Windows 3.1, Windows 95, Windows NT, OS/2, Linux, and a large number of software applications. In addition, many third-party motherboards, along with chipsets from ALI, VIA, SIS, and Intel, have been tested to ensure compatibility. BIOS support is also available from Award, AMI, and SystemSoft. IDT WinChip C6 third-party verification includes Microsoft Certified Compatibility with Windows 95/98 and XXCAL Platinum Certification. The IDT WinChip C6 is a plug-compatible processor to Pentium with MMX Technology and is offered in a 296-pin ceramic pin grid array (CPGA), Socket 7-compliant ceramic package. IDT WinChip C6 leverages the established and low-cost Socket 7 motherboard infrastructure.

The IDT WinChip C6 processor is a 5.4 million transistor device manufactured using IDT's 0.35 micron, four-layer metal CMOS technology. At only 88 square millimeters in size, the IDT WinChip C6 processor is between 30 and 60 percent smaller than comparable Pentium-class processors with MMX technology. The combination of small die size coupled with a simplified CMOS process allows IDT to manufacture the WinChip C6 very efficiently and at a low cost.

For up-to-date information, visit their Web site at www.idt.com.

Rise Technology

Rise Technology has several low-cost chips that are compatible with Intel CPUs and Windows software. Their CPUs are based on the 100MHz Super7 bus. They are also developing a CPU that is compatible with the Celeron Socket 370 processor. Their mP6 CPUs range in speed from 333MHz up to 433MHz. They have a 256K on-chip L2 cache.

Rise Technology's CPUs have a very low power consumption and are ideal for laptops as well as low-cost desktop systems. For up-to-date information, visit their Web site at www.rise.com.

How CPUs Are Made

Designing and creating a CPU or an integrated circuit is a very complex procedure. Basically, a large, high-powered workstation and computer-aided design (CAD) software may be used for the early design. The transistors and circuit paths are actually drawn to scale. The design may then be printed out on a very large piece of paper. Once the design is checked for accuracy, it is reduced by several magnitudes, then photographed. The negative image is then transferred to a silicon die. Then, using acids and photoengraving procedures and methods, portions of the die are etched away. The photographic image has now become a CPU made up of transistors and circuits in the silicon die. The CPUs are etched onto a thin slab of silicon about 6 to 8 inches in diameter. Several CPUs can be etched onto a single slab. The chips go through several stages of processing. At the end of the processing, the individual CPUs are cut and separated. They are then tested and selected.

A lot of money is involved in manufacturing CPUs. An article in *Electronic Buyers News* calculated that it costs about $30 for each Celeron manufactured with the 0.25 process. When manufacturers switch over to the 0.18 process, they will be able to get more CPUs from each slab, so the cost should drop to about $13 per CPU. The Pentium II and III cost a bit more because they have more transistors and require more space. Therefore, they cannot get as many CPUs from each slab. Except for the selecting and testing, a 550MHz CPU should cost no more than a 400MHz chip. But before you decide to go into the CPU business, remember that the above description is very much simplified. The actual cost of setting up an advanced CPU manufacturing facility may be 2 billion dollars or more.

The Price of Speed

Here are some current prices of a few Intel CPUs:

Celeron 333MHz	$100
Celeron 400MHz	$149
Celeron 466MHz	$209
Pentium II 333MHz	$158
Pentium II 400MHz	$229
Pentium II 450MHz	$314
AMD K6-III 450MHz	$259
Pentium III 450MHz	$332
Pentium III 500MHz	$585
Pentium III 550MHz	$880

Note the wide variation in prices as the speed goes up. The prices will be much lower by the time you read this.

Overclocking

CPUs are usually all made from the same die and slab of silicon. For some reason, some of the chips may be able to perform at a higher speed than others. The vendor usually tests and selects these chips and sells them for a premium. Quite often the vendor does not take the time to test all the chips. They usually throw them all in a bin after selecting out as many as needed to fill the orders for the higher speeds. It is quite possible that a large number of the chips will perform at the higher speeds. Especially after the first few runs, most of the bugs are worked out and the yield becomes much greater.

Of course, manufacturers want to sell as many as they can at the higher price. But they can sell a lot more of the lower-speed chips. You can therefore save a bit of money by buying a 450MHz and setting the motherboard jumpers so that it runs at 500MHz. Here are some recent prices from one company: for the Intel Pentium III 450MHz, $332, and for the Intel Pentium III 500MHz, $585. For just 50MHz of more speed, they charge a difference of $253. That could be quite a lot of savings if the 450MHz will work at 500MHz. And configuring it to do so is a very simple procedure.

Most motherboards have jumpers or switches to set the CPU and bus speed to match whatever CPU that is being used. It is usually some fraction of the internal speed. Refer to Table 3-1. A Pentium III at 450MHz operates internally at 450MHz and externally at 100MHz, so the jumper setting would be for 4.5. To run it at 500MHz, the setting would be for 5. For 550MHz, the setting would have to be for 5.5. You can try the higher speed, boot up the computer, and if it works, you have saved some money. If it refuses to boot, then you will have to set the jumpers back to the original setting. Figure 3-3 shows some white jumpers that were used to configure this motherboard for 450MHz (4.5X) CPU and 100MHz (100M) bus speed. To overclock this system, you could move the jumper to 5X for 500MHz. If this didn't work, you could try increasing the bus speed to 112MHz.

Of course, to be able to do this, you need the motherboard documentation that shows the jumpers and switches. This should not cause any harm to your system, but it will void your warranty if the company finds out. You can bet that Intel and the other vendors do not want you to

overclock. They want to sell you the chips at the higher prices. There is a rumor that they have put a lock on some of the chips so that they will not operate at a frequency higher than what is stated on the chip.

My AMD 450MHz motherboard has a set of jumper pins that can be set for anything from 166MHz up to 550MHz. I tried to overclock my AMD 450MHz by setting the multiplier to 5. The initial screen came on and said that it was running at 500MHz, but the system then froze and refused to complete the boot up. I set the jumpers back to 4.5 and it still works fine. So no harm was done.

What's in a Number?

At one time, we only had two types of CPUs and systems: the original IBM PC (for personal computer) and later the XT (for extended technology). Soon after, IBM introduced the AT (for advanced technology). Most people eventually called it 286 because it used the 80286 CPU. The 286 was followed by the 386, then the 486. Several companies began to make clones of the 286, 386, and 486 CPUs. This did not make Intel very happy. They went to court and sued the companies for using their designations but found that they could not copyright the CPU numbers. As mentioned, the next logical CPU number should have been 586, but since they couldn't copyright it, they called it the *Pentium*, which is copyrighted. The copyright issue didn't bother the clone makers. AMD came out with a 586 and Cyrix with a 5x86. To match the Pentium Pro, Cyrix came out with a 6x86. Intel introduced the Pentium II with MMX technology; Cyrix introduced their M2 and AMD their K6. The clones are usually a few steps behind Intel, but, eventually, they are usually able to match anything that Intel produces—and at about 25 percent less in cost.

Basic Characteristics of CPUs

Table 3-1 shows some of the characteristics of some of the early Intel CPUs and the newer ones.

Addressable Memory

Note that the 386, 486, and Pentium can address up to 4GB, or 4,000,000,000 bytes of memory. The Pentium III can address 16 times more, or 64GB. Many of the Pentium II and III motherboards are now designed to accept up to 2048MB of RAM or 2GB.

TABLE 3-1

CPU
Characteristics.

CPU	Freq.	Volt	Bus	Addr.	Mem.	Cache	Xsistors	Date
8088	4.77	5V	8bit	20bit	1MB	no	29 k	6/79
286	6	5V	6bit	24bit	16MB	no	134 k	2/82
386	16	5V	32bit	32bit	4GB	no	275 k	10/85
486	25	5V	32bit	32bit	4GB	8K	1.2 mil	4/89
486DX2	66	5V	32bit	32bit	4GB	8K	1.2 mil	3/92
486DX4	99	5V	32bit	32bit	4GB	16K	1.6 mil	2/94
Pentium	60	5V	32bit	32bit	4GB	16K	3.1 mil	3/93
Pentium	75	3.3V	32bit	32bit	4GB	16K	3.3 mil	3/94
Pent. Pro	150	2.9V	32bit	36bit	64GB	16K	5.5 mil	9/95
Pent. II	333-450	1.8V	32bit	36bit	64GB	32K	7.5 mil	5/97
Celeron	333-466	1.8V	32bit	36bit	64GB	32K	7.5 mil	4/98
Pent. Xeon	400-450	1.8V	32bit	36bit	64GB	32K	7.5 mil	4/98
Pentium III	400-550	1.8V	32bit	36bit	64GB	32K	7.5 mil	1/99

A few years ago, Gordon Moore, while chairman of Intel Corporation, noticed a very definite CPU trend. Table 3-1 above basically shows what he observed. Note that the 286 had 125,000 transistors, more than three times the 29,000 in the XT. Very soon the 386 was introduced with 275,000 transistors, which more than doubled the 286, then the 486 with 1.2 million, then soon after the Pentium with 3.1 million and then the Pentium Pro with 5.5 million. The present Pentium generation (P6) has 7.5 million transistors. The next generation will have over 10 million. The trend is that every 18 months or so, the number of transistors and computing power more than doubles. Another trend is that as the power goes up, the price goes down, which is great news for us consumers.

In the chart above, the CPU operating frequency listed is the introductory value. Intel was usually rather conservative in the operating frequency recommended. In every case, soon after introduction, the frequency was revised upward. Even the old 8088 was eventually boosted up to as high as 10MHz. The 286 was introduced to run at 6MHz, but very soon many were running it at 8MHz, then as high as 12MHz. Near the end of its reign, some were running it as high as 25MHz. The 386 was introduced to operate at 16MHz. Almost overnight, people were boosting it up to 20MHz. Eventually, it was revved up as high as 40MHz. When the 486 was introduced it operated at 25MHz, so some of the 386 CPUs actually ran faster than some of the new 486s. But because of the internal design and number of transistors, the 486 could still outperform a 386 that was running faster.

The first Pentium operated at 60MHz, but before long it was revised so that it ran as high as 200MHz. At the present time the Pentium III can run as fast as 550Hz. It may eventually run as high as 700MHz. We have certainly come a long way since that first XT that ran at 4.77MHz.

CPU Frequency and Motherboard Speed

When a software program is run, the program is copied from a hard disk or some other source and loaded into RAM. (Actually, it is dynamic RAM that is most often used, or DRAM.) To process the data, the CPU runs back and forth to the DRAM, brings parts of the data into the CPU, processes it, and sends it back to DRAM. After the processing is completed, the data is sent back to the hard disk, the printer, or wherever it is needed. The speed at which the CPU operates internally and the external speed used on the motherboard to run back and forth to the DRAM may or may not be the same. The internal operating frequency may be 1x, or up to 5.5x more than the external motherboard speed. There are usually jumpers or switches on the motherboard that can be used to set the external and internal frequency or speed of the particular CPU.

Table 3-2 shows the memory bus speeds for several Pentium CPUs.

Each equivalent version of the Celeron would have the same configurations.

TABLE 3-2
Memory Bus
Speed.

CPU Type	Int. Freq.	x	Ext. Speed
Pentium 60	60MHz	1x	60MHz
Pentium 66	66MHz	1x	66MHz
Pentium 75	75MHz	1.5x	50MHz
Pentium 100	100MHz	1.5x	66MHz
Pentium 120	120MHz	2x	60MHz
Pentium 133	133MHz	2x	66MHz
Pentium 150	150MHz	2.5x	60MHz
Pentium 166	166MHz	2.5x	66MHz
Pentium 180	180MHz	3x	60MHz
Pentium 200	200MHz	3x	66MHz
Pentium II	233MHz	3.5x	66MHz
Pentium II	266MHz	4x	66MHz
Pentium II	300MHz	4.5x	66MHz
Pentium II	333MHz	5x	66MHz
Pentium II	350MHz	3.5x	100MHz
Pentium II	400MHz	4x	100MHz
Pentium II	450MHz	4.5x	100MHz
Pentium III	450MHz	4.5x	100MHz
Pentium III	500MHz	5x	100MHz
Pentium III	550MHz	5.5x	100MHz

Memory Bus

Note that the 60MHz system processes the data internally at 60MHz and externally to RAM memory also at 60MHz. The Pentium 90MHz, 120MHz, 150MHz, and 180MHz operate internally at those frequencies but externally at 60MHz. The Pentium 75MHz operates internally at 75 and externally at 50MHz. The Pentium 66MHz, 100MHz, 133MHz, 166MHz, and 200MHz operate internally at those frequencies but externally at 66MHz. Many of the motherboards have jumpers so that they can be configured for whatever speed of installed CPU. One reason the systems don't operate faster going back and forth to RAM is that very high frequencies are difficult to control. The longer the distance and the length of the bus, the more problems. At very high frequencies, two circuit paths alongside one another will have a capacitance and an inductance. It is possible that the contents or signals on one circuit would be picked up by the adjacent circuit. It takes extremely careful and costly engineering to design high-frequency circuits. Cyrix has systems that will operate externally at 75MHz, which is faster than any of the Intel systems. By the time you read this, Intel will probably have systems that will operate externally between the CPU and the RAM at 100MHz.

Remember that the memory bus is not the same as the bus for peripherals. Many of the peripherals, especially the Industry Standard Architecture (ISA)-type boards and components, may still operate at 8 or 10MHz. Because of this limitation, several new faster bus systems were developed: the Micro Channel Architecture (MCA) by IBM, the Enhanced Industry Standard Architecture (EISA), the Video Electronics Standards Association (VESA), Local Bus (VLB), and the Peripheral Component Interconnect (PCI).

Only the PCI has survived. All of the other systems are now obsolete. Newer special systems have been developed that surpass the speed of the PCI for certain applications such as the Accelerated Graphics Port (AGP) for faster graphics and the Ultra DMA/33 for faster hard disk access.

Despite the improved buses, few of them can feed data to the CPU fast enough to keep it busy.

Cache Systems

One solution to the high-frequency problem is to build a cache system as near the CPU as possible. Often when a program is being processed, the

CPU may use blocks of the same data over and over. If a cache is set up nearby to hold this data, then the processing speed can be improved. Having the cache nearby is so important that, beginning with the 486, a small Local 1 (L1) cache of 8KB was built onto the same die as the CPU. Beginning with the 486DX4, the internal L1 cache was doubled to 16KB.

All of the Pentiums have the 16KB L1 cache. The Pentium II and III have two 16K L1 caches.

In addition to the L1 cache, all systems beginning with the 486 also have a L2 cache on the motherboard, as close to the CPU as possible. The L2 cache may be from 256KB and up to 512KB or more. Beginning with the Pentium Pro, Intel put the L2 cache about as close as it could possibly be to the CPU. They installed it in the same package very near the CPU. The cache must be very fast, at least 15 nanoseconds (ns). The fastest standard DRAM is about 60ns. For the faster systems, static RAM (SRAM) is often used. The SRAM systems require six to seven times more transistors than DRAM. The Pentium III L2 cache for 512KB requires 31 million transistors.

Chipsets

The CPU needs support for several functions such as for direct memory access (DMA), the interrupts, the timer, and the clock generator. In early systems, these were all separate chips installed on the motherboard. Now many of the support chips are integrated into a single set, such as the Intel 440BX, 440EX, 440LX, and 440GX. Intel has recently introduced a new 810 chipset for the Celeron. When choosing a motherboard, it is very important to choose one that will work with your CPU. See Chapter 2 for more information about chipsets.

CPU Competition

It is rather interesting to note some of the dates for the introduction of the new CPUs. Note that from the introduction of the 8088 in 1979 to the 286 in 1982 was three years. It was also about three years after this that the 386 was introduced in 1985 and a little over three years before the 486 was introduced in April of 1989.

At about this time, AMD and Cyrix Corporation introduced CPUs that were Intel clones. Up until this time, Intel had no competition.

They were selling every CPU that they could make. There was little incentive to spend a lot of money to build new fabrication factories. Such a factory may cost as much as 2 billion dollars or more.

Ordinarily, Intel would develop a product, then leave it on the market as long as it was still selling well. They would milk it as long as possible, even though they may have had more powerful and better products on hand. No one can dispute the fact that it was good business. But after Intel was presented with a little competition beginning in 1991, suddenly one or more new products have been introduced every year since. Quite often new products are introduced even though the old ones were still selling well. But as soon as a competitor showed any sign of taking a bit of the market, Intel would immediately switch to the new product. Then high-cost ad campaigns would be instituted to try to convince everyone that the old product was no longer a good buy, even though just a few months earlier, they were trying to convince everyone that this product was the best buy in the world. In any case, the competition has been good for us consumers. Besides having a greater choice of products, they are much less expensive. I paid $4450 for my first 486 motherboard, which operated at 25MHz. A motherboard with a Pentium III 500MHz costs less than $900 today, about one-fifth of what I paid for my old 486 CPU and motherboard. Besides the lower price, the new CPU is over 20 times faster.

CPU Sockets

Intel has designed several sockets for the motherboard. Most of the later sockets are the Zero Insertion Force (ZIF) type. Some of the pin grid array (PGA) sockets were designed for 238 pins up to 387 pins. The sockets are simply called Socket 1 through 8. Table 3-3 shows various sockets.

Socket Standardization

Most of the sockets have the socket number on them, but in some cases it is very lightly molded onto the socket. For Sockets 7 and 8, the VRM means voltage regulator module. The Pentium CPUs may operate at different voltages anywhere from 3.3V down to 2.5 or lower. The low voltage for the CPU must be well regulated, clean, and devoid of spikes.

TABLE 3-3

Standard CPU Sockets.

Socket #	# Pins	Voltage	CPUs
Socket 1	169	5V	486SX, 486DX, 486DX2, 486DX4 OverDrive
Socket 2	238	5V	486SX, 486DX, 486DX2, 486DX4 OverDrive, 486 to Pentium OverDrive
Socket 3	237	5V/3.3V	486SX, 486DX, 486DX2, 486DX4 OverDrive, 486 to Pentium OverDrive
Socket 4	273	5V	Pentium 60/66, Pentium 60/66 OverDrive
Socket 5	320	3.3V	Pentium 75-133, Pentium 75+ OverDrive
Socket 6		Not used	
Socket 7	321	VRM	Pentium 75-200, Pentium 75+ OverDrive, AMD, Cyrix, IDT, Rise Technology
Socket 8	387	VRM	Pentium Pro
SEC Slot 1	242	VRM	Pentium II, III, Celeron
Socket 370	242	VRM	Celeron

The Pentium MMX, AMD K6, and Cyrix M2 all use the standard Socket 7. These CPUs can be used on any of the motherboards with the standard Socket 7. Intel created a new socket, the single edge connector (SEC) Slot 1 for their Pentium II-type CPU. AMD and Cyrix were not too happy because this created a separate proprietary standard. Some have accused Intel of acting like IBM when they created their proprietary MCA system.

The original Celeron CPUs were mounted on a circuit board for Slot 1. But it adds to the cost of the CPU. To lower cost, they designed a Socket 370 for the Celeron. New production will be in the Socket 370 configuration.

Why Lower Voltage?

Heat is an enemy of transistors and other semiconductors. The more transistors, the higher the frequency, the more current required, the more wattage used, and the more heat generated. Watts used is equal to the amount of current times the voltage. So the lower the voltage, the less wattage used and the less heat to worry about. Another reason to use less voltage is that the etched lines between the transistors are

Figure 3-4
A fan and heat sink
assembly for Socket 7
CPUs.

becoming thinner and thinner, some as thin as 0.18 microns, or 18 millionths of an inch. That would be several times smaller than a human
hair. The connecting lines are made thinner in order to crowd more transistors into the limited space. Because it wouldn't take much for a voltage to break through the thin lines and short out, the voltage is carefully
regulated and fans and heat sinks are used to dissipate the heat. The
early XT, 286, 386, and 486 did not need heat sinks or special cooling.
Even though they all used 5 volts, the fewer transistors and lower frequency did not generate enough heat to cause a problem. The later 486
DX2 and DX4 did require extra heat sinks and fan cooling. Figure 3-4
shows a fan and heat sink for a Socket 7 CPU.

ZIF Sockets

Almost all motherboards now use the Zero Insertion Force (ZIF) sockets
for the CPU. These sockets have a lever that when raised allows the
chip to be easily removed and replaced. The ZIF socket has split contacts for the pins from the chip. A lever opens the socket contacts so that
the chip just falls in. When the lever is closed, the contacts are forced
together so that they make intimate connection with the pins. In the
early days, there were very few occasions or need to remove and replace
a CPU. Often, the CPU was soldered into the socket. But today there

Figure 3-5
A ZIF socket.

are so many different CPUs and so many options that the ZIF socket is a necessity. Figure 3-5 shows a ZIF socket with an older Pentium CPU. Figure 3-6 shows the backside of a CPU designed for Socket 7.

Whether it is the old-style socket or the ZIF, you must note carefully where pin 1 is located. The chip will usually have a corner cut off to indi-

Figure 3-6
A Socket 7 and the backside of a CPU. The pen points to the corner with slant pins and contacts—pin 1 is in this area.

cate pin 1. Again, you should be aware that it may be more cost-effective and less expensive to buy a new motherboard and CPU rather than install a CPU upgrade. Some of the clone motherboards are very inexpensive. Be sure to check all of your options.

Of course, with the Slot 1, you don't need a ZIF-type system.

Resources

For more information on any of these CPUs, contact the companies below:

AMD Corp.
    One AMD Place, P.O. Box 3453
    Sunnyvale, CA 94088-9968
    408-749-5703
    http://www.amd.com

Cyrix Corp.
    P.O. Box 853917
    Richardson, TX 75086-3917
    214-968-8388
    http://www.cyrix.com

Intel Corp.
    2200 Mission College Blvd.
    Santa Clara, CA 95052
    408-765-7525
    http://www.intel.com

For latest press releases from Intel, point your browser to:

www.intel.com/pressroom/archive/releases/DP050797.htm

Benchmarks

An early benchmark was the Norton System Information (SI) that came with Norton's utilities. It provided a measure for a system's throughput, including processing speed and the speed of some peripherals. The Norton SI reference 1.0 is based on the original IBM XT, which had a CPU frequency of 4.77MHz. Later systems are measured against this reference. My 486DX2-66 system measures 42.4, which means that it is over 42 times faster than the original XT. The 66MHz frequency of the 486 is just a little over 13 times faster than the XT at 4.77MHz, but the newer technologies and operation of the CPU system yield over 42 times better performance.

There are several other benchmarks. Whetstones measure arithmetic operations. Dhrystones measure millions of instructions per second, or MIPS. WinBench executes on top of Windows and gives WinMark measures. Other benchmarks have been developed by organizations such as the Ziff-Davis Labs. They do a lot of testing for the system reviews that are reported in their various magazines. The Intel Comparative Performance (iCOMP) index rating provides a simple relative measure of microprocessor performance. It is not a system benchmark, but a test intended to help nontechnical end users decide which Intel CPU best meets their needs. The iCOMP is based on both 16- and 32-bit CPU performance processing integer, floating-point, graphics, and video performance. The higher the iCOMP index, the higher the relative performance.

History

One of the first CPUs was the 4004, introduced by Intel in 1971. It had 2300 transistors, a fantastic amount at that time. It ran at a blazing 1MHz. The next-generation Pentium from Intel will have over 10 million transistors and can operate at frequencies above 700MHz. Comparing the early 4004 to some of the CPUs today is about like comparing a World War I biplane to the Space Shuttle.

For several years, Intel was the sole manufacturer of the CPU for the IBM-compatible-type machines. Now there are several companies making them. Though Intel still has well over 80 percent of the CPU market, they have to constantly be on their toes in order to retain this share. The competition has helped keep the prices down and has spurred the companies to develop newer and better products.

Upgrading

At one time, the motherboard and CPU were sold as a single unit. In some cases, the CPU was actually soldered to the motherboard. But no more. Today, many of the motherboards are designed so that you may use a large number of different CPUs with them. So a good upgrade strategy may be to simply pull out the old CPU from the motherboard and replace it with a newer one. However, there may be a problem with this simple upgrade. Some of the older motherboards were designed before we had the newer and faster CPUs. So many of them may not have the jumpers or means to configure them for the speed and voltages of the newer CPUs.

More about upgrading in Chapter 12.

Which CPU System Should You Choose?

Asking *which* CPU system is almost like asking how high is up. You should choose the system that will best accomplish whatever you need to do. However, what you need to do today may not be the same as what you need to do tomorrow. Therefore, I suggest that you choose the biggest and most powerful system that you can afford.

It would appear that the AMD Athlon is the fastest and most powerful at the moment. Of course, Intel will not let that stand for long.

When I first fired up my new 500MHz Pentium III, I was so happy, trying it out, lovingly exploring all of its nooks and crannies. It was much like a new marriage. During the honeymoon, many couples are hard-pressed to keep their hands off each other. But the honeymoon eventually ends, and the couple may start taking each other for granted. They may even start thinking that the grass looks greener on the other side of the fence and head for divorce court and a new mate. You should be aware that whatever system you choose will be practically obsolete by the time the honeymoon is over. Alas.

4

Memory

Memory is one of the most critical elements of the computer. There are several types of memory. This chapter will discuss the more important types that you will need.

Computing as we know it would not be possible without memory. I know that you want to get started, so here is a bit about the kind of memory you will be using. The latter part of this chapter goes into memory basics, how it operates, and how it is arranged.

Types of Memory Modules

You should have received a manual or some documentation with your motherboard telling you what type of memory you should use and how it should be installed. Types of memory include standard dynamic random access memory (DRAM), Fast Page Mode, extended data out (EDO) DRAM, and synchronous DRAM (SDRAM). Your motherboard documentation should tell you what you can use.

DRAM SIMMs

The primary memory chips used in PCs are DRAM. The older PCs reserved about one-fourth of the motherboard area for memory chips. The early boards used 64KB chips. (64KB is 64×1024, or 65536 bytes.) It took nine chips to make 64KB, and that is all that some of the motherboards had. Later they developed 256KB chips, and up to 640KB was installed on some motherboards.

Some of the older motherboards have 64MB single in-line memory modules (SIMMs) that allow the installation of up to 256MB on a motherboard in less space than it took for the original 64KB. The SIMM sockets may be located anywhere on the different motherboards.

The older systems required one set of chips for parity. The 72-contact SIMMs were usually designated as 1×36, which is 4MB, 2×36 for 8MB, 4×36 for 16MB, or 8×36 for 32MB. Most newer systems don't use parity, so they now use only eight chips. The designations would be 1×32 or $n \times 32$.

Again, the SIMM chips are obsolete. Newer motherboards are designed for DIMM chips, which can pack much more memory onto a small circuit board.

DIMMs

Dual in-line memory modules (DIMMs) are very high-density, fast-memory chips. Because they require less space for the same amount of memory, DIMMs have become the standard chip of choice. SIMMs have either 30 or 72 contacts. DIMMs may have 72 contacts, but most of the newer ones have 168 pins. The motherboard has to be designed to accept the chips. Figure 4-1 shows two 32MB SIMMs and two dual-contact 64MB DIMM modules.

Figure 4-1
Two 32MB SIMMS in
top photo and two
64MB DIMMS in
lower photo.

Figure 4-1
Two 32MB SIMMS in top photo and two 64MB DIMMS in lower photo.

Fast Page Mode

Fast Page Mode DRAM is faster than standard DRAM. It works on the principle that once an address has been accessed, it will access the following next. Fast Page Mode works well with a large cache.

Extended Data Out (EDO)

As CPUs keep getting faster and faster, developing DRAM chips that can keep up is becoming increasingly difficult. A type of DRAM being manufactured by Micron Technology (208-368-4000) is called extended data out (EDO). It operates about 10 percent faster than ordinary DRAM and is still fairly reasonable in cost. Conventional DRAM requires two wait states for accessing and refreshment times. Due to its architecture, EDO only needs one wait state. EDO also uses a wider bandwidth during the address select so that there are fewer cache misses. The motherboard must be designed to accept the EDO DRAM.

Burst EDO (BEDO)

An advanced type of EDO memory is burst EDO (BEDO). Its design and architecture requires zero wait states to read or write. BEDO DRAM will increase system efficiency by as much as 13 percent or more.

Synchronous DRAM (SDRAM)

Another type of memory is synchronous DRAM (SDRAM). SDRAM should not be confused with SRAM, which is static RAM. The DIMM chips shown in Figure 4-1 are SDRAM assemblies rated at 10ns. The fastest standard DRAM is 60ns. The SDRAM system couples the operation of the memory very tightly to the processor clock. At this time not all motherboards will accept SDRAM. The Pentium II motherboards made by Intel accept it, but my Micronics Pentium II cannot use it. I tried it, and my system will not boot up. Several companies are manufacturing SDRAM. It is very fast and comparatively inexpensive. Some believe that it will eventually displace standard DRAM chips and be the choice for the main memory.

RIMMs

Intel has invested a lot of money into a system called Rambus DRAM (RDRAM). The modules are called Rambus In-Line Memory Modules, or RIMM. This is a very fast memory system that can operate at 800MHz. At the present time, we don't have any CPUs that can operate that fast, but we should have some that approach that speed within a short time. This memory will be used for the very high-end machines.

PC-133

At the present time the PCI systems operate at a maximum of 66MHz. Eventually they will operate at 133MHz. Several companies are exploring the possibility of a new DRAM PC-133 standard as an alternative to

RDRAM. At this time, there have been several problems getting RDRAM to market. Some companies want to institute the PC-133 standard in the interim, and several companies are gearing up to make PC-133-compliant synchronous DRAMs in both 64-MB and 128-MB densities.

DDR SDRAM

Another fast-memory system is the Double Data Rate-Synchronous DRAM (DDR-SDRAM). DDR-SDRAM transfers data twice as fast. AMD, Cyrix, and several of the chipset companies are supporting efforts to have it become a standard.

Memory Slots

Some of the older motherboards may have two or more slots for 72-contact SIMMs and two or more 168-contact slots for DIMMs. Figure 4-1 shows a couple of 32MB SIMMs in the upper photo and a couple of 64MB DIMMs in the lower photo. The SIMM and DIMM chips are usually mounted on a small board that is plugged into the special slots. SIMMs and DIMMs are very easy to install. They usually have cutouts so that they can only be installed properly. The SIMMs are laid in the slot on a slant, then pulled forward until the retaining latches lock them in. To remove a SIMM, just press on the latch assembly on both ends. The SIMMs are obsolete, but some of the less expensive Socket 7 motherboards are still using them. There are also millions of older computers in operation that still use them, so many vendors still sell them.

If you are building or buying a new system, the motherboard will have DIMM slots. Figure 4-2 shows a DIMM module being installed. To install the DIMMs, just press them into the slot straight down. When seated properly, the two latches on each end can be closed.

Memory must be configured in banks. Most motherboards are designed for four banks: bank 0, 1, 2, and 3. Check your documentation that came with your motherboard. You must fill the lowest-numbered bank before filling other banks. If you have one of the older systems that use SIMMs, you must install the SIMMs in multiples of two. For instance, for 64MB, you would have to install two 32MB modules. The bank designations may be different on motherboards from different vendors. Some motherboards may designate bank 0 on one side of the

Figure 4-2
A DIMM module
being installed.

Figure 4-2
A DIMM module
being installed.

socket assembly; others may designate the other side. The modules can be of different speeds but must be of the same size or capacity. If a slower speed is installed, the system will operate at the speed of the slowest module.

Most DIMM chips are now designed for either the 66MHz bus systems or for the 100MHz bus systems. Of course, the 100MHz will operate in the 66MHz systems, but the slower 66MHz will not operate in the 100MHz. Most of the newer and more powerful systems now operate at a bus speed from the CPU to the main memory at a speed of 100MHz.

How Much Memory Do You Need?

The answer to the question of how much memory you need is, all that you can afford. You can probably get by with as little as 32MB, but you should get used to twiddling your thumbs while running many programs. You may have a very fast CPU, but if you don't have enough memory, it will sit idle for much of the time.

You have several options as to how much memory and how it is installed and configured. Check your documentation or motherboard manual. For your new fast machine, don't even think of buying anything less than 64MB. I recommend 128MB. For some high-end applications, you may need at least 256MB. (My first computer had 64KB of memory. I was very happy when my next one had 256KB. It really makes me appreciate the advances that have been made in the last few years. I can buy 128MB of memory today for less than 128KB cost a few years ago.)

Basics

The rest of this chapter deals with memory basics. If you are an old pro, you may want to skip it. The PC uses two primary types of memory: ROM and RAM.

ROM

Read-only memory (ROM) is memory that cannot be altered or changed. The principal use of ROM in PCs is for the basic input/output system (BIOS). The BIOS contains routines that set up the computer when we first turn it on. It facilitates the transfer of data among peripherals. The ROM programs are usually burned into erasable programmable read-only memory (EPROM) chips. The ROM BIOS for an early XT could be programmed onto a 128KB chip. The 486 ROM BIOS needs 512KB. It is possible to print out the programs stored in ROM. To give you some idea of how much 512KB is, the entire text in some of my earlier books was less than 512KB. The ROM BIOS on a Pentium III motherboard is stored in flash memory. It takes about 2MB.

RAM and DRAM

If we open a file from a hard disk or a floppy, the files and data are read from the disk and placed in random access memory (RAM). When we load in a program, be it word processing, a spreadsheet, database, or whatever, we will be working in the system RAM. If we are writing, programming, or creating another program, we will be working in RAM. Actually, it is dynamic RAM, or DRAM. *Random access* means that we can find, address, change, or erase any single byte among several million bytes.

We can also randomly access any particular byte on a floppy or hard disk. We cannot randomly access data on a magnetic tape system, however. The data on the tape is stored sequentially. In order to find a particular byte, we would have to run the tape forward or backward to the proper area. Being able to randomly access the memory allows us to read and write to it immediately. It is somewhat like an electronic blackboard. Here we can manipulate the data, do calculations, enter more data, edit, search databases, or accomplish any of the thousands of tasks that software programs allow us to do. We can access and change the data in RAM very quickly.

RAM memory is an essential element of the computer. Of course, if you are working on a large file, you will need a lot of RAM. If you are using Windows and you don't have enough RAM, some portions of the file may be loaded onto a special area of the hard disk and used as a swap file.

RAM Volatility

An important difference in ROM and RAM is that RAM is volatile. That is, it disappears if the machine is rebooted or if you exit a program without saving it. If there is a power interruption to the computer, even for a brief instant, any data in RAM will be gone forever.

You should get in the habit of saving your files to disk frequently, especially if you live in an area where there are power failures due to storms or other reasons. Many of the software programs now will automatically save open files to disk at frequent intervals. Of course, if the file is saved to disk, a power failure will not affect it.

How RAM Is Addressed

Each byte of memory has a separate address. The cells in the memory bank could be analogous to the "pigeon holes" for the room keys of a large hotel. They would be arranged in rows and columns so that the pigeon holes would correspond to each room on each floor. If the hotel had 100 rooms, you could have 10 rows across and 10 down. It would be very simple to find any one of the 100 keys by counting across and then down to the particular room number. Memory addressing is a bit more complicated than the hotel pigeon holes, but with just 20 address lines (2^20), any individual byte out of 1 million bytes can be quickly accessed. One byte is also called a *word*, so the old 8-bit XTs can only address one word at a time. The 16-bit 286 can address two words, 32-bit 386 and 486 systems can address four words, and the 64-bit Pentium can address eight words at a time.

The CPU and the RAM Bus

As mentioned, the CPU is the brains of the computer. Almost everything that happens in a computer must travel over a bus path and go through the CPU. Say you have a very fast and powerful Pentium. You will probably have several plug-in boards and peripheral components. The peripheral components will communicate with the CPU over a 16-bit bus at about 8MHz. But data that moves between the RAM and the CPU has its own special memory bus. Data moves back and forth on the bus between the RAM and CPU at some fraction of the CPU speed or frequency, usually at 66MHz for older systems or at 100MHz for newer systems.

The amount of work that a computer accomplishes depends on how fast it can process data. There may be billions of bits in a software program. It may take a lot of shifting and adding and moving around to process the program. The faster the computer can handle these billions of iterations, the better.

One of the critical factors that determines the speed of a computer is the time that is spent shifting the data back and forth from the CPU and RAM. The width of the path, or bus, between the CPU and the RAM is a critical factor in the operating speed of the computer. The original PC had an 8-bit memory bus connected to the CPU. The bus was doubled to 16 bits for the 286 CPU. It was doubled again to 32 bits for the 386 and 486 CPUs. For the Pentium II the bus width is 64 bits. Some designers have developed a 64-bit bus going in one direction to the CPU and another 64-bit bus returning from the CPU.

The computer technology has come a long way in just a few short years. The bus has been likened to a highway. If there are only eight bits, it can be compared to a single-lane highway and will be rather slow. Twice as many cars can get through on a two-lane highway, and four times as many if there are four lanes. If there are eight lanes, or a 64-bit system, the traffic can really whiz along.

A Brief Explanation of Memory

Computers operate on binary systems of 0s and 1s, or off and on. A transistor can be turned off or on to represent the 0s and 1s. Two transistors can represent four different combinations: 1) both off; 2) both on; 3) #1 on, #2 off; and 4) #1 off, #2 on. A bank of four transistors can represent 16 different combinations. With eight transistors, we can have 256 different combinations. It takes eight transistors to make 1 byte. With them you can represent each letter of the alphabet, each number, and each symbol of the extended American Standard Code for Information Interchange (ASCII). With eight lines, plus a ground, the eight transistors can be turned on or off to represent any single one of the 256 characters of the ASCII code.

As mentioned, each byte of memory has a separate address. Returning to our hotel analogy, memory is similar to a large hotel's pigeon holes for the room keys. One megabyte of memory would require many more pigeon holes or cells. But with just 20 address lines and one ground line, any individual byte can be quickly accessed. Actually, it would be 2^20 or 2 to the twentieth power, which would equal 1,048,576 bytes.

Programs that Stay in RAM

In the DOS era, besides the application programs that were loaded into the 640KB of RAM, there were certain DOS system programs that stayed in RAM at all times. These are programs such as command.com and the internal commands. There are over 20 internal commands such as COPY, CD, CLS, DATE, DEL, MD, PATH, TIME, TYPE, and others. Under DOS these commands were always in RAM and were available immediately. The config.sys file and any drivers that you may have had for your system were also loaded into RAM. There were several others such as SideKick that were loaded into RAM and stayed there. They were called terminate-and-stay-resident (TSR) programs.

For instance, my copy of Norton Utilities is loaded into memory each time I boot up. Microsoft Office 97 is also loaded into memory. If you are running Windows 95 or 98 and would like to see what programs are in memory, just press Ctrl + Alt + Del, and the list of programs in memory will come up. (Be careful that you only press Ctrl + Alt + Del once. If you press it twice, it will reboot the computer.)

Quite often when you install a program, it will tell you to make sure that no other programs are running at the same time. If you would like to delete any of the programs from memory, just use the mouse or arrow key to highlight the program, and press Enter. You cannot delete Microsoft Explorer; if you do, it will shut the computer down.

All of these things contributed to the utility and functionality of the computer and made it easier to use. But, unfortunately, they took big bites out of our precious 640KB of RAM. There may have been less than 400KB left for running applications after loading all these memory-resident programs. There were many programs that would not run if you had less than 600KB of free RAM.

Windows 95 and 98 have now solved most of those problems. They can load several programs in extended memory above the 640KB. These programs can then be available at any time. Windows 95/98 also allow us to have several programs open at the same time. We can be working on one in the foreground and have another running in the background. Of course, this requires lots of memory.

Cost of Memory

As I've said, I don't like to talk about cost because it changes so quickly. Here is what I wrote a few years ago about the cost of DRAM:

> Although the 386 and 486 can address 4GB of RAM, without special software DOS will not let you access more than 640KB. (Incidentally, 4GB of DRAM, in 1MB SIMM packages, would require 4096 modules. You would need a fairly large board to install that much memory. It would also be rather expensive. At $35 per megabyte, 4096 modules would cost $143,360.)

You can buy memory today for less than $1 per megabyte. I just bought 128MB, two 64MB DIMM chips, for $100. So you could install 4GB for less than $4000, down from $143,360. What a fantastic change in just a few years.

Another change is that 128MB DIMMs are quite common. With these chips, you would need only 31.25 modules to make 4GB. Eventually, you will be able to buy 256MB DIMMs. Memory prices are still coming down. By the time you read this, the prices will be even lower. One reason for lower prices is that most newer systems use the eight-chip non-parity system. Most older systems used the nine-chip parity system. The extra chip added to the cost.

Virtual Memory

In its virtual memory mode, the 386, 486, and Pentium class CPUs can address 64 terabytes (TB), or 64 trillion bytes, or 64,000,000,000,000 bytes. Virtual memory is a method of using part of a hard disk as RAM. Many large programs will not run unless the entire program resides in RAM. So the program can be partially loaded in the available RAM and the rest of it in a virtual RAM section of the hard disk. Of course, having to access the disk for data can slow the processing down considerably, but it is one solution. The virtual disk system must be implemented by the operating system.

How Memory Is Arranged

The early PCs used dual in-line pin (DIP) chips with two rows of 8 pins, or 16 pins total. The DIP chips used up a lot of motherboard real estate. It takes nine chips of whatever type memory is designated. For instance, for 64KB, it takes eight 64KB $\times$ 1 bit chips plus one 64KB $\times$ 1 bit chip for parity checking. If they are 256KB chips, it takes eight 256KB $\times$ 1 bit chips, plus one 256 $\times$ 1 bit chip for parity checking. Even with the high-capacity SIMMs, it still takes nine chips to make up the designated memory. For 1 megabyte, it takes eight 1024 $\times$ 1 bit chips plus one 1024 $\times$ 1 bit chip for parity. For a 4MB SIMM, it takes eight 4096 $\times$ 1 bit chips plus one 4096 $\times$ 1 bit chip for parity. The same system is used even for the $n \times 36$ SIMM chips. Sometimes, instead of having nine individual chips, they may have three or more integrated into a single chip. So you may see some SIMMs with only three chips in the module.

I know this is a bit confusing, so here is a brief chart:

$$64KB = 64KB \times 1 \text{ bit} + 64KB \times 1 \text{ bit for parity}$$

$$256KB = 256KB \times 1 \text{ bit} + 256KB \times 1 \text{ bit for parity}$$

$$1MB = 1024KB \times 1 \text{ bit} + 1024KB \times 1 \text{ bit for parity}$$

$$4MB = 4096KB \times 1 \text{ bit} + 4096KB \times 1 \text{ bit for parity}$$

Figure 2-6 in Chapter 2 shows two different motherboards, a large standard-size 286 at the left and a Pentium at the right. To illustrate how much space the DIP chips require, there are four rows of DIP chips in the top right corner of the 286. There are a total of 36 of the chips to make one megabyte. The four white SIMM 72-contact sockets on the left center of the Pentium motherboard can accept up to 128MB. The DIP chips were rather difficult to install. It was very easy to install them backwards in the socket or to bend one of the pins so that it did not make contact. Over a period of time, some of the DIP chips could actually creep up out of the socket.

SIMM chips are very easy to install. They have a cutout on one end so that they can only be inserted one way. Just lay the assembly slantwise in the socket, then push it to an upright position. A projection on the socket fits into a small hole on each end of the SIMM board when the SIMMs are inserted in the socket. Spring-loaded clamps on each end locks the assembly in place. To remove the assembly, press on the clamps on each end.

Memory Problems

Although SIMM chips are very easy to install, it is possible to have a module that is not seated properly. If this happens, the computer may not boot up. The screen may be completely blank with no error messages or any indication of the problem.

I had a whole lot of problems when I tried to replace my old Cyrix 100MHz with the Tyan motherboard and the AMD 233MHz CPU. I have four 8x2 chips for a total of 32MB on my old board. It seemed to work fine. Memory check was okay each time I booted up. But I had a blank screen when I tried to boot up with the new motherboard and CPU. I checked the SIMMs to make sure they were seated properly. Then I tried again and again. Sometimes it would boot up, but then it would tell me that it had a fatal error and would shut down.

I reinstalled everything back in my old Cyrix motherboard, and it worked fine. I reinstalled it in my new motherboard, and it booted up once in a while, but then dropped out. Once when I got the blank screen upon boot up, I checked the SIMMs again, but thought that maybe my monitor adapter might be bad. I replaced it with a spare, but I still had a blank screen. I removed two of the SIMMs, or one bank of memory, and everything worked fine. I replaced one of the SIMMs with one of the two that I had removed, and sure enough, I had a blank screen.

Evidently, one of the contacts on the chip was bad or the chip itself had an intermittent defect. It took me half a day of frustration to find it.

Parity

The old DIP chips have two rows of 8 pins, or 16 pins total. It requires nine chips of whatever type memory is designated. As mentioned, for 64KB, it took eight 64KB $\times$ 1 bit chips plus one 64KB $\times$ 1 bit chip for parity checking. If 256KB chips were used, it took eight 256KB $\times$ 1 bit chips, plus one 256 $\times$ 1 bit chip for parity checking.

For the older systems that still use parity, even with the high-capacity SIMMs, it still takes nine chips to make up the designated memory. For a 4MB SIMM, it takes eight 4096 $\times$ 1 bit chips plus one 4096 $\times$ 1 bit chip for parity checking. The nine chips would all be on the one small SIMM plug-in board. The same system is used even for the $n \times 36$ SIMM chips. The Macintosh systems do not use the parity checking chip, so they have only the 8 $\times$ whatever the SIMM designation. Most of the newer systems no longer use the parity system.

As mentioned, memory must be configured in banks. Most motherboards are designed for four banks: banks 0, 1, 2, and 3. Check the documentation that came with your motherboard. You must fill the lowest-numbered bank before filling other banks.

Because memory is interleaved on most systems, you must install the SIMMs in multiples of two. You cannot intermix SIMMs of different values. For instance, for 16MB, you would have to install two 8MB modules. If you install a single module instead of the required two, the computer may not boot up. The screen may be completely blank. Interleaved memory is discussed in more detail below.

Caution! It is possible to have a module that is not seated properly. If this happens, the computer may not boot up. The screen may be completely blank with no error messages or any indication of the problem.

If the chips are not installed in their proper banks, you may get one long continuous beep. Or the computer may not boot up. Be sure to check your motherboard documentation.

Flash Memory

A few years ago, Intel developed flash memory, which is similar to erasable programmable read-only memory (EPROM). AMD and several other companies now also manufacture it. Flash memory is fairly slow compared to DRAM and SRAM, so it can't replace them. But it can be equivalent to hard disk memory. The hard disk is a mechanical device that will eventually wear out or fail. The flash memory is strictly electronic and should last several lifetimes.

A disadvantage is that flash memory is still rather expensive and limited in the amount of memory that can be installed on a card. Most all motherboards now use flash memory for the BIOS chip. The BIOS can be updated electronically by floppy disk or by a modem from a BBS or over the Internet.

Video RAM

Video RAM (VRAM) chips are a bit different than DRAM chips. They are special memory chips that are used on the better (and more expensive) monitor adapter cards. The VRAM chips are unusual in that they have double ports so that they can be accessed and refreshed at the same time. A new memory standard, Unified Memory Architecture (UMA), is being used on many of the high-end graphics and video accelerator adapters. Many of the faster video cards now have as much as 32KB or more of VRAM.

Printer Memory

Your laser printer probably came with a minimum amount of memory or about 512KB. A laser printer determines where each dot on a printed page should be, then prints the whole page. Most printers require memory that is installed on special proprietary boards. You may need to add more memory for better printing speed. Most lasers will perform much better if they have a minimum of 2MB.

Memory Chip Capacity

The size and speed of the chip is usually printed on the top of the chip. For instance, a 256KB chip at 150ns might have the manufacturer's logo or name and some other data. But somewhere among all this would be "25615." The 15 indicates 150ns (the zero is always left off). A 1MB 100ns chip might have "102410."

The chips are usually arranged in banks or rows of nine. Almost all ISA computers use an extra ninth chip for parity checking. This chip checks and verifies the integrity of the memory at all times. It is usually the same type of chip as the eight that are used to make up the bank. The Macintosh systems don't use this chip, and some experts say that it is a waste of memory to use it on the ISA systems.

The XT and early 286 motherboards had their RAM memory usually located in the front right corner of the motherboards. They all used the DIP type of chips. To make 640KB, most boards filled the first two banks, banks 0 and 1, with 256KB chips, which would equal 512KB. The next two banks, 2 and 3, were then filled with 64KB chips to make 128KB for a maximum 640KB.

Many of the early 286 and 386 systems filled all four banks with 256KB DIP chips for a total of 1MB. Although the 286 was capable of addressing 16MB with special software, for most ordinary uses, it was still limited to 640KB. Boards that had the extra 384KB could use it for a RAM disk, print spooling, or for other extended memory needs with the proper software. Until Windows 95, the 386, 486, and Pentium was limited to 640KB without special software that could take advantage of extended memory.

The Need for More Memory

One of the upgrades that you probably need is more memory. For some applications, you may need to buy several megabytes more. In the old days we got by fine with just 64KB of memory. Many of the new software programs such as the spreadsheets, databases, and accounting programs require a lot of memory.

If you bought a new motherboard through mail order, you may have received it with 0K memory. You probably know that 0K does not mean "okay," it means zero KB memory. The price of memory fluctuates quite a lot. Ads are sometimes made up and placed two or three months before the magazine comes out. Because of the fluctuating prices, some vendors will not advertise a firm price for memory, so they just specify 0K. Besides, if they included the price of the memory, it might frighten you away. They usually invite you to call them for the latest price.

The good news for us consumers is that memory prices are dropping every day.

Things to Consider before You Buy Memory

You'll need to consider type, size, speed, and other factors before buying memory. You should buy the type that is best for your computer. Be sure to check your motherboard documentation.

Dynamic RAM (DRAM)

Dynamic RAM is the most common type of memory used today. Each memory cell has a small etched transistor that is kept in its memory state, either on or off by an electrical charge on a very small capacitor. Capacitors are similar to small rechargeable batteries. Units can be charged up with a voltage to represent 1s or left uncharged to represent 0s. But those that are charged up immediately start to lose their charge. So they must be constantly "refreshed" with a new charge. Steve Gibson, the developer of SpinRite, compares the memory cell capacitors to a small bucket with a hole in the bottom. Those buckets, or cells, that represent 1s are filled with water, but it immediately starts leaking out through the hole. So it has to be constantly refilled. You don't have to worry about filling those buckets, or cells, that represent 0s.

Also, each time a cell is accessed, that small voltage in the capacitor flows through a transistor to turn it on. This drains the charge from the capacitor, so it must be refreshed before it can be accessed again. In our bucket of water comparison, when the cell is accessed, the bucket is turned upside down and emptied. So if it represents a 1, it must be refilled immediately. Of course, it takes a finite amount of time to fill a bucket or to place a charge on a capacitor. If the memory cell has a speed of 70ns, it may take 70ns, plus the time it takes to recycle, which may be 105ns or more, before that cell can again be accessed.

In older systems, a computer could spend 7 percent or more of its time just refreshing the DRAM chips. Newer systems may spend less than 1 percent of its time refreshing the memory.

Refreshment and Wait States

The speed of the DRAM chips in your system should match your system CPU. You might be able to install slower chips, but your system would have to work with wait states. If the DRAM is too slow, a wait state will have to be inserted. A wait state causes the CPU and the rest of the system to sit and wait while the RAM is being accessed and then refreshed. Wait states could deprive your system of one of its greatest benefits, speed.

A Waste of Time

If the CPU is operating at a very high frequency, it may have to sit and wait one cycle, or one wait state, for the refresh cycle. The wait state might be only a millionth of a second or less. That may not seem like much time, but if the computer is doing several million operations per second, it can add up.

It takes a finite amount of time to charge up the DRAM. Some DRAM chips can be charged up much faster than others. For instance, the DRAM chips needed for an old XT at 4.77MHz could take as much as 200ns or billionths of a second to be refreshed. Some of the newer and faster systems use DRAM chips that operate at 10ns. The Pentium III CPUs may operate internally as high as 550MHz, but externally over the memory bus to DRAM at a speed of 100MHz.

Interleaved Memory

Most of the older systems that used SIMMs used interleaved memory to prevent having to insert wait states. The memory had to be installed in multiples of two. You could install two banks of 512KB, 2MB, 4MB, 8MB, 16MB, 32MB, 64MB, or 128MB of memory.

One-half of the memory would be refreshed on one cycle, then the other half. If the CPU needed to access an address that was in the half already refreshed, it would be available immediately. This can reduce the amount of waiting by about half.

Most of the newer DIMM systems do not have to be installed in pairs.

Static RAM (SRAM)

Static RAM (SRAM) is made up of actual transistors. They can be turned on to represent 1s or left off to represent 0s and will stay in that condition until they receive a change signal. They do not need to be refreshed, but they revert back to 0 when the computer is turned off or if the power is interrupted. They are very fast and can operate at speeds of 10ns or less.

A DRAM memory cell needs only one transistor and a small capacitor. It takes a very small amount of space for a DRAM cell. Each SRAM cell requires four to six transistors and other components. So SRAM is much more expensive than DRAM. In older systems, the SRAM chips are assembled in the DIP-type package, so they are physically larger and require much more space than the DRAM chips. Because of the physical and electronic differences, SRAM and DRAM chips are not interchangeable. Newer motherboards have the SRAM integrated into a single very large-scale integrated (VLSI) chip.

Cache Memory

A cache system can speed up computer operations quite a lot. When running an application program, the CPU often loops in and out of certain areas and uses portions of the same memory over and over. A cache system is usually made up of very fast memory chips such as SRAM that can store the often-used data so that it is quickly accessible to the CPU. The data that is moved back and forth between the CPU and RAM are electrical on and off voltages. The electrons move at almost the speed of light. Still, it takes a finite amount of time to move a large amount of data. It takes even more time to access the RAM, find the data that is needed, then move it back to the CPU.

The computer can also be slowed down considerably if it has to search the entire memory each time it has to fetch some data. If this often-used memory is stored in the cache, it can be accessed by the CPU very quickly. A good cache can greatly increase the processing speed. The Pentium CPU has a built-in 16KB Level 1 (L1) cache in among its 3.1 million transistors. This cache helps considerably, but a good, fast external L2 cache can help speed things up even more. The speed and static characteristics of SRAM make it an excellent device for memory cache systems.

The Pentium III CPU has a 16KB L1 cache, but it also has a 512KB or a 1MB L2 cache nearby in the same enclosure. The Pentium III Xeon CPU may have a 2MB L2 cache.

Hit Rate

A well-designed cache system may have a "hit rate" of over 90 percent. This means that each time the CPU needs a block of data, it will find it in the nearby fast cache. A good cache system may increase speed and performance considerably.

Level 1 and Level 2 Caches

A Level 1 (L1) cache is one that is built into the CPU. This makes the cache very close and fast. The 486 was the first CPU with an internal L1 cache. Intel built in an 8KB cache among the 1.2 million transistors in the CPU. They increased the L1 cache to 16KB in the 486DX4 and all of the Pentium class CPUs. The L1 cache allows the CPU to access memory that is often used without having to travel outside to the external RAM. Because of the short distance and the high-speed transistors, the L1 cache operates at the same internal speed as the CPU. Many CPUs operate externally two to three times slower than the internal speed. The 486 and Pentium CPUs also use a Level 2 (L2) or external cache made up of fast SRAM located on the motherboard. The speed and static characteristics of SRAM makes it an excellent device for memory cache systems.

But again, it takes a finite amount of time for the data to move from the CPU over the bus at an external frequency to the SRAM cache. The Pentium Pro lessened this problem by building an L2 cache in the same enclosure as the CPU. The L2 cache is closely coupled to the CPU and communicates with it over a very short 64-bit interface or special bus at the internal CPU frequency. The L2 cache will either be 256KB or 512KB. A cache made up of SRAM transistors is very fast, but it requires lots of transistors. It takes six transistors for each bit of SRAM, so a 256KB cache requires 15.5 million transistors; 512KB requires 31 million. It only takes one transistor for each bit of DRAM, so 256KB would require 2.6 million transistors and 512KB would need 5.2 million.

The 486 has an 8KB cache system built into the chip; the 486DX4 and the Pentium CPUs have two 8KB caches. This built-in cache gives the CPUs about a 90 percent hit rate. The 486DX also has a math coprocessor in among the 1.2 million transistors in this chip; the 486SX does not have a math coprocessor.

It takes a large number of transistors for a cache, even one as small as 8KB. The Cyrix Company built in a 1KB cache on their 486 clone. They claim that this still gives them an 80 percent hit rate. Cyrix also left the coprocessor off their 486 clone, but they package an external coprocessor with each CPU. By reducing the number of transistors on their CPU, they made the chip to be the same size as the 386 CPU.

▰ ▰ ▰ Write-Through and Write-Back

After the data is processed, it is returned to RAM. The write-through system simply sends the data back to RAM. System operations are delayed while the data is being written back to RAM. The delay may be only microseconds, but if you are processing a lot of data, it can add up. The write-back system keeps the data in the cache until there is a break in operations, then writes the data to RAM.

▰ ▰ ▰ CMOS

The complementary metal-oxide semiconductors (CMOS) use very little power to keep the data alive. They are actually SRAM transistors that store your system setup. Several of the computer features that are configurable, such as the time, date, type of disk drives, and other features that can be changed by the user, are stored in CMOS. You should take a pad and write down all of the features stored in your CMOS setup. For instance, if you lose the data in your CMOS and you don't know what type of hard drive is in the setup, you will not be able to access your data on the hard drive.

A lithium or a rechargeable battery keeps the data alive when the computer is turned off. If your computer is not used for a long period of time, you may have to reset the time. If you have to reset the time quite often, you may need a new battery. The early IBM AT used batteries that only lasted a couple of years. The batteries were soldered onto the motherboard and were very difficult to change. Most motherboards today have lithium batteries that last about 10 years.

Why the 640KB Limit?

When DOS was first introduced in 1981, 1 megabyte of memory was an enormous amount. It was believed that this amount would be more than satisfactory. After all, many of the CP/M machines were getting by fine with just 64KB of memory. So DOS was designed to operate with a maximum of 1 megabyte. Of this 1 megabyte, 640KB would be used for running programs and applications. The other 384KB was reserved for purposes such as the BIOS, the video control, and other special hardware control. This 384KB is called the *upper memory area* and is divided up into blocks called *upper memory blocks*, or UMBs.

Sometimes when I tried to load and run a program, I got an error message "Not enough memory," or "Insufficient memory." But I had 32MB of DRAM in my computer. I knew that the program that I was trying to run was less than 500KB. So why couldn't I run it if I have 32MB?

The reason was simple. The program that I was trying to run was a DOS-type program that could not handle extended memory. It was limited to the 640KB of conventional memory. But if the program is only 500KB, why couldn't it run in the 640KB?

The reason is when the computer was booted up, COMMAND.COM and several other internal DOS commands were loaded into that 640KB. In addition, any terminate-and-stay resident (TSR) programs were also loaded into the 640KB. Any drivers for special devices such as a fax modem, a CD-ROM, or other device drivers listed in my CONFIG.SYS and AUTOEXEC.BAT were also loaded into the conventional memory. After all of this stuff was loaded, there may have been less than 400KB left. So if the program was larger than 400KB, it would not run.

The DOS internal commands and many TSRs are loaded in memory at all times. These commands can be invoked by just a few keystrokes from any directory. There are about 75 DOS commands. About 30 of them are internal commands, such as COPY, DEL, MD, CD, and TYPE. In many of the early versions of DOS, these were all separate commands. But later versions of DOS incorporate them all into COMMAND.COM. They were always loaded and immediately available. If you wanted to run one of the external commands, such as FIND or DISKCOMP, you had to go to the DOS directory and load them.

Tremendous improvements have been made in computer technology since the original PC. The 640KB barrier is not really much of a problem today. Windows 95/98, Windows NT, and IBM's OS/2 are not limited to the 640KB barrier. When running programs designed for Windows, these systems will let you use all of the RAM that is available if it is needed.

Flash Memory

You will probably want a laptop or notebook computer for the times when you are on the road. If you do buy one, it should have the PC Card (originally called PCMCIA) connectors for flash memory. Intel developed flash memory, which is similar to erasable programmable read-only memory (EPROM). Flash memory is fairly slow compared to DRAM and SRAM, so it can't replace them. Flash memory is often installed on small plug-in cards about the size of a credit card. The cards are ideal for use on laptop and notebook computers. When first introduced, the cards were quite limited in the amount of memory that could be stored on a card. But cards are now available that can store several megabytes. They can be a good substitute for a hard disk on small notebook computers.

PC Card

The Personal Computer Memory Card International Association (PCMCIA) adopted a standard of connectors so that several products can be used with laptop and notebook computers. Most laptop and notebook computers now include the PC Card connectors so that flash memory and other peripherals can be installed.

There are several advantages of the PC Cards over a hard disk in a laptop. The hard disk is a mechanical device that will eventually wear out or fail. The PC Card flash memory is strictly electronic and should last several lifetimes. But the flash memory is still rather expensive and limited in the amount of memory that can be installed on a card. Using flash memory and the PC Card standard, companies have developed several other peripherals for the laptop and notebook computer, including high-speed modems and network adapters. In addition, a flash floppy has been designed that can store from 2MB up to 100MB. Some desktop PCs are installing PC Card sockets so they can take advantage of the technology. It makes downloading or transferring data back and forth to a laptop easy.

IBM has developed a microdrive hard disk that weighs about one-half ounce. It can store 340MB and can fit in one of the laptop's PC Card slots.

Video RAM (VRAM)

Video RAM, or VRAM, chips are a bit different than DRAM chips. They are special memory chips that are used on monitor adapter cards. They are especially optimized for graphics.

Printer Memory

Your printer will probably come with a minimum amount of memory. Most printers require memory that is installed on special proprietary boards. You will need to add more memory for better printing speed.

Buying Chips

Buying chips that are faster than what your system can use only costs you extra money. It doesn't hurt to use faster chips, or even to intermix faster ones with slower ones.

If you plan to upgrade the memory in an older system, you may have trouble finding the older chips. The older systems used the dual in-line package (DIP) chips. Make sure that you buy only the type that will fit in your system. For instance, the 64KB and 256KB DIP chips have 16 pins; the 1MB chips have 18. Some memory boards have both 256KB and 1MB sockets interlaced so that you can use either size chip. The DIMM chips are the type of chip used most often today. But you cannot use a DIMM module unless your motherboard is designed for it.

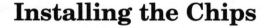 # Installing the Chips

Caution! Electrostatic voltage.

Before handling your memory chips, or any electronic components, the first thing that you should do is to discharge any electrostatic charge that may have been built up on you. If you have ever walked across a carpet and gotten a shock when you touched a door knob, then you know that you can build up static electricity. It is quite possible to build up 3000 to 5000 volts of static electricity in our bodies. So if we touch a fragile piece of electronics that normally operates at 5 to 12 volts, we can severely damage it. We can discharge this static electricity from our bodies by touching any metal that goes to ground. The metal case of the power supply in your computer is a good ground if it is still plugged into the wall socket. The power does not have to be on for it to connect to ground. You can also touch an unpainted metal part of any device or appliance that has three wires and is plugged into a socket. We should always discharge ourselves before we touch any plug-in board or other equipment where there are exposed electronic semiconductors.

Memory chips and most other critical electronic components come in a special packaging. Before unwrapping any component, one of the first things that you should do is to discharge any static electric charge that you may have on you. This is especially important if you are working in an area where there is carpet. Touch some metal object such as a lamp that is plugged into an outlet to discharge yourself of any static electricity.

Floppy Drives
and Disks

The Floppy Evolution

Floppy disks were all we had in the early days. Some PCs had a single floppy drive. Almost all of the early drives used single-sided floppy disks that were from 140KB to 180KB. It was a great leap forward when IBM introduced a PC with two floppy drives that could handle double-sided floppy disks. The first double-sided floppy disks could be formatted to a whopping 160KB on each side for a total of 320KB. Later, 360KB systems were introduced. Even if you were fortunate enough to have a PC with two floppy drives, doing any kind of computing involved an endless amount of disk swapping and took forever to get anything done.

My first computer had two single-sided 140KB drives. It was slow and required a lot of disk swapping. Once, I wrote a book with my 140KB single-sided floppy disks. Since I had only 64KB of memory, any program that I used had to be on a floppy disk. The entire WordStar program (an early word processor) was on one 140KB disk. That disk had to be in slot A, and a blank 140KB disk was inserted in slot B for writing and saving your data.

Floppy systems have come a long way since those early days; from 140KB single-sided systems to 320KB double-sided systems, then 360KB, then 1.2MB, 1.44MB, 2.88MB, and now even 120MB and 200MB on a floppy disk.

Up until just a few years ago, the majority of all software programs came to us on floppy disks. But those programs were fairly small. In a compressed form, most of them didn't require more than four or five 1.44MB floppies. Many software programs today may be over 100MB. Even in a compressed format, this would take a large number of floppies.

Most companies are now using CD-ROMs to distribute their software. For the last couple of years, I have not had to buy any 1.44MB disks. I just erased and used the floppies sent out by America Online. I subscribe to lots of computer magazines, and almost every one of them had an AOL disk with it every month. But lately they are sending out CD-ROMs. A blank CD-ROM may cost as little as 7 cents. And it can be stamped out much quicker than making a floppy copy. I may eventually have to buy some floppy disks, but I don't use them that often anymore.

I don't think that the CD-ROM will ever completely replace the floppy disk. Floppy disks can do many things that a CD-ROM can't do such as making archive copies of small programs, backing up small files from a hard disk, or moving a small program from one computer to another. The floppy system will be around for a long time.

1.44MB Floppy

The 1.44MB floppy drives are very inexpensive at this time. I recently bought one at a swap meet for $17. I didn't need it, but for that price, it was worth it to just have it on hand for use as a spare. I have had several 1.44MB $3\frac{1}{2}$-inch drives become defective. Just as Murphy's Law predicts, it always happens at a most inopportune time.

I still have a 1.44MB $3\frac{1}{2}$- and a $5\frac{1}{4}$-inch floppy combination drive installed in one of my old computers, as shown in Figure 5-1. I have a lot of old $5\frac{1}{4}$-inch floppy disks, but I can't remember the last time I used the $5\frac{1}{4}$-inch drive. Although it can read and write to the 1.2MB and 360KB formats, both formats are as obsolete as the Model T Ford.

At one time we had to buy a rather expensive controller card for our floppy drives. The controller interface is now built in on motherboards as a set of 34 upright pins. The motherboard will usually have some sort of label or marking. Most of the newer motherboards now have keyed

Figure 5-1
Combination $3\frac{1}{2}$- and $5\frac{1}{4}$-inch 1.44 MB drive.

shells around the upright pins so that the cable connectors can only be plugged in the proper way. Unless the pins have a shell around them, the cable connector can be plugged in backwards on these pins. If you do so, it will immediately erase and destroy any data on a floppy disk that you try to run. When you plug in the cable, make sure that the different-colored stripe on one side of the cable goes to pin 1 on the motherboard.

The LS-120 SuperDisk

A floppy disk drive system called the LS-120 SuperDisk may hasten the demise of the 1.44MB floppy as we know it. The LS-120 SuperDisk is a combination of magnetic and laser optical technologies. It can read or write to any 1.44MB diskettes. But to use the 120MB, you need to buy special preformatted diskettes. You can write to these 120MB diskettes and rewrite to them as many times as you want. With the LS-120 there may be no need to upgrade to a larger-capacity hard disk. With several 120MB floppies, you would never run out of space. A disadvantage, of course, is that the file that you need will no doubt always be on the other floppy disk. At the present time, cost for the special 120MB disks is $12 to $20 each. Figure 5-2 shows an LS-120 SuperDisk drive.

Compaq Computer Corp. was one of the original developers of the system. Several of the Compaq systems now have the LS-120 as standard equipment. In addition, several laptop computers now have the LS-120 floppy disk as standard equipment.

Figure 5-2
An LS-120 SuperDisk drive. It can store 120MB on the special disk on the left. It can also read and write to the 1.44MB floppy on the right.

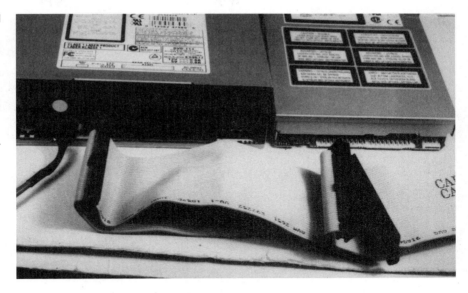

Figure 5-3
The rear of the LS-120 SuperDisk showing the IDE connector and cable. On the left is an IDE CD-ROM drive. The cable can connect both units.

The 120MB floppies are specially formatted with laser technology. They use a standard head for reading and writing to the 1.44MB disk, but they use a different head for reading and writing to the 120MB disks. The high-capacity drives can work off the IDE or SCSI interface or as an external drive on your parallel printer port. Figure 5-3 shows the IDE connector on the rear of the LS-120 SuperDisk. It is shown alongside an IDE CD-ROM drive to the left. The IDE cable can be used to connect both drives.

The following information is from the OR Technology Web site at www.ortechnology.com:

The a:DRIVE from OR Technology was designed to replace the floppy disk drive. While its outward appearance is almost indistinguishable from that of its floppy technology counterpart, the a:DRIVE achieves 120MB of storage when used with LS-120 media. At the same time, the a:DRIVE is downward compatible with current 3.5-inch floppy disk technology. It can read and write to both 720KB and 1.44MB diskettes, providing an upward-migration path for millions of personal computer users and the billions of diskettes they own. As its name indicates, the a:DRIVE can be used as a bootable drive in any system in which it is installed. From the start, OR Technology created the 1-inch-high a:DRIVE with this purpose in mind. Extensive development has optimized the device for internal use as an integral system component. It was designed to be the ideal form, fit, and function replacement for the floppy disk drive. The a:DRIVE is an advanced technology product, yet so familiar you already know how to use it. OR Technology has worked closely with Microsoft Corp. and Compaq Computer Corp. developing standards to enable the operating system, the computer system, and the a:DRIVE to work together. Both Windows 95/98 and Windows NT operating systems have now been updated to recognize the a:DRIVE as a bootable drive in both 120MB and 1.44MB mode. To accomplish this, changes were required to the system BIOS.

In addition, OR Technology has been active in the ATAPI standards committee, developing the necessary protocol for devices that read and write. As a result, the a:DRIVE is ATAPI-compatible and can be attached to the same internal IDE cable the hard disk drive uses. Unlike alternative technologies, the compact a:DRIVE meets current industry standards established for floppy disk drive and floppy diskette form factors. It can be easily configured for use in standard notebook or desktop PC drive bays.

LS-120 drives use MIG (metal-in-gap) heads for superior resolution and reliability. The drives spin the media at higher speeds. When LS-120 diskettes are used, access is five times faster than a standard floppy disk drive. When 720KB or 1.44MB diskettes are used, the drive is three times faster.

Identifying Location

Just as with a common floppy disk drive, track identification is determined by the information that is written magnetically on the track. LS-120 drives use the same file allocation table and cluster address system as ordinary floppy disk drives.

However, the LS-120 drive is smarter. In addition to doing all that a floppy disk drive can do, it contains integrated circuits that keep track of everything and tell the drive where to go to get information. A defect management table on each disk and error correction capabilities in the drive are unique to LS-120 technology. The drive can identify errors and correct them. Corrections are made for small imperfections in the data or disk wear from use. Like tape drives and hard disk drives, the LS-120 floppy disk drive uses error correction code, enabling the drive to pack data closer together and accurately recover it. The media has also been updated with new stainless steel shutters for durability and an advanced hub for improved reliability. Everything has been done to ensure quality in manufacturing and use. For example, while the optical system assembly performs many complex tasks, it is a relatively simple component, measuring only $\frac{1}{4}$-inch high. A lens array combines the hologram with diffractive and refractive lenses into a single piece. Tiny but simple optical lenses, like those in a microscope, a disposable camera, or a pair of sunglasses, are used, along with other easily obtainable parts. In comparison to floppy disk technology, LS-120 technology is mechanically simplified, making it even more reliable.

The a:DRIVE looks and is used exactly like the familiar, durable, reliable floppy disk drive it replaces—it's just better suited to the needs of today's computer users.

The Optic System

At the heart of the optic system is a hologram. Held on the tip of your finger, it looks like a tiny piece of square-shaped glass. It contains a two-dimensional image developed from a complex computer optimization program that took into account light efficiency, thermal dynamics, and geometry constraints.

A laser diode, just like those found in compact disc drives, provides the light source that illuminates the hologram. As light passes through the hologram, it forms a pattern of six spots. Three of these spots are used to position the head on LS-120 media, and three are used to position the head on 720KB or 1.44MB floppy diskettes. Each set of three spots contains two "striped" spots and a single spot without stripes. The striped spots are actually made up of seven individual pin points of light, which give the spot a striped appearance.

As light leaves the hologram, a lens focuses the spots. A mirror bounces the light in two directions: up to the surface of an LS-120 disk as it spins parallel to the optic system and down to a photo encoder.

On the media, the seven stripes of light are projected over seven tracks and provide tracking information. The nonstriped spot, known as a *modulation spot*, measures variations in the servo pattern etched on the media so that the intensity of light making up the striped spots can be adjusted on the fly.

The interaction of the spots with the LS-120 media provides the tracking information required to write data accurately on tracks that are 10.2 microns wide. Understanding how the spots and media work together can be aided by taking a closer look at the unique attributes of LS-120 media.

LS-120 Media

The media inside the LS-120 diskette shell is manufactured from a PET (polyethylene terathalate) substrate and uses a dual-layer coating of high-density metal particle (MP) for high coercivity. The media is thinner (.0025-inch in comparison to .003-inch) than that found in traditional floppy diskettes and provides better head-to-media contact.

At the factory, one surface of the LS-120 diskette is laser-etched with a precise servo pattern. The laser etching is not constant, but intermittent, producing tracks that are "stitched" instead of being continuous stripes. The process creates 900 concentric circles with tracks that vary in length from 43 to 77 microns depending on their location. Shorter tracks are closer to the hub or center of the media, while longer tracks reside at its edge. The distance between all tracks is equal regardless of location. The optical track pitch is 20.4 microns wide including a 2-micron-wide laser-inscribed mark surrounding magnetic tracks. (From track edge to next track edge, measurement begins with a 1-micron-wide half-stitch, 8 microns of data, another 2 microns of laser mark, and another 8-micron track bordered by a final half-stitch. At this point the period starts all over again.) The stitches contain the tracking information, while the magnetic tracks contain the data. LS-120 technology optimizes the amount of space where data can be stored, unlike alternative technologies that rely on magnetic servo.

The laser servo data is written in between the data tracks, in an area that is typically used for guard bands, instead of taking up valuable data space. As a result, 20 to 30 percent more data can be written using laser servo in comparison to magnetic servo. In addition, the servo information on LS-120 media is indelible. This feature enables users to bulk-erase and reformat disks easily for additional use.

Here is some information from the Imation Company at www.imation.com, which also markets the LS-120:

No matter how you use your computer, one thing is certain: the number and size of the files you deal with is constantly increasing. Hard drives have had to grow to gigabyte size to make room for huge applications that eat up more and more hard drive space.

But the 3.5-inch diskette hasn't kept up. At 1.44MB, it often can't even hold an entire business presentation. And you need hundreds of them to back up that gigabyte drive.

The SuperDisk diskette is a single 3.5-inch diskette that holds 120MB. That's 83 times the capacity of a conventional 1.44MB disk.

Technical Specifications

1. The SuperDisk LS-120 drive is compatible with both the SuperDisk diskette and standard 3.5-inch diskettes. Users get the benefits of increased removable storage without adding a second drive.

2. A SuperDisk diskette looks, feels and works just like a conventional diskette so users will be more comfortable with it. For IT professionals,

you can give your users the storage they want without any additional training.

3. The SuperDisk diskette holds as much data as 83 conventional 1.44MB diskettes.

4. The SuperDisk diskette has a read/write latch just like a conventional diskette so it is write-protectable. Users can easily protect their work from being overwritten.

5. Mobile users will be able to get the benefits of 120MB of removable storage without having to carry an extra drive or giving up their ability to read their old disks.

At the present time, the LS-120 SuperDrives are selling for about $75. The preformatted special 120MB floppy disks are selling for $10.

The 200MB Floppy Drive

The Sony Company and Fuji Film Company have developed a 200MB floppy drive, shown in Figure 5-4. Here is a press release:

Sony Corporation and Fuji Photo Film Co., Ltd. have jointly developed "HiFD,"* a new 3.5-inch floppy disk system with a 200MB (both sides) storage capacity. This is the largest capacity floppy disk system.

Figure 5-4
Sony 200MB floppy.

---

*HiFD is an abbreviation of "High Capacity Floppy Disk."

In recent years, the rapid increase in the processing power of personal computers and the large increase in size of data handled have led to growing demand for a new high-capacity data recording system that is more efficient and has a fast data transfer rate. Because the current 3.5-inch floppy disk is a convenient, easy-to-use recording medium that has wide penetration around the world, the ability to continue using the data accumulated on this medium in the future is also required of such a system. In order to meet these demands, Sony and Fujifilm have developed the new HiFD 3.5-inch floppy disk system by combining the technologies of both companies to achieve a next-generation high-capacity floppy disk system that features 200MB storage capacity, 3.6MB/sec transfer rate, and backward read-and write-compatibility with current 3.5-inch floppy disks. Sony and Fujifilm plan to introduce this system in spring 1998. The two companies have already received support for the basic specifications of the system from Alps Electric Co., Ltd. and TEAC Corporation. In the future, Sony and Fujifilm will propose the specifications of the system to a wide range of PC and drive manufacturers.

Sony and Fujifilm have achieved this industry-pioneering task based on the magnetic recording technology that each company possesses. In 1980, Sony developed the 3.5-inch floppy disk system which is widely used in computers throughout the industry. In 1992, Fujifilm developed its Advanced Super Thin-Layer and High Output Metal Media technology (ATOMM technology), which has contributed to the realization of many high-capacity magnetic recording systems. In addition, both companies have been steady suppliers of high-quality recording media products for many years.

HiFD: Main Characteristics

1. *High capacity of 200MB*

   A high-capacity floppy disk with a 200MB recording capacity has been achieved through the use of a newly developed super-thin layer coating metal disk and a dual discrete gap head.* This disk can easily handle large files such as digitized audio and video data. (Current 3.5-inch floppy disks (2HD) have recording capacity of 1.44MB when formatted.)

2. *High data transfer rate and quick access*

   Through high linear recording density and high disk rotational speed of

---

*Dual discrete gap head. The head used in the drive for this system features both a narrow gap for 200MB high-density recording and a wide gap for current 3.5-inch floppy disks.

3600 rpm, a maximum 3.6MB/sec transfer rate is achieved. Also, through use of a dual discrete gap head, which is a flying-head type* similar to those used in hard disk drives, and a high-speed head actuator with VCM (voice coil motor), quick access speed is possible. [Current 3.5-inch floppy disks (2HD) have data transfer rates of approximately 0.06MB/sec.]

3. *Read/write-compatibility with current 3.5-inch floppy disks*
In order to achieve read-and write-compatibility with current 3.5-inch floppy disks, a "dual discrete gap head" has been used. In drives that use the HiFD system, data can be read from current 3.5-inch floppy disks (2DD/2HD), and data can also be written to such disks. This ensures the continued utility of current 3.5-inch floppy disks widely used.

4. *High reliability*
Through development of a new structure in which head-loading is done softly, wear on the disk is reduced. Also, through the error correction scheme, high data reliability is ensured. Furthermore, the cartridge uses a new shutter that makes it difficult for dust to enter into the disk.

Specification outline
Recording capacity: 200MB (both sides) (formatted); 240MB (both sides) (unformatted)
Disk diameter: 86 mm
Track pitch: 9 micrometers
Track density: 2,822 tpi (111 tpmm)
Linear recording density: 72–91 KBpi (2.83–3.58 KBmm)
Modulation/Demodulation method: PRML[†] (16-17 code)
Transfer rate: Maximum 3.6MB/sec

HiFD Problems

Although the Sony HiFD has a 200MB capacity compared to the SuperDisk's 120MB, it may have a difficult time in becoming the standard. The LS-120 SuperDisk had about a two-year head start on the

---

*Flying head. Because the head is flying slightly due to the rotation of the disk when reading or recording, the disk and the head do not come in contact. The result is a long life and high reliability because the erosion due to wear on both the head and the disk is reduced in comparison with a contact head.
[†]PRML is an abbreviation of "Partial Response Most Likelihood."

Sony HiFD. The SuperDisk also has some big names backing it, such as Compaq, one of the developers and users. So a lot of companies and users have already made the SuperDisk their choice. The HiFD did finally get to the stores in early 1999, but the devices had some problems and all were recalled. The problems should be fixed, and they should be back in the stores by the time you read this.

The cost is another problem that may prevent many people from choosing the HiFD. At the present time, the cost of the HiFD is about $200; the SuperDisk is about $75. Also, at the present time, the HiFD can only be used as an external parallel device with a transfer rate of only 600KB/s. They are working on an internal IDE model that will have a transfer rate of 3.5MB/s. It should be available by the time you read this. Conversely, the SuperDisk is available as a parallel device, an internal IDE, or internal SCSI device.

Obsolete Drives

The 5-¼-inch drives and disks are as obsolete as the horse and buggy. The 3-½ inch 1.44MB drives are also obsolete in many ways, but many vendors are still installing them on new systems. One reason is because they are so inexpensive. For just a few bucks more, you can install an LS-120 SuperDisk 120MB drive that does everything the 1.44MB drive does and a whole lot more.

How Floppy Drives Operate

The rest of this chapter tells a bit about how floppies operate and goes into a bit of the history of floppies. Computers rely to a very large extent on magnetism. Magnetic lines of force can be produced when voltage is passed through a coil of wire that is wrapped around a piece of iron. The amount of magnetism produced varies enormously, depending on such factors as the voltage level, the number of turns of wire, the properties of the iron core, the frequency of the voltage, and many, many other factors.

Conversely, voltage can be produced when a coil of wire is passed through a magnetic field. So we can use voltage to make magnetism or use magnetism to make voltage.

The floppy drive spins a disk much like a record player. The floppy disk is made from a type of plastic material called *polyethylene tereph-thalate*. This is coated with a magnetic material made primarily of iron oxide. It is similar to the tape that is used in cassette tape recorders. The drive uses a head, which is basically a piece of iron with a coil of wire around it. The iron core for the head is shaped somewhat like a C. When voltage is passed through the coil of wire, a magnetic field is produced between the ends of the C. The space between the ends of the C may be very small and is called the *gap*. The head records (writes) and plays back (reads) the disk much like the record/playback head in a cassette tape recorder.

There is a considerable difference in the methods of recording on a tape recorder and digital recording. When audio is recorded, the sound waves cause a diaphragm to vibrate in a microphone. Attached to the diaphragm is a magnet that moves in and out of a coil of wire because of the sound vibrations. The movement of the magnet in the coil of wire generates a voltage that goes up and down to exactly match the up and down vibration of the sound. This sine wave analog voltage is then amplified and fed to the tape record head. The record head responds with a voltage or current output that is a replica of the original sound. The varying current from the head magnetizes the tape with an exact replica of the original sound. When the tape is played back, as the magnetized image on the tape passes by the head, it causes a voltage to be produced that is a replica of the original sound. Of course, the voltage produced by the magnetism on the tape is very small, so it must be amplified. Placing a small voltage on the base of a transistor can cause it to turn on and amplify or create a much larger replica of the small original voltage.

The voltages in the tape recorder are alternating current; that is, they vary up and down. Most of the voltages used in computers are direct current, usually 3 to 5 volts DC. Transistors, which act like a switch, can be used to turn the direct current on and off. When the current is on, it can represent a 1. When it is off, it can represent a 0. A transistor can be switched on and off millions of times per second.

When the head on a disk drive writes or records on the iron oxide surface, a pulse of electricity causes the head to magnetize that portion of track beneath the head. A spot on the track that is magnetized can represent a 1. If the next spot of the same track is not magnetized, it can represent a 0. When the tracks are read, the head detects whether each portion of the track is magnetized or not. If the spot is magnetized, it creates a small voltage signal to represent a 1, or a 0 if it is not magnetized.

Computers operate with a very precise clock rate based on internal crystal oscillators. If a voltage remains high for a certain length of time, it can represent two or more 1s. If it is off for a certain length of time, it can represent two or more 0s.

The floppy disks are divided into several concentric tracks. Each track is then divided into sectors. This system allows us to find any particular item on the track. It is amazing to me that the head can find any one byte on a floppy disk that may have over a million bytes. It is even more amazing that the same system can find any one byte on a hard disk that may have over 2 billion bytes, or 2GB.

On a 1.2MB floppy disk, 80 tracks are laid down at the rate of 96 tracks per inch. So each track occupies $\frac{1}{96}$ of an inch, or about .0104 inches wide. The record current that passes through the heads may vary considerably. A stronger current may even magnetize adjacent tracks. To prevent this, the actual recording part of the head is only about one-third as wide as the track width. There are two erase heads on each side behind the record head; the erase heads extend to the full width of the track. As the record head lays down the square waves that represent 1s and 0s, the erase heads trim any signal that may have exceeded the normal width of the track. These side erase heads form guard bands between each track.

More about tracks and disk formats later in the chapter.

The Virtual Drive

DOS reserves the letters A and B for floppy drives. If you have only one drive, you can call it A and B. For instance, you can say, "copy A: to B:". The drive will copy whatever is in the drive, then prompt you to insert a disk in drive B:. Of course, you could have said "copy A: to A:" and gotten the same results.

High-Density Drives and Disks

By just looking at a 360KB and a 1.2MB drive, you wouldn't be able to tell which was which. The main distinction between the two involves magnetic and electrical differences. The 1.2MB drive has an oersted (Oe) of 600, the 360KB has an Oe of 300. The higher Oe means that the material requires a higher head current for magnetization.

In order to store 1.2MB on the floppy, 80 tracks on each side of the disk are laid down. Each of these tracks are divided into 15 sectors, and 512 bytes can be stored in each sector. These 80 tracks are just half as wide as the 40 tracks of a 360KB disk. The 1.2MB drives switch to a lower head current when writing to the 360KB format.

The 3½-inch 1.44MB and 720KB drives also look very much alike. The main difference is that the 1.44MB drive usually has a small microswitch that checks for the square hole in the right rear corner of the 1.44MB disks. The 1.44MB drives will read and write to the 720KB format, as well as to the high density. The 720KB drive is as obsolete as the 360KB.

The All-Media or Combination Floppy Drive

The 1.2MB drive system is also obsolete. But you may have several 1.2MB disks with small programs on them. I have about 500. I may never use them, but I just hate to throw them away. If you have several 1.2MB disks, you might consider buying a combination drive. Most older systems never had enough bays. Many of the desktop cases only provided three or four bays to mount drives. You may not have had space to mount two floppies, two hard drives, a tape backup drive, and a CD-ROM.

The CMS Enhancements Company, (714-222-6316) noted this problem. They created an All-Media floppy drive by combining a 1.2MB and a 1.44MB floppy drive into a single unit. The 5¼-inch part of the drive can handle 5¼-inch 360KB and 1.2MB floppies; the 3½-inch part handles 720KB and 1.44MB floppy disks. The combination drive requires only a single drive bay. The two drives are never both used at the same time, so there is no problem. They can even share most of the drive electronics.

Teac, Canon, and several other companies also manufacture the combo drives. But they are practically obsolete now, so you may have trouble finding one.

Disk Drive Motors

Disk drives have two motors. One motor drives the spindle that rotates the disk. Then a stepping motor, or actuator, moves the heads back and forth to the various tracks.

Spindle Motor

If you have an older computer, then no doubt you have a 5¼-inch 360KB floppy drive, or maybe two such drives. If they are very old, they may be full height, or about 3½-inches high. If they are original IBM drives, then they probably have a plastic or rubber O-ring for a drive belt from the motor to the disk spindle. The O-ring deteriorates and stretches with time. The speed of the disk is very critical. When the O-ring stretches, the speed will slow down, and the spindle might not even turn at all.

I replaced an IBM 5¼-inch 360KB floppy drive in 1985 because it kept giving me errors in reading floppies. It cost $425 for a new IBM drive. A 5¼-inch drive today costs about $25. I didn't realize it at the time, but I could have just replaced the O-ring. Most of the newer drives use direct-drive motors. Modern floppy drives use a direct drive where the spindle is just an extension of the motor shaft.

The motors are regulated so that the speed is usually fairly constant. The speed of the old 5¼-inch 360KB floppy drive is 300 rpms. The 5¼-inch 1.2MB drive rotates 360 rpms, even when reading and writing to a 360KB disk. All of the 3½-inch floppy drives rotate at 300 rpms.

Head Actuator Motor

The head actuator motor is electronically linked to the file allocation table. If a request is received to read data from a particular track, say track 20, the actuator motor moves the head, or rather heads, to that track. Floppy drives have two heads, one on top and one on the bottom. They are connected together and move as a single unit.

Several large companies, such as Sony, Toshiba, Fuji, and Teac, manufacture the floppy drives. Each company's prices are within a few dollars of the others. Most of them are fairly close in quality, but there may be minor differences.

On some of the older drives, a fairly large actuator stepping motor is used to position the heads. It is very quiet and works smoothly as it moves the heads from track to track. A steel band is attached to the shaft of the stepper motor and to the heads that move the heads in discrete steps across the disk. It can find and stop on any track.

The actuator stepping motors on the combo drives are small cylindrical motors with a worm screw. The motors groan and grunt as they move the heads from track to track. Other than being a bit noisy, they have worked perfectly. The heads are mounted on the worm screw, and as the motor turns, the heads move in and out to access the various tracks. If the software tells the motor to go to track 15, it knows exactly how far to move the heads.

If the worm screw becomes worn, or the steel band on the 1.2MB drive that is attached to the actuator motor shaft becomes loose or out of adjustment, the drives may not be able to find the proper tracks. If the hub of the disk you are trying to read has become worn or is not centered exactly on the cone spindle, the heads may not be able to find a track that was previously written, or one that was written on another drive.

If your heads are out of alignment, you can write and read on your own machine, since you are using the same misalignment to write and read. But another drive may have trouble reading a disk recorded with misaligned heads.

Cost of 1.44MB Drives

I recently went to a weekend computer swap meet here at the Los Angeles County Fairgrounds and bought a 1.44MB drive for $17.95. I didn't really need one, but at that price, it makes a good backup spare. I like to keep spare components so that if something goes bad, I can easily replace it.

Floppy Controllers

A floppy drive must have a controller to tell it when to turn on, and to go to a certain track and sector. In the early days the controller was a large board full of chips. Later, some manufacturers integrated the floppy disk controller (FDC) onto the same board as the hard disk controller (HDC). These were large, full-length boards that were rather expensive at about $250. Now the floppy drive controllers are usually built into a single VLSI (very large-scale integration) chip and integrated with a hard disk controller or Integrated Drive Electronics (IDE) interface. Now the FDC and the IDE hard disk interface are often built in on the motherboard. These motherboards usually have a set of upright pins for the flat ribbon cable connectors. There will usually be pins for the floppy drives, for

IDE hard drives and CD-ROMs, and for a short printer cable to a back panel connector, as well as pins for COM1 and COM2 for short cables to back panel connectors for the mouse.

The older controller boards had an edge connector for the cable. Later boards had two rows of pins for the connector. Be very careful when plugging in the cable connector. Look for pin 1 on the board, and make sure that the different-colored wire goes to that side. If the cable is plugged in backwards, the floppy disk will not work properly. If you try to boot up, the floppy drive will erase portions of the boot section of the floppy disk. You will no longer be able to boot up with the disk. I know that this happens because I have made this stupid mistake. Fortunately, I had a backup boot disk.

Drive Select Jumpers

It is possible to have four different floppy drives connected to one controller. The floppies will have a set of pins with a jumper so that each drive can be set for a unique number. The pins may be labeled DS0, DS1, DS2, and DS3, although some manufacturers label them DS1, DS2, DS3, and DS4. The vast majority of systems use only two drives. These jumpers also let you determine which drive is A: or B:. In most cases, you will use them as they come from the factory and never have to worry about these jumpers. Most drives are received with the second set of pins jumpered, which means they are set for drive A:. If you install a second floppy drive, it will also have the second set of pins jumpered just like the A: drive. Don't change it. Since the floppy cable has some twisted wires in it, the controller automatically recognizes it as drive B:. This can be confusing, and you may or may not get any documentation at all with your drive. Fortunately, they usually work fine as received from the factory.

Combination drives usually have small jumper pins near the miniature power cable connector. The combos have two columns of pins, one for each drive. There are six pins in each column, and four pins in each column are jumpered. Again, you should never have to reset or bother with these pins. The two drives share a single controller cable connector. If you want to use the $5\frac{1}{4}$-inch drive as drive A:, then plug the end of the cable with the twisted wires into the cable connector. If you want the $3\frac{1}{2}$-inch 1.44MB drive to be drive A:, then plug in the middle connector that has no twists. Again, fortunately, there is usually no need to move the jumpers.

Data Compression

Data compression can double your disk capacity. It can be used on floppy disks as well as hard disks. Compression can be the least expensive way to increase disk capacity.

Differences between Floppy Disks

The 5¼-inch 360KB and the 3½-inch 720KB disks are called double-sided double density (DS/DD). The 5¼-inch 1.2MB and the 3½-inch 1.44MB are called high-density (HD). The 3½-inch double-density disks are usually marked DD; the high density are usually marked HD. The 5¼-inch 360KB and the 1.2MB disks, however, usually have no markings. They look exactly alike, except that the 360KB usually has a reinforcing ring or collar around the large center hole. The high-density 1.2MB disks do not have the ring.

Figure 5-5 shows a 1.2MB floppy in the upper left, a 360KB in the upper right, a 1.44MB in lower left, and a 720KB in the lower right. The 360KB disk shown in the upper right has a white collar or ring; most of the new disks have a black ring.

Figure 5-5
Some floppy disks: 1.2MB (5¼), 360KB (5¼), 1.44MB (3½), 720KB (3½).

One of the major differences between the 720KB and the 1.44MB is that the high-density 1.44MB has two small square holes at the rear of the plastic shell, while the 720KB has only one. The 3½-inch drive has a small media sensor microswitch that protrudes upward. If it finds a hole on that side of the disk, it knows that it is a 1.44MB disk. If there is no hole, it is treated as a 720KB.

When looking at the back side of the two disks, you'll note that the square hole on the right rear of the shell has a small black slide that can be moved to cover the hole. Another small microswitch on the drive protrudes upward and checks the hole when the disk is inserted. If the hole is covered, the switch is pressed downward, allowing the disk to be written on. If the hole is open, the switch protects the disk so that it cannot be written on or erased. The 3½-inch write-protect system is just the opposite of the system used by the 5¼-inch disks. They have a square notch that must be covered with opaque tape to prevent writing or unintentionally erasing the disk. (Incidentally, you must use opaque tape. The 5¼-inch system uses a light to shine through the square notch. If the detector in the system can see the light through the notch, then it can write on the disk. Some people have used clear plastic tape to cover the notch, with disastrous results.) There might be a time when you would want to make a disk copy of a 720KB and all you have are 1.44MB. Or for some reason, you may want to use a 1.44MB as a 720KB. You can cover the hole with any kind of tape, and it will format as a 720KB.

360KB and 1.2MB

Although the 360KB and 1.2MB disks look exactly alike except for the hub ring on the 360KB, there is a large difference in their magnetic media formulation. Several materials such as cobalt or barium can be added to the iron oxide to alter the magnetic properties. Cobalt is added to increase the oersted (Oe) of high-density floppy disks. Barium is used for the 2.88MB extra high-density (ED) disks. Oe is a measure of the resistance of a material to being magnetized. The lower the Oe, the easier it is to be magnetized. The 360KB has an Oe of 300; the 1.2MB is 600 Oe. The 360KB disks are fairly easy to magnetize or write to, so they require a fairly low head current. The 1.2MB is more difficult to magnetize so a much higher head current is required.

The 1.2MB system can switch the current to match whatever type of disk you tell the system you are using. If you place a 360KB floppy in a

1.2MB drive and just type FORMAT, it will try to format it as a 1.2MB. However, it will find several bad sectors, especially near the center where the sectors are shorter. These sectors will be marked and locked out. The system may report that you have over a megabyte of space on a 360KB disk. This disk could be used in an emergency, for instance, to move data from one machine to another. But I do not recommend that you use such a disk for any data that is important. The data is packed much closer together when it is recorded as 1.2MB. Since the 300 Oe of the 360KB disks are so easy to magnetize, it is possible that nearby data may be affected. The data may migrate and may eventually deteriorate and become unusable.

720KB and 1.44MB

The $3\frac{1}{2}$-inch disks have several benefits and characteristics that make them superior to the $5\frac{1}{4}$-inch disks. The 720KB disk can store twice as much data as a 360KB in a much smaller space. The 1.44MB can store four times as much as a 360KB disk in the same small space.

The $3\frac{1}{2}$-inch floppy disks have a hard, plastic protective shell, so they are not easily damaged. They also have a spring-loaded shutter that automatically covers and protects the head opening when they are not in use.

The $3\frac{1}{2}$-inch systems are much more accurate than the $5\frac{1}{4}$-inch systems in reading and writing. The $5\frac{1}{4}$-inch drive systems have a cone-shaped hub for the large center hole in the disks. If the disks are used for any length of time, it is possible for the hole to become stretched or enlarged. If the disk is not centered exactly on the hub, the heads will not be able to find and read the data.

The $3\frac{1}{2}$-inch floppies have a metal hub on the backside. This gives them much greater accuracy in reading and writing, even though the tracks on the $3\frac{1}{2}$-inch systems are much closer together.

One-Way Insertion

It is possible to insert a $5\frac{1}{4}$-inch floppy upside down, backwards, or sideways. When I first started using computers, I inserted a floppy that had the original software on it into a drive. I waited for a while and nothing happened. Then I got the error message, "Not ready reading drive A. Abort, Retry, Fail?" I almost panicked. I thought for sure that I had destroyed the software. Finally, I discovered that I had inserted the floppy upside down. I was still scared that I had damaged the disk, so I did what I should have done when I first got the program. I made a disk copy backup of the disk. I found that the software was still okay.

Fortunately, you can't actually damage a disk by inserting it upside down. You can't read it because the small hole that tells DOS where track 1 begins is on the wrong side. And, of course, you can't write to it or format because of the small hole and also because the write-protect notch is on the other side.

The 3½-inch disks are designed so that they can only be inserted properly. They have arrows at the left top portion of the disks that indicate how they should be inserted into the drive. They also have notches on the backside that prevent them from being completely inserted upside down.

The 720KB 3½-inch disks may have an Oe of 600 to 700. The 1.44MB may have an Oe of 700 to 720. The Oe of the extra high-density 2.88MB disks may be about 750.

The 360KB and 720KB disks are both obsolete.

Disk Format Structure

Tracks

A disk must be formatted before it can be used. This consists of laying out individual concentric tracks on each side of the disk. If it is a 360KB disk, each side is marked or configured with 40 tracks, numbered from 0 to 39. If it is a 1.2MB, 720KB or 1.44MB, each side is configured with 80 tracks, numbered from 0 to 79.

The tracks have the same number on the top and bottom of the disk. The top is side 0 and the bottom is side 1. When the head is over track 1 on the top, it is also over track 1 on the bottom. The heads move as a single unit to the various tracks by a head actuator motor or positioner. When data is written to a track, as much as possible is written on the top track, then the head is electronically switched and it continues to write to the same track on the bottom side. Electronically switching between the heads is much faster and easier than moving them to another track.

Cylinders

If you could strip away all of the other tracks on each side of track 1 on side 0 and track 1 on side 1, it would be very flat, but it might look like a cylinder. So if a disk has 40 tracks, such as the 360KB, it has 40 cylinders; the 1.2MB and 1.44MB have 80 cylinders.

Sectors

Each of the tracks are divided up into sectors. Each track of the 360KB is divided into 9 sectors, each of the 1.2MB tracks are divided into 15 sectors, each of the 720KB tracks are divided into 9 sectors, each of the 1.44MB tracks into 18 sectors, and the 2.88MB tracks into 36 sectors. Each sector can contain 512 bytes. Multiplying the number of sectors times the number of bytes per sector times the number of tracks times two sides gives the amount of data that can be stored on a disk. For instance, the 1.2MB has 15 sectors times 512 bytes times 80 tracks times two sides would be $15 \times 512 \times 80 \times 2 = 1,228,800$ bytes. The system uses 14,898 bytes to mark the tracks and sectors during formatting, so there are actually 1,213,952 bytes available on a 1.2MB floppy.

Figure 5-6 shows how the tracks and sectors are laid out on a floppy disk.

Clusters or Allocation Units

DOS allocates one or more sectors on a disk and calls it a *cluster* or *allocation unit*. On 360KB and 720KB disks, a cluster or allocation unit is two sectors. On the 1.2MB and 1.44MB disks, each allocation unit is one sector. Only single files or parts of single files can be written into an allocation unit. If two different files were written into a single allocation unit, the data would become mixed and corrupted.

File Allocation Table (FAT)

During formatting, a file allocation table (FAT) is created on the first track of the disk. This FAT acts like a table of contents for a book. Whenever a file is recorded on a disk, the file is broken up into allocation units. The head looks in the FAT to find empty units, then

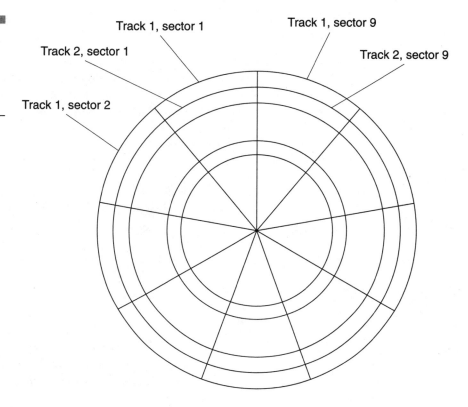

Figure 5-6
A diagrammatic
representation of
how tracks and
sectors are laid out
on a floppy disk.

records the parts of the file in any empty units it can find. Part of the file may be recorded in sector 5 of track 10, part in sector 8 of track 15, and any place it can find empty sectors. It records the location of all the various parts of the file in the FAT. With this method, parts of a file can be erased, changed, or added to without changing the entire disk.

TPI

The 40 tracks of a 360KB is laid down at a rate of 48 tracks per inch (TPI), so each of the 40 tracks is $\frac{1}{48}$ of an inch wide. The 80 tracks of the high-density 1.2MB is laid down at a rate of 96 TPI, so each track is $\frac{1}{96}$ of an inch. The 80 tracks of the 3½-inch disks are laid down at a density of 135 per inch, or .0074 inches per track.

Read Accuracy

The 5¼-inch disks have a 1⅛-inch center hole. The drives have a spindle with a conical hub that comes up through the disk center hole when the drive latch is closed. This centers the disk so that the heads will be able to find each track. The plastic material that the disk is made from is subject to environmental changes and wear and tear. Because the conical spindle might not center each disk exactly, head-to-track accuracy is difficult with more than 80 tracks. (If you have trouble reading a disk, it might be off-center. Removing and reinserting the disk might help.) Most of the 360KB disks use a reinforcement hub ring, but it probably doesn't help much. The 1.2MB floppies do not use a hub ring. Except for the hub ring, the 360KB and 1.2MB disk look exactly the same.

If your drive consistently has trouble reading your disks, or especially reading disks recorded on another machine, the heads may be out of alignment. The steel band or worm screw from the actuator motor that moves the heads may have slipped or become worn. So the actuator or head positioner may not be able to move the heads to the proper track. It is possible to have the heads realigned, but it is time-consuming and expensive. Computer service time may cost from $50 up to $100 or more per hour. It would probably be much less expensive to scrap the drive and buy a new one.

The 3½-inch disks have a metal hub on the back that is used to center the disks. The tracks of the 3½-inch floppies are narrower and greater in density per inch. But because of the metal hub, the head-tracking accuracy is much better than that of the 5¼-inch systems.

Some Differences between Floppies and Hard Disks

Hard disks have very accurate and precise head-tracking systems. Some hard disks have a density up to 3000 or more tracks per inch, so much more data can be stored on a hard disk.

Floppy disks have a very smooth lubricated surface. They rotate at a fairly slow 300 rpms. Magnetic lines of force deteriorate very fast with distance. So the closer the heads, the better they can read and write. The floppy heads are in direct contact with the floppy disks.

TABLE 5-1

Capacities of
Various Disk Types.

Disk Type	Tracks per Side	Sectors/ Track	Unformatted Capacity	System Use	Available to User	Max. Dirs
360KB	40	9	368640	6144	362496	112
1.2MB	80	15	1228800	14898	1213952	224
720KB	80	9	737280	12800	724480	224
1.44MB	80	18	1474560	16896	1457664	224
2.88MB	80	36	2949120	33792	2915328	240

Hard disks, on the other hand, rotate at speeds from 3600 up to 7200 rpms. The heads and surface would be severely damaged if they came in contact at this speed. So heads "fly" over the surface of each disk, just a few millionths of an inch above it.

Comparison of Floppy Disks

Table 5-1 shows some of the differences in the various types of floppy disks. Notice that the maximum number of root directories is the same for the 720KB, the 1.2MB, and the 1.44MB. The 2.88MB has four times the capacity of the 720KB yet allows only 16 more root entries. This means that you can enter 240 different files on a 2.88MB disk, but if you try to enter one more, it will not accept it, even though you may have hundreds of unused bytes.

The reason is that the DOS file allocation was designed for this limited number of files. There is an easy way around this problem. Just create subdirectories, like those created on a hard disk. Just type MD for "make directory." If necessary, you can even make subdirectories of the subdirectories.

Formatting

Formatting with Windows 95 is much easier. Just point your mouse to the My Computer icon and click. All of your drives will be shown. Point to whichever one you want to format and click to highlight it. Then select File. You will be given several options, one of which is to format a disk.

For those who might still be using an older version of DOS but have a 1.2MB for the A: drive, to format a 360KB disk with the 1.2MB drive, type FORMAT A /4. To format a 1.2MB disk, you only have to type FORMAT A:. If you insert a 360KB disk, it will try to format it to 1.2MB, and it will probably find several bad sectors. To format a 720KB disk on a 1.44MB B: drive, type FORMAT B: /f:720. To format a 1.44MB disk, just type FORMAT B:.

The FORMAT command in newer versions can take a very long time before it starts. It searches the floppy disk, then will save unformatted information on the disk. If you decide later that you want to unformat the disk, just type UNFORMAT. But for most cases, I don't want to unformat a disk, especially if it is one that has never been formatted before. You can speed up the formatting process by typing FORMAT A:/U. This performs an unconditional format. If the disk has been formatted before, you can type FORMAT A:/Q. This gives you a quick format by just erasing the first letter of the files in the file allocation table of the disk.

Cost of Disks

All floppy disks are now quite reasonable. The 1.44MB are so inexpensive that many companies are sending out demo disks, press releases, and junk mail on 1.44MB floppies. I usually erase them and reuse them. I feel it is my duty to recycle. One Internet company sent out several million copies of their sign-up software. I got so many copies of their software that I didn't have to buy any floppies for some time.

There are several discount mail-order floppy disk stores. Check the computer magazines for ads. Some companies are selling 1.44MB preformatted disks for as little as 20 cents apiece. These are real bargains. At one time I paid as much as $2.50 each for 360KB floppy disks.

CHAPTER 6

Choosing a Hard Disk Drive

This chapter covers some of the different types of hard drives and some of the hard disk drive basics. Formatting hard drives will be discussed in Chapter 12 after the system is assembled.

What Should You Buy?

You have the option of a very large number of different types and capacities of disks to choose from. Of course, what you choose will depend on what you need to do with your computer and how much you want to spend. I recommend that you buy two drives, ideally, a large-capacity Enhanced Integrated Drive Electronics (EIDE) and a similar Small Computer System Interface (SCSI). But a similar SCSI drive will be a bit more expensive. In addition, if you don't already have a SCSI interface board, you will have to buy one. Except for some of the very high-end type of applications, there is very little if any difference in the SCSI and the IDE systems. The SCSI systems are usually more expensive than the equivalent IDE drives. If you don't have a lot of money, you can do very well with two IDE drives. They are relatively inexpensive.

The reason for having two drives is for backup purposes. You never know when disaster may strike. Disk drives are very reliable nowadays. But they are mechanical devices, and some of them do crash. You should always have your critical files backed up. You can easily and quickly copy and back up files to another hard disk. Figure 6-1 shows two Western Digital hard drives, a 13GB hard disk on the left and a 20.4GB on the right. Both of these drives will be attached to the same cable.

Figure 6-1
A 13GB hard drive on the left and a 20.4GB drive on the right.

Figure 6-2
Jumpers that configure the drive as master or slave.

Figure 6-2 shows the jumpers that tell the system which one is master and which one is slave.

If you have two IDE drives, there is very little chance that both of them would crash at the same time. If you have an IDE and a SCSI, there is even less of a chance that both would crash at the same time.

Ultra DMA/66

Most new drives are now manufactured to the Ultra DMA/66 specifications. This means that they can transfer data at a rate of 66MHz. Unfortunately, many of the motherboards will not let them operate at this rate. In fact, you can't even format these drives without special software that turns off the 66MHz function. Western Digital has such software at their Web site (www.westerndigital.com). If you buy a new hard drive, with it you should receive some installation instructions. Western Digital provides a large, comprehensive installation guide with about 60 pages that can tell you just about everything you need to know about hard disks. Many of the mail-order dealers and those at swap meets do not provide any instructions at all.

Western Digital, Maxtor (www.maxtor.com), Quantum (www.quantum.com), Seagate (www.seagate.com), and most of the other major manufacturers provide instructions on their Web sites.

Ultra DMA/66 Promise Controller Cards

Promise Technology (www.promise.com) has developed several controller cards that will allow you to use the new Ultra DMA/66 hard disks on just about any PC. (See Figure 6-3.) Their Ultra66 card vastly improves the throughput of a hard disk made to the Ultra DMA/66 specifications. Standard EIDE drives operate at a maximum of 16.7Mbps. The Ultra ATA 33 operates at 33Mbps, the Ultra Wide SCSI operates at 40Mbps, and the Ultra DMA/66 operates at 66Mbps.

Again, it is possible to disable the Ultra DMA/66 functions of a hard disk and install it as a standard EIDE. But look at the speed that is being sacrificed.

Figure 6-3
The Promise Ultra66
Controller.

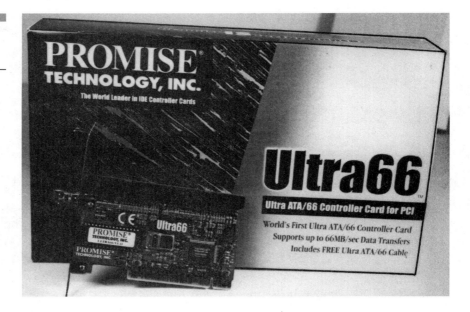

The Ultra66 also has an onboard BIOS that supports drive capacities up to 128GB. The BIOS of many motherboards designed before late 1998 could not recognize a hard disk larger than 8.4GB.

The Ultra66 is designed so that four IDE devices can be attached to it. This leaves your standard motherboard connectors free so that four other IDE devices could be installed. It is quite possible to have eight or more IDE devices, such as two or more hard drives, a standard CD-ROM, a recordable CD-R, a DVD, an LS-120 SuperDisk, a ZIP drive, a tape backup, a scanner, and several other IDE devices. The Ultra66 controller is a Plug and Play device and is very easy to install.

At this time, Promise Controllers sell for around $50.

Promise Low-Cost RAID

Promise Technology also has a FastTrak controller that will let you set up an IDE RAID system. (RAID is an acronym for "redundant array of independent disks"). Ordinarily, RAID systems use SCSI hard disks and controllers and are rather expensive. The new Ultra DMA/66 disks are actually faster than the SCSI and are less expensive. Here is an example from a recent ad in the *Computer Shopper* from TC Computers (www.tccomputers.com or 1-800-677-9781): A Western Digital 18GB IDE drive with 2MB of cache is advertised at this time for $326, and a SCSI 18GB with 2MB of cache from the same company, Western Digital, is advertised at $755, more than twice as much. You can be sure that the prices will be different by the time you read this.

With the Promise FastTrak controller, you can control four IDE drives. (See Figure 6-4.) They can be set up so that two of them can be used for striping. Striping allows you to write every other track to the other drive. For instance, one drive would write or read track 1-3-5; the second one would read or write track 2-4-6. Striping essentially doubles the speed of the disk read and write. Hard disks are never as fast as the electronics, so anything that can double and speed up the throughput is great.

You can also set up two drives to mirror each other. This is one of the better ways to make backups. The same data is written to both disks at the same time. If one of them fails, the other one will still have all of the data. An ideal system would be to have four hard disks, two for striping and two for mirroring.

If you are in a business and have to make sure that your data is

Figure 6-4
The Promise FastTrak
controller that can
control four IDE
drives—excellent for
small RAID and
backup.

backed up, this is one of the better ways to do it. This system is also ideal for the small office/home office (SOHO) or even a home user.

Capacity

When you consider capacity, buy the biggest you can afford. You may have heard of Mr. C. Northcote Parkinson. After observing business organizations for some time, he formulated several laws. One law says, "Work expands to fill up available employee time." I propose a parallel law that paraphrases Mr. Parkinson's immutable law: "Data expands to fill up available hard disk space."

Just a short time ago, 200MB was a large disk. But that was before Microsoft and other companies began developing "bloatware" programs that required 200MB or more for a single program. Office 97 requires 191MB for a full installation. So don't even think of buying anything less than 8GB. Better yet would be 10GB minimum and even better would be two 10GB or two 20GB. New software programs have become more and more friendly and offer more and more options. Most of the basic application programs that you will need such as spreadsheets, databases, CAD programs, word processors, and many others will each require 40MB to 80MB of disk storage space.

Seagate and several other companies now have drives with over 50GB at very reasonable prices.

Cost

Most of the major hard disk drives are fairly close in quality and price. My recommendation is to buy the highest-capacity drive that you can possibly afford. I recently bought a 20GB hard drive for $315. That is less than $16 per gigabyte—an absolutely fantastic price. About three years ago, I paid $750 for a 1.05GB hard drive. I would not have believed that it was possible for a precision piece of machinery like this to be sold for any less. You will be able to buy similar drives for even less by the time you read this.

IDE- or ATA-Type Drives

The most popular drives today are those with EIDE, often just called "IDE." They are also sometimes referred to as ATA (for Advanced Technology Attachment) drives because they were first developed for use on the 286 AT. The drives are similar to the SCSI drives in that all of their controller electronics are integrated on the drive. You do not need a controller card such as those required by the older MFM, RLL, and ESDI drives, but you do need an interface. The interface will be a set of upright pins on the motherboard.

The IDE drives are less expensive than the SCSI. One major difference is that the IDE interface may cost nothing because it is usually built in on all new motherboards. A SCSI controller may cost from $80 up to $600 or more.

The newer IDE drives are designed for the Ultra DMA/66 specification.

SCSI

At one time SCSI drives were usually reserved for larger-capacity and faster drives. But now the IDE drives are equivalent in almost all respects. Most companies who manufacture IDE drives also make identical SCSI drive models. The built-in electronics on the two drives are very similar. As mentioned, SCSI stands for "Small Computer System Interface." It is called "small computer" because when it was first proposed, the big iron mainframes ruled the computer world. However, the desktop PCs were proliferating, and there was a real need to be able to connect various peripherals to these PCs. It was a very ambitious undertaking. There wasn't even a standard among the PCs at that time. You can imagine the problems in trying to devise a standard that would work with several nonstandard machines. In addition, this standard would have to work with several different peripherals from different companies. We now have strict SCSI standards. Devices that conform to the SCSI standard have most of their controller functions built into the device. The different devices may be two or more SCSI-type hard disk drives, one or more CD-ROM drives, a scanner, a tape backup unit, or other SCSI products.

A SCSI board can be an interface for up to seven different intelligent devices to a computer. SCSI devices are called *logical units*. Each device is assigned a *logical unit number* (LUN). The devices have switches or jumpers that must be set to the proper LUN. If you have several SCSI devices attached to your system, you should keep a list of the LUNs used. This will make it easier to know what number to assign a new device. Ordinarily, your system will look for the C: drive or floppy A: drive to boot your computer. Usually, the system will assign drive letters to any IDE drives that are present, then the SCSI. If you have only SCSI drives and will be using one as a boot drive, you should assign it a lower LUN number than any other devices so that it will be loaded first.

The IDE and SCSI drives have most of the disk controlling functions integrated onto the drive. This makes a lot of sense because the control electronics can be optimally matched to the drive.

The equivalent SCSI and IDE hard drives made by most companies are physically the same size. They both use the same type of zone bit recording and rotational speed. The only difference in the two is the onboard electronics.

SCSI systems need a host adapter, or interface card, to drive them. SCSI interfaces are rather complex. Some of the older systems were very difficult to set up. The newer systems are the Plug and Play (PnP) variety and are very easy to install.

Some of the newer motherboards may have the SCSI interface built in. There will be a set of pins or a connector for the SCSI cable.

Removable Disk Drives

Several companies manufacture removable disk drives, and there are several different models and types.

The Iomega 100MB and 250MB Zip Floppy Disks and Drives

The Iomega Zip drive uses a $3\frac{1}{2}$-inch disk that is similar to a floppy. Over 10 million of the original 100MB drives were sold. Figure 6-5 shows one of the 100MB drives and a couple of 100MB disks. The newer 250MB drives (see Figure 6-6) are backward compatible so that the older 100MB disks can still be used. This system is fairly inexpensive.

Here is part of a press release from Iomega:

> The high-capacity Zip 250 drives and disks are the answer for burgeoning file-size demands that are being driven by the exponential growth of computer applications, the emergence of audio and video files, and the proliferation of Web downloads. The new internal ATAPI Zip 250 drive provides high performance with simple, affordable system integration and compatibility.

Figure 6-5
An Iomega 100MB Zip drive with $3\frac{1}{2}$-inch disks.

Figure 6-6
A 250MB Iomega Zip drive. Can also read and write to 100MB disks.

The drive fits into a conventional PC drive bay, connects to an internal power supply, and includes a full suite of value-added software applications.

The internal ATAPI Zip 250MB drive is available at an estimated street price of $169.95 (U.S.), with disks available at an estimated street price of $16.65 (U.S.) each, when purchased in a six-pack. The internal ATAPI Zip 250 drive includes one Zip 250MB disk, IomegaWare software and Norton Zip Rescue software, the easiest way to rescue your PC when it does not start properly. Also included is RecordIt software, the coolest way to record and play back voice and audio on a computer from a Zip disk or hard drive.

The new Zip 250MB drive is an extension to Iomega's popular line of Zip 100MB drives and disks. The Zip 250 drive uses new Zip 250 disks, but also reads and writes to Zip 100MB disks. Zip 100MB drives and disks are also available worldwide through most major distributors, retailers, and catalogs. Iomega Zip drives and genuine 100MB and 250MB Zip disks offer an easy-to-use solution for consumers to move, protect, use, share, and back up information.

Iomega can be reached at 1-800-MY-STUFF (800-697-8833), or on the Web at http://www.iomega.com.

The Iomega 40MB Clik! Disk and Drive

Here is an Iomega press release about Clik!:

> The Clik! PC Card Drive offers the ultimate in portability for mobile customers. The Clik! PC Card Drive fits inside the PC card slot, which is common in most notebook and sub-notebook computers shipping today. It's lightweight, extremely easy to carry, and comes ready to use with no extra cables, which eliminates the need to carry external storage backup. Using 40 megabyte Clik! disks, the Clik! PC Card drive offers unlimited backup and expandable, portable storage options for road warriors who rely on their notebook PCs.
>
> **Availability and Pricing**
> The Clik! PC Card Drive is available worldwide through retail outlets, catalog and Iomega's Web site at www.iomegadirect.com. The Clik! PC Card Drive is currently available in the United States for an estimated street price as low as $199.95 (U.S.) and 40MB Clik! disks are available at an estimated street price as low as $9.99 (U.S.) each when purchased in a 10-pack. The Clik! PC Card Drive ships with the drive, disk, protective carrying case, and software.
>
> **About Clik! Drives and Disks**
> The Clik! PC Card Drive joins two members of Iomega's Clik! portable storage family, the Clik! Drive for Digital Cameras and the Clik! Drive Plus bundle. The Clik! Drive for Digital Cameras and the Clik! Drive Plus are ideal storage companions for today's portable products, from digital cameras and handheld personal computers to notebook PCs. They also enable easy access to a desktop computer. In addition to the Clik! PC Card Drive, the Clik! Drive for Digital Cameras and the Clik! Drive Plus are designed to offer unlimited, portable storage through 40MB Clik! disks.
>
> The Clik! disk holds 40MB of data and fits in the palm of your hand. The Clik! drive, about the size of a mouse, works with just about every handheld digital device and desktop product on the market. Clik! is the connection between your handheld devices and your PC.
>
> *Digital Camera*   Clik! disks let you store up to 40 high-res (megapixel) images or hundreds of low-res images. A Clik! disk becomes your digital "roll of film," releasing you from the PC to take pictures wherever you choose.
>
> *Handheld PC (HPC)*   Clik! disks let you bring more of your desktop to your palmtop. Clik! disks let you store a number of color Microsoft PowerPoint presentations or graphic-heavy spreadsheets or hundreds of word documents, e-mails, and attachments.

Personal Digital Assistant (PDA)   On one Clik! disk you can store thousands of addresses or hundreds of notes, faxes, and e-mails.

Smart Phone   The Clik! removable storage disk gives you the capacity to store up to 4 hours of voice messages or hundreds of e-mails.

Global Positioning System (GPS)   Store maps and e-mails on one Clik! disk. And Clik! disks offer you unlimited, inexpensive (under $10 MSRP), removable storage.

Personal Projector   Clik! disks let you store approximately 25 color, ten-page, PowerPoint presentations with graphics. Clik! disks offer you unlimited, inexpensive (under $10 MSRP), removable storage.

IBM's Microdrive

IBM has the world's smallest hard drive. The 340 microdrive weighs 16 grams, which is just a bit more than a half ounce. It measures 1.68 inches by 1.43 inches by 0.19 inches. It can hold up to 340MB of data, or the equivalent of 200 standard floppy disks. The drive comes with a PC Card adapter and field case and will cost about $499.

The microdrive can be used for storage for digital cameras, handheld computers, personal digital assistants, and notebook computers. The storage disk will also be used in future generations of digital audio devices for portable MP3 players. Diamond Multimedia Systems announced that future versions of its Rio MP3 devices will include the IBM hard drive, which will allow listeners to store several hours of CD-quality music.

The drive is small enough to fit into a PC Card-type slot on laptops. Many laptops use Lexar Media's CompactFlash on PC Cards. It is expected that the Microdrive will give CompactFlash a lot of competition. The maximum flash memory for a type II card is 96MB compared to the 340MB of the microdrive. The CompactFlash is a bit less expensive at $300 compared to the $499 for the microdrive.

Parallel Port Hard Drives

Many of the drives listed above are available as parallel port models. As such, they can be used with laptops or any computer with a parallel port. These drives are great for backup, for removal and security and for data transport. They come in several capacities from 100MB up to 1GB or more and are great for backup or for adding a second hard drive.

Since these drives plug into the computer's only parallel port, the hard drives usually provide a parallel port connector for the printer. Most of them come with a small transformer power supply.

Magneto-Optical Drives

Magneto-optical (M-O) drives are a combination of the magnetic and optical technologies. Magnetic disks, especially floppies, can be easily erased. Over a period of time, the data on a magnetic disk, whether hard or floppy, will gradually deteriorate. Some critical data must be renewed about every two years.

If a magnetic material has a high coercivity, or a high resistance to being magnetized, it will also resist being demagnetized. (Coercivity is measured by oersteds—Oe). But the higher the Oe, the more current that is needed to magnetize the area. A large amount of current may magnetize a large area of the disk. In order to pack more density, the magnetized area must be very small.

The Oe of a material decreases as it is heated. Most materials have a Curie temperature whereby the Oe may become zero. By heating the magnetic medium with a laser beam, a very small current can be used to write data to a disk. The heated spots cool very quickly and regain their high coercivity. The disks can be easily written over or changed by heating up the area again with the laser beam.

The most popular M-O drives at this time have a capacity of 128MB and 256Mb. The M-O disks will have a minimum lifetime of more than 10 years without degradation of data.

A short time ago there were several companies who made M-O type disks and drives, such as SyQuest and Avatar. Except for Iomega, most of the companies who manufactured M-O drives have now gone out of business. One reason is because of the recordable CD-ROMs, or CD-Rs. The CD-Rs are less expensive and easier to use. Another big factor is that there was no compatibility between M-O-type drives. If you recorded a disk on one company's drive, it could not be played on another company's drive. The CD-Rs all conform to the CD-ROM standards.

These drives use a patented combination of magnetic (magneto) and laser (optical) technologies, along with removable disks. These combined technologies enable M-O drives to provide excellent reliability, high data-storage capacity, high performance, with conformance to a single worldwide standard. The drives are available in standard 5.25-inch half-height format and external enclosures as well.

Since the disks are read and written with a non-contact optical head, there's never a head crash as with hard disk drives. The disks are made of high-strength polycarbonate plastic, the same material as bulletproof glass. The data layer is kept very safe between a sandwich of polycarbonate. Also, the disks are rated for more than a 50-year data storage life, far longer than hard disks and magnetic tape.

Because the data in an M-O disk is well protected under the disk's near-indestructible polycarbonate surface, it isn't affected by contamination. An M-O disk isn't affected by stray magnetic fields because data is written with a combination of laser and magnetic power. Without this combination, data cannot be altered.

A single low-cost optical disk can hold 5.2GB of data. Depending on size (2.6GB or 5.2GB), and ordered in quantity, a disk may cost from $35 to $75 each.

Optical disks and drives comply with the ISO (International Standards Organization) standards. Compliance with these standards ensures that any ISO disk can be used with anyone's ISO drive. This feature eliminates reliance on single-source suppliers and guards against premature obsolescence. It also enables users to exchange data and disks with greatest confidence of compatibility

The drives are fast enough to be used just like a hard drive. Unlike tape or CD-R disks, users can work on complex projects right on their M-O drive, just like a hard disk. In desktop publishing, digital audio, digital video, electronic photography, and CAD/CAM applications, the files are very large and work is very project-oriented. Users can't afford to keep all jobs on one hard drive. But with M-O, they can keep each project on its very own disk.

M-O Applications

Video and Audio Editing   These applications both require very large amounts of reliable storage. Users can edit directly on the disk easily using a low-cost disk for each project. The disks are tough, so users don't fear losing many hours of work through an accident.

Desktop Publishing and Photo Editing   This application is also very project-oriented with fairly large files (5 to 50MB or more for each file). Again, users can edit directly on the M-O drives as if they were a hard drive. With the M-O drives' ISO compatibility, it's easy to send the disk out for final hard copy output.

Document Imaging Managing document information is a large and growing application. Handwritten, drawn, or typed pages are critical to health care, insurance, legal, engineering, manufacturing, shipping, and many other markets. A single 2.6GB M-O disk can hold well over 40,000 scanned pages—more than a four-drawer file cabinet! Using an optical disk, one jukebox can hold the contents of a very large room full of file cabinets. The M-O drives work right out of the box with the most important PC platforms, but they do require a SCSI adapter.

A recent ad in *Computer Shopper* lists a 2.6GB Maxoptix drive for $1049 and a 5.2GB drive for $1519. The difference is that the 5.2GB system is faster and has a larger buffer. The 5.2GB is compatible with the 2.6GB disks. The disks cost from $35 to $75, depending on size and quantity.

A Few M-O Models

Fujitsu DynaMO The Fujitsu DynaMO 640 (800-626-4686, or www.fcpa.com), is a 640MB magneto-optical drive. DynaMO magneto-optical drives provide reliable, removable storage for graphics, multimedia, large documents, or file backup—nearly anything that requires high-capacity storage is ideal for magneto-optical. DynaMO drives are available in internal and external versions, and offer cartridges that are impervious to dust, magnets, moisture, and X-rays. The DynaMO family reads and writes to all previous media sizes (128, 230, and 540MB) and connects to any PC or Macintosh system.

The Iomega Jaz Drive The Iomega Jaz Drive from the Iomega Company (800-697-8833, or www.iomega.com) is a drive that originally used 1.07GB magneto-optical cartridges. They now have 2GB cartridges. It is a SCSI device. If you have a laptop with SCSI, it can be plugged in externally. Cartridges are less than $100 each. The Jaz drive is very fast and is great for backing up data.

Recordable CD-ROMs (CD-Rs)

Several companies now offer drives that can record CD-ROM discs. When first introduced, the CD-R recordable drives cost up to $10,000. There are some that are available today for less than $200. The CD-

ROM blank disc can hold up to 600MB of data. This is a great way to back up or archive data and records that should never change. The blank CD-ROM discs cost $1 to $2 each, so if you want to change some of the data, just change the data and record it onto another disc.

CD-Rs may have different speeds. Some of the less expensive drives may record at 2x; the more expensive ones will record at 4x or 8x. I have a Plextor 8/20. This means that it can record at 8x and play back at 20x. My Plextor can record a 72-minute music CD in about 10 minutes.

All of the CD-Rs will also play back standard CD-ROM or music CD discs. The CD-Rs may play back at 6x and up to 20x.

An ideal setup would be to have a standard CD-ROM drive or a DVD and a CD-R. You could then copy other CD-ROM discs or music CDs. When buying blank recordable discs, you should buy those designated

Figure 6-7
A CD-R CD-ROM
recorder.

for the speed of your CD-R. In addition, unlike magnetic media that deteriorates or can be erased, data on a CD-ROM should last for many, many years.

My Plextor is a SCSI drive. An IDE drive would have been less expensive, but if you have an IDE CD-R and an IDE CD-ROM, it can cause problems if you are copying from one to the other. Figure 6-7 shows my Plextor 8/20 with the SCSI controller and cable. This controller has a mini 50-pin connector for an external drive. SCSI controllers can control up to seven devices.

There are several different types of SCSI cables and connectors, as shown in Figure 6-8. If you install a SCSI drive, make sure that you get the proper cable.

Figure 6-8
Different types of
SCSI connectors.

■ The end of the SCSI cable that attaches to the SCSI card in the PC can be one of several configurations, depending on the card. The most common types of connectors that may be on the SCSI card are shown below.

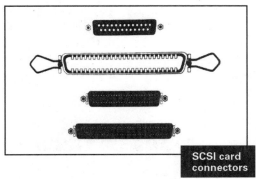

SCSI card connectors

■ The end of the SCSI cable that connects to the scanner must be a high-density mini 50-pin connector, shown below.

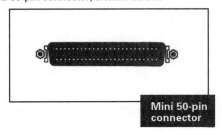

Mini 50-pin connector

Figure 6-9
Blank CD-R discs.
Note that the blank
discs should be certi-
fied for the speed of
your drive.

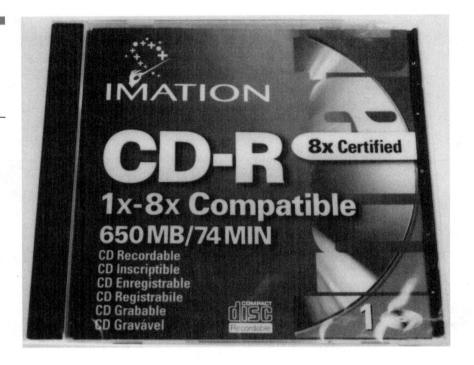

Figure 6-9 shows a blank CD-R disc. Note that the blank discs should be certified for the speed of the CD-R drive.

Chapter 8 contains more information about CD-ROMs.

Advantages of Removable Disk Drives

Following are some of the advantages of removable disks or cartridges.

Security

There may be data on a hard disk that is accessible to other people. If the data is sensitive data, such as company design secrets or personal employee data, the removable disks can be removed and locked up for security. After all, you wouldn't want anyone seeing just what salary the boss was getting or what his or her golf score might be.

Unlimited Capacity

With enough disks or cartridges you will never have to worry about running out of hard disk space. If you fill one cartridge, just pop in another and continue.

Fast Backup

One reason people don't like to back up their data is that it is usually a lot of trouble and takes a lot of time, especially if you are using tape backup. It may take several hours to back up a large hard drive onto tape. However, it may take only seconds or minutes to back up the same data onto a removable drive. A big advantage of the removable cartridge backup is that the data can be randomly accessed; a tape backup can only be accessed sequentially. If you want a file that is in the middle of the tape, you must run through the tape to find it.

Moving Data to Another Computer

If you have two or more computer systems with the same type of removable drives, you can easily transfer large amounts of data from one machine to another. It is possible to send the data on a disk or cartridge through the mail to other locations that have the same type system.

Multiple Users of One Software Copy

Most people don't bother to read the License Agreements that come with software. And who can blame them? The agreements may be two or more pages long, in small type, and filled with lawyer-type jargon.

Essentially, most of them simply say: "You are granted the right to use one copy of the enclosed software on a single computer." But supposing that you have several computers in an office. Some of the people may be doing nothing but word processing most of the time. Others may be running databases or spreadsheets. Occasionally, these users may have need to use one of the other programs for a short time. If these users all have standard hard disks, then legally, you need a separate copy of all of the software used on the computers. Some software programs may cost from $500 up to $1000 or more. If you have several computers in an office, providing individual packages for each machine can be quite expensive. It would be a little less expensive to buy licenses for each computer. If these computers had removable disks, then a copy of a software program could be installed on the cartridge and the cartridge could be used on the different machines whenever needed.

Some Disadvantages of Removable Disk Drives

Following are disadvantages of removable drives.

Limited Cartridge Capacity

Many of the removable cartridges have a capacity of only 100 to 250MB. At one time that was a whole lot of storage space. But that may not be enough to store all of the data that you need to operate some of today's large programs. And according to Murphy's law, there will always be times when you need to access a file that is on another cartridge. If you only have one removable drive, it could be a problem. If they are SCSI drives, you could install up to seven of them. Of course, data compression can be used with all of the removable disks as easily as on hard disks.

Several companies now make CD-ROM jukeboxes that may have up to a dozen or more drives that could be accessed.

Cost of Disks and Cartridges

Another disadvantage is that the removable drives may cost a bit more than a standard hard drive. A cartridge may cost from $10 to over $100. But if you consider that, with enough cartridges, the capacity is unlimited, the cost may be quite reasonable.

The CD-R blank discs are very reasonable at $1 to $2 each. Most cartridges only store 100MB to 250MB. The CD-R discs can hold up to 650MB. The cost to store data on a CD-R is very minimal.

Need for Accessible Bays

If you intend to buy an internal system with removable cartridges, you will need to access it from the front panel. If you have a system that has a limited number of bays that are accessible from the outside, it may be a problem. Some desktop cases only have four bays: two accessible bays for floppy disk and CD-ROM drives and two internal bays for hard disks. If your system does not have enough bays, you might consider buying a larger case, perhaps a tower case. A case and power supply will cost from $35 to over $100 for the large tower case with a 325-watt power supply. Many of the tower systems have from five to eight bays. It is very easy to transfer a system from one case to another.

The external drives with removable disks usually cost a bit more than the internally mounted drives. The extra cost is because of the need for the power supply and drive case.

Access Speed

Still another disadvantage is that some of the removable drives are a bit slower than most standard hard drives. The M-O drives are especially slow because it takes time to heat the area with the laser. But if you don't mind waiting a few milliseconds, it shouldn't be too much of a problem.

Data Compression

The capacity of all of the hard drives mentioned above can be doubled by using data compression with them. Windows 95/98 comes with a utility called DriveSpace that can compress data on hard drives and on floppies. Before Windows 95, MS-DOS, IBM PC DOS, and DR DOS all had a disk compression utility. Stacker, from Stac Electronics, was one of the most popular standalone compression utilities. Microsoft and Stac Electronics are now partners. The DriveSpace utility is the result of that partnership. Using data compression is certainly inexpensive and easier than installing a second, or larger, hard disk. But as the cost of hard disk drives are now very reasonable, rather than compress your data, you may sleep better at night if you install a larger hard disk.

Floppy and Hard Drive Similarities

A hard disk drive is similar to a floppy disk drive in some respects. Floppy drives have a single disk; the hard drives may have an assembly of one or more rigid disks. The hard disk platters are coated with a magnetic plating, similar to that of the floppy disks. Depending on the capacity, there may be several disks on a common spindle. A motor turns the floppy spindle at 300 rpms; the hard disk spindle may turn from 3600 rpms up to 10,000 rpms.

There will be a read/write head on the top and one on the bottom of each platter or disk. On floppy disk systems the head actually contacts the disk; on a hard disk system the head "flies" just a few millionths of an inch from the disk on a cushion of purified air. If the head contacts the disk at the high speed at which it turns, it would cause a "head crash." A crash can destroy the disk, the head, and all the data that might be on the disk.

Formatting

You cannot use a floppy disk or a hard disk unless it has been formatted. Formatting divides the disk up into partitions, tracks, and sectors so that any information on the disk can be instantly found and accessed. Formatting of hard disks will be discussed in detail in Chapter 12.

Tracks and Sectors

Like the floppy disk, the hard disk is formatted into several individual concentric tracks. A 1.44MB floppy has 80 tracks on each side; a high-capacity hard disk may have 3000 or more tracks. Also like the floppy, each hard disk track is divided into sectors, usually of 512 bytes. But the 1.44MB floppy system divides each track into 18 sectors; a hard disk system may divide each track into as many as 84 sectors.

Clusters and Allocation Units

A sector is only 512 bytes, but most files are much longer than that. Therefore, DOS lumps two or more sectors together and calls it a *cluster* or *allocation unit*. If an empty cluster is on track 5, the system will record as much of the file as it can there, then move to the next empty cluster, which could be on track 20. DOS combines sectors into allocation units depending on the capacity of the hard disk. For a 100MB disk, DOS combines four sectors, or 2048 bytes, into each allocation unit; for 200MB, each allocation unit is composed of eight sectors, or 4096 bytes.

File Allocation Table

The location of each part of the file and which cluster it is in is recorded in the file allocation table (FAT) so the computer has no trouble finding it. Usually the larger the hard disk partition, the more sectors are assigned to each cluster or allocation unit.

A 500MB hard disk would actually have 524,288,000 bytes. Dividing this number by 512 bytes to find the number of actual sectors gives us 1,024,000 sectors. If each allocation unit is made up of four sectors, there would only be 256,000 of them; if eight sectors are used, then the operating system would only have to worry about the location of 128,000 allocation units. If it had to search through 1,024,000 entries in the FAT each time it accessed the hard disk, it would slow things down considerably. The FAT is updated and rewritten each time the disk is accessed. A large FAT would take a lot of time and disk space.

On one of my older machines, I had a 500MB hard disk that was divided into three logical disks: a 100MB and two 200MB. The 100MB used four sectors per allocation unit, so it has 51,219 clusters or allocation units. The 200MB used eight sectors per allocation units, so they each have 51,283 allocation units, about the same number as the 100MB disk.

The FAT is very important. If it is damaged or erased, you will not be able to access any of the data on the disk. The heads just wouldn't know where to look for the data. The FAT is usually written on track 0 of the hard disk. Because it is so important, a second copy is also made near the center of the disk so that if the original is damaged, it is possible to use the copy.

A 500MB disk is not nearly enough nowadays. I recently removed this disk and I gave it to a nephew. I replaced it with a 20GB drive.

DOS 3.3 and earlier versions could only handle hard disks up to 32MB. I paid $600 for a 40MB hard disk, but could only use 32MB of it until I bought DiskManager special software.

DOS 4.0 and later versions of DOS and Windows allowed large-size partitions up to 2GB. Windows 98 will allow hard disks up to several hundred gigabytes. Windows 95/98 will allow you to format very large disks as a single partition, or to make very large partitions in large disks. At the DOS C: prompt, when you type FDisk, this message will come up:

```
This version of Windows includes improved support
for large disks, resulting in more efficient use of disk
space on large disks, and allowing disks over 2GB to be
formatted as a single drive.
IMPORTANT: If you enable large disk support and
create any new drives on this disk, you will not be able to
access the new drive(s) using other operating systems,
including some versions of Windows 95 and Windows
NT, as well as earlier versions of Windows and MS-DOS.
In addition, disk utilities that were not designed explicitly
for the FAT32 file system will not be able to work with
this disk. If you need to access this disk with other
operating systems or older disk utilities, do not enable
large size drive support.
Do you wish to enable large disk support? (Y/N) [N].
```

Unless your business or situation needs a very large single drive, I would recommend not using the large-disk support. If you have a large drive, such as a 20GB drive, or even two such drives, you can format them as several 2GB logical drives.

If there are several partitions on a disk and one of them fails, you might be able to recover the data in the other partitions. If your disk is one large partition and it fails, you may not be able to recover any of the data, especially if the FAT is destroyed. Norton Utilities can be set up to make a mirror image of the FAT. If the primary FAT is destroyed, you can still use the mirror image.

One of the disadvantages of creating large logical drives is that the larger the drive, the more sectors are used to create each cluster or allocation unit. Remember that a sector is 512 bytes. If you have a lot of small files, it may waste a lot of disk space. Table 6-1 shows how DOS and Windows set up the allocation unit size.

The figures in Table 6-1 are for FAT 16 systems, which use 16 bits to store the FAT entries. One reason for making the clusters or allocation

TABLE 6-1

*Cluster or
Allocation Sizes.*

Partition Size	Cluster Size
16MB-128MB	2KB (4 sectors)
128MB-256MB	4KB (8 sectors)
256MB-512MB	8KB (16 sectors)
512MB-1GB	16KB (32 sectors)
1GB-2GB	32KB (64 sectors)

units larger was to cut down on the amount of space that the FAT would need to be stored. Also remember that the larger the number of FATs that the system has to search, the more it slows down the system. But we now have much faster systems and much more disk space. So a version of Windows 95 released in 1996 and Windows 98 gives you the choice of using a FAT32 system. The FAT32 system allows more FATs to be stored and allows very small clusters.

Cylinders

Just like the floppy, each same-numbered track on the top and bottom of a disk is called a *cylinder*. Since a hard disk may have up to 10 or more platters, the concept of cylinders is even more realistic. Incidentally, some of the BIOS chips in some of the older computers would not allow you to install a hard disk that had more than 1024 cylinders and 63 sectors, which is about 504MB. It was possible to install a disk larger than 500MB by using special driver software such as DiskManager from the Ontrack Corp. Windows 98 will now let you install hard disks that have over 50GB.

Head Actuators or Positioners

Like the floppy, a head motor, or head actuator, moves the heads from track to track. The head actuator must move the heads quickly and accurately to a specified track, then detect the small variations in the magnetic fields in the specified sectors. Some of the older hard disks used a stepper motor similar to those used on floppy disk drives to move the head from track to track. Most all hard disks now use a voice coil type of motor, which is much smoother, quieter, and faster than the stepper motors.

The voice coil of a loudspeaker is made up of a coil of wire that is wound on a hollow tube attached to the material of the speaker cone. Permanent magnets are then placed inside and around the outside of the coil. Whenever a voltage is passed through the coil of wire, it will cause magnetic lines of force to be built up around the coil. Depending on the polarity of the input voltage, these lines of magnetic flux will be either the same or opposite the lines of force of the permanent magnets. If the polarity of the voltage—for instance, a plus voltage—causes the lines of force to be the same as the permanent magnet, then they will repel each other, and the voice coil might move forward. If they are opposite, they will attract each other, and the coil will move backwards.

Most of the better and faster hard disks use voice coil technology with a closed-loop servo control. They usually use one surface of one of the disks to store data and track locations. Most specification sheets give the number of heads on a drive. Since all the heads are on the same spindle, they all move as one. When the servo head moves to a certain track and sector, the other heads follow. Feedback information from the closed servo loop positions the head to the exact track very accurately.

Figure 6-10 shows a Seagate hard drive with the cover removed to

Figure 6-10
A hard drive with the cover removed (courtesy Seagate).

show the heads and disks. The voice coil actuator is the section in the top left corner of the drive. It can quickly and accurately swing the arm and head to any track on the disk.

Speed of Rotation and Density

As the disk spins beneath the head, a pulse of voltage through the head will cause the area of the track that is beneath the head at that time to become magnetized. If this pulse of voltage is turned on for a certain amount of time, then turned off for some amount of time, it can represent the writing or recording of 1s and 0s. The hard disk spins much faster than a floppy, so the duration of the magnetizing pulses can be much shorter at a higher frequency.

The recording density depends to a great extent on the changes in magnetic flux. The faster the disk spins, the greater the number of changes. This allows much more data to be recorded in the same amount of space. Most hard disks spin at a rate between 3600 to 7200 rpms.

Seagate's Cheetah spins at 10,000 rpms. They have two models: a 1-inch-high model with four platters has a capacity of 4.55GB, and a 1.6-inch-high model with eight platters has a capacity of 9.1GB. The Quantum Atlas is also 1.6 inches high and has a capacity of 9GB, but it has 10 platters. With the two extra platters, it should have more capacity than the Seagate, but the Quantum spins at 7200 rpm.

Areal density is the number of bits per inch times the number of tracks per inch. The areal density continues to be improved. At the present time, some manufacturers are achieving 1 billion bits per square inch. Within a couple of years, it should reach 10 billion bits per square inch.

Timing

Everything that a computer does depends on precise timing. Crystals and oscillators are set up so that certain circuits perform a task at a specific time. These oscillating circuits are usually called *clock circuits*. The clock frequency for the old standard modified frequency modulation (MFM) method of reading and writing to a hard disk is 10MHz per second. To write on the disk during 1 second, the voltage might turn on for a fraction of a second, then turn off for the next period of time, then back on for a certain length of time. The head sits over a track that is moving at a constant speed. Blocks of data are written or read during the precise timing of the system clock. Because the voltage must go plus or zero—that is, two states—in order to write 1s and 0s, the maximum data transfer rate is only 5 megabits per second (5Mbps) for MFM, just half of the clock frequency.

The RLL systems transfer data at a rate of 7.5Mbps. Some of the ESDI drives have a transfer rate of 10Mbps or more. (Note that these figures are *bits*; remember that it takes 8 bits to make 1 byte). The SCSI and IDE systems may have a transfer rate as high as 10 to 13 megabytes (MB) or more. So a SCSI or IDE system that can transfer 10 megabytes per second (10MBps) is 8 times faster than a 10Mbps EDSI.

You have probably seen representations of magnetic lines of force around a magnet. The magnetized spot on a disk track has similar lines of force. To read the data on the disk, the head is positioned over the track and the lines of force from each magnetized area cause a pulse of voltage to be induced in the head. During a precise block of time, an induced pulse of voltage can represent a 1; the absence of an induced pulse can represent a 0.

Pulses of voltage through the head will cause a magnetic pulse to be formed that magnetizes the disk track. When reading the data from the track, the small magnetic changes on the recorded track cause voltage to be produced in the heads. It is a two-way system. Forcing voltage through the heads causes magnetism to be produced; bringing a magnetic field into the area of the head when reading can cause voltage to be produced.

Head Spacing

The amount of magnetism that is placed on a disk when it is recorded is very small. It must be small so that it will not affect other recorded bits or tracks near it. Magnetic lines of force decrease as you move away from a magnet by the square of the distance. So it is desirable to have the heads as close to the disk as possible.

On a floppy disk drive, the heads actually contact the diskette. This causes some wear, but not very much, because the rotation is fairly slow and the plastic disks have a special lubricant and are fairly slippery. However, heads of the hard disk systems never touch the disk. The fragile heads and the disk would be severely damaged if they made contact at a speed of 3600 to 10,000 rpms. The heads fly over the spinning disk just microinches above it. Hard disks are sealed, and the air inside them is purified. The air must be pure because the smallest speck of dust or dirt can cause the head to crash. You should never open a hard disk.

Speed or Access Time

Speed or access time is the time it takes a hard disk to locate and retrieve a sector of data. This includes the time that it takes to move the head to the track, settle down, and read the data. For a high-end, very fast disk, this might be as little as 9 milliseconds (ms). Some of the older drives and systems required as much as 100ms. An 85ms hard drive might have been fine for an old slow XT. A 9ms drive may not be fast enough for a Pentium II. Some of the newer drives have an access time of less than 6ms.

Disk Platters

The surface of the hard disk platters must be very smooth. Because the heads are only a few millionths of an inch, or microinches, away from the surface, any unevenness could cause a head crash. The hard disk platters are usually made from aluminum, which is nonmagnetic, and lapped to a mirror finish. They are then coated or plated with a magnetic material. Some companies are using tempered glass as a substrate for the platters. The platters must also be very rigid so that the close distance between the head and the platter surface is maintained. The early 5¼-inch hard disks had to be fairly thick to achieve the necessary rigidity. Being thick, they were heavy and required a fairly large spindle motor and lots of wattage to move the large amount of mass.

If the platter is made smaller, it can be thinner and still have the necessary rigidity. If the disks are thinner, then more platters can be stacked in the same area. The smaller disks also need less power and smaller motors. With smaller-diameter disks, the heads don't have to travel as far between the outer and inner tracks. This improves the access time tremendously.

You should avoid any sudden movement of the computer or any jarring while the disk is spinning because it could cause the head to crash onto the disk and damage it. Most of the newer hard disk systems automatically move the heads away from the read/write surface to a parking area when the power is turned off.

Physical Sizes

One of the first hard drives I ever owned was a full-height 10MB drive. *Full-height* meant that it was over $3\frac{3}{4}$ inches high, 6 inches wide, and 8 inches deep. The original full-height floppies were the same size. Later, they developed half-height drives for both hard drives and floppies. The drives were physically large and clunky and operated at a very slow 100ms. They were also expensive. A 20MB hard disk cost as much as $2500. (And that was back in the days when $2500 was worth about three times what it is today.) You can buy a 20GB hard disk today for about $300. A modern 20GB drive is only 1 inch high, 4 inches wide, and 6 inches deep, yet it has 1000 times greater storage capacity, operates 10 times faster at about 10ms, and is $2200 less expensive than a large 20MB was 10 years ago. If you weren't around in those early days, you can't begin to appreciate the advances in the technology. We have come a long, long way.

One of the reasons they can make the hard disks smaller now is because they have developed better plating materials, thinner disks, better motors, and better electronics.

Zone Bit Recording

There are several reasons why the old hard drives were physically so much larger than the newer drives. The old MFM drives divided each track into 17 sectors. A track on the outer edge of a 5¼-inch platter would be over 15 inches long if it were stretched out. You can determine this by using the simple math formula for pi (3.14159) times the diameter. So 3.14159 × 5.25 is 16.493 inches in length. A track on the inner portion of the disk may only be 1.5 inches times pi, or 4.712 inches in length. The MFM system divided each track into 17 sectors, no matter whether it was 16 inches long or only 4 inches long.

It is obvious that you should be able to store more data in the outer, longer tracks than in the short, inner tracks. That is exactly what the newer drives do. One reason the newer drives can be made so much smaller with so much more capacity is that they use *zone bit recording* (ZBR). The platters are divided up into different zones depending on the area of the disk platter. The inner tracks, which are shorter, may have relatively few as sectors. There is an increased number of sectors per track toward the outer, longer tracks.

Rotational Speed and Recording Density

The recording density or bits per inch (bpi) for each zone changes from the inner tracks to the outer tracks. The reason for this is that the speed at which the inner tracks pass beneath the heads is faster than that of the outer tracks.

The overall drive speed is still another way of increasing the amount of storage. The old MFM drives spun at 3600 rpms. The newer drives have a rotational speed of 6300 and up to 10,000 rpms or more. One big factor in the amount of data that can be recorded in a given area is the frequency of the changing 0s and 1s and the speed of the disk. The higher the speed of the disk, the higher the recording frequency can be.

Of course, the rotational speed of the disk is also one of the factors that determines the seek, access, and transferal time. If you want to access data on a certain track, the faster the disk rotates, the sooner that sector will be available for reading.

The hard disk technology has improved tremendously over the last 10 years.

Mean Time between Failures (MTBF)

Disk drives are mechanical devices. If used long enough, every disk drive will fail sooner or later. Manufacturers test their drives and assign them an average lifetime that ranges from 40,000 up to 150,000 hours. Of course, the larger the figure, the longer they should last (and the more they cost). These are average figures, much like the figures quoted for a human lifespan. The average man should live to be about 73 years old. But some babies die very young, and some men live to be over 100.

Likewise, some hard disks die very young; some older ones become obsolete before they wear out.

I have difficulty accepting some of the manufacturer's MTBF figures. For instance, to put 150,000 hours on a drive, it would have to be used 8 hours a day, every day, for over 51 years. If they operated a drive for 24 hours a day, 365 days a year, it would take over 17 years to put 150,000 hours on it. Since hard drives have only been around about 10 years, I am pretty sure that no one has ever done a 150,000-hour test on a drive.

Near Field Recording (NFR)

The TeraStor Company of San Jose is working on a new technology called Near Field Recording (NFR). It combines facets of the magneto-optical technology and standard hard disk technology. It will be able to store over 20GB on a plastic disk about the size of a CD-ROM. TeraStor can be contacted at 408-324-2110, or at www.terastor.com.

IBM's GMR Read Head

IBM has developed a giant magnetoresistive (GMR) read head that can double the capacity of hard disks. They are twice as sensitive as a standard head and can read 2.69GBits per square inch areal density. They will be used on an IBM $3\frac{1}{2}$-inch disk that can store 16.8GB.

How the times have changed. I was ecstatic when I got my first hard drive with 10MB. Physically, the new $3\frac{1}{2}$-inch IBM drive is about half the size of my early hard drive. The smaller IBM drive can store 1680MB, compared to only 10MB for my early full-size drive. And they say there are only seven wonders in the world.

Cables and Connectors

The standard SCSI cable is a 50-wire, flat-ribbon cable. The standard connectors are Centronics types, but some devices may have a small, miniature connector. Most devices have two connectors in parallel for attaching and daisy chaining other devices. I have a Future Domain host adapter that has a miniature connector for external devices. In order to attach my Epson 800 Pro scanner, I had to buy a cable with the miniature connector on one end. It cost almost $40. I found out later that there are adapters for this purpose that cost about $5. Try some of the cable companies that advertise in *Computer Shopper* and other computer magazines.

Not all of the 50 wires in a flat-ribbon cable are needed for data. Many of the wires are ground wires placed between the data wires to help keep the data from being corrupted. The better, and more expensive, cables are round cables with twisted and shielded wires. This type of cable may be necessary for distances greater than 6 feet.

You should be aware that the advertised price of a SCSI device usually does not include an interface or cables. It may not even include any software drivers. Be sure to ask about these items whenever you order a SCSI device.

Installation Configuration

If you are only installing a single IDE drive, the installation may be very simple. The drive should have jumpers set at the factory that makes it drive 1, or master drive. Check your documentation and the jumpers, then just plug the 40-pin cable into the drive connector and the other end into a set of pins on the motherboard. Most motherboards now have keyed shells around the upright pins so that the cable can only be plugged in properly. If your motherboard does not have the shell, you must make sure that the colored side of the ribbon cable goes to pin 1 on the drive and on the interface.

If you are installing a second IDE drive, you will need to set some jumpers so that the system will know which drive to access. When two IDE drives are installed, the IDE system uses the term "master" to designate the C:, or boot, drive and the term "slave" to designate the second drive. The drives usually come from the factory configured with the jumpers as a single or master drive. If the drives are not configured properly, you will get an error message that may tell you that you have a hard disk or controller failure. You will not be able to access the drives. There were no standards as to how the early IDE drives should be configured. Different manufacturers used different designations for the pins and sometimes different functions for the pins. So it was difficult, or sometimes impossible, to install and configure two different early IDE drives in a system.

Later, a group of IDE manufacturers got together and agreed on an IDE standard specification. They called the specification Common Access Method AT Attachment, or CAM ATA. Almost all IDE drives now conform to this specification. You should have very little trouble connecting drives made by different companies, or drives of different capacities, if they conform to the CAM ATA specifications. Most later models have three sets of pins for jumpers for configuring the drive as a single drive, for a master and slave, or for a slave.

Some drives have pins that can be jumpered so that they will be read-only. This is a type of write protection that is similar to write-protecting a floppy. This could be used on a hard disk that had data that should never be changed or written over.

You should have received some documentation with your drive. Figure 6-2 shows the small configuration jumper pins on a Western Digital IDE drive. Your drive may be different. If you don't have the configuration information, call the company or dealer. You may also visit the company's Web site, as most all companies now have Web sites, along with e-mail addresses of the various departments within the company. Following are a few of these:

Conner Peripherals
 URL: www.conner.com
 Tech support phone: 408-438-8222
 Tech support fax: 408-438-8137
 Fax back support: 408-438-2620
 Automated support: 800-732-4283
 Conner Peripherals is now a subsidiary of Seagate.

Iomega Corp.
 URL: www.iomega.com
 Tech support: 801-629-7610

Fujitsu
 URL: www.fcpa.com
 Tech support phone: 800-626-4686
 Fax back support: 408-428-0456

Maxtor
 URL: www.maxtor.com
 Tech support phone: 800-2-Maxtor or 800-262-9867
 Tech support fax: 303-678-2260
 E-mail: Technical Assistance@Maxtor.com

Micropolis
URL: www.micropolis.com
Tech support phone: 818-709-3325
Tech support fax: 818-709-3408
Fax back support: 800-395-3748
E-mail support: tom~earthlink.net

Quantum
URL: www.quantum.com
Tech support phone: 800-826-8022
Tech support fax: 408-894-3282
Fax back support: 800-434-7532

Samsung Electronics America
URL: www.samsung.co.kr
Tech support phone: 800-726-7864
Fax back support: 800-229-2239

Seagate
URL: www.seagate.com
Tech support phone: 408-438-8222
Tech support fax: 408-438-8137
Fax back support: 408-438-2620
Automated support: 800-732-4283

Western Digital
URL: www.wdc.com
Tech support phone: 507-286-7900
Fax back support: 714-932-4300

Sources

Local computer stores and computer swap meets are a good place to find a disk drive. You can at least look them over and get some idea of the prices and what you want. Mail order is a very good way to buy a hard disk. However, keep in mind that you may not get any documentation if you buy a hard disk at a swap meet or even from mail order. Ask for the manuals. Of course, all of the major manufacturers have Web sites where you can find all of the specifications and jumper settings. In addition, there are hundreds of ads in the many computer magazines. Check the list of magazines in Chapter 19.

Backup: Disaster Prevention

Making backups is a chore that most people dislike, but if your data is worth anything at all, you should be making backups of it. You may be one of the lucky ones and never need it. But there are thousands of ways to lose data. Data may be lost due to a power failure or a component failure in the computer system. In a fraction of a second data that may be worth thousands of dollars could be lost forever. It may have taken hundreds of hours to accumulate, and it may be impossible to duplicate it. Yet many of these unfortunate people have not backed up their precious data.

Most of these people are those who have been fortunate enough not to have had a major catastrophe. Just as sure as we have earthquakes in California, if you use a computer long enough, you can look forward to at least one unfortunate disaster. But if your data is backed up, it doesn't have to be a catastrophe.

By far, most losses are the result of just plain dumb mistakes. I have made lots of mistakes in the past. And no matter how careful I am, I will make mistakes in the future. When the poet said, "To err is human," he could have been talking about me. And, possibly, thee.

Write-Protect Your Software

Most software now comes on CD-ROMs, but a few programs still come on floppy disks. When you buy a software program on a floppy disk, you should make a disk copy of the program and store the original away. If you should ruin the copy, you can always make a new copy from the original. But the very first thing you should do before you make a disk copy is write-protect the original floppies. It is very easy to become distracted and write on a program diskette in error. This would ruin the program. The vendor might give you a new copy, but it would probably entail weeks of waiting and much paperwork.

If you are using 3½-inch diskettes, you should move the small slide on the left rear side so that the square hole is open. The 3½-inch write-protect system is just the opposite of the 5¼-inch system. The 3½-inch system uses a small microswitch. If the square hole is open, the switch will allow the diskette to be read, but not written on or erased. If the slide is moved to cover the square hole, the diskette can be written on, read, or erased. It takes less than a minute to write-protect a diskette. It might save months of valuable time.

.BAK Files

There are functions in many of the word processors and some other programs that create a .BAK file each time you alter or change a file. The .BAK file is usually just a copy of the original file before you changed it. Most word processors and other programs such as spreadsheets and databases can be set up to automatically save any file that you are working on at certain times when there is no activity from the keyboard. If there is a power outage, or you shut the machine off without saving a file, chances are that there is a backup of it saved to disk.

Unerase Software

One of the best protections against errors is to have a backup. The second-best protection is to have a good utility program such as Norton's Utilities from Symantec. Windows 95/98 also have undelete utilities. These programs can unerase a file or even unformat a disk. When a file is erased, the system goes to the FAT table and deletes the first letter of each filename. All of the data remains on the disk unless a new file is written over it. If you have erased a file in error, or formatted a disk in error, *do not do anything to it until you have tried using a recover utility*. To restore the files, most of the utilities ask you to supply the missing first letter of the filename.

Delete Protection

I assume that you are using Windows 95 or 98 now. If you delete a file, it is sent to the recycle bin. If you decide later that you still need that file, you can go search through the bin and recover it. The recycle bin may take up a lot of disk space. If you have don't have a lot of spare disk space, you may have to go to the recycle bin every so often and dump certain files that you know you won't need, or dump the entire bin.

If you delete just portions of a file while revising it, the original may still be saved in the recycle bin. If you decide that the revision is not what you wanted, you may be able to recover the original and start over. I have Norton Utilities installed. Norton also has a recycle bin that has a few more utilities than the one that comes with Windows 95/98.

Every few minutes, my word processor automatically saves copies of the file I am working on. Of course, every time it saves a file, it deletes the earlier version and sends it to the recycle bin. As an example, I just checked the Norton recycle bin for this file that I am currently working on. There are several versions of this file in the bin. The bin gives the exact time that the file was updated and saved. I could go back and recover any of those earlier versions.

The early versions of MS-DOS made it very easy to format your hard disk in error. If you happened to be at the C: prompt and typed FORMAT, it would immediately begin to format your hard disk and wipe out everything. Later versions would not do a format unless you specified a drive letter.

The early versions of DOS would also let you copy over another file. If two files were different, but you told DOS to copy one to a directory that had the file with the same name, the original file would be gone forever. Windows 95 now asks if you want to overwrite the file.

Jumbled FAT

The all-important file allocation table (FAT) was discussed in the previous chapter about disks. The FAT keeps a record of the location of all the files on the disk. Parts of a file may be located in several sectors, but the FAT knows exactly where they are. If for some reason track 0, where the FAT is located, is damaged, erased, or becomes defective, then you will not be able to read or write to any of the files on the disk. Because the FAT is so important, a program such as Norton Utilities can make a copy of the FAT and store it in another location on the disk.

Every time you add a file or edit one, the FAT changes. So these programs make a new copy every time the FAT is altered. If the original FAT is damaged, you can still get your data by using the alternate FAT. Norton Utilities from Symantec (408-253-9600, or www.symantec.com/nu/index.html) is an excellent utility software package. If you accept the defaults when installing Norton Utilities, it causes Norton to scan your disk and analyze the boot record, FAT, directory structure, and file, as well as check for lost clusters or cross-linked files. It then reads the FAT and stores a copy in a different place on the hard disk.

The Reasons for Smaller Logical Hard Disks

Early versions of DOS would not recognize a hard disk larger than 32MB. Windows 95/98 can now handle hard drive capacities up to several gigabytes. Most programs seem to be designed to be installed on drive C:. You could have a very large drive C:, but if this large hard disk crashed, you might not be able to recover any of its data.

When formatting a disk, the FDISK command allows you to divide it up and partition it into as many as 24 logical drives. If the same disk was divided into several smaller logical drives and one of the logical sections failed, it might be possible to recover data in the unaffected logical drives.

Partition Magic and Partition-It

You can think of a partition much like a room with four walls. When the house was built, some of the rooms may have been very small. It is sometimes possible to knock out some of the walls and make the room larger. You can do something similar with the partitions on your hard disk.

You are probably using a hard disk that has already been formatted and has lots of data on it. Normally, the only way to change the size of the drive partitions is to back up everything, then use FDISK to resize it and then reformat it. Both Partition Magic and Partition-It will let you resize the partitions on your hard drive without having to back up all the data. It will automatically move the data, resize the partition, and move the data back into it.

A very fast way to back up is to copy the data from one logical drive partition to another. This type of backup is very fast and very easy. But it doesn't offer the amount of protection that a separate hard drive would offer. Still, it is much better than no backup at all.

Head Crash

As mentioned, the heads of a hard disk "fly" over the disk just a few microinches from the surface. They have to be close in order to detect the small magnetic changes in the tracks. The disk spins from 3600 rpms on some older drives and up to 10,000 rpms on some of the newer drives. If the heads contact the surface of the fast-spinning disk, it can scratch it and ruin the disk.

A sudden jar or bump to the computer while the hard disk is spinning can cause the heads to crash. Of course, a mechanical failure or some other factor could also cause a crash. You should never move or bump your computer while the hard disk is running.

Most of the newer disks have a built-in safe-park utility. When the power is removed, the head is automatically moved to the center of the disk where there are no tracks.

The technology of hard disk systems has improved tremendously over the last few years. But hard disks are still mechanical devices. And as such, you can be sure that eventually they will wear out, fail, or crash.

I've worked in electronics for over 30 years and am still amazed that a hard disk will work at all. It is a most remarkable mechanical device made up of several precision components. The mechanical tolerances must be held to millionths of an inch in some devices, such as the flying head and the distances between the tracks. The magnetic flux changes are minute, yet the heads detect them easily and output reliable data.

Despite all of the things that could go wrong with a hard disk, most hard disks are quite reliable. Manufacturers quote figures of several thousand hours mean time between failure (MTBF). However, these figures are only an average, so there is no guarantee that a disk won't fail in the next few minutes. If a disk should fail and you get it repaired, it should last as long as their guarantee says before it fails again.

Crash Recovery

Despite the MTBF claims, hard drives do fail. There are lots of businesses who do nothing but repair hard disks that have crashed or failed. A failure can be frustrating, time-consuming, and make you feel utterly helpless. In the unhappy event of a crash, depending on its severity, it is possible that some of your data can be recovered one way or another.

There are some companies who specialize in recovering data and rebuilding hard disks. Many of them have sophisticated tools and software that can recover some data if the disk is not completely ruined.

Ontrack Data International

If it is possible to recover any of the data, Ontrack Data International's data recovery program can probably do it. They can send you a floppy disk that can help in the event of a crash or disaster. Here is some information from their Web site:

Diagnose a Data Loss Directly on Your Computer!
When you lose your valuable computer data, every second that passes equals time, money and effort lost to you or your company. Ontrack Data Advisor software reduces expensive downtime by providing you with an instant diagnosis of your data loss situation. Ontrack Data Advisor software will investigate your desktop, laptop or notebook computer to deter-

mine what is preventing you from accessing your data. This keeps your downtime to a minimum, helping you resume normal business functions as quickly as possible.

Powerful Tools Provide a Comprehensive System Analysis

Ontrack Data Advisor software includes a complete set of hard disk drive and system diagnostic tools. These tools assess the read abilities of your hard disk drive and determine if your drive is electromechanically stable. These tools also analyze your file systems and file structures, check your system memory, scan for computer viruses and more. Contained on a bootable diskette, Ontrack Data Advisor software can even diagnose your system when it cannot boot on its own!

The First Component of the Patent-Pending Ontrack Remote Data Recovery Process

Ontrack Data Advisor software is the first component of Ontrack Remote Data Recovery services, currently in development. This patent-pending process will allow Ontrack to perform remote data recoveries via communication link based on the test results provided by Ontrack Data Advisor software. It is yet another way to bring you the fastest data recovery services available.

Ontrack Data Recovery and Ontrack Data International
   6321 Bury Dr.
   Eden Prairie, MN 55346
   Phone: 800-872-2599
   www.ontrack.com

DriveSavers

Here is information from another disk recovery company, DriveSavers:

At DriveSavers we believe the customer comes first. You'll never have to leave a voice mail message when you call us during normal business hours, and our helpful customer service staff will provide you with immediate assistance. You can even speak directly to the engineer working on your recovery to learn about the nature of your data loss and how to prevent future occurrences.

What to Do Before You Call DriveSavers

If your disk is crashed, you can try the following suggestions before you contact DriveSavers. This document covers a few of the many kinds of problems that can occur when data recovery may be necessary.

The "Oops" Factor

Sometimes cables just wiggle loose. It's a good idea to check your cables when there's a problem accessing your drive. It's a good idea to do this anyway. Be sure to shut the system off and check both the power cable and ribbon cable(s). Make sure their connections are all secure. If need be, you can pull them off and then put them back on to be certain there's a secure connection.

The Disk Exhibits Unusual Noises (Clicking, Grinding, or Metal Scraping)

This typically indicates a serious hardware problem such as a head crash or major media damage. In such a case it is best to copy all accessible data from the drive immediately. The longer the drive runs in this condition, the more damage can occur making the data irretrievable. It is best to send the drive directly to DriveSavers so we may disassemble it in a special clean-room environment and extract the data for you.

Using Utility Programs

Use utility programs with caution. They are best used to clean up minor problems on drives that have already been backed up. These programs can do a fine job of helping you out of a tight spot...or they can "fix" your data beyond recoverability! If you do use one of these, please heed the following cautions.

Utility programs like Symantec's Norton Utilities and ScanDisk allow you the opportunity to save "undo" files if the repair doesn't work out. It's very important because saving an undo file can help you back out of a bad "fix". Save your undo file to a floppy disk, not your hard disk. It's a good idea to have a few formatted diskettes handy for the program to write to.

If your drive is sounding or acting "funny" in any way, it's extremely important that you avoid the use of these utilities altogether. These symptoms can include any rattling, buzzing or scraping sounds the disk drive might be emitting. In these circumstances, it's best to back up your data immediately or shut the drive down, as further use may well cause damage. If the drive is completely crashed, your best chance for recovery is to contact us here at DriveSavers.

"Invalid Drive Specification" Error Message

A common problem that occurs, especially with older systems, is a system's propensity to lose track of its CMOS drive setup. When you turn on your system, it goes through its memory countdown, etc., and then just sits there, asks for a system disk, or drops into BASIC (on true-blue IBM systems). When you put in a boot floppy and ask for drive C:, you get the "invalid drive specification" message.

In such a circumstance, first check your CMOS setup. Most systems will allow you to enter the CMOS setup at startup time with a keystroke or two, such as [Del], [Esc], or [Ctrl]-[Esc]. Some systems, such as Compaq, NEC, Mitsubishi, and many laptops and notebooks, require a setup or diagnostic diskette to change the CMOS drive setting. Tab to the appropriate field for drive settings and enter in the correct settings for your drive. (It's a good idea to keep these settings on a note attached to your computer for future reference.) Most modern systems will let you "Auto" sense the drive. This will usually be successful. You should then reboot your PC. If this works, great! Back up your system and get a replacement battery from your dealer. If not, it may be time to give DriveSavers a call.

Removable Cartridge or Other SCSI Drive Gives "Invalid Drive Specification" Error

If a removable cartridge (SyQuest, magneto-optical, or Iomega) or SCSI hard disk refuses to mount, the device driver may be damaged, or the CONFIG.SYS file may have been changed. Look for lines in your CONFIG.SYS files that look something like: "DEVICE=ASPIDISK.SYS".

If no such line exists, check the manual or README file on your installation disk for the cartridge drive or SCSI Host Adapter manual. Try another cartridge that is known to be good. This will help you identify whether the problem is with the cartridge or the drive mechanism. If the same problem occurs with another cartridge, check that your SCSI cables are firmly attached and the termination is correct.

You might also isolate the drive on the SCSI bus by disconnecting other devices. With most systems, the first SCSI drive must have a SCSI ID of 0 (zero), and the first removable media drive must have a SCSI ID of 2.

DriveSavers—Multi-Platform Data Recovery
400 Bel Marin Keys Boulevard
   Novato, CA 94949
   Phone: 800-440-1904 or 415-382-2000
   Fax: 415-883-0780
   www.drivesavers.com

Another company who specializes in recovery is as follows:

Total Recall
   2462 Waynoka Rd.
   Colorado Springs, CO 80915

Cost of Recovery

The cost for recovery services can be rather expensive. But if you have data that is critical and irreplaceable, it is well worth it. It is a whole lot cheaper to have a backup. There are several companies who specialize in data recovery. Look for them in computer magazine ads.

Preventing Hard Disk Failures

During manufacturing, the hard disk platters are coated or plated with a precise layer of magnetic material. It is almost impossible to manufacture a perfect platter. Most all hard disks end up with a few defective areas after being manufactured. When the vendor does the low-level format, these areas are detected and marked as bad. They are locked out so that they cannot be used. But there may be areas that are borderline-bad that won't be detected. Over time, some of the areas may change and lose some of their magnetic characteristics. They may lose some of the data that is written to them.

There are several companies that manufacture hard disk utilities that can perform rigorous tests on the hard disk. These software programs can exercise the disk and detect any borderline areas. If there happens to be data in an area that is questionable, the programs can usually move the data to another safe area.

The ScanDisk command basically does what some of the standalone utilities do. It does a surface test of the hard disk and will report on any areas that are questionable. It can move any data from those areas to safer areas. It will then mark the questionable areas as bad. The bad areas are listed in the FAT just as if they were protected files that cannot be written to or erased.

A Few Reasons Why People Don't Back Up and Why They Should

Here are a few of the lame excuses used by some people who don't back up their software:

Don't Have the Time

This is not a good excuse. If your data is worth anything at all, it is worth backing up. It takes only a few minutes to back up a large hard disk with some of the newer software. It may take just seconds to copy all of the files to a directory on another logical drive of the disk or to another hard drive.

Too Much Trouble

It can be a bit of trouble unless you have an expensive tape automated backup system or a second hard disk. If you back up to floppies, it can require a bit of disk swapping, labeling, and storing. But with a little organizing, it can be done easily. If you keep all of the disks together, you don't have to label each one. Just stack them in order, put a rubber band around them, and use one label for the first one of the lot.

True, it is a bit of trouble to make backups. But if you don't have a backup, consider the trouble it would take to redo the files from a disk that has crashed. The trouble that it takes to make a backup is infinitesimal.

Don't Have the Necessary Disks, Software, or Tools

If you use floppy disks, depending on the amount of data to be backed up and the software used, it may require 50 to 100 disks. But it may take only a few minutes and just a few disks to make a backup of only the data that has been changed or altered. In most cases, the same disks can be reused the next day to update the files.

Failures and Disasters Only Happen to Other People

People who believe this are those who have never experienced a disaster. There is nothing you can say to convince them. They just have to learn the hard way.

Outside of ordinary care, there is little one can do to prevent a general failure. It could be a component on the hard disk electronics or in the controller system. Or it could be any one of a thousand other things. Even things such as a power failure during a read-write operation can cause data corruption.

Theft and Burglary

Computers are easy to sell, so they are favorite targets for burglars. It would be bad enough to lose a computer, but many computers have hard disks that are filled with data that is even more valuable than the computer.

Speaking of theft, it might be a good idea to put your name and address on several of the files on your hard disk. It would also be a good idea to scratch identifying marks on the back and bottom of the case. You should also write down the serial numbers of your monitor and drives. I heard a story where a man took a computer to a pawn shop. The dealer wanted to see if it worked, so he turned it on. A name came up on the screen that was different from the name the man had given to the dealer. He called the police, and the man was arrested for burglary. The owner of the computer was very happy to get it back. He was also quite fortunate. Most burglaries don't have a happy ending.

Another good idea is to store your backup files in an area away from your computer. This way, there would be less chance of losing both computer and backups in case of a burglary or fire. You can always buy another computer, but if you had a large database of customer orders, files, and history, how could you replace that?

An article in a recent issue of *Information Week* says that PC theft has increased over 400 percent in the last few years. (*Information Week* magazine is free to qualifying subscribers. See Chapter 19 for the address.)

Archival Reasons

Another reason to back up is for archival purposes. No matter how large the hard disk is, it will eventually fill up with data. Quite often, there will be files that are no longer used or they may only be used once in a great while. I keep copies of all the letters that I write on disk. I have hundreds of them. Rather than erase the old files or old letters, I put them on a disk and store them away.

Data Transfer

There are often times when it is necessary to transfer a large amount of data from one hard disk on a computer to another. It is quite easy to use a good backup program to accomplish this. Data on a disk can be used to distribute data, company policies and procedures, sales figures, and other information to several people in a large office or company. The data can also be easily shipped or mailed to branch offices, customers, or to others almost anywhere. If more companies used disks in this manner, we could save thousands of trees that are cut down for paper.

Types of Backup

There are two main types of backup: image and file oriented. An image backup is an exact bit-for-bit copy of the hard disk copied as a continuous stream of data. This type of backup is rather inflexible and does not allow for a separate file backup or restoration. The file-oriented type of backup identifies and indexes each file separately. A separate file or directory can be backed up and restored easily. It can be very time-consuming to back up an entire 40MB or more each day. But with a file-oriented-type system, once a full backup has been made, it is necessary only to make incremental backups of those files that have been changed or altered.

Once the first backup is made, all subsequent backups only need to be made of any data that has been changed or updated. Most backup programs can recognize whether a file has been changed since the last backup. Most of them can also look at the date that is stamped on each file and back up only those within a specified date range. So it may take only a few minutes to make a copy of only those files that are new or have been changed. And, of course, it is usually not necessary to back up your program software.

You do have the original software disks safely tucked away, don't you?

Windows 95 Backup Accessory

Windows 95/98 has a very good built-in backup program. To use it, push the `Start` button, then choose `Programs`, then `Accessories`, then `System Tools`, then `Backup`. The Microsoft Backup Wizard will be displayed. Then just follow the simple directions.

Backup Software

Several companies make backup software. One very good program is from Seagate Software, 840 Cambie St., Vancouver, BC V6B 4J2, Canada, Tel: 604-681-3435. (They are not the same Seagate Company who makes hard drives.) This program allows a complete backup and restore onto tape. The software can be set up to do an automatic backup at whatever time you choose.

Tape

There are several tape backup systems on the market. Tape backup is easy. However, it can be relatively expensive: $250 to over $500 for a drive unit and $10 to $20 for the tape cartridges. Some of them require the use of a controller that is similar to the disk controller. Therefore, they will use one of your precious slots, but there are some SCSI systems that can be daisy-chained to a SCSI controller. There are also enhanced IDE tape systems that can be controlled by an EIDE interface.

Unless the tape drives are external models, they will also require the use of one of the disk mounting areas. Since it is only used for backup, it will be idle most of the time.

Some available tape systems run off the printer parallel port. These systems don't require a controller board that takes up one of your slots. Another big plus is that it can be used to back up several different computers by simply moving it from one to the other. In addition, several companies are now manufacturing tape systems that attach to a universal serial bus (USB).

Like floppy disks, tapes have to be formatted before they can be used. But unlike a floppy disk, it may take over two hours to format a tape.

You can buy tapes that have been preformatted, but they cost quite a bit more than the unformatted tapes.

Tape systems are rather slow as well, so the backups should be done at night or during off hours. Most systems can be set up so that the backup is done automatically. If you set it on auto, you won't have to worry about forgetting to back up or wasting the time doing it.

Another disadvantage of tape is that data is recorded sequentially. If you want to find a file that is in the middle of the tape, it has to search until it finds it. Since disk systems have random access, they are much, much faster than tape both in recording and reading.

Despite any disadvantages, tape can be one of the ways to do a complete backup. If your hard disk ever crashes, you will need a complete backup in order to restore all of your files and programs. Most files today are so large that you cannot even use a 100MB or even 200MB disk to make a complete backup.

Here are some tape products, along with the companies who manufacture them:

Iomega Ditto Max
   Iomega Corp: 888-446-6342

Onstream SC30 and DI30
   Onstream: 800-759-4621

Tecmar Travan NS20
   Tecmar Technologies:800-422-2587

Removable Disks

One of the better ways for data backup and for data security is to back up to a disk that can be removed and locked up. There are several different systems and companies that manufacture such systems.

The Iomega Zip Drive

The Iomega Zip drive uses a $3\frac{1}{2}$-inch disk that is similar to a floppy. But this $3\frac{1}{2}$-inch disk can store 100MB or 250MB. At this time, Zip drives cost less than $150, and the disks cost less than $15. With a few disks, you would never have to worry about running out of hard drive space. The Zip system is ideal for backup or for any type of data storage.

The LS-120MB SuperDisk

Compaq, 3M, and Matsushita-Kotubuki Companies have developed a 120MB floppy system. The very high-density drives are downward-compatible so that they can also read and write to the 720KB and 1.44MB format. These drives are ideal for backup. Several vendors are now offering the high-capacity floppy drive. For more details, refer back to Chapter 5.

Sony 200MB Floppy System

The Sony Corporation and Fuji Film have developed a 200MB floppy system. It is also discussed in Chapter 5.

Again, the floppy systems are fine for partial backups, but in most cases, they cannot be used for a complete backup of all your files and programs. You need a very large hard disk or a tape system.

Magneto-Optical Drives

The magneto-optical drives (M-Os) are rather expensive, but the removable cartridges are fairly low cost. They are a good choice for use as a normal hard drive and for backup.

Pinnacle Micro (800-553-7070) has several removable M-O drive systems that are almost as fast as a standard hard disk. The cartridges can be erased and rewritten up to 10 million times.

Flex

One of their drives is called Flex. It harnesses the power of DVD technology to provide a high-capacity, multifunction storage device that writes to 5.2GB removable cartridges, and reads eight different CD and DVD formats.

Pinnacle Micro's Flex drive provides 5.2GB of rewritable storage on one low-cost removable cartridge. Files can be added, edited, and deleted just as they are with a floppy disk. Flex provides an ideal solution for backup and archiving, or distributing large amounts of data in an inexpensive, rewritable format.

A standard magnetic disk begins to deteriorate almost immediately after it has been recorded. It should be refreshed every two or three years. M-O disks have a lifetime of up to 100 years without degradation of data.

Another system from Pinnacle Micro, the Apex, would also be ideal for backing up or archiving a large amount of data.

Apex 4.6GB Optical Hard Drive

Pinnacle Micro's Apex model is another very good choice for backup. The Apex 4.6GB drive offers one of the highest capacities available in removable 5.25-inch storage.

Pinnacle's optical storage solutions are ideal for financial, legal, medical, publishing, networking, multimedia, engineering, government, and other data-intensive and archiving applications.

According to the company's literature, Pinnacle's optical media has a 100-year shelf life. It has a virtually unlimited number of reads and writes without data loss. It is highly resistant to magnetic fields, heat, and contamination; immune to head crashes; and shock resistant.

See Chapter 6 for more on magneto-optical drives and for other M-O products.

Recordable CD-ROM (CD-Rs)

As mentioned in the previous chapter, when they first came out, recordable CD-ROM systems were very expensive, at about $10,000. Many companies are now selling recordable CD-ROM systems for less than $300, and the prices are still dropping. If you have a lot of data that needs to be permanently backed up, a CD-ROM can store over 650MBs. An advantage of CD-ROM over magnetic systems is that data on a CD-ROM will last for many years. Magnetic data deteriorates and may become useless within 10 years. Unlike the magnetic systems, the data on a CD-ROM cannot be erased, changed, or altered. If the data needs to be changed, just record it onto another disc. The blank discs cost from $1 to $2 each.

Pinnacle Micro's RCD 6X24 is a powerful 6x writer/24x reader recordable CD system that can store up to 650MB or 74 minutes of audio. With this CD technology you can create custom CDs in approximately 10 minutes or read any CD-ROM title at 24x speed.

The RCD 6X24 is available in both internal and external configurations for both PC and Mac. With its 5.25-inch half-height form factor, the internal RCD 6X24 can fit into any open drive bay. Another option is the unique compact design of the external RCD 6X24, making it perfect for desktop use.

Users can create CDs in many popular formats using different CD-authoring packages available from third-party software partners such as Adaptec (Easy CD-Creator and Direct CD for PC), or Adaptec (Toast for Mac).

DVD

Some say that DVD means "digital video disc," others that it means "digital versatile disc." It certainly is versatile. There are several versions of DVD that are much like the CD-ROM. Some are recordable, and some are rewritable. DVD-RAM is a DVD that can read and write to DVD-RAM discs. It can store up to 2.6GB on each side of a disc. The special disc can be erased and written over again and again—similar to a hard disk. The DVD-RAM is ideal for backing up large amounts of data. It is much better than tape because the data can be randomly accessed. They are also much faster than tape.

Chapter 8 discusses CD-ROM and DVD technology in greater detail.

WORM

Write once, read many (WORM) are laser optical systems that are similar to recordable CD-ROMs. One difference is that the WORM systems usually have larger discs and can store up to several gigabytes.

They are great for backing up and archiving data. With a good document management system and a scanner, vast amounts of paper files can be stored on a WORM. This type of system even has earned an acronym, COLD, which means computer output to laser disc. A WORM recording should last for over 100 years. Ordinarily, even paper will deteriorate in less time.

Keep in mind, however, that WORMs have been practically obsoleted by the DVD-RAM systems.

Second Hard Disk

The easiest and the fastest of all methods of backup is to have a second hard disk. It is very easy to install a second hard disk. An IDE interface can control two high-capacity hard disks; the EIDE interfaces can control up to four hard drives. You can add as many as seven hard drives to a SCSI interface.

A good system is to have an IDE drive for the C: boot drive and one or more SCSI drives. You can back up several megabytes of data from one hard drive to another very easily and quickly. The chances are very good that both systems would not become defective at the same time. So if the same data is stored on both systems, it should offer very good RAID-like protection.

At one time tape backup systems were much less expensive than a hard disk, but the cost of hard disks have come way down. One of the advantages of using a hard disk for backup is that, unlike tape, any file is available almost immediately.

Ultra DMA/66 Promise Controller Cards

Promise Technology (www.promise.com) has developed several controller cards that will allow you to use the new Ultra DMA/66 hard disks on just about any PC. Their Ultra66 card vastly improves the throughput of a hard disk made to the Ultra DMA/66 specifications. Standard EIDE drives operate at a maximum of 16.7Mbps. The Ultra ATA 33 operates at 33Mbps, the Ultra Wide SCSI operates at 40Mbps, and the Ultra DMA/66 operates at 66Mbps.

Again, it is possible to disable the Ultra DMA/66 functions of a hard disk and install it as a standard EIDE. But look at the speed that is being sacrificed.

The Ultra66 also has an onboard BIOS that supports drive capacities up to 128GB. The BIOS of many motherboards designed before late 1998 could not recognize a hard disk larger than 8.4GB.

The Ultra66 is designed so that four IDE devices can be attached to it. This leaves your standard motherboard connectors free so that four other IDE devices could be installed. It is quite possible to have eight

IDE devices, such as two or more hard drives, a standard CD-ROM, a recordable CD-R, a DVD, a ZIP drive, a tape backup, a scanner, and several other IDE devices. The Ultra66 controller is a Plug and Play device and is very easy to install.

At this time, Promise controllers sell for around $50.

RAID Systems

RAID is an acronym for redundant arrays of inexpensive disks. There are some data that is absolutely critical and essential. In order to make sure that it is saved, data is written to two or more hard disks at the same time. Originally, five different levels were suggested, but only three levels—1, 3, and 5—are in general use today.

Some RAID systems allow you to hot swap or pull and replace a defective disk drive without having to power down. You don't lose any information because the same data is being written to other hard disk drives.

To prevent data losses due to a controller failure, some RAID systems use a separate disk controller for each drive. A mirror copy is made of the data on each system. This is called *duplexing*. Some systems use a separate power supply for each system, and all systems use uninterruptible power supplies.

RAID systems are essential for networks or any other area where the data is critical and must absolutely be preserved. But no matter how careful you are and how many backup systems you have, you may still occasionally lose data through accidents or some other act of God. You can add more and more to the backup systems to make them fail-safe, but eventually you will reach a point of diminishing returns.

Depending on how much is spent and how well the system is engineered, the system should be system fault tolerant (SFT)—that is, it should remain fully operational regardless of one or more component failures.

Promise Low-Cost RAID

Promise Technology also has a FastTrak controller that will let you set up an IDE RAID system. Ordinarily, RAID systems use SCSI hard disks and controllers and are rather expensive. The new Ultra DMA/66 disks are actually faster than the SCSI and are less expensive.

With the Promise FastTrak controller, you can control four IDE drives. They can be set up so that two of them can be used for striping. Striping allows you to write every other track to the other drive. For instance, one drive would write or read track 1-3-5, and the second one would read or write track 2-4-6. You can also set up two drives to mirror each other. This is one of the better ways to make backups. The same data is written to both disks at the same time. If one of them fails, the other one will still have all of the data.

If you are in a small business and have to make sure that your data is backed up, this is one of the better ways to do it.

LapLink

Traveling Software's LapLink allows you to connect two computers together and access either one. It is very simple to use the parallel port cables that come with the package and transfer files from one computer to the other. LapLink allows you to update only those portions of a file that have changed. If you are updating or backing up files that are already on the disk, it takes very little time.

LapLink can also be used over a modem. If you are on the road and need to back up a laptop, you can easily send the data back to the desktop.

Uninterruptible Power Supplies

Uninterruptible power supplies (UPS) are very important to back up. If you have a power failure or brownout while working on a file, you could lose a lot of valuable data. In areas where there are frequent electrical storms, it is essential that you use a UPS. The basic UPS is a battery that is constantly charged by the 110V input voltage. If the power is interrupted, the battery system takes over and continues to provide power long enough for the computers to save the data that might happen to be in RAM, then shut down.

Several companies manufacture quite sophisticated UPS systems for almost all types of computer systems and networks. Of course, for a single user, you only need a small system. On a network or for several computers, it will require a system that can output a lot of current.

Here are just a few manufacturers of UPS systems:

American Power Conversion
   www.apcc.com
   888-289-APCC, ext. 8172

Best Power Technology
   800-356-5794

Sola Electric
   800-289-7652

Tripp-Lite Mfg.
   312-329-1777

Again, if your data is worth anything at all, it is worth backing up. It is much better to be backed up than to be sorry.

CD-ROM and DVD

As you probably know, CD-ROM is an acronym for compact disc read-only memory. Today, CD-ROM drives are an essential part of computers. Most computers now sold have a CD-ROM as standard equipment. It has become as necessary as a hard disk drive. Almost all software programs now come on CD-ROM discs. (Note that the CD-ROM discs are spelled with a *c*, as opposed to hard and floppy disks, spelled with a *k*.) It makes you wonder how we got along without them for so long.

CD-ROM systems offer some very important benefits to the individual end user for entertainment, education, business, and industry. There are thousands and thousands of CD-ROM disc titles that cover just about every subject imaginable.

I will briefly describe some of the systems here, then go into a bit more detail later in this chapter.

CD-ROM Drives

It would be impossible for me to try out and test all the CD-ROM drives that are on the market. But I subscribe to a lot of magazines that have test labs to do evaluations. In most cases, there is really not that much difference in similar models from different companies. In some instances, one drive may have a fraction of a second better statistics than another. But I don't worry too much about fractions of a second. Since most of the similar-model drives are equivalent, the first thing I look at is cost. One of the best ways to look for CD-ROM drives and do some comparisons, is to visit the company's Web pages. Of course, you should expect to find a lot of PR hype at the company Webs, praising their products.

Some fantastic improvements have been made in CD-ROM technology. In fact, some CD-ROM drives are now almost as fast as a hard disk.

CD-R Drives

At one time the CD-R recordable drives were very expensive at $10,000 or more. You can now buy a very good system for less than $200. Most of the major manufacturers are now making them. Some of the blank discs sell for less than $1 each. The CD-R is a write-once device. If you need to change something, just slip in another blank disc and burn a new version.

More about CD-R later in the chapter.

CD-RW

The CD-RW will let you record over or rewrite over previously written data, much like a hard disk system. You can now buy a CD-RW for less than $200.

More about CD-RW later in the chapter.

DVD Drives

There has been some confusion as to what "DVD" stands for. Originally, it was said that it meant "digital video disc." Many people now say it stands for "digital versatile disc." This is a much better term because DVD drives can do much more than handle video. They are truly very versatile.

DVD drives will read and play back all of the CD-ROM discs. DVD drives are not much more expensive than the standard CD-ROM drives. There should be several on the market for less than $100 by the time you read this. The one major difference between CD-ROM and DVD is that some of the CD-ROM drives now operate up to 50x; the DVD drives are still limited to about 6x. Still, if you can only afford one CD drive, I recommend that you buy a DVD drive.

DVD-RAM

A DVD-RAM drive can read and write to special DVD discs. It can store up to 2.6GB on each side of a disc. The special disc can be erased and written over again and again—similar to a hard disk. The DVD-RAM is ideal for backing up, storing, or archiving large amounts of data.

Here are just a few companies who make CD-ROM and DVD drives. To find out more about their products, just access their Web sites.

Creative Labs
408-428-6600
www.creativelabs.com

Denon Electronics
973-575-7810
www.del.denon.com

Diamond
800-468-5846
www.diamondmm.com

Hi-Val
www.hival.com

JVC Company
800-252-5722
www.jvc.com

Mitsubishi
800-332-2119
www.mitsubishi.com

NEC
800-632-4636
www.nec.com

Panasonic
800-742-8086
www.panasonic.com

Pioneer
800-444-6784
www.pioneerusa.com

Plextor
800-886-3935
www.plextor.com

Samsung
800-726-7864
www.samsung.com

Sony
800-352-7669
www.sony.com

TEAC
800-888-4293
www.teac.com

Toshiba
800-678-4373
www.toshiba.com

UMAX
800-562-0311
www.umax.com

Hi-Val and some of the other companies listed above will sell direct to you from their Web site.

Sample Specification

Here are some specifications from Creative Labs' Web site (www.creative.com) to give you an idea of what is available.

Creative Labs 48x Internal CD-ROM Drive

Maximum data transfer rate of 7,200KB/second

100ms or better average access time

Integrated cache RAM

Front-panel headphone jack, volume control, busy indicator, and close/eject button

Front-loading, motorized tray design

Enhanced IDE interface for increased performance

Works with the following disc formats: CD-Audio, CD-ROM, CD-ROM XA, CD-I, Photo CD, CD-R, Video CD, CD Extra, and CD-RW

Supports DMA (direct memory access) mode for faster transfer rates and decreased CPU utilization

Horizontal and vertical installation and operation

Sound Blaster Live! Value

Wave-table synthesis

E-mu Systems EMU10K1 music synthesis engine

64-voice polyphony with E-mu's patented 8-point interpolation technology

512-voice polyphony PCI wave-table synthesis

48 MIDI channels with 128 GM- and GS-compatible instruments and 10 drum kits

Uses SoundFont technology for user-definable wave-table sample sets; includes 2MB, 4MB, and 8MB sets; load up to 32MB of samples into host memory for professional music reproduction

Effects Engine

Supports real-time digital effects like reverb, chorus, flanger, pitch shifter, or distortion across your audio source

Capable of processing, mixing, and positioning audio streams using up to 131 available hardware channels

Customizable effects architecture allows audio effects and channel control

Full digital mixer maintains all sound mixing in the digital domain, eliminating noise from the signal

Bass, treble, and effects controls available for your audio sources

Environmental E-mu 3D Positional Audio Technology

User-selectable settings are optimized for headphones or two to four speakers

Accelerates Microsoft DirectSound and DirectSound3D

Support for Environmental Audio property set extensions

Creative Multi Speaker Surround technology places any mono or stereo sound source in a 360° audio space

Creative Environments—user-selectable DSP modes that simulate acoustic environments like Hall, Theater, Club, etc. on the sound source

Hollywood-quality, 32-bit digital audio engine

User-selectable from 8- to 16-bit rate and from 8kHz to 48kHz sampling rate

All sound sources are handled with 32-bit precision for highest-quality output

Analog and digital I/O modes supported

Hardware full-duplex support enables simultaneous record and playback at 8 standard sample rates

Utilizes AC97 audio codec

On-board connectors for microphone in, line-in, line-out (front), line-out (rear), joystick port, auxiliary in, Digital CD in, telephone answering device in, MPC-3 (ATAPI) CD Audio in, and MIDI interface/joystick port

Works with these standards: Microsoft Windows NT 4.0, Windows 95/98, General MIDI, PCI v.2.1 compliant, Sound Blaster PCI, Environmental Audio Extensions, Microsoft DirectSound, Microsoft DirectSound3D and derivative technology; Plug and Play, and MPC3

Sound Blaster SBS20 speakers

Designed by Cambridge SoundWorks

10 watts per channel (PMPO); magnetically shielded

Creative Labs

Following is some information from Creative Labs' Web site concerning their products.

Blaster CD-RW 4224

Blaster CD-RW 4224 lets you do it all—distribute large graphics and database files with clients, send copies of your vacation photos to friends and family, put all your favorite songs on one CD, or share the latest independent MP3 music with your friends.

With easy-to-use software, simply drag-and-drop your files to a blank CD or copy the whole disc, and you're ready to go. Store up to 650MB of data or over 74 minutes of audio on each CD, write CD-Rs at 4X and CD-RWs at 2X speeds, and read CD-ROMs at up to 24X. Blaster CD-RW looks, installs, and works like a CD-ROM, so not only can you create CDs, you can play audio CDs, run popular applications, or read other CD-R and CD-RW discs.

For the smart way to create CDs that you can use everywhere, Blaster CD-RW is the only answer.

Blaster DVD-ROM 6X

With Blaster DVD-ROM 6X, today's demanding interactive programs are no obstacle for your PC. The Creative PC-DVD 6X drive transfers CD-ROM data at up to 24X speeds and DVD-ROM data at up to 6X speeds. The Creative PC-DVD 6X drive technology supports multiple DVD-ROM and CD-ROM formats including CD-R and DVD-R, and accesses up to 17GB of DVD data.

You can upgrade the Blaster DVD-ROM with the optional Creative Dxr3 DVD Decoder Board, and you'll have a blast with high-resolution DVD movies and engrossing DVD titles. See vibrant, cinema-quality DVD video and hear surround-sound Dolby Digital (AC-3) audio through your PC or your TV.

Dolby Digital (AC-3) 5.1 channel audio requires Cambridge SoundWorks DeskTop Theater 5.1 speaker system or an amplifier/receiver with Dolby Digital coaxial input, and Dolby Digital (AC-3) supported applications.

Creative DVD RAM

Creative PC-DVD RAM drive and disc conform to the latest finalized DVD-RAM Book (version 1.0), published by the DVD Forum. DVD will be the converging standard for all media in the near future. Virtually all types of media, including movies, PC software titles, and audio will soon be delivered in DVD format. Thus, your removable storage device should demand full compatibility with DVD.

Viewing DVD-Video (movies) with the PC-DVD RAM drive requires an optional Creative Dxr3 Decoder (sold separately).

DVD-RAM uses UDF (Universal Disk Format) filing system format, the same as DVD-ROM. Files can be dynamically added, just as how they are added to your hard disc. Buffer under-runs, a notorious and common problem with CD-R, are virtually eliminated. And because DVD-RAM and DVD-ROM use the same filing system, DVD-RAM will work with newer generation DVD-ROM drives that support Type 1 and Type 2 DVD-RAM media.

Huge Storage Space at a Low Cost   Creative PC-DVD RAM offers storage space of up to 5.2GB per cartridge (double-sided). With one cartridge alone, you can store as many as 5,200 full-color digital pictures (640x480, 24 bit/pixel); or 230 minutes of MPEG-2 compressed theatrical quality video; or more than 8 hours of CD-quality audio (44.1kHz, 16-bit). Creative PC-DVD RAM comes bundled with a 5.2GB DVD-RAM disc cartridge.

Fast Data Transfer Speed   Creative PC-DVD RAM provides 1,385 KB/second (1x) read/write for DVD-RAM, equivalent to 9.5x CD-R write. The PC-DVD RAM drive also reads DVD-ROM data at 2,700 KB/second (2x) and CD-ROM data at up to 3,000 KB/second (20x).

Some Definitions

The Dolby Digital Decoder mentioned in the Creative Labs info above refers to special audio that is on many of the new DVD discs. The DVD players have a pair of composite audio output jacks for Dolby Surround signal. You need a Dolby Pro Logic decoder. They also have music tracks. Many DVD discs come with a 5.1-channel Dolby Digital AC-3 audio sound track that has separate channels for left, center, and right surround sound. This format requires an AC-3 decoder.

Figure 8-1 shows a Creative Labs 6X DVD and a Dxr3 Decoder board.

Figure 8-1
A Creative Labs 6X DVD and a Dxr3 DVD decoder board.

Figure 8-2
The Cambridge four small speakers and a large woofer for excellent sound.

Figure 8-2 shows the Cambridge four small speakers and a large woofer for surround sound.

Toshiba

Here is some information from Toshiba's Web site (www.toshiba.com) about some of their products.

ATAPI Half-Height (IDE) DVD-ROM Drive

Toshiba's leadership in DVD-ROM continues with the new SD-M1202 DVD-ROM drive. The SD-M1202 takes DVD to a new performance level with 4.8X transfer for DVD and 32X for CD-ROM—that's twice as fast as first-generation DVD-ROM. Beyond performance, the SD-M1202 boasts all the capabilities which have made DVD-ROM the technology of choice for computer system manufacturers: compatibility with all DVD-ROM and CD-based media, including CD-R and CD-RW, plus support for full-motion MPEG-2 video and Dolby Digital Surround Sound AC-3 audio.

CD-R compatible
Reads up to 17GB DVD Disc

4.8-max data transfer
135ms avg random access
256 KB buffer

DVD-RAM Drive

For industry standard, high-capacity rewritable optical storage, look no further than Toshiba's SD-W1101 DVD-RAM drive. Toshiba's RAM drive combines high storage capacity of 5.2GB with unprecedented performance to benefit a range of applications including multimedia development, backup and data archiving. The SD-W1101 DVD-RAM drive conforms to all DVD industry standards to ensure media interchangeability with other DVD-RAM drives.

Rewritable 2.6GB single-sided and 5.2GB dual-sided
Reads DVD-ROM, DVD-R, and all CD-ROM media
1350KB/sec DVD-RAM write and read
270ms avg random access DVD-RAM write
180ms avg random access DVD-RAM read

Toshiba's SD-W1001 (SCSI) DVD-RAM drives represent the next generation of random access rewriteable storage technologies. Toshiba's DVD-RAM stores an unprecedented 2.6GB to 5.2GB of data on a DVD-RAM disc that is the same physical size as a standard CD. DVD-RAM, because of its high-capacity storage and the durability of the media, is perfectly suited for multimedia, backup, data archiving, data storage, and small-group software distribution.

Rewritable 2.6GB Single-Sided and 5.2GB Dual-Sided
Reads DVD-ROM, DVD-R, and all CD-ROM media
1352kbps DVD-RAM write and read
270ms avg random access DVD-RAM write
170ms avg random access DVD-RAM read

MPEG-2 Decoders

If you plan to watch movies on your PC or TV, you will need an MPEG decoder card. MPEG is an acronym for Moving Pictures Experts Group. MPEG is a method of compressing video so that it is more manageable. Ordinarily, one frame of a movie may require about 25MB. MPEG-2 delivers 30 frames of video playback per second with a variable compression ration as high as 200:1. Broadcast-quality video can be achieved with a 30:1 compression ratio. MPEG-2 will also support MPEG-1 playback. MPEG-2 works by removing redundant signal information during compression and reassembles this data during playback through the use of I-frames, B-frames, and P-frames. MPEG-2 is utilized for DVD, HDTV, and DBS video.

Many of the DVD kits come with the MPEG-2 decoder. Otherwise, Creative Labs and most of the manufacturers listed earlier in the chapter carry them.

DVD Players

Several of the major companies who make CD-ROMs also make DVD players. These can be attached to a TV set and allow you to watch movies in high resolution. The DVD players usually have some very high-fidelity, built-in sound amplifiers. They are very good for a home entertainment system.

What Should You Buy?

Some DVD drives are now selling for around $100. They can read all of the CD formats. The best system would be to have a DVD and a DVD-RAM: the DVD to play and the DVD-RAM to copy CDs, CD-ROM discs, or data from a hard disk.

Both DVD and DVD-RAM systems are available in fairly low-cost IDE interfaces. But if both devices are being used, there may be some interference as they both try to access the system through the IDE interfaces. It would be better if one of them, preferably the DVD-RAM, is a SCSI device.

CD-ROM Titles

A short time ago, CD-ROM disc titles were very expensive. But every day brings more and more competition. There are just too many titles to even try to review them in a book like this. Several CD-ROM magazines and PC magazines are available to help you be aware of what is out there. Here are just a few:

New Media Magazine
  800-253-6641
  www.hyperstand.com

This magazine is sent free to qualified subscribers. Almost any person with a business connection can qualify.

EMedia Professional
  800-806-7795
  e-mail:emediasub@online.com
  www.online.com/emedia

Because of the thousands of companies who are producing CD-ROM titles, the enormous amount of competition is forcing the prices down. Some CD-ROM titles that cost as much as $100 a few months ago can now be bought for as little as $5 to $10. And the prices are still going down. It is great for the consumer.

Home Entertainment

A large number of the CD-ROM and DVD titles are designed for entertainment for both young and old, including arcade-type games, chess, and other board games. In addition, there are titles for music, opera, art, and a large variety of other subjects. Many of the titles are both educational as well as entertaining.

Home Library

At the present time, only one side of the CD-ROM discs are used for recording, but this single side can hold over 650MB of data. Some DVD discs can store as much as 17GB by using both sides. You can have a multitude of different programs on a single CD-ROM disc and a world of information at your fingertips. More books and information can be stored on just a few CD-ROM discs than you might find in an entire library. A 21-volume encyclopedia can be stored in just a fraction of the space on one side of a single CD-ROM disc. When data compression is used to store text, several hundred books can be stored on a single disc. It may take only seconds to search through an entire encyclopedia or through several hundred books to find a subject, sentence, or a single word.

An Easier Way to Learn

Text, graphics, sound, animation, and movies can be stored on CD-ROM discs. We have several avenues to the brain. The more avenues used to input information to our brain, the easier it is to learn and to remember. We can learn by reading. But we can learn much better if sound is added to the text. We have all heard the old saying that a picture is worth a thousand words. It is so very true. We learn much better and retain more if graphics and motion are added. Rather than trying to remember just dry text, the many advantages of CD-ROM can make learning fun and pleasurable. Schools can use CD-ROM for teaching. Businesses can use CD-ROM to train their personnel.

Lawyers

Lawyers may have to spend hours and hours going through law books to find precedents, to find some of the finer points of the law, or to find loopholes. A few CD-ROM discs could replace several law clerks.

Health and Medicine

The human body is a fantastic machine. There is more written about medicine and computers than any other subject. Several CD-ROMs have been published for the home user such as the Family Doctor, published by Creative Multimedia Corp. (503-241-4351), the Mayo Clinic Family Health Book, published by Interactive Ventures, (507-282-2076), and several others.

A doctor must keep abreast of all of the scientific advances, new drugs, and treatments. A busy doctor can't possibly read all of the published papers. A CD-ROM can help. The American Family Physician is the official journal of the American Academy of Family Physicians. It is available from the Bureau of Electronic Publishing at 800-828-4766. The A.D.A.M. (for Animated Dissection of Anatomy for Medicine) Software Company (800-755-2326) has developed several discs that show the various parts of the anatomy, both male and female. This CD-ROM is a very good way for students and families to learn about the human body. If you are a bit prudish, you are given an option to cover certain parts of the anatomy with fig leaves.

How CD-ROM Works

The CD-ROM system was first developed by Sony and Philips using lasers for recording and playing back music. (LASER is an acronym for light amplification by stimulated emission of radiation.) Almost all CD-ROM drives can also play music compact discs. Most of the drives have a plug for ear phones and an audio connector on the back so that it can be plugged into a sound card. You can set up a very good hi-fi system using a CD-ROM and a computer. Basically, music compact disc systems are quite similar to CD-ROM systems, but CD-ROM drives are usually more expensive.

When a CD-ROM disc is created, a powerful laser is turned on and off in response to data 0s and 1s which burns holes in the disc material. When the beam is switched on to create a hole it is called a *pit*; when left off, the area of the track is called a *land*. When played back, a laser beam is focused on the track. The pits do not reflect as much light as the lands, so it is easy to distinguish the digital data.

High Sierra/ISO 9660

The Philips and Sony companies developed the audio CD in 1982. It wasn't long before the importance of the technology was recognized and adopted for CD-ROMs.

It was a fast-growing technology, but there were no standards. Every company wants to make their products a bit different, so there were several different formats. In 1985 a group of industry leaders, including Microsoft, met at a hotel in Lake Tahoe to hammer a set of standards. The standard that they devised defined the table of contents and directory structure. It also defined the logical, file, and record structures. Microsoft provided their Microsoft Compact Disc Extensions (MSCDEX) software, a driver that allows DOS to access the CD-ROM through conventional DOS commands. All CD-ROMs used in PCs use the Microsoft MSCDEX driver. Every time a CD-ROM is installed and used, a small license fee is paid to Bill Gates. (This is just one of the ways that Bill Gates has earned his $100 billion. In mid-1998 he only had $50 billion.)

There were several other specifications adopted at this meeting. Since they were meeting at Tahoe, which is in the Sierra Mountain range, they called the new standard the High Sierra Specification. The specification was later adopted, with minor modifications, by the International Standards Organization as ISO 9660. Unless otherwise stated, most all CD-ROM drives and discs conform to the ISO 9660. Besides the standards set forth in ISO 9660, several other standard specifications have been developed.

There are thousands of pages of specifications in each of four books. Some books are more than 1 foot thick. The specifications were originally issued in books with different colors, and the standards have been named for the color of the original book. Sometimes a disc will have specifications from two or more books. For instance, if the disc contains text, audio, and graphics it may conform to specifications from the Red Book, the Yellow Book, and the Green Book. The Red Book sets forth the standards for audio or compact disc digital audio (CD-DA).

The Yellow Book sets forth the ISO 9660 standards for storing files that can be translated to DOS, Apple, or Amiga files. The Microsoft MSCDEX drivers are used to accomplish the translation. The Green Book covers CD-Interactive (CD-I) and CD-ROM extended architecture (CD-ROM/XA). The Orange Book covers write once, read many (WORM) drives and magneto-optic (M-O) drives. It also covers the multisession PhotoCD-type drives.

How the Discs Are Made

Data that is to be stored on a CD-ROM disc is usually assembled and organized, then copied onto a large-capacity hard disk. The data can be copied onto the large hard disk from floppies, hard disks, tape, or almost any medium. A table of contents, an index, error detection, and correction and retrieval software are usually added to the data. A one-off disc can be made from the organized data. A CD-ROM recorder similar to the Philips CCD 521 can be used to make this first test disc. The disc can be tested and tried and if it meets the client's specifications, then the data will be laser-etched onto a glass master disc. All of the duplications will come from this disc.

All CD-ROM discs are pressed much like the vinyl phonograph records. But a disc that is pressed from the original master would be a mirror image of it. The pits and the lands on the copy would be just the reverse of those on the master. To make it identical to the master, a copy of a copy is made. The pits and lands are then in the proper order. The first copy of the master is called a *mother*. Then a working copy of the mother is made, which is called the *father*. Virgin blank discs are pressed against the father to make all of the commercial discs.

The blank discs are 120 millimeters in diameter (about $4\frac{3}{4}$ inches) and are made from a polycarbonate plastic. Each blank disc costs less than $1. After being pressed, the discs are coated with reflective aluminum. This coating is 1 micron thick. The discs are then coated with a thin layer of lacquer to prevent oxidation and contamination. The same process is used for both audio compact discs and CD-ROM discs.

Laser Color

As you probably know, white light encompasses all of the colors of the rainbow. Each color has its own frequency of vibration; the slower frequencies are at the dark-red end. The frequencies increase as the colors move toward the violet end.

The particles that make up ordinary light are incoherent—that is, they are scattered in all directions. Lasers are possible because a single color of light can be sharply focused and amplified. All of the particles of one color are lined up in an orderly, coherent fashion.

The laser effect can be obtained from several different gases and materials. Most of the present CD-ROM lasers use light at the lower-frequency dark end of the spectrum, such as the red or yellow. The Samsung Company has developed a green laser that has a shorter wavelength and higher frequency. They claim that by using this laser and their proprietary compression techniques, they can store up to 110 minutes of the MPEG-2 video on a disc, five times as much as usual. (As mentioned, MPEG is an acronym for Moving Pictures Experts Group, who developed a set of methods for video compression.)

An experimental blue laser has also been developed that will have an even higher frequency than a green laser. At this writing, neither the green nor the blue have been incorporated into available units. A hard disk may have several thousand separate concentric tracks, with each track divided into several sectors. Usually, each sector can store 512 bytes. A CD-ROM disc has a single spiral track that begins in the center and winds out to the outer edge. If the track was stretched out, it would be several miles long. The track is similar to the groove on a phonograph record, except that the groove on a phonograph record begins on the outer edge and winds to the center. (An old question is, how far does the needle on a phonograph travel when it plays a large record? The answer is, about 6 inches.) The needle moves from the outer edge to the center while the record spins beneath it. The same thing happens when you play a CD-ROM or DVD.

The long spiral track of a CD-ROM disc is divided into about 270,000 sectors, each sector with 2048 bytes. The sectors are numbered and given addresses according to the time in minutes, seconds, and hundredths of a second. For instance, starting from the center, the first sector is 00:00:00, and the second sector is 00:00:01.

Remember that the hard disk has a head actuator motor that moves the head to the various concentric tracks. The CD-ROM has a similar small motor that moves the laser beam to whatever sector on the spiral track is to be read. The laser beam is mounted on a rail and moves smoothly to whatever section is needed. Figure 8-3 shows a CD-ROM drive that has been opened. The pen points to the small laser-light assembly that moves back and forth on the rails beneath the spinning disc. It can move to any sector of a track very quickly.

Figure 8-3
A CD-ROM drive that has been opened. The pen points to the laser assembly that moves on the rails.

Rotational Speed

The CD-ROM uses a system that constantly changes the speed of the drive. The drive electronics speeds the disc up or slows it down, depending on what area of the disc it is reading. The original 1x drive spins at about 200 rpm and up to 530 rpm. This is called *constant linear velocity* (CLV). The double-speed 2x CD-ROMs rotate at 400 rpm to 1060 rpm; the quad-speed drives double these figures again from 800 to over 2000 rpm; 6x ranges from 1200 to over 3000 rpm; 8x ranges from 1600 to over 4000 rpm.

At 4000 rpm, there may be quite a lot of vibration from the spindle motor. The plastic disc is somewhat flexible. At the higher speeds a slight imbalance can cause the spinning disc to wobble and vibrate. Even if the label is not properly placed on the disc, it can cause an imbalance at the high speed. This may cause errors in reading the small pits and lands.

Because of its importance, several companies have developed label printing machines and installers. Many people are now using CD-recordable machines to make their own CD-ROMs. Here are some companies who sell CD labeling kits:

Mediastore
   800-555-5551
   www.mediastore.com

The Mediastore also sells CD-R recorders, CD-blanks, and other electronic products.

One-Off Label System
   800-340-1633
   www.oneoffcd.com

NEATO CD Labeler Kit
   800-648-6787

CD-R Gold Label Applicator
   800-255-4020

PressIT CD Labeling Kit
   800-203-6727

Prosource
   800-903-1234

For other dealers and components, check the several CD-ROM magazines that are available.

The Speed Limit

Because of vibration and other problems, when they came out with the 8x speed, many people thought that this was the absolute speed limit. But technology does not stand still. Despite the title of this section, there does not seem to be any speed limit. We now have 52x units, and there will be even faster ones tomorrow that are almost as fast as a hard disk. Actually, the discs will not rotate much faster than the 12x speed. They achieve the transfer rate of a higher speed without spinning that fast by using a combination of *constant linear velocity* (CLV) and *constant angular velocity* (CAV). The 1x and 2x speed drives are as obsolete as the 360KB floppy drives. Just a short time ago, double-speed drives were selling for over $400. No one is even making 2x speed today. Some of the fastest CD-ROM drives are selling for less than $100. A 40x drive was advertised in a recent *Computer Shopper* for $64. It will be less by the time you read this. Figure 8-4 shows a 32x CD-ROM, a bit of a slowpoke compared to some of today's speedsters.

Figure 8-4
A 32x CD-ROM—
a slowpoke
compared to some
speedsters today.

Transfer Speed

The transfer speed, or the amount of time that it takes to read a track on the original 1x and all of the audio CDs, was 75 sectors per second. A sector is 2048 bytes (2KB). Multiplying 2048 by 75 gives us 150KB per second. Doubling the speed of the 1x drive doubles the transfer rate to 300KB per second. A quad-speed drive will transfer data at 600KBps; the 6x speed drives can transfer data at 900KBps. Faster transfer times allow video and motion to be displayed in a smooth fashion. The faster drives can read all of the CD-ROM discs that the slower drives can read, but at a faster rate.

Audio files must still be played back at the 150KB rate. With audio, the speed must drop down to the original speed of 200 to 530 rpms.

Data Buffers

The faster drives usually have a fairly large buffer system, which also helps to smooth out video and motion and speed up the transfer rate. The buffer memory is located on chips on the drive. The firmware (software embedded on chips) portion of the buffer system decides which information will be used most often and stores it in the buffer. For instance, the contents of the disk directory may be stored in the buffer. Many of the newer drive systems have from 128KB up to 2MB of DRAM for cache memory buffers.

Access or Seek Time

The access, or seek, time is the time necessary to move the laser head to find a certain block or sector on the spiral track and begin reading it. The original MPC specification was that the drive should be able to find any block in 1000 milliseconds (ms) or 1 second. Most of the older drives had access times of 300 to 400ms.

The faster rotational speed yields a faster access speed, but not in direct proportion. For instance, the best quad-speed drives have an access rate of 150ms. The best eight-speed drive still has a rate of 150ms. The best 12- to 24-speed drives are a little better, at 90ms.

Generally speaking, the transfer rate or speed is more important than the access speed. In most cases, the transfer rate is proportional to the rotational speed.

CD-ROM Differences

There are several different types of CD-ROM drives. Some mount internally, some externally. Some use SCSI for an interface; others use an enhanced IDE interface. And, of course, they vary in speed. Prices also vary considerably. The external drives may cost up to $100 more than an internal because they need a power supply and cables. As always, what you should buy depends on what your needs are.

Interface Systems

Some of the earlier systems had their own proprietary interface. Often, the interface was built in on sound cards. Most drives sold today are IDE (Integrated Drive Electronics) drives; a few are for the more-expensive SCSI interface. The IDE interface is built in on all motherboards today. If you are buying a SCSI drive, keep in mind that the interface card and cable may not be included in the price of the system. Read the ads carefully if you are buying by mail order.

The interface card will be plugged into one of the bus slots. Before plugging the card in, make sure that any jumpers or switches on the board are set properly. The board must be configured so that it does not conflict with the address or interrupt request (IRQ) of any of your other devices. Check your documentation. In addition, always turn your computer off before unplugging or changing the settings of any card. Never plug in or unplug a card, cable, or device while the power is on.

If your system does not conform to the Plug and Play (PnP) specification, a CD-ROM drive interface may be difficult to set up and configure. It must be set to a specific IRQ and memory address location. If the board conflicts with any other device in your system, it will not work.

Enhanced IDE Interfaces

The Enhanced IDE (EIDE) interface can handle up to four devices. (Most people just call it IDE.) This can be any combination of IDE hard drives and IDE CD-ROMs or IDE backup tape drives. The IDE CD-ROM systems are considerably less expensive than the SCSI. Your motherboard will have a built-in IDE interface.

The IDE may also be called an ATA interface.

SCSI Interfaces

More and more companies are now manufacturing drives for the SCSI interface. If you have other SCSI products such as a SCSI hard drive or tape backup, you already have an interface card. The SCSI interface cards can drive up to seven different devices, preventing you from having to install separate interfaces for each device and using up those precious slots. Most SCSI devices have two connectors: one for the input cable and an identical connector for the next item. If you don't already have a SCSI interface, you may have to pay $100 to $200 extra for the interface. Again, these interfaces would plug into the 16-bit ISA slots and operate at 8 to 10MHz. If you are doing high-end work, you may want to buy a faster and more expensive PCI SCSI interface.

Parallel Printer Port

The parallel printer port has become a popular method to attach peripherals. It all started with tape backup drives that could be attached to one system, then removed and used on another. Soon, many hard disk drives were doing the same thing. This system saves time and money because you don't have to open the system or buy an interface board or controller. In addition, the peripheral can be used on multiple machines.

Some companies are now using the parallel printer port for attaching CD-ROMs—a very easy way to go.

Multidisc Systems

Even though you have over 650MB on a disc, there will be many times when it doesn't have the programs or information that you need at the moment. For instance, I have a telephone directory of the whole country on five CD-ROM discs from PhoneDisc (800-284-8353). Each disc covers a certain section of the country. Ordinarily, to change discs, you have to eject the disc and put a new disc in.

To solve this type of problem, several companies have developed multidisc systems. Panasonic has a 12x Big 5 system that holds five CD-ROM discs. You can then switch to any one of the five. Following are a few other companies who make multidisc systems. Call them for a brochure or visit their Web sites.

Alps Electric
    800-825-2577
    www.alpsusa.com

NEC Technologies
    800-632-4636
    www.nec.com

Panasonic Computer Peripherals
    800-742-8086
    www.panasonic.com

Pioneer New Media
    800-444-6784
    www.pioneerusa.com

Smart & Friendly Co.
    800-959-7001
    www.smartandfriendly.com

In addition, there will probably be many more companies who offer multidisc systems by the time you read this.

Multidrive Systems

Several companies manufacture multidrive systems for network servers and other high-end users. Of course, anything that is high end is usually highly expensive. They may have 4 to 14 drives or more and may cost from $2000 up to $18,000 or more.

Here are some of the companies who offer multidrive systems:

JVC
    800-828-1582
    www.jvc.com

Logicraft
    800-308-8750
    www.logicraft.com

Meridian
    800-755-8324
    www.mtc.com

NSM Jukebox
    630-860-5100
    800-238-4676
    www.nsmjukebox.com

Plasmon IDE
    612-946-4100
    www.plasmon.com

JVC has several changers and network devices. Their CL-100 CD-Library gives you access to 100 different discs. In addition, the NSM Mercury Jukebox gives you access to up to 150 discs.

Build Your Own Multidrive/Multidisc System

You can build your own system and save a bundle. The cost of CD-ROM drives are coming down every day. Just a short time ago, I paid over $400 for a 2x drive. I recently bought a 32x for less than $50. They will no doubt be less than that by the time you read this. Your Pentium III or Socket 7-type motherboard with the built-in IDE interfaces allows you to easily install four IDE devices, and there can be any mix of CD-ROM drives or hard drives in your system. If you buy one of the Promise controller boards, you can have as many as eight IDE devices. I talked about the Promise boards in Chapter 6. You can also check out their Web site at www.promise.com.

As mentioned earlier in the chapter, if you need more CD-ROM drives, you can set up a SCSI system and have up to seven drives. By plugging a second SCSI adapter into the first adapter, you could add six drives on the first adapter, then seven on the second adapter. Theoretically, you could have up to 49 units on SCSI adapters. There aren't any CD-ROMs available at the moment for universal serial bus (USB), but there will probably be several by the time you read this. The USB system will allow up to 128 peripherals to be attached. That would probably be all that you could possibly need, especially if you have a small office/home office (SOHO).

Some multidisc drives are selling for just a little more than $300. (Prices quoted are for comparison only and will be less by the time you read this.) You can put together a system with three or four of the multidisc drives for a whole lot less than $18,000, or even less than $2000.

Tray Load

Many of the early CD-ROM drives used a caddy to load the discs. They were more expensive to build, and you had to have several caddies on hand or stop and load the disc in a caddy each time you wanted to use the disc. The caddy has a clear-plastic hinged cover. The caddy encloses the disc and protects it from dirt and dust and unnecessary handling. When the caddy is inserted into the drive, a metal sliding door moves to one side for the head access. It is similar to the sliding door on 3½-inch floppies.

Most all of the CD-ROM drives now come with a tray to hold the disc. You push a button and the tray comes out, then you drop the disc in with the label facing up and push the tray back in.

Note: You should be very careful in handling the discs to prevent fingerprints, scratches, coffee stains, or other damage to the bright side of the disc. Try to handle them by the edge.

You may have heard this story: When the CD-ROM drives with the tray first came out, one company got a call to their tech support. The guy said that his coffee holder had broken and wanted to know how he could get it repaired. The technician had no idea what the guy was talking about. He questioned him a bit more and finally found out that the guy was using the CD-ROM tray as a coffee holder.

CD-ROM Recorders (CD-R)

There are several companies who are now manufacturing CD-ROM recorders. As mentioned previously, when they were first introduced, they were very expensive, at around $10,000 for a system. Some companies are now offering CD recorders for less than $200. The blank discs cost from $1 to $2 at this time. When buying blank discs for CD-R and CD-R rewriteables, you must buy blank discs that are specified according to speed of device—4x needs 4 speed; 8x needs 8 speed; and so on.

In 1989, Taiyo Yuden of Japan developed an organic dye that could be combined with a reflective gold plating on a blank disc. A laser could then be used to burn pits in the disc, and it would have the same qualities of a standard CD-ROM disc. In addition, this disc offered the capability of multisession—that is, data can be added from time to time. When a disc is stamped out at a factory, nothing further can be added. The data on the recordable disc has the same reflective characteristics as that of a standard CD-ROM.

Recordable CD-ROMs have several advantages. If only one or two discs are needed, they can be made for the cost of the media. In addition, the disc is available immediately; you might have to wait for a week or more to have a disc made up at a factory. Of course, if a large number is needed, then it would be better to have a factory master made to replicate them. But even then, it would be advisable to record a single disc, check it for accuracy and content, then have a master made. Another reason to record the disc in house is to guarantee the security of the data. Recording a small number of discs in house from time to time is much less expensive than having them mastered and replicated.

Some large businesses have huge databases of customers, invoices, prices, and other information. Businesses may also have large parts catalogs that must be updated frequently. They can use a single disc to replace parts catalogs. A CD-ROM disc can store millions of part numbers, descriptions, drawings, cost, location, and any other pertinent information.

In addition to paperwork records that are stored, some businesses must keep and archive important records that should never be changed. If the records and data are stored on magnetic tape and floppy disks, they could be lost or destroyed. The magnetic properties of tape, floppy, and hard disks may gradually deteriorate, and the data may be good for less than 10 years. It is also very easy for magnetic material to be erased, either accidentally or purposefully. A CD-ROM disc should last for 75 to 100 years or more. It is much, much easier to search and find an item on a CD-ROM disc than on a backup tape or in a stack of paperwork.

Large organizations may have acres of file cabinets overflowing with paper. Some studies have shown that 90 percent of the files are never looked at again after they are stored. What a terrible waste of space and paper. If businesses replaced the millions of file folders and cabinets with CD-ROM discs, they could regain millions of square feet of office space. We could also save thousands of trees if businesses saved documents electronically or on CD-ROM discs instead of putting everything on paper.

CD-ROM discs are an excellent way to make backups and to store and archive data. The technology also makes it very easy to share large files with other computers, whether across the room, across the country, or across the world. The discs can be shipped for a very nominal price, and you won't have to worry too much about the data being erased or damaged.

CD-ROM discs can be read by any standard CD-ROM drive. Most of the CD-ROM recordable systems record at 4x or 8x. Faster systems are being developed and will be available by the time you read this. They can usually record at a fairly low speed but play back at a higher speed. With an 8x CD-R, you could record 74 minutes of music in about 10 minutes. With a 4x CD-R, it would take take about twice that much time. Most CD-R systems will let you have multisession recording. If you don't have enough data to completely fill a disc, you can record as much as you have, then come back later and record more. This is also the system used for photo CDs.

When you send data to CD-R, it will probably be from a hard disk. Either the hard disk or the CD-R should be SCSI. If both drives are IDE, there may be some conflict and cause a slowing of data transfer. There won't be as much of a problem if both of them are SCSI.

Organizing Data

There are systems that can be used to scan information into a computer and then compress it. The information can then be indexed, so that any item can be quickly found and accessed, and then be stored on a CD-ROM disc; a write once, read many (WORM) disc; or other storage device.

COLD (computer output to laser disc) is a recent acronym that describes this process. With a good COLD system and the proper hardware and software, millions of documents can be placed on a few small discs. To learn more about this technology, you can subscribe to the following imaging magazines, which are free to qualified subscribers:

Imaging Business Magazine
  301-343-1520

Advanced Imaging
  445 Broad Hollow Rd.
  Melville, NY 11747-4722

Managing Office Technology
  1100 Superior Ave.
  Cleveland, OH 44197-8092

If you are in any kind of business at all, you should be able to qualify. Several other magazines are listed in Chapter 19.

Here are just a few of the many companies who offer recordable CD-ROM systems:

Alos
  800-431-7105
  www.alosmc.com

CMS Enhancements
  800-327-5773
  www.cmsenh.com

Consan Storage
  800-229-3475
  www.consan.com

Creative Labs
  800-998-5227
  www.creativelabs.com

DataDisc
  800-328-2347
  www.datadisc.com

DynaTek Automation
  800-461-8855
  www.dynatek.ca

Eastman Kodak
  800-235-6325
  www.kodak.com

Hewlett-Packard
  800-810-0134
  www.hp.com/go/storage

JVC
  714-261-1292
  www.jvcinfo.com

Microboards Tech.
  800-646-8881
  www.microboards.com

MicroNet Tech.
  714-453-6100
  www.micronet.com

Optima Tech.
  800-411-4237
  www.optimatech.com

Philips Proffesional
  800-235-7373
  www.pps.philips.com

Pinnacle Micro
  800-553-7070
  www.pinnaclemicro.com

Pioneer New Media
  800-444-6784
  www.pioneerusa.com

Plasmon
  800-451-6845
  www.plasmon.com

Smart & Friendly
  800-366-6001
  www.smartandfriendly.com

Sony
  800-352-7669
  www.sel.sony.com

TEAC America
  213-726-0303
  www.teac.com

Several companies manufacture blank discs for the CD-R systems. The ProSource Company (800-903-1234) offers blank discs from several companies. The discs may cost from $1 to $2 each. They also have several other items that are needed, such as labels and label applicators.

Installing CD-ROM Drives

Following are step-by-step instructions on installing a CD-ROM drive.

Step 1. Remove the Computer Cover

There are two main types of CD-ROM drives at this time: IDE and SCSI. The first step in installing any of these drives is to remove the cover from your computer. Then make sure that you have a standard $5\frac{1}{4}$-inch bay that is accessible from the front panel. Figure 8-5 shows my Plextor 8/20 being installed in an open bay beneath my Pioneer DVD.

Once the drive is in the bay, use two small screws on each side to mount the drive to secure it.

Step 2. Set Any Jumpers or Switches

You should have received some sort of documentation and installation instructions with your drive. If you are installing more than one IDE

Figure 8-5
Installing a CD-R in a bay beneath a DVD.

Figure 8-6
Figure 8-6
The rear of an IDE
CD-ROM. The 4 pins
on the right are for
the power cable. The
main 40-wire cable
connector is in the
center. The two small
jumpers configure it
as slave or master.
The small cable is the
audio cable that
connects to the
sound board.

CD-ROM drive or an IDE hard disk on the same cable, they must be configured as master and slave.

IDE CD-ROM Drives   Most Pentium-type motherboards have a secondary IDE interface built in as a set of upright pins. The IDE interface can support up to four devices. Set any jumpers or switches necessary, then follow instructions below for plugging in cables and boards. The IDE CD-ROM drives come with driver software, so they are fairly easy to install.

Figure 8-6 shows the rear of an IDE CD-ROM. The four pins in the connector on the right are for the power cable. The 40-pin connector is for the main ribbon cable. The connector is keyed so that it can only be plugged in properly. The two white jumpers configure the drive as a master or slave. The small cable on the left is the audio cable. The other end plugs into the sound board.

SCSI CD-ROM Drive   You may have up to seven SCSI devices installed, but each device must be assigned a logical unit number (LUN) between 0 and 7. The LUN is usually determined by a set of jumpered pins. Check your documentation. If you already have other SCSI devices installed, you must determine which LUNs are assigned to them and configure the CD-ROM drive for a number not being used.

Step 3. Install the Cables

There should be two sets of 40 upright pins on the motherboard for IDE devices. One set will be marked "primary" and the other set "secondary." The primary set is used for the hard disk that will be the boot drive and a second hard drive if you have one. The CD-ROM will use the secondary pins. The IDE CD-ROM drives should have a flat 40-wire ribbon cable—the same type used for IDE hard drives. It should have a connector on each end and one in the middle. Some motherboards provide a shell around the pins with a cutout so that the cable can only be plugged in properly. Without the shell, the connector can be plugged in backwards. Make sure that the colored wire on the ribbon cable goes to pin 1 on the motherboard.

For SCSI drives, you will have a 50-wire ribbon cable that connects to the back of the CD-ROM and then to a SCSI interface board. Most SCSI interface boards have provisions for two cable connections. If you have more than two SCSI devices, you may need to buy a cable with two or more connectors in the center.

Like the IDE cables, the SCSI flat-ribbon cable will also have a different-colored wire on one side. This wire will go to pin 1 of the connectors. Most SCSI connectors will have a shell with a square slot on one side. The cable connector will have a square elevation that fits in the slot so that they can only be plugged in correctly. Otherwise, look for an indication of pin 1 on the CD-ROM drive and on the interface board. If you plan to use your CD-ROM drive with a sound card, and I strongly recommend that you do, you will have to install a small audio cable.

Figure 8-7 shows a 50-pin SCSI connector on a CD-ROM drive. To the left of this connector are jumper pins for setting the logical unit number of the drive. You can have several SCSI drives. The jumpers are similar to those on the IDE drives that configure them as a master or slave. The SCSI drives can be configured for LUN 0 to 7. There is also a small connector for attaching the audio cable.

Step 4. Install the Drive Power Cable

Plug in one of the four-wire power cables to the drive. The connector can only be plugged in one way.

Figure 8-7
A 50-pin SCSI
connector. To the left
of the connector are
jumper pins for LUN
configuration. To the
left of those pins are
pins for audio cable.

Step 5. Install the Software Drivers

All of the drives should come with some sort of installation and driver software, usually on a floppy disk. The vendor may not provide it unless you ask for it. Windows 95/98 now has most CD-ROM drivers, so you may not need the drivers from the vendor.

If you have other SCSI devices already installed, then you probably have SCSI driver software such as the Corel SCSI. If not, you should contact your vendor for SCSI driver software. Once the SCSI software is installed, it will automatically recognize the new drive when you boot up.

Step 6. Test the System

Test the system with a CD-ROM disc. If everything works, then reinstall the computer cover.

Sources

There are several companies and vendors for CD-ROM and DVD-ROM drives, and thousands of CD-ROM disc titles. Several DVD-ROM titles are currently available and there will be lots more of them very soon. Just look in any computer magazine and you will see dozens of ads. Also, check the magazines listed earlier in the chapter.

Monitors and Adapters

You will need a good monitor to go with your new system. What you intend to use your computer for may determine what type and size monitor to buy. You must also consider what type of adapter to buy. You may have a very expensive monitor, but it won't do you much good unless you have a good adapter to drive it. Remember that you will spend all of the time you are at the computer looking at the monitor, so buy the biggest and best monitor you can afford. Try to get the best.

Lots of 15-inch monitors are available now at very reasonable prices. I recently bought one for $150. For just a few dollars more, you can get a 17-inch or a 19-inch model. Even the 20- and 21-inch models are fairly reasonable now.

Following are several companies who manufacture large-screen monitors:

ADI Systems
  800-228-0530
  www.adiusa.com

CTX International
  800-888-2120
  www.ctx.com

Eizo Nanao Technologies
  800-800-5202
  www.eizo.com

Mitsubishi Electronics America
  800-843-2525
  www.mitsubishi-display.com

Princeton Graphic Systems
  800-747-6249
  www.prgr.com

Sampo Technology
  770-449-6220
  www.sampotech.com

Sony Electronics
  800-352-7669
  www.sony.com/technology

ViewSonic
  800-888-8583
  www.viewsonic.com

You can call the companies and ask them to send a brochure. Or better yet, visit their Web sites for information and specifications. ViewSonic, and many of the other manufacturers, have lots of information on their Web sites for those who may be new to monitors. They also list some of the features that are desirable in choosing a monitor.

Flat-Panel LCD Monitors

Manufacturers are making bigger and bigger liquid crystal displays (LCD; also called thin-film transistor, or TFT) for laptops. They are also now making them for desktop computers. These monitors use a liquid crystal sealed between two pieces of polarized glass. The polarity of the liquid crystal is changed by an electric current to vary the amount of light that can pass through. Because they require a separate transistor for each pixel, LCDs are still rather expensive. Depending on the size of the display or monitor, it may require several million transistors.

If some of the transistors prove to be defective after the panel has been made, there is no way to repair it; there will be a blank spot in the screen wherever the defective transistor is. If there are only three or four defective transistors and if they are not clumped together, it may not be noticeable. But if there are several in one area, the screen must be rejected. Because there are a large number that are rejected, prices are driven up.

Several companies have developed LCD panels, from 12 inches to as large as 20 inches measured diagonally. Some may be as thin as 2.5 inches up to about 7 inches deep and weigh about 20 pounds. They can sit on the desktop or they can easily be hung on a wall. The LCD panels support 24-bit color at a resolution of 1280 × 1024. They require no special adapter, but of course they work best with the better ones. Figure 9-1 shows a flat-panel monitor.

Many people worry about the radiation from the monitor. There are over 25,000 volts bombarding the backside of the monitor face constantly. However, no good evidence that radiation produced by a monitor can be harmful has come to light. Still, a few companies have made a lot of money selling special shields for the monitor. The LCD uses a very low voltage, so there is not any concern about radiation.

The bad news is that at this time a 20-inch LCD monitor costs about $4000. A couple of years ago, they were over $8000. They will eventually become more reasonable, and some companies have smaller LCDs for less cost. Presently, a 15-inch LCD may cost from $900` and up to $1500. Prices will be different by the time you read this.

There are some companies who are manufacturing rear-projection screen monitors. Using lenses and mirrors, a fairly small LCD screen can be projected onto a much larger screen at the same resolution. They

Figure 9-1
A flat-panel monitor.

would work on the same principle used by the large rear-projection television screens. Several companies who make monitors also manufacture LCD projection devices for presentations. So they have much of the technology needed.

We are now becoming more and more energy conscious. Most of the cathode ray tube (CRT) monitors are real wattage hogs. Although most now have an energy-saving mode, they may still require from 100 to 175 watts. Conversely, the largest LCD monitors may only require 40 watts.

The standard output of most video adapters is analog for the standard CRT. Most of the LCD panels are digital, so they have to take the analog signal and convert it to digital. New standards and new adapters will allow digital output.

The basic CRT technology is over 100 years old. There doesn't seem to be much room for further improvements. Eventually, the LCD technology will replace the CRT for most applications.

Here are some LCD models, along with the contact information for the companies who make them:

AcerView F51
  800-379-2237
  www.acerperiperals.com

ADI MicroScan 6L
  800-228-0530
  www.adiusa.com

Advan AGM15T
  888-786-1688
  www.advancorp.com

Argon TP15
  310-727-5500
  www.argontechnologies.com

Compaq TFT 5000
  800-345-1518
  www.compaq.com

Dell 1500FP
  800-388-8542
  www.dell.com

Hitachi SuperScan LC150
  800-441-8300
  www.nsa-hitachi.com

IBM T55D
  800-426-7255
  www.ibm.com/pc/us
    /accessories/monitors

Mag Innovision LT541C
  800-827-3998
  www.maginnovision.com

NEC Technologies
  800-632-4636
  www.nectech.com

Nokia 500Xa
  415-331-4244
  www.nokia.com

Number Nine DFP
  888-744-7373
  www.sgi.com/go/flatpanel

Panasonic Panaflat LC50S
  800-742-8086
  www.panasonic.com/alive

Princeton DPP560
  800-747-6249
  www.prgr.com

Sony CPD-L150
800-352-7669
www.sony.com/displays

Toshiba TekBright 50D
800-867-4422
www.toshiba.com

ViewSonic VPA150
800-888-85832
www.viewsonic.com

USB Monitors

Many of the new monitors—both the standard CRTs and the newer LCDs—are now able to connect to the computer by the universal serial bus (USB). You will also be able to connect your keyboard, mouse, scanner, printer, and any of several other peripherals to the USB bus. Instead of having seven or eight cables going to the computer, everything will be attached to the USB, and it will be the only connection. Many newer monitors may act as a USB hub and provide up to five or more connections for a USB-compatible device.

Choosing a Monitor

As with any component, the primary determining factor for choosing a monitor should be what it is going to be used for and the amount of money you have to spend. Try to get a good 15-inch as a minimum. If you can afford it, buy a large 21-inch monitor with super-high resolution and a good adapter board to drive it.

Monitors are usually long-lived. I have a 19-inch Sampo TriSync that is over 12 years old. I also have a 21-inch ViewSonic that is six years old. Both monitors are still going strong. These monitors were very expensive at the time I bought them, but they have been well worth the cost.

The cost of monitors has dropped tremendously. A recent ad in *Computer Shopper* lists some ViewSonic monitors for the following prices:

15 inch	.28mm	$153
17 inch	.26mm (USB)	$320
19 inch	.26mm	$456
21 inch	.25mm	$829

The prices are higher for some models. The overall prices will probably be less by the time you read this.

An article in *PC Computing Magazine* said that a 19-inch monitor can increase productivity over a 17-inch, claiming that a 19-inch monitor can save over $4640 in a one-year period. They also said that the 19-inch provided a productivity boost for almost all types of applications. So even if you have to eat beans for a few days, save your money and buy the biggest you possibly can.

Look for monitors with a refresh rate of at least 72Hz or higher. Look for a dot pitch of at least 0.26mm; 0.24mm is even better, but may be more expensive. The resolution should be at least 800 × 600; 1024 × 768 is better.

Make sure the controls are near the front and easily accessible. The stated screen size of a TV screen and a monitor is very misleading. Remember that the stated size is a diagonal measurement, and even the actual diagonal measurement may seem less than the stated screen size because there is a border on all four sides of the screen. The usable viewing area on my 21-inch ViewSonic monitor is about 15 inches wide and about 11 inches high. The measurements on my old Sampo 19-inch monitor are just fractions of an inch smaller than those of the 21-inch ViewSonic model.

One of the reasons that the screen is not as large as stated is because the screen is markedly curved near the edges on all sides. If you include this curved area, the screen will measure the stated size. But the curved area can cause distortion, so they are masked off and not used.

If you expect to do any kind of graphics or CAD/CAM design work, you will definitely need a good large-screen color monitor with very high resolution. A large screen is almost essential for some types of design drawings so that as much of the drawing as possible can be viewed on the screen.

You will also need a high-resolution monitor for close-tolerance designs. For instance, if you draw two lines to meet on a low-resolution monitor, they may look as if they are perfectly lined up. But when the drawing is magnified or printed out, the lines may not be anywhere close to one another.

Most desktop publishing (DTP) is done in black-and-white print. The high-resolution paper-white monochrome monitors may be all you need for these applications. These monitors can usually display several shades of gray. ("Paper-white" refers to monitors that display characters in black against a pure-white background.)

Normally, most monitors are the landscape type—that is, they are wider than they are high. Many of the DTP monitors are the portrait type; they are higher than they are wide. Many of them have a display area of $8\frac{1}{2} \times 11$ inches. Instead of 25 lines, they will have 66 lines, which is the standard for an 11-inch sheet of paper. In addition, many have a phosphor that will let you have black text on a white background so that the screen looks very much like the finished text. Some of the newer color monitors have a mode that will let you switch to pure white with black type.

What to Look For

If possible, go to several stores and compare various models. Turn the brightness up and check the center of the screen and the outer edges. Is the intensity the same in the center and the outer edges? Check the focus, brightness, and contrast with text and graphics. There can be vast differences even in the same models from the same manufacturer.

Ask the vendor for a copy of the specs. Check the dot pitch. For good high resolution, it should be no greater than 0.28mm, even better would be 0.26mm or 0.24mm. Also check the horizontal and vertical scan frequency specs. For a multiscan, the wider the range, the better. A good system could have a horizontal range from 30kHz to 40kHz or better. The vertical range should be from 45Hz to 70Hz or higher.

Controls

You might also check for available controls to adjust the brightness, contrast, and vertical/horizontal lines. Some manufacturers place them on the back or some other difficult area to get at. It is much better if they are accessible from the front so that you can see what the effect is as you adjust them.

Glare

If a monitor reflects too much light, it can be like a mirror and be very distracting. Some manufacturers have coated the screen with a silicon formulation to cut down on the reflectance. Others have etched the screen for the same purpose. In addition, some screens are tinted to help cut down on glare. If possible, you should try the monitor under various lighting conditions.

If you have a glare problem, several supply companies and mail-order houses offer glare shields that cost from $20 up to $100.

Cleaning the Screens

Since there are about 25,000 volts of electricity hitting the backside of the monitor face, it creates a static attraction for dust. This can distort and make the screen difficult to read. Most manufacturers should have an instruction booklet that suggests how the screen should be cleaned. If you have a screen that has been coated with silicon to reduce glare, you should not use any harsh cleansers on it. Usually, plain water and a soft paper towel will do fine.

Monitor Radiation

Almost all electrical devices emit very low frequency (VLF) magnetic and electrical fields. There have been no definitive studies that prove that this radiation is harmful to a person. In some cases, the emissions are so weak that they can hardly be measured. However, the government of Sweden developed a set of guidelines to regulate the strength of emissions from video display terminals (VDTs).

Several people in this country are also concerned that the VDT radiation might be a problem, so many monitor manufacturers now add shielding to control the emission. If you are worried about VDT emissions, look for monitors that are certified to meet MPR II specifications.

Incidentally, if you use a hair dryer, you will get much more radiation from that than from a monitor.

Green Monitors

The monitor may use 100 to 150 watts of energy. The EPA Energy Star program demands that the energy be reduced to no more than 30 watts when they are not being used. I sometimes sit in front of my monitor for 10 or 15 minutes, doing research, or more likely, with writer's block. All this time the monitor is burning up lots of watts of energy. Many of the new monitors meet the Energy Star specifications, so when there is no activity, they go into a sleep mode where they use very little energy. A small amount of voltage is still applied to the monitor, and it will come back online almost immediately.

Software for Monitor Testing

If you are planning to buy an expensive high-resolution monitor, you might want to buy a software program called DisplayMate for Windows from SONERA Technologies (908-747-6886 or www.displaymate.com). It is a collection of utilities that can perform several checks on a monitor. It lets you measure the resolution for fine lines, the clarity of the image, and distortion. It also has gray and color scales, and a full range of intensities and colors. The software can actually help tweak and fine-tune your monitor and adapter. The setup also helps a person set the controls for the optimum values. About 40 percent or more of the cost for a computer system is for the monitor. It could be well worth it to test the monitor first.

The following are statements from the DisplayMate Web site at www.displaymate.com:

> DisplayMate has been the leader in video utility software for years—without equal. If you've ever read a monitor review in a computer magazine, the editors were probably using DisplayMate Professional, our comprehensive DOS-based video hardware diagnostic. In fact, every single major U.S. computer magazine uses it! DisplayMate is recognized worldwide as the benchmark standard for image quality in PC video.
>
> DisplayMate has won a Best of Show award at COMDEX and has been selected as one of the Best Utilities by the Editors of *PC Magazine*.
>
> Now, DisplayMate for Windows has taken a giant leap forward by pioneering *Monitor Enhancement Technology* that can improve or correct most of the problems that our earlier state-of-the-art diagnostic programs detected.
>
> **How DisplayMate for Windows Works**
> DisplayMate for Windows includes an Expert System and online database that contains everything our leading experts know about improving a mon-

itor's image and picture quality. You look at a special programmed series of test screen images and follow the easy step-by-step instructions that are shown on-screen for correcting or improving the problem you're experiencing. The expert advice is even customized to your particular video system. DisplayMate for Windows assumes no prior video knowledge and is designed for both video novices and experts alike.

First you'll go through our precision "Set Up Program," which produces top-notch image quality right away. We'll show you how to properly set every control on your monitor and video board to its optimum value.

Then our "Tune-Up Program" actually improves image quality through expert manipulation of monitor and video board controls. DisplayMate will improve sharpness and contrast, reduce certain forms of geometric distortion, minimize or eliminate annoying moiré patterns, and improve color and gray-scale accuracy. Once you get used to a perfectly tuned display, you'll want to use DisplayMate for Windows regularly—daily if you have critical eyes or critical applications and weekly to correct for the inevitable drift of hardware with time.

So Advanced that We Guarantee It Will Work for You
SONERA Technologies guarantees that DisplayMate's revolutionary Monitor Enhancement Technology will make any monitor look better than it ever has before. A really good analogy is that DisplayMate will do for your monitor what a Diagnostic Test Center does for your car: use advanced technology to expertly bring it up to top performance.

Runs under ALL PC Operating Systems
DisplayMate for Windows automatically configures itself to run under Windows 95/98, Windows 3.1x, and Windows NT. Plus it also runs under OS/2 and on Apple Macintoshes and UNIX Workstations using Soft Windows or Virtual PC. The DisplayMate Utilities are designed to help you achieve the highest possible image quality and picture quality on any computer monitor, LCD display, video projector, television, HDTV, or any type of display device that can be connected directly or indirectly to a computer. DisplayMate guarantees to improve the image and picture quality on any display.

You can use DisplayMate to compare and evaluate displays you're thinking of buying. Our video diagnostic products will thoroughly test, including your entire video system for performance and compatibility, the monitor, video board, and video BIOS. DisplayMate's rich set of color and gray-scale patterns are also essential for accurate printer set up and calibration.

DisplayMate is the only utility in the world that is devoted to monitors and video boards. The product is easy to use. There is no learning time.

DisplayMate works by presenting a slide show of special highly sensitive test screen images. You simply look at them and follow the easy step-by-step instructions and expert online advice and guidance. The result is a complete video system Tune-Up with your display performing at its absolute best.

Here are some monitor tips that can be found at the DisplayMate Web site:

1. *How Picky Are You?*   No video display is perfect, including the best and most expensive monitors, so be prepared to accept some compromises in image and picture quality. Remember, you may be looking at that monitor for several thousand hours! Every single major computer magazine in the USA uses DisplayMate to test and evaluate monitors.

   You can gain similar insight into monitor performance and capabilities by taking along a copy of DisplayMate when you go monitor shopping.

2. *Know What Bothers You the Most*   Different people are bothered by different image quality imperfections. It's important to identify the ones that bother you, and then prioritize them. The most common problems that bug people include: color misregistration, fuzzy image, moiré patterns in the image, geometric distortion, tilted image, flicker, glare, and screen reflections.

   Look for monitors with controls that can adjust the imperfections that bug you the most: for example, look for convergence controls if color misregistration is at the top of your list.

3. *The More Controls on Your Monitor the Better*   Monitors are now coming with more and more end-user accessible controls that allow you to adjust and correct problems in the image.

   Besides the mandatory Brightness, Contrast, Size, and Position controls, you may find Focus, Convergence, Tilt, Pincushion, Keystone, Moir, Color Temperature, RGB Color Drive and Cutoff, and Manual Degaussing controls.

   Advanced controls found on only a few monitors include: Dynamic Focus, Dynamic Convergence, Color Purity, Pincushion Phase, and Pincushion Balance. They're all very useful. The more controls you have, the better the image and picture quality on your monitor will be.

   Don't worry if you don't know how to adjust some of the more obscure controls, DisplayMate can show you how.

4. *Watch Out for Sample-to-Sample Variations*   There is generally a significant sample-to-sample variation between monitors of the same make and model, even among the best brands. Monitors are actually

delicate precision analog instruments. They are affected by variations in components, assembly, and factory calibration. They are also particularly affected by how much they bounce around during shipment and handling. If you're buying from a store rather than mail order, then check out the actual monitor you're getting with DisplayMate before you pay for it and take it home. If you're buying mail order, then try to get an exchange capability in case there is a problem.

5. *Carefully Set All the Controls on Your Monitor and Video Board* Many users don't know how to adjust some of the controls on their monitor or video board. If you don't take the time to properly set every control, then they'll actually make matters worse rather than better.

   DisplayMate includes specialized Test Patterns to precisely adjust every one of the controls to its optimum value. Detailed online information and instructions explain what to look for and what to do. For example, setting the Brightness and Contrast Controls is straightforward, but requires four separate Test Patterns in DisplayMate to do it accurately. The payoff is obtaining an optimum gray-scale with optimum contrast.

6. *Take Advantage of the Inherent Image Quality Trade-Offs Between Controls* Most of the monitor's image parameters are interdependent. Changing one control will often directly or indirectly affect another. While this is a complication, it's also an opportunity, because some things can be improved at the expense of others, based on your own preferences.

   For example, the higher you set the refresh rate, the lower the image flicker, but the fuzzier the image is likely to appear due to limitations in video bandwidth. Setting the refresh rate to the highest values allowed by your monitor and video board is not likely to be the best visual compromise setting.

   DisplayMate tells you which are the important trade-offs and provides Test Patterns that let you decide what the best overall visual compromises are. There are hundreds of suggestions on improving image quality.

7. *Make Sure You Get a Sharp Video Board* Image quality and image sharpness vary significantly among video board brands and models. Try out different boards with the same monitor to compare the differences.

8. *Keep the Monitor in Good Tune* Many users will set the controls as best as they can when the monitor and video board are first installed, and then forget about them. Monitors drift as they warm up, they'll drift a bit during the day, and they'll age over a period of weeks and months.

Environmental factors such as room lighting are also important, and can vary because of changing sunlight. How often you need to adjust the monitor controls depends upon how stable your hardware is, the nature of your application, and how discriminating you are. Once you become aware of image quality issues, you'll become sensitized to them. Things that you glossed over or tolerated before will no longer be acceptable.

3D Video Cards

If you do a lot of game playing, a 3D graphics card will make the games much more realistic. But 3D graphics cards are also needed for animation, simulation, 3D Web authoring, CAD, and other graphics applications. The 3D cards need a lot more memory than a standard graphics card—at least 8MB for games and at least 8MB for good CAD work. Most of the faster cards have up to 32MB of memory onboard.

Vendors usually provide one or more drivers for the cards and provide updated drivers that can be downloaded from their Web sites. The 3D cards will provide good 2D as well as 3D.

Much of the newer software for games and animation is now 3D. In order to display 3D images, it takes billions of calculations per second. An assembly line, called the 3D pipeline, does the number crunching. To create the illusion of motion, the 3D pipeline must process a new stream of data for each individual scene. An object's position must be recalculated each time it is moved. The geometric data is processed by the CPU, then passed back to the video card. The CPU also calculates the surface color of each object.

Most of the videocards now have a large amount of onboard memory that helps ease the strain placed on the CPU. You can understand why the more powerful and faster CPUs are better for graphics, images, and games. AMD's 3Dnow! and Intel's SSE Instructions help speed up the calculations.

Here are some 3D software companies:

Caligari Corp.
  800-351-7620
  www.caligari.com

MetaCreations
  800-846-0111
  www.metacreations.com

Microsoft 3D Movie Maker
  800-426-9400
  www.microsoft.com

NewTek Lightwave 3D
  800-843-8934
  www.newtek.com

Several companies make 3D adapters. Below are a few companies and some of their cards. These cards were tested and reviewed in a recent issue of *Maximum PC*.

ATI All-In-Wonder
905-882-2600
www.atitech.com

Hercules Terminator
800-532-0600
www.hercules.com

Diamond Stealth and Viper
800-468-5846
www.diamondmm.com

Guillemot Maxi Gamer Xentor
888-893-2648
www.guillemot.com

Matrox Millenium G400
800-301-1408
www.matrox.com

3Dfx Voodoo 2 and 3
888-367-3339
www.3dfx.com

Figure 9-2 shows an ATI All-In-Wonder board with TV, video, and graphics all in one board.

Here are a couple of virtual reality products:

SimulEyes VR
Stereo Graphics
800-746-3937

Virtual I-Glasses
Virtual I-O
800-646-3579

Figure 9-2
The All-in-Wonder adapter board. It has TV, video, and graphics.

There are many other companies who are working on 3D hardware and software. To find them, check out magazines such as the *New Media Magazine*, *CD-ROM Today*, and *Virtual Reality*. In addition, the *Maximum PC Magazine* (800-274-3421, or www.maximumpcmag.com) devotes a lot of space to graphics and games. Almost every issue has several reviews of the fast video boards needed to run these applications.

See Chapter 19 for addresses.

PCI Bus Adapters

Most motherboards now have three or four PCI connectors and three or four ISA plug-in slot connectors. You could use an old 8- or 16-bit ISA adapter on your new computer, but it would be about like hitching up a horse to pull a Cadillac. The PCI bus adapters are much faster than the older graphics and accelerator boards, and they can communicate with the memory bus at 33MHz. The ISA I/O systems are limited to the 8- or 16-bit bus and operate at a speed of 8MHz to 10MHz no matter how fast the CPU is. The old ISA systems are obsolete.

Some Windows, most graphics, and many other applications require a lot of interaction with the CPU. All of the faster adapters are now made for the PCI or the AGP.

AGP Adapters

Accelerated Graphics Port (AGP) adapters are usually equivalent to the PCI adapters. One of the prime uses for AGP is for high-end graphic designers. The other major use is for games. Games are big business, especially 3D games. It takes a lot of memory and CPU power to make them realistic. Most of the newer motherboards will have a special slot for the AGP.

The PCI bus can become quite crowded with so many boards now designed for them. A lot of traffic, especially if it has to communicate with the CPU, can slow things down. Intel developed the AGP to relieve some of the traffic. It is dedicated to communication between the CPU and the video chipset. The original version operates at 2x, or 66MHz. Newer 4x versions run at 133MHz. Some burst activities will allow it to run at 533MHz.

Video Accelerator Boards

The fixed-function cards have accelerator chips with several built-in graphics functions. Because they have built-in functions, they can handle many Windows-type graphics tasks without having to bother the CPU. Newer and better boards are being developed every day to meet the strenuous demands of multimedia for digital video, 3D technology, and full-motion video. Most of these boards are available for the AGP and PCI bus. The graphics accelerator boards can handle graphics and play digital video from several different formats such as Indeo, Motion JPEG, and MPEG. (JPEG is a set of standards set up by the Joint Photographers Experts Group; MPEG is a similar set of standards set up by the Moving Pictures Experts Group. Both standards concern compression of video and motion pictures.)

Video Memory

Having memory on the adapter board saves having to go through the bus to the conventional RAM. Some adapter boards even have a separate plug-in daughterboard for adding more memory. An AGP or PCI accelerator card with lots of onboard memory can speed up the processing considerably.

You should have at least 2MB of memory to display 256 colors in 1024 × 768 resolution. Of course, the more colors displayed and the higher

Figure 9-3
A Diamond Viper 550 AGP 2X video card with 16MB of S DRAM memory.

the resolution, the more memory is required. Many of the cards now come with 16MB or more of video RAM (VRAM) memory on board. The VRAM chips look very much like the older DRAM DIP memory chips, but they are not interchangeable with DRAM. The DRAM chips have a single port; they can only be accessed or written to through this port. The VRAM chips have two ports and can be accessed by one port while being written to in the other. This makes them much faster and a bit more expensive than DRAM. If you expect to do lot of heavy graphics, the VRAM is worth it.

Sources

There are hundreds of adapter manufacturers. I hesitate to mention models because each manufacturer has dozens of different models with different features and resolutions. And they are constantly designing, developing, and introducing new models. I have used several different models of the Diamond adapters and think they are one of the best.

Several computer magazines have tested adapters from the following companies and rated them to be among the best. Call the companies for brochures and more information.

ATI Technologies
   905-882-2600
   www.atitech.ca

Boca Research
   561-997-6227
   www.bocaresearch.com

Diamond Multimedia Systems
   800-468-5846
   www.diamondmm.com

Matrox Graphics
   800-361-1408
   www.matrox.com

Number Nine Imagine 128
   800-438-6463
   www.nine.com

Orchid Technology
   510-683-0300
   www.orchid.com

STB Powergraph 64
   214-234-8750
   www.stb.com

Adapter Software

Most adapter cards will work with any software that you have. But many adapter vendors provide special software drivers that are necessary for high resolution and speed with certain applications. Make sure that the adapter has drivers for all popular graphics type software.

MPEG Boards

The Moving Pictures Experts Group (MPEG) devised a specification for compressing and decompressing graphics and video. Ordinarily, a single frame in a moving picture requires about 25MB to digitize and store. The MPEG system allows a compression up to 100-to-1, so it is possible to store as much as 72 minutes on a 650MB CD-ROM.

Several companies have developed plug-in boards that will allow you to capture and play back video from several different sources such as a VCR, camcorder, CD-ROM, TV, laser disc, and others. Some cards have built-in sound systems, and some can even be supplied with a TV tuner so that you can watch TV on your monitor. One such card is the ATI All-In-Wonder. Visit their Web site at www.atitech.com.

There are now many feature movies that have been compressed to the MPEG specifications. With an MPEG board, you can watch the movies on your high-resolution monitor. It is possible that as the MPEG system becomes more widespread, the PC may become the home entertainment center.

Here are a few companies who manufacture MPEG boards. Call them for brochures and information or visit their Web sites.

Creative Labs
  800-998-1000
  www.creativelabs.com

Diamond Multimedia System
  800-468-5846
  www.diamondmm.com

Genoa GVision DX
  800-934-3662
  www.genoasys.com

Orchid Kelvin MPEG
  510-651-2300
  www.orchid.com

Sigma Real Magic Rave
  510-770-0100
  www.realmagic.com

Using a TV as a Monitor

For some applications such as presentations or playing some games, it would be nice to have a large screen such as a 32-inch TV or even a large projection-type TV to use as a monitor. You can't just plug your PC output into a TV and have it work; however, there are adapter boards that will let you do it. The ATI Technologies All-In-Wonder graphics board will let output to a TV and even bring a TV signal back to the PC.

The All-In-Wonder is a full-featured 2D/3D video accelerator that will work on your standard monitor or on a TV. It has a TV tuner so that you can watch TV on your standard monitor. This board will also accept the output of a VCR for your standard monitor. (Remember that you should not expect the resolution of a TV to be equal to even the poorest monitor.) There are other companies who manufacture similar graphics boards that will allow you to use the TV. Here are some Web sites:

ATI Technologies
    All-In-Wonder
    www.atitech.com

STB Systems
    TV PCI
    www.stb.com

Matrox Graphics
    Rainbow Runner
    www.matrox.com

Wireless Keyboards

If you are using a TV as a monitor, you may want to be a few feet away from it. Most keyboards have about a 4-foot cable. Several companies make wireless keyboards that work off the same principle as the TV remote controls. The Silitek Corp. (www.silitek-corp.com) has one that is rather inexpensive. Wireless Computing (www.wireless-computing.com) also has a wireless keyboard; however, it is a bit more expensive.

Monitor Basics

Many different types of monitors are available with many different sizes, qualities, and of course, prices. In this section, we will discuss a few monitor basics to help you make a better decision in buying your monitor.

The CRT

A monitor is similar to a TV. The main component is the cathode-ray tube (CRT) or picture tube. In some respects, the CRT is like a dinosaur that is left over from the vacuum tube era. Before the silicon age of semiconductors, vacuum tubes operated almost all electronic devices.

Like all vacuum tubes, CRTs use enormous amounts of power and generate lots of heat. Vacuum tubes have three main elements: the cathode, the grid, and the plate. These elements correspond to the emitter, the base, and the collector of the transistor. In a vacuum tube, the cathode is made from metallic material that causes electrons to be boiled off when heated. The filament is made from resistive wire similar to that used in lightbulbs. Also, very much like lightbulbs, the filaments burn out, which causes the tube to fail. Burned-out filaments are the single greatest cause of failure in vacuum tubes. The filaments of computer CRTs are designed a bit better now, so that they don't burn out as often as in the early days.

If a positive direct current (DC) voltage is placed on the plate of a vacuum tube, the negative electrons boiled off from the heated cathode will be attracted to the plate. A control grid is placed between the cathode and plate. If a small negative voltage is placed on the grid, it will repel the negative electrons and keep them from reaching the plate. Zero voltage or a small positive voltage on the grid will let them go through to the plate. As the analog voltage swings up and down on the grid, it acts as a switch that allows a much larger voltage to pass through the vacuum tube.

A voltage as small as a millionth of a volt on the grid of a vacuum tube can create a much larger exact voltage replica on the output of the plate. With the proper voltages on the emitter, base, and collector, a transistor operates much like a vacuum tube, acting as a switch or as an amplifier. A vacuum tube can take a small signal and amplify it.

A vacuum tube may be quite large, requires a lot of space and energy, and produces a lot of heat. A transistor can amplify the same signal, but it requires much less power and space and produces very little heat. The Pentium III has over 7.5 million transistors in a very small enclosure. If you had 7.5 million vacuum tubes, it would fill a large warehouse.

Like the vacuum tube, the CRT has a filament that heats up a cathode to produce electrons. It also has a grid that can shut off the passage of the electrons or let them pass through. The corresponding plate of the CRT is the back of the picture screen, which has about 25,000 volts on it to attract the electrons from the cathode. The back of the screen is coated with a phosphor. Because of the high attracting voltage, the electrons slam into the phosphor and cause it to light up and glow.

A very small, thin beam of electrons is formed. This electronic beam acts very much like a piece of iron in a magnetic field. If four electromagnets are placed around the neck of the CRT—one on top, one on the bottom, and one each side—the beam of electrons can be directed to any area of the screen by varying the polarity of the voltage fed to the electromagnets. If we wanted the beam to move to the right, we would increase the plus voltage on the right magnet. If we wanted the beam to move up, we would increase the plus voltage on the top magnet. With these electromagnets, we can move the beam to any spot on the screen.

The small input signal voltage on the grid of the CRT turns the electron beam on and off to cause portions of the screen to light up. The beam can be caused to move and write on the screen just as if you were writing with a pencil. Alphabetic characters or any kind of graphics can be created in an exact replica of the input signal.

The present day CRTs are like ancient dinosaurs. Many laptops and notebook computers have excellent color screens using transistors. The active matrix-type uses millions of transistors, one to light up each individual pixel. Eventually the large, low-energy LCD screens will be inexpensive enough so that the CRT will become obsolete. Even the television CRTs will be replaced with flat screens that can be hung on a wall.

Monochrome vs. Color

In a monochrome TV or monitor, there is a single "gun" that shoots the electrons toward the back of the screen. Color TVs and color monitors are much more complicated than monochrome systems. During the manufacture of the color monitors, three different phosphors—red, green, and blue (RGB)—are deposited on the back of the screen. Usually a very small dot of each color is placed in a triangular shape. If you use a magnifying glass and look at a color monitor or color TV, you can see the individual dots.

The different phosphors used to make color monitors are made from rare earths. They are designed to glow for a certain period of time after they have been hit by an electron beam.

In a color TV or monitor, there are three guns, each shooting a beam of electrons. The electrons from each gun have no color. But each gun is aimed at a particular color—one to hit only the red dots, one the blue dots only, and one the green dots. They are very accurately aimed so that they will converge or impinge only on their assigned color dots. To make sure that the beams hit only their target, the beam must go through the holes of a metal shadow mask. Being hit by stray electrons causes the shadow mask to heat up. The heat may cause fatigue and loss of focus. Many of the newer monitors use shadow masks made from Invar, an alloy that has good heat resistance.

By turning the guns on or off to light up and mix the different red, green, and blue dots of phosphor, any color can be generated. The Sony Trinitron monitors and TVs use a system that is a bit different. Its three guns are in a single housing and fire through a single lens. Instead of a shadow mask, the Trinitron uses a vertical grill that allows the beams to pass through. The Trinitron system was actually invented in this country, but no one in the TV industry was interested until Sony adopted it.

Dot Pitch

If you look closely at a black-and-white photo in a newspaper, you can see that the photo is made up of small dots. There will be a lot of dots in the darker areas and fewer in the light areas. The text or image on a monitor or a television screen is also made up of dots very similar to the newspaper photo. You can easily see these dots with a magnifying glass. If you look closely, you can see spaces between the dots, much like the dots of a dot-matrix printer. The more dots and the closer together they are, the better the resolution. A good high-resolution monitor will have solid, sharply defined characters and images.

The more dots and the closer together they are, the more difficult it is to manufacture a CRT. The red, blue, and green dots must be placed very accurately and uniformly in order for their specific electron beam to hit them. The amount of space between these dots is referred to as the *dot pitch*. Most standard monitors will have a dot pitch of 0.28 millimeters (mm). The better monitors will have dots that are as close as 0.24mm. Some of the low-cost color monitors may have them from 0.39mm up to 0.52mm. Such monitors may be all right for playing games, but they wouldn't be very good for anything else.

Pixels

Resolution is also determined by the number of picture elements (pixels) that can be displayed. A *pixel* is the smallest unit that can be drawn or displayed on the screen. Although a pixel can be turned on or off with a single bit, to control the intensity and color depth, it may take several bits per pixel.

The following figures relate primarily to text, but the graphics resolution will be similar to the text. Most monitors are designed to display 80 characters in one row or line across the screen. By leaving a bit of space between each row, 25 lines of text can be displayed from top to bottom.

The old color graphics monitor (CGA) could display 640 × 200 pixels. If we divide 640 by 80, we find that one character will be 8 pixels wide. There can be 25 lines of characters, so 200/25 = 8 pixels high. The entire screen will have 640 × 200 = 128,000 pixels. The EGA has 640 × 350, so each cell is 8 pixels wide and 14 pixels high. The Video Electronics Standards Association (VESA) chose 640 × 480 to be the VGA standard and 800 × 600 to be the Super VGA (SVGA) standard. For SVGA it is 800/80 = 10 pixels wide and 600/25 = 24 pixels high. Many of the newer systems are now capable of 1024 × 768, 1280 × 1024, 1664 × 1200, and more. With a resolution of 1664 × 1200, we would have 1,996,800 pixels, or almost 2 million pixels, that could be lit up. We have come a long way from the 128,000 pixels possible with CGA.

Painting the Screen

To put an image on the screen, the electron beam starts at the top left corner. Under the influence of the electromagnets, it is drawn across to the right of the screen, lighting up a very thin line as it moves. Depending on what the beam is depicting, it will be turned on and off by the grid as it sweeps across the screen. When the beam reaches the right side of the screen, it is turned off and sent back to the left side. It drops down a bit and begins sweeping across the screen to paint another line. On a TV set, it paints 262.5 lines in 1/60th of a second. These are all of the even-numbered lines. It then goes back to the top and inter-laces the other 262.5 odd-numbered lines in between the first 262.5. It does this fairly fast, at a frequency of 15,750Hz. (15750/60 = 262.5). So it takes 1/30th of a second to paint 525 lines. This is called a *frame*, so 30 frames are written to the screen in one second.

When we watch a movie, we are seeing a series of still photos flashed one after the other. Due to our persistence of vision, it appears to be con-tinuous motion. It is this same persistence of vision phenomenon that allows us to see motion and images on our television and video screens.

Scan Rate

Obviously, 525 lines on a TV set, especially a large screen, leaves a lot of space in between the lines. If there were more lines, the resolution could be improved. At the time this is being written, the FCC and the TV industry is trying to decide on a standard for a High-Definition Television (HDTV) that would have from 750 to about 1200 lines at 30 frames per second.

At 750 lines, it would paint 375 lines in 1/60th of a second and 750 in 1/30th of a second. For 750 lines, the horizontal frequency would be 22,500Hz. For 1200 lines, the horizontal frequency would be 36,000Hz.

The Vertical Scan Rate

The time that it takes to fill a screen with lines from top to bottom is the *vertical scan rate*. This may also be called the *refresh rate*. The phosphor may start losing some of its glow after a period of time unless the vertical scan refreshes it in a timely manner. Some of the multiscan, or multifrequency, monitors can have several fixed or variable vertical scan rates. The Video Electronics Standards Association (VESA) specifies a minimum of 70Hz for SVGA and 72Hz for VGA systems.

Multiscan

Multiscan monitors can accept a wide range of vertical and horizontal frequencies. This makes them quite versatile and flexible. Many early multiscans could accept both digital and analog signals. Except for the flat panel, almost all monitors sold today are the analog type.

Adapter Basics

An adapter is just as important as the monitor. You can't just plug a monitor into your computer and expect it to function. Just as a hard disk needs an interface with the computer, a monitor needs an adapter to interface with the computer. Our computer monitors are a bit different than a TV. A TV set usually has all of its controlling electronics mounted in the TV console or case and is assembled and sold as a single unit. A computer monitor may have some electronics within its case, but its main controller, the adapter, is usually on a plug-in board on the PC motherboard. This gives us more versatility and utility because we can use different or specialized adapters if needed.

TVs are usually much less expensive than a comparable-sized computer monitor. One reason is because they don't provide the resolution that a computer monitor does.

Because there are several manufacturers who make monitor adapters, there is quite a lot of competition. This has helped to keep the prices fairly reasonable. Most monitors can operate with several different types of adapters. Adapters may cost as little as $40 and up to $1000 or more. Monitors may cost as little as $150 and up to $3000 or more. It would be foolish to buy a very expensive monitor and an inexpensive adapter, or vice versa. You should try to match the capabilities of the monitor and the adapter.

Most monitor adapters have text character generators built onto the board, making them similar to a built-in library. When we send an *A* to the screen, the adapter goes to its library and sends the signal for the preformed *A* to the screen. Each character occupies a cell made up of a number of pixels. The number of pixels depends on the resolution of the screen and the adapter. In the case of the VGA, if all the dots within a cell were lit up, there would be a solid block of dots 10 pixels wide and 24 pixels high. When an *A* is placed in a cell, only the dots necessary to form the outline of the *A* will be lit up. The process is very similar to the formation of dots by a dot-matrix printer when it prints a character.

With the proper software and graphics adapter, you can place lines, images, photos, normal and various text fonts, and almost anything you can imagine on the screen. Almost all adapters sold today have both text and graphics capability.

Depth

True color usually refers to displays with 15-, 16-, or 24-bit depths. *Depth* means that each of the individual red, green, or blue (RGB) color pixels will have a large amount of information about each color. The 15-bit system will have 5 bits of information for each of the three colors. The 16-bit system may have 6 bits for red, 6 bits for green, and 4 bits for blue or a combination of 5:6:5. The 24-bit system will have 8 bits for each color.

Dithering

If a board doesn't have enough power to display the true distinct colors, it may use *dithering* to mix the colors to give an approximation. Dithering takes advantage of the eye's tendency to blur colors and view them as an average. A printed black-and-white photo uses all black dots, but several shades of gray can be printed depending on the number of black dots per inch. A mixture of red dots with white ones can create a pink image. Gradual color transitions can be accomplished by using dithering to intersperse pixels of various colors.

Anti-aliasing

Some low-resolution systems have a "stairstep" effect when a diagonal line is drawn on the screen. Some adapters have the ability to use anti-aliasing to average out the pixels so that a smooth line appears.

Installation

Installing a monitor and adapter is usually fairly easy. Just plug the adapter board into an empty slot and plug in the monitor cable. Then run whatever software drivers that may have come with the board. Virtually all monitors and adapters now conform to the PnP standard, so they are very easy to install and set up. Windows 95/98 has built-in drivers for most major adapters.

Windows lets you easily customize your display. Just click the right mouse button anywhere on the desktop, then choose Properties. Display Properties has four different tabs: Background lets you set or change the desktop's pattern or wallpaper; Appearance lets you modify the color scheme; Screen Saver and Settings let you change the color depth, resolution, and drivers for the monitor and adapter.

Glossary of Monitor Terms from Princeton Graphics

Note: The following glossary is from the Princeton Graphics Web site at www.prgr.com. This section describes specific terms used to describe monitor characteristics and performance.

Active timing This is defined as the portion of the video signal that carries the actual video information. Surrounding this region is the front porch and back porch.

Actual image size The size of the display on the screen is dependent upon the timing signals provided by the video card. The displayable diagonal linear measurement can vary based on the graphic mode being generated and how the monitor responds to the characteristics of the signal.

Aspect ratio The ratio of height to width. Typical aspect ratio for a monitor is 4 to 3 or 1.33. Example: 640/480 = 1.33.

Bandwidth This is a qualitative term used to describe the monitor's video amplifier potential performance. The higher the pixel rate (or format number), the higher the bandwidth required of the video amplifier.

Barrel An outward bowing of the picture.

Brightness Light output measured at the face plate of the CRT; typically measured in foot-lamberts (fL). A minimum brightness level of 20fL when viewing at full-page size is considered acceptable.

Character matrix The total number of horizontal and vertical spaces required per character.

Color balance The ability of the monitor to show and maintain the same color when switching or varying the intensity of the screen.

Convergence The ability of the electron beam to hit precisely the correct phosphor dot.

CRT This abbreviation stands for Cathode Ray Tube, also known as picture tube or screen. The picture tube in a home TV is also a CRT.

Degauss Removes random color swirls caused by changes in the earth's magnetic field. To avoid putting a strain on your monitor, wait at least 10 minutes before pressing the degauss button a second time.

Diagonal linear measurement "Official" screen size is the diagonal measurement of the CRT before it's mounted in the monitor cabinet. Some monitor CRT category sizes are 14″, 15″, 17″, 19″, and 21″.

Dot pitch The distance between the one phosphor dot and the nearest dot of the same color in the line above or below.

Driver A special configuration file written to control a specific device.

Flicker Lit condition of the display caused by mismatch of phosphor and vertical refresh when the phosphor begins to decay prior to being refreshed giving the display the appearance of "flashing."

Focus Sharpness of a pixel or series of pixels on the CRT face plate. Also measured as the spot size.

High-voltage regulation Ability of the high-voltage to respond to changes in beam current. Good high-voltage regulation means a stable display even when changing between different intensity levels.

Horizontal frequency This indicates how long it takes to scan each of the horizontal lines that make up the display. The unit of measurement is kilohertz (kHz). It is directly related to the number of lines and the vertical refresh (frequency) so that the higher the vertical refresh or the number of lines, the higher the horizontal frequency required.

Interlacing Method of significantly increasing data densities at conventional horizontal scan rates. Half the image is refreshed (every other scan line) to produce a field. Two fields are refreshed at rates of 87Hz, forming one 43.5Hz frame. Causes flicker on the display.

Linearity Comparison of a character size to the size of adjacent characters.

Magnetic field effects The monitor is affected by magnetic fields. If your screen develops wrong colors in areas or the picture becomes distorted, you must check what is near your monitor. If your monitor is positioned near a steel cabinet, on a steel desk or bench, or a steel girder imbedded in a wall or ceiling, then all of these things could be magnetized and therefore interfere with the picture tube's electron beams. Try moving the monitor two to three feet away from the suspected source of magnetic field and see if the picture improves. If the picture only looks colored or distorted during certain times, check if you have any speakers near the monitor, because these could radiate magnetic fields strong enough to distort the picture when they are powered-up.

Maximum viewing area   The actual maximum viewing area is dependent upon the size of the plastic or bezel around the CRT. Typically, the maximum possible for a "17-inch monitor" is actually $15\frac{3}{4}$ inches plus or minus $\frac{1}{2}$-inch. In other words, plus or minus $\frac{1}{4}$ inch at the ends of the diagonal measurement.

OSD   OSD stands for On Screen Display. Most monitors today have on-screen menus that will allow you to configure and manipulate settings.

Moiré   An interference pattern generated by the interaction of the electron beam and the shadow mask.

MPRII   The Swedish National Board for Measurement and Testing (SWEDAC) requires that products sold in Sweden comply with a set of safety standards known as MPRII, that covers the levels of magnetic and electrical fields in both the VLF and ELF ranges. It is worth noting that there are no scientific studies that conclude that measurements above MPRII levels are hazardous. To measure emissions, a sophisticated testing area that screens out background radiation needs to be in place.

   Since distance to the CRT and orientation of the measuring device affects measurement, precise placement of the measuring device is essential and difficult to repeat. For the MPR standards, 48 different locations around the monitor need to be measured. In addition, the actual image displayed can have an impact on emissions so that a given set of measurements may not predict the emissions a user would actually encounter.

Orthogonality   A deviation from the true perpendicular of the vertical.

Parallelogram   A deviation of the sides from the true vertical.

Persistence   Phosphor characteristic consisting of the ability to emit light after excitation current of electron beam is removed.

Phosphor   Chemical compound that emits light while being excited by electrons.

Pincushion   An inward bowing of the video image. All monitors experience slight amount of pincushion distortion. The manufacturer has a guideline on what the specification is for each model. The pincushion changes per resolution and also according to the size of the image. Pincushion is similar to bowing or barrel distortion.

Purity The ability of the electron beam to hit precisely the correct phosphor color dot. If a full page of red color is shown on the display, impurity would result in a purple or greenish color region. This impurity can occur if the shadow mask has been damaged or if the screen has become magnetized. Degaussing the screen may fix the problem.

Real-world screen size Starting out with a 17″ monitor, adding the bezel, and then having a border around the actual video image may result in a diagonal picture size of only 14″. With new technology, there is a way to increase the viewing size but there are some limitations.

Tilt The angle of the CRT with respect to the horizontal mounting bracket of the chassis. Tilt can vary depending on the monitor's orientation to the earth's magnetic poles. Monitor manufacturers orient and align their products in the eastern direction. When the monitor is facing a north/south direction, there may be a slight rotation of the image.

Refresh rates An ergonomic issue that is directly related to long-term ease of use. A higher refresh rate translates to a more "flicker"-free display. Bandwidth, horizontal, and vertical scanning rates depict a monitor's ability to provide a higher resolution and refresh rate.

Resolution The number of pixels or dots per linear distance, dots per inch (DPI).

Uniformity Comparison of one area's brightness to an adjacent area. In general, the brightest part of the image will be in the center area. When moving out to the edges, the intensity of image will vary in a non-linear function. This means that one corner of the screen will not be the same brightness as another corner of the screen. A typical CRT manufacturer's specification may call for up to a 30 percent difference between the center area and the corners.

Vertical frequency This indicates how many times per second the monitor can draw all the lines on an entire screen. A higher vertical frequency or refresh rate will produce less flicker.

ViewSonic Information

Frequently Asked Questions (FAQs)

Here is some good information from the ViewSonic Web site:

1. *What should I look for when monitor shopping?* The main hardware factors to consider are the screen size, the maximum refresh rate a monitor will support at the resolution you wish to run, and the num-

ber and type of image adjustment controls provided by the monitor (also look at the simplicity with which the image can be adjusted). With ViewSonic you have a choice of our E2, Graphics, Multimedia, Professional and ViewPanel Series monitors, in CRT sizes ranging from 14″ to 21″ (13.2″ to 20.0″ viewable screen size). Each series offers a unique range of capabilities and features so you can find a monitor that meets your needs and fits your budget.

When buying a monitor there are, in addition, intangible items that should not be overlooked. These include the warranty and customer support put behind the monitor. ViewSonic carries a three-year warranty (on current production models) and has a highly trained customer support staff who will assist you in getting the most from your ViewSonic product. In addition, we also have our exclusive Express Exchange program to minimize your down-time in the event of a product failure.

Health and safety issues should also be a concern. Although there is no conclusive evidence, studies have indicated that there may be a link between health problems such as increased cancer and complications in pregnancy, and exposure to certain low-frequency electromagnetic fields. All current ViewSonic desktop monitors comply with MPRII radiation standards, and several models also comply with the stricter TCO standard. All of our current models are also FCC-Class B compliant, UL listed, and surpass the U.S. Department of Health and Human Standards requirements for electromagnetic radiation of home-use equipment.

2. *What video card do you recommend for my ViewSonic monitor?* We do not make specific recommendations for video cards; however, the card you choose should match the capabilities of your monitor to get the most for your money. For instance, if you have a 17GS, which will support 1024 × 768 resolution at a maximum refresh rate of 86Hz, you will not want a low-end video card that will not provide at least 75Hz refresh rate at this resolution. To assist you, we have put together a Compatibility Chart that matches our product line with the product lines of several major video card manufacturers.

As far as compatibility goes, there are set timing parameters agreed to by VESA (Video Electronics Standards Association) and other industry norms that both monitor and video card manufacturers adhere to in order to prevent hardware conflicts. All ViewSonic monitors are designed to operate under VESA and industry standard timing patterns.

3. *Which of your monitors can I use on my Mac?* We have several monitors that are Macintosh compatible. Please refer to our Macintosh Compatibility Chart.

4. *Which of your monitors can I use on my workstation?* It depends. If you are working on a Sun Workstation, we do have an adapter available to match Sun's video output. This adapter (part number SW1152) can be ordered directly from ViewSonic at a cost of $14.95.* For other workstations, compatibility is dependent upon the timing of the video signal and the output type.

5. *What type of video inputs will your monitors work with?* All ViewSonic monitors accept analog RGB signals with black at zero volts and white at 0.7 volts. In addition, several models will also operate on a zero-to-one volt range. The horizontal and vertical synchronization signals may be one of three types: separate, composite, or sync-on-green. These timing signals are assumed to be at transistor-transistor logic (TTL) levels (except sync-on-green). All ViewSonic monitors can operate with separate horizontal and vertical synchronization signals. Check your User's Guide or call us to see whether your monitor can also accept a composite or sync-on-green timing signal.

   If the video signal from your computer is as described above, the timing of the signal falls within the VESA or industry standard timing patterns, and the horizontal and vertical scanning rates are within the operating range of your monitor, you should not have any compatibility problems. Also look at the output port of the graphics adapter. If it is a 15-pin mini D-Sub connection, no other adapter is needed. Otherwise, a custom adapter to convert your graphics card output to 15-pin mini D-sub (or BNC if your monitor has the capability) is required.

6. *Should I connect my monitor to a UPS (Uninterruptible Power Supply)?* Probably. If you have a UPS for your computer, you will only want critical equipment connected to it, to prolong backup time if there is an extended power failure. Typically you will want to connect only the computer and monitor to a UPS. Printers draw a lot of power when they are operating, and for the most part are not critical during a power outage. In addition, a good UPS will protect your monitor from dangerous spikes and drops as well as surges and brown-outs experienced in many residential and commercial power lines. If you choose to use a UPS, be sure to size the unit properly for the load it will be supporting.

7. *Can I use a power strip to power my monitor?* Some power strips will protect against most line voltage spikes, but be sure not to run too many devices on the power strip or connect several strips to a single

---

*Price subject to change without notice. Dealer inquiries welcome.

wall outlet. Also, do not use the surge protector as a master switch to turn on your entire system. To avoid possible synchronization problems between your monitor and video card, it is best to turn your monitor on a few seconds before powering up your CPU.

8. *Can I use an extension cable on my monitor's video cable?* Maybe. Low-quality extension cables may cause an echo effect resulting in an outline of images on your screen (called a ghosting effect). The reason being, the connector and added cable length increase the impedance seen by the video signal. This increase in impedance creates a mismatch between the signal that the video card sends and what the monitor receives causing a portion of the signal to "bounce" back and forth in the video cable. We do carry a high-quality, shielded, low-impedance extension cable. However, a single-piece cord is a better solution. Image degradation should be expected with cable lengths of twelve feet or more.

9. *Do I need a Plug & Play video card to use your Plug & Play monitors?* Yes and no. Yes, if you want to take full advantage of a Plug & Play operating system such as Windows 95. No, if you just want a monitor that works and you don't mind configuring your system's video parameters manually. That is to say, our monitors that are Plug & Play compatible do have a Display Data Channel (DDC). If you have a Plug & Play system, the display data will be used. If you do not, the data will be ignored.

10. *Do you have an updated .INF file for Windows 95?* Yes. Download the self-extracting file VSINF.EXE from our file area, decompress it, and run the INSTALL.EXE program to update your Windows 95 monitor .INF file. This program also includes a Display Data Channel test for your monitor and video card.

Troubleshooting

1. *Who do I call if I have questions about, or trouble with my ViewSonic product?* Call us at 1-800-888-8583 from 7:00am to 6:00pm PST, or e-mail us anytime at vstech@viewsonic.com. ViewSonic has a professional, highly trained customer support staff who will work with you to get the most from your ViewSonic product.

2. *When I use my monitor at home the image seems to jump or jitter, but when I try it at my office, the picture is solid as a rock. What should I do?* There are two likely culprits to look for: an unreliable power source and/or electromagnetic interference. First, check your power source. If you are using your computer's power supply or an overloaded power strip, try plugging your monitor into a separate wall socket.

Second, check for electromagnetic interference. Usually this is caused by poorly shielded speakers, transformers sitting next to the monitor, or fluorescent lights hanging too closely above the unit. Another possible source is house wires behind the walls near the back of your monitor. To test for interference, try facing your monitor in different directions, or moving your monitor to a new location. If you are experiencing electromagnetic interference there are shielding devices available. Contact our customer support engineers for more information.

3. *I have color spots on my screen. Is this normal?* No, you should have good color continuity across the entire screen area. Most likely the color spots are caused by magnetic interference. The first thing to try is degaussing your monitor. All ViewSonic monitors automatically degauss when first turned on. If your monitor has a manual degauss, simply activate it. Note, however, that for best result you must wait 30 minutes before redegaussing. If your unit does not have a manual degauss feature, simply turn the monitor off for 30 minutes, then power it back up again.

   If degaussing does not help, or if the spots come back after a little while, try rearranging the equipment near your monitor. Devices with magnetic properties (e.g., speakers and transformers) can affect the purity of your monitor. If color spots persist, give us a call for further assistance.

4. *I'm not getting an image on my monitor, just a scrambled mess. What do I do?* This is a synchronization problem. The first thing to look for is a faulty connection between the computer and monitor. Inspect the cables to make sure no pins are bent or loose. If the cable looks OK contact your video card manufacturer to see what the horizontal and vertical scanning frequencies are of the video card at the resolution you are running. They may be outside the range the monitor is capable of using. If this does not take care of things, try your monitor on another system to see if it is the monitor or video card that is malfunctioning. If it is the monitor, give us a call!

5. *Can I use an extension cable on my monitor's video cable?* Maybe. Low-quality extension cables may cause an echo effect resulting in an outline of images on your screen (called a ghosting effect). The reason being, the connector and added cable length increase the impedance seen by the video signal. This increase in impedance creates a mismatch between the signal that the video card sends and what the monitor receives causing a portion of the signal to "bounce" back and forth in the video cable. We do carry a high-quality, shielded, low-impedance extension cable. However, a single-piece cord is a better solution. Image

degradation should be expected with cable lengths of twelve feet or more.

Other Resources

A monitor is a very important part of your computer system. I couldn't possibly tell you all you need to know in this short chapter. One of the better ways to keep up on this ever-changing technology is to subscribe to one or more computer magazines. They frequently have articles about monitors, and, of course, they also have many ads for monitors and adapters.

Input Devices

Before you can do anything with a computer, you must input data into it. There are several ways to input data: with a keyboard or mouse, or through a scanner, bar code reader, voice recognition program, fax device, main frame, or network. This chapter discusses a few of the ways to input data.

Keyboards

By far the most common way to get data into the computer is by way of the keyboard. For most common applications, it is impossible to operate the computer without a keyboard.

The keyboard is a most personal connection with your computer. If you do a lot of typing, it is very important that you get a keyboard that suits you. Not all keyboards are the same. Some have a light, mushy touch, some heavy. Some have noisy keys; others are silent with very little feedback.

A Need for Standards

Typewriter keyboards are fairly standard. There are only 26 letters in the alphabet and a few symbols, so most QWERTY typewriters have about 50 keys. But I have had several computers over the last few years, and every one of them has had a different keyboard. The main typewriter characters aren't changed or moved very often, but some of the very important control keys like Esc, Ctrl, Prtsc, \ (backslash), the function keys, and several others might shift from keyboard to keyboard. A few years ago, most keyboards had 101 keys. Windows 95 and multimedia functions have caused several more keys to be added. Keyboards may now have up to 109 or more keys. The extra keys provide application shortcuts for Windows 95 and other task functions.

Currently, there are well over 400 different keyboards in the United States. Many people make their living by typing on a keyboard, and many large companies have systems that count the number of keystrokes that an employee makes during a shift. If the employee fails to make a certain number of keystrokes, then that person can be fired. Can you imagine the problems if the person has to frequently learn a new keyboard? I myself am not a very good typist in the first place and I have great difficulty using different keyboards.

There definitely should be some sort of standard. Innovation, creating something new that is useful and needed and makes life better or easier, is great. That type of innovation should be encouraged everywhere. But many times changes are made just for the sake of differentiation without adding any real value or functionality to the product. This applies not only to keyboards but to all technology.

The Windows Keyboards

It appears that we may be nearing a standard of sorts. Most newer keyboards now have three or four extra keys. A couple of these keys probably have the Microsoft Windows logo on them. If you have one of the new keyboards with the Microsoft logos, pressing one of those keys will let you switch from one program to another. It will put the program in the taskbar while you work on the other program. When you are ready to come back to the original program, just point to the program and it will bring you back to the same place you were when you switched. This is a handy utility. Quite often I need to stop writing and look up something on the Internet. I can press one of the Windows keys, access the Web, then come back to exactly where I left off.

Carpal Tunnel Syndrome

Businesses spend billions of dollars each year for employee health insurance. Of course, the more employee injuries, the more the insurance costs. Carpal tunnel syndrome (CTS) has become one of the more common complaints. CTS causes pain and/or numbness in the palm of the hand, the thumb, and the index and ring fingers. The pain may radiate up into the arm. Any movement of the hand or fingers may be very painful. CTS is caused by pressure on the median nerve where it passes into the hand through the carpal tunnel and under a ligament at the front of the wrist. Either one or both hands may be affected. Treatment often requires expensive surgery, which may or may not relieve the pain.

CTS most commonly affects those people who must use a computer for long periods of time. Keying in data is a very important function in this computer age. That is the job of many employees, eight hours a day, every day. CTS is usually caused by the way the wrist is held while typing on the keyboard. There are several pads and devices to help make the typing more comfortable. I have a foam rubber pad that is the length of the keyboard and is about four inches wide and three-quarters of an inch thick. I can rest and support my wrists on this pad and still reach most of the keys. Many of the vendors give them away at shows like COMDEX.

Repetitive strain injury (RSI) is about the same as CTS. Many employees are asking for workers' compensation insurance and taking companies to court because of RSI. At this writing, there are several cases in court against IBM, Apple, and several other large computer manufacturers. CTS and RSI injuries have cost millions of dollars in loss of work days, so it has become a serious problem. In California, for instance, workers' compensation programs were costing millions of dollars. In 1997, a law was passed requiring all employers with more than 10 employees to provide special training to injured workers and others doing similar work. The employers must try to identify and combat potential injury hazards with corrective action. Possible steps are adjusting desks for typists with sore wrists and allowing more rest breaks. The law also encompasses measures for those who may be lifting heavy weights or other repetitive tasks that could be injurious.

Before the computer revolution, thousands and thousands of people, mostly women, sat at a typewriter eight or more hours a day typing on keyboards that are similar to computer keyboards. Yet there were few, if any, cases of CTS or RSI ever reported. It is a disorder that has become prevalent only in the last few years. Last year, 308,200 cases were reported. The reason for the injuries might be that computer keyboards lie nearly flat, whereas typewriter keyboards have more slant and were usually placed at a different height. Another factor may have been that the typewriter limited the typist's speed and repetition. With the computer, some data input workers can do as many as 13,000 keystrokes per hour.

Some of the measures that are suggested to help prevent RSI and CTS are to pause frequently and stretch your hands and upper body. The desk and chair should be adjusted so that both feet rest easily on the floor.

Ergonomic Keyboards

The Key Tronic company developed an ergonomic keyboard for Microsoft. Like most products with a brand name, it is a bit expensive at $99. Several other companies have also developed similar ergonomic keyboards for less than half that price. ALPS Electric (800-825-2577), Cirque Corp. (800-454-3375), and Northgate (800-548-1993) all have Glidepoint keyboards with pads that can take the place of a mouse. They have a square pad below the arrow keys. You use your finger on the pad to move the cursor. To click, just tap the pad with your finger or press one of the three nearby buttons. The Northgate OmniKey is ergonomically shaped with the keys separated and angled like the Microsoft Natural keyboard. Mitsumi (800-648-7864) also has a low-cost ergonomic-shaped keyboard. Figure 10-1 shows a clone ergonomic key-

Figure 10-1
An ergonomic key-
board helps reduce
carpal tunnel
syndrone.

board with a touch pad that is quite similar to the keyboards mentioned above. This clone sells for about half what the Microsoft and other similar brand names cost. It has a PS/2-type keyboard connector, which is much smaller than a standard AT keyboard connector. But it comes with an adapter so that it can be used on either system. The touch pad must be connected to one of the serial ports, just like a normal mouse. This port connector and cable is part of the keyboard cable. Advantages of the touch pad are that it does not have the mouse cable on the desktop and does not require desktop space for a mouse pad. The keyboard has a switch that will allow you to switch off the touch pad and use a standard mouse if you want to. In addition, this clone keyboard has the Windows 95 extra keys. It also has an extra Tab and an extra Backspace key. Most of the other keys are the same as the standard 101 keyboard, but they are angled, separated, and raised in the center. Becoming accustomed to it has taken me a bit of time.

Even though some of the ergonomic keyboards are a bit expensive, they are a lot less expensive than having to go to a doctor for a painful operation that may or may not be successful. Other than surgery, the other alternative is to rest the hands and miss several months of work. If you work for a large company, the company might save money by installing these ergonomic keyboards. As mentioned, many people are now suing the companies for CTS and RSI injuries. (Of course, the insurance companies are increasing their rates to help pay for any damages that may be awarded.)

How a Keyboard Works

The keyboard is actually a computer in itself. It has a small microprocessor with its own ROM. The computerized electronics of the keyboard eliminates the bounce of the keys, can determine when you hold a key down for repeat, can store up to 20 or more keystrokes, and can determine which key was pressed first if you press two at a time. In addition to the standard BIOS chips on your motherboard, there is a special keyboard BIOS chip. Each time a key is pressed, a unique signal is sent to the BIOS. This signal is made up of a direct current voltage that is turned on and off a certain number of times, within a definite time frame, to represent 0s and 1s.

Each time a 5V line is turned on for a certain amount of time, it represents a 1; when it is off for a certain amount of time, it represents a 0. In the ASCII code, if the letter A is pressed, the code for 65 will be generated: 1 0 0 0 0 0 1.

Reprogramming Key Functions

Most word processors, spreadsheets, databases, and other software programs usually designate certain keys to run various macros. A *macro* is a word or several words that can be input by just pressing one or more keys. By pressing a certain key or a combination of two keys, you can input your name and address or any other group of words that you use frequently. These programs also use the function keys to perform various tasks such as moving the cursor, underlining, bolding, and many other functions.

The problem is that there is no standardization. Changing from one word processor or software program to another is about like having to learn a new foreign language. It sure would be nice if you could go from one program to another as easily as you can drive different automobiles.

Keyboard Sources

Keyboard preference is strictly a matter of individual taste. The Key Tronic Company of Spokane (509-928-8000) makes some excellent keyboards and are considered the IBM of the keyboard world; their keyboards have set the standards. The Key Tronic keyboards have been copied by the clone makers, even to the extent of using the same model numbers. Quality keyboards use an etched-copper printed circuit board and keys that switch on and off. The keys of quality keyboards have a small spring beneath each key to give them a uniform tension.

Key Tronic offers several models. Some models even let you change the little springs under the keys to a different tension. The standard is 2 ounces, but you can configure the key tension to whatever you like. You can install 1-, 1.5-, 2-, 2.5-, or 3-ounce springs for an extra fee. They can also let you exchange the positions of the CapsLock and Ctrl keys. The Key Tronic keyboards have several other functions that are clearly described in their large manual. Call them for a copy.

Many of the less expensive keyboards use plastic with conductive paint for the connecting lines instead of an etched-copper printed circuit board. Instead of springs beneath each key, they use a rubber cup. The bottom of each key is coated with a carbon conductive material. When the key is depressed, the carbon allows an electrical connection between the painted lines. The keys are part of, and are attached to, the main plastic board by strips of flexible molded plastic. These low-cost keyboards may have as few as 17 parts, and they work fairly well.

I recently saw new clone keyboards being sold at a swap meet for $10 each. The keyboards looked very much like the Key Tronic 101 key types. The assembly snapped together instead of using metal screws. They also had several other cost-saving features. But there are quite a lot of electronics in a keyboard, and I don't know how they can possibly make a keyboard to sell for $10. At that price, you could buy two or three of them; if you ever had any trouble with one, just throw it away and plug in a new one.

There are several keyboard manufacturers and hundreds of different models with many different special functions. Prices range from $10 up to $400 or more. Look through any computer magazine for the various models.

Specialized Keyboards

Several companies have developed specialized keyboards. I'll list just a few of them here.

Quite often I have the need to do some minor calculations. The computer is great for calculations. Most of the word-processor, database, and spreadsheet programs have built-in calculator functions. But in order to use the calculator, most of these programs require that the computer be on and be using a file. Some keyboards have a calculator built into the number pad. It has a battery so that it can be used whether the computer is on or not.

As mentioned, all newer keyboards now have the extra Windows 95 keys—even the $10 clones that I saw at a swap meet. You don't need the extra keys to run Windows 95, and in fact, I have several older keyboards that work just fine with Windows 95.

The Maxi Switch Company (520-746-9378), NMB Technologies (800-662-8321), and SC&T International (800-408-4084) have multimedia keyboards that come with a microphone, speakers, input jacks, and volume control. Another Key Tronic model has a bar code reader attached to it. This can be extremely handy if you have a small business that uses bar codes. This keyboard would be ideal for a computer in a point-of-sale (POS) system.

If you have been in the computer business for a while, you may remember the PCjr from IBM. It had a wireless keyboard that used an infrared system similar to a TV remote control. The Casco Products Company (800-793-6960) thinks this is still a good idea. They have developed the LightLink, a wireless keyboard that communicates by infrared with a small receiver that plugs into the motherboard keyboard socket. One use for this keyboard is for presentations, since the computer can be operated from across the room.

The Cherry Electrical Products Company (800-510-1689) has developed several different keyboards. They now have one that can accept the Smart Card. The Smart Card is similar to a credit card, except that it has a certain amount of money encoded on it from your bank. Each time you use the card, your purchase is deducted from the card. It has been used in Europe for some time and is expected to become very popular in the United States. The one thing that some people might not like is that you must have the money on the card. With a credit card, you can charge an item and not worry about paying for it until the bill comes. Then you may only have to pay a portion of it, and finance the rest of it.

Some companies have developed a keyboard that has a scanner built into it. This is a particularly handy feature and can save a lot of typing.

Mouse Systems and Other Pointing Devices

One of the biggest reasons for the success of the Macintosh is that it is easy to use. With a mouse and on-screen icons, all you have to do is point and click. You don't have to learn a lot of commands and rules. A person who knows nothing about computers can become productive in a very short time. The people in the DOS world finally took note of this and began developing programs and applications such as Windows for the IBM and compatibles.

Now dozens of companies manufacture mice. Some mice may cost up to $100 or more; others may cost less than $10. What is the difference? The answer is $90. The low-cost mouse does just about everything that most people would need from a mouse. After all, how much mouse do you need just to point and click? Of course, if you are doing high-end-type drafting, designing, and very close tolerance work, then you definitely need one that has high resolution.

The Ball-Type Mice

Most mice have a small, round rubber ball on the underside that contacts the desktop or mouse pad. As the mouse is moved, the ball turns. Inside the mouse, two flywheels contact the ball: one for horizontal and one for vertical movements. The flywheels are mounted between two light-sensitive diodes. The flywheels have small holes in the outer edge. As the flywheels turn, light shines through the holes or is blocked where there are no holes. This breaks the light up into patterns of 1s and 0s, which then control the cursor movement.

Mouse Ball Cleaning

The mouse ball picks up dirt. If the dirt builds up on the flywheel rollers, it may cause the mouse to be erratic or skip and not work properly. On most mice, the ball can be easily removed and the three rollers cleaned. If you turn the mouse over, there is usually a round twist-off retainer plate that allows you to remove the ball. One of the best ways to clean the rollers is to use a cotton swab and alcohol. (I told one woman this, and she asked me whether she should use bourbon or scotch. Either one will work fine, but it would be a terrible waste. I suggest just plain old rubbing alcohol.)

If the rollers have not been cleaned for some time, they may have some caked debris. You may have to take a small knife blade or similar tool to scrape the debris off the rollers. Figure 10-2 shows a disassembled mouse for cleaning the rollers. The pen points to a small roller. Figure 10-3 shows using a cotton swab and alcohol to clean the roller.

Figure 10-2
A disassembled
mouse to clean
rollers—the pen
points to a small
roller.

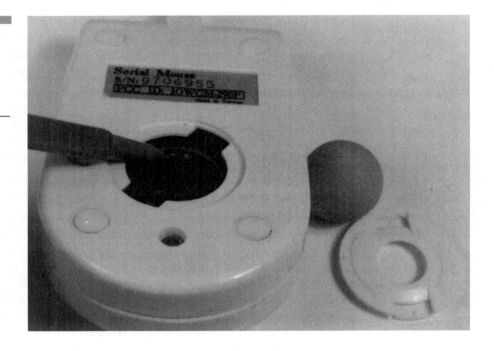

Mouse Interfaces

You can't just plug in a mouse and start using it. The software, whether Windows, WordPerfect, or a CAD program, must recognize and interface with the mouse. So mouse companies develop software drivers to allow the mouse to operate with various programs. The drivers are usually

Figure 10-3
Use a cotton swab
and alcohol to clean
the roller.

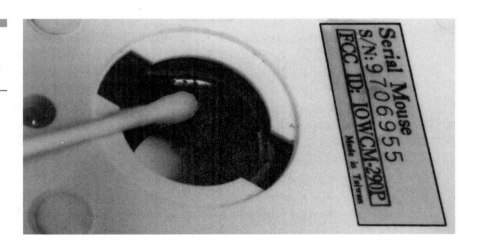

supplied on a disk. The Microsoft Mouse is the closest to a standard, so most other companies emulate the Microsoft driver. Most mice drivers are now included in Windows 95 and 98.

The Microsoft-type mouse plugs into a serial port: COM1 or COM2. This may cause a problem if you already have two serial devices using these ports. DOS also allows for COM3 and COM4, but these two ports must be shared with COM1 and COM2, so they must have special software in order to be shared. Most mice do not like to share COM ports.

The serial ports on some systems use a DB25-type socket connector with 25 contacts. Others may use a DB9 socket with 9 contacts. Many of the mice now come with the DB9 connector and a DB25 connector adapter. The DB25 connector looks exactly like the DB25 connector used for the LPT1 parallel printer port, except that the serial port connector is a male-type connector with pins, and the LPT1 printer port is a female with sockets. Most motherboards now come with upright pins for the COM1 and COM2 and printer connections. Short cables with connectors plug into the upright pins. The connector assembly is then installed in one of the spaces on the back panel.

There may be times when you have a cable that is a male when what you need is a female or vice versa. (A male connector is one that has pins; a female connector has sockets.) You can buy DB25 "gender bender" adapters that can solve this type of problem. If you simply need an extension so that you can plug two similar cables together, straight-through adapters are also available. There are many different kinds of combinations. The Cables To Go Company (800-225-8646) has just about every cable and accessory that you would ever need. The Dalco Electronics Company (800-445-5342) also has many types of cables, adapters, and electronic components.

Before you buy a mouse, you might check the type of serial port connector you have and order the proper type. You can buy an adapter for about $3.

PS/2 Mice

Most of the newer motherboards now have PS/2 connectors for the mouse and keyboard. You can use either connector to plug in the keyboard or the mouse.

The PS/2 connector saves having to use one of the COM ports, but it does require the use of one of the precious IRQs, usually IRQ12. Even the fastest, most powerful computers still only have 16 IRQs, and most

Figure 10-4
Connectors on the
back panel of a
Pentium III. At the top
is the power input
connector. Below that
is a switch for 110V or
220V. Below that are
two round PS/2
connectors for mouse
and keyboard; then
two rectangular USB
connectors. The two
connectors on the left
are for serial ports—
the larger connector
is for the printer, then
small audio connec-
tors and monitor con-
nector. Not shown is
the telephone line for
the modem.

of them are used by the system. If you need to install a sound board, a modem, a mouse, a network card, a SCSI device, or any of many other peripherals, you may not have enough IRQs. There are some devices that will share IRQs, but most of them are rather selfish and don't like to share.

You have two serial ports, COM1 and COM2, on the motherboard. If you don't have a PS/2 mouse, one of ports is needed for that function. Your modem will use the other serial port. The serial ports can share, so COM1 can share with COM3 and COM2 can share with COM4. If you have more than four serial devices, special boards can provide an additional four or more ports.

Figure 10-4 shows the connectors on the back panel of a Pentium III computer. The grill at the top is the fan for the power supply. Next is the grill for the special fan for the Pentium III. The power input connector is at the top; below it is a switch for 110 volts or for 220 volts. Below the switch are two round PS/2 connectors for the mouse and keyboard. Next are two rectangular USB connectors, and below that two serial port connectors and the larger parallel port printer connector. Finally, at the bottom on the left are the audio connectors and on the right is the connector for the monitor. Not shown is the telephone line for the modem.

Wireless Mice

One of the disadvantages of operating a keyboard such as the wireless LightLink mentioned earlier is that you also need a wireless mouse. Several companies have developed wireless mice. They operate with infrared rays similar to the remote control of a TV. Some may operate using a radio frequency such as the wireless mouse made by Mitsumi Electronics (800-648-7864). Logitech (800-231-7717) also has wireless models. Even though they are wireless, they still need a receiver and an interface to connect to a serial port.

Trackballs

A trackball is a mouse that has been turned upside down. Like the mouse, the trackball also requires a serial port. One advantage of the trackball is that you don't need the square footage of desk space that a mouse requires. In addition, trackballs are usually larger than the ball in a mouse, so it is possible to have better resolution. They are often used with CAD and critical design systems.

Constant use of a mouse can also lead to CTS and RSI. Itac Systems (800-533-4822) claims that their ergonomically designed trackball called the MOUSE-TRAK can help prevent those injuries. Several companies manufacture trackballs. Look through the computer magazines for ads. Figure 10-5 shows a trackball.

Touch Screens and Light Pens

Some fast-food places now have a touch screen with a menu of several items. You merely touch the item that you want, and the order is transmitted. The same type system is sometimes found in kiosks in shopping malls and large department stores. Some systems use an image of a keyboard so that you can touch the various keys almost as if you were typing. The touch system is accurate, saves time and money, and is convenient. The touch screen operation is similar to using a mouse and pointing. Most of them have a frame installed on the bezel of the monitor. Beams of infrared light criss-cross the front of the monitor screen.

For ordinary text, most monitors are set up so that they have 80 columns left to right and 25 rows from top to bottom. Columns of beams

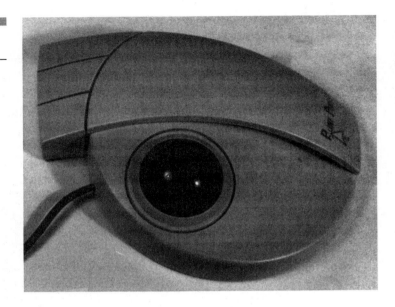

originate from the top part of the frame and pass to the bottom frame. Rows of beams originate from the left portion of the frame and pass to the right frame. If one of the beams is interrupted by an object such as a finger or pencil, the computer can determine exactly whatever character happens to be in that portion of the screen.

Joysticks

Joysticks are used primarily for games. They are serial devices and need an interface. Many of the multifunction boards that have COM ports also provide a game connector for joysticks. Joysticks are fairly reasonable and may cost from $10 up to $30. There are usually several ads for them in magazines such as *Computer Shopper*.

Digitizers and Graphics Tablets

Graphics tablets and digitizers are similar to a flat drawing pad or drafting table. Most of them use some sort of pointing device that can translate movement into digitized output to the computer. Some are rather small; others may be as large as a standard drafting table. Cost may be as little as $150 or as high as $1500. Most graphics tablets and digitizers have very high resolutions, are very accurate, and are intended for precision drawing. Some of the tablets have programmable overlays and function keys. Some will work with a mouse-like device, a pen light, or a pencil-like stylus. The tablets can be used for designing circuits, for CAD programs, for graphic design, for freehand drawing, and even for text and data input. The most common use is with CAD-type software. The Wacom Technology Corp. also has a digitizer pad that uses a cordless, batteryless, pressure-sensitive pen.

Most of the tablets are serial devices, but some of them require their own interface board. Many of them are compatible with the Microsoft mouse systems.

Several companies have developed pressure-sensitive tablets, including Wacom, who has developed several different models. Wacom tablets use an electromagnetic resonance system. This allows the use of a special stylus that requires no wires or batteries. The tablet has a grid of embedded wires that can detect the location of the stylus and the pressure that is applied. The tablets sense the amount of pressure and may draw a thin line or a heavy line in response.

The tablets can be used with different graphics software programs to create sketches, drawings, designs, and art. Here are some of the companies who manufacture pressure-sensitive tablets:

Wacom Technology
800-922-6613

Communication Intelligence Corp.
800-888-9242
http://cic.com

Kurta Corp. (part of Altek Corp.)
602-276-5533
www.kurta.com

Summagraphics (part of GTCO CalComp)
800-337-8662
www.gtcocalcomp.com

Wacom Technology
800-922-6613
www.wacom.com

Call the companies for brochures or more information or visit their Web sites.

Digital Cameras and Products

There are several companies who manufacture digital cameras. The digital photos can be easily input to the computer, then various software packages will let you edit, crop, touch up, or do just about anything you want to the photo. One of the companies who provides software for this purpose is Adobe Systems (www.adobe.com).

The early digital cameras were very expensive and had rather poor resolution. But prices have come way down. You can buy a camera with 2 million pixel resolution for about $300, similar to what a good 35mm would cost. The megapixel resolution now approaches that of film. Film is not quite obsolete, so don't throw your 35mm camera away just yet. However, digital cameras have several advantages over film. One of the advantages is the cost of film. It may cost $3 or more for a roll of film, then you have to take it to a store and pay $8 to $10 to have it developed. Some stores will have the film ready in about an hour; for other stores, you may have to wait two or three days to get the photos back.

Digital cameras have lenses, shutters, view finders, and most everything that a 35mm has except film. Instead, the photos or images are recorded in flash memory or on a floppy disk. (I expect that the new half-ounce 340MB microdisk from IBM will be installed in several digital cameras.) Digital cameras work by focusing light through the lens. The image hits light-sensitive components, such as charge-coupled devices, and a small voltage is generated for each of the colors such as red, green, or blue. The camera's electronics convert the generated voltage into a digital format of 0s and 1s and stores the result in the memory system.

Many digital cameras have a small built-in LCD screen so the results can be viewed immediately. If you don't like the shot, erase it and do it over. The photos can then be downloaded to a hard disk or to a recordable CD-R disc, or printed out on any of several inkjet printers. Of course, once the photos or images are in digital format, you can edit, crop, rotate, change colors, and do a thousand other marvelous things with them.

All of the companies who manufacture digital cameras have Web sites with lots of information about their products. I can't possibly give you all the information you need in this book. Log on to their Web sites for more specifications and information.

Here are a few companies who have digital cameras:

Agfa Corp.	www.agfahome.com
Canon	www.ccsi.canon.com
Casio	www.casio.com
Epson	www.epson.com

Fujifilm	www.fujifilm.com
Hewlett-Packard	www.photosmart.com
Kodak	www.kodak.com
Konica	www.konica.com
Leica Camera	www.leica-camera.com
Minolta Corp.	www.minoltausa.com
Nikon	www.nikon.com
Olympus	www.olympus.com
Toshiba	www.toshiba.com

Digital "Film" for Standard 35mm Cameras

The IMAGEK Company (www.imagek.com) has developed a digital cartridge that looks very much like a standard 35mm roll of film. It is dropped into the film cavity of a standard 35mm camera and provides 24 digital images. The images can then be downloaded to a computer, and the cartridge is ready to be used again.

Here are a couple of frequently asked questions as posted on their Web site:

Who Benefits from Using EFS-1 and Why?

EFS-1 benefits all photographers using conventional 35mm cameras due to its affordability, ease-of-use, and its rapid capture of stunning quality images. EFS-1 enables the non-digital photographer to seamlessly enter the world of digital photography. IMAGEK provides the digital photographers the ability to expand their capabilities using their high-quality camera bodies, lenses, and accessories.

What Is the Marketplace for EFS-1?

The initial market for the EFS-1 is the millions of high-quality 35mm camera owners. In the U.S. alone over 20 million SLRs have been sold since 1983. IMAGEK is targeting this existing customer base. The sheer volume of these existing high-quality camera systems and the desire of their owners to use the systems they have grown to know and trust underpins a large potential market for IMAGEK.

The EFS-1 will be able to instantly put digital photography in the hands of these camera consumers. (A recent study by International Data Corp. and the Future Image Report projects that more than 3 million digital cameras will be sold in 1998; industry analysts are now predicting 6 million units sold in 2000.) IMAGEK sees a widespread and fast-growing market for digital image capture and is giving photographers a seamless method to step up to digital.

My Opinion

I like the idea of using one of my good 35mm cameras. One of the disadvantages is that I would not have the ability to immediately look at the photos such as the LCD screen provided with most digital cameras. However, I do believe that the advantage of being able to use my Minolta 700SI camera for both digital and film is a great idea.

Digital Video Cameras

Digital video cameras will let you record motion and most of them will also let you take still photos. Sony (www.sony.com) has a DCR-TRV900 that will even let you use 8mm tape or the digital system. It seems to offer the best of all worlds.

Here are some other companies who have digital video cameras:

Canon
800-652-2666
www.canondv.com

Hitachi
800-225-1741
www.mpegcam.com

JVC
973-315-5000
www.jvc-america.com

Panasonic
800-211-7262
www.panasonic.com/video

Sharp Electronics
800-237-4277
www.sharp-usa.com

Digital Imaging Software

Many digital cameras come with some software that will allow you to edit, reshape, manipulate, or do just about anything you want to your photos or images. Here are a few of the more popular ones:

Adobe PhotoDeluxe   www.adobe.com

Corel Print House Magic Deluxe   www.corel.com

LivePix   www.livepicture.com

MGI PhotoSuiteII   www.mgisoft.com

Microsoft Picture It! 99   www.microsoft.com

Ulead Photo Express 2.0   www.ulead.com

View Your Photos on TV

Avicor Incorporated (800-604-5700, or www.avicor.com) has developed what they call a "digital photo album" that will let you view your photos and images on TV. It is about the size of a large book and can sit on top of your TV or VCR. The Avicor Album has connections for input from several different digital cameras and output to the TV or VCR and uses a $3\frac{1}{2}$-inch floppy disk for storage. It comes with a remote control so that you can scan through your photos and choose the ones to view.

This system would be ideal for anyone making a presentation using a large-screen TV.

Scanners and Scanner Products

Scanners with optical character recognition (OCR) software can scan a line of printed type, recognize each character, and input that character into a computer just as if it were typed in from a keyboard. A beam of light sweeps across the page, and the characters can be determined by the absorption and reflection of the light. One problem with early scanners was that they could only recognize a few different fonts and could not recognize graphics at all. The machines today have much more memory, and the technology has improved to where the better scanners can recognize almost any font or type. You can reduce a mountain of printed data that may fill several file cabinets into a few files on a hard disk.

The scanners will also digitize photos, line drawings, and blueprints, and let you place them on a hard disk. Any of these items could also be sent over the Internet. If you need a few copies of an item, you can use the scanner to copy the item, then print it out.

Scanners have been around for several years. When they first came out, they cost from $6000 to more than $15,000. Three years ago, I paid $800 for a full-page flatbed scanner. I can buy an equivalent scanner today for $150. In fact, many full-page flatbed scanners are now selling for as low as $50. A series of technological breakthroughs have allowed the lower costs. One of the breakthroughs is the use of charge-coupled devices (CCDs). Some of the less expensive scanners use a contact image sensor (CIS), a single chip that handles many data-processing functions.

As mentioned, scanners now have the ability to recognize a large number of fonts, and they can copy and digitize color graphics and images. Most of the scanners come bundled with several software packages. Nearly all of them come with OCR software for recognizing fonts and text. One of the better OCR software packages is OmniPage Pro, which is discussed later.

Many of the inexpensive scanners have a resolution of 24-bit color. Some that may be a bit more expensive have 30- to 36-bit resolution. The 36-bit resolution means that it is possible to have 12 different bits of information for each of the three primary colors. Some high-end, very high-resolution scanners that are needed for color graphic image processing and publishing may cost from $12,000 up to $95,000.

The flatbed scanners have a glass panel that is similar to those found in copy machines. The sheet to be scanned is laid on the glass panel, and the machine sweeps the scanning heads across the sheet from top to bottom. Scanners have a lot in common with copy machines, printers, and fax machines. Many companies manufacture multifunction machines that include the capability to scan, copy, print, and fax. These machines will be discussed in more detail in Chapter 15.

If you do a lot of presentations, some of the scanners have an additional device that will let you make transparencies from 35mm film. Another feature provided by some is a tray paper feeder.

Figure 10-6 shows a Hewlett-Packard 6200C USB scanner. The USB cable is shown on top of the scanner.

Figure 10-6
An H-P 6200C USB scanner. The USB cable is on top of the scanner.

Personal Scanners

Several companies are manufacturing small-page, pass-through compact scanners such as the Logitech PageScan shown in Figure 10-7. This little scanner is quite versatile. It attaches to the parallel port of the computer, so it doesn't need a separate board. It can scan in text, drawings, or even photos into the computer. If you need a copy of a page, scan it into the computer, then print it out. It can input printed text, signatures, drawings, or graphic images to a fax/modem board or to a hard disk.

The PageScan can also handle color fairly well, but of course, the resolution is not as good as the more-expensive flatbed scanners. If you happen to be on the Internet, you can scan in a photo of yourself and send it to someone as e-mail. For photos sent over the Internet, the lower resolution is fine.

What to Look for When Buying a Scanner

What to look for will depend on what you want to do with your scanner, and of course, how much you want to pay. There are several manufacturers of scanners and hundreds of different models, types, resolutions, bus types, and prices. The less-expensive scanners may have a resolution of only 300 dots per inch. But they may use interpolation software that fills in the spaces between the dots to give two or three times the true resolu-

Figure 10-7
The Logitech PageScan. It is quite versatile.

tion. As you might expect, some ads may list the interpolated resolution in large type and the true resolution in small type (if it is mentioned at all).

The specifications usually list two numbers, such as 600 × 1200. The first figure usually means that the scanner is reading the image pixels at 600 dots per inch (dpi) horizontally. The 1200 means that the scanner lens moves down 1/1200th of an inch to read the next horizontal line. The higher the resolution, the more memory or disk space it will require. Even at 300 dpi by 300, you would have 90,000 dpi. Depth of color will also make the file much larger. A color image may require 24 times as much disk space as the same image in black-and-white.

The more-expensive color scanners can capture all three colors in one pass. They may also scan at a 36-bit color depth with 12 bits of information about each of the three primary colors—red, green, and blue.

Most all systems now conform to the TWAIN specification. The word *TWAIN* is an acronym for "technology without an interesting name." (Mark Twain would have appreciated this acronym.) It is an application programming interface (API) specification that was jointly developed by Aldus, Caere, Eastman Kodak, Hewlett-Packard, and Logitech. A different device driver is needed for each of the hundreds of different printers. Before TWAIN, you needed a different device driver from every manufacturer for each model and type of scanner. TWAIN helps to standardize some of the device drivers. (We really need something like TWAIN for printers.)

Interfaces

Some of the more-expensive scanners still use the SCSI interface. To install a SCSI unit, you must have a SCSI card. To install one, you must take the cover off the computer, find an empty slot, set the logical unit number (LUN) of the device, then install the software.

In addition, several companies now offer very good scanners that attach to the USB port. Setting these scanners up is simple. Just plug in the cable and install the software. Several companies also offer models that plug into the parallel port or printer port of your computer. These scanners are about as easy to install as the USB units. They usually have a pass-through connector so that the printer can still be plugged in. Keep in mind, however, that the parallel units may not have the speed and resolution of some of the SCSI or USB units.

There are many manufacturers of scanners and, of course, many different prices. Here are just a few companies who make scanners:

Acer
   800-369-6736
   www.acerperipherals.com

Agfa
   888-281-2302
   www.agfahome.com

Canon Computer Systems
   800-652-2626
   www.ccsi.canon.com

Epson
   800-463-7766
   www.epson.com

Hewlett-Packard
   800-722-6538
   www.scanjet.com

Microtek
   800-652-4160
   www.microtekusa.com

Pacific Image
   310-618-8100
   www.scanace.com

Plustek
   800-685-8088
   www.plustekusa.com

UMAX
   800-562-0311
   www.umax.com

Visioneer
   800-787-7007
   www.visioneer.com

There are several other companies as well, and many different models. Check out the ads in any of the computer magazines listed in Chapter 19.

OCR Software

The OCR capabilities of a scanner allow it to recognize each character of a printed document and input that character into a computer just as if it were typed in from a keyboard. Once the data is in the computer, a word processor can be used to revise or change the data, then print it out again. Faxes are received as paper graphical documents; however, it requires a lot of disk space to store a fax. An OCR scanner can convert faxes to digital text, which takes up much less disk space. Some OCR software programs such as OmniPage Pro support over 100 different scanners. In most cases, such programs can match text to the original fonts and can read degraded text by reading it in context. OmniPage Pro also has a large internal dictionary that helps in this respect and yields excellent OCR accuracy. It can automatically convert scanned text into any of the most popular word-processor formats. OmniPage Pro also has the Image Assistant, an integrated 24-bit color editor for graphic editing. OmniPage Pro 6.0 is one of the better OCR packages available. If you have any earlier version of OmniPage or WordScan, you can upgrade for a nominal sum.

Once data is entered into a computer, it can be searched very quickly for any item. Many times I have spent hours going through printed manuals looking for certain items. If the data had been in a computer, I could have found the information in just seconds. Several companies have developed advanced software to work with their scanners, and in some cases, those manufactured by other companies.

Here is part of a press release from the Caere Company:

Caere, the worldwide leader in optical character recognition (OCR) technology, has introduced OmniPage® Pro 9.0, a major upgrade to the world's best-selling OCR application. The new version improves overall OCR accuracy with several new features including support for color documents, the ability to identify and maintain tables in word processors, improved recognition of spreadsheets, and enhanced format preservation. In addition, Version 9.0 comes bundled with Caere's PageKeeper® Standard document management software to easily organize and retrieve scanned and electronic documents. The latest version of OmniPage Pro makes significant strides in improving recognition and satisfying users' needs.

The goal of OCR software is to accurately reproduce scanned pages in the user's word processor or other text-based application while retaining all elements of the original pages including text, graphics, tables, layout, etc. Character accuracy is one of many factors that contributes to overall OCR accuracy. Other factors such as format retention (i.e., the ability to maintain the look and feel of a document) play important roles in OCR accuracy as well. OmniPage Pro provides over 99% character accuracy on good-quality original documents. Version 9.0 improves overall OCR accuracy by building on the superior character accuracy with new features such as support for tables and color graphics, a new spreadsheet mode, and others.

New Color Support OmniPage Pro now supports scanning and loading color pages. Version 9.0 displays color graphics in all views (thumbnail, image, and text) and maintains color graphics in the user's word processor or other text-based application. For example, if a user scans in a magazine page with color graphics, that user can view the document in its original layout and color, open the graphics in any image editor, and make changes to the graphic. Changes will be reflected in OmniPage and in the word processor.

New Output of Table Objects Version 9.0 can identify tables and save them as table objects in Microsoft Word and Corel WordPerfect. The software automatically detects gridded tables (tables with lines dividing rows and columns) and even enables users to indicate when a non-gridded table should be saved as a table object as well.

New Spreadsheet Recognition Capabilities   OmniPage Pro 9.0 features a new spreadsheet mode for better handling of spreadsheet documents. It has improved recognition of spreadsheets for output to Excel and other spreadsheet applications by better maintaining proper alignment of text and numbers within rows and columns.

Improved Handling of Single-Column Documents   Version 9.0 is better at automatically parsing single-column documents. This improvement is extremely important for documents such as legal pleadings, which are single column documents but include a column of numbers next to each line of text. The column of numbers can confuse competitor OCR applications, which re-create these pages as multiple column documents and separate the row number identifiers from the text. This improvement is also important for documents that include single column text mixed with a non-gridded table or other single column areas with varying paragraph widths.

Better Handling of Reversed-Out Text   Detection of reversed-out text (light text on a dark background) as text has improved dramatically. This improvement is particularly helpful for users who scan magazine-style pages, which often include reversed-out text.

PageKeeper Standard Document Management Software Included

Caere's document management application enables users to organize, use, and retrieve documents on their PCs. PageKeeper Standard (street price $39) is included with OmniPage Pro 9.0. It is the first document management application to comprehensively organize both scanned pages and electronic documents (such as Word, Excel, and Web pages) in a single desktop. As a result, scanner users can easily manage all of their documents, including those scanned into OmniPage Pro, within a single application. (Additional information on PageKeeper Standard is available at the Caere website: www.caere.com.)

OmniPage Pro 9.0 and PageKeeper Standard are very closely integrated. For example, documents scanned into OmniPage Pro can be automatically added to PageKeeper, providing an easy way for users to organize and retrieve these documents. OmniPage Pro is also available on PageKeeper's Application Toolbar, which enables users to launch a scanned page directly into OmniPage Pro 9.0. Likewise, scanned pages stored in PageKeeper can be loaded into OmniPage Pro with a single click.

Fast OCR on Pentium III and MMX PCs   OmniPage Pro is optimized for the extended MMX instruction set. Users will see a 15% speed improvement over non-MMX systems.

More Comprehensive OCR Wizard   Version 9.0 provides an enhanced OCR Wizard that asks new questions to improve OCR results, giving users access to more options for OCR. For example, users are now prompted to identify the scanning mode and choose from color, grayscale, or black and white. Also, the OCR Wizard enables users to select languages in the document. With the OCR Wizard, users can also improve accuracy by indicating when pages include tables or reversed-out text.

New Re-sizeable OCR Proofreader   OmniPage Pro's OCR Proofreader (formerly Check Recognition) works like a spell checker and enables the user to verify OCR results while viewing the relevant portion of the original image. Version 9.0 now provides the ability to re-size the OCR Proofreader so the user can see more of the original image while proofreading.

Improved Support for Multifunction Devices (MFDs)   Version 9.0 better handles multiple-page documents scanned using MFDs like the HP OfficeJet. Users are able to load a multiple page document into the MFD document feeder and automatically scan all pages at once.

COLD

About 10 years ago, just about everyone began installing computers in their offices. There was lots of excitement about the forthcoming age of the paperless office. But instead of reducing the large stacks of paper, the amount of paper increased. The reason was that most people insisted on having paper printouts along with the files on disk. A discouraged vice-president of a large company made the observation that we would probably see paperless offices at about the same time we had paperless bathrooms. He was right, but we are making a bit of progress. Most large companies have thousands of file cabinets overflowing with memos, manuals, documents, and files that must be saved. Most of the documents will never be needed again. But from time to time, a few items stored in these files must be retrieved. Even with a good indexing system, it may take lots and lots of time to find a particular item. A good filing system and document management system using scanners, OCR, and a Computer Output to Laser Disc (COLD) system can be very helpful. Acres of file cabinets can be replaced by just a few small optical discs. As an added bonus, a good COLD system can help you find and retrieve any document within seconds.

The recordable CD-R systems DVD-RAM have just about made the COLD systems obsolete. The CD-R and DVD-RAM may be less expensive, and they are more standardized than the WORM systems often used with COLD.

Business Card Scanners

If you depend on business cards to keep in contact with prospective buyers or for other business purposes, you may have several Rolodexes full of cards. Or you can take each card and enter the information into your computer database. There is an easier way. Some companies have developed card scanners that can read the information off a business card and input it to a computer.

At this time they are still a bit expensive, but if you depend on business cards, they are well worth it. Like most computer products, the prices will come down very soon.

Here are some companies who offer business card scanners, along with their products:

CyperScan 1000
  CypherTech, Inc.
  408-734-8765

Scan-in-Dex
  Microtek Labs
  800-654-4160

Cognitive BCR
  Cognitive Technology
  415-925-2367

CardGrabber
  Pacific Crest Tech.
  714-261-6444

Large-Format Scanners

Several companies manufacture large-format scanners that are similar to the large plotters. They may be up to 4 feet wide and stand about 3 feet high. The scanners can be used to copy and digitize blueprints, CAD, architectural drawings, and even large signs and color images. These type of scanners are rather expensive and are often used with high-end workstations. Here are two companies who manufacture them:

The WideCom Group
  905-712-0505
  www.widecom.com

Vidar Systems
  703-471-7070
  www.vidar.com

Voice Recognition Input

Another way to input data into a computer is to talk to it with a microphone. Of course, you need electronics that can take the signal created by the microphone, detect the spoken words, and turn them into a form of digital information that the computer can use. The early voice data input systems were very expensive and limited. One reason was that the voice technology required lots of memory. But the cost of memory has dropped considerably in the last few years, and the technology has improved in many other ways. Eventually, voice input technology will replace the keyboard for many applications.

Voice technology usually involves "training" a computer to recognize a word spoken by a person. When you speak into a microphone, the sound waves cause a diaphragm, or some other device, to move back and forth in a magnetic field and create a voltage that is analogous to the sound wave. If this voltage is recorded and played through a good audio system, the loudspeaker will respond to the amplified voltages and reproduce a sound that is identical to the one input to the microphone. A person can speak a word into a microphone, which creates a unique voltage pattern for that word and that particular person's voice. The voltage is fed into an electronic circuit, and the pattern is digitized and stored in the computer. If several words are spoken, the circuit will digitize each one of them and store them. Each one of them will have a distinct and unique pattern. Later when the computer hears a word, it will search through the patterns that it has stored to see if the input word matches any one of its stored words.

Of course, once the computer is able to recognize a word, you can have it perform some useful work. You could command it to load and run a program or perform any of several other tasks. Because every person's voice is different, ordinarily the computer would not recognize the voice of anyone who had not trained it. Training the computer might involve saying the same word several times so that the computer can store several patterns of the person's voice. Some of the new systems will now recognize the voices of others who have not trained the computer.

Uses for Voice Recognition

Voice recognition can be used by many professionals such as doctors, nurses, lawyers, reporters, loan officers, auditors, researchers, secretaries, business executives, language interpreters, and writers. It can be used for letters, reports, and complicated business and technical text.

I have very poor handwriting; in fact, I can't even read my own writing once it gets cold. Thank God for the computer. But doctors are notorious for their bad handwriting. I am amazed that pharmacists can decipher some of the prescriptions I have seen. Deciphering a doctor's writing can be the difference between life and death. Doctors also have to write reports for medical records. Ordinarily, the written report is then typed up and stored in the patient's folders. Of course, there are times when it is impossible for the transcriptionist to decipher the doctor's reports. Many doctors are now using voice input to directly type the report into a computer. Pharmacists should band together and insist that doctors voice recognition to type out their prescriptions.

Computer voice recognition is also very useful whenever you must use both hands for doing a job but still need a computer to perform certain tasks. In addition, voice recognition is useful on production lines where the person does not have time to manually enter data into a computer. It can also be used in a laboratory where a scientist is looking through a microscope and cannot take his or her eyes off the subject to write down the findings or data. Or perhaps lighting must be kept too dim to input data to a computer manually. In other instances, the person might have to be several feet from the computer and still be able to input data through the microphone line or even with a wireless mic. The person might even be miles away and be able to input data over a telephone line.

Voice recognition and a computer can help many of those who have physical limitations to become productive and independent. There are also a few systems that will allow a person using English to call someone who speaks a different language, and the spoken conversation can be instantly translated and understood. The system would recognize the spoken word, then use computerized speech to translate it for the parties. So the parties would actually be talking to a computerized mechanical interpreter. The same type of system has been built into small handheld foreign language interpreters. Speak an English word into the machine, and it gives you the equivalent spoken foreign word. In addition, many luxury automobiles now come with cellular phones with voice-activated dialing. This lets the driver keep his or her eyes on the road while the number is being dialed.

The designers of computers are constantly looking for new ways to differentiate and improve their product. In the very near future you can be sure that many of them will have voice recognition built in. Chips that use very large-scale integration (VLSI) are combining more and more computer functions onto single chips, making computers smaller and smaller. We now have some very powerful computers that can fit in a shirt pocket. One of the big problems, however, is that there is not room for a decent keyboard. To fit, the keys have to be very small. Some keyboard systems use a stylus to press each key. Others may let you use a single finger to type on the keyboards. Even then if your fingers are very large, you may end up pressing two keys at once. A solution would be to build in voice recognition so that the keyboard would not be needed.

Limitations

For most systems, the computer must be trained to recognize a specific, discrete, individual word. So the computer vocabulary is limited to what it is trained to recognize, the amount of memory available, and the limitations imposed by the software and hardware.

Many basic systems are available today that are very good at recognizing discrete words. But ordinarily, when we speak, many words meld together. There are some systems that can recognize continuous speech, such as Naturally Speaking from Dragon Systems (800-437-2466, or www.dragonsys.com) and ViaVoice from IBM (800-426-3333, or www.software.ibm.com/is/voicetype).

Another problem is homonyms, or words that are pronounced the same and sometimes spelled the same, but that have different meanings. For instance, *him* and *hymn* are pronounced the same but have very different meanings. Another instance is the words *to*, *too*, and *two*. In addition, many people misspell and confuse the words *there* and *their*, *your* and *you're*, and *it's* and *its*. Also, a lot of our words have multiple meanings, such as *set*, *run*, *round*, *date*, and many, many others.

One of the solutions to this problem would be to have software and hardware with enough intelligence that it could not only recognize the words but recognize the meaning due to the context in which they are used. That requires more intelligence than some human beings have.

Security Systems

The voice of every person is as distinct and different as fingerprints. Voiceprints have been used to convict criminals. Since no two voices are alike, a voice recognition system could be used to practically eliminate the need for keys. Most automobiles already have several built-in computerized systems. You can be sure that sometime soon you will see autos that have a voice recognition system instead of ignition keys. Such a system could help reduce the number car thefts and carjacking.

A voice recognition system could also be used for any place that required strict security. If they installed voice recognition at Fort Knox, they could probably eliminate many of their other security measures. In most of the older systems, the computer had to be trained to recognize a specific word. Memory limitations and computer power was such that the vocabulary was quite limited. Today we have computers with hundreds of megabytes of memory and lots of power. Since every word is made up of only 42 phonemes, several companies such as IBM, Verbex Voice Systems, and Dragon Systems are working on systems that will use a small sample of a person's voice that contains these phonemes. Using the phonemes from this sample, the computer could then recognize any word that the person speaks.

Basic Systems

Verbex Voice Systems has developed a fairly sophisticated system that can almost obsolete the keyboard. Their Listen system for Windows uses special software and a 16-bit plug-in board with a digital signal processor (DSP) on it. After a bit of training, this system can recognize continuous speech. Of course, it is still not perfect, so there are times when you will have to slow down to discrete words and make corrections for words it does not understand. Call Verbex at 800-275-8729, or visit the Verbex Web site at www.verbex.com for more information and current pricing.

Digital Voice Recorders

The Olympus D1000 Digital Voice Recorder comes with IBM's ViaVoice software. It creates a whole new category of voice recorder and uses Intel's Flash Memory 2MB Miniature Card. It is a great solution for the mobile worker, as well as for the small office/home office (SOHO) and other businesses. The following information is from the Olympus Web site (www.olympusamerica.com):

> Users can dictate memos, reports, and other types of correspondences into the Olympus D1000 Digital Voice Recorder, where it is stored on the Flash Memory Miniature Card. The audio is then transferred to the PC, where

IBM's ViaVoice dictation product converts the recorded voice into text that can be edited, formatted, or printed, just like any word processor file.

The D1000 is shipped with a cable, a carrying case, a customized version ViaVoice, a 2MB Intel Flash Memory Miniature Card, and a PC adapter card. The removable miniature card and the Olympus PC adapter card (for PCMCIA slots) allow users to easily move audio files to a PC and conveniently share information with coworkers. The cable is for installation and enrollment of a customized version of ViaVoice. An optional Miniature Card reader/writer is available for desktop computer users.

The D1000 comes loaded with many features, including a removable flash memory card, overwrite recording, insert recording, and LCD information display. It has an ultra compact design, measuring a mere $4.7 \times 1.81 \times .091$ inches and weighing only 6 oz. with batteries. It easily fits in the pocket.

You can record in Standard or Long modes, by setting the REC TIME switch. Standard recording is 16 minutes with a 2MB card and 33 minutes with a 4MB card. Long recording is 34 minutes with a 2MB card and 72 minutes with a 4MB card. If using ViaVoice, you must be recording in the Standard mode. The D1000 comes standard with one 2MB card. Additional 2MB and 4MB cards can be purchased for increased storage.

Depending on the incoming speech activity, a unique algorithm called SCVA is incorporated dynamically, selecting one of two bit rates. This new SCVA (Silent Compression Voice Activation) allows you to save additional memory space by coding silence at a lower bit rate.

Large LCD Panel for Message and Operating Mode Display
Message editing made easy with three edit features: Over-Write, Insert, and Erase. Digital recording accommodates an Insert Recording feature not possible in analog recording. The Insert Recording feature is comparable to the ability to add text in word-processing software, creating a natural and efficient way to edit voice recordings. The Erase feature allows you to erase each file, part of a document, or the whole card. The Write Protection feature can be used for the entire card or for each file to prevent accidental erasure.

Files can be transferred to any laptop or desktop PC which has a PCMCIA slot. An optional Miniature Card reader/writer is available for desktop computer users. Fast-forward control will gradually speed up playback to 96 times normal speed, but will stop automatically at the end of the file.

ViaVoice Transcription is a customized version of the IBM ViaVoice using the speech engine of ViaVoice Gold.

Some Other Features With ViaVoice, you don't need to leave a brief pause between words. You talk naturally, and it types.

- *Type Eyes-free and Hands-free.* With ViaVoice, there is no need to stare at the screen or pound away at the keyboard. Just talk, it types! When you're finished with your text, then go back and make corrections.
- *Dictate into SpeakPad.* SpeakPad is ViaVoice's optimized speech recognition word processing environment. From SpeakPad, text may be transferred to any application, on any operating system that supports the cut and paste facility.
- *Dictate into MS Word.* With IBM ViaVoice a user may dictate directly into the Microsoft Word, word processing environment.
- *Play Back Your Dictation.* The system offers complete audio playback of a word, sentence or the entire text. This unique feature allows you to make sure that sounds and words match.
- *Train Incrementally.* ViaVoice allows users to train in small, easy steps. Try the first 50 sentences in the enrollment (training) process; it will take less than 30 minutes and will significantly increase your dictation accuracy.
- *Add Your Own Words.* ViaVoice ships with a 22,000 word base vocabulary and the ability for you to add 42,000 of your own words.
- *Learn Continuously.* ViaVoice adapts to you as you adapt to using it. The system continuously learns how you say and use words. If you dictate, correct and update, your dictation accuracy will just keep on getting better and better!
- It can be used as a standard audio recorder.

Figure 10-8 shows the small Olympus D1000 digital recorder. With this system, you need a line-in support. It is 100 percent compatible with Sound Blaster.

Computers and Devices for the Disabled

Having physical limitations can be worse than being in prison. It can be boring and depressing. Several computer devices have been developed that can help give people with disabilities a bit of freedom, allowing them to live more fulfilling, productive lives.

Just because they have a physical impairment doesn't mean that they have a brain impairment. Nature often compensates. For instance, the hearing and tactile senses of many blind people is much more acute than those who can see. There are devices that allow the blind, the deaf,

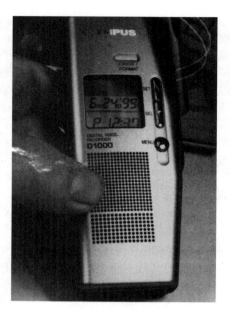

Figure 10-8
The Olympus digital
voice recorder.

the quadriplegic, and other severely disabled persons to communicate. One example is special braille keyboards and keyboards with enlarged keys for the blind. The EyeTyper from the Sentient Systems Technology of Pittsburgh, PA, has an embedded camera on the keyboard that can determine which key the user is looking at. It then enters that key into the computer. Words Plus of Sunnyvale, CA, has a sensitive visor that can understand input from a raised brow, head movement, or eye blinks.

The Speaking Devices Corp. (408-727-5571) has a telephone that can be trained to recognize an individual's voice. It can then dial up to 100 different numbers when the person tells it to. The same company has a tiny earphone that also acts as a microphone. These devices would be ideal for a person who can speak but cannot use his or her hands. Devices for the disabled can allow many people to lead active, useful, and productive lives. Some have become artists, programmers, writers, and scientists. IBM has a number of products, called the Independence Series, that are designed to aid those people with physical disabilities. They have a DOS-based utility, AccessDOS, that can be used to add functions to the keyboard, mouse, and sound boards. Call IBM at 800-426-4832 for more information.

Windows 95 also has a bit of help for disabled persons. Click on the Start button, highlight Settings, click on Control Panel, then double-click on Accessibility Options. You will see several window tabs: `StickyKeys` lets you press one key at a time instead of having to press two or three such as Ctl, Alt, Del, and `FilterKeys` tells Windows 95 to disregard keystrokes that are not held for a certain length of time; `SoundSentry` lets you substitute a visual cue for an audible alert, and `ShowSounds` can be used with programs that use digitized speech to display captions on screen; `Display` is an option that allows you to select colors, fonts, and high contrast; `MouseKeys` lets you control the cursor with the numeric keypad instead of a mouse; `SerialKey` option makes it easy to attach special equipment to the serial port.

Braille

I correspond frequently on the Internet with a friend who has been blind since early childhood. He has a computer with a braille reader and printer, along with a text-to-speech (TTS) recognition program. He has not ever considered his blindness to be a handicap. He figures that he can do almost anything that anyone else can do. Here is his signature:

> bud keith Ph.D., blind cross-country skier, tandem biker, returned Peace Corps volunteer and retired civil servant, currently surviving prostate cancer in arlington virginia.

Despite all of his problems, he has never lost his sense of humor. Sometimes he becomes a bit philosophical about how his blindness can allow him to see things so much better and differently than others. He is a delightful person to know.

One thing that his text-to-speech program will not do is recognize graphics. Someone sent him a drawing of a turkey on Thanksgiving, and he said his program went crazy trying to recognize it.

Here are some other companies who supply devices for people with disabilities:

Wrist and Arm Supports

Bucky Products	800-692-8259
DeRoyal/LMB	800-541-3992

Miniature Keyboards

InTouch Systems	800-332-6244
TASH	800-463-5685

Programmable Keyboards

Don Johnston	800-999-4660
IntelliTools	800-899-6687

On-Screen Keyboards

Don Johnston	800-999-4660
Words+	800-869-8521

Wands and Pointers

Extensions for Independence	619-423-1478
North Coast Medical	800-821-9319

Electronic Pointers

Ability Research	612-939-0121
Madenta	800-661-8406

Switches

AbleNet	800-322-0956
Toys for Special Children	800-832-8697

Touch Screens

Edmark	800-426-0856
MicroTouch Systems	800-642-7686

Voice Recognition

Dragon Systems	800-825-5897
Speech Systems	303 938-1110

Speech Technology Magazine is a free magazine to qualified subscribers. If you are in any kind of business that involves speech, you can probably qualify. Call 203-834-1430 for information and a qualifying form, or e-mail Speechmag@aol.com.

Several organizations can help in locating special equipment and lend support. If you know someone who might benefit from the latest technology and devices for people with disabilities, contact these organizations:

AbleData	800-344-5405
Accent on Information	309-378-2961
Apple Computer	408-996-1010
Closing the Gap, Inc.	612-248-3294
Direct Link for the Disabled	805-688-1603
Easter Seals Systems Office	312-667-8626
IBM National Support Center	800-426-2133
American Foundation for the Blind	212-620-2000
Trace Research and Development Center	608-262-6966
National ALS Association	818-340-7500

Some of these organizations will be glad to accept your old computers. Of course, you can write it off your income tax as a donation. You will be helping them and yourself. And you will feel better helping someone else.

11

Communications

One of the most important abilities enjoyed by humans is our many ways to communicate. Since the first time that someone yelled at the top of his or her lungs or beat on a hollow log, we have been constantly striving to improve our methods of communicating. We have come a long way since that first human yelled or beat on the hollow log. Today, we have more means of communicating than at any time in history. We can easily communicate with someone on the other side of the world and don't even have to raise our voices.

The reason for communications is to share information for pleasure, for health, for business, and for every aspect of our daily lives. One of the worst punishments of all is to be ostracized, or forced out of a group by common consent. When the ancient Greeks wanted to punish someone or ban them from the community, they ostracized them. They voted by depositing fragments of *ostrakon*, Greek for *shell*, hence *ostracize*. We all need to communicate.

Some people think that today we have too much information—that it is overwhelming. In order to try to keep up with this industry, I subscribe to over 25 computer magazines. I also spend a lot of time on the Internet and have at least 50 messages every day. It is truly almost overwhelming. Someone has coined the term "infoglut." Whether you like it or not, the infoglut is going to continue to grow. What we all need is enough information to be able to determine what we need without being overwhelmed. If only there were some way to separate the wheat from the chaff without having to sift through it all.

Telephones

Telephones are one of the most important communications devices ever invented. It can be a critical part of our personal life, as well as for almost all business. By adding a modem to your computer, you can make the telephone even more useful and important. You can use your computer and the telephone line to access online services, bulletin boards, for telecommuting, for the Internet, and to communicate with anyone else in the world who also has a computer and modem. Many modem boards are now integrated with fax capability. A modem board with a fax may not cost much more than the modem alone. Communicating by fax is fast and efficient.

Reaching Out

There are about 400 million computers installed in homes, offices, and businesses worldwide. About half of them have a modem or some sort of communications capability. This capability is one of the computer's most important aspects. A short time ago, if your computer had a modem, you could access over 10,000 electronic bulletin boards in the United States. But the Internet has just about made them obsolete. Every business in the country that is of any size now has a Web site. This World Wide Web is much better than a bulletin board. In addition, electronic mail (e-mail) has almost made snail mail obsolete. You can send an e-mail across the street or to anywhere in the world in just seconds. It may take the post office days or weeks to deliver the same message.

The Internet can also provide up-to-the-minute stock market quotations, as well as a large number of other online services, such as home shopping, home banking, travel agencies, business transactions, many databases, data services, and even dating services.

There may be times when you need to send a signature, blueprints, or a form to be filled out. A fax machine can send it in about the same time that it takes for e-mail to be delivered.

For some types of work, a person can use a modem and work from home. Telecommuting is a whole lot better than commuting by car and sitting in traffic jams on the crowded freeways and breathing poisonous exhaust fumes.

Communications covers a wide range of activities and technologies. Many books have been written that cover all phases of communications. Just a few of the many technologies will be discussed in this chapter.

The Internet and World Wide Web

One of the hottest topics at the moment is the Internet and World Wide Web (WWW). The Internet is so important that Chapter 14 is devoted to it.

Modems

A *modem* is an electronic device that allows a computer to use an ordinary telephone line to communicate with other computers that are equipped with a modem. *Modem* is a contraction of the words *modulate* and *demodulate*. The telephone system transmits voice and data in analog voltage form. Analog voltages are sine waves that vary continuously up and down. Computer data is usually in a digital voltage form, which is a series of on and off square wave voltages. Check back to Figure 1-5 to see what a sine wave and square wave look like.

The modem takes the digitized bits of voltage from the computer and modulates, or transforms, it into analog voltages in order to transmit it over the telephone lines. At the receiving end, a similar modem will demodulate the analog voltage and transform it back into a digital form.

Transmission Difficulties

Telephone systems were originally designed long before we had the ability to digitize the signals. Analog sine wave voltage was all that we had at the time. They were originally designed for voice and have a very narrow bandwidth. A person with perfect hearing can hear 20 cycles per second, or hertz (Hz), all the way up to 20,000Hz. For normal speech, we only use about 300Hz up to 2000Hz.

Telephone analog voltages are subject to noise, static, and other electrical disturbances. Noise and static takes the form of analog voltages. So does most of the other electrical disturbances such as electrical storms and pulses generated by operating electrical equipment. The analog noise and static voltages may be mixed in with any analog data voltages that are being transmitted. The mixture of the static and noise voltages with the data voltages can corrupt and severely damage the data. The demodulator may be completely at a loss to determine which voltages represent data and which is just noise.

Baud Rate

These problems, and the state of technology at the time, limited the original modems to about 5 characters per second (cps), or a rate of 50 baud. [We get the term *baud* from Emile Baudot (1845–1903), a French inventor.]

Originally, the *baud rate* was a measure of the dots and dashes in telegraphy. It is now defined as the actual rate of symbols transmitted per second. For lower baud rates, it is essentially the same as bits per second. Remember that it takes 8 bits to make one alphanumeric character.

Just as we have periods and spaces to separate words, we must use one start bit and one stop bit to separate the on/off bits into characters. A transmission of 300 baud would mean that 300 on/off bits are sent in one second. For every 8 bits of data that represents a character, we need 1 bit to indicate the start of a character and 1 bit to indicate the end. We then need another bit to indicate the start of the next character. So counting the start/stop bits, it takes 11 bits for each character. If we divide 300 by 11, it gives us about 27 cps. Some of the newer technologies may actually transmit symbols that represent more than 1 bit. For baud rates of 1200 and higher, the cps and baud rate can be considerably different.

There have been some fantastic advances in the modem technologies. A few years ago, 2400-baud systems were the standard. Today they are obsolete. The industry leaped over the 4800 and 9600 baud systems to the 14.4K systems (*K* is shorthand for Kbps, or kilobits per second), then doubled to the 28.8K, then 33.6K and now the 56K.

When two modems communicate, both the sending and receiving unit must operate at the same baud rate and use the same protocols. Most of the faster modems are downward compatible and can operate at the slower speeds. Since the advent of the Internet and e-mail, there is not much need to directly access another computer with a modem. Almost everyone has an e-mail address.

If you use a modem frequently, a high-speed modem can quickly pay for itself. We have sure come a long way since those early 50-baud standards.

56K Modems

Originally, the Public Switched Telephone Network (PSTN), a fancy name for our Plain Old Telephone System (POTS), was analog. Over the past few years, once the telephone message gets from your telephone line to a central office, in most instances it is converted to digital information and transmitted by radio relay to the next station. When it gets to the central office closest to where you are calling, the digital message is converted back to analog data and transmitted by wire to the telephone.

The 56K is a bit misleading. It is possible to download files from the Internet at close to 56Kbps, but the fastest you can upload a file is the standard 33.6Kbps. One reason for the limitation is the fact that the data has to be converted or modulated from digital to analog when sending, then converted back to digital or demodulated on the receiving end. A man named Shannon came up with a law that states that the maximum possible speed over the Public Switched Telephone Network was 35Kbps. In addition, a federal regulation limits the amount of power that can be sent over the PSTN. The higher speeds require higher voltages, and higher voltages may cause crosstalk or interference with other messages on adjacent lines. Under ideal conditions, the maximum speed is about 53Kbps.

An all-digital network would allow much greater speeds. Digital voltages are not affected by noise or static. The modern telephone networks send and receive digital data between central stations. But your telephone line to the central station is still analog.

On the download side, Internet service providers and large companies can install special equipment that can bypass the analog loop and send it as digital data directly to the central office. It still must come from the nearest central office as analog data to your modem, then be converted back to digital for the computer. If the lines are dirty and noisy between the central station and your computer, you may not be able to enjoy the full 56Kbps transmission. Even with the best conditions, you may never get more than 48Kbps. Like the standard systems, whenever a high-speed connection is not possible, the 56K systems fall back to the next lower speed that is reliable. So you shouldn't be surprised if it drops to as low as 28.8Kbps at times. Figure 11-1 shows a 56K modem.

The Integrated Services Digital Network (ISDN) is faster than the 56K systems. You can have two 64K systems, for a total of 128K. But it requires an expensive special line installation and a fairly high monthly fee.

One good thing about the 56K technology is that you do not have to have new lines installed and there is no increase in telephone charges.

Figure 11-1
A 56K modem.

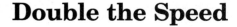

Double the Speed

Diamond Multimedia (www.diamondmm.com) has developed a single board with two 56K modems on it. Using two phone lines, you can double the speed. Some testers have got up to 105Kbps with this system on the downstream side. This is almost as fast as ISDN and a whole lot less expensive.

At this time, Diamond is selling the modems for $149.95 with a $50 rebate, so that the final cost is 5 cents less than $100. The big problem is that many of ISPs are not set up to let you use the dual modem. Before you buy one, make sure that there is a local ISP who will let you use it.

Here is some more information about the dual modem from Diamond's Web site:

SupraSonic II Dual Line Modem

The SupraSonic® II with Shotgun™ technology integrates two 56K modems on one board for speeds of up to 112K! Plus, it's designed with the new 56K ITU standard (V.90) and K56flex for widespread ISP support. The SupraSonic II works over two ordinary phone lines to deliver this amazing speed without monopolizing the use of your second phone line. Featuring Voice Priority, the SupraSonic II "senses" incoming calls (voice, fax, etc.) and allows them to ring through on your second line. It also allows the user to manually release or add a second phone line to the Internet connection by simply clicking on a software button.

Some of the features are: Flash ROM upgradeable, Bandwidth-on-Demand, Caller ID, Distinctive Ring, Shotgun technology, and Voice Priority.

How to Estimate Connect Time

You can figure the approximate length of time that it will take to transmit a file. For rough approximations of cps, you can divide the baud rate by 10. For instance, a 33.6K modem would transmit at about 3360 cps. Look at the directory and determine the number of bytes in the file. Divide the number of bytes by the cps to get a rough approximation. For instance, to transmit a file with 336,000 bytes at 3360 bytes per second, it would take about 100 seconds.

Protocols

Protocols are procedures that have been established for exchanging data, along with the instructions that coordinate the process. Most protocols can sense when the data is corrupted or lost due to noise, static, or a bad connection. It will automatically resend the affected data until it is received correctly. The protocol transmits a block, or packet, of data along with an error-checking code, then waits for the receiver to send back an acknowledgment. It then sends another packet and waits to see if it got through okay. If a packet does not get through, it is re-sent immediately. Both the sending and receiving modems must use the same protocol and baud rate. However, the faster modems are able to shift down and send or receive at the lower speeds.

ITU Recommended Standards

Because the communications industry is very complex, there have not been many real standards. There are many different manufacturers and software developers, and, of course, all of them want to differentiate their hardware or software by adding new features.

A United Nations standards committee was established to help create world-wide standards. If every country had different protocols and standards, communicating would be very difficult. The original committee was called the Comité Consulatif International Téléphonique et Télégraphique (CCITT). The name has now been changed to International Telecommunications Union (ITU). This committee has representatives from over 80 countries and several large private manufacturers. The committee makes recommendations only. A company is free to use or ignore them. But more and more companies are now adopting the recommendations.

All ITU recommendations for small computers have a *V* or *X* prefix. The V series is for use with switched telephone networks, which is almost all of them. The X series is for systems that do not use switched phone lines. Revisions or alternate recommendations have *bis* (second) or *ter* (third) added.

The V prefixes can be a bit confusing. For instance, a V.32 modem can communicate at 4800 or 9600 bits per second (bps), and it can communicate with any other V.32 modem. A V.32bis can communicate at 14,400 bps.

The V.32bis standard is a modulation method and is not a compression technique. The V.34 standard is for 28.8K modems. A V.42bis standard is a method of data compression plus a system of error-checking. A V.42bis can communicate with another V.42bis at up to 57,600 bps by using compression and error-checking.

Low-Cost Communication Software

If you buy a modem or modem/fax board, many companies include a basic communications program. If you subscribe to one of the large online services such as AOL or Prodigy, they provide special software for their connections. Netscape and Microsoft Internet Explorer are well known as browsers, but they also handle e-mail and have several other utilities.

Basic Types of Modems

There are two basic types of modems: the external desktop and the internal. Each type has some advantages and disadvantages. For the external, a disadvantage is that the unit requires some of your precious desk space and a voltage source. It also requires an external cable from a COM port to drive it. The good news is that most external models have LEDs that light up and let you know what is happening during your call.

The external and most of the internal models have speakers that let you hear the ring or a busy signal. But the internal modem may have a very small speaker, and you may not even be able to hear the dial tone and the ringing. Some external models have a volume control for the built-in speaker.

The internal modem is built entirely on a board, usually a half or short board. The good news is that it doesn't use up any of your desk real estate; the bad news is that it uses one of your precious slots. It also does not have the LEDs to let you know the progress of your call. Of course, not being able to see the LEDs flashing may not be that important to you. The only thing most people care about is whether it is working or not. The fewer items to worry about, the better.

External modems may cost up to $50 or more than an equivalent internal modem. By far, the most popular modems are the internal types. The external modems may also require an external 110V power source. This type of modem is practically obsolete.

Hayes Compatibility

One of the most popular early modems was made by Hayes Microcomputer Products. They became the IBM of the modem world and established a de facto standard. Currently, there are hundreds of modem manufacturers. Except for some of the very inexpensive ones, almost all of them are Hayes-compatible.

Installing a Modem

The first thing to do when installing a modem (or any device) is to check your documentation to see if there are any jumpers or switches needed to configure the device. There probably will not be any. The older modems usually had jumpers or small switches that had to be set to enable COM1, COM2, COM3, or COM4. Under Windows 95/98 and Plug and Play devices, there may be no jumpers to set.

Find an empty slot and plug the board in. The older modems used the Industry Standard Architecture (ISA)-type 16-bit boards. Most all modems today use the PCI slots.

Normally, most systems only allow for two ports: COM1, which uses IRQ4 and COM2, which uses IRQ3. But COM1 and COM3 can share IRQ4, and COM2 and COM4 can share IRQ3 if the software or hardware will allow it. Before Plug and Play, one of the biggest problems of installing serial-type hardware such as network cards, mice, modems, fax boards, sound cards, serial printers, plotters, and other serial devices is that there just aren't enough IRQs. All of our computers, even the most powerful Pentium III, only have 16 IRQs, and most of them are reserved for other uses. The Plug and Play specifications automatically select the best way for the device to be installed. The specifications have eliminated a lot of problems.

The IRQs (interrupt requests) cause the BIOS and CPU to stop whatever they are doing and give their attention to the current request. The

TABLE 11-1

IRQ Arrangement

IRQ No.	Users
0	Timer click
1	Keyboard
2	Second 8259A
3	COM2: COM4
4	COM1: COM3
5	LPT2
6	Floppy disk
7	LPT1
8	Real-time clock
9	Redirected IRQ2
10	(Reserved)
11	(Reserved)
12	(Reserved)
13	Math coprocessor
14	Fixed disk
15	(Reserved)

IRQs have a hierarchical arrangement so that the lower-numbered IRQs have priority. Table 11-1 shows how my IRQs are arranged.

It is permissible to use any of the IRQs marked "Reserved" for things like sound boards and network cards, but serial devices such as mice and modems must be connected to one of the COM ports. A PS/2 mouse does not use a COM port, but it does require an IRQ, usually IRQ12. If you are using Windows 95/98 and want to see how your IRQs are assigned, click on the My Computer icon, then click on Control Panel. Now click on the System icon, then the Device Manager tab. This will bring up a list of all the items in your computer. At the top of the list is Computer. Double-click on Computer, and it will show you a list of all your IRQs that are being used. (It will not show those that are not currently being used.) Some that may be open are 10, 11, 12, and 15. If you are installing an external modem, you must go through the same procedure to make sure the COM port is accessible and does not conflict. If you have a mouse, a serial printer, or some other serial device, you will have to determine which port they are set to. You cannot have two serial devices set to the same COM port unless you have special software that will allow them to share the port. It is not always obvious that an interrupt is in use.

It is a crying shame that even the fastest, most powerful computers still only have 16 IRQs and most of them are used by the system. If you need to install a sound board, a modem, a mouse, a network card, a SCSI device, or any of many other peripherals, you may not have enough IRQs. There are some devices that will share IRQs, but most of them are selfish and don't like to share.

Plug and Play (PnP)

All motherboards today will have a Plug and Play (PnP) BIOS. Almost all devices are now manufactured to the PnP specifications. When you plug in a board, Windows will check to determine which IRQs are free and automatically set itself so that there is no conflict. But it is not always that easy. When the Pentium II first came out, I bought the fastest one available, a 266MHz Intel Pentium II. I also bought a 233MHz AMD K6 and a Cyrix 6x86MX PR200. Until this time I had been using a 120MHz Pentium system. I removed the Pentium motherboard and installed the new motherboard with the Cyrix 6x86MMX PR 200.

Everything worked great except for my modem. I opened the Windows 95 Control Panel and clicked on Modems. A window came up and said that my modem, a Diamond SupraExpress 33.6, was installed. I clicked on the tab marked Diagnostics. A display showed that the modem was connected to COM3, Interrupt 11, address 3E8. I then clicked on More Info. A message was displayed saying that Windows would test the modem. Then an error message was displayed that said, "The modem failed to respond. Make sure it is properly connected and turned on. If it is an internal modem and is connected, verify that the interrupt for the port is properly set."

On my old motherboard, the modem had been set for COM1. But COM3 should have been okay. I didn't know why it would not work. I was a bit unhappy: I had wasted a whole day trying different combinations to install the modem. I thought there might be something wrong with the new motherboard, so I tried the modem on my Intel 266MHz Pentium II. It would not work there either. I then thought that perhaps I had somehow damaged the modem when I removed it from the

120MHz motherboard. So I installed it again on the old motherboard, and it worked perfectly.

I then thought that perhaps the modem was just not capable of working at the higher frequencies. I called the long-distance support number, and after pushing about 15 different buttons for choices and options, I was put in a queue for technical support. I was told that I would have to wait about 20 minutes for a technician.

When the technician finally came on, he had me go back to the Control Panel and check the `Modem`, `Diagnostics`, and `More Info` areas that I had already checked. He then had me click on the `System` icon, then on `Device Manager`. Then he had me click on `Modem`, then on my `SupraExpress 336i`. A window came up, and he had me click on `Properties`. Another window came up, and he had me click to delete the check on `Automatic Settings`. He then had me click on `Change Settings`, then on `Resources`. A window came up that said "Edit Interrupt Requests."

The interrupt, number 11, that was presently being used was displayed. Below it was a box that said this interrupt was not conflicting with any other interrupt. But evidently it was lying. At this point you can enter a specific interrupt number, or you can use the up-down arrows to install any interrupt that is not being used. Interrupt 15 said it was free and would cause no conflicts. I said okay to 15, then went back and clicked on `Modems` and `Diagnostics`. Then I had Windows try to communicate with the modem. Again, an error message came up that the modem was not responding. I went back to `Systems` and `Device Manager`, then to `Change Settings`; I then selected interrupt 12. I went back to `Modems` and `Diagnostics`, then to `More Info`, and I had Windows try to communicate with the modem. Even though the box had said there was no conflict, I still got an error that said the modem failed to respond.

I went back to `Systems` and `Device Manager` to try the one remaining IRQ that was free, number 10. This one worked like a charm. I still have no idea why the others did not work. Windows said that they were free and that there was no conflict. I believed Windows when it first told me that there was no conflict with interrupt 11, which Windows had automatically assigned to the modem. I also believed it when it told me that there was no conflict with interrupt numbers 15 and 12 also. But again, Windows was lying. It was only telling the truth when it said there was no conflict on IRQ number 10. Because I believed it when it said there was no conflict with the automatically assigned IRQ11, I thought there must be some other problem. Therefore I never thought to try the other IRQs.

But I still had one more problem. My AOL and Prodigy software was set for a modem that operated on COM1. This one was now operating on COM3. It was fairly easy to use the Setup option on the AOL and Prodigy sign-on screens and reassign the modem COM ports from COM1 to COM3.

There are not quite as many problems with Plug and Play today, but most of the major companies have to maintain an extensive help desk for technical support. At one time, technical support was free. Now most companies charge for it. Today even toll-free calls are no longer available for many companies. If you have to wait a half-hour just to speak to a support technician, the toll charges can mount up.

Connecting to the Line

There should be two connectors at the back end of the modem board. One may be labeled "Line in" and the other "Phone." Unless you have a dedicated telephone line, you should unplug your telephone, plug an extension into the modem line, then plug the telephone into a jack marked "Phone."

After you have connected all of the lines, turn on your computer and try the modem before you put the cover back on. Quite often I have installed something, put the cover back on, and then found it would not work. So I would have to remove the cover and try to find out what I did wrong. Now I always try a new device before buttoning up the computer.

Unless you expect to do a lot of communicating, you may not need a separate dedicated line. But you may need some sort of switching device, such as those from Command Communications (800-288-6794). They have several different devices that can recognize an incoming voice, modem, or fax signal and route the call.

Fax/Modem Software

Most fax/modems come with several communication software packages. One time, the fax/modem that I had been using for the last couple of years died on me. I bought a new one and installed it, along with some communication software that came with it. It screwed up my system completely. I could no longer access Prodigy or CompuServe. I sweated for half a day before I discovered that the included software was terminate-and-stay-resident (TSR). It loaded itself into memory each time I booted up. With that software in memory, I could not access CompuServe or Prodigy. I only had 8MB of RAM memory at that time. I now have 128MB, so the TSR probably wouldn't make much difference on this system.

You can find out if there are any TSRs loaded into memory on your computer when in Windows by pressing Ctrl+Alt+Delete once. (If you do it twice, it will shut the computer down.) This will show you a list of any TSR programs in memory. You can then highlight them or point to them with the mouse, then press Enter, and they will be closed. However, be sure not to close Explorer, or your computer will shut down.

There are thousands of little things that can go wrong. PnP will go a long way to help solve some of the problems, but it can't possibly solve all the potential problems.

Viruses

A few years ago, you could access a bulletin board and download all kinds of good public domain or shareware software. You never had to worry about the software destroying your data. But later a few sick psychopaths created computer viruses. These scum, these @#$%$##*& no-good pieces of slime create virus programs with the purpose of harming someone that they don't even know. They get no monetary rewards for creating viruses. Evidently, their reward is the pleasure they get from destroying data or work that may have taken years to accomplish.

Several viruses and worms have been posted on the Internet. They are usually hidden in an attachment that has to be downloaded onto your hard drive. Ordinarily, you can't get a virus just by opening and reading your e-mail.

There are all kinds of people in this world. But I cannot imagine why anyone would be so mean and dastardly as to harm someone they don't even know. I wouldn't condone it, but I might be able to understand doing harm to someone as revenge for some wrong they had received. But the no-good &**&$@# people who write viruses seem to get their jollies by harming people they have never met or will never know. (*Note:* The &**&$@# is shorthand for some very dirty words that can't be used in a book like this.)

A computer virus is not a living thing. It cannot harm you—only the data in a computer or on a disk. But you may have invested a large part of your life creating that data. A computer virus is usually a bit of program code, hidden in a piece of legitimate software. The virus is usually designed to redirect, corrupt, or destroy data. It may resemble an organic virus in that it can cause a wide variety of virus-type symptoms in the computer host.

The virus code may be written so that it can replicate or make copies of itself. When it becomes embedded on a disk, it can attach itself to other programs that it comes in contact with. If your system has a virus and a file is copied onto a floppy disk, it could come away with a hidden copy of the virus.

Infected software may appear to work as it should for some time. But eventually, it may contaminate and destroy many of your files. If a virus gets on a workstation or network, it can infect all of the computers in the network.

Here is some reliable antivirus software and their manufacturers:

Norton AntiVirus from Symantec	www.symantec.com
PC-cillin from TouchStone	www.checkit.com
McAfee Antivirus	www.mcafee.com

Visit their Web sites for information and downloads.

The U.S. Department of Energy has established the Computer Incident Advisor Capability (CIAC). It has lots of information about viruses. There are over 20,000 viruses, some just slight variations of an original. The CIAC lists some of the more infamous of them. Visit their Web site at http://ciac.llnl.gov.

Many of the companies who provide antivirus software and tools have Web sites with lots of information about what a virus is, the types of viruses, and how they operate. These sites, along with other virus information pages, can tell you all you need to know about viruses, worms, and Trojan horses:

Symantec Antivirus Research Center	www.symantec.com/avcenter/
Dr. Solomon's Virus Central	www.drsolomon.com/vircen/
DataFellows Virus Information Center	www.datafellows.com/vir-info/
Stiller Research Virus Information	www.stiller.com/
Virus Bulletin Home Page	www.virusbtn.com/
Joe Well's Wild Lists —Viruses in the Wild	www.virusbtn.com/WildLists/

NIST Virus Information Page	csrc.nist.gov/virus/
McAfee Virus Pages	www.mcafee.com/
Sophos Virus Information Page	www.sophos.com/virusinfo/
Trend Micro Virus Encyclopedia	www.antivirus.com/vinfo/vinfo. html
AVP Virus Encyclopedia	www.avpve.com/

Virus Hoaxes

A group has surfaced recently who are almost as bad as the virus writers. These are people who broadcast virus hoaxes. A person has to have a good knowledge of programming and computer technology to be able to write a computer virus. It takes no technical knowledge to be able to devise a virus hoax. Once the hoax has been posted on the Internet, others with good intentions pick it up and rebroadcast it.

A hoax that has been on the Internet several times is that if you read a certain e-mail, it will infect your system. Many have started chain letters about the phony viruses. Just reading your e-mail will not affect your system. When you open e-mail to read it, you are reading it from an Internet service provider's server. Unless you download the e-mail to your own hard disk, it remains on the ISP server. The hoaxes have become so prevalent that many of the antivirus companies have placed information about them on their Web pages. (Of course they also provide information about real viruses.) In addition, the U.S. Government Department of Energy's CIAC Web site compiles a list of the virus hoaxes and updates them often. Visit the Web site at http://ciac.lln.gov.

Online Services

Online services provide forums for help and discussions, mailboxes, and a large variety of information and reference services. A caller can search the databases and download information as easily as pulling the data off his or her own hard disk. They also have phone service to most areas in the larger cities, so there is not even a toll charge. They have an impressive list of services, including home shopping, home banking, airline schedules and reservations, stock market quotations, a medical bulletin board, and many others.

See Chapter 14 for more about the Internet.

Banking by Modem

Many banks offer systems that will let you do all your banking with your computer and a modem from the comfort of your home. You never again have to drive downtown, hunt for a parking space, then stand in line for a half-hour to do your banking.

Intuit (415-322-0573) developed Quicken, an excellent financial software program. Intuit also offers CheckFree, a service that allows you to pay all of your bills electronically. Or you can print your checks from your computer on a laser printer. (This requires special checks that are imprinted with your account number in magnetic ink.) CheckFree costs about $10 a month. But if you spend about four hours a month paying bills, the $10 is not very much compared to the time spent. Another advantage to CheckFree is that the bills are paid automatically, but not until they are due. This lets your account accrue interest until the last moment. If you ordinarily write a lot of checks, CheckFree and Quicken can quickly pay for themselves.

Intuit is also the developer of TurboTax, one of the better software packages for doing your taxes. This company offers some of the most complete financial software available for your computer system. With a good financial program, you can get rid of the shoe boxes full of canceled checks. It can also make the onerous task that occurs on April 15 each year a bit easier to accomplish.

Facsimile (Fax) Machines

Facsimile (fax) machines have been around for quite a while. Newspapers and businesses have used them for years. The early machines were similar to the early acoustic modems. Both used foam-rubber cups that fit over the telephone receiver/mouthpiece for coupling. They were very slow and subject to noise and interference.

Fax machines and modems have come a long way since those early days. A page of text or a photo is fed into the fax machine and scanned. As the scanning beam moves across the page, white and dark areas are digitized as 1s and 0s, then transmitted out over the telephone lines. On the receiving end of the line, a scanning beam moves across the paper. The dark areas cause it to print as it sweeps across the paper. The finished product is a black-and-white image of the original.

When a text file is sent by modem, the digitized bits that make up each character are converted from digital voltage to analog voltage. A modem sends and receives bits that make up each character. A fax machine or board sends and receives scanned whole pages of letters, graphics, images, signatures, and so on. Since a modem recognizes individual characters, a computer program can be sent over a modem but not over a fax. A fax sends and receives the information as digitized graphic data. A modem converts the digital information that represents individual characters into analog voltages, sends it over the line, then converts it back to individual digital characters.

There are times when a modem or fax is needed. Both units cannot be in use at the same time on the same phone line. However, a single phone line can be used for both fax and modem if they are not used concurrently.

Millions of facsimile machines are in use today. There are very few businesses that could not benefit from the use of a fax. It can be used to send documents that include handwriting, signatures, seals, letterheads, graphs, blueprints, photos, and other types of data around the world, across the country, or across the room to another fax machine. Overnight mail services may cost from $8 to $10 or more. A fax machine can deliver the same letter for about 40 cents and do it in less than three minutes. Many software programs will let you delay sending a fax until late at night to get the best rates. Depending on the type of business and the amount of critical mail that must be sent out, a fax system can pay for itself in a very short time. If you have a fax/modem board, it may be even less expensive to send e-mail.

Most of the early fax machines used thermal-type paper for printing. The thermal paper does not provide very good resolution, and it fades when exposed to light. Most of the fax machines today use inkjet or laser technology and print on plain paper. They are usually a bit slow, but almost all of the fax machines can be used as a copier. In fact, fax machines have a lot in common with copy machines, scanners, and printers. Several companies have added these features to their machines so that one multifunction machine can do the work of several.

Fax/Modem Computer Boards

Several companies have developed fax systems on circuit boards that can be plugged into computers. Most of the fax boards are now integrated with a modem on the same board. The modem and fax combination costs little more than either board separately. This combination also saves having to use an extra plug-in slot. For some time, the standard baud rate for fax transmissions was 9600. Many of the newer fax/modem boards are now capable of a 14,400 speed for faxes. However, just like the modem connections, both the sender and receiver must be operating at the same speed. Also like the modem, the fax can shift down to match the receiver if it is slower.

Fax Software

One of the better fax software packages is WinFax Pro 9.0 from Symantec (www.symantec.com). It will let you print a fax to a modem or to a printer. You can store attachments to be added to a fax, and you can have multiple phone books for fax recipients and many other utilities and functions.

Most fax software allows the computer to control the fax boards. Using the computer's word processor, letters and memos can be written and sent out over the phone lines. Several letters or other documents can be stored or retrieved from the computer's hard disk and transmitted. The computer can be programmed to send the letters out at night when rates are lower.

The computer fax boards have one disadvantage. They cannot include information such as signatures, graphics, or drawings that are not in the computer. But with a scanner, this information can be stored as a file on a hard disk, then added to a document that is to be faxed. With the proper software, a computer can receive and store any fax. The digitized data and images can be stored on a hard disk, then printed out.

Fax-on-Demand

Several companies have set up fax machines that can supply information to you 24 hours a day. You simply call them with your voice phone, tell them what documents you want, give them your fax number, and the documents will be sent immediately. Most of the companies have a catalog that lists all of their documents and the document number. You should first ask to have the catalog faxed to you. You can then determine which documents to order.

The FaxFacts Company (708-682-8898) publishes a small booklet that lists several companies who have the fax-on-demand or faxback capability. They list things such as medical, computers, travel, trade shows, and many more categories.

Most faxback information is free, but some companies, such as Consumer Reports (800-766-9988), ask for a credit card number and charge a fee for articles you request. Here are just a few of the other companies who offer faxback or fax-on-demand (when you call, ask for their new users instructions and navigation map):

Borland TechFax	800-822-4269
Cyrix Direct Connect	800-215-6823
IBM	800-426-4329
Novell Support Line	800-638-9273
Symantec Corp.	800-554-4403

If you prefer, most will send the information to you by mail rather than by fax.

FAX/Modem/Phone Switch

Having the modem and telephone on the same line should cause no problems unless someone tries to use the telephone while the modem is using it. Life will be a lot simpler though if you have a switch that can detect whether the incoming signal is for a fax, a modem, or voice. Fax and modem signals transmit a high-pitched tone, called the CNG (CalliNG) signal. A fax/modem switch can switch and route the incoming call to the proper device.

You should be aware that there are a few old fax systems that do not use the CNG signals. My Command Communication system will let me manually transfer the call in that case. There is another solution for those who have machines without the CNG signal. The telephone company can set up two or more numbers with different and distinctive rings on a single line. The Command Communications switchers can be programmed to recognize the distinctive ring and route the call to the proper device. In addition, the South Tech Instruments Company (800-394-5556) has a FoneFilter device that can recognize the distinctive rings and route the call to a fax, modem, or answering machine. Of course, there is a charge by the telephone company for the extra numbers added to your line. At this time, in the Los Angeles area, it costs $7.50 to set up a separate distinctive ring on your line and then $6 a month thereafter. This is still less expensive than adding a second line.

Command Communications (800-288-6794) has several different model switchers that are suitable for homes, small offices, and large businesses. They have connections for a telephone answering device (TAD), telephone extensions, a fax machine or fax board, and a connection for an auxiliary device or modem. The alternative to a switcher would be to install a dedicated telephone line for the fax machine, another line for the modem, and another line for voice. If you don't do a lot of transmissions by fax and modem, you can get by with a single telephone and a good switcher. It can pay for itself many times over. Many of the standalone fax machines have a built-in detector that can determine if the incoming call is for voice or fax.

Telephone Outlets for Extensions

You need a telephone line or extension to hook up a computer modem or a fax. You may also want telephone outlets in several rooms, at one or more desks, or at another computer. You can go to almost any hardware store, and even some grocery and drug stores, and buy the telephone wire and accessories needed. But you may have trouble running telephone wires to the computer, desks, and other rooms. It can be a lot of work cutting holes in the walls and running the wires up in the attic or under the floor.

There is a much simpler way. Just use the 110V wiring of the building. The Phonex Company (801-566-0100) developed special adapters that plug into any wall plug outlet. It requires at least two adapters: one for the telephone input line and another for where you want the extension. More adapters can be plugged into any other 110V outlet to provide as many telephone extensions as needed. Or if you need an extension in another location, just unplug an adapter and plug it into another nearby wall outlet. You could even use a standard electrical extension cord and a Phonex adapter to provide a telephone extension.

Electronic circuitry in the adapters blocks the AC voltage from getting into the telephone lines, but allows voice and data to go through. The device is being marketed and sold by Comtrad Industries (800-704-1211).

Combination Devices and Voice Mail

Fax machines, copiers, printers, and scanners all have a lot in common. Several companies are now taking advantage of this commonality and offering combination devices. Some companies are starting to use color for fax. If you have one of the combination devices with a color scanner, Laser Today International (415-961-3015) has software that will let you send and receive color faxes.

If you don't already have an all-in-one machine, the Compex International Company (800-626-8112) has a combination fax, scanner, printer, and copier. The Speaking Devices Corporation (408-727-2132) has a unit with a fax, a fax/phone switch, a scanner, voice mail, and Caller ID. In addition, Boca Research (561-997-6227) has a multimedia voice modem that has up to 1000 password-protected voice and fax mailboxes, as well as private and public fax-on-demand, remote message and fax retrieval, professionally recorded greetings and voice prompts, and personalized greetings for individual mailboxes.

Tiger Software (800-888-4437) publishes a catalog that has hundreds of software and hardware items. They advertise the Vomax 2000, which is a fax, voice, and modem system. It has 1MB of digital storage, which can store up to 20 minutes of voice-mail messages or up to 50 sheets of faxes. It also has message forwarding so that it can call another number and play your messages. In addition, this device can call your pager and relay messages. Call Tiger Software for a catalog and more information.

AnyWhere Associates (617-522-8102) has software that allows you to send e-mail to faxes. Cylink (408-735-5800) and Syntel Sciences (800-499-1469) have software that lets you encrypt faxes so that your nosey neighbor will not be able to read them.

Telecommuting

Millions of people risk their lives and fight frustrating traffic every day. Many of these people have jobs that could allow them to stay home, work on a computer, then send the data to the office over a modem or a fax. Even if the person had to buy his or her own computer, modem, and fax, it might still be worth the investment. You could save the cost of gasoline, auto maintenance, and lower insurance. Thousands are killed on the highways; telecommuting can be a life saver. In addition, being able to work from home is ideal for those who have young children, for people with disabilities, or for anyone who hates being stuck in traffic jams.

Another very big plus for those working at home is that he or she can be an "open-collar worker"—unlike a "blue-collar worker" or a "white-collar worker." Many women spend thousands of dollars buying new outfits so that they can wear a different one to work each day of the week. They can save that money (and on dry-cleaning bills) if they work at home. Men won't save as much because few people notice if they wear the same clothes more than once a week. (A man can wear the same shirt two or three times in the same week if he wears a tie so that no one can see the ring around the collar. This is one of the best reasons I know of for wearing a tie.) If you are working at home, you can wear any old clothes as often as you like. If you are living alone, you don't have to wear anything at all (but you probably should remember to put on a robe or something when answering the door for the UPS or FedEx delivery person).

There are several technological tools, such as modems/fax/voice/whatever machines, remote access software, conference calling software, cellular telephones, and many other goodies that can make working from home almost like being at the office. A telecommuter can have a first-class virtual office in a bedroom or den. A plus for the company is that they will be saving office space, parking space, and less wear and tear on the coffee machine.

There are a few disadvantages, however. You may miss the face-to-face interaction of your coworkers. In some cases, you may be overlooked when it comes time to hand out raises and perks. Out of sight, out of mind. You might also be required to wear a beeper and stay close to a telephone or computer, making you feel like you are on a short leash.

But the advantages far outweigh the few disadvantages. Telecommuting and virtual offices will be adopted by more and more companies.

Remote Control Software

If you are on the road or working from home and have a computer at the office, it is often necessary to access the data on that computer. There are several software packages that will allow you to connect from remote locations. You can be sitting in a distant hotel room or at a PC at home and dial up a computer at the office. You can take control across a phone line or across a network and work just as if you were sitting in front of the office computer, reviewing documents, updating files, editing reports, doing print-outs, or downloading files.

LapLink

For many years, LapLink (800-343-8088) has had one of the best ways to connect a laptop to a desktop or to connect any two computers together. Their software usually comes with a cable for linking computers together. LapLink for Windows 95/98 still does all the good things it did in the past; in addition, it is now one of the better ways to remotely access and connect two or more computers. It has SmartXchange and will let you transfer only those files that have been changed. You can also update a file by sending only that portion of it that has changed, which can save a lot of connect time. You can connect via cable, modem, Internet, a network, or even with infrared. It comes with a cable for the parallel port or for a serial port.

Here are a few other software packages for remote control:

Norton pcAnywhere from Symantec	www.symantec.com
Compaq Network Products	www.compaq.com/products/networking/
Close-Up from Norton Lambert	www.nortonlambert.com/

You should be able to find the above software at most software stores or find them listed in software catalogs such as the MicroWarehouse (800-367-7080) or DellWare (800-847-4051).

Of course, all of these packages will only work if the computer is turned on and booted up. Server Technology Inc. (www.servertech. com/) has a product called Remote Power On/Off + Aux. This device plugs into the power line between the computer and the wall plug. The telephone line plugs into this device. When the device detects an incoming call, it will automatically turn on and boot up the PC. When the call is ended, it can turn off the PC. It can even let you reboot if the computer hangs up for some reason. Some companies bundle Remote Power On/Off with Symantec's pcAnywhere and other remote software.

It is available from DellWare, MicroWarehouse, and other discount catalog stores.

Telephony

There have been some important advances in computers and telephones in the last few years. Even greater changes can be expected soon. All of the items listed below can be used in a large business or a small office/home office (SOHO). The SOHO has become a very important element of business today.

Computer Telephony is a magazine that is devoted entirely to telephone computer technology and computer-telephone integration (CTI). The magazine is free to qualified subscribers. If you work for a company or for yourself and use a telephone or computer, then you can probably qualify for a free subscription. Call 800-677-3435 and ask them to send you a qualifying form.

The telephony business has become so important and widespread that Computer Telephony Conferences and Expositions are being held twice a year. The conferences are sponsored by *Computer Telephony* magazine. At these shows they have hundreds of vendors displaying and demonstrating the latest computer and telephone technology, plus dozens of informative seminars. For the next show date and location, call 800-677-3435.

Another free magazine that deals with telephony is *InfoText* (218-723-9437). A free catalog that is devoted to telephone products is Hello Direct. A current issue has 72 pages full of descriptions of telephone-related products, such as all kinds of telephones, headsets, computer and telephone integration products, and many other items. A couple of items actually do away with a standard telephone. The telephone line is plugged into your computer, then with a headset and microphone, you can use a mouse to point to an address list or to dial the number by pressing the keys of the keyboard. There are several different models with different features.

The products sold through Hello Direct are rather expensive, but they have many items that are difficult to find elsewhere. Hello Direct is at 800-444-3556. Call them for a catalog.

Universal serial bus (USB) is a new standard that will allow telephones and other telephone technologies to be connected to computers and operate at up to 12MB per second. Several modems are now USB-capable.

Several companies provide hardware and software for interactive voice response (IVR) that can be used in many different business functions. The computer industry is rife with hundreds of acronyms. The computer-telephone integration portion of the industry has greatly increased the number.

Telephone Conference

It is very simple to have a telephone conference with as few as two persons or as many as several hundred. In a conference call, everyone on the line can talk to anyone else on the line. You can do teleconferences from anywhere: home, a small office, a large office, or even a pay telephone booth.

U.S. Robotics (800-949-6757) has developed a PC-adaptable conference speakerphone, the ConferenceLink CS 1500. It can be connected to a computer as a speakerphone for teleconferences, for videoconferencing, or for use in Internet telephony applications.

Fax Conferences

If you have a fax machine, you can send out a graphics design, plans, or any number of business papers. Then you can have other persons review the material, make changes or sign it, and return it. You can also have an interactive meeting with others in the same building, or almost anywhere in the world, over a simple telephone line. One disadvantage is that it is not in real time. You have to send the fax then wait for a reply.

Modem Teleconferences

With a computer modem, you can have a desktop conference. You send data, graphics, and other materials over the telephone line to other computers over a local-area network (LAN), whether in the same building or almost anywhere in the world. Other persons sitting at their computers, can view the text data, spreadsheets, graphics, and other materials. The persons can change the material or interact with the other persons on the line in real time.

Education by Modem

Several universities, colleges, and specialized training facilities are using telecommunications to offer many different courses. Some courses may lead to degrees; others may be for specialized training for a large company. You could sit at home in front of your computer and take a course from a college or training facility on the other side of the country. (These services are discussed at greater length in Chapter 17.)

National Telephone Directories

As I've mentioned, I live in the Los Angeles area. In Los Angeles and Orange Counties, there are over 100 suburban cities with over 12 million people. Can you imagine a single telephone directory that would list all of these people? Or how about a telephone directory that would list all of the millions of people in New York? Or Boston? Or San Francisco? Believe it or not, there are such directories. And these directories are smaller than one that you might find in a small town. These national directories are small because they are on CD-ROM discs.

The ProPhone, from New Media Publishing (617-631-9200) has seven CD-ROM discs: six discs for the White Pages and one disc for businesses in the United States. There is over 600MB of data on each disc, which lists the telephone numbers, the address, and zip codes. The separate disc for business makes it very easy to look up a company anywhere in the country.

The PhoneDisc from Digital Directory Assistance (800-284-8353) only has five CD-ROM discs. It has over 90 million listings of residences and businesses. It does not have a separate business disc, but lists businesses along with the general population in the White Pages. Not every person in the country is listed on the discs. And, of course, many people move and change phone numbers.

Most phone companies only update their directories once a year. But these CD-ROM disc directory companies do quarterly updates. Once you are a registered owner, the updates are very reasonable.

If you are in a business where you have to contact a lot of people, you need these two directories. You may also need them if you live in the Los Angeles area.

In addition, a very good Web site for finding people or businesses is www.anywho.com. Of course, you can use any of the search engines to find people and businesses or almost any subject. Some of the most popular are www.yahoo.com, www.altavista.com, www.excite.com, and www.hotbot.com.

ISDN

ISDN is an acronym for Integrated Services Digital Network. Most of the ISDN networks are made up of fiber-optic cable. Eventually, the whole world will have telephone systems that use this technology. It will be a system that will be able to transmit voice, data, video, and graphics in digital form rather than the present analog. When this happens, we can scrap our modems.

ISDN is already installed in several cities. But don't throw your modem away just yet. The new service may not be available at all locations for some time. It will be rather expensive.

Cable Modems

At the present time, ISDN allows modems to operate at up to 128Kbps. But it is not nearly as fast as communicating over coaxial cable, which can operate at up to 10Mbps. Many Internet Web sites have lots of graphics. It may take several megabytes to create a good graphic image. In addition, over the Plain Old Telephone Service (POTS), it may take several minutes to download a graphic. With a cable modem, it only takes seconds. Cable modems allow download or downstream speeds up to 1.5Mbps, and allow upstream speeds of about 300Kbps. Cable modem service cost will vary depending on the number of hours used, from $29.95 up to $129.95.

Congress has just passed a law giving cable and TV companies the right to enter the phone business and vice versa. You can expect to see a lot of competition from the cable and telephone companies for your business. Motorola (www.mot.com), 3Com Corp. (www.3com.com), and several other companies are busy making new cable modems.

To find out if cable modem service is available or will be available in your area, visit these Web sites:

www.home.net/home

www.convergence.com

www.mediaoneexpress.com

Asynchronous Digital Subscriber Line (ADSL)

Asymmetrical digital subscriber line (ASDL, sometimes called "loop" or simply DSL) is a system that uses the ordinary telephone lines for high-speed transmission, up to 1.5Mbps. The system has been available for several years, but very few systems have been installed. It does require some special electronics, and not many phone companies have installed the necessary equipment.

Another reason why many have not been installed is that the end user must be within 18,000 feet (about 3½ miles) from the telephone company's central office. There may also be problems with some of the older wiring. But some systems *are* being installed. The cost of the service may vary. The service may offer 1.5Mbps downstream and about 256Kbps upstream to 768Kbps for about $60 per month. Call your local phone company to see if it is available in your area.

Sources

I have not listed the names and manufacturers of modems and faxes because there are so many. Look in any computer magazine and you will see dozens of ads. A recent copy of *Computer Shopper* had ads for about 200 modem/fax boards from several different companies.

One modem company that I do want to mention, however, is U.S. Robotics. They manufacture a large variety of modems, especially the high-end, high-speed type. They will send you a 110-page booklet that explains about all you need to know about modems. For the free booklet, call 800-342-5877.

You should also subscribe to several of the computer magazines listed in Chapter 19. A good magazine that is free to qualified subscribers is *Telecommunications*. Almost anyone can qualify (especially if you fudge a little on the questionnaire form). For a qualification form, call them at 617-769-9750 or write to *Telecommunications*, P.O. Box 850949, Braintree, MA 02185.

Upgrading an Older PC

You can do several things to an older computer to make it run better. Some of them are adding more memory, adding a new motherboard, and adding new hard drives and other peripherals.

Why You Should Do It Yourself

There are shops and several mail-order stores that will upgrade your computer for you. Of course, these stores cannot stay in business unless they make a profit, so it can be a bit expensive. It can also take a lot of time and cause a considerable amount of problems.

First, you have to find someone who will do it for you at a reasonable price. Then you have to lug the computer down to the shop during business hours. Or you can package it up and send it off to a mail-order store.

If you send it via mail for an upgrade, there can be a problem of communications. Just what do you want done to your computer? How much do you want to spend? How busy is the shop or mail-order store? How reliable is the shop? Can you get a firm price for the total cost and a date as to how soon they can get it back to you? How long can you wait for it? If the shop is very busy, it might take longer than promised to get it out.

What If It Is Too Old to Upgrade?

Your computer is never too old to be enhanced or upgraded in some manner. You can add a new monitor, large-capacity hard drive, and many other peripherals to almost any of the older computers. However, I hate to say this, but depending on what type of upgrade you want or what you want to do with your computer, it might be better to buy a new computer. You can buy a less expensive one, then add to it to suit your needs.

If you decide that you don't want to upgrade your older computer, what do you do with it? You might decide to try to sell it. But you probably won't be able to sell the computer for what you think it is worth. The computer that you paid $2500 for a few years ago may not be worth $100 today. Besides, you might not want to go through the bother and hassle of advertising and selling it, especially if you live in a city like Los Angeles. A news story reported that a gang would go to the house of a person who had advertised a computer for sale. The gang would tie the person up, then take all of the computers and software that they could find. It would be bad enough losing a computer, but it would be disastrous if I lost all of my software.

If you live near a larger city, there may be computer swap meets every so often. Usually there will be a consignment table at these meets where you can sell your old hardware. But don't expect to make a lot of money off your old components.

Still another alternative is to pass it on to a relative or someone who is just getting started in computers. Or you can keep it and use it for word processing, for a dedicated printer server on a network, or for voice mail.

There are several DOS software packages that work very well on the 286, such as WordPerfect 6.0, WordStar 7.0, Microsoft Works, dBASE IV, and thousands of other perfectly good programs. Most of the standard DOS programs also run very well on an XT. The DOS programs will run a bit slower on an XT or 286 than they would on a Pentium III, so you may have to wait a few seconds or a few minutes. If you are not exactly wealthy, perhaps you can afford to waste a bit of time rather than spend money for an upgrade.

Another alternative might be to donate your old computer to a school, church, or charitable organization. Depending on your tax situation, you might come out ahead by donating it and deducting it as a gift on your income tax return.

Upgrading to a New Hard Disk

It seems like every program wants to be loaded on drive C:. Pretty soon it will be bursting at the seams. There are some programs that are temporarily loaded onto the hard disk while being run, especially if you don't have a lot of memory. If you don't have enough space on your hard disk, you will not be able to run the programs.

Parallel Printer Port Drives

One of the easiest ways to upgrade to a new hard disk is to install one of the drives that plug into the printer port. You will be able to plug the drive cable into the port. There will be an extra connector for the printer cable so that both can be plugged into the same port.

Most of these drives have removable cartridges, such as the 250MB Zip Drive from Iomega (801-778-1000, or www.iomega.com). Iomega also has some large drives up to 2GB.

IDE Drives

If you have a fairly new system, you will have provisions for hooking up four IDE drives. This can be four hard disks, or better yet, two hard disks, a DVD drive, and a CD-R drive. There will be two sets of upright pins on the motherboard for connecting the IDE drives. One set will be marked "Primary" and the other will be marked "Secondary." You will also have two 40-wire flat-ribbon cables. The cable will have a connector on each end and one in the middle. One end of the cable will be connected to one CD-ROM or hard disk, then another IDE drive can be connected to the middle connector. The cable is then connected to the upright pins on the motherboard. See Figure 12-1. The hard disk drives should be connected to the primary set of pins. The CD-ROMs or other IDE devices should be connected to the secondary set of pins.

On the rear of the drive will be small jumpers, as shown in Figure 12-2. These jumpers will be used to configure each drive. The two drives on the primary set of pins will be configured as primary master and slave. The master drive on this cable should have drive C:, which is your boot drive. The two drives on the secondary set of pins will be configured as secondary master and slave. The two drives may be a CD-ROM, a DVD, a CD-R, a DVD-RAM, a hard drive, or any other IDE device.

Figure 12-1
Connecting an IDE drive cable to the motherboard.

Figure 12-2
The pen points to the small jumpers used to configure the drive as a master or slave.

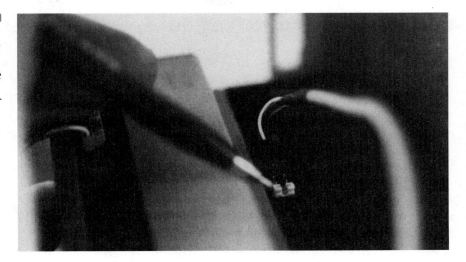

A DVD drive will allow you to play DVD movies, CD-ROM discs, and music CDs. A CD-R recordable CD-ROM drive will let you record other CD-ROM discs or music CDs, or let you store up to 650MB of backup data. The CD-R will also read standard CD-ROM discs and music CDs.

An excellent upgrade would be to install an LS-120 SuperDisk drive. This IDE drive can read and write to all your 1.44MB floppies. It can also read and write to specially formatted 120MB floppies. With enough of these 120MB floppies, you may never need a larger hard disk.

SCSI Drives

If you already have a SCSI (pronounced *scuzzy*) board for a SCSI device, you can easily add a second SCSI device. If not, you will need to buy a SCSI host adapter. You can attach six SCSI devices to the host. The devices will have a set of jumper pins so that each device can be set to a logical unit number (LUN). The devices can be hard drives, CD-ROM or DVD drives, scanners, or any other SCSI device.

A SCSI hard drive is usually a bit more expensive than an equivalent IDE drive. But it may be a good idea to have one or more of both types. You can use one to back up your critical data. Hard disks do fail, but it is not likely that both would fail.

If you install a DVD drive and a CD-R drive, it is better that one of them is a SCSI drive. If both are IDE drives, there may be some interference when copying from one to the other.

Formatting and Transferring Files

You probably have lots of files on your old hard disk that you want to save. Before you can even think of transferring any files or even using your new computer, the hard disk must be partitioned and formatted.

You may have bought your hard drive from a dealer who has already formatted it and installed Windows 98 on it. It is great if it has already been done, but if it has not been done, then you must do it. Instructions for partitioning and formatting a hard disk are given in Chapter 13.

Once the hard disk or disks have been formatted, you can install software or transfer software from your old machine. If you have lots of floppies, you can copy it all onto floppies and transfer it to your new system's hard disk. But it can take a whole lot of time and be a lot of trouble. Besides, some programs and files will not fit on a 1.44MB floppy. This is a good reason to have something like the Zip 250MB drive that plugs into a printer port. You could plug it into your old system, copy all the files, then plug it into your new system, and transfer it.

Another disadvantage in copying files is that Windows 95/98 adds many files to your programs, even if they are DOS programs. Many of them are hidden and scattered all over your disk. It is almost impossible to copy them all.

LapLink

LapLink was mentioned in the previous chapter as a way to remotely access another computer, but it's also one of the best solutions to transfer files. LapLink, from Traveling Software (800-662-2652, or www. travsoft.com) has software and cables that will allow you to plug into the printer connection of each computer, then easily transfer all your files. Once you have connected the cables, the software allows you to see the entire directories on both machines. You can just point the mouse and click on a file or whole directory, and it will be immediately transferred to the other computer.

LapLink was originally developed for transferring data back and forth between laptop and desktop computers. But they have improved the software tremendously. It can even be used over modem for remote file transfers. The software can also let you set up a very simple network by connecting two computers with the furnished cabling.

DriveCopy

Another solution for transferring data from one hard drive to another is to use the DriveCopy software from PowerQuest (801-226-8977, or www.powerquest.com). When you buy a new hard disk, DriveCopy will let you easily copy everything to the new drive and make a much larger drive C:. It will maintain your file and directory structure so that your new drive will operate the same as the old one. (You will appreciate the extra disk space.) You can then reformat your old drive and use it as a second drive or as a backup for your critical files.

Buying a Used Computer

You may find some very good bargains in buying a used computer. You can then upgrade it to suit your needs. Look around your area and check the classified ads.

If you work for a large company, chances are that they are in the process of buying new, more powerful systems to meet their added business needs. (A basic law, based on Parkinson's laws, is that the need for more and larger computer systems grows in a logarithmic fashion each year that the company is in business whether or not the business increases.) Try to find out what the manager of the computer procurement department is doing with the old computers. Some companies pass them down to secretaries and other people who are low on the totem pole. Many companies will sell them to their employees for a good price. Talk to the manager and remind him or her how much goodwill that such a practice can buy for the company.

Buying a Bare-Bones System

Several companies advertise bare-bones systems. A bare-bones system usually includes a case, power supply, motherboard, and a CPU. Sometimes it will include memory and a monitor adapter. The price will depend primarily on the CPU that you choose. The bare-bones bundle will usually be less than what it would cost to buy each component separately. Here is an example from a recent ad in *Computer Shopper* from AlphaCom (800-822-8864, or www.alphacompc.com):

Pentium II motherboard with 440BX chipset

Celeron 400MHz CPU with 128KB L1

8MB video card

56K fax modem

1.44MB floppy drive

Mini mid-tower case

All this for $269. You could also include other CPU options. A 400MHz Pentium II CPU added $91 to the basic kit. There is really not that much difference in a 400MHz Celeron and a 400MHz Pentium II. They also offered other options such as an equivalent kit with Cyrix or AMD CPUs for a somewhat lesser cost. In addition, an AMD K6-3D 400MHz was available for $209, as well as a Cyrix 333MHz CPU with the basic kit for $155.

If you bought the items separately from the same company for the AMD K6-3D 400MHz barebone, it would cost $273, as opposed to $209 for the kit. I hate to quote prices because they will change tomorrow. The good news is that the prices will no doubt be lower.

There are not too many companies who advertise bare-bone kits today. So it may be hard to find them. Look in the computer magazines listed in Chapter 19. As with all ads, you have to read them carefully to make sure what they include. Bare-bones systems usually do not include a floppy or hard disk, keyboard, mouse, and other essential things that you will need.

Upgrading to a New Computer

I hate to admit it, but there are some companies who advertise computer systems for less than what it costs to build one. The vendors can offer low-cost machines by purchasing in high volume at good discounts. Some companies are building "white boxes" for other vendors. They assemble computers with no name and usually ship them in a white box with no brand name. The vendors can then add their names to the units if desired.

Keep in mind that some of these low-cost machines may not have all that you would like in a computer. But you can always add to it. If you bought a bare-bones system or a low-cost new machine, you may have a modem, a floppy drive, a hard disk drive, a CD-ROM, a printer, or any of several other components and boards that you would like to install in your new machine.

In most cases, you can just install them, plug them in, and let Windows recognize and install the software. In some cases, you may have to go to the BIOS setup and tell it what you have installed. Most systems will give you the opportunity to run the BIOS setup when you first turn on the computer. Usually you have to press a key such as Del or a combination of keys to display the setup. You can then set the time and date, tell the system what type of floppy drives you have, and input the hard drive information. (This may not be necessary for some drives, since most of the BIOS systems today can automatically recognize a hard drive's characteristics.) You will be given several other options for setting up and configuring your system. You should have received some documentation that will explain them.

If you are transferring a CD-ROM drive, the software from your old disk should be copied onto your new hard disk. If not, you should have the original software that came with the drive so that you can install it.

If you are transferring a CD-ROM, floppy drive, or hard drive from an older machine to the new one, leave the cables connected to the drives. The other end of the cables will be connected to the motherboard. There will be sets of pins for the floppy drive and for the IDE drives. On older motherboards, when plugging the connectors onto the upright pins, you had to make sure that the colored-wire side was connected to pin 1 on the motherboard. Almost all motherboards now have a keyed shell around the pins so that the connector can only be plugged in properly. If there is no shell around the pins, there is usually some marking on the motherboard. Ordinarily, if the upright pins are side by side, pin 1 on the floppy connection, pin 1 on the IDE connection, and pin 1 on the printer connection will all be in the same direction. For instance, in most cases, if pin 1 on any connector is toward the rear of the motherboard, pin 1 on all connectors will be toward the rear.

Be very careful, however. If there is no keyed shell, it is very easy to plug the connectors in backwards. If so, you could possibly damage the drive or the motherboard electronics. It is also possible to plug the connector in so that some of the pins are outside the connector.

Again, most of the newer motherboards have a shell around the upright pins. They have a cutout that is keyed so that the connectors can only be plugged in properly. Figure 12-3 shows a 40-wire connector that shows the elevated key. A cutout in the shell is around the set of pins.

Figure 12-3
A 40-wire IDE connector showing the elevated key. It fits in the cutout of a shell around a set of pins.

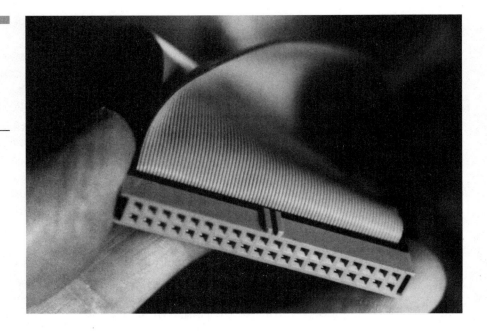

Minor Upgrades

Even if you just bought it yesterday, in many ways your computer is obsolete. There is no way it could have all the things that could be installed in it. There are hundreds of ways that a computer can be configured and upgraded. Computers are made up of various components that just plug together. You can add hundreds of different boards, components, and peripherals to a computer.

When we speak of upgrading, we usually think about hardware; but software upgrades are every bit as important. We will discuss some of the essential software in Chapter 16.

Memory Upgrade

When a program is being processed or operated on, it is loaded into dynamic random access memory (DRAM). Most programs today are very friendly, but the friendlier they are, the larger they are. So you will need a lot of DRAM. One very useful feature of Windows 95/98 is that it lets you have two or more programs open and running at the same time. You can go from one to the other, swap files, compare and edit, and much more. Quite often I will open a file, then log onto the Internet, and if I see something I like, I just highlight, press Ctrl + C to copy it, then go back to my open file and press Ctrl + V to paste in my file.

If you are working with large programs, you need lots of memory. Upgrading to more memory is one of the better ways to upgrade any computer. You can never have too much. Most programs today need at least 32MB of DRAM to run well, but the more you have, the better. At one time memory was rather expensive, but the prices have dropped considerably in the last few months. My first little Morrow Computer in 1983 had a whopping 64KB of memory. I just installed 128MB in my AMD K6-III 450MHz system. It cost me $100, or 78 cents per megabyte of fast memory. Memory will probably be even less expensive by the time you read this.

Just a few years ago, 128MB of memory would have cost thousands of dollars. A few years ago, none of the motherboards were big enough to install that much memory. The 640KB of memory on a 286 required about one-fourth of the entire large motherboard using dual in-line-package (DIP) memory. When single in-line memory modules (SIMMs) were developed, they were able to cram more memory into a smaller space. We now have dual in-line memory modules (DIMMs) that can hold 128MB of memory on a single small board.

Adding memory is very easy—just open your computer and plug in the new memory. Before you rush out to buy more memory, open your computer and check to see what kind you have installed. If you have a manual, that may also tell you. You will need to buy the same type. If you have an older computer, it is possible that you have rather slow and outdated memory. It will be perfectly okay to install faster memory. At one time there was a large differential in cost for the faster memory and the slower. Today there is very little difference.

You may never need all the memory you have available, but it is nice to have. It is something like having a car with a 427-hp engine. You may never need all that horsepower, but it sure feels good to have it when you do need it. You may not ever need all you memory, but if you ever run large programs or have several programs in memory at the same time, it is sure nice to have it when you do need it. Installation is easy. Just lay them in the slot, and pull them forward until the latches on each end lock them in. There are cutouts on the SIMMs so that they can only be installed properly. SIMMs are practically obsolete now. They have been replaced by the more-dense DIMMs. Some motherboards will have slots for both SIMMs and DIMMs. You must use one or the other.

Figure 12-4
Installing a 64MB
DIMM module.

Figure 12-4 shows a 64MB DIMM module being installed. Refer back to Chapter 4 for more memory and installation instructions.

Upgrading the CPU

One of the best upgrades is to install a new motherboard and CPU. I hesitate to mention this, but you may not have to buy a new motherboard if your old one has a Socket 7 for the CPU. (The different types of CPU sockets were discussed in Chapter 3. Also see Table 12-1 below.) You might be able to install a new AMD K6, Cyrix 8x86MX, or an IDT Centaur C6 CPU. This would be a fairly inexpensive way to move up to a more powerful computer. But before you rush out and buy a new CPU, make sure your motherboard can handle it. The newer CPUs operate at different frequencies and at different voltages. Newer motherboards have jumpers that can be used to configure them for voltage and frequency of just about any CPU. Some of the older motherboards were designed and built before the newer CPU frequencies and voltages were adopted.

TABLE 12-1

CPU, Socket, and
Chipset
Specifications

CPU	Socket No.	Chipset
Intel 75-233MHz	7	Intel 430TX
AMD, Cyrix, IDT	7	Intel 430TX
Pentium Pro	8	Intel 440LX
Pentium II	SEC 1	Intel 440BX
Celeron	SEC 1	Intel 440LX or BX
Celeron (FPPGA)	370	Intel 440LX or BX
Pentium III	SEC 1	Intel 440BX
Pentium III (FPPGA)	370	Intel 440BX
Pentium Xeon	SEC 2	Intel 440EG
AMD Athlon (K7)	Slot A	AMD Special

CPU Sockets

Matching the right motherboard with the CPU is very important. All
this talk about sockets may be a bit confusing, so Table 12-1 may help.

Replacing the Motherboard

Upgrading an older computer to a Pentium III or AMD Athlon is not
much different than upgrading any other computer. It is even easier and
much less expensive to upgrade to one of the CPUs that uses the motherboards with Socket 7. The AMD K6, Cyrix 6x86MX, and IDT Centaur
C6 all use the Socket 7 motherboards. Figure 12-5 shows a Socket 7-type
motherboard. You can upgrade an old computer, whether a 486, a 386, or
even a 286, to a fast and powerful top-of-the-line Socket 7 clone or a
Pentium III by replacing the motherboard.

Keep in mind, however, that if you are upgrading to a newer Socket 7
clone motherboard, you may not be able to use your old case. Some of
the newer motherboards have the keyboard, serial, and printer port connectors all in a group for an opening in the back of the case. Most of the

Figure 12-5
A Socket 7
motherboard.

newer motherboards also have a couple of USB ports. The older cases
would not have an opening for those connectors.

One other problem: Most of the newer motherboards now have the
ATX-type connector for the power supply. You probably will need to
buy a case with your new motherboard. The power supply usually
comes with the case. A case and power supply may cost from $40 to
over $100.

You will still be able to use your old hard disks, floppy disk, keyboard,
and other peripherals. Most of the new motherboards also come with the
PS/2-type connectors for the mouse and motherboard. You may have to
buy a new keyboard and mouse or buy some adapters so that you can
use the PS/2-type connectors. The adapters may cost from $3 to $5. They
are available from Dalco (800-650-066), Cables to Go (800-297-2843), or
Cables Plus (888-794-9600). The standard keyboard connector is much
larger than the PS/2 type.

You should be able to use almost all of your other boards and peripherals. Of course, you may want to buy more memory chips and perhaps a

higher-capacity hard drive. All PCs are very similar in the way they are assembled. They are all very simple.

Pentium III Motherboard or AMD Athlon

If money is no object, then you should buy a Pentium III 550MHz CPU and motherboard. Or better yet, an AMD Athlon, 600MHz motherboard and CPU. You can hope that with systems like these, it would be some time before they became obsolete. But the industry changes, sometimes overnight.

At the moment, there is little software that can take full advantage of the speed and power of the latest systems. Software development always lags behind the hardware. Another big factor is that these CPUs and motherboards will be rather expensive. You can probably buy two 400MHz AMD K6-III or Celeron CPUs and motherboards for what one Pentium III 550MHz or Athlon 600MHz would cost.

A Bit of History

The original Pentium was introduced in March 1993 and had 3.1 million transistors. It operated at either 60 or 66MHz. It was a fantastic advance at that time. The Pentium 75+ was introduced in March of 1994. It had 3.3 million transistors and originally operated at 75MHz, but was soon boosted to 100, 120, 150, and then 200MHz. The Pentium Pro was introduced in September 1995 and had 5.5 million transistors. Originally, it operated at 150MHz, but was soon boosted to 200MHz. Intel redesigned some of their 166MHz and 200MHz Pentiums and added a set of 57 multimedia extension (MMX) instructions to the chip.

The MMX technology gave new life to the Pentium. It ran most normal software programs much faster. Those programs, such as graphics, video, and multimedia written to take advantage of the MMX, could be processed much faster. For the next generation, the Pentium II, Intel added the 57 MMX instructions to the CPU. The fastest Pentium Pro ran at 200MHz. The Pentium II originally ran at 233MHz, then 266MHz, and now up to 450MHz.

Back to Reality

Realistically, for most applications, the 450MHz AMD and 466MHz Celeron CPUs will do just about everything the Pentium III will do—and for a whole lot less money. If you are really strapped for money and don't mind waiting a few microseconds for a program to be processed, they are practically giving away the AMD and Celeron CPUs. A recent ad in *Computer Shopper* listed these prices:

AMD K6-2	333MHz	$71
Celeron	333MHz	$83 (has 128KB L2 cache)
AMD K6-2	400MHz	$90
Celeron	400MHz	$109 (has 128KB L2 cache)

Note that the Celeron and all Pentium IIs and IIIs have integrated L2 cache nearby in the same enclosure. The Celeron will only have 128KB of L2 cache; the Pentium II and III may have 512KB and up to 1MB of L2 cache. Most Socket 7 motherboards have from 512KB to 2MB of L2 cache. The vendors may not advertise the amount of cache on the motherboard. Ask about the L2 cache if you are ordering a Socket 7 motherboard for an AMD, Cyrix, or IDT Centaur CPUs.

These low-cost motherboards and CPUs will do just about everything you need to do. This is especially so for the small office/home office (SOHO) and small businesses. Owning a Pentium III or AMD Athlon is almost like owning an expensive automobile that can go 150 miles an hour, but there is no place where you could drive that fast except on a racetrack. At this time, unless you have some high-end applications, you might be much better off upgrading to the low-cost motherboards and CPUs. You could then invest the money saved on peripherals and other goodies.

If you can get by with a CPU that is not quite as fast, you can save a lot of money. Again, prices listed are for comparison only. They will be less by the time you read this.

Steps to Replace a Motherboard

Caution! Before you handle any of your boards or chips, be sure to discharge yourself of any static electricity. You can build up an electric charge on your body of 3000V to 4000V. You may have experienced a shock after walking across a carpet and then touching a doorknob. Most of the transistors and semiconductors in your computer and peripherals are very fragile. You could fry them if you are not careful.

To discharge yourself, just touch any metal object that has a power cord plugged into a wall outlet.

Step 1. Remove the Cables from the Rear Panel

If you are fairly new to computers, you should use some masking tape or some way to label all the cables and connectors on the back panel. You might also take a felt-tip pen and make a slash on the panel connector and cable connector. Make the slash at different areas of the connectors. All you will have to do then is to match up the slash marks when you reconnect the cables. You will probably have only four or five cables connected to the rear panel. In most cases, the connectors will all be different, so reconnecting them will be no problem.

With the new motherboards, the connectors may look different. You should get some kind of documentation that shows the various connectors.

Step 2. Remove the Case Cover

To replace the motherboard, unplug the power cord and remove the case cover. The case may have six to eight screws to hold it in place. The screws are usually in the back along the edge of the case cover. If it is a tower case, you will probably see four screws near the top of the case. These screws are to hold the power supply in place. Do not remove them.

If it is a desktop case, the power supply screws will be located in the right rear corner. Again, remove only the screws that hold the cover in place. For the tower cases, the cover will usually slide off to the back. For the desktop, it will probably slide off to the front.

The newer cases may have only two screws. Most of them now have plastic latches with only one or two screws to hold the cover on. You may have to look closely to see where the latches are. You can just press on them to release them.

Step 3. Make a Diagram

Once the cover is removed, make a drawing of where all the boards are plugged in and the cables that are connected to the boards. Once you have made your diagram, remove the boards and power cables that are plugged into the motherboard. Label and remove the several wires that go to the speaker and the front panel.

Step 4. Disconnect Cables and Remove the Boards

Disconnect all of the cables and plug-in boards from the motherboard. If possible, leave the cables connected to the plug-in boards. For most of the cables, the other ends will be connected to your disk drives. There should be no reason to disconnect the drives or remove them. Just lay the cables and boards aside. See Figure 12-6.

Figure 12-6
Attached cables.

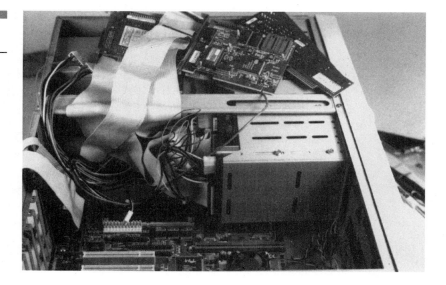

Step 5. Remove the Motherboard

For the older motherboards, there will probably be a single screw in the front of the motherboard and one in the rear, usually in the center. Once the two screws are removed, pull the motherboard toward you. It has plastic standoffs that fit in the slots of the case. When you pull the motherboard toward you, the slots are wide enough to allow you to lift the motherboard out. Figure 12-7 shows the backside of the motherboard, the slots, and the white plastic stand-offs.

The early XT motherboards used nine copper stand-offs and screws to hold the motherboard. Later models used plastic stand-offs and only two screws. Most of the new cases have gone back to screws. The cases have

Figure 12-7
The backside of
a motherboard.

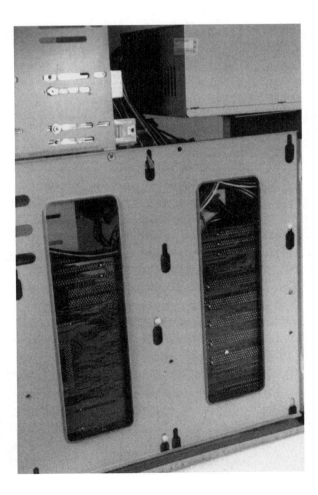

Figure 12-8
A new case and
motherboard
showing elevated
screw holes for the
motherboard.

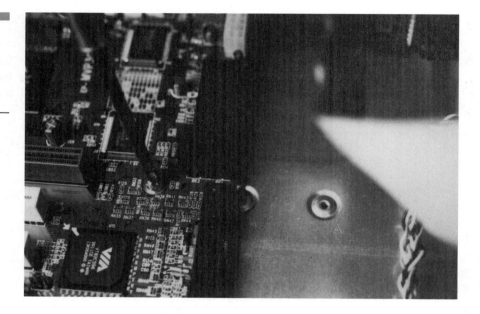

small, threaded elevations for the screws. You can see the elevated screw holes in Figure 12-8.

Step 6. Configuring the New Motherboard

Before installing the new motherboard, make sure that all of the jumpers and any switches have been set properly for the CPU that you are going to use. Jumpers are small, black shorting bars that fit over two adjacent pins. They are usually quite small. If your fingers are normal size, it would be almost impossible to handle the jumpers. I have a pair of needle-nose pliers just for moving jumpers. It is very important that you get some kind of documentation with your motherboard. Most of them today can be configured to work with dozens of CPUs. The jumpers can be set for the CPU voltage, for the CPU frequency, for the type and size of memory, and several other functions. Without the documentation, it is almost impossible to set the jumpers properly to configure a motherboard.

You should install your memory before installing the motherboard. It may be a bit difficult to get to the memory slots once the motherboard is installed. Again, check your documentation. The memory slots are called *banks*. The first bank is usually numbered 0. You must fill the lowest-numbered bank first. In older systems, SIMM memory is also usually installed in pairs. The DIMM memory on the newer motherboards usually does not have to be installed in pairs. Again, check your documentation.

Once the jumpers have been set, remove the plastic stand-offs from your old motherboard and install them on your new one. You will need a pair of pliers to remove the plastic stand-offs. They are flared so that when they are pushed through the hole in the motherboard, two sections flare out to hold them in place. If you do not have a pair of pliers handy, you can take a low-cost ballpoint pen, such as a Bic, and remove the pen. You can then press the plastic shell down over the flared stand-off, allowing you to remove it easily.

There will be several holes in the motherboard and in the case. Find the proper holes, and drop the motherboard stand-offs into them. Push the motherboard until the stand-offs are in the narrow part of the holes. The two screw stand-offs at the front center and rear center should now be visible.

Place a screw in the rear center of the board and one in front. If you have one of the newer motherboards that use all screws, line the motherboard up so that the screw holes are visible, and install the screws.

Having a magnetized Phillips screwdriver will be very helpful to hold the screws and get them started. You can magnetize a screwdriver by rubbing it with a magnet, such as those used to hold the kids' drawings on the refrigerator door. Most hardware stores also sell them. They also have screwdrivers that have clips to hold a screw until it is started.

Be very careful with a magnetic screwdriver around any of your floppy disks. It can ruin them.

Step 7. Reinstall Boards and Cables

Once the motherboard is in place, reinstall all the boards and cables. The first thing to connect is the motherboard power. If you have one of the old style systems, your motherboard power supply will be a set of two cables. They are usually marked P8 and P9. There are six wires in each connector. They can be plugged in improperly. If you do so, you may severely damage the electronics on your motherboard. When plugged into the motherboard properly, the four black wires will be in the center.

If you have an ATX power supply, it can only be plugged in properly. Some motherboards may have both the ATX-type connector and the old-style power connector.

You will have to plug in the hard and floppy disk cables in the upright pins on the motherboard. Some motherboards will have a shell around these pins so that the cable can only be plugged in properly. You may also have sets of upright pins for the printer and mouse cables. These short cables have a bracket on one end that mounts in the back panel for external connections. Most newer motherboards have the mouse and serial printer ports attached to the rear of the motherboard. Because of this, these motherboards may not fit in your old case. Of course, you could take a hacksaw or tin snips and make an opening for these ports rather than buy a new case. Since it is in the back of the computer, nobody is going to see it.

If your motherboard does not have the keyed shells around the upright pins, you will have to make sure the cables are plugged in properly. There should be an indication on the motherboard as to which is pin 1. Your flat-ribbon cables will have a different-colored wire on one side—either red, black, blue, or red stripes—that indicates pin 1. Make sure that the side with the different-colored wire goes to pin 1 on the motherboard.

You will also have upright pins for the wires to the small speaker and for the several wires for the front panel LEDs. Figure 12-9 shows some of the small cables and connectors for the front-panel LEDs. They plug

Figure 12-9
Some connectors for the front-panel LEDS. They plug into upright pins on the front of the motherboard.

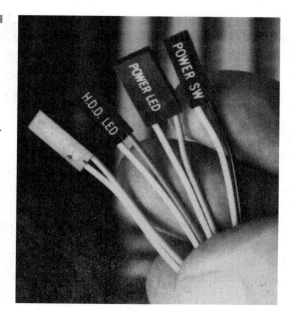

into upright pins on the front of the motherboard. If you left the boards connected to the cables, reinstalling them should be no problem. The ISA boards can be plugged into any ISA slot, and the PCI boards into any PCI slot.

After all the cables and boards are installed on the motherboard, connect all the cables to the back panel. You should have a power cord, a keyboard cable, and a cable for the monitor, printer, and mouse. You should also have a telephone line to the modem and a wire for your speakers from the sound card.

Step 8. Turn on the Power and Test It Out

Check to see that everything is connected properly, then turn on the power. Your new system should boot up immediately. If it works okay, you can replace the cover. Then congratulate yourself for saving a bundle on your new computer—and learning a lot about it.

There Is No End to Upgrade Possibilities

Some of the other important and easy upgrades are as follows:

- *New modem* If you are still using an old modem that is less than 33.6K, it will help to move up to a 56KB unit. It is very easy to install. Just pull out the old one and install the new one. Some are very inexpensive now. Windows 95/98 will usually recognize the new Plug and Play devices and automatically install them.

- *New monitor* Monitors have come way down in price. I recently bought a 15-inch monitor for $150. The bigger 19- and 21-inch ones are still $400 to $700.

- *Accelerated graphics card* A faster AGP card or accelerated graphics PCI card will make your monitor more enjoyable. Some of the older Socket 7 motherboards did not have an AGP slot, but the PCI equivalent card will work fine. If you want to play DVD movies on your computer, the accelerated graphics card should have an MPEG-2 decoder.

- *New sound system* You will need a good sound system to enjoy DVD movies on your computer. Creative Labs and several other companies offer very good sound systems.

■ *New scanner*   A scanner can save you a whole lot of time. You can scan in articles, photos, or almost anything into your computer. The scanner digitizes the items so that they can then be edited, modified, and sent to others as e-mail.

■ *New color printer*   Some of the new inkjet printers are fairly inexpensive yet can print out photos or images that have near-photographic quality.

■ *Digital camera*   Take photos of your family and friends, and install them on your hard disk. Use the color printer to print them out. If you happen to be in a business such as real estate, you could take digital photos of the properties, store them on your hard disk, and display them to potential buyers.

■ *New software*   If you are still limping along on Windows 95, or worse yet, Windows 3.1, you should definitely upgrade to Windows 98. It will make life a lot simpler. There are hundreds of other very important software packages that can help you cope. You also definitely need an antivirus program. The Norton System Works has an antivirus program and lots of other utilities.

There are many other things that you can do to improve and enhance the performance and capabilities of your computer. It is impossible to list them all, partly because new devices, hardware, and software are being developed and introduced every day. We could never have a complete list.

Assembling Your Computer

This chapter is primarily about assembling a computer from scratch. It lists the recommended components and how to assemble them. This chapter also explains how to format and configure hard disks once they are installed.

Needed Components

You should have all of your components ready for installation. Here is a list of what you should have:

Case and power supply

Motherboard

CPU and cooling fan

Hard drive

Floppy drive

CD-ROM drive

Monitor

Monitor adapter

Sound card

Modem card

Keyboard

Mouse

IDE cables

Floppy drive cables

CD-ROM drive audio cable

Windows 95 or Windows 98 software

A boot-up floppy disk

Tools

Before you start, gather all of your components and tools. You will need a Phillips and a flat-blade screwdriver and a pair of long-nose pliers. The long-nose pliers will be needed to place the small configuration jumpers over pins. If you don't have a pair of long-nose pliers, you can use a pair of tweezers.

Static Electricity Warning

Caution! Before touching any of the components, make sure that you discharge yourself of any static electricity. If you have ever walked across a carpeted room and gotten a shock when you touched a doorknob, then you know what static electricity is. It is possible for a person's body to build up as much as 3000V or more of static electricity. If you touch any of the sensitive electronic components, that static electricity could be discharged through them. This static electricity could destroy or severely damage some of the fragile components.

Discharging Yourself

When you touch a metal doorknob, you can discharge the static electricity. A much better discharge occurs if you touch something that goes directly to ground, such as a water pipe. Since you probably don't have a water pipe near your computer, the next best thing is to touch a bare metal part of your computer.

Most boards and components will have a static-electricity warning label on the packaging, as shown in Figure 13-1. The plastic bag that

Figure 13-1
Warning label on a plastic bag.

WARNING!
Static Sensitive
Components

This device may be damaged by extremely small amounts of static electricity. Before you open this bag, be sure to touch an unpainted metal surface, such as your computer frame, to discharge any static build up that you may have accumulated.

most electronic parts come in is made of a material to protect the part from static electricity. In most cases, you have to break that warning label in order to open the package. Again, it is a good idea to discharge yourself by touching something that is metal and grounded before handling any electronic component or board, especially if you have walked across a carpeted room.

Assembly Steps

When I assemble a computer, I usually gather all of the components and assemble them on a benchtop or kitchen table. I then turn on the power and try it before I install it in the case. If there is any problem or trouble, it is fairly easy to find it while it is still in the open state. Note that the backside of motherboards and other plug-in boards have sharp projections from the cut and soldered component leads. I usually lay a couple of newspapers on the table or benchtop to prevent scratching or marring of the surface.

Detailed steps for assembly are listed below, but in a few words, here is a basic benchtop assembly: Plug the power-supply cables into the motherboard. If you are using the old-style power supply, make sure that the four black ground wires are in the center. If you are using an ATX-type motherboard and power supply, which is recommended, there will be a keyed socket, and the cable connector can only be plugged in properly. Next, connect the keyboard, the floppy drives, the hard disk drives, and the monitor. Then apply power, boot the computer up, and see if it works.

Motherboards, Case, and Power Supply

The AMD K6, the Cyrix 6x86MX, and the IDT Centaur C6 are designed to use motherboards with the CPU Socket 7. To save a bit of typing, when I speak of the Socket 7-type CPUs, I will just call them Socket 7 clones. Note that the Intel Pentium MMX CPUs are also designed for motherboards with Socket 7. Figure 13-2 shows a Socket 7. This is also a

Figure 13-2
A socket for Socket 7 CPUs.

Zero Insertion Force (ZIF) socket. On the lower side of the socket is a lever. When it is raised, it opens all of the contacts so that the CPU can be easily inserted. When lowered, the lever causes the contacts to tightly grip the pins of the CPU.

The Intel Pentium II and III are mounted on a small board. Intel calls the board a Single Edge Contact, or SEC. The SEC plugs into a motherboard with a Slot 1 connector. Figure 13-3 shows the long, horizontal slot near the top of the motherboard. The Pentium III and heat sink assembly are near the bottom of the photo.

Benchtop Assembly

Quite often, I go through all the steps listed below, except that I do not install the disk drives and motherboard into the case until I know that everything works right. It is much easier to find a mistake or something not connected right if it is out in the open. It will not hurt to run the system outside the case.

Figure 13-3
Slot 1 is the long,
horizontal slot in the
upper part of the
motherboard.
A Pentium III and a
heat sink are in lower
part of the photo.

Figure 13-3
Slot 1 is the long, horizontal slot in the upper part of the motherboard. A Pentium III and a heat sink are in lower part of the photo.

Configuring the Motherboard

If you bought your motherboard and CPU as a unit, the jumpers on the motherboard may already be set and configured for your CPU. But you should use your documentation and check to make sure.

If you bought a Socket 7 CPU separately, then you must use the motherboard manual that came with it and set all the jumpers for that particular CPU. Dozens of different CPUs can be used with the motherboards. The jumper blocks are very small, so you will need long-nose pliers or tweezers to install them. Figure 2-7 in Chapter 2 shows some jumpers.

The small jumpers are used to configure the motherboard for CPU voltage, for frequency, bus speed, memory type and voltage, and several other functions. Be very careful when setting the jumpers. For instance, most motherboards offer an option of several different CPU core voltages. Some motherboards offer settings for as many as 16 different voltages, from 2.0 to 3.5 in steps of 0.1V. If the voltage is set too high, it may burn up the CPU.

Installing a CPU in Socket 7

Installing a CPU in a Socket 7 motherboard is very easy. Just lift the Zero Insertion Force (ZIF) lever, and drop the CPU into the socket. You will notice that there may be a dot on one corner of the CPU and the corner may be cut at an angle. This will indicate pin 1. Find pin 1 on the socket, and drop the CPU in. Be very careful; the pins are very fragile. The CPU will not drop in unless the pins are lined up properly. Once the CPU drops in, pull the lever down and then install the fan on top of the CPU. The fan usually has a clip that fits over the projections on the socket. Figure 3-4 in Chapter 3 shows a fan and heat sink assembly.

If you are installing a Pentium III, you must first install a cradle, or retainer, on the motherboard to hold the CPU assembly. Figure 13-4 shows the CPU and heat sink assembly mounted in the Slot 1 and supported by the upright cradle on each end. Since it rises so high above the motherboard, the motherboard is usually shipped with it uninstalled. It is installed over the Slot 1 connector. Four screws hold it in place.

The Pentium III CPU and heat sink are separate items. The assembly is quite different than the Pentium II assembly shown in Figure 13-5. The Pentium II had very little heat sink material, but it had an individual fan. The Pentium III has lots of heat sink, but it depends on a large fan mounted on the back panel of the case for cooling. Figure 13-6 shows the large fan inside the grill for the Pentium III cooling.

It has been reported that Intel is going to abandon Slot 1 for the Pentium III and start producing Pentium in the flat, plastic pin grid

Figure 13-4
The CPU and heat sink assembly mounted on motherboard.

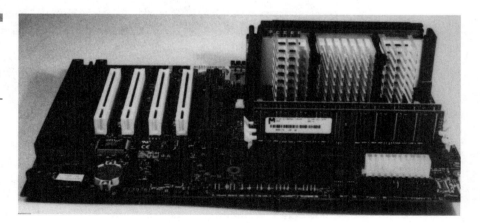

Figure 13-5
A Pentium II CPU
assembly—compare
to Figure 13-4.

Figure 13-6
A large fan is inside
the grill which pro-
vides cooling for the
Pentium III assembly.

array package, such as that used for the Celeron. It would fit in a socket
that is similar to the Socket 370. This setup would certainly save a lot of
cost in assembly labor and parts.

Memory Installation

You should next install the memory chips. Once the motherboard is
installed, the memory slots are often in an area that is difficult to get to.

It is therefore usually much better to install the memory on the motherboard before installing the motherboard in the case.

The memory slots, or banks, may not be plainly labeled. Use your motherboard documentation to determine which banks to fill. The lowest-numbered bank, usually 0, must be filled first.

Memory is very easy to install. The slots are keyed so that the chips can only be installed correctly. For SIMMs just lay the assembly slantwise in the slot and pull it toward you until the retainers on each end snap.

The DIMMs are installed a bit differently than the SIMMs. The SIMMs are laid in the socket on a slant, then pulled up until they are latched in place. The DIMMs are pressed straight down until the holders on each end can be closed. Figure 13-4 shows two 64MB DIMMs installed in front of the Pentium III heat sink assembly.

Make sure the memory chips are seated properly. If one is not properly seated, the computer will not boot up. Usually when something is wrong, the computer will give you an error beep. If the memory is not seated properly or is defective, you may not get an error beep or any message at all. The monitor screen may be black.

Motherboard Stand-offs

When you buy a case, you will usually get a plastic bag with any screws and stand-offs that will be needed. The old XT used brass stand-offs to mount the motherboard in the case. Beginning with the 286, most motherboards used white, plastic stand-offs. Most of them also used one or two brass stand-offs to make sure the motherboard made good ground contact with the case. Most of the new motherboards and cases have now gone back to screws. Instead of stand-offs, the motherboard sits on raised threaded projections on the floor of the case.

Your motherboard will have several holes for securing it. You may not need to use all the holes. You should lay the motherboard in the case and see which holes line up with the screw holes of the raised projections.

Installing the Drives

Here is a copy of an e-mail that I received:

<Dear Mr Pilgrim,
   I intend to build a computer and have purchased your book. There's just

one thing I need to know. I am building a midi tower so do I just turn everything sideways or is it more complicated than that?>

At first I thought it was a bit humorous. But then I realized that there are a whole lot of things that I take for granted that a person who is new to computers would not know.

I am sure that he was mostly concerned about the disk drives, which can be mounted on the side. You could even mount them upside down, but it is not recommended. One of the 20MB hard drives in my new Pentium III is standing up on end right behind the front panel. My second hard drive is mounted in the old-fashioned, traditional way just above it. See Figure 13-7.

For some hard drives, it may be difficult to determine which is the right side up. The top will usually have a cover over it. The bottom may have some exposed electronic components.

Before the drives are installed, they must be configured. If you are only installing a single IDE drive, the installation may be very simple. The drive probably has jumpers that were set at the factory that makes it

Figure 13-7
Note that the hard disk drive in the lower right corner is standing on end. The one above it is mounted in the traditional way.

Figure 13-8

Figure 13-8
Two IDE CD-ROM drives—note the small white jumpers that configure them as master and slave.

drive 1 or the master drive. Figure 13-8 shows the back of two CD-ROM drives. Note the small white jumpers that configure them as either master or slave. Also note the small audio cables from each unit.

Figure 13-9 shows a 40-wire ribbon cable being connected to an IDE drive. The cable will have three connectors—one end plugs into the pins on the motherboard marked "Primary." You connect the two hard disks to the other two connectors. The disks can be connected to the end or middle connector. It doesn't matter which connector, because the jumpers determine which is the master and slave. Of course, if you only have one hard disk, you only use one connector.

The connectors on the 40-wire ribbon cable are usually keyed. The drive connectors have a shell around the connector with a cutout so that they can only be plugged in properly. The pins on the motherboard usually have a keyed shell around them. If there is no shell around the pins, you must make sure that the colored-wire side of the ribbon cable goes to pin 1.

When two IDE hard drives are installed, the C:, or boot, drive must be the master and the slave will be the second drive. The drives usually come from the factory configured with the jumpers as a single or master

Figure 13-9

Connecting the 40-wire ribbon cable to the IDE drives. The connectors are keyed so they can only be plugged in correctly. The four pins on the right are for the 4-wire power connectors. They can only be connected properly.

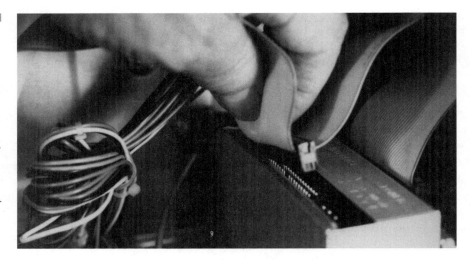

drive. If the drives are not configured properly, you will get an error message that may tell you that you have a hard disk or controller failure. You will not be able to access the drives.

There will be a second set of upright pins on the motherboard for IDE drives that will be marked "Secondary." If you install more than two IDE drives, such as CD-ROMs, they will be installed on the secondary pins. Again, one of the two drives should be configured as a master and the other as a slave. To recap: You can have a master and a slave on the primary set of pins and a secondary master and slave on the second set of pins.

If you are installing a SCSI hard drive or SCSI CD-ROM drive, you will have to set some jumpers on the drive to assign a logical unit number (LUN) to each device. The jumpers are usually on the rear of the drive, similar to those on the IDE drives. You should take care of the jumpers before installing the drives. The cables for the SCSI drives usually have a keyed shell around the connector so that they can only be connected properly. Not many motherboards have the SCSI interface built in, so you will probably have a plug-in board for the SCSI host interface. The cable from a SCSI hard disk will be connected to the SCSI host interface. The cable may have one or more connectors in the middle for other SCSI devices. The interface board will also probably have an external connector on the back panel for any external SCSI devices such as a scanner.

Bench Test

As mentioned, I usually hook everything up on the bench and try it out before I install it in the case. If I have made an error or did not connect something properly, it is much easier to find. Once I am sure it works okay, then I install it in the case.

Install in the Case

I usually leave the cables connected to the drives when I install them in the bays. There is not much room between some of the drives and the power supply. The power supply is the rectangular box in the top left corner in Figure 13-7.

The four pins in the right corner of Figure 13-9 are for the 4-wire power cables for the drives. They can only be plugged in properly.

Most cases are like that shown in Figure 13-7. Most of them will have bays that will accept five or more $3\frac{1}{2}$-inch drives. Two or more of these bays will be accessible from the front panel. In the top section there is usually room for three or four bays for $5\frac{1}{4}$-inch drives, such as a CD-ROM, CD-R, and DVD drives, or even the old $5\frac{1}{4}$-inch floppy drives. These bays will be accessible from the front panel. Of course, you don't need front-panel access for the hard drives.

The screw holes in almost any drive can match up with the mounting slots of the drive bays. You should use two screws on each side of the drive. Be careful not to over-tighten the screws. The frames of most drives are made from soft cast aluminum and will strip out very easily. Also be very careful not to use screws that are too long. If too long, they may protrude into the electronics on the drive. Figure 13-10 shows screws being inserted to mount a hard disk drive in a bay.

Install the Plug-in Boards

Once all the cables are connected, install the plug-in boards. I have a SCSI board for one of my hard drives. I also have an adapter board for the monitor, a sound board, and a modem/fax board.

Most of the Pentium II and III motherboards use a PS/2-type small connector for the keyboard and mouse. Either connector can be used for the PS/2 mouse or the keyboard. Many of the new keyboards have this

small connector. Sometimes the keyboard will have the old-style larger connector and a PS/2 adapter so that it can be used on either system. If you are buying a new keyboard, make sure that it has the PS/2-type connector. If you already have a standard keyboard and mouse that you want to use, it is possible to buy PS/2 adapters.

If you want to use your standard mouse, it can be connected to COM1 or COM2. The only benefit of the PS/2 mouse is that it does not use one of the COM ports, but it does require the use of one of the precious IRQs.

Here is a chart showing the difference in the wiring in the standard keyboard and mouse connector pins and the PS/2 connector pins:

Signal	Std. Pin	PS/2 Pin
Clock	1	5
Data	2	1
Ground	4	3
+5 VDC	5	4
Not used	3	2 & 6

As you can see, there is a difference in the pin assignments for the two systems. An adapter will have the wires crossed and be wired so that the proper signal will be present on the proper pin.

The adapters are available from most major computer stores or from several of the companies who specialize in cables and connectors. The adapters may cost from $3 to $5 each. Here are some companies who carry adapters:

ABL Electronics
  800-726-0610
  sales@ablcables.com

Cables to Go
  800-506-9605
  www.cablestogo.com

Dalco
  800-650-0666

QVS Computer Connectivity
  800-622-9606

There are several other similar companies. Look for ads in computer magazines. Call for a catalog.

The motherboard may also have two sockets for the universal serial bus (USB). This bus can allow up to 128 peripheral components to be daisy-chained and attached. Some of the available peripherals are monitors, mice, keyboards, scanners, disk drives, and modems. There will be lots more of them in a very short time. The USB has many advantages over the SCSI bus. The cable companies listed above also carry cables and connectors for the USB system.

Connecting the Wires for the Front-Panel LEDs

There will be several upright pins on the front of the motherboard, as well as twisted pairs of wires that are connected to the front-panel LEDs that power on and monitor hard disk activity. There are pins for connection to the speakers, pins for reset, and pins for connection to an infrared port.

Most earlier cases had twisted pairs of wires with connectors that were not well marked. It was often difficult to trace the twisted wires back to the various LEDs and switches. Quite often I never bothered to connect the wires to the motherboard.

Turn on the Power and Boot Up

Make one last check to see that all the cables are connected properly. I often try out new boards and parts. Quite often I will install something, then reassemble everything, put the cover back on, and then find that it doesn't work. Sometimes it is because I did not check my cables or didn't do something that I should have. So when I install something new, I usually try it out first to make sure it works before I replace the cover. Often I just leave the covers off my computers. Other than the messy look, it doesn't cause any problem. Actually, in addition to saving me time and trouble, leaving the covers off allows the system to run cooler.

The FCC would not be too happy with me, but the computer does emit some radiation. If it is near a TV set, it may cause interference on some channels. However, it is a very weak signal and should not cause any real problems. (At times it seems that the FCC hasn't got much to do. I have seen agents at COMDEX go to different booths, pick a system at random, and test it for any stray radiation. The vendor can be fined if it does not pass the tests.)

If it appears that all the cables and jumpers are set properly, turn on the power and boot up. You will need a floppy disk that can boot up your system. If you are using Windows 95/98, you should have a 3½-inch floppy boot disk. This floppy disk should also have the FDISK and FOR-MAT programs on it that are needed to format the hard disk. The steps below explain the format operation.

Formatting a Hard Disk

Once you have assembled your computer, you need to format and load your software on your hard disk—or perhaps, two hard disks. You can't do anything with your hard drives until they have been formatted. Windows 95/98 comes on a CD-ROM disc that can hold up to 650MB of data. It has hundreds of help topics and files. But you won't find any help for formatting a hard disk. Even the small manual that comes with Windows 98 does not even mention formatting. Here is Windows 98's entire help file for formatting a floppy disk from their CD-ROM:

To Format a Disk
1. If the disk you want to format is a floppy disk, insert it into its drive. Otherwise, skip to step 2.

2. In **My Computer** or in the right pane of Windows Explorer, click the icon for the disk you want to format.
3. On the **File** menu, click **Format**.

Notes
- Do not click the disk icon, because you can't format a disk if it is open in **My Computer** or Windows Explorer.
- Formatting a disk removes all information from the disk.
- You cannot format a disk if there are files open on that disk.

There is no mention at all about formatting a hard disk. I don't understand why Microsoft neglected this very important aspect of computing. I suppose they expect you to buy your system with the hard disks already installed and formatted. But what if you wanted to add a second hard disk? You just have to buy a book like this one to find out how to format it. You may have trouble finding a book that tells you how to format a hard drive. I have books by Peter Norton, Scott Mueller, and lots of other books, but none of them give the detailed instructions you need to format a new hard drive.

The Purpose of Formatting

Formatting organizes the disk so that data can be stored and accessed easily and quickly. If the data was not organized, it would be very difficult to find an item on a large hard disk. I have about 3000 files on my two hard disks. Those files are on tracks and sectors that are numbered. A file allocation table (FAT) is set up to record the location of each track and sector on the disk.

A brief analogy of disk organization would be a developer of a piece of land. He would lay out the streets and create blocks. He would then partition each block into lots and build a house on each lot. Each house would have a unique address. A map of these streets and house addresses would be filed with the city. A track would be analogous to a street, and a sector number would be similar to a house number.

The FAT is similar to an index in a street atlas or a book. When a request is sent to the heads to read or write to a file, it goes to the FAT, looks for the location of that file, and then goes directly to it. The heads can find any file, or parts of any file, quickly and easily.

Formatting is not something that is done every day, and it can be rather difficult in some cases. One reason the disks do not come from the manufacturer preformatted is that there are so many options. If you have a 20GB hard disk, you will probably want to divide or partition it into two or three different logical disks.

For the old MFM (modified frequency modulation) drives, one reason manufacturers did not preformat the drive is that there were so many different controller cards. The controller cards are usually designed so that they would operate with several different drives from different companies.

The First Step

You must have a floppy startup disk. If you have installed Windows 95/98 on another system, it prompted you to make a startup disk. You can use that disk to format your new drive. If you don't have such a disk, ask your vendor to provide one. The floppy disk should have COMMAND.COM, FDISK, FORMAT, SYS, CONFIG.SYS, AUTOEXEC.BAT, and MSCDEX. Insert the Startup disk into the floppy drive and turn on the power. At the A: prompt, type FDISK.

FDISK allows you to partition the drive into one or more logical drives. Your first drive should be your primary DOS system drive, or drive C:. You can only have one active primary drive in the system, so all other logical drives will be extended DOS drives.

FDISK Options

FDISK means "fixed disk," or it could also mean "format disk." It is a DOS command on the startup boot disk. You will not be able to use a hard disk until it has been partitioned with FDISK, then high-level formatted.

DOS uses all of the alphabet letters for disk drives. It reserves A: and B: for floppy drives and C: for the boot drive. So if you have a very large disk, you can make up to 23 other logical partitions, or drive D: through Z:.

Using FDISK can be a bit confusing. Windows 95/98 comes on a CD-ROM disc that has a lot of help files. But the help for FDISK is as scant as the help they give for formatting a hard disk. In fact, they don't even list FDISK in their index. (Microsoft Press is a division that primarily prints books about how to use Microsoft software. If their manuals were well written, you would not need to buy an extra book to learn how to use the software. If I were a cynical or distrustful person, I might think that the Microsoft manuals are deliberately poorly written so that you have to buy some of their books about the software.)

The older MFM, RLL, and ESDI hard disks had to have a low-level and a high-level format. Newer drives have the low-level format done at the factory. Many of the newer BIOS systems have a utility for doing a low-level format, but you should not use it on an IDE or SCSI drive that has already been low-level formatted.

When you type FDISK, if you are using MS-DOS 6.2 or a later version, this message will be displayed:

```
FDISK Options
Current Fixed Disk Drive: 1
Choose one of the following:
1. Create DOS partition or Logical DOS Drive
2. Set active partition
3. Delete Partition or Logical DOS Drive
4. Display partition information
5. Change current fixed disk drive
```

[Option 5 is only displayed if you have more than one drive.]

```
Enter choice: [1]
Press ESC to exit FDISK
```

If you choose 1 and the disk has not been prepared, a screen like this comes up:

```
Create DOS Partition or Logical DOS Drive
Current Fixed Drive: 1
Choose one of the following:
1. Create Primary DOS partition
2. Create Extended DOS partition
3. Create logical DOS drive(s) in the Extended DOS partition
Enter choice: [1]
Press ESC to return to FDISK Options
```

If you want to boot from your hard drive (I can't think of any reason why you would not want to), then you must choose 1 to create a primary DOS partition and make it active.

If you choose 1, a prompt will come up and ask:

```
Do you wish to use the maximum size for a Primary DOS Partition and
  make the partition active (Y/N) ?[Y]
```

If you type Y for yes, the entire drive will be made into one large C: drive. If you answer N, it will display the maximum disk size and ask what percentage or number of megabytes to assign as the primary drive. You can type in 50 percent or any number of megabytes. You can make the whole drive a single partition, but it is better to have two or more partitions.

After you create the primary partition, press Esc, and this same screen will be displayed again:

```
Create DOS Partition or Logical DOS Drive
Current Fixed Drive: 1
Choose one of the following:
1. Create Primary DOS partition
2. Create Extended DOS partition
3. Create logical DOS drive(s) in the Extended DOS partition
Enter choice: [2]
Press ESC to return to FDISK Options
```

Since you have already created the primary partition, choose option 2 to create an extended DOS partition. This will show the amount of space that is left over from the primary drive assignment. If you have a 20GB drive and you assigned 5GB for the primary, you would have 15GB left for other partitions.

You cannot partition the drive at this point. Accept the figure given. If you try to partition the drive, whatever you choose will be all that you can use. For instance, with option 2, if you have 15GB left and you try to divide it into two 7.5GB partitions, it will figure that the entire extended drive is to be only 7.5GB. You will not be able to use the other 7.5GB. You must tell it to use the 15GB that is available.

Next, press Esc to return to the options, then choose option 3, Create Logical DOS Drives in the Extended DOS partition. You can now divide this partition into as many drives as you want.

It will now tell you how much space is available for the extended partition. The default is the maximum amount of space shown. If you want to accept it and have a single primary drive and a single extended drive, just press Enter. Otherwise, type the number of megabytes or a percentage desired. If you type a percentage number, follow with the percentage symbol, for instance, 50%. Continue creating logical drives until the entire disk is assigned.

You can press Esc and delete and revise any of the partitions that you have created.

Installing a Second Hard Disk

If you are installing a second hard disk, you will see this display when you enter the FDISK command:

```
FDISK Options
Current Fixed Disk Drive: 1
```

```
1. Create DOS partition or Logical DOS Drive
2. Set active partition
3. Delete Partition or Logical DOS Drive
4. Display partition information
5. Change current fixed disk drive
```

[Option 5 is only displayed if you have more than one drive.]

```
Enter choice: [5]
Press ESC to exit FDISK
```

You will choose option 5 to change drives. Use the same procedure listed above for the first drive. Note that the primary partition is only on the C: drive and it contains the Boot utility. You cannot create a primary partition on the second drive. Use the options to create more logical drives just as you did on the first drive.

High-Level Format

After the FDISK options have been completed, return to drive A: and high-level format drive C:. Because you want to boot off this drive, you must also transfer the system and hidden files to the disk as it is being formatted. You must therefore use a /S to transfer the files. Type:

```
FORMAT C: /S
```

DOS will display a message that says:

```
WARNING! ALL DATA ON NON-REMOVABLE DISK DRIVE C: WILL BE LOST!
Proceed with Format (Y/N)
```

If you press Y, the disk light should come on, and you might hear the drive stepping through each track. After a few minutes, it will display:

```
Format complete
System transferred
Volume label (11 characters, ENTER for none)?
```

You can give each partition a unique name, or volume label, if you wish to.

You can test your drive by doing a warm boot by pressing Ctrl + Alt + Del. The computer should reboot.

Now that drive C: is completed, if you have other partitions or a second disk, format each of them. Use the same procedure as above, but do not transfer the boot files (/S) to the other partitions and drives.

Helpful Utilities for Transferring Files and Increasing Disk Space

I'd like to take a little time out in the assembly process to mention a few utilities that can help you partition your hard disk and organize and transfer files. Each of these programs is reasonably priced and quite handy.

DriveCopy

You may have just bought a new hard drive to add to your system, perhaps because your C: drive is bursting at the seams. It seems that every program wants to be loaded on C:. A hundred megabytes can be used up in a hurry. It would be nice to be able to just copy all of the files from drive C: onto a new, much larger drive. But Windows 95 has all kinds of hidden files that must be copied along with the parent files. Besides that, you need to create new directories before you can copy files into it. It can be quite time-consuming.

DriveCopy from PowerQuest will do all of the work for you in a very short time. The program is rather inexpensive and is well worth the money. Contact PowerQuest at www.powerquest.com, or at 801-226-8977.

PartitionMagic

In addition to DriveCopy, PowerQuest Corporation also makes PartitionMagic. PartitionMagic 3.0 lets you resize your drives and reclaim wasted disk space. It will also let you safely boot and run multiple operating systems and organize and protect your data.

You want to get the most out of your hard drive; however, up to 40 percent of your hard drive may be totally wasted because of inefficient storage methods. PartitionMagic 3.0 increases your usable disk space by shrinking large FAT partitions and restructuring cluster sizes to reclaim up to hundreds of megabytes of lost disk space.

Contact PowerQuest at www.powerquest.com, or 801-226-8941.

Partition-It

Partition-It is another relatively inexpensive utility that will let you partition large hard drives into smaller, more manageable drives. Partition-It can do this without your having to back up. It is all automatic. It scans the drive and calculates what the optimum cluster size should be for maximum storage.

Partition-It was created by Quarterdeck Corp. It has now been acquired by Symantec (www.symantec.com).

LapLink

If you have just built a new computer and need to transfer files from your old one, one of the best ways to do it is to use LapLink from Traveling Software. It will transfer all the directories and files and save an enormous amount of time.

As the name implies, LapLink was first developed for connecting laptops to a desktop to transfer information and data. But LapLink also has several other excellent utilities. The software comes with cables so that you can connect two computers together through the printer ports. The cables could be used as an inexpensive peer-to-peer type of network.

For more information, contact Traveling Software at 800-527-5465, or www.travsoft.com.

Install in Case

If you have assembled your computer on the benchtop and everything works okay, turn the power off and install it in the case. Turn the power on and check it again to make sure it still works, then install the cover.

Installing an AMD Athlon CPU on a Motherboard

Below are some very detailed instructions from AMD (www.amd.com) as to how the Athlon CPU should be installed on the motherboard.

Intel had very few instructions for the Pentium II and Pentium III. Note that the Athlon looks a bit like the Pentium II shown in Figure 13-5.

AMD Athlon Processor Installation Guide
For PC enthusiasts, VARs, small businesses, and others needing to build the ultimate performance PC—AMD proudly presents the AMD Athlon™

processor....The innovative AMD Athlon processor with 3DNow!™ technology brings industry-leading unsurpassed performance to PC systems running the extensive installed base of x86 software. This processor is Microsoft® Windows® compatible and offers seventh-generation 64-bit design features that distinguish it from previous generations of PC processors. AMD Athlon processor innovations include a nine-issue superscalar architecture optimized for high clock frequency, a superscalar pipelined floating-point unit, 128 Kbytes of on-chip level-one (L1) cache, a programmable high-performance backside L2 cache interface, and the 200-MHz Athlon system bus with support for scalable multiprocessing. These features provide industry-leading performance for Windows 95, Windows 98, and Windows NT™ operating systems. Before installing your new AMD Athlon processor, please review this installation guide in its entirety.

Recommended Configuration

The AMD Athlon processor is a leading-edge high-performance processor that requires high-end components to ensure that it will operate at maximum efficiency. Do not attempt to install the AMD Athlon processor with an inadequate power supply, memory, or other supporting components.

[Table 13-1 shows the minimum and recommended AMD Athlon processor components. Additional information is available on the AMD Web site at www.amd.com/athlon/config.]

[Specifications for additional peripheral devices, software, and components are available on the AMD Web site at the address given above.]

The AMD Athlon processor module and motherboard have sensitive electronic components that can be easily damaged by static electricity. We recommend that you leave the processor in its original packaging until you are ready to install it. The installer should only touch the processor case or the attached heatsink and fan assembly. The installer should not touch

TABLE 13-1

AMD
Recommended
AMD Athlon
Processor
Components

Component	Minimum	Recommended	Comments
Power supply	250-watt ATX	300-watt ATX	—
PC enclosure	Mid-size ATX	Full-size ATX	A fan should be installed in back wall of enclosure.
Memory	64MB	128MB	DIMMs must be PC100, Rev.1 8ns or faster.

Source: *AMD Athlon Processor Installation Guide.*

the processor board edge connector. We recommend that unpackaging and installation be done on a grounded, anti-static mat, and that you should wear an anti-static wristband grounded at the same point as the anti-static mat (preferably the personal computer chassis). When the processor module is removed from its package, place it on the anti-static mat.

Unpacking Your Processor

Take a moment to inspect the package for obvious damage due to shipping or handling. Be sure that no noticeable damage exists before proceeding. You should have the following items in your processor package:

- AMD Athlon processor module with heatsink and fan assembly attached
- AMD Athlon Certificate of Authenticity
- AMD Athlon Processor Installation Guide
- Warranty card
- Heatsink support assembly

If you are missing any of these items, contact your local distributor for a replacement.

Installation Procedure

The following step-by-step procedure must be followed to successfully install the AMD Athlon processor in the personal computer system motherboard.

Note: In order to ensure successful operation of the AMD Athlon processor, AMD strongly recommends selecting a motherboard from our website. The motherboards that have been tested and verified for use with the AMD Athlon processor can be found at the following URL: http://www.amd.com/athlon/config.

1. While wearing the grounded anti-static wristband, place the motherboard on the anti-static mat as shown in Figure 13-A1.
2. Open the processor module box, remove the AMD Athlon processor module, and place it on the anti-static mat oriented as shown in Figure 13-A2.
3. If there is a heatsink support assembly on your motherboard as shown in Figure 13-A3, go to step 6. The heatsink support assembly is a black plastic assembly. If there is not a heatsink support assembly, go to step 4.
4. Remove the ziplock bag containing the heatsink support assembly from the processor module box and disassemble the heatsink support assembly so that the four parts are as shown in Figure 13-A4. The two pins are used to secure the heatsink support to the motherboard. The

Figure 13-A1
Motherboard on anti-static mat.

Figure 13-A2
AMD Athlon processor module removed.

heatsink support clip will be used later to secure the heatsink to the heatsink support.

5. Install the heatsink support on the motherboard as shown in Figure 13-A5.

The support will only fit on the board in one orientation because the

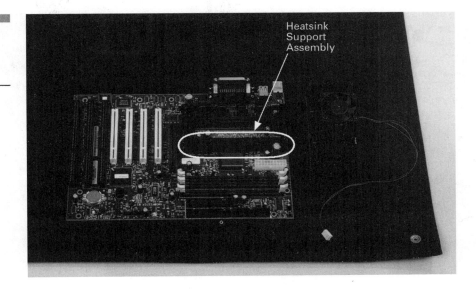

Figure 13-A3
Heatsink support
assembly on
motherboard.

Heatsink
Support
Assembly

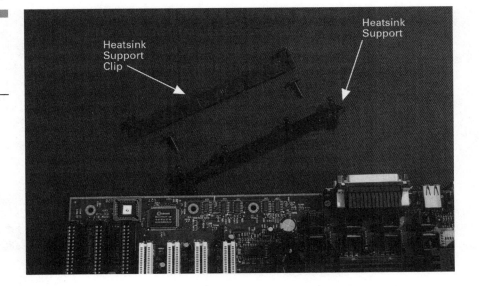

Figure 13-A4
Disassembly of
heatsink support
assembly into four
parts.

Heatsink
Support
Clip

Heatsink
Support

two legs of the support are different sizes and the holes on the motherboard only accept the support oriented in one direction.

After installing the heatsink support on the motherboard, secure
the support to the motherboard by pressing the two small plastic pins
down through the legs of the heatsink support.

Go to step 7.

Figure 13-A5
Installation of
heatsink support on
motherboard.

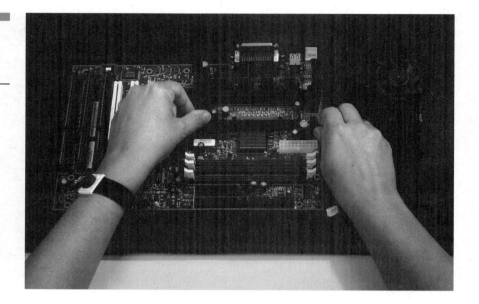

Figure 13-A6
Removal of clip from
heatsink support.

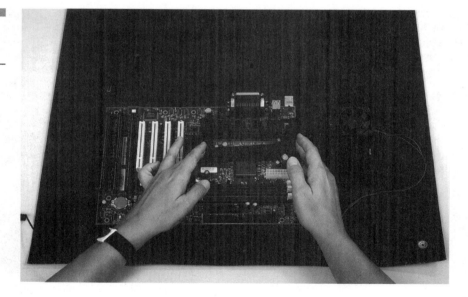

6. If the heatsink support is already installed on the motherboard, you
   must remove the heatsink support clip from the heatsink support. The
   heatsink support clip is shown in Figure 13-A4.

   Depress the plastic levers on the end of the heatsink support clip
   and remove the clip from the heatsink support on the motherboard as
   shown in Figure 13-A6.

7. If the motherboard has folding processor module guides installed, move the processor module guides to the open position as shown in Figure 13-A7.
8. Press the processor module retention latches in until they click into the retracted position as shown in Figure 13-A8.

Figure 13-A7
Moving the processor module guides to the open position.

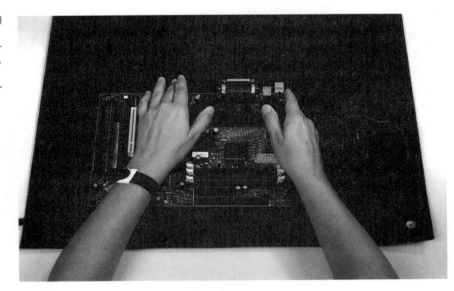

Figure 13-A8
Pressing processor module retention latches into retracted position.

9. Install the heatsink support clip between the first and second rows of pins at the bottom of the heatsink as oriented in Figure 13-A9. The openings of the locking slots on the heatsink support clip should be facing upwards.

10. Slide the processor module into the processor module guides as shown in Figure 13-A10.

Figure 13-A9
Installation of heatsink support clip at bottom of heatsink.

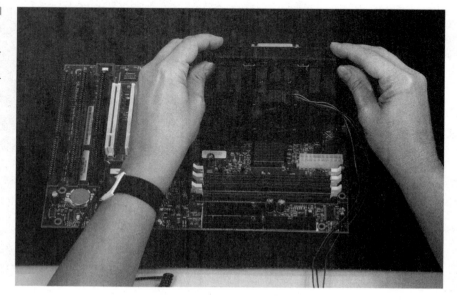

Figure 13-A10
Sliding processor module into processor module guides.

11. Firmly seat the processor module into the motherboard connector as shown in Figure 13-A11.
12. Lock the processor module in place by pulling the processor module latches out as shown in Figure 13-A12.

Figure 13-A11
Seating of processor module into motherboard connector.

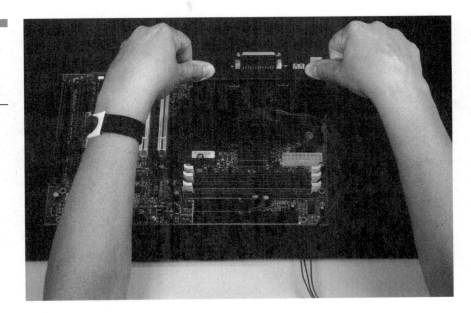

Figure 13-A12
Locking processor module in place.

13. Slide the heatsink support clip onto the grooves on the heatsink support as shown in Figure 13-A13. The clip should snap into position.
14. Consult your motherboard users manual for the location of the fan power socket. Insert the fan power plug into the appropriate socket on the motherboard as shown in Figure 13-A14. The plug is keyed to ensure proper polarity.

Figure 13-A13
Sliding heatsink support clip into heatsink support.

Figure 13-A14
Inserting fan power plug into motherboard socket.

Figure 13-A15
Correctly installed
AMD Athlon
processor.

15. Figure 13-A15 shows a correctly installed AMD Athlon processor module.
16. Install the motherboard in the PC enclosure.
17. Install additional components on the motherboard as required.
18. Ensure that nothing is restricting the airflow through the processor fan/heatsink assembly.

Anything laying across the top of the fan, such as a disk drive cable, will not allow the processor to be properly cooled and may result in damage to the processor.

Congratulations! You have successfully installed your new AMD Athlon processor.

If You Need Help

If you need technical assistance with the installation of your new processor, or if you have technical questions about its operation, you can obtain E-mail addresses and technical support phone numbers on our support website at the following URL: http://www.amd.com/support/support.html.

In the United States, technical support is available at the following phone number: 408-749-3060.

Congratulations

Go ask your spouse or somebody to pat you on the back and congratulate you. You deserve it.

The Internet

Never before in the history of the world has there been so much information available. Almost all of it is no further away than your fingertips. The one thing that makes it possible is the Internet and World Wide Web (WWW). The Internet started off as a government project in 1973 with the Advanced Research Projects Agency (ARPA), an agency of the Department of Defense (DoD). It was a network designed to facilitate scientific collaboration in military research among educational institutions. ARPAnet had some similarities to peer-to-peer networking. It allowed almost any system to connect through an electronic gateway.

Internet Service Providers (ISPs)

The ARPAnet is no longer primarily concerned with military research. It is now known as the Internet. It is possible to access the Internet or WWW from several of the larger online services, called Internet service providers, or ISPs. Some of the biggest are Prodigy (800-776-3449), America Online, or AOL (800-827-6364), Microsoft Network (800-386-5550), and CompuServe (800-848-8199). (Note that CompuServe is now a part of AOL.)

Besides the large online service providers, there are hundreds of smaller Internet service providers (ISPs). The Los Angeles California edition of the *Computer Currents Magazine* lists several local ISPs each month. They have an overall listing of over 200 ISPs in the greater Los Angeles area. There are several thousand in the entire country. The smaller ISPs connect to a network of national service providers (NSPs).

At one time, the larger online companies had similar hourly or monthly rates to the smaller ISPs. The smaller ISPs began cutting their rates in order to attract customers. The larger companies then began cutting their rates to match the small companies. Most of the small ISPs in the Los Angeles area charge $20 a month for unlimited hours. Some are as low as $10 or $12 per month. Now almost all of the large companies offer a flat rate of $19.95 to $21.95 per month for unlimited usage. This is an excellent example of competition working to our benefit.

But the lowered rates and unlimited time have caused some problems. Before the unlimited time was instituted, a person would watch the clock and get on and get off as quickly as possible. Now they can log on and chat or surf for hours because of the flat rate.

AOL instituted a very aggressive ad campaign and signed up over 8 million subscribers. Unfortunately, this was more than they could handle. Many people spent hours trying to get online, only to get a busy signal. They have since increased the number of phone lines, but it can still be difficult to get on at certain times of the day. AOL recently took over CompuServe and their 3 million subscribers. It is estimated that AOL now has over 15 million subscribers.

Many people go online after they have their dinner, so it may be difficult to sign on to AOL during the hours from 5 P.M. until 10 P.M. This usually isn't too much of a problem with most of the other ISPs.

Voice and Video on the Internet

Several companies are now making software and hardware that will let you use voice over the Internet. The telephone companies are a bit worried. If a person can make a long-distance call to anywhere in the world by just dialing a local access number, then the telephone companies may stand to lose some money. But some of the voice systems require that the ISP have special equipment. The ISP then usually charges for calls made. At the present time, the voice quality is not as good as the Plain Old Telephone System (POTS).

Diamond Multimedia (www.diamondmm.com) has developed a kit that allows you to send voice and video over the Internet. The $199 kit includes a camera, microphone, hardware, and software to make this all possible. Some of the Internet voice phone systems require that you have an ISP with specialized equipment. The ISPs then charge 12 cents a minute or more for using the Internet for voice. But the Diamond video and voice does not require that the ISP provide any special equipment. It can be used just as if you were using your modem for the Internet. Several other companies have developed similar video and voice systems.

Browsers

Since there is such a large amount of information on the Internet, search and browsing software is essential. The two most popular navigational software browsers are NetScape and Microsoft Internet Explorer 5.0. Both of these browsers are free.

Modems and Access Numbers

At the time when there were only three or four major providers, most people were using 1200- and 2400-baud modems. It took quite a lot of time for downloads or to send messages. When 14.4K modems came out, the companies figured that they would be losing a lot of money because the people would not be online as long. To make up for the lost revenue, if you used a high-speed modem, they charged you extra. Now there is no difference in the charge for faster modems. The access numbers that you call must be able to handle the faster modems.

Most companies have been very good at providing numbers for the faster modems. Of course, they also still provide numbers for the older 14.4K and even the old 2400-baud systems. Most faster modems will drop down and operate at the lower speed. Since you are paying a flat monthly rate anyway, it may actually be advantageous to use a 14.4K number even if you have a much faster modem. Getting on during the busy hours might be easier. If you are just chatting or sending a short e-mail, it won't make much difference what speed you use. But if you are browsing the Web sites, especially if there is a lot of graphics, then you definitely need a fast modem.

When you sign up with most of the companies, they will ask for your telephone area code and number, then provide a list of numbers in your area. They will list them by speed, such as 28.8K, 14.4K, and even 2400 baud. The major ISPs now offer 56K or X2 service in many cities. You are usually allowed to choose two numbers—a primary number and an alternate number. If the primary number that you choose is busy, then usually the software will have the modem try the alternate number. Hopefully, the numbers offered will be toll-free. If the numbers offered require a toll charge, you will have to pay it. Unfortunately, there are some parts of the country that do not have local service. It might be in your best interest to check with several ISPs to find out if there are any local numbers available.

AOL has improved their service, and I seldom have a problem getting online. One reason I chose AOL is because I do a lot of traveling. I usually take my laptop along. Some of the ISPs have very few outlets. I have been able to find a local AOL telephone number wherever I go. When I had accounts with some of the other ISPs, I often had to pay a large toll charge to access the Internet.

If you are still using an older modem and you do a lot of downloading of graphics or you access a lot of Web sites with graphics, it might be a good idea to buy a 56K modem. If you are on AOL, to find out if the X2 or 56K is available in your area, go to AOL Keyword: X2. You will then be prompted to type in your area code, state, and city. A list of access numbers in your area will be displayed. Those that are 56K will have an X2 beside the number.

Modems operate by taking the digital signals from the computer, then turning them into analog signals for transmission over the phone lines. There are several factors that limit the speed of analog signals. One big factor is noise and static, which are analog-type signals. Digital signals are not affected by noise and static. When using high-speed modems, the standard analog signal is sent to the main router. The signal is then broken up into packets and transmitted digitally to the next station, where it is again converted back to analog. This analog signal is then fed to your modem, which converts it back to digital.

So the signal is converted from digital to analog, then to digital, then back to analog, then back to digital. The Integrated Service Digital Network (ISDN) will make life a lot better. But its installation has been very slow in most cities and it is rather expensive. ISDN is discussed a bit more later on in this chapter.

Free ISP

Unlike the other Internet service providers, the Juno Online Services Company (800-654-JUNO, or www.juno.com) provides Internet service without charging a monthly fee. They can do this because they have signed up several advertisers. If you are on a tight budget and don't mind a few commercials, Juno could be all that you need. They don't offer all of the goodies that you would find on AOL, but they provide e-mail and most of the other essentials.

You can access anyone on the Internet or WWW from any of the online providers or ISPs. Unfortunately, if you travel a lot, you may not be able to find a local number for a smaller ISP. The larger companies have local numbers near most cities.

Services

There is something on the Internet for everyone. There are encyclopedias, up-to-the-minute news, people chatting with one another, online romance, and X-rated photos and talk. You can post notes or send e-mail. You can send a message to anyone in the world for just the cost of the dial-up connection and your hourly rate from the ISP. I recently sent several e-mail messages to a friend in England for less than it would have cost me to send a letter. It is as easy to chat with someone in Australia or France or England as it is to chat with your next-door neighbor.

Search Engines

At this moment, there are over 3 million Web sites on the Internet. With this vast amount of information, it would be almost impossible to find a specific item without a search engine. There are several good search engines that you can use for free to find things on the Internet. The search engine companies have hundreds of employees who search the various Web sites, then create categorized databases. The databases can quickly spit out locations of almost anything you are looking for, from aardvark to zygotes. They have encyclopedias that you can read on line for free. They have hundreds of sites for information on the various diseases and treatments. They have sites for travel and games and entertainment. Some of the most popular are the hundreds of sites for pornography. There is something for everyone on the Internet.

You can search for companies, for people, for almost anything imaginable.

Some of the most popular search engines are www.yahoo.com, www.altavista.com, www.excite.com, www.hotbot.com, and www.lycos.com. There are several others. These utilities are free. Just type the address in, and a search form will come up. Type in what you are looking for, and a list of the items found will be displayed. Most of the found list will be in blue, indicating a hyperlink. Just click on the blue type, and you will be sent to that site. If one of the engines does not find what you are looking for, try one of the others.

One search engine that I use often is www.anywho.com. This engine can find just about anyone or any business that is listed in any telephone book anywhere in the country. It can give you their address, phone number, and a lot of other info.

Another good one is www.whowhere.com. If they don't find who or what you are looking for, they can do a live search, much like a private detective. The live search will cost money, which can be charged to a credit card. If you are looking for a long-lost boyfriend or for someone who may have skipped out owing you money, it may be worth the cost.

Help Wanted Ads

If you spend a lot of time looking through the help wanted classified section of your paper, you might be better off searching the Internet. You can download a free program from www.wantedjobs.com and use it to search for you. You specify your state, your job category, and enter various keywords. The program then goes out and searches several sites for jobs that match your requirements. (If you are looking for a job as CEO of a large corporation, there probably will not be too many offers.)

Shopping on the Internet

There are very few businesses who do not have a Web site. You may not need a search engine or address for most of them. For the larger companies, to access their Web site, just type www.companyname.com.

Ordinarily, most businesses have distributors and retail stores. Now many of the companies have gone to direct marketing. You can buy anything from an automobile to a computer to furniture directly from the manufacturer. I recently bought an AnyPoint home network system from Intel over the Internet. Of course, many of the distributors and retailers are not too happy with this new marketing ploy. Some of the larger companies have decided that if you can't beat them, join them. Of course, the competition is great for the consumer. And often the price of the item is less than if you went to the store, especially if you order something from out of state. California charges $8\frac{1}{2}$ percent sales tax. Even if I have to pay shipping charges, it is usually less than what the sales tax would be.

Another benefit is that I do not have to fight the traffic and drive downtown to look at the item. Also, I can access several sites and compare prices without leaving my computer.

A word of caution, however: The vast majority of people are good and honest, but when you get a lot of people communicating with one another, there will always be a few who will try to take advantage of others. Today, a lot of people are using the Internet for business purposes. Most of them are reputable business people and have something of value to offer. But again, there are a few who will do or say anything in order to get their hands in your pocket. Just be careful and watch your wallet.

As mentioned, there is something on the Internet for everyone. Most sites have search software that can help you find almost anything on their site. Some have links to the other major search engines that can search the whole Net. A *link,* or *hyperlink,* is usually an address of another Web site. It is usually shown in blue type. Just point to it with your mouse and click on it, and it will send you there.

Major ISPs

All of the major companies offer chat rooms, Instant Messaging, home pages, member searches, and many other services. Many offer private chat rooms where two or more people can go to chat or discuss anything they want to behind closed doors. One reason AOL is so popular is because of their many chat rooms and areas. They also offer a "buddy list" feature. You can add your friends to this list, and whenever one of them signs on, it will show up on the list. You can then send an Instant Message (IM) to the buddy, and it will reach him wherever that person is. You can even ask to locate the member. It will tell you if the buddy is in a private room or a chat room or just online doing IMs. If that person is in a chat room, it will ask if you want to join him or send him an IM.

AOL has made this Instant Message utility available so that anyone on any other network can send and receive Instant Messages to any member of AOL. If you have a friend on another network, just have her point her browser to www.aol.com and download the free software. I have been a member of Prodigy for over 10 years. It is fine for e-mail and a few business-type things, but it can't come close to AOL for fun and games. To its credit, Prodigy has changed quite a lot. They still have the old Classic Prodigy, but they now have Prodigy Internet. Classic Prodigy has an old, very slow browser. Prodigy Internet uses Netscape for a browser. They added a few features to Netscape that make it look a little bit like AOL. Most of the larger service systems offer either Netscape or Microsoft Explorer with their programs. They have more or less become the two standards.

AOL and several other services will let you choose a unique screen name. On AOL I am simply Apilgrm. If I get tired of using that name, I can have up to five aliases. I can log on as someone else, play out any fantasies, and do it anonymously. I don't have to worry that my dignity or reputation will be marred by something that I might say or do, because no one would know it was me. No matter how mousy or wimpy one is in real life, one can assume any identity, persona, or personality they may want and play out their wildest fantasies.

The downside of the anonymity is that there are always people who will become absolute asses. They may be crude and rude and disruptive. It can sometimes take all the fun out of it. Some of them will join a chat room and use special programs they have created that will completely take over the screen and prevent anyone from participating. The

Senior Scene room on AOL seems to be a favorite target. It is suspected that the culprits are younger people just showing off. AOL usually provides a host to facilitate the chat sessions. The host may remind the person of the rules of "netiquette," but it may not dissuade some of them. Of course, these people can be reported to the AOL Terms of Service (TOS) Advisors, and the culprit will be warned or even denied service. But the disruptive people usually hit and run, so it is difficult to catch them.

These people are a lot like those who write virus programs to harm other people. I believe that they are sick. They take great pleasure in causing pain to others who they have never met. AOL has many, many different chat rooms for various topics. In addition to the Senior Scene room, there is a married with children room, a lesbian room, a twenty-something room, and many, many more. Often there are as many as 20 to 25 people in these rooms. When one fills, the host will open another one similar to the one that is filled.

It is not required, but members are invited to post a profile of themselves. This is a brief statement: whether you are male or female, your interests, and anything else you would like to say about yourself. Of course, no one is going to verify the statements, so some of them may be just a bit exaggerated. The names of the members who are in a room is displayed in a box alongside the chat screen. You can double-click on any member's name, and a box comes up that will let you read their profile.

The Internet can be dangerous to some marriages. Although it is strictly fantasy, some spouses take a very dim view of their mate having a cyber-affair with someone else. I heard of one woman who didn't trust her husband. She went next-door and used her friend's computer. She signed on with an assumed name and made up a very sexy profile. She then sent IMs to her husband and enticed him into a private room. After leading him on to see just how far he would go, she stopped, went home, and confronted him. It very nearly led to a divorce. I read once that someone had determined that there were 726 sins. But that was before cybersex. There must be many more than that now.

Lest you get the wrong idea, AOL and the Internet is not all just sex. Many lasting friendships are made on the Internet. It is a godsend to many lonely people, especially those who can't sleep at night. There are also informational and special-interest groups who can meet on the Internet. Some services do require legitimate identification. One such place is the Well (www.well.com).

Internet Addiction

There is one other disadvantage of the Internet: the potential for addiction. The Canadian Medical Association and the University of Pittsburgh have defined a disorder they call Internet Addiction Disorder (IAD). They claim that it is a maladaptive pattern of Internet use that can lead to clinically significant impairments and increased levels of distress. They say it may be as serious as alcoholism.

I know one woman who has been on the Internet for about six months. Her telephone company bills her by the minute. One month she logged 12,000 minutes. She has used her keyboard so much that the most-used letters, e, a, s, c, d, l, n, and several others are completely worn off.

A recent item in the news concerned a woman divorcee who was arrested and charged with child endangerment. She had locked her three young children in a separate room while she chatted and surfed the Internet for hours. The children were dirty and hungry and neglected. Her ex-husband had often found them in this condition when he came to pick them up for his weekend visits. He finally turned her in for child neglect.

A support group, much like the Alcoholics Anonymous, has been formed to help people. Of course to participate, you have to be on the Internet. (This is something like an AA member taking a bottle along with him to a meeting.) If you would like to find out more about the Internet Addiction Disorder Support Group, point your browser to www.iucf.indiana.edu/~brown/hyplan/addict.html.

E-Mail

To me, one of the most useful and worthwhile benefits of the Internet is e-mail. It is so much better than snail mail in dozens of ways. An e-mail message is almost instantaneous. And it is cheap. You can send hundreds of e-mail letters for less than the cost of one 33-cent stamp. E-mail that you receive can be answered immediately, saved to a hard disk, printed out, or deleted. I subscribe to several health-related sites. Besides personal messages, I usually get 100 or so health messages in my mailbox every day. I have set up directories and files on my hard disk for the messages that I want to save. I usually save them in a wordprocessor format. If you compose a message offline with an older word processor, you may have to convert it to ASCII-type format before it can be sent. You may not have to worry about this with many of the modern word processors. You don't have to do any conversion with word processors such as Word 2000 for Windows, WordPerfect for Windows, and Lotus.

Most of the e-mail programs designed for the Internet have several management tools. Eudora (www.eudora.com) is a very powerful e-mail program. It can receive your messages, separate them, and automatically send them to various folders and directories. Eudora has multiple formatting tools to let you send or receive stylized text, fonts, graphics, sound bites, videoclips, or any data file. In addition, Eudora lets you read and compose mail offline. It also has a built-in spelling checker. Eudora has a lot more utilities and functions than the e-mail programs that come with AOL, Prodigy, or CompuServe. But unfortunately, Eudora will not work with these large companies. It works fine with most of the smaller ISPs such as Juno.

E-Mail, Privacy, and Internet Crime

Most ISPs provide the subscriber with a certain amount of hard disk space on their servers. When you open your mail, you will be reading it from their server hard disk. You can download the message, print it out, delete, or change it, but the original still remains on the ISP server hard disk.

For the ordinary person, that should be of no concern. But there are millions of people on the Internet, and of course, there are a few who commit crimes. The law enforcement agencies are particularly concerned with pedophiliacs, adults who prey on young children. There is a federal law against child pornography. Of course, it is very easy to send photos over the Internet. The photos may be legal in other countries, but if a person in the U.S. downloads them, it can be a criminal offense.

It is possible to log on to the Internet under many different guises. No one can see you or know much about you. Law officers have often logged onto the Internet pretending to be a young person. In one case, an officer pretended to be a young 13-year-old girl. A man made a date with her and flew all the way across country to meet her. Imagine his surprise when he met a law officer instead.

A review of over 100 warrants issued to search AOL files showed that most of them involved pedophiles, stalkers, and harassers. Here are a few other cases as reported in a local paper:

A woman posed as a man and formed a relationship with a 15-year-old girl.

A custodian of a cathedral was charged with setting fire to the church. He claimed that he was online at the time, but the records proved otherwise.

A sheriff's department dispatcher was found to be in collusion with a suspect by sending him e-mail.

A man was suspected of inciting a riot against a Nike store with his e-mail.

Another important issue on the Internet is hate mail and hate crimes. Agents have been able to use the Internet to investigate and convict several people for these crimes, even of murder.

In order for law enforcement officials to view records on an ISP hard disk, they must have sufficient reason and must convince a judge to give them a search warrant.

AOL says it generally keeps unread e-mail on their system for 28 days and mail that has been read for two days. But they offer the option of keeping it longer. One man charged with possessing child pornography opted to have his mail stored for a longer period. Some of the images they found in his file were over six months old. And, of course, the person can download it to her or his own computer hard disk. Even if the person erases a file from a personal hard disk, it may still be recoverable.

If you have not violated any laws, then your privacy probably will not be violated.

J-Mail and Spamming

One of the disadvantages of being connected to the Internet is being bombarded with junk e-mail, or j-mail. The reason there is so much j-mail is because it is so cheap and easy to send. There are organizations who are selling lists of e-mail addresses. You can get over a million addresses for as little as $25 and up to $100. You could send a message to every one of those million people for less than the cost of a single postage stamp. *Boot magazine* is a new computer magazine that is rather irreverent and much like the old hippie-type stuff. One of their writers, Tom Halfhill, said in one issue, that if just 3 percent of the people who get the j-mail respond, it would be enough to give the direct mail marketer an orgasm.

There are no laws against spamming, the sending of unwanted e-mail (usually commercial). Even if there were, they would probably be unenforceable. The crush of spam material can clog a small ISP and even some of the larger ones. I have gotten unwanted mail on AOL, but when I reply and try to complain to the sender, it is sent back to me as undeliverable. They have ways of sending the stuff without revealing their whereabouts.

There are a few resources on the Web to fight back. Net Services, at http://www.compulink.co.uk/~net-services/span/, offers Spam Hater, a free program to combat spam. This program analyzes the spam; extracts a list of addresses of relevant Postmasters, and prepares a reply; allowing you to choose legal threads or insults; or insert your own message. If required, it will also append a copy of the spam. It then places the reply in a mail window ready for sending. The program also includes a tool to help keep you out of spammers' databases, contains context-sensitive help (you right-click on the item), shows a sample of the spam it's analyzing, generates a WHOIS query to help track the perpetrator, and generates a TRACEROUTE query to help track the perpetrator's provider.

Another site tells you how to track down spammers yourself: The site also contains a link to a commercial program, called Spamicide (cost is $45), which lets you cut down on the amount of spam you view by automatically moving spam into a Trash folder.

One small ISP has sued one of the companies, but it has not gone to court yet. The spammers are making so much money that they will gladly pay any fine and continue doing business as usual. One way to stop them would be to ignore them and not buy their products.

Connections

As mentioned, you should try to find the fastest modem possible. Technology does not stand still. Newer and faster methods are being developed every day.

ISDN

ISDN technology is about the fastest available at the moment. But you need a special ISDN modem, and the ISP must be able to interface with ISDN. Another disadvantage is that it is not available in all areas of the country. Even where it is available, it can be rather expensive and may cost from $25 to over $200 extra on your phone bill. However, if you are a large business that does a lot of videoconferencing and other business over the telephone and Internet, it may be well worth it.

Asymmetric Digital Subscriber Line (ADSL)

ADSL is a very fast line that can provide data at a speed as high as 6.14Mbps (megabits per second). That is about 200 times faster than a 28.8Kbps modem. It will be ideal for videoconferencing, video-on-demand, networking, fax, and voice. It is still being tested and developed, but it should be available in some parts of the country by the time you read this. The original hardware will cost about $300 to $500. The original service will cost about $100 a month.

Cable Modems

Some companies have developed cable modems that can operate off the cable lines. They can operate as high as 10Mbps. The hardware cost may be $300 to $500 and cost an extra $30 to $40 a month on your cable bill.

Cable TV Internet

If you can't afford a computer and a modem, there are a few companies who have developed keyboards and set-top boxes that will let you access the Internet over your cable TV. Instead of a computer monitor, it uses the TV screen. The keyboard uses a wireless infrared system similar to that used in the standard TV remote controls. These systems will do most of what you can do with a computer as far as the Internet goes. You can surf the Internet, access all the Web sites, send and receive e-mail, perform financial transactions, search for desired information, and visit chat rooms.

Of course, you may not have many of the advantages of a computer such as a hard disk, a printer, a scanner, or a CD-ROM drive. Another disadvantage is that most of them are very slow. If you have been exposed to a fast computer, using one of the set-top boxes may not satisfy you.

Most of the systems require you to purchase the set-top boxes and keyboards for a nominal price. Then to access the Internet, it usually costs about $29.95 for unlimited hours.

Here are some companies who provide set-top boxes:

Inter-Con/PC
612-975-0001

Interactive Media Systems
408-245-8283

Interlink Electronics
800-340-1331

NetLink Sega Saturn
800-733-7288
www.sega.com

Philips Magnavox Internet TV
888-813-7069
www.magnavox.com

Web-i
www.pmpro.com

WebTV
888-772-7669
www.sony.com

Distance Learning

The California State Universities, and I am sure several others, are using the Internet for teaching courses. It doesn't matter where you are; you can sign up for a course and receive college credit for it just as if you were sitting in class. Anyone can access the classes, but to receive credit, you may have to pay some fees and actually go to the classroom for tests. Quite often when I was attending the San Jose State University, I would try to get a class, but it was filled. I was just out of luck. It made it very difficult if it was a class that was required for graduation. With the Internet, there will be no problem of denial because of filled classes. Another problem that I faced was that I was working full-time and had to take my classes when I could arrange them around my work schedule. I sure wish Internet classes had been available at that time. With the Internet, you can do your class work at any time that suits you.

You might be surprised to know that the company who published the book you are holding also provides significant distance-learning opportunities. Point your browser to www.mhcec.com or call 888-649-8648, ext. 2621. McGraw-Hill World University is fully accredited as a distance education provider.

Online Catalogs and Bookstores

The McGraw-Hill Online Catalog and bookstore at www.mcgraw-hill.com/books.html, has 9000 in-print titles in areas such as business, computing, engineering, science, and medicine from imprints such as Osborne, Schaum's, International Marine, and Ragged Mountain Press. The catalog includes all titles published by the McGraw-Hill College Division, with titles to be added from the recently acquired Irwin, Dushkin, and WCT publishing units.

Warning: The following is an unabashed commercial. Of course, you will find all of the books that I have written in the McGraw-Hill bookstore. Be sure to look for the Save a Bundle series. A good book about the Internet, published by McGraw-Hill, is *The Internet for Everyone: A Guide for Users and Providers* by Richard Wiggins.

Many books have been written about the Internet. Some very good ones can be found in the McGraw-Hill Bookstore listed above. Or you can contact Osborne/McGraw-Hill at 800-227-0900 or www.osborne.com, and they will send you a current catalog.

Another excellent place to buy books online is at www.amazon.com. Amazon claims that they are the world's largest online bookstore, and have an excellent search engine to sift through the enormous database. Amazon also offers music CDs, video and DVD titles, games, and electronics. Most recently, they've added an online auction area. Another large online store is Barnes and Noble (www.barnesandnoble.com). This site also sells music CDs, along with magazines and software. Both stores carry all of my books. They have a search engine that can quickly locate any book that they carry. If you search on *Pilgrim,* you will see all of the computer books that I have written. (They even carry my *Revolutionary Approach to Prostate Cancer.*)

Internet Magazines

Most computer magazines have at least one article about the Internet in each issue. There are also several magazines devoted entirely to the Internet. Most of the magazines have reviews and listings of Web sites. The magazines can be very helpful in telling you where to look for something. Here are a few Internet magazines:

■ *Maximum PC Magazine* gives you the option of receiving a CD-ROM disc each month with lots of reviews of computer products and programs and games. I enjoy the magazine for its new ad fresh outlook. Their Web site is at www.maximumpcmag.com. If you would like to subscribe, call 800-274-3421 or send e-mail to: subscribe@maximumpc.com.

- *Internet World*—P.O. Box 7461, Red Oak, IA 51591-2461, Tel. 800-573-3062, Internet, Customer service iwservice@iw.com, IW Online, www.iw.com.

- *Yahoo Internet Life* is published by Ziff-Davis. Named for the Yahoo search engine, they have an excellent Web site at www.yil.com. If you would like to subscribe, send e-mail to yil@neodata.com. Yahoo has a page titled "Pretty Strange" that lists odd sites. One of the Web sites they reported as www.pxdirect.com. Here is some information from that Web site:

PX:Direct is one of the few suppliers of authentic inmate uniforms, prisoner restraints, and detention equipment to both the general public and to prisons, jails and other correctional facilities. Every item sold by PX:Direct is the same as that used in state, local and federal prisons, jails and correctional facilities. PX:Direct also supplies everything you need to install an authentic jail cell at your location such as Cell doors, Cell bars, a combination toilet and sink....PC:Direct also offers used jail cell equipment and furnishings. They also have handcuffs, leg irons and prison uniforms.

Sounds like just the thing you need for that rebel teenager.

The magazines are an excellent way to know what is available on the Web. They also have some very interesting and informative articles in each issue.

Your Own Web Page

Many of the large providers such as Prodigy and AOL will give you space on their site for your own Web page. It is usually just a few megabytes. If you want more, it will cost you. Most Web pages of large companies have been constructed by professionals who are familiar with the Hypertex Markup Language (HTML). There are books that can show you how to create your own professional-looking site. WordPerfect 2000 and Microsoft Word 2000 can convert text to the HTML format.

Web Hosting

The Internet magazines have dozens of ads from companies who will set up a Web site for you and give you 20 to 25MB of space. Additional space is usually available in 5MB blocks. They will take care of the business of registering you for one or more domain names. In addition, they will set up unlimited e-mail for you, set up anonymous FTP (File Transfer Protocol), and perform many other services. Most of the companies charge from $19.95 to $25.

If you have a company or larger business, there are professional designers who will develop a complete site for you. For a large job, you may have to bring in an ISP rep, a graphics designer, a programmer, network integrators, and many others. Setting up a large site can be very expensive.

The Corel Company (www.corel.com), offers WebMaster Suite, which can be used to create a professional Web site. The suite contains Web page authoring, Web site management, graphics, database publishing, Web site hosting service, and much more.

Sex on the Web

There has been a lot of concern about young people accessing the many Web sites that feature nudity and sex. Most of the sites ask if the person is over 18 or not. If they say they are under 18, they will not be allowed to access the site. But how many do you suppose will say that they are under 18?

In the Scandinavian countries, they don't worry too much about young people seeing depictions of the sex act. But they do ban young children from movies that have lots of killing and gore. Our children are exposed to an unbelievable amount of killings and blood and guts on television and in the movies. I think the Scandinavians are right. Our government is quite worried about pornography on the Net and has spent a lot of time trying to come up with laws that would control it. They really shouldn't worry too much. Most of the sites will show a fairly modest teaser for free, but if you want to see the good stuff, they ask for a credit card number. So unless your children have their own credit cards, you probably don't have to worry too much.

In addition, AOL provides a parental control. The parent can set the controls for several different age levels. If you are on AOL, go to keyword: Parental Controls. You can have up to five different names on your account. Only the parent can change the parental control levels. Just don't let your kids use your primary name, or they can change the level. There are also several software packages that will scan an incoming message for certain words. If it detects anything that sounds like sex, it will refuse to load.

AOL provides a message board where kids can leave messages. As you might expect, the kids don't particularly like the parental controls.

Emoticons and Abbreviations

There are several ways to communicate with the symbols on the keyboard. You may have to turn your head sideways to the left to see them properly. Here are a few:

- :-)   Happy or a smiley face
- :-o   Writer is surprised
- :-#   Writer's lips are sealed
- ;-)   Winking
- :-@   Screaming
- :-(Frowning or unhappy
- >:->   Angry
- :/)   Not funny
- { }   A hug
- {{{{ HUG }}}}   Lots of hugs
- :*   A kiss
- :**:   Kissing
- :-)*(-:   Also kissing
- :-&   Tongue-tied

Some Shorthand Acronyms

BRB   Be right back, or bathroom break

LOL   Laughing out loud, or lots of love

ROFLOL   Rolling on floor laughing out loud

ROFLMAO   Rolling on floor laughing my ass off

@!#@$$%^&   Dirty words

Another Side of the Net

Dear reader, the following doesn't have much to do with building a computer, but it may help save a life.

One of the better aspects of the Internet is the many health sites that are available. Susan's husband, Tom, had prostate cancer. Tom had gone to his doctor every year for checkups, but the doctor had never done a simple Prostate Specific Antigen (PSA) blood test on him. The PSA test is fantastic. The amount of PSA produced by cancer cells correlate fairly closely to the amount of cancer present. Normally there should be less than 4 nonograms per milliliter (ng/ml). So this test can detect prostate cancer in its early stage.

When Tom started experiencing terrible back pain, they did a PSA test on him. Instead of 4 ng/ml, his PSA was 255 ng/ml. The cancer had spread to his spine and was eroding his vertebrae. Prostate cancer thrives on testosterone, which is produced in the testes. Testosterone production can be blocked either by using expensive drugs or by surgery. The surgical procedure is an orchiectomy, a nice term meaning castration. He chose to have the orchiectomy. But despite the drastic treatment, the prostate cancer continued to spread and erode his lumbar vertebrae. It was causing unbearable pain. He was put on massive doses of morphine, but even that failed to relieve the pain. There are some awful side effects of large doses of morphine. He was constipated, he was unaware of his surroundings most of the time, and he was bedridden. Death seemed imminent.

They lived in a rather remote area and didn't have many friends. Their son set them up with a computer and signed his mother up on the Internet. Susan discovered that there was a site devoted to prostate cancer called the Prostate Problems Mailing List (PPML). There were several doctors and many survivors on the list each day. There was information about a new drug, Novantrone, that Tom's doctor had not heard of. Susan downloaded the information and took it to her doctor, who immediately started Tom on the new drug.

Tom's response was remarkable. He was able to forgo the morphine and with the aid of a cane was able to get around. They visited friends, traveled, and did so many things that seemed impossible just the month before. Tom was able to see his daughter give birth to a new grandson. He was able to go out to restaurants and enjoy good food again. For nine months life was good. He was almost able to forget that he had cancer. But it came back with a vengeance and started growing again. Within a month he went from a man who was full of life into a coma and died.

Susan is absolutely convinced that had she not found the Internet Tom would have died nine months earlier. They would not have been able to enjoy the many precious moments they had in that last nine months. Susan had also discovered that there are many good people on the Internet. She made many cyber friends who offered her love and support and encouragement. When they had the funeral for Tom, hundreds of people showed up at the small church. Some came from all parts of the country. The church was so crowded that some had to stand outside. Most of these people had never met Tom nor Susan, but because of the Internet, they knew both of them very well.

I had prostate cancer myself several years ago. Fortunately, mine was detected in time and I was successfully treated. Along with several medical doctors, I put together a book on prostate cancer, titled *A Revolutionary Approach to Prostate Cancer,* published by Sterling House. It should be available at most bookstores or from www.amazon.com. If you are a man over 40 years old, by all means you should have a PSA test. It could save your life. In 1999 about 40,000 men died from prostate cancer, more than those men killed by AIDS.

If you would like to subscribe to the Prostate Help Mailing List (PHML) or the Prostate Problems Mailing List (PPML), send e-mail to either or both of the following addresses:

PROSTATE-HELP@HOME.EASE.LSOFT.COM

Prostate@listserv.acor.org

Leave the Subject heading blank or insert a dash. For the Message, type Subscribe Prostate, then your first name and last name.

About 43,000 women died from breast cancer in 1999. Here is a good Internet site for breast cancer information:

www:medinfo.org/listserv.html?to_do = interact&listname = Breast-Cancer.

One other site that has some good health information is the http:\\rattler.cameron.edu. This site was set up by Gary Huckabay, a prostate cancer survivor and professor of mathematics at Cameron University.

There is no charge for the subscriptions to any of these sites. In addition, there are many other health sites that are very good. Use a search engine to find them.

Viruses, Chain Letters, and Hoaxes

There are about 20,000 viruses, many of them just variations of another one. The major antivirus companies such as Symantec (www.symantec.com), McAfee Associates at (www.mcafee.com), and Touchstone (www.touchstonesoftware.com) have large databases of the various viruses and have programs to cure the viruses.

A department of the U.S. government called the Computer Incident Advisory Capability (CIAC) maintains a Web site about viruses, chain letters, and hoaxes that have invaded the Internet. The address is http://ciac.llnl.gov/.

Here's some information about viruses from the CIAC Web site:

The online CIAC Virus Database contains the virus descriptions from the current version of the CIAC Virus Update, CIAC-2301. The CIAC virus database contains much of the information we have been able to gather about small computer viruses and Trojans. The purpose of this database is to identify most of the known viruses for the Macintosh and PC, and give an overview of the effects of each virus. This database is revised about twice a year as new virus information becomes available. The current data is shown above.

Please keep in mind that the information in this database is the best information that we have to date, but it is not all based on first hand experience. We depend on many sources of information for this data. Therefore, nothing is guaranteed to be correct. In addition, realize that viruses can change in character as new strains are created by virus writers.

Note: Aliases for the viruses are not cross referenced on this list, but are listed with each virus. Use the Find command on your browser to search this page for a particular virus name.

Also listed here are links to several other virus description databases available over the Internet. If you do not find what you are looking for in our database, try one of these others. You can also check our Internet Hoaxes page or our Chain Letters page to see if the virus you are looking for is actually a hoax or chain letter.

Webster's II defines a chain letter as "a letter directing the recipient to send out multiple copies so that its circulation increases in a geometric progression as long as the instructions are carried out." Chain letters on the Internet can be more than just a nuisance. Because they proliferate geometrically, they can clog networks with billions of pieces of useless correspondence. The chain letters described on CIAC's site are PENPAL GREETINGS!, Make Money Fast, American Online Upgrade, Bud Frogs Screen Saver, A Little Girl Dying, Jessica Mydek, Anthony Parkin, Tickle Me Elmo, Kidney Harvest, PBS and NPR—Petition, Hawaiian Good Luck Totem, and Everything You Never Wanted. You probably have seen one of these or a similar e-mail in your mailbox.

Computer virus hoaxes are not real viruses, but they are almost as bad. They are e-mailed warnings of viruses that do not exist. While they cannot infect systems, they are still time-consuming and costly to deal with. The CIAC site contains a lot of information about such hoaxes, including how to distinguish bogus warnings from real warnings and, once identified, how to deal with them. It also lists several of the most common hoaxes.

The Future

The Internet is still in its infancy, but it is growing faster than the weeds in my front lawn. There are millions of Web pages and thousands more being put up every day. There is just about everything that anyone could possibly want on the Internet. Maybe even more than what you want.

CHAPTER 15

Printers

For the vast majority of applications, a computer system is not complete without a printer. There are several manufacturers of computer printers and hundreds of different models. You will have a vast number of options and choices when choosing a printer.

One of the least expensive printers is the ink-jet. Even ink-jet color printers are very inexpensive. If you have a small office/home office (SOHO), you may want to buy one of the multifunction machines that can print, copy, scan, and fax. If you expect to do a lot of heavy-duty printing, then you should look at laser-type printers. This chapter discusses some of the features and functions of these different types. Almost every printer manufacturer now has a Web site. The sites are frequently updated. I have listed several vendors and their Web sites. Visit their Web sites for more information. All of the computer magazines also have articles and ads for printers. You can easily compare types, models and prices by looking through the magazine ads.

Printer Life Expectancy

Printers usually have a long life. I have an HP LaserJet III that I bought in May 1990. It has a self-test utility that tests and prints out all of the various fonts and graphics that it can do. It also prints out a record of how many pages it has printed. Up until this date, it has printed out 32,250 pages.

I had one major problem. I had to replace the fuser assembly at 26,000 pages at a cost of $120. I thought that it would cost me several hundred dollars to get it repaired. To tell the truth, I was just a little bit disappointed that it didn't cost more to repair it. Deep down, I was looking for an excuse to buy a new printer.

I paid $1695 for this HP LaserJet III printer in 1990. I have bought a total of 12 cartridges at an average of $40 each and I have bought 64 reams of paper at a cost of $5 per ream. Adding up the initial cost, the cost of the cartridges and paper, the cost of the repair, I have spent a total of $2615 to print out 32,250 pages, or about 8 cents per page.

The LaserJet III has a resolution of 300 × 300 dpi (dots per inch). HP and several other manufacturers now have laser printers with 600 × 600 for less than $500. My LaserJet III, though, is built like a Sherman tank. I am not sure that the new lasers would last as long as the LaserJet III. (Although printers usually last a long time, like most other industries, the printer manufacturers constantly work to obsolete the printer that you may already have so that you will buy a new and improved model.)

There have been some fantastic advances in the last few years, however. The new lasers are faster, have much better resolution, and are much less expensive.

Because the models change so frequently, in this chapter when I mention a product, I don't usually mention the model name.

Ink-Jets

Ink-jets are about the least expensive printer you can buy, yet they can produce an output that is close to that of an expensive laser. A disadvantage is that they are much slower than a laser. Hewlett-Packard developed the first ink-jet printer. Now there are many companies such as Brother, Canon, Epson, Lexmark, and several others who are manufacturing ink-jet printers. Some of the companies call them by a different name, such as Canon's Bubble Jet, but they are all basically ink-jets. Most of the ink-jet manufacturers have one or more color models. Those models that can print in color usually have a C in the model number, such as the HP 2000Cse or the Canon MultiPASS C5500.

Ink-jet printers use a system that is similar to the dot-matrix printers. Dot-matrix printers are explained later in this chapter. Look under the heading "Number of Pins" to see how they work. For now, you just need to know that they press pins against a ribbon to create characters and images.

Instead of pressing pins, ink-jets use a matrix of small pores that sprays dots of ink onto the paper. Dot-matrix printers may have from 9 to 24 pins, so the resolution is very poor. Ink-jet printers may have from 48 to 128 or more small jets. Otherwise, the head moves across the paper much like the dot-matrix system.

To print color, ink-jets have three or more color cartridges. Of course, those with a larger number of jets produce more and smaller dots, yielding higher resolution. In addition, most of the ink-jet printers come with software that allows them to use a large number of different fonts.

Like the dot-matrix, the speed of the ink-jets is measured in characters per second (cps). Depending on the model and type of print, the speed can be from 3 to 10 pages per minute.

Most ink-jet printers sold today can print black and color. Ink-jet color printers use a system of three different color-ink cartridges: cyan, magenta, and yellow. Since black is used most often, most of them have a separate large, black cartridge for standard text. Others use the mixture of the three colors to make black which is not as good as having a true black cartridge. As the head moves across the paper, the software can have any of the various colors sprayed onto the paper. The three colors blend to produce any color of the rainbow.

On many of the older printers, if you were printing black and wanted to add some color, you had to shut down and switch to the color cartridges. That is still the way it is done in some of the newer less-expensive printers. Most of the more-expensive newer printers have a slot for each of the various colors. There is no need to shut down and switch cartridges.

It is now possible to buy color ink-jet printers for less than $90. If you only need color occasionally, these machines might be all you need. Kids love color. If you have children, these machines are ideal for them. Even if they break them, it is not such a big deal.

The inexpensive color machines can be rather slow, however. About the best they can do is about 2 pages per minute just printing black text.

Most lasers can print 10 to 20 pages per minute for black text. A color graphics printout may take several minutes on one of the low-cost ink-jets. The more-expensive machines can print 4 to 10 pages of black text per minute, and about 4 to 6 pages in color.

Most of the printers come bundled with several software packages. For some of the low-cost units, the software bundle may be worth more than the cost of the printer.

Ink-Jet Resolution

Some of the low-cost printers have a resolution of 360 × 360 dots per inch (dpi), the more-expensive ones will have 600 × 600, and the better ones have a resolution of 1440 × 720 dpi. A color photo printed 1440 × 720 will approach the resolution of film. In addition, many of the systems will let you download photos and images from a digital camera and print them out.

Cartridge Refills

Black ink-jet cartridges are good for about 700 to over 1000 pages of text. Color cartridges may yield about half this many pages. They must then be replaced or refilled. A new cartridge may cost from $8 up to $38 depending on the type of cartridge and the company.

If you do a lot of printing, the cost of replacement cartridges may eventually add up to more than the original cost of the machine. One reason for the high cost is because they usually have a built-in electronic head assembly. Some systems can warn you when the ink is low in a cartridge; for others, you won't know until it runs out, most probably in the middle of a rush job. It is wise to have a spare cartridge that can be dropped in when a cartridge is depleted. ACSI Bulk Inks (770-925-2616) has refill kits for black and all the colors.

I have an older Canon MultiPASS 2500C ink-jet multifunction printer, copier, and fax machine. The cartridges for it have a small cap in the top that can be pried off so that they can be refilled. For some cartridges, you may have to drill a hole. The hole can then be covered with almost any kind of adhesive tape.

The Global Company (800-845-6225) sends out a computer supplies catalog with hundreds of computer products. They list several printer cartridges for the most popular printers, as well as ink for refills. A bellows-type syringe is used for refilling the cartridges, but almost any type of large-bore syringe would work. There is a sponge inside the cartridge that absorbs the ink. There may be an excessive amount of ink when it is first used, so it is a good idea to make a few copies or use the cartridge a few times to get rid of any excessive ink.

Global Computer Supplies also sells cartridges that have been refilled or remanufactured. The printer manufacturers and vendors advise against using ink to refill the cartridges or using the remanufactured cartridges. They point out that the ink formulations are critical and many formulations are specific to their machines. That may be a good reason not to refill a cartridge, but the other reason the vendors don't want you to do it is because they make a lot of profit off the cartridge sales. For instance, it was reported that Hewlett-Packard has a gross profit from the sale of printers of 33 percent, their gross profit from ink-jet cartridges is 67 percent.

Transparencies for Presentations

If you do any presentations using an overhead projector, the ink-jets can handle transparencies very well. Color ink-jet printers are ideal for creating low-cost colored transparencies for presentations, for graphs, and for schematic plotting and drawings.

Color Ink-Jet Manufacturers

Here are some of the color ink-jet companies and their numbers:

Brother
www.brother.com

Canon Corp.
800-652-2666
www.ccsi.canon.com

Compaq
800-345-1518
www.compaq.com

Hewlett-Packard
800-752-0900
www.hp.com

Lexmark International
800-539-6275
www.lexmark.com

Okidata
800-654-3282
www.okidata.com

Call the companies for brochures and specifications, or check out their Web sites.

In addition, there are several ink-jet and color ink-jet printers that I did not mention with various features, functions, and prices. Look for ads in major computer magazines.

Multifunction Ink-Jet Machines

There are many times in a small office/home office (SOHO) when one needs to make one or more copies or to scan something. A large office can afford to have high-end copiers, scanners, plain-paper fax machines, and printers. But each of these items are rather expensive, and if not used very often, the cost cannot be justified. Besides, in a SOHO, especially one like mine, there just isn't room for all of these separate machines.

Several companies have noted the fact that most of these machines have a lot in common. There are now many multifunction machines that can copy, scan, fax, and print. Most of them can do all these functions in color and most are fairly reasonable in cost when you consider what they can do. Another big plus is that these four-in-one machines take up very little space. Figure 15-1 shows a Brother multifunction six-in-one color ink-jet printer, fax, color fax, color copier, and scanner. I use it mostly for faxing and copying.

The scan can be sent to a computer in color, and it has the optical character recognition (OCR) ability. It is very handy to have. I just retired my old Canon MultiPASS C2500 and replaced it with a Brother MFC-7150C. Here are some of the specifications:

Color Printer

Up to 1440 × 720 dpi resolution

Up to 6 ppm mono/4 ppm color print speed

Video Frame printing from your VCR, camcorder, or digital camera

Windows GDI and Epson emulation

200-sheet paper cassette

Bidirectional parallel cable included

Includes Brother Automatic Email Print software

Works with Windows 3.1, 3.11, 95/98, Windows NT Workstation 4.0, or MS-DOS (Epson emulation)

Figure 15-1
My Brother multifunction device.

Color Copier

Makes a color copy right at your desk, including color transparencies

Copies photos, charts, and graphs from 2.8″ × 5″ up to 8.5″ × 14″ originals

No need to turn your PC on. Copies are made directly on the MFC 7150C.

Up to 720 × 720 dpi resolution

Preset Copy Reductions: 93%, 87%, 75%, 50%

Preset Copy Enlarge: 120%, 125%, 150%, 200%

Manual copy reduction/enlargement in 1% increments from 50% to 200%

Multi-copying up to 99 copies (black & white)

Color Scanner

Scan color or B/W originals

Up to 1200 × 1200 dpi (interpolated)

256 Gray Scale / 24-bit color

Includes Visioneer PaperPort and Xerox TextBridge OCR

Works with Windows 3.1, 3.11, 95/98, Windows NT Workstation 4.0

Twain compliant

Plain-Paper Fax

20-page auto document feeder

14.4Kbps fax modem

2MB memory (100 pages for out-of-paper reception)

Broadcasting up to 130 locations

Dual Access and Quick Scan

Fax/Tel Switch, Caller ID, and Distinctive Ring Detection

80-station auto dialing

Simultaneous Operation allows you to receive and send faxes while printing

Color Fax

Send/Receive color faxes (via your PC) between other MFC-7100-series users with included Info Imaging 3D FaxSpeed software

Fax and Group number storage

Broadcasting from your PC

Includes NetCentric PC Internet Fax Software for low-cost, per-page faxing over the Internet (Requires Internet access and an Internet fax service provider account)

Works with Windows 3.1, 3.11, 95/98, Windows NT Workstation 4.0

Video Capture

Capture video frames from a digital camera, VCR, TV, LaserDisc player, or camcorder

Make copies of video frames directly with copy button, or capture the frame into your PC

Use the captured frames for printing, faxing, to save in a file or to manipulate the image within software

Uses a standard NTSC video input jack

Works with Windows 3.1, 3.11, 95/98, Windows NT Workstation 4.0

Software Included

Visioneer software for document filing, annotation, and instant linking to other applications

Xerox TextBridge for Optical Character Recognition

My Marketing Materials software with templates and formats to let you create everything you need for your business

Kai's Power Goo lets you bend, twist, distort, and stretch photos and images. Can even turn photos into cartoon characters. Great fun for kids.

Many of the multifunction machines from other companies come with similar functions and software.

Multifunction Laser Machines

All of the machines above use ink-jet technology. Most of the same companies who make ink-jet multifunction machines also make laser multifunction machines. Here are a couple that use laser technology. The laser technology provides better resolution and speed but does not provide color (more on laser technology coming up). These machines are comparably priced to some of the ink-jet multifunction machines. They provide laser printing, copying, scanning, and fax functions.

Brother International
800-284-4357
www.brother.com

Canon LS6000
800-652-2666
www.ccsi.canon.com

Panasonic Company
201-348-9090
swww.panasonic.com

Wide-Format Printers

There are several companies who make wide-format color printers that can print such things as large posters, signs, banners, point-of-sale (POS) displays, trade show materials, advertisements, business and presentation graphics, and billboards. Most of the printers can print on 36-inch-wide cut sheets or on roll sheets as long as 50 feet. Usually the paper has to be specially coated. Most of the printers use a high-resolution ink-jet technology. The cost of these printers range from $6000 up to $20,000. Figure 15-2 shows a wide-format printer.

Using standard silk-screen techniques or large four-color printers to make a large poster or banner may cost from $1000 up to $6000 or more. The same poster can be printed on a wide-format ink-jet printer for $200 to $300 or less.

Another type of wide-format printer uses an electrostatic process with special cyan, magenta, yellow, and black (CYMK) toners. The special paper is electrostatically charged, and the toners adhere to the charged areas. The high-speed printers have a very high resolution that is suitable for life-size posters and banners, or for several types of signs. The signs and posters can be used in exterior areas where they can withstand temperature changes and sun and rain. The electrostatic printers are rather expensive at $30,000 to $100,000.

Most wide-format printers use a raster image processor (RIP), which is a software controller. The RIPs act as color and ink control managers, and handle enlargement, rotation, tiling and paneling, previewing, screening, and other tasks. The RIP software is made by several different companies, so it is not all the same.

Figure 15-2
A wide-format printer.

Here are three companies who offer wide-format printers:

CalComp
714 821-2100
www.calcomp.com

ColorSpan
800-390-8261
www.colorspan.com

Hewlett-Packard
800 367-4772
www.hp.com

Laser Printers

The Hewlett-Packard LaserJet was one of the first lasers. It was a fantastic success and became the de facto standard. There are now hundreds of laser printers on the market. Most of them, even IBM's, emulate the LaserJet standard. Laser printers are a combination of the copy machine, computer, and laser technology. They have excellent print quality, but they have lots of moving mechanical parts and were rather expensive originally. Many of them are now quite reasonable. I paid $1695 in 1990 for my LaserJet III. It only has a resolution of 300×300 and a maximum of 8 pages per minute. I can buy a laser printer today with 600×600 resolution and 10 pages per minute for less than $300. I am amazed that a precision instrument such as this can be so inexpensive.

Laser printers use synchronized, multifaceted mirrors and sophisticated optics to write the characters or images on a photosensitive rotating drum. The drum is similar to the ones used in repro machines. The laser beam is swept across the spinning drum and is turned on and off to represent white and dark areas. As the drum is spinning, it writes one line across the drum, then rapidly returns and writes another. It is quite similar to the electron beam that sweeps across the face of a TV screen or computer monitor one line at a time.

The spinning drum is sensitized by each point of light that hits it. The sensitized areas act like an electromagnet. The drum rotates through the carbon toner, and the sensitized areas become covered with the toner. The paper is then pressed against the drum, and the toner that was picked up by the sensitized areas of the drum is left on the paper. The paper then is sent through a heating element where the toner is heated and fused to the paper.

Except for the writing to the drum, this is the same thing that happens in a copy machine. Instead of using a laser to sensitize the drum, a copy machine takes a photo of the image to be copied. A photographic lens focuses the image onto the rotating drum, which becomes sensitized to the light and dark areas projected onto it.

Engine

The drum and its associated mechanical attachments is called an *engine*. Canon, a Japanese company, is one of the foremost makers of engines. They manufacture them for their own laser printers and copy machines, and for dozens of other companies such as Hewlett-Packard and Apple. There are several other Japanese companies who manufacture laser engines.

Low-Cost Laser Printers

Because of the large number of companies manufacturing laser printers, there is lots of competition, which is a great benefit to us consumers. The competition has driven prices of both lasers and dot-matrix printers down. It has also forced many new improvements. Until recently, most laser printers had a resolution of only 300 $\times$ 300 dots per inch (dpi). Most lasers now have a resolution of 600 $\times$ 600. Some have a 1200 $\times$ 1200 dpi. Some laser printers are now selling for less than $300.

Memory

If you plan to do any graphics or desktop publishing (DTP), you will need at least 1MB of memory in the machine. Before it prints the first sheet, the printer loads the data into its memory and determines where each dot will be placed on the sheet. Of course, the more memory, the faster and better.

Not all lasers use the same memory configuration. For some machines, you must buy a special plug-in board for the memory. Check the type of memory that you need before you buy. Several companies offer laser memories. Here are a couple:

ASP   800-445-6190

Elite   800-942-0018

In addition, look in computer magazines for ads from other companies.

Page-Description Languages

If you plan to do any complex desktop publishing, you may need a page-description language (PDL) of some kind. Text characters and graphics images are two different species of animals. Laser printer controllers are somewhat similar to monitor controllers. The monitor adapters usually have all of the alphabetical and numerical characters stored in ROM. When we press the letter *A* from the keyboard, it dives into the ROM chip, drags out the *A*, and displays it in a precise block of pixels wherever the cursor happens to be. These are called *bitmapped characters*. If you wanted to display an *A* that was twice as large, you would need a complete font set of that type in the computer.

Printers are very much like the monitors and have the same limitations. They have a library of stored discrete characters for each font that they can print.

With a PDL, the laser printer can take one of the stored fonts and change it, or scale it, to any size you want. These are called *scalable fonts*. With a bitmapped font, you have one typeface and one size. With scalable fonts, you may have one typeface and an infinite number of sizes. You can print almost anything that you want with these fonts if your system can scale them.

Speed

Laser printers can print from 4 to over 20 pages per minute depending on the model and what they are printing. Some very expensive high-end printers can print over 40 pages per minute.

A dot-matrix or ink-jet printer is concerned with a single character at a time. The laser printers compose and then print a whole page at a time. With a PDL, many different fonts, sizes of type, and graphics can be printed. But since the laser must determine where every dot that makes up a character or image is to be placed on the paper before it is printed, the more complex the page, the more memory it will require and the more time needed to compose the page. It may take several minutes to compose a complex graphics. Once composed, it will print out very quickly.

A PDL controls and tells the laser where to place the dots on the sheet. Adobe's PostScript is the best-known PDL.

Resolution

Most lasers now print 600 × 600 dpi resolution, which is very good. But it is not nearly as good as 1200 × 1200 dpi used for typesetting in standard publications. LaserMaster has models that can print at 1200 × 1200 and some that go as high as 1800 dpi. They also have upgrade kits for the HP LaserJet III and LaserJet4 that can increase the resolution to 1200 dpi. Call LaserMaster at 800-327-8946 for details and brochures.

Maintenance

Most of the lasers use a toner cartridge that is good for 3000 to 5000 pages. The cost of an original cartridge is about $75. Several small companies are now refilling the spent cartridges for about $30 each. It may be a good idea to keep an extra cartridge as a spare. The toner cartridge is sealed, so it will last for some time on the shelf. I had a cartridge go out on a weekend when I was working on a tight deadline. Most stores that sell cartridges were closed. Since then, I keep a spare on hand.

Most laser printers keep track of the number of sheets that have been printed. If you have an HP LaserJet, you can use the front panel buttons to run a self-test. This tells you the configuration, how much RAM is installed, font cartridges installed, type of paper tray, how many pages have been printed, and several other tests.

When the toner gets low, most lasers will display a warning message in the digital readout window. Or if the print is very light, the toner may be low. If you remove the toner cartridge, turn it upside down, and shake it vigorously, sometimes you can get a few more copies out of it. This may help until you can get a replacement.

Of course, there are other maintenance costs. Since these machines are very similar to the repro copy machines, they have a lot of moving parts that can wear out and jam up. Most of the larger companies give a mean time between failures (MTBF) of 30,000 up to 100,000 pages. But remember that these are only average figures and not a guarantee.

Most of the lasers are expected to have an overall lifetime of about 300,000 pages. In the last nine years, I have printed out 32,250 sheets. Still have a long way to go.

Paper

There are many different types and weights of paper. Almost any paper will work in your laser. But if you use a cheap paper in your laser, it could leave lint inside the machine and cause problems in print quality. Generally speaking, any bond paper or a good paper made for copiers will work fine.

Colored paper made for copiers will also work fine. Some companies are marking copier paper with the word "laser" and charging more for it. The lasers will accept paper from 18 lb up to 24 lb easily. I have even used 67-lb stock for making up my own business cards. It is a bit heavy for wrapping around the drums, and it jams once in a while. Some lasers use a straight-through path, so the heavier paper should not cause any problems in these machines.

Many of the laser printers are equipped with trays to print envelopes. Hewlett-Packard recommends envelopes with diagonal seams and gummed flaps. Make certain that the leading edge of the envelope has a sharp crease.

Labels

The Avery Company (818-858-8245) and a few others make address labels that can withstand the heat of the fusing mechanism of the laser. There are also other specialty supplies that can be used with your laser. The Integraphix Company (800-421-2515) carries several different items that you might find useful. Call them for a catalog.

Here are some other companies who make small special printers for labels:

P-Touch PC
Brother International
800-284-4357

CoStar LabelWriter
Costar
800-426-7827

Smart Label
Seiko Instruments
800-688-0817

Color Laser Printers

Several color printers are available, costing from less than $2000 up to $20,000 or more. The QMS ColorScript Laser 1000 was one of the first true laser color printers. It cost about $10,000. A much faster QMS today costs about $3200.

The color lasers blend four different color toners—black, cyan, magenta, and yellow—to print out color. The drum is sensitized for each color, and that color toner is transferred to it. Once all of the colors are applied to the drum, it then prints out on ordinary paper or on transparencies.

Most of the color laser printers have PostScript, or they emulate PostScript. The Tektronix Phaser CP can also use the Hewlett-Packard Graphics Language (HPGL) to emulate a plotter. These color printers can print out a page much faster than a plotter.

One of the early disadvantages of the color lasers was not only the cost of the machine, each page cost a considerable amount. Thermal wax cost about 45 cents per page, dye-sublimation could cost up to $2.75 per page. Most of this cost was for the ribbons and wax rolls that were used by the color machines. The cost of a color page today ranges from 6 cents to as much as 11 cents per page.

The Lexmark Optra Color can print out 12 color or 12 black text pages per minute. Most of the other printers are rather slow for color. Panasonic can only print 3 color pages per minute, but 14 per minute in black text. Hewlett-Packard Color LaserJet can print 6 pages of color and 24 pages of black text per minute.

There will be several other color printers on the market soon. Because there is lots of competition, prices are coming down. Here are just a few companies who have color laser printers:

Fargo Electronics
800-258-2974
www.fargo.com

Hewlett-Packard
800-257-3783
www.hp.com

Lexmark
800-539-6275
www.lexmark.com

NEC
800-632-4636
www.nec.com

Panasonic
201-348-7000
www.panasonic.com

QMS
800-523-2696
www.qms.com

Color Photo Printers

Digital cameras are now becoming quite reasonable in price, and many people are buying them. Besides storing these photos on a hard disk or CD-ROM, many people would like to have hard copies. Fargo Electronics (800-327-4622) has developed the FotoFun, a small printer that uses their dye-sublimation to print out color photos up to a 4 × 6 trim. The FotoFun can also print color postcards or transfer photos to coffee mugs and other materials.

Nikon Electronic has developed a dye-sublimation color photo printer they call the Coolprint. It also is limited to about 4 × 6 prints.

Plotters

Plotters can draw almost any two-dimensional shape or design under the control of a computer. The early plotters were a bit like a robot. An arm selected a pen. The pen could be moved from side to side, while at the same time, the sheet of paper could be moved from top to bottom. The computer could direct the pen to any point across the paper and could move the paper up or down for any point on an X-Y axis. The motors were controlled by predefined X-Y coordinates. They could move the pen and paper in very small increments so that almost any design could be traced out.

Values could be assigned of perhaps 1 to 1000 for the Y, or vertical, elements and the same values for the X, or horizontal, elements. The computer could then direct the plotter to move the pen to any point or coordinate on the sheet.

The newer plotters use ink-jet technology instead of pens. This makes them a lot faster. The different-colored ink cartridges can be activated much quicker than moving an arm to a rack, selecting a pen, and then replacing it and selecting another.

Plotters are ideal for such things as printing out circuit board designs, architectural drawings, making transparencies for overhead presentations, graphs, charts, and many CAD/CAM (computer-aided design/computer-aided manufacturing) drawings. All of this can be done in many different colors. The different colors can be very helpful if you have a complex drawing such as a multilayered motherboard, since a different color can be used for each layer.

There are several different-sized plotters. Some desktop units are limited to only A- and B-sized plots. There are other large floor-standing models that can accept paper as wide as 4 feet and several feet long. Many of the floor-standing models are similar to the wide-format ink-jet printer/plotters. In addition, there are many good graphics and CAD programs available that can use plotters.

One of the disadvantages of the early plotters was that they were rather slow. There are now some software programs that allow laser printers to act as plotters. Of course, they are much faster than a plotter, but except for the colored printers, they are limited to black-and-white. Most of the laser printers are also limited to the A-size, or $8\frac{1}{2} \times 11$ inches.

Dot-Matrix Printers

I wrote in one of my earlier books that the dot-matrix was practically obsolete. I was very wrong. Some of the best hotels still use them to print out your bill. Thousands and thousands of businesses still depend on them for all kinds of uses. The dot-matrix may be obsolete when it comes to office letter-writing and fancy reports, but there is still lots of life left in the dot-matrix for many other things.

Dot-matrix printers are fairly low-priced, but they are limited in fonts and graphics capability. The laser printer speed is measured by the average number of pages per minute it can print. The speed of dot-matrix printers is measured by the characters per second (cps) they can print. They can print much faster in the draft mode than in the near letter quality (NLQ) mode. There are some high-end dot-matrix line printers that can print a whole line at a time. Some of them can print up to 1000 lines per minute. In order to get the high speed, some dot-matrix printers may have four or more heads, with each head printing out a different line.

Advantages of Dot-Matrix Printers

One of the distinct advantages that dot-matrix printers have over the lasers is their low cost. Some dot-matrix printers cost less than $150. Of course, there are some high-end dot-matrix printers, such as the very fast line printers, that may cost close to $10,000.

There are many applications where a dot-matrix printer is needed to accomplish a task. Wide, continuous sheets are necessary for some spreadsheet printouts. My LaserJet can't handle anything wider than $8\frac{1}{2}$ inches. Wide sheets are no problem with the wide carriage on some of the dot-matrix printers.

Another advantage is the number of sheets that can be printed. Most lasers have from 100 to 250 sheet bins. The dot-matrix can print up a whole box of 5000 sheets of fanfold continuous sheets. (It has been my experience though, if you start a job that requires a lot of printed sheets, as long as you stand there and watch the printer, it will work perfectly. If you walk away and start doing something else, the printer will immediately have a paper jam or some other problem. This is probably one of Murphy's many laws.)

In addition, many offices and businesses still use multiple-sheet forms. A laser printer can't handle these forms, but a dot-matrix can easily print them. The dot-matrix can also print on odd sizes, shapes, and thicknesses of paper.

The U.S. Post Office has adopted a Postnet bar code that helps sort and speed up mail. If you look at some of the envelopes that you receive in the mail, you may see the Postnet bar codes below the address. Many of the companies that send out bulk mail use this code. Several of the dot-matrix printers have the Postnet bar code built in; others offer it as an option. If you do a lot of mailing, the Post Office may give you a discount if the envelopes have the Postnet code on them.

Maintenance Costs

Maintenance costs of dot-matrix printers are usually much less than that for lasers and ink-jets. The main costs for a dot-matrix is to replace the ribbon about every 3000 sheets. A dot-matrix ribbon may cost from $3 to $10. A laser toner cartridge also lasts for about 3000 sheets and may cost from $30 to $75 to replace.

Number of Pins

There are still a few 9-pin dot-matrix printers being sold today, but most people are buying those with a 24-pin print head. The 24-pin head has much better resolution and may cost only a few dollars more. The 24-pin printer forms characters from two vertical rows of 12 pins in each row. There are small electric solenoids around each of the wire pins in the head. An electric signal causes the solenoid to push the pins forward. Dot-matrix printers are also called "impact printers" because the pins impact against the ribbon and paper. The solenoids press one or more of the various pins as the head moves in finite increments across the paper so that any character can be formed.

Here is a representation of the pins if it were a 7-pin print head and how it would form the letter *A*:

```
1  o                      o
2  o                    o   o
3  o                  o       o
4  o                o           o
5  o                o   o   o   o
6  o                  o           o
7  o                  o           o
```

The print head moves from left to right. The numbers on the left represent the individual pins in the head before it starts moving across the paper. The first pin to be struck would be number 7, then number 6, then 5, 4, 3, 5, and 2, then 1, 2, and 5, then 3, 4, 5, 6, and then 7. Ink-jet printers use a similar system to print characters and images.

A 24-pin head would be similar to the 7-pin representation above, except that it would have two vertical rows of 12 pins, side-by-side, in each row. The pins in one row would be slightly offset and lower than the pins in the other row. Since the pins are offset, they would overlap slightly and fill in the open gaps normally found in a 9-pin system.

Except for the few specialized uses listed above, the dot-matrix can be considered obsolete.

Installing a Printer or Plotter

Most IBM-compatible computers allow for four ports: two serial and two parallel. No matter whether the printer is a plotter, dot-matrix, or laser, it will require one of these ports. Most printers use the parallel port LPT1; most plotters use a serial port.

If the parallel port is used, normally the cable can only be about 10 feet long. There are special devices that will allow longer cables to be used. Parallel printers usually use a Centronics-type connector on the printer end.

Printer Sharing

Ordinarily, a printer will sit idle most of the time. There are some days when I don't even turn my printer on. There are usually several computers in most large offices and businesses. Almost all of them are connected to a printer in some fashion. It would be a terrible waste of money if each computer had a separate printer that was only used occasionally. It is fairly simple to make arrangements so that a printer or plotter can be used by several computers.

Sneakernet

One of the least expensive methods of sharing a printer is for the person to generate the text to be printed out on one computer, record it on a floppy diskette, then walk over to a computer that is connected to a printer. If it is in a large office, an old 386 or 486 clone could be dedicated to running a high-priced laser printer.

It doesn't matter whether the person carrying the floppy disk is wearing sneakers, brogans, or wing tips, the "sneakernet" is still one of the least expensive methods of sharing printers.

Switch Box

If there are only two or three computers and they are fairly close together, you can use a simple switch box to switch between the computers. If you use a simple switch box and the computers use the standard parallel ports, the cables from the computers to the printer should be no more than 10 feet long. Parallel signals will begin to degrade if the cable is longer than 10 feet and could cause some loss of data. A serial cable can be as long as 50 feet.

If an office or business is fairly complex, then there are several electronic switching devices available. Some of them are very sophisticated and can allow a large number of different types of computers to be attached to a single printer or plotter. Many of them have built-in buffers and amplifiers that can allow cable lengths up to 250 feet or more.

Printer-Sharing Device Sources

Here are a few of the companies who provide switch systems. Call them or visit their Web site for their product specs and current price list:

Belkin Components
310-515-7585
www.belkin.com

Black Box Corp.
412-746-5530
www.blackbox.com

Digital Products
800-243-2333
www.digprod.com

Wireless Connections

Many of the Pentium class and later motherboards now have an infrared (IrDA) built-in port. The IrDA systems are similar to TV remote controls. The IrDA ports can be used to connect keyboards, notebook computers, and printers. The JetEye from Extended Systems Company (800-235-7576) is two small devices—one plugs into the parallel printer port on the computer and the other plugs into the printer connector.

The Merrit Computer Products Company (800-627-7752) has a different type of wireless printer sharing kit. Instead of IrDA it uses a radio frequency. The system can support up to 16 computers and 4 printers.

Network Printers

Almost any printer can be attached to a network and called a network printer. But several companies make fast, high-end, heavy-duty laser printers specifically for networks. The prices may range from less than $1000 to more than $30,000. Many of the printers come bundled with special network printer management software and internal network interfaces. The print speed may range from 12ppm to 60ppm. Some of them are capable of duplex printing or printing on both sides of the paper. The resolution may be from 300 dpi to 1200 dpi. They may come with several different page description languages (PDLs) such as PostScript, Hewlet-Packard HPGL, Intellifont, or True Image. They may have a paper tray that can hold as many as 3000 sheets.

Here are some of the companies who manufacture network printers:

Dataproducts Corp.
 800-980-0374
 www.dataproducts.com

Digital Equipment Corp.
 800-777-4343
 www.digital.com

Hewlett-Packard
 800-752-0900
 www.hp.com

Kyocera Electronics
 800-232-6797
 www.kyocera.com

Lexmark International
 800-891-0331
 www.lexmark.com

QMS Inc.
 800-523-2696
 www.qms.com

Xerox Corp. \
 800-349-3769
 www.xerox.com

Visit their Web sites or call the companies for more information.

Green Printers

The entire industry is under pressure to produce energy conservation products. The federal government will no longer buy computer products that do not meet Energy Star standards.

Printers, especially laser printers, are notorious for being energy hogs. Hewlett-Packard and most of the other manufacturers are designing newer models that go into a "sleep mode" after a period of inactivity. Ordinarily, it takes from 20 to 30 seconds for a printer to warm up. Some of these models maintain a low-voltage input so that they can warm up almost instantly.

Progress

If you mention Johann Gutenberg, most people think of the first printed Bible. Actually, Gutenberg developed the movable print and started the printing of the Bible, but he ran out of money. He borrowed from Johann Fust, and when he couldn't repay the loan, Fust took over the printing press and completed printing the Bible. So it was Fust who was first to print the Bible. There is a copy of this Bible in the British Museum.

If Gutenberg were around today, you can bet that he would be quite pleased with the progress that has been made in the printing business. We have come a long way since 1436.

16

Essential Software

Why Bill Gates Is a Billionaire

You cannot operate a computer without software. It is equally as necessary as hardware. Software is merely instructions that tells the hardware what to do. Computers are dumb. They will only do what the software tells them.

Off-the-Shelf and Ready-to-Use Software

To make your computer functional and useful, you will need a few basic programs. I can't possibly list all of the software that is available for the Pentium III or AMD Athlon. There is more software, already written and immediately available, than you can use in a lifetime. The software companies are constantly revising and updating their software. There are off-the-shelf programs that can do almost everything that you could ever want to do with a computer.

There are several categories of software programs that you will need. At the top of the list is an operating system such as Windows 95/98. But you will also need things like word processors, databases, spreadsheets, communications and graphics programs, and utilities. Depending on what you intend to use your computer for, there are hundreds of other software programs for common and special needs.

Cost of Software

Unfortunately, it may cost more for the software to run a computer than for the hardware to build one. Hardware prices have consistently dropped over the years. An equivalent computer that cost $5000 in 1992 now sells for about $1500. A version of Windows 3.1 cost about $100 in 1992; an equivalent version of Windows 98 now costs $189.99. (If you can prove that you purchased Windows 95, you can upgrade to Windows 98 for $89.95.) There are thousands and thousands of hardware manufacturers. The competition keeps the prices low. But the major software company is Microsoft, which has no competition.

Of course, there are other companies who manufacture software, but again, not many of them have any competition.

Note that I list prices several times in this chapter. Prices listed are for comparison only. They will be different by the time you read this. If it is software, it will probably be higher; if hardware, it will be lower.

Software prices may not vary much from vendor to vendor. In most cases, for the major software packages, every vendor will charge the same price, right down to the penny. You know that the vendor is given a certain amount of profit for each software package, and you know that each vendor has different overhead costs. How is it that each vendor decides on the same price to charge? Automobile dealers usually have a suggested list price, but you can often haggle with them and get a different price. Not so with the software vendors. The government could probably make a good case of price fixing against many of the vendors.

If you look through the catalogs listed below, you will find that the prices for software are usually the same in most all of the catalogs. Order all of the catalogs and do your own comparisons.

Surplus Software

The software business is somewhat like the soap business. The software companies and soap companies have to come out with a new and improved version every year. Quite often, the new and improved versions don't perform much better than the old ones did. Or it may do things for which you have no need. Like most people, I never use all of the capabilities of my software.

When a new version of a software program is released, quite often there are quite a lot of software packages that were not sold. The Surplus Software Company was established to buy up the outdated software and offer it to the public at a huge discount. They did a fantastic amount of business. However, their days were numbered, as we'll soon see.

Live Upgrades

Most of the major software companies offer a discount if you upgrade an older program to a new one. Here's an example of what was possible just a couple years ago:

You could buy Lotus SmartSuite Release 2.1 for $44.99. This package had Lotus 1-2-3 spreadsheet, Lotus Approach database, Lotus Ami Pro word processor, Lotus Freelance Graphics presentation software, and Lotus Organizer for Personal Information Management. Or you could spend $25 more and get Lotus SmartSuite 96 for $69.99 from Surplus Software. This software had everything listed in Release 2.1, but was updated to the latest 1996 release. In addition, SmartSuite 96 had Lotus ScreenCam, which was screen recording software that let you create and distribute custom audio/visual communications. You could probably do just about all that you could ever want to do with SmartSuite 96, but if you really had to have the latest, you could get SmartSuite 97. It was listed in a discount magazine for $439.99. But you could get SmartSuite 97 for only $137.99 as a live upgrade. A live upgrade is a previous version of the same product. So if you bought the SmartSuite 96 version from Software Surplus for $69.99 and sent in proof of your purchase, you could buy SmartSuite 97 for only $137.99 as a live upgrade. Your total cost would have been $69.99 plus the $137.99, or $207.98. You would have saved $232.01.

Competitive Upgrades

If you had an older copy of WordPerfect, the proof of purchase could be used to upgrade to a new version of Word for Windows. Or you could use an older copy of Word for Windows to upgrade to a new version of WordPerfect. The Surplus Software Company had several of these older versions that could be used as upgrades to save you a whole lot of money.

Several companies who had competing products, such as databases, spreadsheets, graphics programs, utilities, and others, offered the same competitive upgrade prices.

Proof of Purchase for Upgrade Discount

At one time they were very lax in the requirements for proof of purchase and offered quite a bit of latitude. Often they would ask for the title page from the original manual for proof of purchase. The software companies had no use for the older used copies. They would just clutter up their stores. You could keep the old software and the rest of the manual. The proof of purchase varied among the different software publishers. A person may have been required to provide one or more of four general types of proof of purchase or ownership listed below:

1. The title page of the user manual.

2. A copy of a sales receipt or invoice.

3. The serial number of the software program.

4. A photocopy of the original program disk.

Wow! Look at the loopholes. A person could get a title page from a friend who has an older copy of a software package you wanted to buy. If you belonged to a user group, there were always people who would lend you the title page of their user manual, or give you a copy of their invoice or serial number, or let you make a photocopy of the original program disk.

It didn't take the software companies very long to see all the ways that this system could be abused. And didn't take them long to come up with a solution to overcome the lax requirements for the upgrade price.

End of a Very Good Thing

Surplus Software was doing such a fantastic business it attracted the Egghead Software Company (800-753-7877, or www.egghead.com). Egghead bought Surplus Software, but the surplus business was just too good to last. The software companies, especially Microsoft, are not dumb. They recognized the loopholes. Whenever a new version of software is now released, the older versions are taken off the shelves and sent back to the manufacturer to be destroyed.

Current Upgrade Practices

The software companies have not abandoned their upgrade practices, however. Most of the magazines and catalogs will advertise a software package for a very low price in large bold type. Then in small letters it will usually say "Upgrade Price." They don't ask for any proof that you have a previous version. They will gladly sell you the upgrade product at the discount price. But if you do not have an earlier version, you will not be able to use the product. When you attempt to install the upgrade version, the software will first check if you have an earlier version on your computer. If you don't, you won't be able to install the new version.

Microsoft Office 2000

There are several different versions of the Microsoft Office 2000 suite. The full Premium Office 2000 has the following products in the suite; the other products will not have all of these packages:

- *Word 2000*   Wordprocessor; improvements include expanded Web menus, full-fidelity HTML conversion, 24-bit color, floating tables, and wraparound text for charts
- *Excel 2000*   New Web capabilities, chart components, enhanced PivotTable options, and improved database connectivity
- *Outlook 2000*   Messaging and collaboration client with Web short-cuts
- *Microsoft Internet Explorer 5.0*   Improved Web browser and more
- *NetMeeting Conferencing Software*   Tools for conferencing
- *Publisher 2000*   Desktop publishing program with design wizards and templates for print and Web
- *Microsoft Small Business Tools*   Helpful programs and tools for any small business
- *PowerPoint 2000*   Presentation graphics program
- *Access 2000*   New data access pages, SQL Server integration, programmability, worldwide support, and Jet database engine environment
- *FrontPage 2000*   Web site creation and management tools; supports two-way collaborative environment
- *PhotoDraw 2000*   New business graphics software with tools and templates
- *Essential Development Tools*   For program developers

All of the items above are in the Microsoft Office 2000 Premium product. The other packages have products as listed below:

	Word	Excel	Outlk	Expl 5	NetMeet	Pub	Sm Bus	Pwrpt	Access	FrontPg	Photo	Dev
Premium	Yes	Yes	Yes	Yes	Yes	Yes	Yes	Yes	Yes	Yes	Yes	Yes
Profess.	Yes	Yes	Yes	Yes	Yes	Yes	Yes	Yes	Yes	No	No	No
Small Bus.	Yes	Yes	Yes	Yes	Yes	Yes	Yes	No	No	No	No	No
Standard	Yes	Yes	Yes	Yes	Yes	No	No	Yes	No	No	No	No
Developer	Yes	Yes	Yes	Yes	Yes	Yes	Yes	Yes	Yes	No	Yes	Yes

Here are some prices:

Premium full version—$759.95

Upgrade Premium version—$379.95

Professional full version—$569.95

Upgrade Professional version—$289.95

Small Business full version—$469.95

Upgrade Small Business version—$189.95

Standard full version—$469.95

Upgrade Standard version—$189.95

Developer full version—$949.95

Upgrade Developer version—$379.95

WordPerfect Office 2000

WordPerfect Office 2000 also has several versions, all of them less expensive than Microsoft Office 2000. Here are the products that it contains:

- *WordPerfect 9*   Wordprocessor
- *Quattro Pro 9*   Spreadsheet
- *Corel Presentations*   Presentation tools
- *CorelCentral*   Personal information manager
- *Office 2000SDK*   Software development kit
- *Adobe Acrobat Reader*   For portable documents
- *VBA Tools*   Scripting tools
- *Trellix 2*   Web publisher
- *Dragon Naturally Speaking*   Voice recognition program
- *Corel Print Office*   Desktop publishing program
- *NetPerfect*   Intranet management
- *Paradox 9*   Database

Corel has three versions of their WordPerfect Office 2000. The Professional package contains all of the products above. The Voice-Powered package contains all of the items above except for NetPerfect and Paradox 9. Their Standard version contains all of the items except for Dragon Naturally Speaking, Corel Print Office, NetPerfect, and Paradox 9.

Here is a bit more about WordPerfect Office 2000:

- Application icons, toolbars, and dialog boxes are standardized.
- Has the latest productivity tools, but preserves your macros, training, and legacy files.
- Install-As-You-Go lets you install only portions as needed.
- Enhanced Scrapbook manages clipart images across WordPerfect 9, Quatrro Pro 9, and Corel Presentations.
- RealTime Preview shows changes before applying them.
- WordPerfect 9 has new browser-style navigation buttons.
- Trellix 2 converts files to HTML. Lets you create interactive documents and publish to the Web and intranets.
- Paradox 9 is more visually oriented, with a new table designer.
- Quattro Pro 9's dynamic cross tab reports and analyzes and summarizes large amounts of data.
- Corel Presentations 9 has new Image tools for special effects.
- Increased compatibility with third-party programs, including Microsoft Office and Lotus SmartSuite documents.

Here are the prices at this writing:

Professional full version—$359.95

Upgrade Professional version—$189.95

Voice-Powered full version—$319.95

Upgrade Voice-Powered version—$139.95

Standard full version—$289.95

Upgrade Standard version—$99.95

Competitive Discounts

Except for a few packages, most companies have now stopped giving competitive discounts. One competitive upgrade that is currently advertised in a couple of the software catalogs is Adobe Illustrator 8.0. If someone has CorelDraw or Macromedia FreeHand, they can buy Adobe Illustrator for $189.98. Otherwise, the package costs $359.98. If the person has an earlier version of Adobe Illustrator, they can do a live upgrade to the 8.0 version for $118.98.

You must have the older version on your computer hard disk in order to install upgrades such as Adobe Illustrator or from Windows 95 to Windows 98. The same is true for upgrading from Microsoft Office 97 to Office 2000. The software will check your system, and if you do not have the earlier version, you will not be able to install the upgrade. The upgrade software may be similar in every way to the full version, except that the upgrade will check your system first for proof of the earlier version.

You might think that you should uninstall a previous version of software to make room for the new one. But don't do it. If the older software is not there, you will not be able to install an upgrade. Usually the upgrade just writes over the older version.

Shareware and Public-Domain Software

Remember that there are excellent free public-domain programs that can do almost everything that the high-cost commercial programs can do. Check your local bulletin board, user group, or the ads for public-domain software in most computer magazines. There are also some excellent shareware programs that can be registered for a nominal fee.

Software Catalogs

There are several direct-mail discount software companies. If you are undecided about what you need, call the companies for a catalog. Many of the companies who send out catalogs sell both software and hardware. They usually have very good descriptions of the software and hardware, along with prices. In a book like this, I just don't have the available space to describe the software and hardware like the catalogs do.

The catalogs are an excellent way to get prices and basic facts about software. You should be aware that some of the companies are not exactly discount houses. You might find better prices at your local store or in some of the computer magazines.

You should also note that some of the catalogs do not have a date on them. They usually have some sort of unintelligible code near the mailing address. If you order from one of the catalogs, they will ask you for the code. They will then charge you the price listed in that particular catalog.

Prices of software and hardware change almost overnight. So if you don't have the latest catalog and you order, you may not be paying the latest price. Here are just a few of the companies who will send you their software catalogs:

Computer Discount Warehouse (CDW)
800-726-4239
www.cdw.com

DellWare
800-847-4051
www.dell.com

Desktop Publishing (DTP Direct)
800-325-5811

Egghead
800-344-4323
www.egghead.com

Elek-Tek
800-395-1000

Global Software & Hardware
800-845-6225
www.globalcomputer.com

JDR Microdevices
800-538-5000
www.jdr.com

MicroWarehouse
800-367-7080

The PC Zone
800-258-2088
www.zones.com

Shareware Express
800-346-2842

Software Spectrum
800-787-1166

Tiger Direct Com
800-756-8443
www.tigerdirect.com

Essential Software Needed

As mentioned, I can't possibly list all of the thousands of software packages available. The computer magazines listed in Chapter 19 often have detailed reviews of software. And of course, they usually have many advertisements for software in every issue. Briefly, following are some of the essential software packages that you will need.

Operating Systems Software

Windows 95/98

The only real choice you have is Windows 98. If you still have Windows 95, you can get by. If you wait a while longer, Windows 2000 will be out.

I spent a lot of time trying to learn DOS. (DOS is an acronym for Disk Operating System.) One of the problems with DOS was that it was hard to learn. It had over 50 commands, but I hardly ever used more than 15 or 20 of them. One reason that the Macintosh was so popular was that you didn't have to remember a lot of commands. Just use the mouse and point-and-click.

Just about the time I was getting pretty good at using DOS, Microsoft came out with Windows 3.1. It helped a whole lot. But again, about the time I got pretty good at using it, Microsoft came out with Windows 95. I used Windows 95 for over three years. There was still a lot that I hadn't learned when they came out with Windows 98. It really wasn't that much different than Windows 95. Within a short time I will have to start learning Windows 2000.

Having to start learning all over again every time a new program comes out is almost like having to learn a new language every so often. It sure would be nice if they could choose a system and stay with it. Being a Pilgrim, I know that progress does not stand still.

UNIX and Linux

UNIX has been around for some time. It has been used primarily for servers and high-end workstations. Linux is a fairly new product that is similar to UNIX. It was first developed by Linus Torvalds in Finland as a free public-domain product. He made the code public so that anyone can use it and revise it.

Linux is a multi-user, multitasking operating system that runs on many platforms, including Intel processors. It interoperates well with other operating systems, including Apple, Microsoft, and Novell.

The Linux operating system is freely available. It can be copied and redistributed without fees or royalties. The source code for Linus is available on the Internet to anyone who wants it. The Red Hat (888-733-4281, or www.redhat.com) will sell you a software version for a very nominal sum. It comes with manuals and other information that you may need. For additional information, see www.linuxresources.com.

At the present time, not too many applications have been developed for Linux. But there are many programmers working on new ones. Unfortunately, it will probably never have as many applications as Windows. It would sure be nice to have an alternative that would offer a bit of competition.

Here is a press release about a Linux suite from the operating system's manufactures, S.u.S.E., Inc. (www.suse.com):

Oakland, California S.u.S.E., Inc. announced the release of Linux Office Suite 99—a comprehensive software package that combines the latest in Linux technology with some of the most powerful, user-friendly applications on the open-source market. S.u.S.E.'s Linux Office Suite 99 includes a spreadsheet, word processor, presentation graphics, database, fax program, and many other critical business applications. "Serious computer users have been calling for an integrated, 'out-of-the-box' office suite for Linux for quite some time," said Scott McNeil, president of S.u.S.E. North America. "Truly, Linux now has an office suite competitive with Microsoft Windows products. S.u.S.E.'s Linux Office Suite is affordable, functional, and easy to use." Linux Office Suite 99 comes with the latest version of Applixware 4.4.1, which includes Applix Words, Spreadsheets, Graphics, Presents, and HTML Author, as well as Applix Data and Applix Builder. Applixware's latest release delivers a new filtering framework that has been optimized for document interchange with Microsoft Office 97. In addition, Linux Office Suite 99 integrates Applixware with the powerful ADABAS D 10.0 database system, enabling users to import data from the ADABAS D database into Applix Spreadsheets. Linux Office Suite 99 also contains the KDE and GNOME graphical desktops, S.u.S.E. fax, the personal edition of the backup utility ARKEIA 4.0, the popular GIMP graphics program, and many other features.

Linux Office Suite is compatible with S.u.S.E., Red Hat, Caldera, and other popular versions of Linux. Users who need to install Linux for the first time can do so quickly and easily with the base system of S.u.S.E. Linux 5.3 that is included with the Office Suite.

S.u.S.E.'s Linux Office Suite 99 is scheduled to ship on October 12, 1998. Ordering information is available at 1-888-875-4689 and on S.u.S.E.'s web site at http://www.suse.com. The Linux Office Suite will also be available through most major computer retail outlets and other resellers at a suggested retail price of $ 79.95.

More information on S.u.S.E, Inc. is available at www.suse.com. Their street address and phone number are as follows:

580 Second Street, Suite 210
  Oakland, CA 94607
  510-835-7873

Many people think that Linux is a better product than Windows. Besides that, it is free. The Linux Journal (888-665-4689, or www.linuxjournal.com) has very good articles about Linux every month. You can read most of them online, or you can subscribe online.

Word Processors

The most used of all software are word processors. At one time there were literally dozens of word processor packages, each one slightly different than the other. It amazed me that they could find so many different ways to do the same thing. All of the major word processor programs come with a spelling checker and a thesaurus. They usually also include several other utilities such as a calculator, communications programs for your modem, outlines, desktop publishing, print merging, and many others. Most of them are now bundled into a suite such as Microsoft's Office 2000 and Corel's WordPerfect Office 2000.

Unfortunately, Microsoft has steamrollered over most of the word processors with their Word for Windows. WordPerfect is just barely holding on, and Lotus Word Pro is practically dead.

WordStar

At one time, WordStar was the premier word processor and number one in its field. But it lost a lot of its luster and was displaced by others such as WordPerfect and Microsoft Word.

I started off with WordStar 3.0 on my little CP/M Morrow with a hefty 64KB of memory and two 140KB single-sided disk drives. It took me some time to learn it. I used it for so long that I could almost do it in my sleep. It was like second nature to me. I tried several other word processors and found that most of them required almost as much time as it would take to learn a new language. It is a proven fact that the older one gets the more difficult it is to learn a new language. I don't have a lot of free time. WordStar did all I need to do. In fact, WordStar, like most other programs, has lots of utilities and functions that I never used. I have been forced to abandon my old friend and come into the twentieth century. Using WordStar today is almost like trying to communicate in Latin. It is now as obsolete as the 360KB floppy drive. Alas, how the mighty have fallen.

WordPerfect

WordPerfect displaced WordStar as the most popular word processor in the world. It simplified several functions and made word processing a lot easier. WordPerfect now comes as part of Corel's WordPerfect Office 2000 suite.

Microsoft Word

Microsoft Word for Windows is part of Microsoft's Office 2000 suite. It is now the number-one word processor in the world.

Lotus Word Pro

Lotus Word Pro is a part of the Lotus SmartSuite. It has all the equivalent tools found in Office 2000. IBM bought the Lotus products and had hoped to be able to offer some competition to the Microsoft products. Unfortunately, even with Big Blue behind them, Lotus has not done well.

Database Programs

Database packages are very useful for business purposes. They allow you to manage large amounts of information. Most programs allow you to store information, search it, sort it, do calculations and make up reports, and perform several other very useful functions.

Most of the database programs are now parts of suites such as Microsoft's Office 2000, Corel's WordPerfect 2000, and IBM's Lotus SmartSuite.

Suites

One of the best ways to buy software now is to buy a suite. A suite usually costs much less than buying each package separately. The suites usually have the most important items, such as a word processor, a spreadsheet, and a database. They may also have items such as presentation software, personal information manager (PIM), financial managers, groupware, e-mail, and Web tools. The software in the suite packages are integrated so that they will all work together.

Sometimes, a whole suite of programs will cost about the same as a single program. Some of the suites have so many utilities and goodies that you could easily get lost trying to find and use them all.

Most word processors come with a dictionary and thesaurus, but they are usually quite limited. Most of them have a spelling checker. In Microsoft Word 7.0, which came with Office for Windows 95, if you type in a word that isn't in the dictionary, it will offer one that it thinks is what you meant. If you typed in zzzz, Microsoft Word will tell you that it isn't in the dictionary and offer the suggestion of sex. This was posted on the Internet, and a lot of people thought it was rather funny. The newer versions simply says that it is not in the dictionary and do not offer any suggestion. (Evidently, Bill didn't think it was funny.)

Microsoft has a Web page at www.microsoft.com/office that can help in some cases if you have problems. They list the latest news about Office and have a list of frequently asked questions (FAQs). But if you are like me, I never seem to be able to find an answer to my questions at a site like this. And there is almost no chance of getting to speak to a live person about your problem.

Utilities

Utilities are essential tools that can unerase a file, detect bad sectors on a hard disk, diagnose problems, unfragment, sort, and perform many other tasks.

Norton Utilities

Norton Utilities was the first, and is still foremost, in the utility department. Norton is currently a part of Symantec and can be contacted at www.symantec.com. Here is some information about their Norton SystemWorks:

Norton SystemWorks gives you five powerful Symantec utilities in one convenient package—at a great value. They work together to both fix and prevent system problems. And Norton SystemWorks is flexible, providing customization and automation so all users can take advantage of Norton SystemWorks' features. Norton AntiVirus offers the world's most popular and most powerful anti-virus capabilities.

Norton Utilities is the industry leader in fixing and preventing computer problems. Norton CleanSweep is the most complete PC hard drive cleanup software on the market. Norton CrashGuard protects against system crashes and screen fixes. Norton Web Services gives you easy access to the latest virus definitions, hardware drivers, and software updates.

- *Norton 2000 Bios Test & Fix* Scans your computer, applications, and data for potential Year 2000 problems.
- *Norton Ghost* The complete solution for backing up or cloning entire hard drives and creating exact reproductions down to the last byte

Comprehensive Solution Everything you need to keep your computer working, in one integrated solution. Complete versions of the following products:

- Norton AntiVirus
- Norton Utilities
- Norton CleanSweep
- Norton CrashGuard
- Norton Web Services
- Norton 2000
- Norton Ghost

TouchStone's CheckIt 98

Touchstone (www.touchstonesoftware.com) has some very good diagnostic software. Here is some information from their Web site:

CheckIt 98 offers one of the quickest and most thorough evaluations of your PC's hardware. If you're experiencing problems, or you want confirmation of your system's configuration and performance, CheckIt's QuickCheck will give you all the answers. For more in-depth analysis of your system, CheckIt's exhaustive tests thoroughly examine your individual hardware components. If information is what you need, CheckIt provides details on core components and all of your key peripherals. With so much testing and diagnostic power, CheckIt 98 can answer your questions and help you solve problems quickly.

CheckIt offers real hardware tests that examine the user's system with their System Tuneup.

- Includes hardware tests for: motherboards, hard drives, memory, and modems
- Includes system information for every PC component, even advanced technology like USB, Infrared, and PCMCIA
- Offers automatic crash recovery by backing up critical Windows and system files

CheckIt 98 runs Windows utilities automatically and unattended. It's the easiest way possible to remove unneeded and temporary files, clean up your Start Menu, and improve Windows load times.

CheckIt 98's TroubleShooter can answer your questions and help you solve problems quickly. It automatically flags problems and gives you real-world advice to solve them. You can also select from a list of common problems to help you deal with system crashes, BIOS error codes, boot problems, and more.

It backs up your critical Windows and System files so you can restore your computer to working order after a crash. You can back up to your hard drive, a floppy or a Zip drive, and restore them under Windows or DOS.

CheckIt 98 has individual diagnostic tests for your key hardware, including Motherboard, Drives, Memory, Modem, and Ports.

CheckIt adds convenience to Windows 98 and Windows 95 by placing Windows utilities in one place for easy access.

System Spy tells you what's changed in your system, so you can easily identify where problems started.

CheckIt 98's Video Calibration tool helps you troubleshoot, correct and enhance your computer's display.

You'll see all of the detailed information on your core components and key peripherals, including new information on advanced power management, USB, infrared, and PCMCIA.

FastMove

A technician or advanced user's best friend, FastMove! offers quick and easy file transfer. Perfect for setting up new PCs, or for moving files between a desktop PC and a notebook computer.

- Includes a fast parallel file transfer cable
- One-button ease of use

Directory and Disk Management Programs

There are dozens of disk management programs that help you keep track of your files and data on the hard disk, find it, rename it, view it, sort it, copy it, delete it, and perform many other useful utilities. They can save an enormous amount of time and make life a lot simpler.

XTree for Windows

XTree was one of the first and is still one of the best disk management programs available. I use it to view my files, then delete unnecessary ones. I also use it to copy and back up files from one disk or directory to another. It will also let you order the files by date or alphabetically. (I often look at the date stamp so I know which files are the latest.) It has many other excellent features. I don't know how anyone can get along without XTree. XTree is a part of the Symantec Companies (www.symantec.com). Symantec, the provider of Norton Utilities, has a large number of excellent software products.

PKZIP

PKZIP has been around for many years and is still one of the most used and useful tools available. PKZIP allows you to compress files so that they take up less space on a floppy disk or hard disk. A ZIP file takes much less time to download or upload to the Internet. PKZIP lets you save or archive files that are not used very often in compressed form to save hard disk space. PKZIP, available from PKWARE at 414-354-8669 or www.pkware.com, is the de facto standard for most all compression software today.

Miscellaneous Software Programs

There are many programs for applications such as accounting, statistics, finance, graphics, and many others. Some are very expensive; others are very reasonable.

CorelDRAW

CorelDRAW can be used for such things as drawing, illustration, page layout, charting, animation, and desktop publishing and presentations. It has word processing, OCR, over 5000 drag-and-drop symbols and shapes, over 18,000 clip art images, over 750 fonts, and many other features and utilities. Corel has several other excellent software packages. Call them for a brochure at 613-728-3733, or check out their Web site at www.corel.com.

Here's an interesting side note: Corel honored Hedy Lamarr by placing a photo of her on their issue of CorelDRAW 8. (See Figure 16-1.) Hedy is most famous for swimming in the nude in a film called *Ecstasy*, made back in 1933. The scene was taken from about a half-mile away. Today the film would not even get an R rating, but at that time it was scandalous.

Not many know it, but during WWII Hedy invented a secret communication system and holds patent number 2,292,387. This system was a frequency-skipping system so that broadcasts could not be intercepted unless you had the code.

Figure 16-1
Hedy Lamarr:
beautiful actress and
inventor.

CorelSCSI

CorelSCSI is a program that has software and several SCSI drivers that work with most major SCSI host adapters such as Always, DPT, Ultrastor, and Adaptec. In addition, it has itBACk, a software program for unattended backup and Corel tape backup software. It also has several other programs and utilities.

For information, contact the Corel Corp. at 613-728-3733, or at www.corel.com.

UnInstaller for Windows

When a program for Windows is installed on your computer, it copies pieces and portions into several different areas. If you decide later that you don't want that application, you can use DOS to delete the program. But it will not delete all references to the program. Every time you load Windows, it may hunt for that program, then tell you that it can't find it.

Even some demo programs load themselves into several areas that are difficult to clean out. Use the DOS EDITOR command and look at the WIN.INI sometime. You may find references there to programs that you erased months ago. These leftover bits and pieces can clutter up your disk considerably.

UnInstaller from McAfee can track down all of the different parts of a Windows program and delete them. Even if you are a Windows pro, the UnInstaller can save you time. You can contact McAfee at www.mcafee.com. (UnInstaller was originally published by MicroHelp. The product was then acquired by CyberMedia, which, in turn, was acquired by McAfee.)

Money Counts

Money Counts is a very inexpensive program that can be used at home or in a small business. With it you can set up a budget, keep track of all of your expenses, balance your checkbook, and perform several other functions. It's available from Parsons Technology at 800-223-6925, or at www.parsonstech.com.

It's Legal

It's Legal is software that helps you create wills, leases, promissory notes, and other legal documents. Parsons Technology has several other very good low-cost software packages. Contact them at 800-223-6925 or at www.parsonstech.com.

WillMaker

WillMaker from Nolo Press (510-549-1976, or www.nolo.com) is a low-cost program that can help you create a will. Everyone should have a will, no matter what age you are or how much you own. Many people put it off because they don't want to take the time, or they don't want to pay a lawyer a large fee. This inexpensive software can help you easily create a will that can prevent many family problems.

We don't like to think about this sort of thing, but it happens to everyone, sooner or later.

Living Trust Maker

Living Trust Maker is also from Nolo Press. It is a program that every family should have. Even if you have a will, it is possible that it could end up in probate court. You may have heard some of the horror stories about how probate can take several years to settle and the costs can completely eat up all of a large estate. A living trust can avoid probate and its lengthy and costly processes.

Ordinarily, a living trust requires a lawyer and can be relatively expensive. With the Nolo Press Living Trust Maker, you can create your own living trust without a lawyer. The program allows you to fashion the trust to your unique needs. The software guides you through the process, but it comes with a large user guide and legal manual that can explain and answer most of your questions. Nolo Press has free technical support if you have any problems.

Nolo Press has several other books and software. Call them for a catalog at 510-549-1976, or access them online at www.nolo.com.

Family Tree Maker

Many people are curious about their ancestors. The computer has made it possible to do searches and dig up all kinds of facts about our forefathers and foremothers. The Broderbund Company has a Web site at www.familytreemaker.com that will let you search online for millions of people. It has records of just about everyone who has ever been issued a birth certificate, death certificate, marriage license, or most any other record. Broderbund also sells software that will let you make charts and other things necessary for a family tree record.

I just did a search on the Web site for "Pilgrim," and it came back and told me that there were over 13,500 pages with the name "Pilgrim" mentioned. I have a niece who is into family tree stuff. She made up a booklet of our immediate family. I wrote this for the cover of her booklet:

When you search my family tree
Please don't search it diligently
Cause I'm afraid that you may find
A monkey hiding in that tree.

I might also add that one may find some cattle rustlers or a few other unsavory characters hanging from my tree. :-)

Software for Kids

One of the big reasons to have a home computer is for the kids. If you have children and you don't have a computer, then they are at a disadvantage. In today's society a child needs all the help he or she can get in order to make it as an adult. A computer is absolutely essential to help in the very important early training. There are thousands of software programs—commercial, shareware, and public domain—that have been developed for children. Most of the software catalogs listed earlier in the chapter have software listings for children.

A good example of a children's educational program is the Smithsonian Institution Dinosaur Museum from the Software Marketing Corporation (602-893-2042). Many of the programs such as this come on CD-ROMs. The program is in 3D, so a pair of plastic 3D video glasses comes with it.

KidSoft Magazine (800-354-6150) has reviews of dozens of software packages for kids.

Software Training

Most software manuals are very poorly written. You can usually tell how bad the manuals are by the number of books written telling you how to use the software. Microsoft is the largest software publisher in the world. They also have a very large book publishing house, Microsoft Press. They publish hundreds of books each year to help people learn to use the software they publish. (A cynical person might suspect that Microsoft publishes poor user manuals so that they can sell more books.)

There are also several companies who conduct training classes and seminars for learning some of the most popular software. These seminars may cost several hundred dollars for a one- or two-day session. I can't learn enough in one or two days to justify the cost of some of the seminars. If you pay $500 or $600 for a software package, you shouldn't have to spend another $500 or $600 to learn how to use it.

One of the better ways to learn software is by using videotapes. The ViaGrafix Company (800-842-4723, or www.viagrafix.com) has about

200 different videotape courses. They have tapes on all of the most popular software and even some that is not so popular. You should be able to find a tape for almost any program imaginable. They even have instructional tapes on networking, telecommunications, programming, and much more. You can view the tapes at your leisure and learn at your own pace. Call them for a catalog. In addition, ViaGrafix now has several training programs on CD-ROM, which is even better than a videotape because it offers hands-on learning.

There is one company that takes out full-page ads in local newspapers and offers a free videotape of any of several programs. They ask for a credit card number to pay a nominal sum for shipping. When you receive the tape, there will be a notice in very small print that says they will ship additional videotapes on a regular basis for a cost of $39.95. I get a lot of mail, so I don't read everything as closely as I should. I began getting a new videotape every month. I finally read the small print. I was rather unhappy with this company and felt that this was almost fraudulent because I did not order the tapes. Now I read the invoices more closely.

LapLink for Windows

If you do any traveling, it is almost essential that you have a laptop computer. Or if you work in an office, it is very convenient to copy data from a desktop PC to a laptop to bring work home. But transferring files and data from the PC to the laptop then back to the PC can sometimes be a problem. For many years, Traveling Software (800-662-2652, or www.travsoft.com) has been foremost in providing software and cables specifically for this purpose.

They have now developed several new utilities that make file transfer faster and easier. With their programs, you can now use a modem to tie into the office PC or a network so that you can work at home, update your files, or access your e-mail while traveling.

[The PCs are connected with the supplied cables by using the LPT1 parallel printer ports, the COM serial ports, by modem, by wireless devices, or over a network such as Novell.] Using the cables and software, two computers can be tied together in a very low-cost type of network. If you own a laptop, or work in an office with two or more computers, you could probably save a lot of time with LapLink for Windows. In addition, if you have just bought a new computer and want to transfer your old data to it, Laplink is one of the best ways I know to do so.

EULA—One Reason Bill Gates Is a Multibillionaire

In mid-1998, it was reported that Bill Gates was worth over $50 billion. In mid-1999, it was reported that his worth had doubled to $100 billion. Yet he is not happy and wants to make more and more.

One reason he is so wealthy is the End-User License Agreement (EULA). If you have ever installed any software, this is a contract that you have probably agreed to many times, but most likely have never taken the time to read. You had to agree to the contract, or the software would not load. Following is a EULA from Microsoft. Most EULAs from other companies are pretty much the same.

END-USER LICENSE AGREEMENT FOR MICROSOFT SOFTWARE

IMPORTANT—READ CAREFULLY: This End-User License Agreement ("EULA") is a legal agreement between you (either an individual or a single entity) and the manufacturer ("PC Manufacturer") of the computer system ("COMPUTER") with which you acquired the Microsoft software product(s) identified above ("SOFTWARE PRODUCT" or "SOFTWARE"). If the SOFTWARE PRODUCT is not accompanied by a new computer system, you may not use or copy the SOFTWARE PRODUCT. The SOFTWARE PRODUCT includes computer software, the associated media, any printed materials, and any "online" or electronic documentation. By installing, copying or otherwise using the SOFTWARE PRODUCT, you agree to be bound by the terms of this EULA. If you do not agree to the terms of this EULA, PC Manufacturer and Microsoft Corporation ("Microsoft") are unwilling to license the SOFTWARE PRODUCT to you. In such event, you may not use or copy the SOFTWARE PRODUCT, and you should promptly contact PC Manufacturer for instructions on return of the unused product(s) for a refund.

Software PRODUCT LICENSE

The SOFTWARE PRODUCT is protected by copyright laws and international copyright treaties, as well as other intellectual property laws and treaties. The **SOFTWARE PRODUCT is licensed, not sold**. [Bolding and underline was added by author for emphasis.]

GRANT OF LICENSE

This EULA grants you the following rights:

Software. You may install and use one copy of the SOFTWARE PROD-UCT on the COMPUTER.

Storage/Network Use. You may also store or install a copy of the computer software portion of the SOFTWARE PRODUCT on the COMPUTER to allow your Storage/Network Use.

You may also store or install a copy of the computer software portion of the SOFTWARE PRODUCT on the COMPUTER to allow your other computers to use the SOFTWARE PRODUCT over an internal network, and distribute the SOFTWARE PRODUCT to your other computers over an internal network. However, you must acquire and dedicate a license for the SOFTWARE PRODUCT for each computer on which the SOFTWARE PRODUCT is used or to which it is distributed. A license for the SOFT-WARE PRODUCT may not be shared or used concurrently on different computers.

Back-up Copy. If PC Manufacturer has not included a back-up copy of the SOFTWARE PRODUCT with the COMPUTER, you may make a single back-up copy of the SOFTWARE PRODUCT. You may use the back-up copy solely for archival purposes.

DESCRIPTION OF OTHER RIGHTS AND LIMITATIONS

Limitations on Reverse Engineering, Decompilation and Disassembly.

You may not reverse engineer, decompile, or disassemble the SOFT-WARE PRODUCT, except and only to the extent that such activity is expressly permitted by applicable law notwithstanding this limitation.

Separation of Components

The SOFTWARE PRODUCT is licensed as a single product. Its component parts may not be separated for use on more than one computer.

Single COMPUTER

The SOFTWARE PRODUCT is licensed with the COMPUTER as a single integrated product. The SOFTWARE PRODUCT may only be used with the COMPUTER.

Rental

You may not rent or lease the SOFTWARE PRODUCT.

Software Transfer

You may permanently transfer all of your rights under this EULA only as part of a sale or transfer of the COMPUTER, provided you retain no copies, you transfer all of the SOFTWARE PRODUCT (including all component parts, the media and printed materials, any upgrades, this EULA and, if applicable, the Certificate(s) of Authenticity), and the recipient agrees to the terms of this EULA. If the SOFTWARE PRODUCT is an upgrade, any transfer must include all prior versions of the SOFTWARE PRODUCT.

Termination

Without prejudice to any other rights, Microsoft may terminate this EULA if you fail to comply with the terms and conditions of this EULA. In such event, you must destroy all copies of the SOFTWARE PRODUCT and all of its component parts.

UPGRADES

If the SOFTWARE PRODUCT is an upgrade from another product, whether from Microsoft or another supplier, you may use or transfer the SOFTWARE PRODUCT only in conjunction with that upgraded product, unless you destroy the upgraded product. If the SOFTWARE PRODUCT is an upgrade of a Microsoft product, you now may use that upgraded product only in accordance with this EULA. If the SOFTWARE PRODUCT is an upgrade of a component of a package of software programs which you licensed as a single product, the SOFTWARE PRODUCT may be used and transferred only as part of that single product package and may not be separated for use on more than one computer.

COPYRIGHT

All title and copyrights in and to the SOFTWARE PRODUCT (including but not limited to any images, photographs, animations, video, audio, music, text and "applets," incorporated into the SOFTWARE PRODUCT), the accompanying printed materials, and any copies of the SOFTWARE PRODUCT, are owned by Microsoft or its suppliers. You may not copy the printed materials accompanying the SOFTWARE PRODUCT. All rights not specifically granted under this EULA are reserved by Microsoft.

DUAL-MEDIA SOFTWARE

You may receive the SOFTWARE PRODUCT in more than one medium. Regardless of the type or size of medium you receive, you may use only one medium that is appropriate for the COMPUTER. You may not use or install the other medium on another computer. You may not loan, rent, lease, or otherwise transfer the other medium to another user, except as part of the permanent transfer (as provided above) of the SOFTWARE PRODUCT.

PRODUCT SUPPORT

Product support for the SOFTWARE PRODUCT is not provided by Microsoft or its subsidiaries. For product support, please refer to PC Manufacturer's support number provided in the documentation for the COMPUTER. Should you have any questions concerning this EULA, or if you desire to contact PC Manufacturer for any other reason, please refer to the address provided in the documentation for the COMPUTER.

U.S. GOVERNMENT RESTRICTED RIGHTS

The SOFTWARE PRODUCT and documentation are provided with RESTRICTED RIGHTS. Use, duplication, or disclosure by the Government is subject to restrictions as set forth in subparagraph (c)(1)(ii) of the Rights in Technical Data and Computer Software clause at DFARS 252.227-7013 or subparagraphs (c)(1) and (2) of the Commercial Computer Software— Restricted Rights at 48 CFR 52.227-19, as applicable. Manufacturer is Microsoft Corporation/One Microsoft Way/Redmond, WA 98052-6399.

FOR THE LIMITED WARRANTIES AND SPECIAL PROVISIONS PERTAINING TO YOUR PARTICULAR JURISDICTION, PLEASE REFER TO YOUR WARRANTY BOOKLET INCLUDED WITH THIS PACKAGE OR PROVIDED WITH THE SOFTWARE PRODUCT PRINTED MATERIALS.

If you buy a book like this one, you can write in it, you can give it away or sell it, or you can do just about anything you want to with it. It is yours. But no matter how much you pay for software, you do not own it. You only paid for a license. And you signed a binding agreement that severely limits what you may do with that software.

Summary

I can't possibly mention all of the fantastic software that is available. There are thousands and thousands of ready-made software programs that will allow you to do almost anything with your computer. Look through any computer magazine for the reviews and ads. You should be able to find programs for almost any application.

How Your Computer Can Help You

You may be a young person who has not yet made up your mind as to what career to pursue. A recent *U.S. News and World Report* listed 20 of the hottest jobs at this time. Most of them require some knowledge of computers. Nearly all require a college degree, some experience, and quite often, a lot of luck.

Even if you have a career, but you are not too happy with it, you may want to switch. Here are some of the jobs from the list:

1. *Accounting*   May include internal auditor, CPA consultant, and corporate tax manager

2. *Arts and Entertainment*   Includes actor, choreographer, and computer animator

3. *Banking and Finance*   Includes bank branch manager, collections specialist, credit analyst, financial analyst, investment banker, loan review officer, and mortgage lender.

4. *Communications*   Includes TV news reporter, TV news producer, PR account executive, and publicist

5. *Education*   Includes teachers for math, science, computer science, and chemistry

6. *Telecommunications*   Includes wireless software programmer, telephone operator, telephone company service representative, telephone technician, cable service representative, and cable technician

7. *Trades*   Includes truck driver, painter, welder, carpenter, electrician, and heavy machine operator

8. *Travel and Hospitality*   Includes airline reservations agent, travel agent, restaurant manager, and menu consultant

9. *Engineering*   Includes computer engineer, mechanical engineer, civil engineer, petroleum engineer, and chemical engineer

10. *Environment*   Includes environmental consultant, Sierra Club regional field representative, forest ecology consultant, industry toxicologist, and natural resources economist

11. *Health Care*   Includes medical doctor, medical assistant, dietitian, speech therapist, registered nurse, nurse practitioner, pharmacist, and optometrist

12. Public Services   Includes therapeutic recreation specialist, firefighter, police officer, and mail carrier

13. *Sales*   Includes electronics specialist, software sales, sales rep, and sales account manager

14. *Social Work*   Includes grief specialist, home health care social worker, geriatric social worker, marriage counselor, and child protective services social worker

15. *Management*   Includes manager supply chain, logistics, marketing manager, and management consultant

16. *Medicine*   Includes cosmetic dentist, family practice MD, psychi-

atrist, allergist/immunogist, pediatrician, internist, pathologist, anethesiologist, Ob-Gyn, radiologist, and surgeon

17. *Personal Services*   Includes professional organizers, wedding consultant, landscaper, pool service, and day care provider

18. *Human Resources*   Includes human resources specialist, human resources consultant, affirmative action consultant, recruitment manager, and benefits director

19. *Internet/New Media*   Includes data control technician, Webmaster, online content manager, and audio engineer

20. *Law*   Includes business expert attorney, IRS attorney, and intellectual-property attorney

Some Uses and Applications

There are many, many applications and ways to use your computer. I can't possibly list them all, but in this chapter, we'll discuss just a few of the possibilities.

Preparing Résumés

There are few people who can't use a good résumé. It is one of the better ways to get your foot in the door if you are looking for a job. Many of the larger companies are now using scanners to create databases of all of the résumés that are sent to them. They can then have the computer search for whatever qualities they are looking for at the moment.

To make sure your résumé gets into their computer, you should use a good printer with a standard font to create it. In order to find out what the companies are looking for, look in the want ads from major companies to see what keywords are used. List your strongest and best skills first. Don't hide them in the middle of a long list.

Several books and software programs are available that can help you create a good résumé. Here are a couple of books:

Be Your Own Headhunter Online by Pam Dixon, published by Random House.

Electronic Résumé Revolution by Joyce Lain, published by John Wiley & Sons.

In addition, a good program is WinWay Resume 4.0 from WinWay Corp. (800-4WINWAY, or www.winway.com). This low-cost program with an estimated street price of $39.95, comes on a CD-ROM and is full of good information. It will not only help you write a good réumé, it will also help you find a job.

Features include automatic résumé and letter writing, contact management, interview simulation, and salary negotiation. The CD-ROM has over 12,000 job descriptions to help you tailor your résumé and cover letter. You can even use the program to link to the Internet: It lets you send your résumé as e-mail and helps you to find jobs via the Internet.

If you are looking for a job, the cost of this program may be one of the best investments you can make. They even offer a 30-day money-back guarantee.

Distance Learning

Many of these jobs require a degree in computer science. Most local colleges and universities now offer many computer courses. There are several colleges and universities who now offer home study courses or distance learning over the Internet. Check the courses offered by the McGraw-Hill World University at www.mhcec.com, or call 1-888-649-8648, ext. 2621.

Some colleges and universities offer college credit courses over local TV channels, usually the public broadcasting channels (PBS). This type of learning can be a fantastic alternative to driving to class, trying to find a parking spot, then sitting in class at a certain time. If the class is offered on TV, you can use a VCR to record it, then watch it when you have the time, or watch it several times in order to learn it. If it is on the Internet, you can usually download the lessons to your hard disk and study when you have time. It is a great way to learn and get a college or university degree.

Setting Up a Home Office

SOHO, an acronym that has recently been created, stands for small office/home office. Many businesses can be operated from a home office.

Several advantages in having a home office are no commuting, no high office rent, ability to take care of young children at the same time, and ability to set your own hours. More and more businesses are allowing their employees to work from home and telecommute, as many jobs can be done from home as easily as at a big office.

There are several computer programs that let you connect your home computer to an office computer. A modem and the Internet may be all you need.

A Note on Home Office Deductions

If you have a home office for a business, you may be able to deduct part of the cost of your computer from your income taxes. You may even be able to deduct a portion of your rent, telephone bills, and other legitimate business expenses.

I can't give you all of the IRS rules for a home office, but there are several deductions available if you use a portion of your home exclusively and regularly to operate your business. These deductions may include portions of your real estate taxes, mortgage interest, operating expenses (such as home insurance premiums and utility costs), and depreciation allocated to the area used for business. You may even be able to deduct a portion of the cost of painting the outside of your house or repairing the roof.

Note: You should be aware that the IRS looks very closely at any deductions for a home office. I had my two-car garage converted into an office and claim deductions for a home office every year. I have been audited twice and each time have had to pay more because they disallowed some of my deductions. I didn't mind so much having to pay more, although I still think my deductions were legitimate. But what really cost me was the large amount of time and trouble and worry. The next time they audit me, and I am pretty sure they will, I am going to ask them how much. If it is within reason, I will just write out a check. It will be much less expensive than having to go through the hassle of trying to explain and justify my deductions.

Before you deduct these expenses, I recommend that you buy the latest tax books and consult with the IRS or a tax expert. There are many, many rules and regulations, and they change frequently. For more information, call the IRS and ask for Publication #587, *Business Use of Your Home.* Look in your telephone directory for the local or 800 number for the IRS.

Here is another recommendation: Whether you have a home office or not, keep good records. I have been rather sloppy in keeping records in the past. But after being audited twice for a home office, I am a changed man.

Quicken

I now use Quicken from Intuit to keep track of all my expenses. Quicken is very easy to use. The data from this program can be imported into TurboTax, which can help make the onerous tax time task a bit easier. Check out Intuit's Web site at www.quicken.com.

Accounting

If you own a SOHO, some accounting skills are a must. Many small businesses can't afford to hire full-time accountants. Instead, many hire accountants on a part-time basis to keep their books and accounts in order. There are also several good software programs that can be used for do-it-yourself accounting. The Computer Associates Company (516-324-5224) has several good accounting programs for both small and larger businesses. Check their Web site at www.cal.com.

Another low-cost accounting package is Peachtree Accounting for Windows. Check their Web site at www.peach.com.

Also check the mail-order catalogs listed in Chapter 19 for more accounting and other software.

Preparing Taxes

Congress and the IRS change the tax rules every year. Each year they become more and more complicated. It is almost impossible for the ordinary person to be aware of, comprehend, and understand all of the rules and regulations. Some of the rules are even difficult for the IRS to sort out.

If a person works at a single job and has a single source of income, the forms are fairly simple. But if you have several sources of income or a small business, preparing your taxes can be a nightmare. It is an impossible task for many people, and they must hire a tax preparer. Many of the tax preparers charge from $50 to over $100 dollars an hour.

Just to give you an indication of how profitable tax preparation can be, the H&R Block Company owned CompuServe. They recently sold it to AOL for several million dollars.

Fortunately, since you have a computer, it may not be necessary for you to pay a tax preparer to do your taxes. Several tax programs are available that can do the job for you. Unless you have a very complicated income, it can be done quickly and easily. In many cases, the cost of the program would probably be less than the cost of having a tax preparer do your taxes just once.

Besides doing your own taxes, most of these programs will allow you to set up files and do the taxes of others. Many of the software companies offer tax preparation programs for professional tax businesses, but usually at a much higher price.

All of the programs operate much like a spreadsheet, in that the forms, schedules, and worksheets are linked together. When you enter data at one place, other affected data is automatically updated. Most of them have a built-in calculator so that you can do calculations before entering figures.

In addition, many of the programs allow "what ifs" calculations to show what your return would look like with various inputs. Most companies also have software for state income taxes, and most allow you to print out IRS forms that are acceptable.

Following is a brief review of one of the better-known programs.

TurboTax

TurboTax from the Intuit Company (www.intuit.com) is an excellent program and is fairly easy to install and learn. It starts out with a personal interview about your financial situation for the past year. It then lists forms that you might need. Based on the present year's taxes, it can estimate what your taxes will be for next year. It is continuously updated to the latest IRS rules and regulations.

You can't expect a person, even CPAs and IRS employees, to remember all the rules and regulations. People have called several of the IRS clerks with questions. Conflicting answers would be given about 50 percent of the time. If you accept the answer to a question from an IRS clerk, and it happens to be a wrong answer, guess who is at fault?

Since TurboTax has the latest rules and regulations in the software, it is probably more trustworthy than the average IRS clerk. It can probably do more for you than many CPAs and is a lot less expensive. Quicken, mentioned earlier and also from Intuit, is a financial software program that is an ideal adjunct to TurboTax. You can use Quicken to keep track of all of your financial records, then at the end of the year, the records can be directly imported into the TurboTax program.

Electronic Filing

The IRS is now accepting electronic filing from certain tax preparers and companies. Eventually, you should be able to complete your taxes from one of the above-mentioned programs, then use your modem to send it directly to the IRS. This, of course, saves you a lot of time and will save the IRS even more. Ordinarily the IRS has to input the data from your return into their computers by hand. Can you imagine the amount of time saved if they can receive it directly into their computers? So the IRS encourages electronic filing.

Electronic filing also offers advantages to you. Here are just a few:

■ Faster refund (up to three weeks faster)

■ Direct deposit of the refund

■ More accurate return resulting in fewer errors

■ IRS acknowledges receipt of the return

■ It reduces paperwork

■ Saves IRS labor, and therefore, taxpayers' money

Some people have used electronic filing to file false claims for refunds. You can be sure that from now on the IRS agents will be checking to make sure that no one is filing refund claims for their cat or dog. There are still some limitations. For more information, call 800-829-1040 and ask for the Electronic Filing Coordinator. Or check with your local IRS office to see if electronic filing is possible in your area.

Other Tools of the Trade

The following items are some other tools that can go very well with your computer in business uses.

Smart Cards

Smart Cards are similar to the standard credit cards. One major difference is that they are programmed or loaded with a certain amount of cash from your account. Each time you use the card to pay for an item, a Smart Card reader deducts the amount of cash from the card.

Smart Cards have been used for some time in Europe and have recently been approved for use in China. They have been a bit slow to catch on here, but they are expected to be very popular within the next few years.

Besides storing the equivalent of cash on the card, there is room for several other things such as one's health history and a large assortment of other critical data.

Point-of-Sale Terminals

Point-of-sale (POS) terminals are usually a combination of a cash drawer, a computer, and special software. They provide a fast customer checkout, credit card handling, auditing, and security. They also reduce paperwork and provide efficient accounting. By keying in codes for various items, the computer can keep a running inventory of everything that is sold. The store owner can immediately know when to reorder certain goods. A POS system can provide instant sales analysis data as to which items sell best, buying trends, and of course, the cost and the profit or loss.

There are several POS systems. A simple cash drawer with a built-in 40-column receipt printer may cost as little as $500. More-complex systems may cost $1500 and more. Software may cost from $175 up to $1000. But they may be able to replace a bookkeeper and an accountant or at least make their jobs easier. In most successful businesses that sell goods, a POS system can easily pay for itself. Here are a few POS hardware and software companies:

Alpha Data Systems	404-499-9247
CA Retail	800-668-3767
Computer Time	800-456-1159
CompuRegister	314-365-2050
Datacap Systems	215-699-7051
Indiana Cash Drawer	317-398-6643
Merit Dig. Systems	604-985-1391

NCR Corp.   800-544-3333

Printer Products   617-254-1200

Synchronics   901-761-1166

Bar Codes

Bar codes are black-and-white lines that are arranged in a system much like Morse code's use of dots and dashes. By using combinations of wide and narrow bars and wide and narrow spaces, any numeral or letter of the alphabet can be represented.

Bar codes were first adopted by the grocery industry. They set up a central office that assigned a unique number, a Universal Product Code (UPC), for just about every manufactured and prepackaged product sold in grocery stores. Different sizes of the same product have a different and unique number assigned to them. The same-type products from different manufacturers will also have unique numbers. Most large grocery stores nowadays sell everything from automobile parts and accessories to drugs and medicines. Each item has its own bar code number.

When the clerk runs an item across the scanner, the dark bars absorb light and the white bars reflect the light. The scanner decodes this number and sends it to the main computer. The computer then matches the input number to the number stored on its hard disk. Linked to the number on the hard disk is the price of the item, the description, the amount in inventory, and several other pieces of information. The computer sends back the price and the description of the part to the cash register, where it is printed out. The computer then deducts that item from the overall inventory and adds the price to the overall cash received for the day.

A store may have several thousand items with different sizes and prices. Without a bar code system, the clerk must know most of the prices, then enter them in the cash register by hand. Many errors are committed. With bar codes, the human factor is almost eliminated (unless, of course, the wrong information was originally entered into the system). The transactions are performed much faster and with almost total accuracy.

At the end of the day the manager can look at the computer output and immediately know such things as how much business was done, what inventories need to be replenished, and what items were the biggest sellers. With the push of a button on the computer, he or she can change any or all of the prices of the items in the store.

Bar codes can be used in many other ways to increase productivity, keep track of time charged to a particular job, track inventory, and so on. There are very few businesses, large or small, that cannot benefit from the use of bar codes.

There are several different types of bar code readers or scanners. Some are actually small portable computers that can store data, then be downloaded into a larger computer. Some systems require their own interface card, which must be plugged into one of the slots on the computer motherboard. Some companies have devised systems that can be inserted in series with the keyboard so that no slot or other interface is needed. Key Tronic has a keyboard with a bar code reader as an integral part of the keyboard.

If you are interested in bar code and automatic identification technology, there are two magazines that are sent free to qualified subscribers:

ID Systems
174 Concord St.
Peterborough, NH 03458
603-924-9631

Automatic I.D. News
P.O. Box 6158
Duluth, MN 55806-9858

Call or write for subscription qualification forms. Almost everyone who has any business connections can qualify.

Bar Code Printers

There are special printers that have been designed for printing bar code labels. Labels can also be printed on the better dot-matrix and on laser printers. Several companies specialize in printing up labels to your specifications.

Networks

If you have a SOHO with two or more computers, you probably need to connect them in a network. You may think that hooking up a network would be very complicated. Some systems are, but to hook up two to four computers can be very simple. Windows 98 helps make it simple. It has built-in software to recognize a network card and configure the system. All you need is a network interface card (NIC) for each unit, a length coaxial cable to connect the computers, and BNC connectors. The BNC connectors on the end of the line should have terminating resistors.

Instead of the BNC connectors, there are some NICs that are designed for the RJ-45 connector. These NICs do not need the terminating resistors.

Types of Networks

The term *network* can cover a lot of territory. Some networks are worldwide—for example, the telephone system. Some computer networks only connect two or three computers; others have thousands tied together.

Networks are made up of two major components: hardware and software. The hardware may consist of boards, cables, hubs, routers, and bridges. There are several different companies who supply network operating software (NOS). The main ones are Novell, Microsoft, and IBM.

A few standards exist so that the hardware and software from the major companies are compatible. For instance, software from either Novell or Microsoft will work on boards and systems from several different vendors and manufacturers.

There are several different types of networks, such as local-area networks (LANs), wide-area networks (WANs), zero slot types, peer-to-peer types, and client/server types. A LAN is usually a system within a single building, plant, or campus; it may include several different types of systems. A WAN connects areas that are geographically separate.

A *zero slot network* is usually two computers tied together with a cable through their serial or parallel ports. Special software can allow access of the hard disk of each unit. Files can be viewed, copied, and transferred between computers. It is a very inexpensive way to share resources. A disadvantage is that it may be limited to a maximum of 115,000bps (bits per second), which is relatively slow. Another disadvantage is that the distance between the two computers may be limited to about 50 feet.

As mentioned, LapLink from Traveling Software (800-527-5465 or www.travsoft.com) is very good if you need to tie a couple of computers together in a small office.

A *peer-to-peer network* may be rather sophisticated. It requires a network card in each computer and requires special software. Depending on the type of system, it may operate from 1MHz up to 10MHz or more. A peer-to-peer network is distinguished from a client/server network in that the computers on this type of network communicate with each

Figure 17-1
An Ethernet network
interface card.

other rather than with a large file server. They can share and transfer files and utilize the resources of all the computers on the network. Figure 17-1 shows a NIC and cabling for a peer-to-peer network; it could also be used to connect computers on a client/server-type network.

In a *client/server network*, one computer is usually dedicated as the server. A Pentium III- or AMD Athlon-type computer is ideal as a file server. It can have a very large hard disk that contains all of the company's files and records.

The individual computers attached to the server are called *clients* or *workstations*. The workstations can access the files and records and change or alter them as necessary.

A client/server network offers several advantages to the company. They only have to buy software for one machine. They do have to pay for a license for each of the networked computers, but it costs much less than having to buy software for each machine.

A network can keep all of the records and data in one place. This can allow close control of the updating and revisions of the data. In addition, a network may allow communication between each of the networked computers. It may also allow the users to share a single printer, fax, modem, or other peripherals.

RAID

One disadvantage with a network server is that if the main server goes down, the whole system is down. The data and records must also be routinely backed up. For critical data, it may be necessary to have a redundant array of inexpensive disks (RAID) that would automatically make two or more copies of all data. A less-expensive-type system would be to use a couple of large IDE hard disks and a couple of SCSI hard disks. Since they use different interface controllers, there is less chance that both of them would fail.

Promise Low-Cost RAID

Promise Technology has a FastTrak controller that will let you set up an IDE RAID system. Ordinarily, RAID systems use SCSI hard disks and controllers and are rather expensive. The new Ultra DMA/66 disks are actually faster than the SCSI and are less expensive.

With the Promise FastTrak controller, you can control four IDE drives. They can be set up so that two of them can be used for striping. Striping allows you to write every other track to the other drive. For instance, one drive would write or read track 1-3-5; the second one would read or write track 2-4-6. Striping essentially doubles the speed of the disk read-and-write. Hard disks are never as fast as the electronics, so anything that can double and speed up the throughput is great.

You can also set up two drives to mirror each other. This is one of the better ways to make backups. The same data is written to both disks at the same time. If one of them fails, the other one will still have all of the data. An ideal system would be to have four hard disks—two for striping and two for mirroring.

If you are in a business and have to make sure that your data is backed up, this is one of the better ways to do it. But this system is ideal for the small business or even a home user.

UPS

For critical data, it is also necessary that the server be supplied with an uninterruptible power supply (UPS). A UPS is essential in areas where there is frequent lightning and electrical storms. It is also necessary in areas where there are wide variations in the electrical supply where there may be "brownouts." The American Power Conversion (APC) Company (800-800-4272, or www.apcc.com) has some excellent UPS systems. They can supply you with a system for a single user or for a fairly large network.

It is possible that in some older houses and even in businesses, there can be wiring faults. When an outlet is wired, if it is a two-wire outlet, it should have a long slot and a shorter slot. If you remove the outlet and look at how it is wired, it should have a white wire going to the longer slot and a black or other colored wire attached to the shorter slot. The white wire is ground and should be attached to a water pipe or some other ground at the fuse box. If it is a three-wire outlet, which should be standard for all newer installations, the long slot should have the white ground wire and the short one should have the hot black or other-color wire. The U part of the outlet may have a single bare copper wire that is also attached to ground at the fuse box.

Of course, if the outlet is miswired, it can be dangerous and deadly. A miswired outlet can also cause grounding problems among your systems.

NOS

Of course, the company will need network operating software (NOS). Novell is the leader in both software and network interface cards (NICs). Windows NT can also be used as a NOS. There are several companies that provide NOS and NICs for small networks. LANtastic from the Artisoft Company (602-670-7326) is one of the better-known suppliers. Novell also has Novell Lite for small networks. The Microsoft Windows 98 can also be used for small networks.

There are three main methods, or topologies, of tying computers together: Ethernet, Token Ring, and Star. Each system has some advantages and disadvantages. The Ethernet system is the most popular.

Home Networks

Here is some information from Intel (www.intel.com) about AnyPoint:

The AnyPoint *Home Network* uses your home's existing phone lines to pass data among your PCs. See Figure 17-2. The Parallel Port model plugs into each PC's parallel port, and to a nearby wall phone jack. Included software handles communications among your PCs, and between the PCs and the

Figure 17-2
A module that makes
two or more
computers into
a network using
telephone lines.

Internet. With the AnyPoint Home Network installed, you can simultaneously access files, surf the Internet (if you have an Internet service
provider account), print documents, and play multi-user games from any
PC in your home.

Phone lines provide a great foundation for a home network. Phone lines
also help enable simple, convenient home networking, since they eliminate
the need for special network wiring. And, you can still make and receive
phone calls while printing, accessing files, or playing multi-player games
across the AnyPoint Home Network.

The AnyPoint Home Network lets you connect your home PCs by simply plugging into your existing phone jacks and using a regular phone line to send data. That's convenient, because Intel research shows that the average home has 4 to 5 phone jacks, and that the rooms that are most likely to have a PC—bedrooms, kitchens, and family/TV rooms—are also the most likely to have a phone jack.

The AnyPoint Home Network is designed to be compliant with the Home Phoneline Networking Alliance 1Mbps (megabit-per-second) specification for phoneline networking. It operates in a specific frequency range on the phone lines, allowing the home network to share the line with other services like voice calls, fax transmissions, and the new high-speed universal asynchronous digital subscriber lines (UADSL).

A Plain Old Telephone Service (POTS), UADSL Internet connectivity and home phoneline networking share the same line by operating at different frequencies. As a result, you can talk on the phone or access the Internet like you ordinarily do, while you or other PC users are playing games, sharing files, and printing across the home network. The only thing you can't do is talk on the phone and access the Internet at the same time—just like you can't now (at least over regular phone lines).

Since your household telephone wiring is essentially a private network within the home, your AnyPoint Home Network helps ensure security for your connected PCs. And, while the home network makes it easy to share devices such as disk drives with other users in the household, there's no obligation to do so. You can easily make devices off limits, or allow other home users to read files but not to edit or delete them.

The AnyPoint Home Network is easy to set up and easy to use. The Parallel Port Model uses your PC's parallel port. There's no ugly network wiring to string and no complicated network configurations to tangle with. Setting up the network is as easy as 1-2-3:

Step 1—No Need to Open Your PC
Plug the AnyPoint Home Network adapter into your PC's parallel port. If you have a printer, plug it into the printer port of the parallel port adapter.

Step 2—No New Wires
Plug the AnyPoint Home Network adapter into a wall phone jack. And plug the adapter into an electrical outlet.

Step 3—Easy Setup Software
Insert the CD and let the Install Wizard quickly and easily help you set up your AnyPoint Home Network. Repeat for each of the other PCs in the house.

That's it—you're ready to go!

An AnyPoint Home Network allows your PCs to send and receive data at up to 1Mbps. That's roughly 18 times faster than a 56Kbps (kilobits-per-second) modem. At this speed, you can share PC resources with ease and play dynamic multi-user games. And, if you have a broadband Internet connection like DSL or cable modem, everyone in the home can share its fast Internet access.

Desktop Publishing

If a company has to depend on outside printing for brochures, manuals, and documents, it may be quite expensive. Desktop publishing (DTP) may save the company a lot of money. There are some high-end DTP software programs such as PageMaker and CorelDRAW that are necessary if you expect to do a lot of DTP. But for many projects, Word for Windows, WordPerfect for Windows, or any other good word-processing program may be all you need.

Ipublish from Design Intelligence is a good, low-cost software program that can be used to publish on paper, on the Web, or for presentations. It is a good program for a small business or for a SOHO. It is very easy to use, even for building HTML Web pages. Check their Web site at www.design.intelligence.com for the latest information. They even offer a 30-day free trial.

Microsoft Publisher, which comes with Office 2000, is also a good program for the SOHO. Check the Microsoft Web site at www.microsoft.com. In addition, WordPerfect 2000 from Corel (www.corel.com) includes a very good program for desktop publishing. Corel also has several excellent graphic and drawing packages. They have clip art and just about everything else that is needed for desktop publishing.

Publishing today may mean more than putting ink on paper. There are now millions of Web sites. Most of them were created with some type of special software. The Microsoft Office 2000 and WordPerfect Office 2000 suites have software that can be used for Web publishing.

You may also need a good laser printer and scanner for DTP. If you plan to do any color work, you will need a color printer and scanner. DTP Direct (800-395-7778 or 800-325-5811) is a catalog that lists several DTP software packages. They also list several hardware DTP products.

The ads in many of the computer magazines don't have much information about the product because the space is expensive. But many of the catalogs such as DTP Direct have a fairly good summary of the various features of the products. Call them for a copy of their catalog.

There are also several good books on DTP. McGraw-Hill publishes several. Check the online McGraw-Hill Bookstore at www.mhcec.com. Also check out Amazon (www.amazon.com) and Barnes and Noble (www.barnesandnoble.com).

There are also several magazines that are devoted to DTP. Almost every computer magazine often carries DTP articles. *Publish* is a magazine that has lots of articles about all kinds of publishing. It also has ads from companies who provide publishing materials, software, and hardware. *Publish* is free to qualified subscribers. For more information, call 800-656-7495.

Presentations

The word *presentation* as used in this chapter has several meanings. A presentation can be used for sales and promotions, for training employees, and for informing employees, and other persons, of such things as policies, benefits, events, changes, updates, and news.

Presentations are not only for businesses. Almost any communication is a presentation. Even a discussion with your spouse about upgrading your computer is a presentation. Every time you have a conversation with a person, you are usually presenting ideas that you want the other person to "buy." There may be no monetary reward if a person buys your ideas, but there may be a substantial reward and sense of satisfaction to your ego.

Whether we realize it or not, most of us are nearly always presenting and selling our ideas. Usually for this type of presentation, we don't need a lot of software and hardware. But for an old-fashioned type of presentation where a person stands up before a group with a projector and pointer, you may need software and hardware for text, graphics, sound, and video. A few years ago software and hardware to accomplish all of this would have required large studios full of equipment and would have cost many thousands of dollars. Today it can be done relatively inexpensively with a desktop multimedia PC.

The Need for Presentations

Presentations are very important business tools for sales, for contract proposals, and for all of the other things listed earlier. Business presentations are also used for reports. Businesses spend billions of dollars each year on presentations to get their message out. But a poor presentation can be a terrible waste of a company's valuable resources. Quite often, it is not the message that is at fault, but the messenger.

Designing a Good Presentation

It is not always the presenter's fault for giving a bad presentation. He or she may not have the proper tools to make a good presentation. There are several new electronic tools, but one of the more important tools is proper training. Few people are born with the charisma that makes them the perfect silver-tongued orator. They don't need to be trained. But if you are like most of us, you may need to learn a few basic rules to become a better presenter.

Presentations are so important that there is a magazine devoted solely them. *Presentation* magazine has lots of articles about presentations, including tips, and lots of ads for presentation products. It is free to those who qualify, and almost anyone in business can qualify. For a qualification form, write to: Presentations, Lakewood Building, 50 South Ninth Street, Minneapolis, MN 55402-9973, or check their Web site, at www.presentations.com.

Whether or not you ever expect to do any professional-type presentations, you should know how to give them. You should know the basic principles of public speaking. One of the best and least expensive ways to learn is through a Toastmasters group. There are usually chapters in most cities. Look in the phone book.

Electronic Notes

If you are giving a talk and need notes, put them on a laptop computer in large type. Have the notes arranged so that each time you press the Page Down key, new notes roll up. Obviously, pressing the Page Up key would then let you easily go back and review. Set the computer on the podium, then glance down now and then at your notes.

Laptops have now become very inexpensive unless you are looking for one with color and an active-matrix display. If you do much public speaking, notes on a laptop are much better than handwritten notes.

Displaying the Presentation

The slide and the overhead projectors are still the most popular display methods. Of course, there is no sound or motion on these systems. With an LCD panel, any image that appears on a computer screen can be projected onto a wall or a large theater-type screen. The output of a computer is plugged into the LCD panel, which is then placed on the bed of an overhead projector system. Whatever appears on the computer screen, appears on the LCD panel, which is then projected onto the screen.

If the computer has a sound board and speakers, a complete presentation with color, sound, and motion is possible.

Many of the LCD panels can be connected to a TV, VCR, or camcorder to project the output onto a large screen. Some of the LCD panel systems may be rather expensive. They have an active-matrix-type screen, the same type of screen used in the more-expensive notebook computers. *Active-matrix* means that they require a separate transistor for every pixel in the panel, which may be several hundred thousand. One reason the active-matrix panels are so expensive is that a single defective transistor makes the whole display panel defective.

There are some less expensive LCD panels that are monochrome but can display several shades of gray. The list prices for the LCD panels start at about $1000, but the color active-matrix may cost from $4000 and go as high as $10,000 or more.

Here are a few companies who manufacture LCD panels.

In Focus Systems	800-327-7231
Proxima Corp.	800-447-7694
Sayett Technology	800-678-7469
Sharp Electronics	201-529-9636
3M Corp.	800-328-1371

Large-Screen TVs

Several companies have developed small devices that allow the output of a computer to be plugged into a large-screen TV. Advanced Digital

Systems (310-865-1432) has the VGA to TV Elite. In addition, Panasonic has developed a 36-inch television screen that is also a computer monitor. It is an SVGA monitor with a resolution of 800 x 600 pixels. Contact Panasonic at www.panasonic.com for more information.

Camcorder Presentations

If you record your presentation on an 8mm tape recorder, you can easily take it with you. The palm-sized camcorders are small, relatively inexpensive, and can be connected to any TV. The 8mm tape cartridges can hold up to two hours of text, graphics, speech, or music and are small enough to fit several in a coat pocket. The camcorders can run off a small battery, so they don't have to have an external power source.

A camcorder can be an excellent presentation tool. Snappy is a small device that lets you capture a single photo from a camcorder, VCR, or TV. Once the single frame is captured on disk, it can be edited, changed, or morphed. For a free demo disk and more information, call Snappy at 800-306-7529.

Digital Cameras

Several companies are now making digital camcorders and still cameras. Some of the digital camcorders, such as the Canon Optura, will let you capture and download single frames or photos. They have all the utilities and benefits of a movie camera plus a still camera.

There are lots of opportunities for business use of this type of camera. Photos taken with a still camera can be downloaded directly to a hard disk. The photos can then be printed out with a color printer. For some applications, even a low-cost color ink-jet printer would do.

Several realty companies in my area take color photos of houses that they have listed. They then have four-color brochures printed up, which they mail to potential buyers. Four-color printing can be very expensive. Besides, by the time the brochures are printed, the house may have already been sold. It would be a lot less expensive and take a lot less time if a person used a digital camera to take photos of the houses for sale, then use an ink-jet printer to print up color brochures.

Rather than using an ink-jet printer, you might want to use one of the more expensive dye-sublimation or color laser printers. Or better yet, use the digital cameras to take photos and download them into a computer. When a customer comes in, he or she can look at several houses without leaving the office.

Some of the digital cameras and printing systems are now close to film-quality resolution. The one-hour photo shops are not yet shaking in their booths, but eventually, the convenience and less cost will have an impact on the film business. Many of the photo shops have started to recognize this fact and now have printers that can print out your digital photos. In addition, many of them will put your photos on a CD-ROM or floppy disk. A local service charges $5 to record a roll of film onto a floppy disk.

At this time, digital cameras are a bit expensive, but they are coming down in price. They are also being improved to provide much better resolution. Following are a few companies who make fairly inexpensive digital cameras that cost from $300 to $1000 at this time. These companies have several different models.

Apple QuickTake	800-538-9696
Casio QV-10	800-962-2746
Chinon ES-3000	800-441-0222
Kodak DC40	800-235-6325
Logitech FotoMan Pixtura	800-231-7717
Dycam DC-10	800-883-9226

Several other companies manufacture cameras that are a bit more expensive. Some of them have very expensive professional digital cameras that cost from $3000 up to $40,000. Here are just a few models:

Dicomed Digital Camera	800-888-7979
Kodak DCS 420, DCS 200	800-344-0006
Leaf Lumina, Leaf DCB II	508-836-5500
Nikon E2	800-526-4566

We are all presenters and salespersons in almost everything we do. We can be much better salespersons if we communicate better.

FireWire

FireWire, also known as IEEE 1394, is a high-speed serial bus that brings new uses to the PC platform. Users will be able to use their PCs to control consumer electronics and PC peripherals, edit audio/video content, link peripherals to the Internet, and much more. FireWire will bring the PC to the family room to provide entertainment, gaming, and learning experiences not possible today.

In the past, PCs and consumer electronics (CE) devices have existed in their own separate worlds. There was almost no interaction between the two. When the two worlds did collide, it was often through low-quality, analog interconnects. People who wanted to make movies with their PC were stuck using expensive, analog video capture cards and NTSC playback mechanisms. FireWire allows full-motion, full-frame digital video to be edited on the PC.

Future PC applications will require a video-speed interconnect. Current PC interconnects such as serial and parallel ports are not ideal for high-quality video streams. They do not have the necessary bandwidth or scalability. Current video capture solutions require expensive, specialized hardware.

FireWire technology is a true plug-and-play interconnect. It allows for up to 63 devices to be connected and disconnected on the fly. This means that you can plug and unplug your camcorder, scanner, or printer without powering down your computer first.

FireWire is a high-speed data pipe, with speeds starting at 100Mbps. Current specifications allow for speeds of up to 800Mbps, and speeds beyond 1600Mbps are in the works. FireWire has sufficient bandwidth for modern video formats, including DV and MPEG II. Because FireWire is an I/O interconnect, no specialized hardware is necessary to capture, edit, and record video over FireWire. Once you have the port on your PC, you have a fully functional video capture solution at your fingertips.

Another Resource

Intel has a Business Guide that has several good suggestions at their site at www.intel.com/businesscomputing/. They offer some business solutions for business users. Of course, they want you to use their technology, but they have some suggestions for reducing the total cost of PC ownership, network management, and business video conferencing products.

For the Kids

One of the better reasons to have a home computer is if you have children. If you don't have a computer for the kids, then you should be ashamed of yourself. You are depriving them of one of the greatest learning tools of all time.

There are lots of software for the kids. One of the better magazines that offers and reviews this type of software is *KidSoft* (800-354-6150). Check other computer magazines for ads as well.

There are several encyclopedias on CD-ROM that are good not only for kids' schoolwork but can also be used as business references. Grolier (www.grolier.com) has an online encyclopedia that is constantly updated. Unlike the old page-bound encyclopedias, you never have to worry about getting a new volume yearly. In addition, the new Collier's Encyclopedia (800-757-7707) has three CD-ROMs full of very comprehensive information.

Summary

There are thousands of different applications for your new computer. We can't possibly list them all. It is a most versatile and fantastic tool.

18

Computer Sound and Music

Sound can be an important part of your computer system. You can run your computer without a sound board and speakers, but you will be missing out on a lot of good stuff. Sound can add a lot more fun, function, and utility to your computer. There are some Windows applications that make great use of sound. The Windows Sound Recorder is an included utility that lets you record, edit, insert, mix, and play sound files that are in the .WAV format. You can add sound annotations to documents such as spreadsheets, or to programs that support object linking and embedding (OLE).

It is possible to run applications with sound with most any 386 or later computer. But it will work best on your Pentium III or AMD Aphlon class computer.

What Sound Board Should You Buy?

What sound board to buy depends on what you want to do and how much you want to spend. If you can afford it, buy the best. Creative Labs is the IBM of the sound world. Almost all sound cards adhere to the Sound Blaster standards they created. Most all new sound boards also adhere to the Windows 95/98 Plug and Play standard. Before Plug and Play, it was sometimes very difficult to install a sound card. Often, jumpers and switches had to be set so that the board would not interfere with other installed devices. I have put in many frustrating hours in the past trying to set up sound boards. Installing them is now fairly easy, since most all of them are manufactured to the Plug and Play specifications. Windows will configure and install them properly.

For sources, look in any computer magazine such as *Computer Shopper, New Media Magazine, PC World, PC Computing, PC Magazine*, or any of the several other computer magazines.

A good audio board should be able to digitally record narration, sound, or music and store it as .WAV files. You should have the option of recording in mono or stereo and be able to control the sampling rate. The board should have chips, called digital-to-analog converters, or DACs, to convert the stored digital signals for analog conversion. It should also have chips, analog-to-digital converters, or ADCs, to convert analog sound to digital signals.

A good board will have a Musical Instrument Digital Interface (MIDI). With MIDI capabilities, you can use the board with MIDI instruments such as piano keyboards, synthesizers, sound modules, and other MIDI products. The board should have an FM synthesis chipset that duplicates the 128 different MIDI voices and 46 percussion instruments. Instead of the synthesized sound, some of the more expensive cards may have samples of actual instruments and use a wave table for synthesis.

In addition, the board should have an audio-mixer function that allows you to control the source and level of the audio signals. The better boards will have tone controls for the bass and treble ranges. The board should also have a joystick port connector, a microphone input, and a speaker output jack.

Speakers

Most sound cards have an output of about 4 watts. That isn't very much, but you're not going to be trying to fill a concert hall. You really don't need much for your computer. You can attach any small speaker, but several companies manufacture small speakers with built-in amplifiers. The speakers are powered by batteries or by power supplied from a wall outlet. They may cost from $10 up to $100 for the larger ones. There are also some high-end high-fidelity systems available. (Of course, "high fidelity" usually means "high cost.") Just a few of the many companies who offer small computer speakers are Labtec, Media Vision, Koss, and Roland. Look through computer magazines for others.

If you use good sound boards and speakers, your computer can be a major component in an excellent high-fidelity system.

Microphones

Many sound boards come with a microphone. The type needed for just voice annotations can be very inexpensive, such as those available from Radio Shack for about $5. If you expect to do any kind of high-fidelity recording, then you definitely need a good microphone. A sound system is only as good as its weakest link. A good microphone may cost from $35 up to $500 or more.

There are two basic types of microphones. The dynamic type uses a diaphragm and a coil of wire that moves back and forth in a magnetic field. The other type is the condenser, or capacitor, microphone. A capacitor is made up of two flat plates. When voltage is applied to the plates, a charged field, or a capacitance, will exist between the plates. The capacitance will depend on the voltage, the size of the plates, and the distance between the plates. If the plates are moved toward or away from each other, the capacity will change. In a capacitor microphone, one plate is fixed and the other is a flat diaphragm. Sound pressure on the flexible diaphragm will move the one charged plate in and out, which causes a change in the capacity and creates a voltage signal that varies exactly with the sound-wave pressure. Capacitor mics can be made very small, such as lapel mics.

Many professional-type microphones sold today are the wireless kind. They have a small transmitter built into the microphone that feeds the sound to a small receiver connected to a nearby amplifier or recorder.

Microphones may also be classified as to their pickup directionality. The omnidirectional type picks up sound from all directions. The bidirectional type picks up sound from the opposite sides of the mic. The cardiod picks up sound in a heart-shaped, unidirectional pattern (*cardi-* is a prefix for *heart*). The unidirectional supercardiod picks up sound on a very narrow, straight-in path. Unlike what you may see rock stars do to a microphone, you don't have to stick it in your mouth to have it pick up your voice.

Music

Computers have made enormous contributions to the creation and playing of music. It has been said that music is the universal language. Everybody likes music of one kind or another. There are many different kinds of music, and it can be used in many different ways. Music can be used to express just about every emotion known to humans. There is music that can make you happy, elated, excited, and exhilarated. There is patriotic and marching-type music that can make you want to stand up and salute. Romantic and passionate music can arouse you and make you feel amorous. Mournful music can make you feel sad and sorrowful. All of this music can be played on your computer.

Not only can you play music through your computer, but even if you know nothing at all about music, you can use your computer to compose and create music. A computer is very good at converting text and graphics into digital data. Music can also be represented as digital data just as easily. Once music is digitized, you can edit it, rearrange it, add new sounds to it, remove certain sounds, or change it in hundreds of different ways. Your new computer, along with the proper software, is an excellent tool for this purpose.

Music software is available from most of the software discount companies. American Music Supply at (800-458-4076, or www.americanmusic.com) has Cakewalk Professional, which is one of the most complete programs for music. Cakewalk lets you record up to 16 tracks; it lets you create music, edit it, print it, and control it in MIDI sequences. Cakewalk is available in several versions.

American Music Supply also has several other software programs such as Band in a Box, Sound Forge, Steinberg Cubase Score, and Music Ace. In addition, American Music has just about every kind of musical instrument known. They will also resell your old equipment or repair it for you.

Call them for a catalog. I was disappointed in their Web site. It doesn't tell you much or list any of the products. Better off to call them.

In addition, there are lots of articles and ads for music software in the music magazines and catalogs listed near the end of this chapter.

Internet Telephone and Video

Making a local telephone call can cost up to 35 cents or more per minute. If it is long-distance or to another country, it may cost a small fortune. I can use my computer to send a message over the Internet to any place in the world for the cost of a local call. That message is being sent using the telephone system. Several companies have developed hardware and software that will let you use the Internet for telephone calls. In some cases, the Internet service providers (ISPs) may have to provide extra hardware at their server. In this case, they may charge extra for phone use, but even then it will be much less expensive than what the telephone company charges.

Some companies have developed low-cost video cameras and other hardware to let you send video over the Internet. Diamond Multimedia (www.diamondmm.com) has a low-cost kit for voice and video over the Internet. They claim that it can be used without having to pay a surcharge because the ISP will not have to install any special equipment.

To use the telephone or video on the Internet, you will need a sound board, a microphone, and speakers.

Teleconferencing

One important reason to have a sound board and speakers in your computer is for voice and data conferencing. Two computers can be linked together on a network in an office or a large campus, or by modem anywhere in the world. Several modems and faxes are now capable of sending and receiving voice and data.

The OfficeF/X from Spectrum Signal Processing (800-667-0018) is a modem/fax, Sound Blaster-compatible sound card, voice mail, and speaker phone. It can distinguish between incoming voice, modem, or fax signals and routes the call appropriately.

Microsoft has developed MS Phone, a telephony application for Windows 95/98 that functions as a telephone, speakerphone, answering machine, PBX, interactive voice response (IVR), and personal assistant. With this application you will be able to use several voice commands to operate your computer.

The AT&T Computer Telephone 8130 connects to a serial port on the computer and provides several functions such as contact management, logging of incoming and outgoing calls, and Caller ID.

Sound, Microphones, and Speakers

Sound is made by the pressure on air created by a vibrating object. The pressure of the vibrations causes the air to move back and forth, creating sound. If a microphone is placed in the vicinity of the sound, it can capture an image of the sound and turn it into electrical impulses. There are several different types of microphones. One basic type has a diaphragm that vibrates due to the pressure of the sound waves. The diaphragm is attached to a coil of wire that moves in and out of the field of a permanent magnet. The movement of the coil of wire in the magnetic field produces an analog voltage that varies according to the vibration of the sound.

We can use electronics to amplify the small signals and cause a loudspeaker to reproduce the original sound. The small signals can also be recorded on tape or on a CD-ROM.

Basically, a loudspeaker is quite similar to the microphone. The speaker has a coil of wire that is attached to the speaker cone. The coil of wire is surrounded by a strong, permanent magnet. Moving a coil of wire through a magnetic field produces a voltage; passing voltage through a coil of wire produces a magnetic field. The polarity of the magnetic field thus created will vary plus or minus depending on the polarity of the voltage.

As the positive and negative pulses of voltage are passed through the coil of wire, it alternately attracts and pulls the coil into the magnet or repels it, pushing the coil and cone outward. The movement of the speaker cone produces pressure waves that are a replica of the original sound waves.

Digital Sampling

Some large mainframe network computers operate by giving each person on a network a small slice of time. This process is called "time-sharing." If the time was divided into millionths of a second, one person may receive a couple of slices, then the next person would get a few slices, then a few millionths of a second later, the first person would get a few more slices of data. It would be done so fast that the person would not realize that the data was being received only part of the time. Hundreds or even thousands of people could be on a single line, all receiving different data, at the same time.

Digitizing an analog voltage is somewhat similar to time-sharing. Digital samples, or slices, are taken of the analog waves. If the number of digital samples per second is rather low, then there can be a lot of unrecorded space between each slice. When played back, the unrecorded space can usually be electronically reconstructed to some degree. But if the sample rate is fairly low, with wide spaces between each sample, the output sound will be somewhat less than high fidelity. The higher the frequency of the sample rate, the more closely the output sound will match the original.

Then why not take higher-frequency samples? Because the higher the frequency of the digital sample rate, the more space it requires to be stored or recorded. High-fidelity digital sound requires a tremendous amount of disk space to store.

Sampling Rates and Bits

Sound can be digitized using 8-bit samples or 16-bit samples. An 8-bit system can chop a waveform into a maximum of 256 steps or $2\wedge8$. A 16-bit system ($2\wedge16$) can save up to 65,000 pieces of information about the same waveform. As you can imagine, the 16-bit system will offer much greater fidelity—but at a greater need for storage space.

Using an 8-bit mode with a sample rate of 11kHz, you will be recording 11,000 bytes of data each second $\times$ 60 seconds, or 661Kb per minute. If you were recording in 8-bit stereo at the same rate, the storage requirement would double to 1.32Mb for one minute. To record in 16 bits stereo at 11kHz, it would be 44,000 $\times$ 60 seconds and would require 2.64Mb for one minute.

Most speech has a frequency range from about 300Hz up to about 6kHz. Sampling at 11kHz and 8 bits is good enough for speech, but it would not be very good for high-fidelity music. Most systems are capable of sampling at 22kHz and 44.1kHz in both monaural and stereo modes. A sample rate for 44.1kHz in monaural would be 82.2K bytes per second $\times$ 60 seconds = 5.292Mb. In stereo it would be doubled to 10.5Mb per minute. One hour of recording at this sample rate would require over 630Mb. Most audio CDs have about 630Mb of storage space and can play for about one hour.

Standard digital sampling rates in the audio industry are 5.0125, 11.025, 22.05, and 44.1kHz.

Why the 44.1kHz Sample Rate?

If we had perfect hearing, we could hear sounds from 20 hertz (Hz), or cycles per second, up to 20kHz. Most of us, especially older people, have a much narrower hearing range. So why should we worry about a 44.1kHz sample rate? This is more than twice the frequency that we could hear even if we had perfect hearing.

Many instruments and other sounds have unique resonances and harmonics that go beyond the basic sounds they produce. These resonances and harmonics are what makes a middle C note on a piano sound different than the same note on a violin or trumpet. Many of the harmonics and overtones of sound are in the higher frequencies. In digital recording, the upper frequency must be at least twice of what you can expect when it is converted to analog. So a 44.1kHz digital signal will produce a 22kHz analog signal.

Resolution

We often speak of the "resolution" of our monitors. The more pixels displayed, the sharper the image and the higher the resolution. We also use "resolution" to describe digitized sound. The higher the sampling rate and the more bits of information about each sound wave, the higher the resolution and the better the fidelity. There is a limit to the resolution of an 8-bit system no matter how fast the sample rate. The maximum samples of a waveform that can be captured by an 8-bit system is 2^8, or 256. Some may think that a 16-bit system would only provide twice the resolution of an 8-bit system. Actually, a 16-bit system can provide 256 times more resolution, or 2^{16}, or 65,536. It is apparent that a 16-bit system can give much better resolution and fidelity than an 8-bit system.

Signal-to-Noise Ratio (SNR)

Analog audio is made up of voltage sine waves that vary up and down continuously. Noise and static is also made up of similar sine waves. Noise and static is everywhere. It is in the air, especially so during electrical storms. It is in our electrical lines and in almost all electronic equipment. It is very difficult to avoid.

The signal-to-noise ratio (SNR) is the ratio between the amplitude of the audio or video signal as compared to the noise component. The SNR is measured in decibels (dB), usually a minus dB. The larger the negative number, the better. Most sound boards, CD-ROM drives, and other sound systems list the SNR on their specifications. Most of the better systems will have at least a 90dB SNR. Since noise is analog voltage, a good digital system will usually have less noise than the analog systems.

Digital Signal Processors (DSP)

One of the things that helps make it possible to get so much music from the sound board is a digital signal processor (DSP). It can be a very large task just to assemble and determine which notes to output from a single instrument. But it can be mind-boggling to try to do it for several instruments.

The central processor unit (CPU) is the brains of your computer. Ordinarily, almost everything that transpires in your computer has to go through the CPU. But there are certain things such as intensive number crunching that can be speeded up with a coprocessor.

The digital signal processor (DSP) chips are quite similar in function to math coprocessors. A DSP can take over and relieve the CPU of much of its burdens. DSP chips can be configured and programmed for several specific tasks such as high-quality audio, or complex graphics and video. The DSP can be used for musical synthesis and many special digital effects.

At one time the DSP chips were rather expensive, but now the chips are quite reasonable. Since they add very little to the cost, more and more manufacturers are adding DSP chips to their sound boards. Before you buy a sound board, check the specifications.

Turtle Beach Systems was one of the first to design and implement the DSP technology on their MultiSound boards. Creative Labs followed soon after with their Sound Blaster 16 ASP. Several other companies are now manufacturing boards with the superior DSP technology. These chips add so much more function and utility to the sound board that eventually every manufacturer will be using them.

■■ ■ ■ Installing a Sound Board

To install a sound board, first turn your computer off and remove the cover. Find an empty slot, and plug the board in. If it is a less-expensive board, it may have been designed for an Industry Standard Architecture (ISA)-type slot. The newer sound boards will be designed for the Peripheral Component Interconnect (PCI) slots.

One of the benefits of CD-ROM and DVD is that they can play sound and music along with the text, graphics, and motion. You can play compact audio discs on most CD-ROM and DVD drives. These drives have a small audio connector on the back panel. A small audio cable is used to connect to the sound board. If you have a CD-ROM or DVD or both, connect the cable, or cables, now. Many of the newer sound boards have two connectors just in case you have more than one CD-ROM installed. The back of the sound board will have connections for a microphone and speakers.

Turn your computer on and see if the system works. If it does, then replace the cover. When you turn on your computer, the BIOS will recognize the board and automatically configure it.

At one time we had to set one or more jumpers or switches on the board for the interrupt request (IRQ) and direct memory access (DMA) before we could install it. Sometimes it took lots of trying, and setting and resetting, before a suitable IRQ and DMA combination was found. If two devices were set for the same IRQ, it caused a conflict.

Most all boards are now designed and manufactured to the Plug and Play (PnP) specifications. You won't have to worry about setting switches and jumpers. The CPU of your computer is always busy and can only be interrupted by certain devices that need its attention. The obvious reason for this is to keep order. If all of the devices tried to act at the same time, there would be total confusion. So computers have 16 interrupt or IRQ lines, and each device is assigned a unique number. They are given a priority according to their ranking number. For instance, if the CPU received an interrupt request from the keyboard, which is IRQ1, and a request from a mouse on IRQ4, the keyboard request would be answered first.

Just as your house has a unique address, areas of RAM memory have distinct addresses. Certain devices use a certain portion of RAM to perform some of their processing.

Before PnP, many of the older boards had built-in diagnostics that could detect a conflict with the IRQ or I/O settings. But still you may have had trouble determining which other device was causing the conflict. To see what devices are being used by the 16 IRQs, in Windows

95/98, you can click on `My Computer`, then on `Control Panel`, then on `System`, then on `Device Manager`, then on `Computer`. It will show all of the IRQs and which components are using them. If you see a yellow symbol on any device, then it is causing some kind of problem.

Musical Instrument Digital Interface (MIDI)

Electronic circuits can be designed to oscillate at almost any frequency. The output of the oscillating circuit is a voltage that can be amplified and routed through a loudspeaker to reproduce various sounds.

In the early 1970s Robert Moog used voltage-controlled oscillators (VCOs) to develop the Moog synthesizer. With a synthesizer you can create synthetic musical sounds that imitate different instruments. The sounds from the early systems didn't sound much like real musical instruments.

Also in the early 1970s John Chowning of Stanford University developed digital FM synthesis. The Yamaha Corporation licensed the technology from Stanford and introduced the first FM digital synthesizer in 1982. Since that time, there have been some tremendous technological advances. Today a person might not be able to discern whether a sound was synthesized or came from a real instrument.

In some instances, the music from a sound board does come from real instruments. Sample notes are recorded from instruments. Under computer control, any of the stored samples can be joined and played back. The notes can be held for a half note, or shortened to a quarter note or for whatever the music requires. Samples from several instruments can all be playing at the same time. The music can sound as if it is being produced by a live 100-piece orchestra. And it all comes from a chip that is about 1 inch square. It is absolutely amazing.

The early VCOs were rather crude. The electronics industry was still in its infancy. There were no integrated circuits. As the electronics industry and technology evolved, newer and better VCOs were developed and incorporated into musical instruments.

The MIDI Standard

There were no standards for the VCOs and new musical instruments. As usual, each vendor's product was a bit different than all others. In 1983 a group of companies got together and adopted a set of standards, which they called the Musical Instrument Digital Interface (MIDI). This was truly a historic agreement for the music industry. MIDI and the advances in electronic technology has made it possible to generate more new music in the last 10 years than was generated in the last 100 years. Synthesized music is not only used for rock and roll but for television commercials, for movies, and for all types of music.

How MIDI Operates

MIDI itself does not produce music. It is only an interface, or controller, that tells other devices such as a synthesizer or a sampler which particular sound to produce. In some respects, MIDI is similar to the old-style piano players that used a punched roll of paper to play.

Briefly, the MIDI specification says that a MIDI device must have at least two MIDI connectors: an input and an output. (These are DIN connectors that are the same type as that used for the computer keyboard connector on the motherboard.) A MIDI device may include adapter cards, synthesizers, piano-type keyboards, various types of instrument pickups, digital signal processors, and MIDI-controlled audio mixers.

One of the great advantages of MIDI is that it allows many different electronic instruments to communicate with each other. When two MIDI instruments are connected, the devices exchange information about the elements of the performance, such as the notes played and how loud they are played. A master keyboard can be connected to two or more MIDI electronic keyboards, or to other MIDI devices. Any note played on the master can be also played on the connected MIDI "slaves." The electronic keyboards can emulate several different instruments. One person playing the master can use the slaves to make it sound as though a very large orchestra is playing.

There are many options available, such as the ability to record the notes played, then play them back or edit and change them.

General MIDI Standard Signals

There are 128 common instrument sound signals for MIDI control; each signal is numbered 1 to 128. (You may also see them numbered 0 to 127.) The standard was originated by the Roland Corporation and is now coordinated by the MIDI Manufacturers Association (MMA).

If the MIDI receives a signal and it is connected to a synthesizer, keyboard, or any MIDI instrument, it will trigger the device to play a note corresponding to the signal number. For instance, a signal on number 3 would cause a honky-tonk piano sound; number 40 would be a violin. Note that there are 16 different instrument classifications. Every eight numbers represents sounds from a basic class of instrument. For instance, the first eight sounds are made by piano-type instruments, the next eight are made by chromatic percussion instruments, then organs, and so on.

There are an additional 46 MIDI note numbers for nonmelodic percussion instruments. These numbers include such things as drums, a cowbell, wooden blocks, triangles, and cymbals.

Synthesizers

The MIDI specification was primarily designed as a standard for controlling synthesizers. It did not specify how a synthesizer should create a sound or what sounds should be created.

The word *synthesize* means to combine or put together. Synthesizers can combine two or more waveforms to form new sounds. There are several types of sound waves or oscillations. Each musical note has a basic oscillation frequency. For instance, the note A2 has a frequency of 220 oscillations per second, or 220Hz. Note E3 vibrates at 330Hz, A4 at 440Hz, and E6 at 660Hz. We could generate pure single-frequency sine waves of each of these notes, but they would be rather dull and uninteresting. The actual notes are a combination of oscillation frequencies.

Even though it has the same basic frequency, if a note is played on different instruments, there will be a distinct difference in the sounds. The note A4 played on a trombone sounds quite different than A4 played on a guitar. They all sound different because they are not pure single sine wave frequencies. The vibrations of a basic note causes other vibrations in the metal of a trombone or the wood of a guitar. These extra vibrations are the timbre that adds tone color to a sound and distinguishes it from a note played on another instrument.

Harmonics

An important cause for difference in sounds is the harmonics created. A guitar string that is plucked to play A4 will vibrate at 440Hz. If you photographed the vibrating string with a high-speed movie camera, then slowed it down, you could see a primary node of vibrations. But there would also be several smaller-sized nodes on the string. These smaller nodes would be vibrating at twice the frequency of the primary node, and some would even be vibrating at four times the primary frequency. The sounds made at the higher frequencies blend with the primary sound to give it tone and color. These higher frequencies are called *harmonics*. Harmonics are even multiples of the fundamental oscillation of a note or its basic pitch.

Envelope Generator

Bob Moog determined that there were four main criteria in each sound: attack, decay, sustain, and release (ADSR). Attack determines how fast the initial sound rises. It may hold at the initial height for a while, then start to decay. Sustain determines how long the sound is audible while a key is held down. Release is the rate at which the sound intensity decreases to zero after the key is released.

The ADSR electronic envelope is used in synthesizers to describe almost any sound.

Wave Tables

FM-synthesized sounds are usually not as good as the sound generated from an actual instrument. The more expensive sound cards and many of the better MIDI instruments use digital samples of real sounds. This requires some memory to store the samples, but actually not as much as you might think. For instance, a piano has 88 notes or keys. But it is only necessary to sample a few notes. Since they are all piano notes, the main difference is the pitch. Middle A, or A4, has a frequency of 440Hz; A2 has a frequency of 220Hz. A sample of a single A can be electronically altered to make it sound like any A on the piano keyboard. So they only need a sample of an A, B, C, D, E, F, and G. With a small sample of each of these notes, any note of the 88 on the piano can be created. It also would not matter whether the note was a quarter note, half note, or whole note. Once the note is simulated, it can be held for as long or as short a time as necessary.

The same type of system would be used to sample notes from other instruments. It would be a little simpler to store notes from other instruments because most of them don't have as many notes as a piano. A piano is one of the few instruments that allows more than one note to be played at the same time.

The samples are stored in ROM. When a note is called for, the sample is read from ROM, placed in RAM, electronically adjusted for whatever note is needed, then sent to an amplifier and loudspeaker.

The more instruments sampled and the more samples that are stored, the more memory that is required, both ROM and RAM. Some high-end keyboards may have 10MB or more of ROM and about 4MB or more of RAM.

Sequencers

Sequencers are a type of recorder that uses computer memory to store information about a performance. Like the MIDI, it does not record the sound itself, but just the information about the sound.

Even if you know nothing at all about music, you can write and compose music with a sequencer that is connected to a synthesizer or other electronic instrument. If you know a little bit about music, you can become an expert composer with a sequencer. Most sequencers are software programs that allow you to create, edit, record, and play back on a hard disk musical compositions in the MIDI message format. The sequencer memorizes anything you play and can play it back at any time. They are similar to multitrack recorders, except that they are much faster because the tracks are on a computer. The computer also lets you do hundreds of things better, quicker, and easier than a tape recorder. A sequencer lets you edit music in thousands of ways that are not possible with a tape machine. With a single MIDI instrument, an entire album can be recorded.

A sequence can be part of a song, a single track of a song, or the whole song. The sequences are laid down in tracks. Several tracks of different instruments can be laid down separately, then all played back together. A single track can be played back and edited or changed. Tracks can be recorded at different times, then blended together. A song or an album can be created by a group even though one may be in New York, one in Los Angeles, or others scattered all over the country. Each member of the group can record their part on a disk, then ship it to a studio, where all of the tracks could be edited and blended together.

Some sequencers allow you to record channels while playing back existing channels. Tracks can be laid down over another track without erasing what is already there. Portions of a track can be erased and new material inserted. The editing capabilities are almost unlimited.

Some synthesizers and keyboards have a built-in hardware sequencer. The built-in sequencer allows you to do many of the same things that sequencer software allows. But a hardware sequencer would not have the capabilities of a computer.

Software for Making Music

Several software packages are available that you can use with your computer to make music. Listed below are just a few.

Cakewalk

Sequencer software such as Cakewalk will let you record in real time as an instrument is being played. Or you can use the step-entry mode and enter one note at a time. The notes can be entered from a computer keyboard or a piano-type MIDI keyboard that is connected to the computer.

The software is intelligent enough to take step-entry notes and combine them with the proper staff notation and timing. Some software will even add the proper chords to the step entry.

Some Windows sequencer software programs are Cakewalk Professional, CommonTime's Cadenza, Passport Designs' Master Tracks Pro, and Midisoft for Windows. Cakewalk has a very good Web site at www.cakewalk.com.

In addition, Cakewalk sells many third-party extras to help you make the most of your Cakewalk product, including Microsoft DirectX-compatible audio-effect plug-ins, hardware, and accessories. Cakewalk has hundreds of different software and hardware items.

Many of the music software programs will also print out music scores. When you consider the modern technology that allows the editing and re-editing of a song until the cut is perfect, you just have to admire the works of some of the early recording artists. They usually didn't get the opportunity to go back and change a mistake or to improve a lick here and there.

Piano Keyboards

It is possible to use a computer keyboard to edit or create music. But it is a lot easier to work with an electronic piano keyboard. Many of the electronic keyboards have built-in synthesizers and MIDI connections. If you are interested in music, one of the magazines that you should subscribe to is the *Electronic Musician* (800-843-4086). They have excellent articles about music and new devices. This magazine is of interest to professional musicians, as well as to amateurs and anyone who enjoys music. They also publish an annual *Digital Piano Buyer's Guide* that is available from the Mix Bookshelf (800-233-9604). The Mix Bookshelf specializes in books for musicians. One book that they carry is *The Musical PC*, edited by Geary Yelton. It is an excellent book for anyone who wants to learn more about music and computers. Another book they carry is *Making Music with Your Computer*, edited by David Trubitt. It would be very helpful to anyone just getting into music. There are also articles in the book that would be of interest to the old pro.

Another magazine for musicians and anyone interested in music is called *Musician* (800-347-6969). It is published primarily for the professional musician, but it is of interest to anyone who enjoys music and wants to keep up with what is happening in the music and entertainment field.

SoundTrek

JAMMER from SoundTrek (800-778-6859, or www.soundtrek.com) allows you to enter a few chords, then choose from over 200 band styles to create professional-sounding songs. Here's some information from their Web site:

> Our products are designed to help you write, record, edit, and arrange music on your PC. JAMMER's intuitive studio interface allows you to record, edit, and arrange your own musical ideas. JAMMER will also give you new ideas and instantly create professional drum tracks, jammin bass lines, innovative rhythms, and even full arrangements of music in a wide variety of styles. No matter what level of musician you are, JAMMER can help you explore musical ideas and expand your creativity in an instant. JAMMER is a powerful production tool, the ultimate accompaniment software, and an endless source of new musical ideas.
>
> You have to experience it to believe it!

SoundTrek is pleased to announce the release of the new Volume 4 Band and Drums Styles and JAMMER Professional v4.0. Download a working demo of this hot new release today!

We encourage you to take our Interactive Guided Tour to get a demonstration of how powerful this software really is. We also encourage you to check out the demo songs and download a JAMMER program demo to play with for a while. You won't believe what you've been missing.

PG Music Company

The PG Music Company (800-268-6272, or www.pgmusic.com) has several versions of Band-in-a-Box. This software lets you type in a few chords and it will supply the rest. It will automatically generate professional quality accompaniment instruments. Here's some information from their Web site:

> This major upgrade includes over 80 new features. Among them, the most amazing new feature is called "Automatic Songs". Simply select the type of song you'd like to hear, and Band-in-a-Box 8.0 will create a complete song in that style, with intro, chords, melody, arrangement and improvisations. It even auto-generates a title for the newly created song! This is HOT! These songs are of professional quality and best of all, they're different every time! And there's much more in 8.0... a new leadsheet window, guitar window, drums display window, long file name support, "undo" option and much more!
>
> PG Music also offers several other music software programs.

Digidesign

Pro Tools III from Digidesign (800-333-2137, or www.digidesign.com) lets you record, edit, process, mix, and master your music. They also have many other products. Visit their Web site for more info.

There are many, many other companies who offer software that can let you make beautiful music with your computer.

Catalogs

You will need music software for your PC. The Soundware Catalog (800-333-4554) lists hundreds of music software programs. They have a comprehensive and detailed description of each program listed. Even if you don't intend to order the program, the descriptions in the catalog can give you a good idea of what is available. Call them for a catalog.

In addition, the Musician's Friend Catalog (800-776-5173), the American Musical Supply Catalog (800-458-4076), and Manny's Mailbox Music (800-448-8478) all have hundreds of musical instruments, supplies, videotapes for training, and books. Call them for catalogs.

Musician Trade Shows

Partly due to the success of the COMDEX shows, there are now lots and lots of trade shows. Here are a couple that you might be interested in.

The National Association of Music Merchants (NAMM) have two large shows each year, usually one near Los Angeles in the winter and one in Nashville during the summer. There are usually hundreds of exhibitors at these shows. You will find just about every imaginable musical product at these shows. They have dozens of rooms where they demonstrate amplifiers and loudspeakers. There will be hundreds of electronic keyboards on the floor, everything from the small toys up to the very expensive grand pianos. They will also have several old-fashioned nonelectronic pianos, all the way from the spinet up to the concert grand. If you are at all interested in music, this is the place to see all that is available. To find out when and where the next NAMM show will be held you can call 619-438-8001.

The Consumer Electronics Show (CES) also presents two large shows each year, a winter show held in Las Vegas during the first week in January and a summer show held in Chicago, usually during the first week in June. This show has several music and musical instrument exhibitors. To find out more about this show, call 202-457-8700.

I hope you all enjoy the sounds of music with your computer.

Component
Sources

How much you save by assembling your own computer
will depend on what components you buy and who you
buy them from. You will have to shop wisely and be
fairly knowledgeable about the components in order to
take advantage of good bargains. It is very difficult to
keep up and know what is going on in this ever-changing industry. As mentioned throughout this book, one of
the best ways to do this is to subscribe to some of the
many computer magazines. You can look through the
magazines and do price comparisons of the various components and systems.

Most of the computer magazines now have Web sites. You may not have to subscribe to get all the information you may need. Another benefit is that most of the magazine Web sites are updated frequently. The way the computer industry changes, some of the articles in the monthly magazines may be obsolete by the time you get them.

Another good way to keep up is to attend the many computer shows and swap meets.

Computer Shows and Swap Meets

I have done a lot of my buying at computer shows and swap meets. There is a computer show or swap meet almost every weekend in the larger cities. Sometimes there are two or three in the Los Angeles area on the weekends. If you live in or near a large city, check your newspaper for ads.

To set up a computer swap, an organizer will usually rent a large building such as a convention center or a large hall. Booth spaces are then rented out to the various local vendors. Most of the booths will have good reputable local business people. Most of the shows have a circus-like atmosphere about them, and I often go just because of this.

One of the best features of the swap meets is that almost all of the components that you will need are there in one place on display. Several different booths will have similar components for sale. I usually take a pencil and pad with me to the shows, then I walk around and write down the prices of the items that I want to buy and compare prices at the various booths. There can be quite a wide variation in the prices.

You can also haggle with most of the dealers at the shows—especially when it gets near closing time. Rather than pack up the material and lug it back to their stores, many will sell it for a lower price.

The Softbank Company (617-433-1500) sponsors the Computer Dealers Exposition (COMDEX). They put on the two of the largest annual computer shows in the country. The spring COMDEX is usually held in Atlanta or sometimes in Chicago. Then a much bigger fall COMDEX is held during November in Las Vegas. The attendance goes up every year. When I first started attending in 1984, they only had about 60,000 people at the show in Las Vegas. They now attract almost a quarter million people for the five-day fall show. Every hotel room in Las Vegas is usually sold out six months before the show. If you can find a room, you can expect to pay two or three times what the room would ordinarily cost. The hotels usually demand a minimum three-night stay.

The Lure of Las Vegas

COMDEX is the most popular show of its kind in the nation. A cynical-type person might say that the large number of people who attend the Las Vegas show may not be there strictly for business. Some might think that some of these people are there because of the other shows and attractions in Las Vegas. But I am sure that the fact that they can write the whole thing off as a business expense never enters their head. In addition to the spring COMDEX, they have now started a New Media Expo, which will be held in Los Angeles in the spring. But since Atlanta and Los Angeles do not have the extra attractions that Las Vegas has, the attendance is usually less than one-fourth that of the Las Vegas show. The Interface Company also puts on international shows in several foreign countries.

Your Local Store

Most of the vendors at the swaps are local businesspeople. They want your business and will not risk losing you as a customer. But there may be a few vendors from other parts of the country. If you buy something from a vendor who does not have a local store, be sure to get a name and address. Most components are reliable. But there is always a chance that something might not work. You may need to exchange it or get it repaired. Or you may need to ask some questions or require some support to get it working.

Most dealers will give you a warranty of some kind and will replace defective parts. If there is something in the system that prevents it from operating, you may not be able to determine just which component is defective. Besides that, it can sometimes take a considerable amount of time to remove a component like a motherboard and return it to someone across town. Or even worse, someone across the country. So if at all possible, try to deal with a knowledgeable vendor who will support you and help you if you have any problems.

Again, computers are very easy to assemble. Once you have bought all of the components, it will take less than an hour to assemble your computer.

Magazines and Mail Order

Every computer magazine carries pages and pages of ads for compatible components and systems that can be sent to you through the mails. If you live in an area where there are no computer stores, or shows, you can buy by mail.

One of the biggest magazines in size and circulation is *Computer Shopper*. It usually has over 1000 tabloid-sized pages. About 90 percent of the magazine is made up of full-page ads for computer components and systems; however, they do manage to get a few articles in among the ads. For subscription information, call 800-274-6384, or check out www.cshopper.com. The *Shopper*, and some of the other magazines, have a categorized list of all the products advertised in the magazine and what page the product is on. A recent issue of *Computer Shopper* had a compilation of 14,000 products, listed in 170 different categories. The *Computer Shopper* Web site has many of the same ads that are found in the magazine. But the ads on the Web site may have a lower price than in the magazine. As mentioned, magazine ads often have to be made up months ahead of time. By the time you see the ad, the prices may have actually changed. The Web site prices are usually up-to-date.

The Computer Shopper Product Index makes it very easy to find what you are looking for. Sometimes they will have several vendors offering the same product. This makes it easy to determine which one offers the better price.

Another reason to use mail order is because it may be less expensive than the local vendors. Local vendors may have their stores in a fairly high-rent district; the mail-order people may be working out of their back bedroom.

In addition, local vendors have to buy their stock from a distributor. The distributor usually buys it from the manufacturer or a wholesaler. By the time you get the product, it may have passed through several companies who each have made some profit. Most of the direct marketers who advertise by mail have cut out the middlemen and passed their profit on to you.

Dell Computer has always been a direct marketer with no fancy showrooms or distributors. Because of this they were able to sell their products for less than IBM, Compaq, and some of the other large companies. But IBM and Compaq and several other large companies are now selling direct. The competition is great for us consumers.

Still another reason why I do a lot shopping by mail is because of state taxes. In California, the state sales tax is as much as 8.50 percent. If I buy a computer system in California for $1000, it will cost me about $85 just for sales taxes. Even if I have to pay shipping charges for mail order, it is usually much less than the sales tax. The states have tried several times to eliminate this loophole and make you pay taxes no matter where you buy, but so far they have been unsuccessful.

Even if they do succeed in taxing you for mail order, considering the advantages of mail order, it may be worth it to pay the extra taxes. I can order from home, which means I don't have to spend half a day fighting traffic to get to the store, then looking for a parking space. I can have mail order delivered directly to my door. If I am in a hurry, and don't mind paying a bit more, I can have it delivered the next day.

Without computer magazines, there would be no mail order, and without mail order, there would be no computer magazines. Ads are the lifeblood of magazines. The subscription price of a magazine doesn't even come close to paying for the mailing costs, so they must have ads to exist.

I don't mind ads. I look at most of them and learn what is available. But most of the magazines have become greedy in trying to see how many ads they can stuff into the magazine. Almost all of them now double the front and back cover and use them for ads. They also place several pages of ads before they list the table of contents. Sometimes it is very difficult to find the contents.

One company started buying several pages of heavy-stock paper and ran photos of cows and other things that have nothing to do with computers. I have no idea at all why it worked, but it is now one of the largest direct-mail companies. Other companies have noted the success and have emulated this company's ads. Any time that something is successful, other companies jump on the bandwagon. The whole idea of the stiff pages is to get you to notice their ads, make it stand out. These ads may stand out, but it makes it very difficult to leaf through a magazine with all the business reply cards and slick ads about cows. This type of advertising must work. Gateway, the company that started the business of stiff pages, is now one of the more successful vendors.

Sorry, advertisers, but the first thing I do when I pick up a magazine with all this heavy stiff page stuff is to tear the ads out and throw them away. They don't make me want to buy their product; they just irritate me.

Honest Ads

Most mail-order vendors are honest. But a few bad advertisers can ruin a magazine. *PC World* has a regular Consumer Watch column. If you have a problem with a mail-order vendor that you can't resolve, write to them. They can usually get it resolved. For *PC World* subscription information, call 800-234-3498. *PC World* is a very good magazine. They also have a very good Web site at www.pcworld.com. They have lots of ads on their site, free downloads, and articles from their magazine.

The magazines have formed the Microcomputer Marketing Council (MMC) of the Direct Marketing Association (6 East 43rd St., New York, NY 10017). They have an action line at 212-297-1393 and police the advertisers fairly closely.

Ordering by Mail

If you decide to order by mail, you should be sure of what you need and what you are ordering. Some of the ads aren't written very well and may not tell the whole story. Ads are expensive, so the advertiser may abbreviate or leave out a lot of important information. If possible, call them up and make sure. Ask what their return policy is for defective merchandise. Also ask how long before the item will be shipped. Be sure to ask for the current price. Again, ads are usually placed about two months before the magazines are delivered or hit the stands. The way prices are coming down, there could be quite a change in cost at the time you place your order. (Of course, if you send them the advertised price, I am sure that they will not refuse it.) A $2 or $3 phone call could save you a lot of time, trouble, grief, and maybe even some money.

Ten Rules for Ordering By Mail

Here are some brief rules that you should follow when ordering by mail:

Rule 1—Look for a street address.

Make sure the advertiser has a street address. In some ads, they give only a phone number. If you decide to buy from this vendor, call and verify that there is a live person on the other end with a street number. But before you send any money, do a bit more investigation. If possible, look through past issues of the same magazine for previous ads. If the company has advertised previously for several months, then the company is probably okay.

Rule 2—Compare other vendor prices.

Check through the magazines for other vendors' prices for this product. The prices should be fairly close. If it appears to be a bargain that is too good to be true, then you know the rest.

Rule 3—Buy from MMC members.

Buy from a vendor who is a member of the Microcomputer Marketing Council (MMC) of the Direct Marketing Association (DMA), or other recognized association. There are now about 10,000 members who belong to marketing associations. They have agreed to abide by the ethical guidelines and rules of the associations. Except for friendly persuasion and the threat of expulsion, the associations have little power over the members. But most of them realize what is at stake and put a great value on their membership. Most who advertise in the major computer magazines are members.

The Post Office, the Federal Trade Commission, the magazines, and the legitimate businesspeople who advertise have taken steps to try to stop the fraud and scams.

Rule 4—Do your homework.

Read the ads carefully. Advertising space is very expensive. Many ads use abbreviations and may not be entirely clear. If in doubt, call and ask. Know exactly what you want; state precisely the model, make, size, component, and any other pertinent information. Tell them which ad you are ordering from, and ask them if the price is the same, if the item is in stock, and when you can expect delivery. If the item is not in stock, indicate whether you will accept a substitute or want your money refunded. Ask for an invoice or order number. Ask the person's name. Write down all of the information, the time, the date, the company's address and phone number, a description of item, and the promised delivery date. Write down and save any telephone conversations, the time, the date, and the person's name. Save all correspondence.

Rule 5—Ask questions.

Ask if the advertised item comes with all the necessary cables, parts, accessories, software, and so on. Ask what the warranties are. Ask what is the seller's return policies and refund policies. Ask with whom should you correspond if there is a problem.

Rule 6—Don't send cash.

You will have no record of a cash transaction. If possible, use a credit card. If you have a problem, you can possibly have the bank refuse to pay the amount. A personal check may cause a delay of three to four weeks while the vendor waits for it to clear. A money order or credit card order should be filled and shipped immediately. Keep a copy of the money order.

Rule 7—Ask for delivery date.

If you have not received your order by the promised delivery date, notify the seller.

Rule 8—Try the item out as soon as you receive it.

If you have a problem, notify the seller immediately, by phone, then in writing. Give all details. Don't return the merchandise unless the dealer gives you a return material authorization (RMA). Make sure to keep a copy of the shipper's receipt or packing slip or some evidence that the material was returned.

Rule 9—What to do if it is defective.

If you believe the product is defective or you have a problem, reread your warranties and guarantees. Reread the manual and any documentation. It is very easy to make an error or misunderstand how an item operates if you are unfamiliar with it. Before you go to a lot of trouble, try to get some help from someone else. At least get someone to verify that you do have a problem. There are many times when a problem will disappear and the vendor will not be able to duplicate it. If possible, when you call try to have the item in your computer and be at the computer so you can describe the problem as it happens.

Rule 10—Try to work out your problem with the vendor.

If you cannot work out a solution with the vendor, then write to the consumer complaint agency in the seller's state. You should also write to the magazine and to the DMA, at 6 E. 43rd St., New York, NY 10017.

 # Federal Trade Commission Rules

Here is a brief summary of the FTC rules:

Rule 1—Must ship within 30 days.

The seller must ship your order within 30 days unless the ad clearly states that it will take longer.

Rule 2—Right to cancel.

If it appears that the seller cannot ship when promised, he or she must notify you and give a new date. The seller must give you the opportunity to cancel the order and refund your money if you desire.

Rule 3—Must notify if order can't be filled.

If the seller notifies you that your order cannot be filled on time, the seller must include a stamped self-addressed envelope or card so that you can respond to the notice. If you do not respond, the seller may assume that you agree to the delay. The seller still must ship within 30 days of the end of the original 30 days or cancel your order and refund your money.

Rule 4—Right to cancel if delayed.

Even if you consent to a delay, you still have the right to cancel at any time.

Rule 5—Must refund money if canceled.

If you cancel an order that has been paid for by check or money order, the seller must refund the money. If you paid by credit card, your account must be credited within one billing cycle. Store credits or vouchers in place of a refund are not acceptable.

Rule 6—No substitutions.

If the item you ordered is not available, the seller may not send you a substitute without your express consent.

Sources of Knowledge

As mentioned throughout this book, there are several good magazines that can help you gain the knowledge needed to make sensible purchases and to learn more about computers. These magazines usually carry interesting, timely, and informative articles and reviews of software and hardware. They also have many ads for computers, components, and software.

Some of the better magazines that you should subscribe to are *Computer Shopper*, *Byte*, *PC Computing*, *PC World*, and *PC Magazine*. Most of these magazines are available on local magazine racks; however, you will save money with a yearly subscription. Besides, they will be delivered to your door.

If you need a source of components, you only have to look in any of the magazines listed above to find hundreds of them. If you live near a large city, there will no doubt be several vendors who advertise in your local paper. Another source of computer information can be found in the several good computer books published by McGraw-Hill.

There are hundreds of computer and computer-related magazines. If you read every one of them, you still will not be able to keep up with the flood of computer information.

Recommended Computer Magazines

Here are just a few of the magazines that will help you keep abreast to some degree.

Audio-Forum
    96 Broad Street
    Guilford, CT 06437

Computer Currents
    5720 Hollis St.
    Emeryville, CA 94608

Computer Graphics World
    P.O. Box 122
    Tulsa, OK 74101-9966

Computer Life
    P.O. Box 55880
    Boulder, CO 80323-5880

Computer Shopper
    P.O. Box 51020
    Boulder, CO 80321-1020

Computer World
    P.O. Box 2044
    Marion, OH 43306-2144

Desktop Video World
    P.O. Box 594
    Mt. Morris, IL 61054-7902

Digital Imaging
    Micro Publishing
    21150 Hawthorne Bld. #104
    Torrance, CA 90503

Digital Video Magazine
P.O. Box 594
Mt. Morris, IL 61054-7902

Electronic Musician
P.O. Box 41525
Nashville, TN 37204-9829

EMedia Professional
462 Danbury Rd.
Wilton, CT 06897-2126
800-806-7795
e-mail:emediasub@onlineinc.com

Home Office Computing
P.O. Box 51344
Boulder, CO 80321-1344

Imaging Magazine
1265 Industrial Highway
Southampton, PA 18966
(800) 677-3435

Internet
P.O. Box 713
Mt. Morris, IL 61054-9965

KidSoft Magazine
718 University Ave. #112
Los Gatos, CA 95030-9958
800-354-6150

LAN Magazine
P.O. Box 50047
Boulder, CO 80321-0047

Maximum PC Magazine
www.maximumpcmag.com
800-274-3421

MicroTimes Magazine
5951 Canning St.
Oakland, CA 94609

Musician's Friend
P.O. Box 4520
Medford, OR 97501

National Association of Desktop Publishers
P.O. Box 11668
Riverton, NJ 08076-7268

Nuts & Volts
430 Princeland Ct.
Corona, CA 91719-1343

PC Computing
P.O. Box 50253
Boulder, CO 80321-0253

PC Magazine
P.O. Box 51524
Boulder, CO 80321-1524

PC Novice
P.O. Box 85380
Lincoln, NE 68501-9807

PC Today
P.O. Box 85380
Lincoln, NE 68501-5380

PC World Magazine
P.O. Box 51833
Boulder, CO 80321-1833

Publish
P.O. Box 51966
Boulder, CO 80321-1966

Repair, Service & Remarketing News
P.O. Box 670
Joplin, MO 64802-0670
(417) 781-9317
Fax (417) 781-0427

Video Magazine
Box 56293
Boulder, CO 80322-6293
(800) 365-1008

Videomaker Magazine
P.O. 469026
Escondido, CA 92046
(800) 334-8152

Virtual City
 P.O. Box 3007
 Livingston, NJ 07039-9922

Virtual Reality
 P.O. Box 7703
 San Francisco, CA 94120
 415-905-2563

Voice Processing Magazine
 P.O. Box 6016
 Duluth, MN 55806-9797

Windows Magazine
 P.O. Box 58649
 Boulder, CO 80322-8649

Free Magazines for Qualified Subscribers

The magazines listed below as free are sent only to qualified subscribers. The subscription price of a magazine usually does not come anywhere near covering the costs of publication, mailing, distribution, and so on. Most magazines depend almost entirely on advertisers for their existence. The more subscribers that a magazine has, the more it can charge for its ads. Naturally, they can attract a lot more subscribers if the magazine is free.

PC Week and *InfoWorld* are excellent magazines. They are so popular that the publishers have to limit the number of subscribers. They cannot possibly accommodate all the people who have applied. They have set standards that have to be met in order to qualify. They do not publish the standards, so even if you answer all of the questions on the application, you still may not qualify.

To get a free subscription, you must write to the magazine for a qualifying application form. Or if you attend one of the larger computer shows such as COMDEX, they will have free samples and qualifying forms. The form will ask questions such as how you are involved with computers, the company you work for, whether you have any influence in purchasing the computer products listed in the magazines, and several others that give them a very good profile of potential readers.

I wouldn't tell you to lie, but it might help you qualify if you exaggerate just a bit here and there—especially when it asks what your responsibilities are for the purchasing of computer equipment. I am pretty sure that they will not send the FBI out to verify your answers.

One way to qualify for most of these free magazines is to become a consultant. There are very few rules and regulations as to who can call themselves a consultant. (You should be particularly aware of this fact if you decide to hire one.)

The list of magazines below is not nearly complete. There are hundreds of trade magazines that are sent free to qualified subscribers. The Cahners Company alone publishes 32 different trade magazines. Many of the trade magazines are highly technical and narrowly specialized.

Advanced Imaging
445 Broad Hollow Rd.
Melville, NY 11747-4722

Automatic I.D. News
P.O. Box 6158
Duluth, MN 55806-9870

AV Video Production &
Presentation
Technology
701 Westchester Ave.
White Plains, NY 10604
914-328-9157

Beyond Computing, An IBM
Magazine
1133 Westchester Ave.
White Plains, NY 10604

Communications Week
P.O. Box 2070
Manhasset, NY 11030

Computer Products
P.O. Box 14000
Dover, NJ 07801-9990

Computer Reseller News
P.O. Box 2040
Manhasset, NY 11030

Computer Systems News
600 Community Dr.
Manhasset, NY 11030

Computer Tech. Review
924 Westwood Blvd. #65
Los Angeles, CA 90024

Computer Telephony
P.O. Box 40706
Nashville, TN 37204-9919
800-677-3435

Data Communications
P.O. Box 477
Hightstown, NJ 08520-9362

Datamation
P.O. Box 7530
Highlands Ranch, CO
80163-9130

Document Management &
Windows Imaging
8711 E. Pinnacle Peak Road,
#249
Scottsdale, AZ 85255

EE Product News
P.O. Box 12982
Overland Park, KS 66212

Electronic Design
P.O. Box 985007
Cleveland, OH 44198-5007

Electronic Manufacturing
P.O. Box 159
Libertyville, IL 60048

Electronic Publishing and Printing
650 S. Clark St.
Chicago, IL 60605-9960

Electronic Publishing
P.O. Box 3493
Tulsa, OK 74101-9640

Electronics
P.O. Box 985061
Cleveland, OH 44198

Enterprise Systems Journal
P.O. Box 3051
Northbrook, IL 60065-3051

Federal Computer Week
P.O. Box 602
Winchester, MA 01890

ID Systems
P.O. Box 874
Peterborough, NH 03458

Identification Journal
2640 N. Halsted St.
Chicago, IL 60614-9962

Imaging Business
P.O. Box 5360
Pittsfield, MA 01203-9788

Information Week
www.informationweek.com
800-292-3642

InfoWorld
P.O. Box 1172
Skokie, IL 60076

Lan Times
122 East, 1700 South
Provo, UT 84606

Lasers & Optronics
301 Gibraltar Dr.
Morris Plains, NJ 07950

Managing Office Technology
1100 Superior Ave.
Cleveland, OH 44197-8092

Manufacturing Systems
P.O. Box 3008
Wheaton, IL 60189-9972

Medical Equipment Designer
29100 Aurora Rd., #200
Cleveland, OH 44139

Micro Publishing News
21150 Hawthorne Blvd. #104
Torrance, CA 90503

Mini-Micro Systems
P.O. Box 5051
Denver, CO 80217-9872

Mobile Office
Subscription Department
P.O. Box 57268
Boulder, CO 80323-7268

Modern Office Technology
1100 Superior Ave.
Cleveland, OH 44197-8032

Mr CDRom
Maxmedia Distributing Inc.
P.O. Box 1087
Winter Garden, FL 34787

Network Computing
P.O. Box 1095
Skokie, IL 60076-9662

Network World
161 Worcester Rd.
Framingham, MA 01701
508-875-6400

New Media Magazine
P.O. Box 1771
Riverton, NJ 08077-7331
415-573-5170

Office Systems
P.O. Box 3116
Woburn, MA 01888-9878

Office Systems Dealer
P.O. Box 2281
Woburn, MA 01888-9873

PC Week
P.O. Box 1770
Riverton, NJ 08077-7370

Photo Business
1515 Broadway
New York, NY 10036

Photo Lab Management
P.O. Box 1700
Santa Monica, CA 90406-1700

The Programmer's Shop
5 Pond Park Rd.
Hingham, MA 02043-9845

Reseller Management
Box 601
Morris Plains, NJ 07950

Scientific Computing
301 Gibraltar Dr.
Morris Plains, NJ 07950

Software Magazine
Westborough Office Park
1900 West Park Dr.
Westborough, MA 01581-3907

Speech Technology Magazine
CI Publishing
43 Danbury Rd.
Wilton, CT 06897-9729
203-834-1430

Sun Expert
P.O. Box 5274
Pittsfield, MA 01203-9479

Telecommunications
P.O. Box 850949
Braintree, MA 02185

▬ ▬ Component and Software Catalogs

Several companies publish special catalogs for components and software through direct mail. Even IBM has gotten into the act. You should be aware that most of these companies charge a bit more than those who advertise in the major magazines. But ads cost a lot of money, so there usually isn't too much information about an advertised product in the magazines. The direct-mail-order companies usually have room in their catalogs to give a fairly good description and lots of information about the product. The catalogs are free. Here are just a few:

Arlington Computer Products
800-548-5105

Black Box Corporation
P.O. Box 12800
Pittsburgh, PA 15241

Compute Ability
P.O. Box 17882
Milwaukee, WI 53217

Computers & Music
647 Mission St.
San Francisco, CA 94105

DAMARK
800-729-9000

DataCom Mall
800-898-3282

Digi-key Corporation
701 Brooks Ave. South
P.O. Box 677
Thief River Falls, MN
56701-0677

Data Comm Warehouse
800-328-2261

Dell Network & Communications
800-509-3355

DellWare
800-449-3355

Digital PCs Catalog
800-642-4532

DTP Direct
800-890-9030

Edmund Scientific Company
101 E. Gloucester Pike
Barrington, NJ 08007-1380

Edutainment Catalog
(mostly kids software)
800-338-3844

Egghead Software
800-344-4323

GlobalComputer
Suppliers
2318 East Del Amo Blvd.
Dept. 64
Compton, CA 90220
800-845-6225

ELEK-TEK
800-395-1000

Global DataCom
800-440-4832

Global Industrial Equipment
800-645-1232

Hello Direct (Telephone products)
800-444-3556

IBM PC Direct
800-426-2968

Image Club Graphics
800-387-9193

JDR Microdevices
2233 Samaritan Drive
San Jose, CA 95124

KidSoft Software Catalog
800-354-6150

MEI/Micro Center
800-634-3478

MicroWarehouse
1720 Oak Street
P.O. Box 3014
Lakewood, NJ 08701-3014

Momentum Graphics Inc.
16290 Shoemaker
Cerritos, CA 90701-2243

Multimedia World
P.O. Box 58690
Boulder, CO 80323-8690

One Network Place
4711 Golf Road
Skokie, IL 60076

Paper Catalog
205 Chubb Ave.
Lyndhurst, NJ 07071

Pasternack Enterprises
P.O. 16759
Irvine, CA 92713

PC Connection
6 Mill Street
Marlow, NH 03456

PC Mall
  800-555-6255

PCs Compleat
  800-385-4522

Personal Computing Tools
  90 Industrial Park Road
  Hingham, MA 02043

Power Up!
  800-851-2917

PrePress
  11 Mt. Pleasant Ave.
  East Hanover, NJ 07936-9925

Presentations
  Lakewood Building
  50 South Ninth Street
  Minneapolis, MN 55402-9973

Projections
  P.O. Business Park Drive
  Branford, CT 06405

Software Spectrum
  800-787-1166

South Hills Datacomm
  760 Beechnut Drive
  Pittsburgh, PA 15205

TENEX Computer Express
  56800 Magnetic Drive
  Mishawaka, IN 46545

TigerSoftware
  800-888-4437

Unixreview
  P.O. Box 420035
  Palm Coast, FL 32142-0035

Public Domain and Shareware Software

There are several companies who provide public-domain, shareware, and low-cost software. They also publish catalogs listing their software. Some may charge a small fee for the catalog. Here are a few of them.

Computer Discount Warehouse	800-330-4CDW
The Computer Room	703-832-3341
Computers International	619-630-0055
Industrial Computer Source	800-523-2320
International Software Library	800-992-1992
J&R Computer World	800-221-8180
Jameco Electronic Components	415-592-8097
MicroCom Systems	408-737-9000
Micro Star	800-443-6103
MMI Corporation	800-221-4283

National PD Library	619-941-0925
Numeridex	800-323-7737
PC Plus Consulting	818-891-7930
PC-Sig 1030D	800-245-6717
The PC Zone	800-258-2088
PrePress Direct	800-443-6600
PsL News	800-242-4775 (cost $24 year)
Public Brand Software	800-426-3475
Selective Software	800-423-3556
Shareware Express	800-346-2842
Software Express/Direct	800-331-8192
Softwarehouse	408-748-0461
Zenith Data Systems	800-952-3099

Computer Books

There are several companies who publish computer books. One of the larger companies is McGraw-Hill (800-262-4729). They also have an online bookstore at www.mcgraw-hill.com/books.html. They have over 9000 titles available in many different categories. It is easy to search for any title or type of book. Computer books from Osborne/McGraw-Hill are also listed there, or you can call them at 800-227-0900. Call them for a current catalog listing of the many books that they publish. I admit that I am a bit prejudiced when it comes to McGraw-Hill books, but I recommend them highly.

You may also access and search the thousands of books at the Amazon online bookstore at www.amazon.com or Barnes and Noble at www.barnesandnoble.com. These stores both claim to be the world's largest online bookstores. They carry all of my books—just do an author search on Aubrey Pilgrim.

20

Troubleshooting and Repairing Your PC

This is one of the longest chapters in this book, but I must tell you that you may not be able to find the answer to your problems here. There are a thousand and one things that can go wrong in a computer, in both hardware and software. This chapter could be 10 times as long and still not cover every possible problem. However, we will cover most of the major problems that you may experience.

When they hear the word "troubleshooting," most people think of hardware problems. But I have had far more trouble with software than with hardware. Software problems may be even more difficult to solve than hardware problems.

Windows 98 can help solve some problems. When I built my 200MHz Pentium Pro, rather than buy all new components, I just upgraded my old 60MHz Pentium. I had two hard disks in the unit: a Maxtor 540MB IDE and a 1.05GB Seagate SCSI. When I attached all of the components to the Pentium Pro motherboard on the benchtop, they all worked perfectly. But when I installed the components in the case and tried to boot up, the Windows 98 screen came up and froze. I rechecked all of my cable connections, made sure that the boards were seated, then tried again to boot up. Again, it got as far as the Windows 98 screen, then froze.

I turned off the power and this time pressed F8 as it was booting up. Out of the options that came up, I chose number 5, "Step-by-step confirmation." This displays each line of the CONFIG.SYS and asks whether you want to load it or not. When it got to the line that loaded my SCSI driver, the system hung up again. So I knew that it must be either my Toshiba CD-ROM or my Seagate hard drive. I disconnected them both, and the system booted perfectly. I then reconnected the CD-ROM, and it booted perfectly. I then switched the connector from the CD-ROM to the hard disk, and it hung again. So evidently, something happened to the hard disk during the time I disconnected it on the bench and installed it in the case.

Of course I was disappointed. I had paid over $700 for this SCSI drive four years ago. I wasn't too concerned about the data on the drive because I had it all backed up on the Maxtor IDE drive. (That is the beauty of having at least two large hard drives.)

I called the Seagate customer service center at 800-468-3472 and was pleasantly surprised to learn that I had a five-year guarantee on this drive. All I had to do was send it in and they would either repair or replace it. A couple of weeks later, they sent me a new drive. Of course, since it was a different drive, none of my data was on it. There was no note or indication as to what the problem had been.

The F8 utility of Windows 95/98 is an excellent tool. Without it, I might not have been able to figure out what was wrong. There are other times when one of my computers will not boot up. But it will usually boot if I use the F8 key and load each item in my CONFIG.SYS and AUTOEXEC.BAT files. I usually expect to see it hang on one of the files or device drivers, but it doesn't. There is probably a good reason why it won't boot normally, but even after 30 years in electronics, I have to admit that there is a whole lot that I do not know.

Finding the cause of the problem is the first step in fixing it. There are several hardware and software diagnostic tools available that can help you find and fix the problems. A few of them will be discussed.

Computer Basics

Troubleshooting will be a little easier if you know just a few electronics basics. Computers are possible because of electricity. Under the control of software and hardware, small electric on/off signal voltages are formed when we type from the keyboard or when data is read from a disk or other input device. This voltage is used to turn transistors on and off to perform various tasks.

An electric charge is formed when there is an imbalance or an excess amount of electrons at one pole. The excess electrons will flow through whatever path they can find to get to the other pole. It is much like water flowing downhill to find its level.

Most electric or electronic paths have varying amounts of resistance, so work or heat is created when the electrons pass through them. For instance, if a flashlight is turned on, electrons will pass through the bulb, which has a resistive filament. The heat generated by the electrons passing through the bulb will cause the filament to glow red-hot and create light. If the light is left on for a period of time, the excess electrons from the negative pole of the battery will pass through the bulb to the positive pole of the battery. Electrons will continue to flow until the amount of electrons at the negative and positive poles are equal. At this time there will be a perfect balance, and the battery will be dead.

A computer is made up of circuits and boards that have resistors, capacitors, inductors, transistors, motors, and many other components. These components perform a useful function when electricity passes through them. The circuits are designed so that the paths of the electric currents are divided, controlled, and shunted to do the work that we want done. The transistors and other components can force the electrons to go to the memory, to a disk drive, to the printer, or wherever the software and hardware directs it to go.

If an electronic circuit is designed properly, it should last several lifetimes. Unlike an electron tube, which has filaments that burn out, there is nothing in a semiconductor or transistor to wear out. But occasionally, too many electrons may find their way through a weakened component and cause it to heat up and burn out. Or for some reason the electrons may be shunted through a path or component where it shouldn't go. This may cause an intermittent, a partial, or a complete failure.

Electrostatic Voltage

Before you touch any electronic component or handle them, you should ground yourself and discharge any electrostatic voltage that may have built up on your body. It is possible for a person to build up a charge of 4000 volts or more of electrostatic voltage. If you walk across a carpet and then touch a brass doorknob, you may see a spark fly and get a painful shock. If you should touch a fragile electronic component, this high voltage can be discharged through the component. It may weaken the component or possibly ruin it.

Most workers in electronic assembly lines wear a ground strap whenever they are working with any electrostatic-discharge-sensitive components. You can discharge yourself by touching an unpainted metal part of the case of a computer or other device that is plugged into a wall socket. The computer or other grounding device does not have to be turned on in order to discharge yourself.

Document the Problem

Chances are, if a computer is going to break down, it will do it so at the most inopportune time. This is one of the basic tenets of Murphy's immutable and inflexible laws.

If it breaks down, try not to panic. Ranting, cussing, and crying may make you feel better, but it won't solve the problem. Instead, get out a pad and pencil and write down everything as it happens. It is very easy to forget. Write down all the particulars—how the cables were plugged in, the software that was running, and anything that might be pertinent. You may get error messages on your screen. Use the PrtSc (for Print Screen) key to print out the messages if possible.

If you can't solve the problem, you may have to call someone or your vendor for help. If you have all the written information before you, it will help. Try to call from your computer, if possible, as it is acting up. If it is a software problem, have your serial number handy. Most organizations ask for that before anything else.

Instruments and Tools

For high levels of troubleshooting, you would need some sophisticated tools and expensive instruments to do a thorough analysis of a system, including a good high-frequency oscilloscope, a digital analyzer, a logic probe, and several other expensive pieces of gear. You would also need a test bench with a spare power supply, spare disk drives, and plug-in boards.

Having a diagnostic card, such as the POST-PROBE or the Ultra-X, along with several of the diagnostic and utility software programs (discussed later in this chapter) would be helpful. It would also be helpful to have a known-good computer with some empty slots so that you could plug in suspect boards and test them.

For high-level work, you would also need a voltohmmeter, some clip leads, a pair of side-cutter dikes, a pair of long-nose pliers, various screwdrivers, nutdrivers, a soldering iron, and solder. In addition, you would need a good workbench with plenty of light over the bench, along with a flashlight or a small light to light up the dark places in the computer case.

Besides the expensive tools and instruments needed for high-level troubleshooting and repair, you would need quite a lot of training and experience.

Fortunately, we don't need the expensive and sophisticated tools and instruments for most of our computer problems. Just a few simple tools and a little common sense is all that is needed for the majority of the problems. Here are some tools that you should have around:

1. You should have a pad and pen near your computer so that you can write down all of the things that happen if you have a problem.

2. You should have several sizes and types of screwdrivers. A couple of them should be magnetic for picking up and starting small screws. You can buy magnetic screwdrivers, or you can make one yourself. Just take a strong magnet and rub it on the blade of the screwdriver a few times. (The magnets on cabinet doors will do, or the voice coil magnet of a loudspeaker.) Be very careful with any magnet around your floppy diskettes. It can erase them.

3. You should have a couple pairs of pliers, including at least one pair of long-nose pliers.

4. You should have a set of nutdrivers. Many of the screws have slotted heads for screwdrivers as well as hexagonal heads for nutdrivers. Using a nutdriver is usually much easier to use than a screwdriver.

5. You may need a pair of side-cutter dikes for clipping leads of components and cutting wire. You might buy a pair of cutters that also have wire strippers.

6. By all means, buy a voltohmmeter. There are dozens of uses for this device. It can be used to check for the wiring continuity in your cables, phone lines, switches, and so on. You can also use a voltohmmeter to check for the proper voltages in your computer. There are only two voltages to check for: 12V and 5V. The newer CPUs require from 2.2 to 3.3V, but usually a voltage regulator on the motherboard or on the CPU socket reduces the 5V supply to the required voltage.

   You can buy a relatively inexpensive voltohmmeter at any Radio Shack or other electronics store.

7. You will need a soldering iron and some solder. You shouldn't have to do much soldering, but you never know when you may need to repair a cable or perform some other minor job.

8. You should also have several clip leads. Clip leads are insulated wires with alligator clips on each end. You can use them to extend a cable or for shorting out two pins or for hundreds of other uses. You can buy them at the local Radio Shack or electronics store.

9. You need a flashlight for looking into the dark places inside the computer or at the cable connections behind the computer.

The chances are very slim that you will ever need these tools unless you are in the repair business. Even then, there will be very few times when you will have to use some of them. Still, it is nice to have them available if you ever do need them.

Solving Common Problems

For many of the common problems, you won't need a lot of test gear. Often a problem can be solved by using our five senses—eyes, ears, nose, touch, and taste. (Actually, we won't be using our taste very often.)

Eyes If we look closely, we can see a cable that is not plugged in properly. Or a board that is not completely seated. Or a switch or jumper that is not set properly. And we can see many other obvious things such as smoke.

Ears We can use our ears for any unusual sounds. Ordinarily, those little electrons don't make any noise as they move through your computer at about two-thirds of the speed of light. The only sound from your computer should be the noise of your drive motors and the fan in the power supply.

Smell If you have ever smelled a burned resistor or a capacitor, you will never forget it. If you smell something very unusual, try to locate where it is coming from.

Touch If you touch the components and some seem to be unusually hot, it could be the cause of your problem. Except for the insides of your power supply, there should not be any voltage above 12V in your computer, so it should be safe to touch the components, even when the power is on. Before touching a component, be sure that you have discharged yourself of any electrostatic voltage.

The Number-One Cause of Problems

If you have added something to your computer or done some sort of repair and the computer doesn't work, something may not have been plugged in correctly or some minor error was made in the installations. If you have added a component, remove it to see if the computer works without it. Never install more than one item at a time. Install an item, then check to see if it works, then install the next one.

By far the greatest problem in assembling a unit, adding something to a computer, or installing software is not following the instructions. Quite often it is not necessarily the fault of the person trying to follow the instructions. I am a member of Mensa, and have worked in the electronics industry for over 30 years. But sometimes I have great difficulty in trying to decipher and follow the instructions in some manuals. Sometimes a very critical instruction or piece of information may be inconspicuously buried in the middle of a 500-page manual.

The Importance of Documentation

You should have some sort of documentation or manuals for all of your computer components and peripherals. You should have a written record of the switch and jumper settings of each of your boards. You should also know what components are inside your computer and how they are configured. The Plug-and-Play components now make it a lot easier, but there are still a lot of items that do not conform to the PnP specifications.

Norton Utilities lets you make a rescue disk that has a copy of your CMOS, boot record, partition tables, AUTOEXEC.BAT, and CONFIG.SYS. This disk is bootable, so it can be used anytime that you may lose your CMOS or any of the other vital information.

What to Do If Your Computer Is Completely Dead

Several software diagnostic programs are available. They are great in many cases. But if the computer is completely dead, the software won't do you any good. If it is completely dead, the first thing to do is to check the power outlet. If you don't have a voltmeter, plug a lamp into the same socket and see if it lights. Check your power cord and the switch on the computer. Then check the fan in the power supply. Is it turning? The power supply is one of the major components that frequently becomes defective. If the fan is not turning, the power supply may be defective. However, the fan may be operating even though the power supply is defective. Do any of the panel lights come on when you try to boot up? Does the hard disk motor spin up?

If there is a short anywhere in the system, the power supply will not come on. The fan won't turn, and none of the drives will come on. The power supply has built-in short-circuit protection, which shuts everything down when the output is shorted. The power supply has four or more cables for the various drives. Unplug the drives one at a time and try the system. If the system works after a drive is unplugged, then you have found the problem. (I hate to say this, but I am pretty sure that one of Murphy's laws dictates that a problem will never be this easy to solve.)

Memory Problems

The SIMM and DIMM chips are very easy to install; however, it is possible to have a module that is not seated properly. If this happens, the computer may not boot up. The screen may be completely blank with no error messages or any indication of the problem.

Cables

You can check any of the cables from the power supply with a voltohmmeter. The power supply will not work unless it has a load, so have at least one disk drive plugged in. There should be +12V between the yellow and black wires and +5V between the red and black. If there is no voltage, then you probably have a defective power supply.

If you hear the fan motor and the panel lights come on but the monitor is dark, check the monitor's power cord, the adapter cable, and the adapter. The monitor also has fuses, but they are usually inside the monitor case. Check the documentation that came with your monitor. You should also check the monitor's brightness and contrast controls. If you have just installed the monitor, check the motherboard or adapter for any switches or jumpers that should be set. In addition, check the documentation of your adapter board. You should also check your CMOS setup to make sure that the BIOS knows what type of monitor you have.

Remove all of the boards except for the monitor adapter and disk controller. Also disconnect all peripherals. If the system works, then add the boards back until it stops. Be sure to turn off the power each time you add or remove a board or any cable. If you have spare boards, swap them out with suspect boards in your system.

CONFIG.SYS and AUTOEXEC.BAT

In the DOS era, you could see your AUTOEXEC.BAT working during bootup. In Windows 98 it is now usually hidden, but it is still working just as it did before. If you have just added a new piece of software and your system doesn't work or it doesn't work the way it should, check your AUTOEXEC.BAT and CONFIG.SYS files. Many programs change these files as they are being installed. These files may have commands and statements that conflict with your new software or system. I try out a lot of different software and systems and have had problems where a statement or command was left in the AUTOEXEC.BAT or CONFIG.SYS file from a system no longer being used. It may ask the computer to perform a command that is not there. It will go off in never-never land and keep trying to find the command or file. You will usually have to reboot to get out.

In Windows 98, you can edit your AUTOEXEC.BAT, CONFIG.SYS, or WIN.INI files by clicking on Start, then Run, then typing SYSEDIT. All of the systems files will be displayed in tiled fashion. Just click on any one in order to edit it.

By pressing F8 while booting up, Windows 95/98 will let you look at each line of the AUTOEXEC.BAT and CONFIG.SYS file and will ask if you want to load it, yes or no. If you say no to a certain line and the system then works, you have found the problem. You can then use the EDIT command and put a REM in front of the offending line in your AUTOEXEC.BAT or CONFIG.SYS file and then see if it works. If so, then you can delete the line or just leave it as a REM just in case you may need it later.

You should always have a "clean" boot disk that has a very lean AUTOEXEC.BAT and CONFIG.SYS on it.

Clearing TSRs from Memory

Windows 98 often loads lots of things in memory and you may not even know it. Quite often when you install a new program, it will set itself so that it will be loaded automatically in memory. As mentioned earlier in the book, such programs are called terminate-and-stay-resident programs, or TSRs. Sometimes the name of the program or its icon may be displayed on the bar at the bottom of the screen. To see what programs are loaded in your memory, press the Ctrl+Alt+Del keys. A list of anything loaded in memory will be displayed. Use the arrow keys or mouse to highlight anything that you don't want to be loaded, then press the Enter key, and it will be deleted from memory.

Microsoft Explorer will always be loaded. You cannot delete it. If you do, the system will shut down.

Windows Start

I recently installed a new larger hard drive with more partitions. In copying the files from the old disk to the new one, some of the files got copied to a different partition. When I booted up my system, I got a message that there was a problem with a shortcut. All I had to do was click OK, and the system would continue to boot up. But it was a bother. I didn't use that program very often, so I just uninstalled it from my hard disk. Uninstalling the program, however, did not uninstall the shortcut. I finally clicked on the Start button and then clicked on Settings, then on Taskbar, then on Start Menu Programs, then on Advanced, and then on Start Menu. I then highlighted the offending shortcut and deleted it.

Drive C:

Every program that you install on your computer will want to be loaded on drive C:. That is the default built into most software. Often you are given the option to install the program on another drive, but a newbie may not realize this. (A newbie is someone new to computers, to the Internet, or almost anything new. It is not meant as a put-down.) If you allow the programs to be loaded on C:, it will soon be completely filled unless you have a very large C: drive.

If you install Windows 98 on your C: drive, it will take up about 80MB, but it doesn't stop there. Every time you load in a new program, even on another drive or in another directory, a large amount of Windows control data will be added to the Windows 98 directory. It is much like the old story about the Arab and his camel: It was a cold night on the desert, but the Arab was nice and warm in his tent. The camel asked his master if he could just put his nose in the tent. The master agreed. But then the camel complained that his head was cold, and could he please put his head in the tent. Again the master agreed. The camel kept it up, and soon his entire body was in the tent and the master was outside.

I have a scan program that will not run unless I have at least 10MB of free space on my C: drive. There are times when Netscape will not let me access some Web sites because I do not have enough free space on one of my computer's C: drive. Therefore, when you set up and format a new drive, make sure that you have a large C: drive. If you have a hard drive of 10GB or more, I would recommend a C: drive of at least 5GB.

If your system is already set up and you are running out of free space, you can try to copy some of the programs to another drive or directory. It will work best if you are able then to uninstall the program and reinstall it. Many of the later programs now come with the uninstall feature. Uninstall clears out all of the hidden portions of the program that is intertwined with Windows 98. Not many of the older programs had the uninstall feature.

Beep Error Codes

Every time a computer is booted up, it does a power-on self test (POST). It checks the RAM, the floppy drives, the hard disk drives, the monitor, the printer, the keyboard, and other peripherals that you have installed. If everything is okay, it gives a short beep, then boots up.

If it does not find a unit, or if the unit is not functioning correctly, it will beep and display an error code. It may beep two or more times depending on the error. If the power supply, the motherboard, the CPU, or possibly some other critical integrated circuit (IC) is defective, it may not beep at all. You can check the beep system by holding a key down while the system is booting up. You may hear a continuous beep. After the boot is complete, the system may give two short beeps and display the message, "Keyboard error. Press F1 to continue."

There are several other beep error codes that are in the system BIOS. Each BIOS manufacturer may use slightly different codes for some of the errors it finds. Some of the beep codes are for fatal errors, which cause the system to hang up completely. The beeps will be arranged so that you may get a beep, a pause, another beep, then three beeps close together, or 1-1-3. This code would indicate that there was a failure in the CMOS setup system. One long and two short beeps, accompanied by a POST code of 400, 500, 2400, or 7400, could mean that there is an error in the CMOS RAM or a motherboard switch setting, or it could indicate a defective video card. A 1-1-4 would indicate that there was an error in the BIOS itself. A continuous beep or repeating short beeps could indicate that the power supply or the motherboard has a fault.

Here are some of the AMI BIOS fatal error beep POST codes:

1 short   DRAM refresh failure

2 short   Parity circuit failure

3 short   Base 64KB RAM failure

4 short   System timer failure

5 short   Processor failure

6 short   Keyboard controller Gate A20 error

7 short   Virtual mode exception error

8 short   Display memory read/write test failure

9 short   ROM BIOS checksum failure

10 short   CMOS shutdown read/write error

11 short   Cache memory error

Here are a couple of non-fatal error beep POST codes:

1 long, 3 short   Conventional or extended memory failure

1 long, 8 short   Display/retrace test failed

Displayed POST Codes

Besides the beep POST codes, there are hundreds of POST codes that may be displayed. The POST codes start with 100 and may go up to as high as 200,000. This does not mean that there are actually 200,000 separate codes. Most of the BIOS designers arrange the codes in blocks. For instance, the 100s have to do with the motherboard errors; 200s with RAM errors; 300s with keyboard errors; 600s with floppy drive errors. Many of the code numbers were designed for systems that are now obsolete, such as the 286 and PS/2. Ordinarily, the codes will not be displayed if there is no problem. If there is a problem, the last two digits of the code will be something other than 00s.

Each BIOS manufacturer develops their own codes, so there are some slight differences, but most of them are similar to the following:

101   Motherboard failure

109   Direct Memory Access test error

121   Unexpected hardware interrupt occurred

163   Time and date not set

199	User indicated configuration not correct
201	Memory test failure
301	Keyboard test failure or a stuck key
401	Monochrome display and/or adapter test failure
432	Parallel printer not turned on
501	Color graphics display and/or adapter test failure
601	Diskette drives and/or adapter test failure
701	Math coprocessor test error
901	Parallel printer adapter test failure
1101	Asynchronous communications adapter test failure
1301	Game control adapter test failure
1302	Joystick test failure
1401	Printer test failure
1701	Fixed disk drive and/or adapter test failure
2401	Enhanced graphics display and/or adapter test failure
2501	Enhanced graphics display and/or adapter test failure

POST Cards

Several companies have developed diagnostic cards or boards that can be plugged into a slot on the motherboard to display the POST codes. If there is a failure in the system, it can tell you immediately what is wrong. If you have eliminated the possibility of a defective plug-in board or a peripheral, then the problem is probably in your motherboard. If the power supply is okay, you could use a diagnostic card such as the POST-PROBE from Micro 2000 (818-547-0125), or the R.A.C.E.R. II from Ultra-X (800-722-3789). (R.A.C.E.R. is an acronym for Real-time AT/XT Computer Equipment Repair.) These two cards are quite similar in the tests that they perform. They can be plugged into a computer that is completely dead except for the power supply, and they will check every chip and component on the motherboard. Each card has a small digital display that lights up a code for the condition of each component.

There are several other POST cards on the market, but some of them are not very sophisticated. The Ultra-X R.A.C.E.R. II has several ROMs that can run over 70 diagnostic tests. Besides displaying the test codes on the plug-in board, the progress of the tests can be displayed on a monitor. If there is a failure in one of the tests, a fault tree will appear that lists, in order, which chips might be at fault. In a computer where several chips interact, it is often difficult to determine exactly which chip might be the problem. The Ultra-X can narrow it down to a very few. At the end of the test, a report can be printed out.

Businesses can lose a lot of money when a computer is down. These diagnostic cards are tools that every professional repair shop and every computer maintenance department should have. It might also be well worth the money for an individual to buy one. If you have to take your computer to a repair shop, at $50 to $100 an hour, the repair could be rather expensive. You will also have to give up some of your time just to take the computer in to the shop. If the shop is busy, it may be some time before you get your computer back.

Diagnostic and Utility Software

Several excellent diagnostic software programs are available. Some of the utilities and tests are quite similar from program to program. Most of them test and report on your system configuration and your system memory. Many perform tests on your hard drives for preventive mainte- nance. Windows 95/98 can do a surface test of your hard disk.

Most BIOS chips have many diagnostic routines and other utilities built in. These routines allow you to set the time and date, tell the com- puter what type of hard drive and floppies that are installed, and specify the amount of memory, the wait states, and several other items. The AMI and DTK BIOS chips have a very comprehensive set of built-in diagnostics. They can allow hard and floppy disk formatting, check the speed of rotation of disk drives, do performance testing of hard drives, and perform several other tests.

Norton Utilities

Norton Utilities from Symantec Corporation (408-253-9600, or www.symantec.com) includes several diagnostic and test programs and essential utilities. One of the programs is Norton Diagnostics (NDIAGS). This tests the memory, the CPU, the DMA controllers, the real-time clock, the CMOS, and the serial and parallel ports.

Software cannot recognize and test the serial and parallel ports unless you have a loopback plug installed. These are 9- and 25-pin connectors that plug into the serial and parallel sockets. Some of the pins in these connectors are shorted out so that the software can recognize them.

The Norton System Works has all the standard utilities, most of which are periodically updated and improved with new releases. Some of the standard utilities are Unerase, Disk Doctor, Disk Test, Format Recover, Directory Sort, and System Information. It also has a very good virus-detection utility.

MicroScope

MicroScope, from Micro 2000 (818-547-0125, or www.micro2000.com) is an excellent diagnostic software tool. It can test the CPU, IRQs, DMAs, memory, hard disk drives, floppy drives, video adapters, and much more. It can search for Network cards and display its I/O and node address. It shows IRQ and I/O addresses and tests memory, displaying available memory space. It also displays CMOS contents and will let you run CMOS setup. In addition, it can run video tests for memory and character sets and perform a read, write, and random seek test of the hard drives. It will even allow you to edit sectors of the hard drive.

MicroScope can be set up to run any or all of the tests continuously. It can be set to halt on an error or to log the error and continue.

CheckIt

CheckIt from TouchStone has long been one of the better diagnostic tools. They have recently revised and improved the programs. Here is some information from their Web site at www.touchstonesoftware.com:

CheckIt version 5 for Windows 98 and CheckIt Professional Edition, the first ever 32-bit hardware troubleshooting utilities, are designed to meet the emerging needs of today's computer users and professional technicians. CheckIt empowers users of all levels by providing powerful tools to help pinpoint and solve computer problems, backup and restore critical system files, install new hardware components, uncover hidden conflicts, and optimize system performance quickly and easily.

CheckIt version 5 features a new approach to troubleshooting that finds problems, and leads the user directly to the tools that can provide the solution. First, QuickCheck tests and locates problems automatically. If a problem is detected, whether it is a hardware glitch, setup conflict, or change in performance, the program's exclusive Troubleshooter guides the user to the tests and information needed to solve it quickly. These include powerful hardware tests, extensive system information, and a fast, easy way to compare system changes.

CheckIt's Find It feature allows users to search for the specific information they need, rather than having to look through pages of system information. In all, CheckIt offers over a dozen comprehensive information displays identifying everything users need to know about their motherboard, memory, modem, drives, video, ports, printer, and Internet connections.

System conflicts, which result from two hardware devices using the same system resources, can be very hard to find. CheckIt monitors all system resources (IRQ, DMA, memory ranges) and the devices using them, highlights the conflicts, and guides the user to the tools needed to resolve them.

Every time a user installs new hardware or loads a new software program, subtle changes are made to critical system files. The changes are often the cause of many types of PC problems. CheckIt's System Spy keeps track of these changes by taking "snapshots" of the system's hardware, critical system files, and performance. The user can then identify the differences by comparing the latest snapshot with a previous one. CheckIt offers real hardware tests that examine the user's system from top to bottom, paying special attention to the devices used most often. At the end of each test, CheckIt produces a report showing exactly what devices have passed and failed. This information is essential for repairing or replacing a component, or for working with a technician. Tests include CheckIt Modem and CheckIt Video, as well as powerful tests for the user's motherboard, drives, memory, ports and CD-ROM.

CheckIt automatically saves Windows Registry and critical system files so users have a recent backup if Windows becomes corrupted.

The new CheckIt Professional Edition provides the best suite of advanced PC diagnostics available. By combining CheckIt for Windows 98, CheckIt for DOS, PC-cillin 3.0 Anti-Virus, special loopback plugs for precise port testing, and a full year of free program upgrades, CheckIt Professional Edition gives professional technicians and power users the capability to solve more in-depth and complex PC problems.

CheckIt for DOS allows users to troubleshoot PCs when Windows won't run. They can access detailed information on a system's hardware, run full diagnostic tests on all key hardware components, and restore critical system files. Users can also generate custom batch tests, and configure the individual test applets for burn-in testing and troubleshooting multiple PCs.

The full version of TouchStone Software's award-winning PC-cillin Anti-

Virus for Windows 98 features 100% guaranteed virus protection, free lifetime pattern file updates, and exclusive MacroTrapd technology to automatically detect and remove both known and unknown strains of destructive macro viruses.

First Aid for Windows Users and PC 911

First Aid for Windows Users from CyberMedia (800-721-7824) is a low-cost program that can spot problems, diagnose them, and then fix most of them automatically. For those it can't fix automatically, it can help you fix them manually. It fixes problems with printing and multimedia, bad INI files, path problems, missing application components, network conflicts, and many others. The software is optimized for several of the well-known brand-name programs such as Microsoft Office, Word, Excel, CorelDRAW, Quicken, Paradox, and many others. In addition, they offer free upgrades to the program that can be downloaded from CompuServe.

PC 911 is a low-cost companion program to First Aid for Windows from CyberMedia. PC 911 keeps track of all changes made to your PC's setup files. Several times in the past I have installed programs that automatically changed my AUTOEXEC.BAT and CONFIG.SYS files to where my system would no longer operate. Recently, a program changed my files so that I was not able to use my word processors. It took me a couple of hours to find the problem. This program could have saved me that time. PC 911 can also help you with conflicts in IRQs and DMAs, as well as with other problems encountered when installing multimedia and other cards.

First Aid and PC 911 can be bought separately, or you can save about one-third by buying them as a bundle. CyberMedia has several other good diagnostic programs and offers frequent upgrades. Call them for the latest information.

Which One Should You Buy?

If I could only afford one program, I would be hard-pressed to choose one. All of them are good tools. Many of them have a few similar utilities, but there are also different utility features in every one of them. I can't possibly list all of the features of the products here. In fact, I can't even list all of the diagnostic products that are available. New ones are being developed daily. Call each company and ask for literature on their products. Also check computer magazines for ads and reviews.

Spares

One of the easiest ways to check a part is to have a good spare handy. If you suspect a board, it is very easy to plug in a known-good one. If your computer is critical to your business and you cannot afford any downtime, then you should have a few spares handy. I suggest that you have a spare floppy disk drive, a space monitor adapter, and a spare keyboard. These items are all fairly inexpensive. Depending on how critical your business is and how important your computer is to it, you might even want to have spares of all your components, such as a motherboard, power supply, and all of your plug-in boards.

You may have some very expensive video adapters, PCI bus interfaces, or other boards that may cost hundreds of dollars. But there are usually some equivalent inexpensive boards for all of the boards in your system. A good PCI graphics high-resolution monitor adapter may cost as much as $300, but you can buy an ISA adapter that doesn't have all of the goodies for about $20. A low-cost board can help pinpoint the problem. If your monitor doesn't light up but it works with a replacement adapter, then you know the probable cause of the problem.

DOS Error Messages

Even with Windows 98, you will still have DOS running in the background for many programs. DOS has several error messages if you try to make the computer do something it can't do. But many of the messages are not very clear. Don't bother looking in the MS-DOS manual for error messages; they are not there. If you are using the IBM PC-DOS and you get an error message, just type HELPn, where n is the first letter of the error message, and an explanation will pop up.

I have dozens of books on DOS, but few of them make any reference to the error messages. One of the better books I have is *DOS: The New Complete Reference* by Kris Jamsa, published by Osborne/McGraw-Hill

(800-227-0900). Another of his books, *DOS Secrets, Solutions, Shortcuts*, also published by Osborne, explains the DOS commands in great detail and the DOS error commands and what to do about them.

Some Common DOS Error Messages

Access Denied

You may have tried to write on or erase a file that was protected. The file may have been hidden or protected by an ATTRIBUTE command. Use the ATTRIBUTE command to change it.

Bad Command or File Name, or File Not Found

You may have made a mistake in typing in the command, or the command or file does not reside in the current directory.

ScanDisk Errors

If you don't shut your computer down properly, the next time you boot up, Windows will automatically run ScanDisk. You should run ScanDisk often. ScanDisk may give you an error that says "*nnn* lost clusters found in *n* chains. Convert lost chains to files Y/N." Reinvoke ScanDisk with the /F (for fix), and the lost clusters will be converted to FILE000n.CHK. These are usually incomplete files. When you delete a file, sometimes portions of it may be left in a sector. Or something may have caused an error in the FAT and caused portions of two different files to be written in a single sector or cluster. The files created by ScanDisk/F are usually incomplete. In most cases, they can be deleted.

General Failure Reading or Writing Drive *n:* Abort, Retry, Fail

This error message might mean that the disk may not be formatted. It is also possible that track 0 on the disk, which stores the FAT, has become defective. Restoring the disk might be possible by using Norton's Disk Doctor (NDD) file on it.

Invalid Directory

If you do a CD (change directory) from the root directory, all you have to type is CD NORTON, or any directory you want to change to, and it will change immediately. If you happen to be in the WordPerfect directory and you type CD NORTON, it will say that it is an invalid directory. If you are in any directory except the root directory, you have to type CD\NORTON or whatever directory. If you type CD/NORTON, using the forward slash instead of the backslash, you will get the same error message.

Nonsystem Disk or Disk Error. Replace and Strike Any Key when Ready

You had a non-bootable disk in drive A:.

Not Ready Error Reading Drive A:
Abort, Retry, Fail

You may have asked the computer to go to drive A:, and it was not ready or there was no disk in the drive.

Software Error Messages

Most software packages have their own error messages. In many cases, the manual will not tell you what the error message means. You will probably have to call the software company to get an answer.

Glitches

There are times when something may go wrong for no apparent reason and the computer may hang up. Glitches can happen when you are running almost any kind of program. Sometimes you can get out of them with a warm boot (pressing Ctrl + Alt + Del). Other times you may have to turn off the computer, wait a few seconds, then turn it back on.

You should remember that anything you are working on is in memory. If you are working on a file that is on your disk, then you still have a copy on the disk, but if it is something that you have just typed in, when you turn off the computer or reboot, anything in memory is gone forever. It is a good idea to save your data to disk every so often while you are working on it. By all means, try to save your work before rebooting, but quite often, if the computer hangs up, there is nothing you can do except to grit your teeth and reboot.

Power Supply

The power supply is one of the most frequent causes of problems. Most of the components in your computer are fairly low power and low voltage. The only high voltage in your system is in the power supply, and it is pretty well enclosed. So there is no danger of shock if you open your computer and put your hand inside it. But you should *never, ever* connect or disconnect a board or cable while the power is on. Fragile semiconductors may be destroyed if you do so.

Semiconductors have no moving parts. If the circuits were designed properly, the semiconductors should last indefinitely. Heat is an enemy and can cause semiconductor failure. The fan in the power supply should provide adequate cooling. All of the openings on the back panel that correspond to the slots on the motherboard should have blank fillers. Even the holes on the bottom of the chassis should be covered with tape. This forces the fan to draw air in from the front of the computer, pull it over the boards, and exhaust it through the opening in the power supply case. Nothing should be placed in front of or behind the computer that would restrict airflow.

If you don't hear the fan when you turn on a computer, or if the fan isn't running, then the power supply could be defective.

Power Supply Connections

Table 20-1 shows the pin connections and wire colors from the power supply.

The 8-bit slotted connectors on the motherboard have 62 contacts: 31 on the A side and 31 on the B side. The black ground wires connect to B1 of each of the eight slots. B3 and B29 have +5 VDC, B5 has −5 VDC, B7 has −12 VDC, and B9 has +12 VDC. These voltages go to the listed pins on each of the eight plug-in slots.

Most of the other contacts on the ISA plug-in slots are for address

TABLE 20-1

Power Supply
Connections

Disk Drive Power Supply Connections

Pin	Color	Function
1	Yellow	+12 VDC
2	Black	Ground
3	Black	Ground
4	Red	+5 VDC

Power Supply Connections to the Motherboard

P8 Pin	Color	Function
1	White	Power good
2	No connection	—
3	Yellow	+12 VDC
4	Brown	−12 VDC
5	Black	Ground
6	Black	Ground

P9 Pin	Color	Function
1	Black	Ground
2	Black	Ground
3	Blue	−5 VDC
4	Red	+5 VDC
5	Red	+5 VDC
6	Red	+5 VDC

lines and data input/output lines. They are not often involved in problems.

Intermittent Problems

Intermittent problems can be most frustrating and maddening. They can be very difficult to find.

If you suspect a cable or a connector, try wiggling it to see if the problem goes away or gets worse. I once spent several hours trying to find the cause of a floppy disk problem. It turned out to be a loose wire in the connector that was just barely touching the contact. A slight vibration could cause the disk drive to become erratic. A wire or cable can be broken and still make contact until it is moved.

You might also try unplugging a cable or a board and plugging it back in. Sometimes the pins may be slightly corroded or not seated properly, or the copper contacts on a plug-in board may become corroded. You can clean them with an ordinary pencil eraser. Sometimes just unplugging and plugging a board or connector back in several times can wipe away the corrosion. In addition, before unplugging a cable, you might want to put a stripe on the connector and cable with a marking pen or nail polish so that you can easily see how they should be plugged back in.

Always write down the positions before changing any switch or knob. Make a diagram of the wires, cables, and switch settings before you disturb them. It is easy to forget how they were plugged in or set before you moved them. You could end up making things worse. Make a mark before turning a knob or variable coil or capacitor so that it can be returned to the same setting if you find out that it didn't help. (**Caution!** Don't ever mark on a circuit board with a pencil. Pencil lead is made from carbon graphite, which makes a good conductor of electricity.) Better yet, resist the temptation to reset these types of components. Most were set up using highly sophisticated instruments. They don't usually change enough to cause a problem.

If too much current flows through a chip, it can get hot and fail. It may only fail at certain times when you are running a particular program. If you suspect a chip and it seems to be warmer than it should be, you might try using a hair dryer and heat it up. If it fails due to the extra heat, then you have found the problem. Be careful that you do not heat up a good chip and cause it to fail.

If a component seemed to be too hot, at one time, we could spray a coolant such as Freon on it. Because of environmental concerns, you may no longer be able to buy Freon. You might try using ice water in a plastic baggie, instead, to cool it. If the component then works properly, you have found your defect.

Some of the diagnostic software will run a system in an endless loop to try to force the system to fail.

Serial Ports

Conflicts in setting up serial port devices can cause a lot of problems. Like the parallel ports, pins for the serial ports are available on any of the bus plug-in slots. The serial ports may be available as a group of 10 pins on the motherboard. Or it may be on a multifunction plug-in board. The serial port may be a male DB25 connector with pins, or it may be a male DB9 connector. The original RS232 specification called for 25 lines. But most systems only use four or five lines, so the DB9 connector with nine pins is more than sufficient. Many of the mice sold today have the DB9 connector.

The serial ports are most often used for a mouse or other pointing device, for modems, for FAX boards, for plotters, for scanners, and for several other devices. DOS supports four serial ports: COM1, COM2, COM3, and COM4. But DOS only has two interrupt request (IRQ) lines for the serial ports: IRQ4 for COM1 and IRQ3 for COM2. So COM3 and COM4 must share the IRQ lines with COM1 and COM2. You will need special software in order to permit sharing. They can share because it is not likely that all four serial devices would be used at the same time.

Windows 98 does a fairly good job of recognizing plug-and-play hardware and setting it up. But it is not perfect. I have still had problems with conflicting hardware. In Windows 98, to see which IRQs are being used, go to `Control Panel`. You can click on `My Computer` or on `Start` from the task bar, then on `Settings`, then on `Control Panel`, then on `Systems`, and then on `Device Manager`. Then double-click on `Computer`. It will show you all the IRQs that are being used.

Software Problems

I have had lots of problems with software. Quite often it is my fault for not taking the time to completely read the manuals and instructions. But I don't usually have the time to read and study every page in the manual when I install a program. Many of the programs are getting easier to run. Microsoft's Plug-and-Play capability will eliminate a lot of problems. But there will still be lots of software problems that you will probably run into.

Many vendors have support programs for their products, whether hardware and software. If something goes wrong, you can call them. Some companies charge for their support and use a 900 telephone number. You are charged a certain fee for the amount of time on the phone. (Maintaining a support staff can cost a lot of money so charging a fee for service is reasonable.)

If you have a hardware or software problem, document it by writing down everything that happens. Before you call, try to duplicate the problem by making it happen again. Carefully read the manual. When you call, it is best to be in front of your computer, with it turned on and with the problem on the screen if possible. Before you call, have the serial number of your program handy. One of the first things they will probably ask is for your name and serial number. If you have bought and registered the program, it will be in their computer system.

Many companies have set up Web sites with answers to frequently asked questions (FAQs). I have never been fortunate enough to find an answer to whatever question I have at the time. Many of them have also set up fax back systems. You call a number for a list of documents available, and they will automatically fax them to you. Again, I have had very little success in getting an answer to any of my problems. But it is a good way to get documentation and answers to the most FAQs.

It seems that everybody in business has now gone to automated telephone answering machines. When you call, usually long-distance, you will be given several options. It may take several minutes to list them all. Press 1 if you want one service, 2 for another, 3 for another, and so on. Then when you get to that number, there will be another five or six options. You might stay on the phone for half an hour and never get to speak to a live person. Or you will be put on hold to wait for the next available person. It can be very frustrating. One of the best investments I have ever made was buying a speaker phone. I can call a number, then push the speaker button and go about my other business while I am on hold.

Most software programs are reasonably bug free. But lots of things can go wrong if the exact instructions and procedures are not followed. In many cases, the exact instructions and procedures are not very explicit. It seems that most software manuals are written by people who know the software very well. But they seem to forget that the person using it for the first time does not know it.

Software companies could save millions of dollars if they produced manuals that were better written to make installation and usage easier. For every major program, there are dozens of books written to help you learn how to use it. Many training programs have been developed to teach people how to use "user-friendly" software. If you spend a lot of money on a program, you shouldn't have to spend a lot more time and money to learn how to use it. Windows 98 is a step in the right direction; it's fairly easy to use right out of the box. But it is a very complex program, and it will take some study, training, and time to learn all of its benefits.

Stupid Problems

I recently bought a SCSI CD-ROM recordable system. I tried for half a day to get it to work. I called the company support line and was on the phone for about a half hour. At the technician's suggestion, I downloaded and installed a couple of new drivers. The unit seemed to work: The panel lights were on, but Windows still would not recognize it. I laid awake for some time that night trying to figure out what was wrong. The next morning, I decided to pull the unit out and try it on the bench. When I pulled it out, I could see immediately what the problem was. The 50-pin SCSI cable connector was not plugged in all the way. I pushed it in to completely seat it, turned on the power, and it worked just like it was supposed to. I felt so stupid for not checking it earlier, but I was sure that it was plugged in properly.

Again, there are 10,000 things that can go wrong—any one of them may cause the system not to work.

User Groups

There is no way to list all of the possible software or hardware problems. Computers are dumb and very unforgiving. It is very easy to plug a cable in backwards or forget to set a switch. Often there is only one way to do something right, but 10,000 ways to do it wrong. Sometimes it is difficult to determine if the problem is caused by hardware or software, or a combination of both. There is no way that every problem can be addressed.

One of the best ways to find answers is to ask someone who has had the same problem, and the best place to find those people is in a user group. If at all possible, join one and become friendly with all of the members. They can be one of your best sources of troubleshooting. Most of them have had similar problems and are glad to help. Many local computer magazines list user groups in their area.

Thank you for buying my book. I wish you all the best. I hope all your problems are easy ones.

GLOSSARY

ACPI   An abbreviation for Advanced Configuration and Power Interface, a utility found on some of the newer motherboards.

active-matrix LCD   A system used for high-resolution liquid crystal diode (LCD) display panels used on color laptop and portable computers. This type of display is fairly expensive, since it requires an individual transistor for each pixel. *See* passive matrix.

adapter card   A printed wiring board with digital circuitry that plugs into connectors on the motherboard of a personal computer, usually performing input/output functions.

ADC   An abbreviation for analog-to-digital converter, an electronic device converting conventional analog audio and video signals to digital form. The digital form can be processed by computer and stored as data on a computer's hard disk drive.

address   The numerical value, usually in hexadecimal format, of a particular location in a computer's random access memory (RAM).

ADPCM   An abbreviation for adaptive differential pulse code modulation. A method of digital waveform sampling encoding the difference between successive samples rather than encoding their actual values (DPCM). The differences are assigned different values based on the content of the sample. ADPCM is the storage format used by CD-ROM XA and CD-1 discs.

ADSL   An abbreviation for asymmetric digital subscriber line, a digital phone line technology that supports high-speed connections using ordinary phone lines. ADSL is asymmetric because the uplink speeds, at about 64Kbps is much slower than the download speeds of up to 6Mbps.

AGP   An abbreviation for Accelerated Graphics Port, a new utility that makes graphics much faster. The port may be a slot on the motherboard, or it may be built into the motherboard.

algorithm   1). A digital set of instructions for solving a problem. 2). The configuration of operators in an FM synthesizer.

amplitude   1). The strength or intensity of sound or signal. 2). The measure of a current's deviation from its zero value.

amplitude modulation   A term describing the interaction of two signals—a carrier and a modulator. The modulation signal varies the amplitude (intensity) of the carrier. In AM radio transmission, the carrier is a medium-frequency signal (550-1550 kHz), and the modulator is the sound signal. In sound synthesis, a low-frequency oscillator modulates a carrier that is the sound's fundamental frequency.

analog   1). A term describing a circuit, device, or system that responds to continuously variable parameters. 2). Generated by hardware rather than by software.

analog-to-digital converter   A circuit that periodically samples a continuously variable voltage and generates a digital representation of its value. Also called an ADC, A-to-D, or A/D converter.

ANI   An abbreviation for automatic number identification, or Caller ID.

ANSI   An abbreviation for the American National Standards Institute. ANSI, in the Windows context, refers to the ANSI character set that Microsoft uses for Windows.

API   An abbreviation for application programming interface. Generically, a method of accessing or modifying the operating system for a program. In Windows, the API refers to the functions provided by Windows 95/98 allowing applications to open and close windows, read the keyboard, interpret mouse movements, and so on. Programmers call these functions "hooks" to the operating systems.

APM and **SMM**   An abbreviation for Advanced Power Management. An API developed by Intel and Microsoft that allows certain programs and operating systems to slow down various hardware components, thereby saving power. SMM is System Management Mode, a group of instructions built into the CPU.

ASCII   Pronounced *ask-ee*. An acronym for American Standard Code for Information Interchange. It is the digital code for displaying alphanumeric characters. It originally consisted of 128 codes, but later it was extended to 254 characters. Some of the characters are smiley faces, playing cards, or music notes. You can see what some of them look like by using the Type command to view almost any .EXE or .COM file.

Most word processors add control characters so that they display bold, underline, page formats, or other characteristics. Text generated on one word processor is usually quite different than that of another. It is almost like a foreign language. But most computers and word processors can handle pure ASCII characters. The control characters can be stripped off so that only ASCII characters are left.

artifact An extraneous sound or effect on an image not present in the source signal and introduced by one of the components in the recording or reproduction chain.

aspect ratio An image's ratio of width to height. Aspect ratio is usually expressed as W:H—*W* being the width and *H* being the height of the image. The aspect ratio of digital images is expressed as the ratio of the number of pixels in each dimension (640:480 for VGA images).

ASPI An acronym for Advanced SCSI Programming Interface. It is the industry standard for SCSI interface cards. If the card conforms to this standard, then several different peripherals from different manufacturers can be used with the card. The Adaptec Company was the original creator of this standard. (*See* CAM.)

ATM 1). Asynchronous Transfer Mode, a wide-band high-frequency protocol for data transmission. 2). Adobe Type Manager, Adobe's system for managing TrueType PostScript fonts. 3). Automated teller machine, where you can get money if you play your cards right.

AVI An acronym for Audio Video Interleaved, Microsoft's application programming interface (API) designed to compete with Apple's QuickTime methodology. AVI techniques provide a software synchronization and compression standard for audio and video signals competing with DVI.

BitBlt Pronounced *bit-blit*. An abbreviation for bit block transfer. An assembly-level function used for copying graphic images in Windows applications from a source to a destination graphic context.

buffer A section of RAM where data is stored temporarily, usually containing data to be edited or inserted.

CAM 1). Common Access Method, a standard that was developed for SCSI devices. It is similar to the ASPI standard except that the interface cards have their own BIOS on board. 2). Computer-aided manufacturing, a type of application used to automate factories.

camcorder A contraction of camera and recorder. The term describes a video camera and videocassette recorder combined into a single handheld unit.

carpal tunnel syndrome Pain and numbness in the hand, wrist, and arm along the path of the medial nerve. It is often caused by the repetitive action of typing on a computer keyboard. Sometimes abbreviated CTS. *See also* repetitive strain injury (RSI).

CAV An abbreviation for Constant Angular Velocity devices, such as computer hard disks and CAV video laser discs. The velocity depends on the distance of the read/write head from the drive spindle. *Compare* CLV.

CCD   Abbreviation for charge-coupled device. An integrated circuit consisting of a linear array of semiconductor photoreceptor elements. CCDs are used to create a bitmapped image. Each photoreceptor creates an electrical signal representing the luminance of one pixel. CCDs are primarily used in scanners, color xerographic printers, and video cameras.

CCITT   An abbreviation for the Consultative Committee International for Telephone and Telegraph communication. CCITT establishes standards for telephone interchange and modems in Europe. Several CCITT standards for communication between modems over telephone networks have been adopted in the United States. The CCITT has been renamed the International Telecommunications Union (ITU).

CD   An abbreviation for compact disc. CDs are the original format for distributing compact optical discs for audio reproduction (CDAudio). This early format was jointly developed by Philips N.V. and Sony Corporation and is described in Philips N.V.'s Yellow Book. Control of Yellow Book CD-ROMs, such as starting and stopping the drive and file selection with your computer, requires Microsoft's MSCDEX.DRV driver.

CD-DA   An abbreviation for compact disc-digital audio, also called "Red Book" audio. CD-A requires compatibility with MPC specification 1.0. It enables interleaving of audio with other types of data, so recorded sound can accompany images. It is usually supplied with the CD-ROM drive when purchased as a component of an MPC upgrade kit. The CD-DA format is defined in the International Electrotechnical Commissions' (IEC) Standard BNNI-5-83-095.

CD + Graphics   A format in which the subchannel(s) of an audio CD contain graphic images that may be displayed on a computer or a television set.

CD-I   An abbreviation for compact disc-interactive. CD-I refers to a class of CDs primarily designed to be viewed on conventional television sets by means of a CD-I player. CD-I players incorporate at least 1MB of memory (RAM), special pointing devices, and remote control systems. CD-I players also may be used for training and other commercial and industrial applications. CD-I formats are covered by Philips N.V.'s Green Book specification.

CD + MIDI   A format in which the subchannel(s) of an audio CD contain data in standard MIDI file format that may be routed to a MIDI

OUT connector and played on external MIDI synthesizers or internally by audio adapter cards.

CD-MO An abbreviation for compact-disc magneto-optical. Magneto-optical CDs and CD-ROMs are capable of multiple use because they can be erased and re-recorded. The standards for CD-MOs are incorporated in Philips N.V.'s Orange Book 1 specification. CD-MO technology is used for high-capacity, 3-1/2-inch "floptical" floppy disks.

CD-ROM An acronym for compact disc read-only memory. CD-ROMs can incorporate both audio and graphic images as well as text files. Philips N.V.'s documentation for this standard has a yellow binding, hence the term "Yellow Book" audio. MPC Specification 1.0 requires multimedia PCs to include a CD-ROM.

CD-ROM XA An abbreviation for CD-ROM eXtended Architecture, jointly developed by Philips N.V., Sony Corporation, and Microsoft Corporation in 1989. CD-ROM XA provides storage for audio and other types of data interleaved on a CD-ROM, enabling access simultaneously.

channel message A MIDI command or data that is sent over a specific MIDI channel.

CHRP Pronounced *chirp*. An acronym for Common Hardware Reference Platform, a set of standards agreed to by Motorola, IBM, and Apple for the PowerPC.

chrominance A term used in television broadcasting to describe the signal (a subcarrier of the basic black-and-white signal) containing the color information in a composite video signal. Chrominance has two components: hue (tint) and saturation (the degree to which the color is diluted by white light). Chrominance is also called "chroma" and is abbreviated as C.

clipping Audible distortion of an audio signal, usually caused by overloading a circuit of transducer.

clock An electronic circuit that generates the pulses used to synchronize bits of information.

CLV An abbreviation for Constant Linear Velocity. The recording technique used with CD-ROMs (and other CD devices) specifying that the velocity of the media at the point of reading or writing remain constant, regardless of the distance from the spindle. CLV devices have a constant data transfer rate. To achieve CLV, the rotational speed of the spindle motor must be inversely proportional to the distance of the read or write point on the media from the spindle video. Laser disc drives are produced in CLV and Constant Angular Velocity models. *Compare* CAV.

codec   An acronym for compression-decompression for video data.

cookie   A piece of information sent by a Web server to a Web browser. If you access certain sites, it will generate a bit of information about you and save it. The next time you access the site, it will remember you and make it easier to access the same information. Some people worry that the information gathered by cookies could be misused and abused.

CP/M   An abbreviation for Control Program for Microprocessors. CP/M was the first operating system for personal computers. Written by Gary Kildall in 1973, it was used by all of the early PCs, such as Osborne, Kaypro, Morrow, and others. In 1980 IBM approached Gary to develop a system for the first IBM PC. IBM later went to Bill Gates, and you know the rest of the story.

cps   1). Cycles per second, such as when describing frequency of an electronic circuit. 2). Characters per second; refers to a printer's (particularly dot-matrix) printing speed.

CTI   An abbreviation for computer telephony integration. Refers to connecting a computer to a telephone switch.

cycle   A single, complete wave; the basic unit of oscillation.

DAC   An abbreviation for digital-to-analog converter. DAC is the electronic device used to convert digital audio and video signals stored on CD-ROMs, DAT, or in computer files to analog signals that can be reproduced by conventional stereo and television components.

daisy chain   The connection of several devices on a SCSI. Also, a network in which data flows from one receiving device's MIDI Thruport to another receiving device's MIDI in port.

DAT   An acronym for digital audio tape. DAT is a process of recording sound in helical bands on a tape cartridge. This process is similar to recording video signals.

default   A parameter value that exists when hardware is turned on or an application is run.

Dhrystones   A benchmark that measures millions of instructions per second (MIPS).

digital-to-analog converter   *See* DAC.

DIN   An acronym for Deutches Institute fur Normalization. DIN is an organization similar to ANSI that establishes and coordinates standards for Germany. It has become the de facto standards bureau for Europe.

DLL   An abbreviation for dynamic-link library. DLL is a file containing a collection of Windows functions designed to perform a specific class of operations. Functions within DLLs are called (or invoked) as necessary by applications to perform the desired operations.

DNS   An abbreviation for Domain Naming System, the Internet system for assigning Internet addresses.

domain name   The unique name of a Web site.

drag-and-drop   A Windows process whereby an icon representing an object, such as a file, can be moved (dragged) by the mouse to another location, such as a different directory, and placed (dropped) in that location. Visual Basic provides drag-and-drop capabilities for control objects.

dongle   A copy protection device that usually plugs into one of the computer I/O ports. Without the specific dongle for that program, it would not run. (The Xircom Company came up with a clever advertising program that featured a full-page photo of a nude Greek statue. In the seventeenth century, a group of people decided that nudity was a terrible thing, even on a statue. So hundreds of statues—priceless works of art—were emasculated. Or as Xircom put it in their ad, they lost their dongle.)

DRAM   An abbreviation for dynamic random access memory. The most popular memory used in PCs.

DSP   An abbreviation for digital signal processing. Although all synthesized sound involves DSP, the term is usually applied to the creation of electronic, acoustic effects such as reverberation, chorusing, flanging, and panning.

DTV   An abbreviation for desktop video. The term describes the production of videotape presentations using the multimedia capabilities of personal computers. DTV implies the capability to edit video tapes by using the playback and record functions of VCRs that can be remotely controlled by a computer.

DVD   An abbreviation for digital versatile (or video) disc.

DVI   An abbreviation for Intel's Digital Video Interactive standard. DVI simultaneously displays compressed video images and sound files. IBM has adopted the DVI standard for its Ultimedia product line. Microsoft adds DVI capability through its DVMCI extensions.

EISA   An abbreviation for Extended Industry Standard Architecture. A bus specification used to interconnect adapter cards employing 32-bit memory addresses or providing multiprocessor capabilities. The EISA standard is now obsolete, although there are several systems still in existence.

Energy Star   The EPA's requirement that PCs implement automatic sleep modes when the item is not being used so as to save energy. Many of the laptop computers have used similar systems for some time. Newer CPUs have a variety of power-saving options.

EPROM   Pronounced *ee-prom*. An acronym for erasable programmable read-only memory. The type of chips usually used for ROM BIOS.

Error-Correction Code (ECC)   A coding system that, in conjunction with an Error-Detection Coding scheme, can reconstruct erroneous data to its original value.

Error-Detection Code (EDC)   A coding system that detects errors in a single byte or in blocks of data. Single-byte errors are caught by parity checkers, such as the ones employed in the PC's memory system. Errors in blocks of data are commonly determined by using techniques such as the cyclic redundancy codes (CRC) used for data transfer by modem. More-sophisticated EDC methods are employed when error correction is required, such as with CD-ROMs.

FAQ   Pronounced as separate letters or as *fak*. An abbreviation for frequently asked questions. Many technical support systems and online services list frequently asked questions. Hopefully, you will find an answer to your question or problem without having to call on the telephone and switch through all the many options.

field   1). In video terminology, one-half of a television image. A field consists of either the even or odd lines of a frame. 2). When used in conjunction with computer databases, a field is a single, distinct element of a complete database record.

filter   A circuit or function that alters a signal's frequency spectrum by attenuating or accenting certain portions.

firewall   Hardware or software that protects a LAN or site from unauthorized access.

FireWire   Apple Computer's proprietary implementation of IEEE-1394. IEEE-1394 is somewhat like the universal serial bus (USB). It is a high-speed bus that can accommodate several devices.

firmware   Software that is embedded in the computer's ROMs or elsewhere in the computer circuitry. You cannot ordinarily change or modify firmware.

FM synthesis A method of generating complex waveforms by modulating the frequency of audio waveforms (carriers) with other waveforms (modulators); frequency modulation.

frame rate In film or video, the frequency at which single frames are shown, usually equal to 24, 25, or 30 frames per second.

frequency The rate of oscillation, which determines pitch, measured in cycles per second, or hertz. *See also* cps and Hz.

FTP An abbreviation for File Transfer Protocol. A TCP/IP protocol for transferring files from one machine to another or from sites on the Internet.

fundamental frequency A sound's primary frequency; the first harmonic.

genlock A contraction of generator locking. A process for synchronizing the video display of a computer to the frame synchronization signal of NTSC, PAL, or SECAM video. This process allows a computer-generated graphics to be viewed on a television set or recorded with a VCR. Genlock capability is required to add computer-generated titling to video productions.

GIF Pronounced *jif*. An acronym for graphics interchange format. GIF is the file format (and extension) storing most graphic images in the CompuServe forum libraries.

global Pertaining to a computer program as a whole. Global variables and constants are accessible to, and may be modified by, program code at the module and procedure level.

gray-scale A description for monochrome (black-and-white) images displayed in various intensities of black. The most common format is an 8-bit gray-scale providing 256 shades of gray. Four-bit gray-scale images with 64 shades are also used.

harmonic A simple component of a complex waveform that's a whole-number multiple of the fundamental frequency.

HDTV An abbreviation for High-Definition Television, a form of television transmission that results in clearer images, especially on large-screen sets. Our present standard is 525 lines swept across the screen from top to bottom. HDTV would increase the number and give much better resolution.

Hi8 An abbreviation for High Band 8-mm, a format developed by Sony Corporation for camcorder videotapes. Hi8 provides the capability of recording PCM digital-audio and time-code tracks in addition to conventional analog audio and enhanced-quality video information.

High Sierra format A name assigned to the predecessor of ISO standard 9660 defining the table of contents and directory structure of CD-ROMs for computer applications. Microsoft's MSCDEX.DRV driver reads the table of contents and directory structure and converts the latter to the structure used by DOS. This function enables you to treat CD-ROM files as if they were located on a conventional hard disk drive.

HMS time Time expressed in hours, minutes, and seconds, usually separated by colons.

HTML An abbreviation for Hypertext Markup Language, a special language used to create Web pages.

http An abbreviation for Hypertext Transfer Protocol; the World Wide Web text-based protocol.

Hz An abbreviation for hertz, the fundamental unit of frequency of audio and radio waves. Hertz was previously called "cycles per second" (cps). Most people can discern sounds that range in frequency from about 20 to 18,000Hz. *See also* cps and frequency.

icon In Windows, a 32- × 32-pixel graphic image, usually in color. An icon identifies the application in the program manager window when the application is minimized and in other locations in the application chosen by the programmer.

interlaced The method of displaying television signals on conventional TV sets and computer images on video display units. Alternative fields of images, making up the even or odd horizontal lines making up the image, are displayed in succession.

interleaved A method for containing sound and video information in a single file but in separate chunks, so digital images and audio signals may be transferred from a file to the computer's memory without delays incurred by CD-ROM seek operations.

IP Internet Protocol, a protocol used to send packets of data over the Internet.

ITU International Telecommunications Union, formerly called the CCITT. A United Nations committee that tries to convince nations and companies to standardize telecommunications devices and protocols. *See* CCITT.

ISA An abbreviation for Industry Standard Architecture, the specification of the connections to plug-in adapter cards with 16-bit memory addressing capability. ISA is the bus structure used in conventional IBM-compatible computers using the 8088, 80286, 80386, and 80486 CPU chips.

ISDN An abbreviation for Integrated Services Digital Network, a digital telephone network that allows much faster communications.

ISO An abbreviation for the International Standards Organization. The ISO is a branch of the United Nations, headquartered in Geneva. ISO coordinates international standards for a wide variety of products and equipment. The CD-ROM standard for tables of contents and file directory entries, originally called the High Sierra format, has been established as the ISO-9660 standard.

ISP An abbreviation for Internet service provider, a company that provides connections to the Internet. Larger ones are AOL, Prodigy, CompuServe, and Microsoft Network, but there are hundreds of small local ISPs. There are well over 200 in the Los Angeles area.

IVRU An abbreviation for interactive voice response unit, a system whereby the computer can play back digitized speech and can accept requests from a Touch-Tone telephone. These systems are now used by many companies to displace live human beings. They save a lot of money for companies because these systems never take a coffee break, go on vacations, or ask for a raise.

JPEG Pronounced *jay-peg*. An acronym for the Joint Photographic Experts Group that has established an industry standard for photographic image compression. The file extension for graphic image files stored with JPEG compression is .JPG.

jumper A small, plastic-enclosed spring clip making an electrical connection between two adjacent square metal pins, usually in the form of a header. Jumpers are used to set device addresses, and interrupt levels, and select other optional features of adapter cards. They are also found on motherboards.

karaoke A musical arrangement designed to accompany an added singing voice. Karaoke can be used to describe a consumer audio or audio-video component equipped with a microphone (and often with digital signal processing). The added singer's voice is combined with the accompaniment and heard through the same speakers.

LAN An acronym for local-area network. A network where several computers may be tied together. The area served may be a single building or several buildings, such as a campus or a company with several buildings.

luminance One of the characteristics defining a color in the Hue-Saturation-Luminance (HSL) system. Luminance is the collective intensity (lightness) of the color defined by hue and saturation. In television broadcasting, the signal containing the black-and-white image is referred to as the "luminance signal."

MFLOPS An abbreviation for millions of floating-point instructions per second.

MIDI Pronounced *middy*. An abbreviation for musical instrument digital interface; a means of communicating musical information among computers and microprocessor-based devices.

MIME An acronym for Multipurpose Internet Mail Extensions. A protocol for sending non-ASCII-type data over the Internet. Such data may be sound, video, and graphics.

MHz Million hertz or cycles per second.

MIPS An acronym for millions of instructions per second, a measure of how fast a CPU operates.

MMX An abbreviation for multimedia extensions. Number extensions added to the Pentium to improve multimedia performance.

MSRP An abbreviation for manufacturer's suggested retail price, usually much higher than the street price.

NAMM An acronym for the National Association of Music Merchants. NAMM is an industry association of music dealers and musical-instrument manufacturers. NAMM hold a yearly exhibition where new MIDI devices and audio components are introduced.

nanosecond One billionth of a second, abbreviated ns. The speed of memory chips is measured in nanoseconds, usually ranging from about 30 to 100. Faster computer clock speeds require memory chips with lower nanosecond response times. 33MHz computers, for instance, use 70 to 80ns memory chips.

NBT An abbreviation for the Next Big Thing, what everybody is waiting breathlessly for. Time and again, NBT has been rumored and hinted at. When it arrives, it will be a real killer app or component.

NLQ An abbreviation for near letter quality. Many printers, especially dot-matrix, can print fairly fast in draft mode. In draft mode, there are usually spaces and jagged edges in the characters. For NLQ printing, more pins in the head are struck so that the characters are better defined.

noninterlaced The preferred method of displaying computer images, usually on a multisynchronous video display unit, in which the image is created by displaying consecutive rather than alternate scanning lines.

OCR An abbreviation for optical character recognition. A system used in scanners to recognize printed text and convert it into digital data.

oscillator A circuit or software that generates voltage signals.

PAL An acronym for Phase-Alternative Line system. PAL is the television transmission standard of Western Europe (except France). PAL displays 625 lines per frame at a rate of 25 frames per second.

palette A Windows data structure defining the colors of a bitmapped image in RGB (red, green, and blue) format.

parallel interface A connection between devices that transfers one or more bytes of information simultaneously. *Compare* with serial interface.

parameter A variable characteristic or value.

passive matrix LCD A system used on the lesser-expensive display panels for color laptops and portables. It uses a single transistor to activate rows and columns of pixels. It is much less expensive than active matrix, but the colors are not as bright as those in the active-matrix systems. See active-matrix LCD.

PCM An abbreviation for pulse code modulation, a means of digitally encoding and decoding audio signals.

PCI An abbreviation for Peripheral Component Interconnect, a system that allows plug-in boards and devices to communicate with the CPU over a 32- or 64-bit high-speed bus.

.PCX The file extension created by ZSOFT Corporation for storing images created by its PC Paintbrush application. PCX bitmapped files can be monochrome or color and are used by many other bitmapped image-creation (paint) and display applications.

photoCD A trademark of the Eastman Kodak Company for its technology and CDs that provide copies of photographic color images in a format compatible with CD-I and CD-ROM XA drives. PhotoCDs are produced from 35mm film images by licensed photo-finishing facilities. These facilities have equipment that can write to the special PhotoCD media.

pipeline In the Pentium, a pipeline is an arrangement of registers within the CPU. They are also called "execution units." Each register performs part of a task, then passes the results to the next register. PCs such as the 486 computer have a single pipeline and can only process one instruction per clock cycle. The Pentium has two pipelines and can process two instructions per cycle.

POP An acronym for Post Office Protocol, the protocol used to send and retrieve Internet e-mail messages.

presentation A multimedia production consisting principally of still images or simple animation covering a single topic.

prosumer A contraction of professional and consumer. Prosumer describes video components, such as camcorders and VCRs, bridging the gap between consumer-grade products and industrial-quality devices.

QIC An abbreviation for quarter-inch cartridge. Magnetic tape used for tape backup.

RAM An acronym for random access memory; a computer's main memory in which data is temporarily stored and that allows the user to enter and retrieve data at will.

RAID An acronym for redundant array of inexpensive disks. When the data is critical, a RAID system of two or more hard disks may be used to mirror each other so that the same data is recorded on each disk.

RBOC An abbreviation for regional bell operating companies, or telephone companies.

Repetitive strain injury (RSI) Pain and numbness to areas of the hand, wrist, and arm. RSI is similar to carpal tunnel syndrome, except that, ordinarily, RSI may occur to any part of the body that is subjected to frequent motion or trauma. The injury usually occurs in tendons and in synovial sheaths that surround the nerves. This injury is sometimes called "repetitive motion injury," which is probably a better term. *See also* carpal tunnel syndrome.

ribbon cable A flat, multiconductor cable having parallel individual conductors that are molded together. One side of the ribbon cable is marked with a printed line, usually blue or red. This line identifies the conductor corresponding to pin 1 of the attached connectors.

RIFF An acronym for the Windows Resource Interchange File Format. RIFF is used in conjunction with Multimedia Extensions (MMX). Depending upon their definition, these files may contain MIDI sequence, sample dump, or system exclusive data; waveform audio files; or data to create graphic images. RIFF is the preferred file format for Windows multimedia files; however, few third-party applications currently create RIFF files, except in Wave format (.WAV files).

RTM What you may hear when you call a company for support, or ask someone for help: Read The Manual.

RTDM Same as above, but a bit more imperative: Read The Damned Manual. Another version that can't be used in nice company is RTFM.

sample To digitally encode an analog signal.

sawtooth wave   A waveform that contains every component of the natural harmonic series; also called a "ramp wave."

scalability   The quality of a multiprocessing operating system that allows a user to run the same application on single-processor and multiprocessor computers.

SCSI   Pronounced *SCUZZY*. An abbreviation for Small Computer System Interface. An interface standard for connecting peripherals to a PC. The standard supports several different peripherals such as hard drives, CD-ROMs, scanners, and other devices. As many as seven different devices can be connected to one interface card.

SDRAM   Synchronous DRAM. A type of DRAM that is synchronized with the CPU. It is much faster than most DRAM and can only be used on motherboards that are designed for it. *See also* DRAM.

SECAM   The acronym for Systeme Couleur avec Memoire. SECAM is the French standard for television transmission (819 horizontal lines per frame displayed at 25 frames per second). SECAM is also the standard for most of Eastern Europe, including the former USSR, and in African countries where French is the most common second language.

seek   To locate a specific byte, sector, cluster, record, or chunk within a disk file.

serial interface   A connection between devices that transfers information one bit after another. *Compare* parallel interface.

signal-to-noise ratio (SNR)   The ratio between an audio or video signal of a specific amplitude (level) and the underlying noise contributed to the signal by a component. Signal-to-noise ratio is expressed in dB or dBr (relative)—a large negative number being preferred.

sine wave   A pure, simple waveform comprised of a single frequency with no overtones. It is a voltage signal that goes positive above zero to a certain height, then back to zero, then negative for a minus voltage, then back to zero. Alternating voltages are sine waves.

slave   A device receiving signals from and controlled by a master device.

SOHO   An acronym for small office/home office.

SMPTE   An type of time code adopted by the Society of Motion Picture and Television Engineers, used to indicate location in time and synchronize playback.

SPEC92   An acronym for systems Performance Evaluation

Cooperative (SPEC). A group of organizations got together in January of 1992 and developed a suite of benchmark programs that effectively measures the performance of computing systems in actual application environments.

SPECint92 An effective benchmark to measure integer application performance.

SPECfp92 A benchmark that measures floating-point performance.

square wave A pulse wave with a 50 percent duty cycle, consisting of odd harmonics only.

SRP An abbreviation for suggested retail price. Sometimes it is called MSRP, or manufacturers' suggested retail price.

streaming The technique used to transfer information from a file structure, such as on a disk or CD drive, to the computer's memory. Streaming takes place in groups of bytes less than the entire file's length, usually processed in memory as a background activity.

stripe A synchronization signal recorded on one track of a multitrack tape recorder.

superscalar Refers to the fact the Pentium architecture has two parallel pipelines. It can process instructions in both pipelines simultaneously, or two instructions per clock cycle.

S-VHS A VHS-format videocassette recorder with S-video capability.

S-Video An abbreviation for super video. S-Video is a video signal with enhanced quality used for recording. S-Video separates the chrominance signal from the luminance signals of composite video.

sync An abbreviation for synchronization.

TCP An abbreviation for Transmission Control Protocol. Usually seen as TCP/IP for Transmission Control/Internet Protocol, this protocol is used on LANs as well as on the Internet. It guarantees reliable delivery by resending any lost packets or corrupted bits and bytes.

.TGA The file extension identifying files created in the format used by Truevision's Targa series of graphic adapter cards.

.TIF An acronym for Tagged Image Format. TIF is a format for storing black-and-white, gray-scale, and color bitmapped images. Developed by Aldus Corporation.

time code A method of identifying the time an event (such as a single motion picture or video frame) occurs in a format that can be understood by a computer.

time stamp   The date and time data attributes applied to a disk file when created or edited. In MIDI files, a time stamp identifies the time MIDI events (such as Note On or Note Off) should occur, so the correct tempo is maintained.

triangle wave   A waveform with strong fundamental and weak overtones, comprised of odd-numbered harmonics only.

trigger   A control signal which indicates the beginning of an event.

truncate   In sampling, to remove recorded data before or after a sample.

TrueType   An outline-based font technology developed jointly by Apple and Microsoft. It creates display and printer fonts in a manner similar to Adobe's PostScript.

TSR   An abbreviation for terminate-and-stay-resident, a term describing software that loads itself into RAM and stays there. It is available at any time, but it may use up a lot of the much-needed 640KB.

twip   Window's smallest unit of graphic measurement. A twip is a twentieth of a point or 1/1,440th of an inch.

typeface   Print or display type of a single design. Typeface is often confused with the term "font," which means a particular size of a typeface. A typeface may be a member of a typeface or type family including related designs with attributes such as bold, Roman (regular), italic, compressed, or extended.

UART   Pronounced *u-art*. An acronym for universal asynchronous receiver and transmitter. It is a chip that processes data through the serial port. For example, it takes 8 bits to make a character. The parallel port can send a whole 8-bit character over 8 lines at one time. To send data over the serial port, the chip takes the digital data and sends it through the port one bit at a time in a serial string. The early UARTs used an 8250 chip, which is rather slow. Newer devices use the 16550, which is much faster. Many of the less expensive multi I/O boards still use the older 8250. To find out what you have, use the DOS MSD command.

UDF   An abbreviation for Universal Data Format. A standard for CD recording.

URL   An abbreviation for Uniform Resource Locator. The name of a site on the World Wide Web, for instance, http://www.pencomputing.com/dim. Ordinarily, the http:// can be omitted.

VESA   An acronym for the Video Electronic Standards Association.

VESA is a group of manufacturers and software developers who create standards for graphic and video display adapter cards.

VLB   An abbreviation for VESA local bus, a system that allows plug-in boards or other devices to communicate with the CPU over a fast 32- or 64-bit bus.

WAVE file   A RIFF (Resource Interchange File Format) file containing PCM waveform audio data, usually with a .WAV extension. Microsoft and IBM have adopted .WAV files as their standard format for multimedia sound applications.

waveform audio   A data type standard of the Windows Multimedia Extensions (MMX). Waveform audio defines how digitally sampled sounds are stored in files and processed by Windows API functions.

wavetable   A term describing the synthesis technique of simulating the sounds of musical instruments with short digitized recordings (PCM samples) of their sounds.

wild card   A character that substitutes for and allows a match by any character or set of characters in its place such as the ? and *.

WinBench   A benchmark for use with Windows.

WinMark   A benchmark for use with Windows.

WORM   An acronym for write-once, read-many. The WORM system uses a laser to write on a special optical disc. CD-WO (the write-once CD standard) is a special type of WORM format.

Write-back cache   A write-back system that only writes data back to the main memory that has been modified.

Write-through cache   A system where all data is immediately written back to memory.

WWW or **World Wide Web**   The Internet that is made up of thousands and thousands of sites and millions of home pages.

YC   An encoding method used in S-Video. In YC, the luminance (Y) and chrominance signals are separated. The chrominance signal incorporates both hue and saturation information.

ZIF   An acronym for Zero Insertion Force. A 238-pin chip like the Celeron requires a large amount of force to insert and remove. It is a fragile device, and the pins can be easily damaged. A ZIF socket has a lever that opens the socket contacts so that the device can be dropped in. When the lever is pressed down, the socket contacts close around the pins.

zoom   To magnify an image on a video display.

INDEX

About the Author

Aubrey Pilgrim (Long Beach, CA) is the author of McGraw-Hill's highly successful Build Your Own series. He is a trusted name among computer do-it-yourselfers.